This book is due for return on or before the last date shown above but it may be renewed by personal application, post, or telephone, quoting this date and the book number.

HERTFORDSHIRE C

COUNTY HALL,

D1348979

L.32

By the same Author

★

MILTON
THE MILTONIC SETTING
SHAKESPEARE'S LAST PLAYS
THE ELIZABETHAN WORLD PICTURE
SHAKESPEARE'S HISTORY PLAYS
POETRY DIRECT AND OBLIQUE
FIVE POEMS 1470-1870
THE POETRY OF SIR THOMAS WYATT
(A Selection and a Study)
SHAKESPEARE'S PROBLEM PLAYS
STUDIES IN MILTON

Edited by the same Author
ORCHESTRA: A POEM OF DANCING
BY SIR JOHN DAVIES
Chatto and Windus

★

THE HOPE VASES
LAMB'S CRITICISM
THE ENGLISH RENAISSANCE:
FACT OR FICTION?

★

With Phyllis B. Tillyard
MILTON, PRIVATE CORRESPONDENCE
AND ACADEMIC EXERCISES

With C. S. Lewis
THE PERSONAL HERESY: A CONTROVERSY

THE ENGLISH EPIC

AND ITS BACKGROUND

BY

E. M. W. TILLYARD, Litt.D., F.B.A.

Master of Jesus College, Cambridge

1954

CHATTO AND WINDUS

LONDON

PUBLISHED BY
Chatto and Windus Ltd
LONDON

★

Clarke, Irwin & Co. Ltd
TORONTO

PREFACE

*I beg the reader's pardon for entertaining him so long with myself:
'tis an usual part of ill manners in all authors, and almost in all
mankind, to trouble others with their business; and I was so sensible
of it beforehand, that I had not now committed it, unless some
concernments of the reader's had been interwoven with my own.*

(Dryden, Preface to Du Fresnoy *De Arte Graphica*)

IT may seem an act of folly to write today on the epic at all, and
especially to do so in a book which, structurally, follows a time
sequence, and, critically, deals with the larger literary properties.
The long poem itself is out of favour; and the suggestive item, not
the large contour, is the typical vehicle of modern poetic emotion.
There is little curiosity about the historical evolution of literature;
and the greatest energy of criticism is directed towards detail, such as
words, sentences, and images, or towards highly concentrated short
poems. Yet, since tastes change, since we may well be due for a
reversal in the ways of criticism, I do not think it foolish to choose an
unpopular topic or to treat it in an unfashionable way.

I was bred a Classic, and in my early years Homer, Virgil, and
Milton were my favourite poets. And I have long been, and still am,
drawn to those writers who have dared to risk everything on one great
work. This attraction has been the basic incentive for making the epic
my theme. Having published my *Milton* in 1930, I began working on
the epic more generally in 1935. I summarised my first results in the
British Academy's Warton Lecture for 1936, the *English Epic Tradition*,
reprinted in my *Miltonic Setting* 1938. But I was held up in my plans
for the present book when I concluded (as others had before) that
Shakespeare's History Plays shared the epic impulse of the Elizabethan
age. I could not include those plays in a book on the epic without
running to extravagant length, and the only thing to do was to treat
them separately. The study of those plays raised the general question
of Elizabethan ideas of order, itself so big as to require separate
treatment. Thus I was constrained to write the *Elizabethan World
Picture* before being free to write on Shakespeare's History Plays, just as
I was later constrained to write on Shakespeare's History Plays before
being free to write on the epic at large. My book on Shakespeare's
History Plays appeared in 1945, and I have at length, in the present
volume, fulfilled the plan roughed out in the Warton Lecture for 1936.

One of the things I hope to have done in this book is to make connections between works not usually related. This process may, at first
sight, look odd. What on earth, the reader may well ask, can the

History of Herodotus, *Piers Plowman*, and Pope's *Iliad* have in common? All I can do is to suggest patience and second thoughts, and to claim that I have made no new connections without thinking them over for a number of years.

In the matter of bulk I have pleased myself, choosing not to be cramped in the treatment of a large subject. Many possible readers will be put off by such length. I wish to remind them that most of my sections on important writers can be read and mainly understood separately. To consider a man as an epic writer often includes considering his general literary worth. I hope that this book, as well as following a theme and telling a story, contains fresh studies of some important works of literature.

I was relieved to find that Sir Maurice Bowra's book on heroic poetry was radically different from mine on the epic. Even when we write of the same works, which is not often, we look at different sides of them. Certain recent books, for instance Sir John Myres's on Herodotus and Professor C. L. Wrenn's on *Beowulf*, were published too late for me to be able to consult.

I must record a debt of encouragement to Mr C. S. Lewis's *Allegory of Love*. Here, I have felt all along, is the kind of book I should like to write: something that includes a great deal of matter, even of detail, but which succeeds in remaining to the last page a book and never degenerates into a compilation. I may not have thus succeeded, but the example of success has been a continuous help towards whatever, in fact, I have achieved.

I owe a special debt of thanks to my wife for making a far better index than I should have had the patience to make on my own resources, and for saving me from many mistakes.

Mr Geoffrey Ivy and Dr Rosemary Freeman read and criticised my chapters on Langland and Spenser respectively. I am indebted to their comments, not only in point of gratitude for the trouble taken but because I found them just and have acted on them.

It is now a quarter of a century since my friend and former pupil, Mr Ian Parsons, asked me to let the firm of publishers to which he belonged see the manuscript of my *Milton*. Through that request Chatto and Windus have published, from then on, almost everything I have written. And I wish to express to that firm and to Mr Parsons in particular my thanks for their courtesy, their good judgement, and for the fair and friendly treatment they have always accorded me.

I wish to thank the Columbia University Press together with the Oxford University Press for their courtesy in allowing me to use their *Works of John Milton* for my quotations from that author. The Johns Hopkins University Press has kindly allowed me to reprint a few sentences from my *English Renaissance: Fact or Fiction?*

E. M. W. T.

CONTENTS

vii

INTRODUCTION

THE NATURE OF THE EPIC

1. THE HEROIC POEM

TILL recently critics used the terms *epic* and *heroic poem* as names for the same thing; and a safe and good way of treating the subject is to continue this practice while limiting and clarifying it. Certainly you must set limits if you are to avoid confusion. Milton knew that *Paradise Lost* was not heroic in the Homeric sense and proceeded to claim that his own, sacred, subject was more, not less, heroic than Homer's or Virgil's. Today we see that his knowledge was truer than his claim. Thanks (in this country at least) mainly to the Chadwicks, we tend to shift the heroic idea from literature in general and to centre it in a particular, early, stage of man's evolution. In accord with this shift heroic poetry ceases to be poetry with a nominally heroic subject and becomes the narrative verse with a heroic subject belonging to the heroic age, at whatever date or in whatever part of the world that age manifested itself. It is eminently a post-Darwinian conception and it is in its own fashion satisfactory today. On it C. M. Bowra wrote his recent book, *Heroic Poetry*.[1]

But if you use the conception you should play fair and not stretch it beyond its proper bounds. It certainly embraces some things in Homer, it might be stretched to embrace some things in Virgil, it certainly does not embrace *Paradise Lost*. If you want, as I do, to consider the literature, heroic in name, that grew out of the genuine heroic ages but was not of them, you have to seek another entry into the subject.

The great age of this kind of English epic was that of the revival of learning. It knew nothing of heroic ages as such and was little versed in the heroic poetry they produced. It considered Homer not less adult a poet than Virgil. It had great confidence in the epic as a literary form and it had some success in producing actual epic poems. It looks as if there were an initial chance of entering my subject through what people thought of it in the days of its greatness. Let me therefore turn to neo-classic theories of the epic form.

[1] London 1952

I

2. NEO-CLASSIC THEORY

Pernassus hill, upon whose Airy top
The Epick *Poets so divinely show,*
And with just pride behold the rest below.
(The Earl of Mulgrave, *An Essay upon Poetry,* 1682)

No one can go far in the history of poetry without recognizing the
power of formal and abstract ideals, especially in the age of the
Renaissance. Of the empty patterns that fascinate the minds of poets
there were two pre-eminent: the Heroic Poem and classical tragedy.
(W. P. Ker)

It is now well known that *Paradise Lost* was no isolated achievement. It represented what many authors, English and foreign, were
trying to do. Where it differed from other seventeenth- or early
eighteenth-century epics was in its success. Now the aim common to
Milton's *Paradise Lost,* Blackmore's *King Arthur,* Courtin's *Charlemagne*
Pénitent, or Voltaire's *Henriade* was more than the simple one of writing
a successful poem in an acknowledged and valued literary form and
of thereby satisfying the motives of ambition or self-expression. It
included more and it was more solemn. For several reasons, and
particularly through the accepted and unchallenged pre-eminence of
Homer and Virgil among the world's poets, the heroic or epic poem
was accounted, axiomatically, the noblest literary form. Every par-
ticle of all the motives that urged the men of the Renaissance to prize
and revere and imitate classical antiquity united in asserting the
value, even the sacrosanctity, of the epic form in its strict classical
manifestation.

But the sense of that sacrosanctity could not consist in, or at least
remain, a timeless and uncircumstantiated adoration of the antique;
inevitably it took its colour from contemporary habits of thought.
One of those habits was patriotism, another had to do with a taste for
abstractions, possibly derived from the Renaissance reverence for
Plato. When nations formed and then recognised themselves, they
became aware at the same time of their own languages. It would
never do to admit that your language, however embryonic at the
moment, lacked the highest potentialities. It followed that when an
author realised, in a small or a great work of literature, a potentiality
of his vernacular, he deserved well of his country. And if the work was
an epic on accredited classical lines, he deserved stupendously. It
was with this ambition of stupendous national desert that Milton
made his plans for a great poem. He decided

to be an interpreter and relater of the best and sagest things among
mine own Citizens throughout this Iland in the mother dialect.

That what the greatest and choycest wits of *Athens*, *Rome*, or modern *Italy*, and those Hebrews of old did for their country, I in my proportion with this over and above of being a Christian, might doe for mine.[1]

About the taste for abstractions it is more dangerous to speak. Perhaps current ideas of kingship furnish an analogy. In earlier times, this or that king had, as the Lord's anointed, been sacred, and so he may have continued to be. But in the seventeenth century the idea of kingship and the awe attached to the abstracted idea reinforced the sanctity of this or that king. Every king embodied the idea, and to embody it worthily was a feat of almost mystical significance. To the thorough-going neo-classic the Rules stood to this or that work in which they were manifested somewhat as the idea of kingship to this or that king. In spite of complaints that the Three Unities forced an author to forgo many cherished beauties, they were principally an *ideal* from whose free and faithful realisation a great good might flow. When Rymer attacked Shakespeare and Fletcher for wrenching their characters away from the type proper to their setting, he believed them to be violating another such ideal. Now the classical form of the epic was yet another. To go against it was sacrilege; to realize it worthily in a work of art an achievement almost superhuman.

Such is part of the setting of *Paradise Lost* or of any other epic or would-be epic written in western Europe in the age of the new learning. It is a strange complex of ideas, some might say perverse, but it is grand. It meant something to its age and it can still strike and entertain us: it is a topic well worth pursuing. But it does nothing to characterize the epic. It tells us that the epic is the noblest form and that to succeed in it is a virtuous act, but it does not tell us the kind of nobility it attains or the conditions of epic success. And when we turn from the high generalisations of the neo-classic critics to their detailed remarks we get less satisfaction. We learn that a noble kind of verse and of language must accompany the nobility of theme and of personages. We hear disputes on supernatural machinery and the propriety of religious subjects. But we do not find any principle to guide us in deciding whether this or that work does or does not make the epic impression. As a matter of history, as a phase of human thought, the general conception of the neo-classic epic is interesting and invites study. But as a help today for finding one's way in the epic writing of the post-heroic ages it is useless.

Now if the neo-classic age cannot help us enter the subject, no other is likely to do so.

What then is to be done? There is still the safe method of defining the epic in external terms alone. I have already indicated how heroic

---

[1] *Reason of Church Government*, ii. Introduction; Columbia Edition, iii. 1. 236.

poetry can safely be so defined. (And here the chance of internal congruities also is good.) With equal safety but with less profit one could group together all the strict Renaissance and neo-classical imitations of the classical epic, linking Vida's *Christiad* with the *Lusiad* of Camoens and Blackmore's *Prince Arthur* with *Paradise Lost*. By so doing you bring a lot of incongruous stuff together; but that is not your responsibility, for you have committed yourself to no more than to a community of formal features. But mere safety may be dull; and when you find that the classification by form does not take you far (seeing that the worthless and the excellent are subsumed under it) and if you still believe that there are features, other than formal, that distinguish some literary kinds, you are not likely to rest satisfied or to forbear seeking a different criterion. I do retain such a belief while admitting that the literary forms that embody the distinguishing features are liable to change. If I am to write of the epic at all, in the way I want, I must begin by saying what I think the distinguishing features of the epic spirit to be.

3. THE EPIC SPIRIT

> *Tel ouvrage est semblable à ces fecons herbages,*
> *Qui sont fournis de prez et de gras pasturages,*
> *D'une haute fustage, et d'un bocage épais,*
> *Ou courent les ruisseaux, ou sont les ombres frais,*
> *Ou l'on void des estangs, des vallons, des montagnes,*
> *Des vignes, des fruictiers, des forets, des campagnes:*
> *Un Prince en fait son parc, y fait des bastiments. . . .*
> *En l'ouvrage Heroique ainsi chacun se plaist. . . .*
> *C'est un tableau du monde, un miroir qui raporte*
> *Les gestes des mortels en differente sorte.*
> (Vauquelin de la Fresnaye, *L'Art Poétique*)

> *But, as a Court or Kings Palace requires other dimensions then a private house: So the Epick askes a magnitude, from other Poems.*
> (Jonson, *Conversations with Drummond*)

Whether or not the reader likes the ensuing account of the epic, he will have to admit that it squares with a modern practice of going outside the bare form or the bare fact and seeking the essential spirit. A. W. Schlegel used the words *classical* and *romantic* in a very simple sense. *Classical* meant ancient Greek and Roman; *romantic* the Gothic that came after. About a hundred years later Middleton Murry declared that 'Romanticism and Classicism are perennial modes of the human spirit.'[1] The tragic has now for a long time been allowed to exist outside the limits of strict tragedy; it has been found in *Beowulf*, *Lycidas*, the *Ancient Mariner*, and *Madame Bovary*: the comic exists in many places outside the comic drama. By such analogy there is warrant enough for refusing to identify epic with the heroic poem and for seeking its *differentia* in matters other than nominal and formal.

To have any value the definition of a literary term must rest on induction; and anyone who has tried to make his own definition and not merely taken one ready made will find that he has been drawing his generalisation from certain (and for the most part unconsciously selected) examples. Experiments with the word *Metaphysical* (in its poetic sense) convinced me that to define it was to generalise on the data of some of Donne's poems. By such a generalisation other metaphysicising poems, whether by Donne or someone else, had been unconsciously measured. Aristotle defined tragedy through the data supplied by a very small number of plays, and in so doing succeeded well enough to invite imitation. The works that first led me to reflect on the spirit of the epic were the *Iliad*, the *Odyssey*, the *Aeneid*, the *Divine Comedy*, the *Lusiad*, and *Paradise Lost*. It was through the conviction of Dante's being as true an epic writer as Virgil that I abandoned any notion of using the heroic subject as a criterion. Finding the *Aeneid* closer in essentials to the *Divine Comedy* than to the *Argonautica* or *Gondibert*, I had to seek a definition of the epic other than the old heroic one. Of course, one must not conceive of the inductive process too simply. It is not a case of drawing conclusions from a limited set of data uninterrupted to the end and then applying those conclusions to works not yet considered. Rather it is a case of passing to and fro between the works you know you will include and those you think doubtful, and allowing each class to influence the other. Thus I soon inclined to include certain novels among the epics. And such inclusion may have affected my general notions. Sometimes the lack of a quality in a work that could not be included might indicate the presence of it (and hence its general desirability) in a work included beyond doubt though not on precisely realised grounds. I did not include the *Book of Job* among the fully authenticated epics because it does not contain enough; nor *Don Quixote*, not because it is in prose but because its construction does not show the human will stretched and sustained to the utmost. And such negative conclusions may have reinforced or even prompted my criteria of wide inclusiveness and sustained will-power. It has therefore been by finding out what works I admit and what reject, and why, that I have gained my conception of the epic.

The first epic requirement is the simple one of high quality and of high seriousness. It is just conceivable, though superlatively improb-

[1] *To the Unknown God* (London 1924) 136.

able, that the other conditions required to give the epic effect could be fulfilled by mediocre means. Hence the need to insist that the writer of epic must use words in a very distinguished way. So to insist excludes from the epic category, as now being characterised, the *King Arthurs* and the *Leonidas's* and all the other inferiorities cast in the traditional form of the heroic poem.

The second epic requirement can be roughed out by vague words like amplitude, breadth, inclusiveness, and so on. Aristotle indicates it with considerable emphasis through his flagrant failure to perceive it in his infamous last chapter of the *Poetics*. Among his reasons for classing the tragic above the epic form is the reason that tragic imitation gains its end in narrower space—τὸ ἐν ἐλάττονι μήκει τὸ τέλος τῆς μιμήσεως εἶναι—and that the concentrated is more pleasurable than the diluted effect. And he asks us to imagine the *Oedipus* of Sophocles expanded to the length of the *Iliad*. Further, he asserts that genuine unity is impossible in an epic, which provides the material for several tragic unities. Taking tragedy, a highly concentrated form, to be the measure of excellence, Aristotle begs the question by calling epic diluted, but, through the very unfairness of so calling it, directs us to that greater amplitude in the epic, that ability to deal with more sides of life, which differentiates it from the tragic drama.

This difference between tragedy and epic, which Aristotle failed to perceive, is simple and fundamental, resting as it does on the physical conditions governing the two forms. A tragedy is limited in length by the physical comfort of a normal audience. Being serious, it will aim at the weightiest effect and it will gain that effect not by crowding everything into a narrow space—that would daze and weary—but by omitting and simplifying. For whatever reason—and the reason is here irrelevant—tragic writers have abbreviated the local and the communal things and have mainly regarded the most general human passions and the individual's concern with his environment, natural, social, or divine: and by presenting experience through the eyes of the individual have been able to turn the limitation of length to the best account. And through that ability acted tragedy has become as it were the home country of certain types of feeling, a home country from which colonies have settled in countries where other types of feeling are characteristic. Thus there is tragic feeling in *Madame Bovary*, but that feeling is not any feeling peculiar to the novel form; it is colonial rather than autochthonous. The peculiar properties of the epic rest, in their turn, on the practical conditions of its performance. Whether a chieftain and his followers in his hall or a band of pilgrims or holidaymakers gathered for some days at a religious festival formed the audience, they wanted or at least tolerated a longer unit than did an audience crowded into the confined space of a theatre. On the side of production mere narrative was less exacting than the complexities of dramatic circumstance and, granted relays of reciters, admitted of great length. And the right retort to the challenge of length is not repetition but variety.

There are different kinds of variety, and not every kind belongs to the epic. An essay by Aldous Huxley, *Tragedy and the Whole Truth*,[1] will help to make the proper distinction. Huxley begins from the passage in the *Odyssey*, Book Twelve, where Odysseus describes how Scylla snatched six of his men from his ship and devoured them at the threshold of her cave as they cried out in terrible struggle,

αὐτοῦ δ᾽ εἰνὶ θύρῃσι κατήσθιε κεκλήγοντας,
χεῖρας ἐμοὶ ὀρέγοντας ἐν αἰνῇ δηιοτῆτι.

Later Odysseus and his men landed in Sicily, ate their supper, and then bewailed their lost fellows. Huxley observes that the intense limited world of tragedy could never have admitted the cool truth to life of the men lamenting only after they satisfied their appetite. Tragedy can exist only through sacrificing what Huxley calls the 'Whole Truth.' And works that admit the Whole Truth are alien to tragedy.

> Tragedy is an arbitrarily isolated eddy on the surface of a vast river that flows on majestically, irresistibly, around, beneath, and to either side of it. Wholly-Truthful art contrives to imply the existence of the entire river as well as of the eddy. . . . In Wholly-Truthful art the agonies may be just as real, love and the unconquerable mind just as admirable, just as important, as in tragedy. . . . But the agonies and the indomitabilities are placed by the Wholly-Truthful writer in another, wider context, with the result that they cease to be the same as the intrinsically identical agonies and indomitabilities of tragedy.[2]

At first Huxley might seem to be thinking of epic in opposition to tragedy; but he ends his essay by finding his 'Whole Truth' principally in modern literature, which has become

> more and more acutely conscious . . . of the great oceans of irrelevant things, events and thoughts stretching endlessly away in every direction from whatever island point (a character, a story) the author may choose to contemplate.[3]

And he goes on to cite Proust, D. H. Lawrence, Gide, Kafka, and Hemingway as authors all concerned with the whole truth; thus ending in very different places from his point of departure in the *Odyssey*.

---

[1] In *Music at Night* (London 1931) 3-18.
[2] *Ib.* 14-15.   [3] *Ib.* 16.

Huxley is quite right in implying that the epic can contain the tragic. Even in the *Odyssey*, usually considered as an epic touching comedy, two at least of the characters who most have our sympathy are subjected to suffering sufficiently acute to rouse their deep passions and to force them like the tragic sufferer to consider their own predicaments in the total world they inhabit. But in another matter Huxley is wrong; and here he can serve us, as Aristotle did, and through his very error point to the truth. His error is to introduce the *Odyssey*, an epic, into his particular modern context, for the epic is alien to the wandering and fortuitous concatenations that Huxley considers typical of recent literature. It will not tolerate amplitude for its own sake; it is not content with an undifferentiated and unorganised display of life's many phenomena. Like tragedy, although its material is ampler, epic must select, arrange, and organise.

But to dwell on this necessity is to leave the present topic for my next; and it is more to the point to consider the five authors Huxley cites as exemplifying his idea of the whole truth as he believes it to be expressed in recent literature. All five—Proust, D. H. Lawrence, Gide, Kafka, Hemingway—are exceptionally introverted, even at times the victims of morbid sensibilities. Anyhow, none of them is near achieving the psychological strength and the healthy balance of mental parts which must mark the writer of epic. (It is in this matter, among others, that tragedy differs from epic. Being narrower and requiring among its first qualities intensity, it is less liable than the epic to be destroyed by the pathological. Swift and Kafka might reasonably ask to be considered tragic writers, but epic writers never.) While at home in large areas of life, the epic writer must be centred in the normal, he must measure the crooked by the straight, he must exemplify that sanity which has been claimed for true genius. No pronounced homosexual, for instance, could succeed in the epic, not so much for being one as for what his being one cuts him off from. Granted the fundamental sanity, the wider the epic poet's mental span, the better. And ideally he should be able to range from the simple sensualities to a susceptibility to the numinous.

The third epic requirement has been hinted already through what I said about fortuitous concatenations. Exuberance, however varied, is not enough in itself; there must be a control commensurate with the amount included. Once again, the clearest illustrations may be from things that fail in the given requirement. The works of Rabelais include a great deal, they may be ample enough. It is their lack of organisation that keeps them remote from the epic. *Don Quixote*, because less remote, illustrates even better. Here at any rate is the true epic range and a superb quality of prose style. And there are passages (and conspicuously the first quarter of the second part) of such weight and density as to bear comparison with those poems I am using unconsciously as criteria. Cervantes must have exerted his will power-fully to have achieved the sustained excellence of these parts. But the work as a whole is not epic because it is governed by no powerful predetermination. Cervantes gathers weight as he writes. Beginning with a pleasant little buccaneering expedition, he insensibly picks up reinforcements on the way until he realises he has collected an army. And he puts that army to fluctuating use. But this is a very different matter from the author's having his strategy settled beforehand and keeping the whole suspended in his mind until composition is complete.

That indeed is the structural ideal: that the whole, however long, should remain fluid and unset till the last word has been written, that the writer should have everything simultaneously in mind and keep it open to modification throughout the process of composition. This must remain an ideal, for no man has possessed the powers of memory and control necessary to fulfil it. Even Dante was inconsistent. And one should not exclude from all possibilities of epic success a work that settles its parts as it goes along, provided it makes one part truly evolve out of the others, provided it retains a general recollection of what has gone before. Such, I conjecture, was the structural method of the *Faerie Queene*.

This insistence on rigorous control and predetermination as necessary in a certain type of poetry is alien to two powerful trends in recent thought. The first is a hostility to the long poem in general: a hostility due partly to theory and partly to the prevalent taste. The theory is that of Poe,[1] which seeks to prove that a long poem is by nature impossible, poetic inspiration being always evanescent and no verse counting as poetry unless written under inspiration. Any so-called long poem, of however high quality, can do no more than consist of a number of short poems connected by verse that is not poetry at all. Poe's theory suited both the French Symbolist poets and those who, like A. E. Housman, had narrowly inspirational theories of poetry. (Housman, in an unpublished paper on Burns, stated that there were six[2] and no more than six lines of poetry in all Burns's works.) And the influence of the theory has extended well into the twentieth century. As to the matter of taste, how should an age which multiplies and abbreviates, which favours many short items in its radio programmes, less time devoted to more subjects in schools, readers' digests, and miniature sermons, take to its heart a long poem calling for sustained concentration?

[1] In his essay, *The Poetic Principle*. Some art criticism shows the same trend: for instance that which cries up Claude's drawings and cries down his elaborate classical landscapes. Of course the drawings are spontaneous in a way the oil-paintings are not; but to make such spontaneity the only test is critical bigotry.

[2] I cannot vouch for the exact figure, having to rely on my memory of hearing the paper read.

The other trend is psychological, that towards valuing the spontaneous, unconscious element in art or in life and towards distrusting the exercise of the conscious will. Aldous Huxley's assertion just quoted, that modern literature is concerned with 'the great oceans of irrelevant things, events and thoughts stretching endlessly away in every direction,' is a good enough illustration.

It is obvious that in writing a long poem or a long highly organised work in prose, the composition of which is perforce extended over years, an author cannot sustain a spontaneous vein of creation. At intervals he will be tempted to break the unity of the original conception and stray after new emotional interests. Spontaneity will not suffice, and the author will have to summon his will to help him abide by the plans he has resolved on. The writing of any poem (except one dictated in dream or trance) needs some effort of the will to control and shape it. But the effort is different in a lyric, a short story, and a play, while only in the most intensely written long works is the will taxed to the utmost. Such sustained writing corresponds to certain phases of the active life. Just as the will may force a man's conduct at a particular time (for instance on an expedition of exploration) to conform to a previously adopted set of resolves, against his present inclinations, so a poet may use his will to suppress new interests and preserve a unity previously resolved on.

Further, in the making of a long poem the will is more than an external driving force; the fact of its exercise and the belief in it become a highly important part of the total experience. Milton speaks of how the Dorian mood of flutes and soft recorders raised

> To highth of noblest temper Hero's old
> Arming to Battel, and in stead of rage
> Deliberate valour breath'd.

But even if Milton had never used the phrase, 'deliberate valour' (which describes my meaning so concisely), his belief in the quality of considered courage, aware of issues, which implies the application of the will, would be apparent from the whole trend of his rhetoric. Moreover, in *Paradise Lost*, as in other genuine epics, the very passages which the will has forced into harmony with the more spontaneously composed ones are significant as declaring the value of the quality to which they owe a large part of their being.

This exercise of the will and the belief in it, which are a corollary of our third epic requirement, help to associate epic poetry with the largest human movements and solidest human institutions. In creating what we call civilisation the sheer human will has had a major part.

Although, for my own purposes, I have dissociated epic from the heroic poem, that is the verse narrative of heroic deeds in the heroic age, I want to insist that the true epic creates a 'heroic impression.'

And that impression has to do with, is a by-product of, the present topic: the control of a large material and the exercise of the conscious will. Heroic poetry often concerns actions in which men know exactly what they are doing and rise through deliberate valour to a great height of resolution. And it is natural enough to attribute the heroic impression to a poem's heroic subject matter. But in fact that impression depends also, indeed ultimately, on the temper of treatment. A heroic theme may encourage a writer to treat it in a sustained, 'heroic' way, to exercise his will to the utmost; but this does not prevent the treatment's being the decisive element. If this is the case with heroic poetry, it follows that literature lacking a heroic subject is not debarred from making the heroic impression. Here Dante is especially apt. His subject is not at all the old heroic one, though certain of his characters, Farinata and Ulysses for instance, may be of the antique heroic cast. But it is not they that make the heroic impression; it is rather the vast exercise of the will which went to the shaping of the whole poem. The *Faerie Queene* fails of the full heroic impression in spite of its chivalrous setting. And it does so because its organisation is rather loose.

Of course, the epic cannot avoid the defects and the risks of its virtues. The freshness of even its most spontaneous parts cannot share the freshness of certain lyrics. Very long time spent in composition may tax the will more than is healthy and make a man grim. This may explain why in his final version of *Piers Plowman* Langland cut down his prologue and deprived it of some of its most charming touches. Of all the epic poets, Homer alone quite escapes the mode's characteristic dangers. But these dangers are negligible in contrast with the possible majesty. There is nothing so exciting and so awe-inspiring in the world of letters as the spectacle of a great spirit daring to risk everything on one great venture and knowing that in its execution he will be taxed to the limit of what a man can endure.

All the same, I know that some readers will never find the epic congenial. There will always be those who think that it is of the very nature of art to be incomplete and to demonstrate in its action the principles of growth. For them it will be a sin to impose unity on work composed over so long a period of time that the author, if he is alive and moving, cannot feel quite consistently throughout. They will think it more natural for a man to empty his changing self into a series of plays or novels or lyrics, where no one of these is definitive but each grows out of its predecessors into something fresh. And they will find these words of Conrad apt to all great creative writing:

> In the body of Mr Henry James's work there is no suggestion of finality, nowhere a hint of surrender, to his own victorious achievement in that field where he is a master. Happily, he will never be

able to claim completeness; and were he to confess to it in a moment of self-ignorance, he would not be believed by the very minds for whom such a confession naturally would be meant. It is impossible to think of Mr Henry James becoming 'complete' otherwise than by the brutality of our common fate whose finality is meaningless— in the sense of its logic being of a natural order, the logic of a falling stone.[1]

It is perfectly true that it suits some writers to have their say in instalments; and no reasonable person would compel them to another method. Others dislike the brokenness of the method more than they like its freedom. They desire a single principle of organisation, the all-inclusive work of art. Each method expresses things denied to the other; and to set up the *Divine Comedy* and the plays of Shakespeare as rivals is unnaturally to narrow the bounds of the human spirit.

The fourth requirement can be called choric. The epic writer must express the feelings of a large group of people living in or near his own time. The notion that the epic is primarily patriotic is an unduly narrowed version of this requirement. Should a country command at some time an exceptionally clear ethical temper, that temper may serve an author well enough. Spenser, for instance, does express the Elizabethan temper successfully in the *Faerie Queene*. But the group-feeling need not be national. Dante is medieval rather than Italian. And it is wise not to bring in nationalism at all. Better, with Lascelles Abercrombie,[2] to look on the epic poet as

accepting, and with his genius transfiguring, the general circumstance of his time . . . symbolizing, in some appropriate form, whatever sense of the significance of life he feels acting as the accepted unconscious metaphysic of the time.

We can simplify even further and say no more than that the epic must communicate the feeling of what it was like to be alive at the time. But that feeling must include the condition that behind the epic author is a big multitude of men of whose most serious convictions and dear habits he is the mouthpiece.

It is in this matter that epic most differs from tragedy. Tragedy cannot lack some imprint of its age, but its nature is to be timeless. It deals with the recurrent human passions and it presents them (having no space to do more) in their bare elements with the least local circumstantiation. It teaches not what it is like to be alive at a certain time but what it is like to be a human being. But though the choric element is necessary to epic and at best adventitious in tragedy, it does not exclude from epic the presentation of those timeless feelings

---

[1] *Notes on Life and Letters* (London 1921) 14.
[2] *The Epic* (London, not dated) 39.

which it is tragedy's privilege to isolate and clarify. Indeed, the greatness of epic will partly depend on the inclusion of such feelings. It is when the tragic intensity coexists with the group-consciousness of an age, when the narrowly timeless is combined in a unit with the variegatedly temporal, that epic attains its full growth.

Lascelles Abercrombie postulates that the epic not only should express the 'accepted unconscious metaphysic' of its age but do so through a clear and authentic story, a story known and already part of the mythology of the audience. I disagree with this further demand. Certainly, the material of the epic should be largely public, but not necessarily in the form of a narrative where the concatenation of sequent events holds a large proportion of the reader's interest. The 'accepted unconscious metaphysic' is the essential starting-point, but the method of conveying it must vary from age to age. When an age holds one kind of opinion on the nature of man, the heroic story may best represent the current metaphysic. But other forms may suit other ages. The Middle Ages regarded man differently and they could not make the heroic story the most serious literary form. Allegory better answered their requirement. In the age of Elizabeth, when the Middle Ages and the new classicism of the Renaissance met, heroic action and allegory combined to express the most serious concerns. In the eighteenth century, prose fiction began potentially to be the best epic medium invading what had been mainly the province of verse. In sum the choric nature of the epic does not dictate any rigidly answering form.

Finally, not every 'accepted unconscious metaphysic' can prompt an epic. If for instance it is predominantly elegiac or nostalgic, it cannot serve. Nietzsche believed tragedy to be possible only in an age of optimism. Epic, in similar fashion, must have faith in the system of beliefs or way of life it bears witness to. The reason for this belongs to other qualities of the epic than the choric. Only when people have faith in their own age can they include the maximum of life in their vision and exert their will-power to its utmost capacity.

4. SCOPE OF THIS BOOK

My main object has been to assemble and to comment on those works of English literature that best embody the epic spirit as I have just described it. But I am interested also in the changes that have occurred in the appropriate embodiments of that spirit and, as described above, in that quasi-mystical conception of the classicising epic dominant in the neo-classic ages. This neo-classic conception ceased to be effective towards the end of the eighteenth century, causing a marked break both in the history of the official epic and in the forms the epic spirit was likely to assume. Here, I was convinced, was the right place to stop even at the cost of omitting certain later works that merit the name epic.

The centre, then, of this book, as I have planned it, is the assembly and the description of the seven English works which, up to the end of the eighteenth century, seem to me most worthily to embody the epic spirit: *Piers Plowman*, the *Faerie Queene*, *Arcadia*, *Paradise Lost*, the *Holy War*, Pope's *Iliad*, and the *Decline and Fall of the Roman Empire*. But I am also interested in some of the near-successes and generally in the interstices between these works. Again, I want to picture the form the epic would have taken in certain vacant ages, had a great enough poet been writing then. I am interested too in the foreign works that helped to form these successful embodiments of the epic spirit in England and in the foreign critics who helped to form the English critics' ideas of the epic kind. A great deal then has accumulated around the seven works that form the core of this book: and most of it demands historical treatment.

I do not think the reader will find it hard to see which of these ends I am pursuing at any one time. Let me give a few instances. I include Douglas's *Aeneid* because, though a translation, it has strong marks of originality and belongs eminently to its age, and further because, though it fails to embody the epic spirit, it is, as it were, on the road to the epic and not to some other destination. I include Berners's *Golden Book of Marcus Aurelius* and Elyot's *Image of Governance* because they seem to me to indicate the form the epic would have taken in the age of Henry VIII had there been a writer capable of the task. I include Cowley's *Davideis* not because it even begins to be a true epic but as a poem, not without merit, written at the dictates of neo-classic epic theory. I include Sidney's *Arcadia* both for its own sake as true epic and for the sake of the critical theory it exemplifies.

It remains to justify certain exclusions and inclusions. There is no reason why the dramatic form, unconfined by the needs of the theatre, should not compass epic significance. And a sequence of acted plays might elude the bounds usually set by those needs. *Faust* and the *Dynasts* are conspicuous examples of nominal drama aspiring to epic height. I have argued elsewhere that Shakespeare's historical sequences are the nearest existing approach to an Elizabethan epic.[1] It might even be claimed that a whole medieval dramatic cycle is worthy to stand by *Piers Plowman*. Whether logically or not, but certainly in the interests of curtailment, I draw the line this side dramatic literature of any kind and confine my examples rigidly to narrative, whether verse or prose.

I hold that in the eighteenth century the epic impulse left poetry for the novel. It was not in Britain that the epic as novel reached its

[1] *Shakespeare's History Plays* (London 1944).

height in subsequent years. But it flourished there sufficiently to constitute a very big topic. Making so big a topic and being largely a new growth, I have excluded it on grounds both of length and of fitness.

I have included history, in a way against my will, my subject being quite heavy enough without it. My reasons have to do both with literary value and with neo-classic theory. Herodotus and Gibbon forced themselves on me as writers who partly fulfilled the epic function. Further, the neo-classic critics constantly bring epic and history together, if only to say that the epic writer must not be too historical. And lastly Gibbon seemed to me directly inspired by neo-classic theories of the epic when he came to consider a subject for historical writing. As a subject for artistic creation, history is uncertain. But at times it presents a favourable shape and, contrary to Aristotle, can form the ground of a literary product no less philosophical than poetry. It can also serve to objectify the feelings of a large group of people. Though not likely to lead to epic, history will never lack the potentiality of doing so, and hence demands inclusion in the present study.

Part One

Classical

CHAPTER I

INTRODUCTORY

TO the creation of the English epic certain classical writings served as a permanent background. They were five poems and one prose work (with a possible second). The poems were Homer's *Iliad* and *Odyssey*, Virgil's *Aeneid*, Lucan's *Pharsalia*, and Statius's *Thebaid*. The prose work was Xenophon's *Cyropedia*, and the possible second was the *Aethiopica* of Heliodorus. These works, not all necessarily epic in the sense in which I use the word, were acknowledged as the classics of epic writing, and when an English writer of the Renaissance or neo-classic periods tried to write an epic he had them consciously or unconsciously in his mind as points of reference. Beyond doubt a book on the English epic and its background should deal with these, while it should be excused from dealing with other writings that might have to figure in a history of the classical epic proper.

There is less reason for writing of Homer than of the other three poets. During most of the period of English literature under review few educated men could read Greek as easily as Latin; and, however much Homer may have meant to the especially learned writers like Daniel and Milton, as a general influence he did not count for so much as Lucan and Statius, let alone Virgil. But as well as being a potent influence on the few in England, Homer has his place in this book as the necessary prelude to Virgil. He set the general pattern of the classical epic once and for all. I shall therefore deal with Homer at some length, but at shorter length than Virgil, who, in fact though not always in repute, was the supreme master.

Herodotus, of whom I have much to say, is in something of the same position as Homer. He was less read and had less influence than Livy and Sallust, but he was the father of history, and of Latin as much as of Greek. That is why I have to include him, but because of his rare merit and because that merit is too little known to the common reader I may have said more about him than strictly I should.

I have tried in this, classical, part to address myself as elsewhere to the non-specialist reader. But, educated a Classic, I may at times and without meaning it have in fact addressed myself to the dwindling company of my fellows. It is indeed difficult to keep one's bearings in a period of transition like the present, when fewer know the originals but many more are getting to know some of the classical masterpieces through translations. Because of this familiarity I have assumed that the educated reader of today will not object to being told something about Herodotus and Lucan and Statius, whom he probably will not know, and reading longer accounts of Homer and Virgil, whom probably he will know in translations.

Though educated a Classic I am not one professionally; but the licence of the general practitioner to add his opinion to that of the specialist holds good for classical as much as for any other literature. The risk of such a licence is plain, but poets are poets and behave as such whatever their date, and the comparisons the wider-ranging amateur brings to bear on some problems usually left to the professionals may hit the truth. And that is why I presume to write on Homer and other classical authors.

Finally there is the matter of tone. The right way to speak of the Classics is to use the same tone as in speaking of any other literature, to treat Virgil as one would treat Chaucer or Milton or Yeats. (Such a way has nothing to do with the affectation of making out that ancient literature is after all so modern.) Dryden was the critic who quite succeeded in following this way. I know that I have failed, but not through ignorance of Dryden's example or through any lack of a wish to use it.

CHAPTER II

HOMER

1. GENERAL

*Ut Aratus ab Iove incipiendum putat, ita nos rite coepturi ab Homero
videmur.* (Quintilian)

WHETHER or not critics have done well to divide epics into the
primitive and mature, using such names as *authentic* and *literary*,
primary and *secondary*, or *recited* and *read*, I need not say. All that
matters here is that I cannot put Homer, after one usual practice,
among the primitives. There are primitive elements in Homer: the
inheritance of the technique of recitation shown chiefly in the stock
phrases, or a piece of subject-matter like Achilles's human sacrifice
at Patroclus's funeral, a practice alien to developed Greece. But these
relics count for little compared with the highly civilised and sophisticated results Homer achieves through them. In fact the *Iliad* and the
Odyssey are much more artificial and typically Greek than they are
primitive and heroic. Their case is much that of Marlowe's *Faustus*,
which is primitive in deriving from the medieval Morality Play and
yet whose dominant character is that of Elizabethan energy and fresh
creation.

C. M. Bowra has written well on the traditional and original
elements in Homer in his *Tradition and Design in the Iliad*:[1] for instance:

> The *Iliad* owes much to tradition, but it has qualities such as no
> tradition can impart, qualities which are lacking in the *Nibelungen-
> lied*. The presence of these qualities separates it sharply from its
> German counterpart, and provides a special problem in elucidating
> its origin. The untraditional elements in the *Iliad* are the elements
> which it shares with other great poetry, and the only explanation
> of their existence is that they are the work of a great poet.

Though Homer's style may contain habits outlived by later epic
writers, it is equal to any task:

> A complicated question of psychology or an unexpected techni-
> cality is mastered with the same ease as the simplest narrative.

C. S. Lewis may be right in recognising a connection between the
pomp that accompanied epic recital at the heroic court and the

---

[1] Oxford 1930. Quotations: 43-4, 132. It is of course possible to concentrate on
the primitive elements in Homer, and this Bowra has done in later books. But to do
so is to forsake the *total* literary view.

stylistic pomp of Milton. But when he sites Homer very centrally in the heroic age, in that mere welter of war, where man had no faith or philosophy but acted darkly his own tragic part, I can only differ. The Trojan War, he thinks, is not the subject of the *Iliad* but is the mere background of the personal stories. And it was not till Virgil with his Roman ideal that the epic assumed a cosmic significance.[1] I maintain, on the contrary, that in spite of primitive relics Homer represents the temper of developed Greece.

Since I shall recur to this topic I shall here confine myself to a single illustration. When, in the last book of the *Iliad*, Priam goes by night to beg Hector's body from Achilles, the tension is extreme till Achilles softens and the two break down into tears, Priam for his son and Achilles for his father, of whom Priam has reminded him. We then know that Priam will get Hector's body back, and the tension is relieved. With the relief comes a vacuum, which could be filled with renewed action or some kind of diversion. Homer chooses diversion: he makes Achilles urge Priam to join him in a meal and gives for reason the precedent of Niobe, who, though Apollo and Artemis had killed all her children, yet did not refuse food when she was tired with weeping

ἡ δ' ἄρα σίτου μνήσατ', ἐπεὶ κάμε δάκρυ χέουσα.
νῦν δέ που ἐν πέτρῃσιν, ἐν οὔρεσιν οἰοπόλοισιν
ἐν Σιπύλῳ, ὅθι φασὶ θεάων ἔμμεναι εὐνὰς
νυμφάων, αἵ τ' ἀμφ' Ἀχελώιον ἐρρώσαντο,
ἔνθα λίθος περ ἐοῦσα θεῶν ἐκ κήδεα πέσσει.[2]

This generalising of Priam's grief by citing the similar fate of Niobe not only tells us of Achilles's exquisite tact, when no longer the victim of his passions, but exhibits a common pattern for the choric songs in Greek tragedy. The Greek habit was not to allow the unhappy instance, just shown on the stage, to remain unassociated; this must be put into proportion by being placed in the context of other similar happenings. This habit has nothing to do with primitive heroic poetry and is above all things Greek.

While a precise date matters little to suit this Greek quality, one late enough to allow continuity of spirit with Pindar, Attic drama, and Herodotus is required. Thus I welcome the recent inclination to advance Homer's date to the mid-eighth century.[3] That Homer

---

[1] *A Preface to Paradise Lost* (London 1944) 15-29.

[2] *Iliad* xxiv. 613-17. 'And she thought of food, when she was tired with weeping. And now somewhere among the rocks in the lonely mountains, on Sipylos, where they say are the beds of the nymphs who dance by the Achelous, there, although turned to stone, she broods over her god-sent griefs.'

[3] E.g. Miss H. L. Lorimer, *Homer and the Monuments* (London 1950) 464, dates the Homeric poems 750-700. From her long survey of the archaeological evidence she concludes that while Homer preserves certain features of the Bronze Age culture, these are much fewer than used to be supposed (452).

belonged to the heroic age he described, living before the first millennium B.C., and was separated from historical Greece by the gap of the Dorian invasions is a notion incompatible not only with the spiritual kinship just illustrated but with Homer's own references to his heroes: that race of men so much more heroic than those of his own day. In fact, Homer treated the departed heroic age much as Shakespeare treated the England of before both Reformation and Wars of the Roses. Shakespeare, writing for Protestants, easily makes the early Catholic world his subject, as when his Henry says before Agincourt:

> *and I have built*
> *Two Chauntries, where the sad and solemne Priests*
> *Sing still for* Richards *Soule.*[1]

And when Shakespeare pictures the chivalric pomp of the lists at Coventry in *Richard II*, though he writes confidently, he knows that the England he describes, with its knightly practices and a genuine antique aristocracy still flourishing, had a glamour remote from the Elizabethan:

> Harry *of* Herford, Lancaster, *and* Derbie,
> *Stands heere for God, his Soveraigne, and himselfe,*
> *On paine to be found false, and recreant,*
> *To prove the Duke of Norfolke,* Thomas Mowbray,
> *A Traitor to his God, his King, and him*
> *And dares him to set forwards to the fight.*[2]

But this confidence in picturing the manner of a past age does not prevent Shakespeare from presenting a very Elizabethan London in *Henry IV* and in the much remoter period of King John that highly topical climber, the Bastard Falconbridge. Such is the mixture of antique and contemporary that can be expected in Homer also.

Next, I find it hard to admit different authors of the *Iliad* and the *Odyssey*. There may be differences of style, but unless they can be proved to be greater than those between, for instance, the *Comedy of Errors* and *Cymbeline*, they are no argument. On the contrary, you expect a poet's style to change over the years. The strongest argument for single authorship is the likeness of general conception. Both include the same areas of existence but in different and contrasted proportions. The *Iliad* is primarily warlike and political, and its men are heroic fighters or statesmen. Such problems as what good it is to fight and how political unity may be achieved are paramount. The *Odyssey* is primarily peaceful and domestic; its politics are local. Odysseus strives for an ordered and settled home life, which he not only re-

---

[1] *Hen. V*, iv. 1. 309-11.
[2] *Rich. II*, i. 3. 110-15.

establishes in Ithaca but witnesses in Phaeacia, his son too having witnessed it in Pylos and Sparta. It also feeds man's appetite for the strange and the fabulous. But each poem covers in a subsidiary way the areas of life which are the other's primary concern. In the *Iliad* Homer is constantly showing his awareness of the peaceful and the domestic: even to the point of insinuating it at the most thrilling moments of warlike action. Thus Achilles and Hector, the one pursuing and the other pursued round Troy walls, pass certain landmarks, including the two fountains, hot and cold; and Homer for a second interposes the picture of the Trojan wives and girls bringing the washing there in the days of peace before the Achaeans came,

ὅθι εἵματα σιγαλόεντα
πλύνεσκον Τρώων ἄλοχοι καλαί τε θύγατρες
τὸ πρὶν ἐπ᾽ εἰρήνης, πρὶν ἐλθέμεν υἷας Ἀχαιῶν.[1]

There is a lot about washing clothes in the *Odyssey*, but Homer shows that in the *Iliad* too he knew just as much about it. When Achilles received his new-made armour from Thetis he gave a great shout to summon the Greeks to war. At this the sailors and the storekeepers, who normally kept by the ships, turned out to watch the army muster.[2] Homer shows by this single touch that he had these civilians in his mind all through the *Iliad*. The same is true about the fabulous. There is much more of it in the *Odyssey*, but there are passages in the *Iliad* (like the story of Bellerophon, who killed the Chimaera, in Book Six) which have just the same fabulous note. In the *Odyssey*, the Trojan War and, after it was won, the fortunes of the Greek chiefs other than Odysseus are never forgotten. The suitors' usurpation is a political matter, and Odysseus is as much the strategist in Ithaca as at Troy. In sum both poems show the cast of one wide-embracing mind, a mind ever preserving the balance between peace and war. Far from assigning them to different authors I should compare them jointly to Arnold Bennett's *Old Wives' Tale* with its contrasted pictures of the two sisters' fortunes.[3]

[1] xxii. 153-6. '(the washing-places) where the wives and fair daughters of the Trojan men used to wash their bright clothes, in the former time of peace, before the sons of the Achaeans came.'

[2] xix. 43-5. I owe my first recognition of this passage's importance to a lecture by D. S. Robertson.

[3] To write thus about the *Iliad* and the *Odyssey* is to contradict the recent opinion of a very influential scholar, Werner Jaeger. In his *Paideia*, Vol. 1 (Oxford 1939) chap. 1, after an admirable account of the ethics of the two poems, Jaeger argues for a widely discrepant date for them on the ground that they mirror two different stages of culture. In this argument he treats the two works not as living poetry but as a mass of dead data. The *Iliad* may indeed include more primitive substance than does the *Odyssey*, but this is precisely the case with *Hamlet* and *As You Like It* respectively. By Jaeger's method of argument Shakespeare could not possibly have written both plays.

2. THE ILIAD

About the poetic excellence of the different parts of the *Iliad*, narrative skill, characterisation, force of style, etc., there is general agreement, and little need be said. However ready-made some Homeric phrases may be, Homer, it is admitted, can put them to effective and, if necessary, new use. He can say just what he wants to say. The first epic requirement is fulfilled.

The question of amplitude and variety has already arisen indirectly. If, as has been pointed out, Homer is both a channel for earlier habits of thought and the fountain-head of very persistent and important later ones, he must achieve one kind of variety. But he is ample also in that he has an eye for everything: nothing escapes it. And that width of vision, comprehending every detail, in no way impairs the man's concentration on the business he has in hand. Shakespeare, and perhaps no other poet, equals him in this union of concentration and flexibility. The first book of the *Iliad* gives in little the prevalent Homeric method. It begins with a display of the most violent passions in the quarrel between Agamemnon and Achilles over the return of Briseis: a scene confined and concentrated in the manner of tragedy. It is followed by a scene of greatly lowered passion but more widely set and pictured with no less intensity, the intensity now concerning the warmth with which the details are apprehended and presented. It represents Agamemnon's two emissaries, coming to Achilles's tent to fetch away Briseis. The details are few, but all necessary, and each stands out with an uncommon clarity like the folds of bare hills lit by the evening sun on a very clear day. The emissaries approach and Achilles was not glad—οὐδ' ἄρα τώ γε ἰδὼν γήθησεν Ἀχιλλεύς. They stand in embarrassment, till Achilles tells them to get on with their business. They are not to blame, but Agamemnon. And when they leave, Achilles goes apart by the sea, to digest his wrongs and to call his mother from the waters to help him. And the very slight elaboration of seascape beyond one consisting of the bare conventional descriptive phrases serves to suggest the aptness of associating a lonely part of the shore and the digestion of grief:

αὐτὰρ Ἀχιλλεὺς
δακρύσας ἑτάρων ἄφαρ ἕζετο νόσφι λιασθεὶς
θῖν' ἐφ' ἁλὸς πολιῆς, ὁράων ἐπὶ οἴνοπα πόντον.[1]

In the picture of the two emissaries, not liking their job and standing embarrassed before Achilles, there is the slightest touch of comedy; and in the subsequent scene on Olympus full comedy emerges. Hera is angry that Thetis and Zeus have been hatching something between

[1] *Iliad*, i. 348-50. 'But Achilles wept and sat down apart, separated from his companions, on the shore of the grey salt-sea, looking over the wide ocean.'

them that she knows nothing of; and Zeus replies that there *are* things he means to keep to himself, though she will be the first to hear anything that he thinks fit to divulge. We are in fact in the social world, where folk quarrel yet somehow in the end conform to an agreed standard of conduct, where Zeus has a hard task in controlling his unruly household of deities and just (but only just) succeeds.

But Homer does more than observe and set forth life's many varieties. He recognises incompatibilities and paradoxes, and like the other great poets he can be on both sides at once. The largest paradox has to do with war and peace, and it takes us to the heart of Homer's philosophy and of the scheme of his poem. First, Homer believes that the works of peace are good and that the sacking of cities is terrible. One of the cities Hephaestus represented on Achilles's shield was at peace, and a bridal procession was in progress. In the torchlight they were leading the brides through the streets, while the bridal song was being sung and young men were whirling in the dance; and the women stood on their doorsteps watching and admiring. Homer is in love with his picture as he is with those of ploughing and vintage.[1] He is equally horrified with the foreboding he puts into Hector's mouth of Andromache led to captivity; Hector, uttering it, prays he may be in his grave before he witnesses the sight and hears her cries.[2] But there is another side, as certain and as unescapable. Honour is another value and it can be won only at the expense of the other value. The best men have to sack cities, for only so is the highest vitality achieved and the shortness of life redeemed.

Homer keeps hinting at this double theme, but does not allow it to become very evident till a third of the way through the poem. It is in the ninth book that he shows us Achilles confronted with the two values between which he had made his choice before coming to Troy.[3] There Achilles, though still implacable to Agamemnon and scornful of his gifts, opens his heart to Odysseus and Ajax, the bearers of Agamemnon's offers, whom he respects. He tells how his mother Thetis foresaw that he could choose between two destinies: that of honour and that of domestic happiness. If he joined the Trojan expedition, he would earn the highest honour but lose his life; if he stayed at home, he would inherit his father's wealth and live long. The ordered domestic life and the sanctity of property: Achilles does not underprize these things. But he made his choice, and, having made it, acted on it thoroughly. He slaved for honour, laying waste twenty-three cities in the Troad for little return. And now, as he told his mother when he called her from the sea near the beginning of the poem, Agamemnon has robbed him of his honour. And so he proposed to go back on his choice and return home to live to old age.

There is not space to enlarge further on Homer's variety in the

---

[1] xviii. 491-6, 541-72.   [2] vi. 450-65.   [3] 395-439.

Iliad. The sum of the matter is that his mind spanned most of life as
then experienced.

Spanning so much, he increased the task of shaping his material.
He fulfilled it principally in two ways: through his hero and through
making his limited plot so pregnant that a few days' fighting implied
the whole course of the Trojan War.

Achilles is not a mere fighter; he draws into himself and unifies all
the scattered references to the morality of his time. He is a man sinned
against, sinning, and repentant. Agamemnon did him a great
wrong. But, in the scene where he spoke of the choice offered to him
between short life with honour and long domestic joy without, he fell
into the great error of refusing Agamemnon's attempt to make
amends. He rejected the Prayers, that were the daughters of Zeus, as
Homer allegorically put it. From that refusal came Patroclus's entry
into battle without Achilles and his death at Hector's hand. That
death brings Achilles back to battle but not to his right mind. He
kills Hector but insults his body, a dreadful crime which the gods
abhor. Only at the very end when Priam goes in person to beg his
son's body does Achilles repent. This repentance is invaluable structurally. It exemplifies that reverence for the agreed decencies of life
which was central to Homer's morality and for a moment at least it
unites the two opposed values of honour and domestic order. To make
my point I must go into a little detail. Priam pursues his dangerous
quest by night. He goes to Achilles's tent with a ransom and performs
the act of a suppliant. In the terms of Homer's earlier allegory,
Prayers, the daughters of Zeus, approach Achilles once more. Priam
in making his plea reminds Achilles of his father, Peleus. This time
Achilles does not fail to reverence the daughters of Zeus. But he does
more. The thought of Peleus, old and childless but for himself, who
is destined soon to die, stirs his sense of pity, which is extended to
Priam, old too and now nearly childless by his own action. At this
culminating place in the poem Achilles learns that the two worlds of
war and home may be seen in a common light. Though Priam is his
enemy, and doubly so because Priam's son killed Patroclus, he applies
to him the emotion of pity, an emotion proper to the domestic life.
He also gets out of the immediate business of war and bereavement to
a position from which he can view all the varieties of experience
together. First he describes Peleus's fortune and misfortune, then
Priam's early wealth and present plight, and between the two
descriptions come the lines

οὐδέ νυ τόν γε
γηράσκοντα κομίζω, ἐπεὶ μάλα τηλόθι πάτρης
ἧμαι ἐνὶ Τροίῃ σέ τε κήδων ἠδὲ σὰ τέκνα.[1]

[1] xxiv. 540-2. 'Nor may I look after him as he grows old, since very far from my
country I am settled at Troy, vexing you and your children.'

For a moment friend and foe are one, as Achilles sees himself the bane of both: of his father by leaving him in his old age, of Priam by killing his sons. Poised on that height, Achilles is the spectator and critic of both the realms between which he had to choose.

The main lines of the structure are majestic and satisfying; and there are signs of the author's bearing the whole in his mind through-out.[1] Homer set himself the difficult task of combining two themes, the whole Trojan War and the personal story of Achilles: difficult, but, if successful, perfect for epic purposes. His method is to begin and end with the two themes intertwined. The anger of Achilles is at once a public disaster and a private passion: the burial of Hector signifies the end of the twelve days' truce which Achilles promised Priam and the end of all Trojan hopes to defend their city—the war is virtually over—as well as the mental regeneration of Achilles. In between, the two themes are often combined, but there are long stretches where one theme (and particularly the first) is to the fore, and the other theme is disengaged, though not absent from the back-ground. The Trojan War was supposed to have lasted ten years, and to give the sense of size and length Homer could not escape including many scenes of fighting. He was interested in military details, but it probably taxed his will-power to the utmost to include so much and yet not to flag. His strategy is to punctuate his fighting with other business, to space it out cunningly; his tactics are to multiply the types of warring acts and to embellish and relieve them by the utmost wealth of simile.

But besides giving in a few days' fighting the sense of a long war, Homer has to imply its course, its beginning, and end. He does so by re-enactment, by prophecy, and by falsification. He re-enacts the beginning of the war at the end of the third and the beginning of the fourth book. There Paris and Menelaus—the two men concerned with the quarrel between Trojans and Greeks—meet in single fight. Menelaus is the stronger and would have killed Paris had not Aphro-dite snatched him away. She carries him to Troy, beautifies him, and brings him and Helen together. Paris, in saying that he now loves her more than at any time since he stole her from Sparta, re-enacts his original theft.[2] Then in the next book Zeus asks the gods whether they had not better spare Troy and let Menelaus take Helen back to Sparta[3]; and he re-enacts in imagination the former days of peace. The beginnings of the war are thus summoned up. Prophecy is

---

[1] This is a general statement. The Dolon episode may be an accretion, and there is something queer about the hurry in which the wall is built in Book Seven. Not that the stylistic differences of the Dolonia *need* prove that it is an accretion. J. T. Sheppard in the *Pattern of the Iliad* (London 1922) 82 ff. points out that it is an interlude between two main sections of the poem, and to such an interlude a difference of style may be appropriate.

[2] iii. 379-448.

[3] iv. 14-19.

frequent. We constantly hear that Troy will fall. Hector, dying, prophesies Achilles's death in the Scaean gates at the hands of Paris and Apollo.[1] Hector, parting from Andromache, has a vision of her carried away captive when Troy falls.[2] Most plainly of all, in Book Fifteen[3] Zeus foretells to Hera the deaths of Patroclus and Hector, from which moment the Greeks will attack continuously till Troy falls. Homer falsifies with fine effect in Book Two. The armies muster as if for the first time, regardless of the war being in its tenth year and of all the losses both sides must in actuality have sustained. The catalogue of the ships and forces, too, is inappropriate to this stage of the war.[4] In Book Three Helen and Priam comment on the Greek chiefs as if they had only just landed. This inappropriateness is no argument for spuriousness or multiple authorship, for it is only factual and not poetical. Homer writes as if the war was in its first year because he wants to create the impression of its whole extent. There is time in twenty-four books for fighters to die or tire, and for the war to grow old. When the fighting begins, forces must be intact and spirits fresh. These are but samples of many touches by which Homer builds up the context of the whole war.

There are many cross-references, and their cumulative effect is very great. One has been cited already, the mention in the last book of Peleus, which links with Achilles's mention of him in the embassy scene in the ninth. And this instance must stand for a great many others I have no room to bring up.

I will postpone treatment of the choric character of the *Iliad* till I have written of the *Odyssey*.

In what I have chosen to say (out of so much that could be said) of the *Iliad* I meant to include enough to impress on the readers the mature art of the poem. There is no question of making allowances. The first epic writing in the western tradition is entirely mature, like a great stream that issues straight out of the side of a mountain. There must indeed have been tributaries, but they are invisible. After the *Iliad* there can be no question of creating a form, only one of modifying it.

3. THE ODYSSEY

Some readers think the *Odyssey* greatly inferior to the *Iliad*. T. E. Lawrence's chilly preface to his translation is a modern example of such an opinion, and Longinus's remark on the *Odyssey*, with its

---

[1] xxii. 358-60. [2] vi. 448-65. [3] 54-71.
[4] For military inappropriateness justifiable on artistic grounds see *Othello*, i. 3. There, the conjectures whether the Turks will go against Rhodes or Cyprus are absurd, because Venice is too far away from the scene of possible action for any decisions taken in Venice to be of the least moment; but it suited Shakespeare to pretend otherwise

fabulous element, being the work of an old man is an ancient one. To both Pope gives the best answer in his postscript to his translation:

> Whoever reads the *Odyssey* with an eye to the *Iliad*, expecting to find it of the same character, or of the same sort of spirit, will be grievously deceived, and err against the first principle of Criticism, which is to consider the nature of the piece, and the intent of its author. . . . The *Odyssey* is the reverse of the *Iliad*, in *Moral, Subject, Manner* and *Style*; to which it has no sort of relation, but as the story happens to follow in order of time, and as some of the same persons are actors in it. Yet from this incidental connection many have been misled to regard it as a continuation or second part, and thence to expect a parity of character inconsistent with its nature.[1]

But Pope recognises common qualities too, and thinks that by comparing these you can judge whether Homer's powers have declined in the *Odyssey*. Comparing the common parts, he says we shall find in each the same vivacity and fecundity of invention, the same life and strength of imaging and colouring, the particular descriptions as highly painted, the figures as bold, the metaphors as animated, and the numbers as harmonious and various.[2] And he thinks that in its way the simple narrative perfection of the *Odyssey* cost Homer as much to achieve as the sublime of the *Iliad*.[3] Here I need do no more than use Pope's authority for asserting that the parts of the *Odyssey* are of high quality and that there is no initial bar to its epic character.[4]

The *Odyssey* embraces the same area of life as the *Iliad*, but it sets out from a different point of the compass and chooses different portions for prolonged occupation. The Greek political unit of Homer's day was the city-state with its not too autocratic king; and however many towns were sacked, the norm was peaceful life in such a city. Whereas the *Iliad* dealt with exceptional happenings and their results, though constantly reminding us of the norm, the *Odyssey* was centred in it. This is clear from the outset. After the opening scene among the gods we are shown Ithaca and how the lawless suitors defy decency and threaten the domestic order. But that order, though threatened, still persists, and it is the moral centre of the poem. Telemachus, Odysseus's heir, is still in occupation of his own house and feels himself responsible for his mother, even if the suitors consume his father's goods. He succeeds in calling a general assembly at Ithaca and in appealing to the people at large against the suitors.

---

[1] 1st Ed. (London 1725-6) 264-5.
[2] *Ib.* 259-60.
[3] *Ib.* 266.
[4] E. V. Rieu, whose plain translation in the Penguin Classics (1946) has won the poem many fresh readers, considers the *Iliad* and *Odyssey* two different but equally good poems (p. viii). He may have helped to counter Lawrence's influential opinion. Mark Van Doren in the *Noble Voice* (New York 1946) thinks the same.

And we gather that the people are on the side of order, though the suitors terrorise them. Anyhow Mentor still has the freedom of speech to blame the people for their lethargy.

There is another touch at the beginning which both confirms the domestic theme and links the *Odyssey* with the *Iliad*. It occurs in the first book during the conversation between Telemachus and Athena in the guise of Mentes. Athena has complimented Telemachus on his bearing and says he indeed resembles his father. To which Telemachus replies:

μήτηρ μέν τέ μέ φησι τοῦ ἔμμεναι, αὐτὰρ ἐγώ γε
οὐκ οἶδ᾽· οὐ γάρ πώ τις ἑὸν γόνον αὐτὸς ἀνέγνω.
ὡς δὴ ἐγώ γ᾽ ὄφελον μάκαρός νύ τευ ἔμμεναι υἱὸς
ἀνέρος, ὃν κτεάτεσσιν ἑοῖς ἔπι γῆρας ἔτετμε,
νῦν δ᾽ ὃς ἀποτμότατος γένετο θνητῶν ἀνθρώπων,
τοῦ μ᾽ ἔκ φασι γενέσθαι, ἐπεὶ σύ με τοῦτ᾽ ἐρεείνεις.[1]

Telemachus yearns for the well-ordered state, with the old, legitimate king, dying among his possessions. But he also recalls by contrast Achilles and his problems as set forth in the ninth book of the *Iliad*. Whereas Peleus had grown old among his possessions and his son had chosen to seek honour in Troy rather than to repeat the pattern set by his father, Odysseus was growing into middle age through all kinds of foreign adventure while his goods were being dissipated and his son, unlike Achilles, was trying to regain the ordered social life. In both poems these elements are the same; they are contrasted not in themselves but in the way they are blended.

When the scene shifts from Ithaca, we witness the quiet routine and the ordered transaction of civilised life in Pylos and Sparta. Even in Phaeacia, where the inhabitants belong to an antique world nearer the gods and where supernatural events are habitual, the prevailing temper is one of domestic order. And the main action consists not only, indeed not principally, in the return of the wandering hero but in re-establishing the domestic and political norm in Ithaca, which though terribly threatened has not quite given way. This great action is completed only in the last book. There we are shown Laertes, now recovered and rejuvenated, joining son and grandson to repel the dead suitors' kinfolk.[2] The proper hereditary norm has been re-established. And in the final heavenly conversation,[3] between Zeus and Athena, it is decreed that Odysseus and the suitors' kin shall be reconciled and he reign in perpetuity. The old mutual goodwill shall be restored.

---

[1] i. 215-20. 'My mother indeed says I am his son. But for myself I am ignorant, for no one ever knew his own father. If only I had been the son of a fortunate man enjoying his possessions when death overtook him! But as it is, he is the most miserable of mortal men, the man, I mean, who they say is my father, now you ask me the question.'

[2] *Ib.* xxiv. 496 ff.   [3] 480-6.

THE ENGLISH EPIC AND ITS BACKGROUND

If the centre of the *Odyssey* is different from the *Iliad's*, so too is the style. I noted how in the first book of the *Iliad* the principal episode, the quarrel between Agamemnon and Achilles, was followed by the subsidiary episode, much quieter but equally intense, of the two heralds fetching away Briseis from Achilles's tent; and I mentioned a slight suggestion of comedy. In the *Odyssey* this vein of quiet, intense description predominates and it answers the mainly social theme. This uncommon clarity of description, where the details are few but necessary and telling to the utmost, is what constitutes the *Odyssey's* basic charm. It depends on powers of observation and enjoyment primitively fresh but wielded by a highly sophisticated art. Here are two samples of Homer's economical clarity in the *Odyssey*. In the last book Odysseus and Telemachus, fearing revenge for having killed the suitors, withdraw from the town and seek out Laertes, now retired from his rule and living a farmer's life in an up-country farm. The context is important: Laertes does not know of his son's return and victory and that there is now no reason for his living in this rough squalor. To Odysseus, now triumphant, the squalor must have appeared doubly pathetic. These things we must bear in mind as we read Homer's description of Laertes on his farm:

> τὸν δ' οἶον πατέρ' εὗρεν ἐϋκτιμένῃ ἐν ἀλωῇ
> λιστρεύοντα φυτόν· ῥυπάοντα δὲ ἔστο χιτῶνα
> ῥαπτὸν ἀεικέλιον, περὶ δὲ κνήμῃσι βοείας
> κνημῖδας ῥαπτὰς δέδετο, γραπτῦς ἀλεείνων,
> χειρῖδάς τ' ἐπὶ χερσὶ βάτων ἕνεκ'· αὐτὰρ ὕπερθεν
> αἰγείην κυνέην κεφαλῇ ἔχε, πένθος ἀέξων.[1]

There is much of the *Odyssey* here in little: the typically human, pathetic situation; the details clear and separate and not too many; the slight comedy of the old man's very forgivable masochism in dressing just a little more miserably than he need, the goatskin hat being (unlike Robinson Crusoe's) more Spartan than the case required. The other passage describes Odysseus, waiting for sleep in beggar's disguise in his own house, hearing the girls of his household who were the suitors' mistresses stealing away to join their lovers. Again, the context is essential, Odysseus has had a terrible day, suffering insults in his own home from the suitors, on whom he is thinking out revenge. The girls' laughter breaks in on an overwrought man.

> ἔνθ' Ὀδυσεὺς μνηστῆρσι κακὰ φρονέων ἐνὶ θυμῷ
> κεῖτ' ἐγρηγορόων. ταὶ δ' ἐκ μεγάροιο γυναῖκες
> ἤισαν, αἳ μνηστῆρσιν ἐμισγέσκοντο πάρος περ,

[1] *Odyssey*, xxiv. 226-31. 'And he found his father alone, in the neat vineyard, breaking up the soil round a vine-stock. He was wearing a dirty tunic, disgracefully patched, his shins bound round with stitched leather gaiters to prevent scratches, with gloves on his hands against the brambles, while on his head, to make matters worse, he had a cap of goatskin.'

THE ODYSSEY

ἀλλήλῃσι γέλω τε καὶ εὐφροσύνην παρέχουσαι.
τοῦ δ᾽ ὠρίνετο θυμὸς ἐνὶ στήθεσσι φίλοισι.[1]

As the final touch to an exhausting day's experience, could anything be more apt?

Of English authors Chaucer comes nearest Homer in this convincing power of description, the power which is so certain of itself that the reader's suspension of disbelief is not merely willing but as instantaneous as the working of the new anaesthetics. This is Canacee retiring from the feast early so as not to spoil her complexion:

> She was ful mesurable, as wommen be;
> For of hir fader hadde she take leve
> To goon to reste soone after it was eve.
> Hir liste nat appalled for to be
> Ne on the morwe unfeestlich for to se,
> And slepte hire firste sleep and thanne awook.[2]

And this is the gigantic stadium Theseus put up for the tournament between Palamon and Arcite:

> The circuit a myle was aboute,
> Walled of stoon and dyched al withoute.
> Round was the shap in manere of compas,
> Ful of degrees, the heighte of sixty pas,
> That whan a man was set on o degree
> He letted not his felowe for to see.[3]

It might be the first grandstand ever to be constructed and Chaucer the first man to see it,[4] but the art has the smoothness of a finished diplomat.

Set against the realism of the domestic norm is the element of the fabulous. And here one must guard against the error of Longinus and of many (if not most) recent readers: that of giving this element a dominant place. Through the way Homer ordered his plot it is obvious that he meant the fabulous element not to dominate but to set off the domestic. The domestic theme is firmly established in the first four books with the troubles of Penelope and Telemachus in Ithaca and Telemachus's journey to the Peloponnese; it remains strong in the scenes on Calypso's island and in Phaeacia, that is for

[1] xx. 5-9. 'So Odysseus lay there unable to sleep, thinking out mischief for the suitors; when out of the women's quarters came the girls whom the suitors had for mistresses, laughing and chaffing among themselves. And his heart was stirred up within him.'

[2] *Squire's Tale*, 362-7. *Be appalled:* 'spoil her complexion.'

[3] *Knight's Tale*, 1887-92. *Letted:* 'prevented.'

[4] I do not mean that Chaucer was being original: cf., for instance, the account of the lists at Constantinople in Mandeville, 'It is made with stages and hath degrees about, that every man may well see and none grieve other' (ed. A. W. Pollard, London, 1900, p. 13).

four more books; and the fabulous element dominates only in Books Nine to Twelve, making indeed a wonderful diversity and variety, but remaining strictly subordinate. A section of antiquity was wiser than Longinus in this matter, for the papyrus finds point to the last four books having been the most popular in Egypt between the third century before and the third after Christ.[1] Of course, there is no denying the enchantment of the wanderings of Odysseus. The point is that it is more than self-valuable. The love of home can never be truly perceived in separation from the other love of freedom to wander and from the desire for change; it can never be truly prized in separation from the chaos and barbarism out of which the domestic pieties were painfully won. Homer gives us the whole picture.

There is another contrast: important both in itself and in the connections it makes with the *Iliad*. Right through the poem the misfortune of Agamemnon and the guilt of Clytaemnestra are compared with the better domestic fortune of Odysseus and with Penelope's virtue; and the action is not complete till Agamemnon in Hades hears from the suitors' ghosts of domestic reunion in Ithaca. That comparison Homer plainly meant to be as important as it is close. We hear of it at the very beginning in the council in heaven, where Aegisthus, Agamemnon, Clytaemnestra, and Orestes all are mentioned. Homer wished us to think of a whole pattern of correspondences: Agamemnon–Odysseus, Clytaemnestra–Penelope, Aegisthus–the suitors, Orestes–Telemachus. Only, in one story the issue is unhappy, the wife is false, and the son has to do an unnatural deed; while in the other the issue is happy, the wife faithful, and the son's deed of violence legitimate. But the two stories are not only parallel, they typify the stories of all the Achaean chiefs who had survived the Trojan War. In fact, the story of Odysseus's return corresponds to the wrath of Achilles in implying a wider context or theme: the combined home-comings of the Homeric heroes.

The *Odyssey* usually passes for a comedy, and rightly. But tragedy is never far off, and we are constantly reassured that the author had it at his call. Telemachus's helpless plight among the suitors is almost intolerable. His growing manhood was constantly being insulted. Penelope's grief for Odysseus is great and prolonged. It culminates in her refusal to acknowledge him when he declares himself; and the lovely passage when her reluctant self-defence breaks barely escapes from tragedy to pathos, like the recognition scenes in *Pericles* and the *Winter's Tale*. Odysseus's longing for home is intense and almost tragic when thwarted for so long. But though intense it is steady and untempestuous: unlike the emotion that corresponds to it in the *Iliad*, the anger of Achilles. Nevertheless, Homer at least twice reassures us that Odysseus too can feel violently as well as obstinately. The first

---

[1] See W. B. Stanford's edition of the *Odyssey* (London 1948) ii. 433.

time is when, having bent his bow, he leaps from his rags, pours out his arrows at his feet, tells the suitors that he will now strike a target which no man yet has struck, and shoots the chief of the suitors, Antinous. The rest, though thinking the blow accidental, are about to set upon him and kill him, when he throws at them his tremendous indictment:

> ὦ κύνες, οὔ μ' ἔτ' ἐφάσκεθ' ὑπότροπον οἴκαδ' ἱκέσθαι
> δήμου ἄπο Τρώων, ὅτι μοι κατεκείρετε οἶκον,
> δμῳῆσιν δὲ γυναιξὶ παρευνάζεσθε βιαίως,
> αὐτοῦ τε ζώοντος ὑπεμνάασθε γυναῖκα,
> οὔτε θεοὺς δείσαντες, οἳ οὐρανὸν εὐρὺν ἔχουσιν,
> οὔτε τιν' ἀνθρώπων νέμεσιν κατόπισθεν ἔσεσθαι·
> νῦν ὑμῖν καὶ πᾶσιν ὀλέθρου πείρατ' ἐφῆπται.[1]

And terror seized them all. And right at the end of the poem, when the suitors' friends and relatives seek revenge, Odysseus becomes a terrific figure, giving a great shout, swooping on them like an eagle, until restrained by a thunderbolt from Zeus.[2] It is almost as if Homer, having rounded off the domestic theme with the union of the three generations in the resistance to the suitors' avengers, wished as a last touch to establish a momentary union with his other great poem.

The *Iliad* is not worse plotted than the *Odyssey*, but the lines of the *Odyssey* are more immediately clear: with the result that the *Odyssey* has supplied the classic shape for the formal epic. Both poems begin at a late stage of the total action, but in the *Iliad* past events are recalled by the unemphatic method of scattered hints. The *Odyssey* by making one of the characters narrate past history established a great precedent. The *Aeneid*, the *Lusiad*, *Paradise Lost* all follow it. The precedent also of making a journey (or journeys) lead to a narrower stage of action was also set by the *Odyssey*. Here the resemblance with *Paradise Lost* is particularly close.[3] In the *Odyssey* the various travels converge in the narrow stage of the palace hall in Ithaca, after which the scene expands somewhat to include the island. In *Paradise Lost* the various travels from Hell and Heaven converge in Adam's garden, after which the scene, though never expanding to its old dimensions, includes the earth. But the Odyssean analogy is not confined to the formal epic. The journey is a simple and universal symbol of human life; and the voyager, of man living his normal span. The stock phrase 'soul-Odyssey' unconsciously testifies to the fact of this symbol and to the instinct to see it in Homer. Man's pilgrimage was a great medieval

[1] xxii. 35-41. 'You dogs, you never thought I should come back from the people of Troy; and so you wasted my household goods, you forced the maid-servants to sleep with you. You wooed my wife behind my back though I was still alive, fearing neither the gods in high heaven nor any retribution that might fall on you from men. And now, for all of you, your fate is sealed.'

[2] xxiv. 537-9.

[3] On this topic see a letter from D. S. Robertson in the *Times Literary Supplement*, 4 May 1940.

theme: so it is the *Odyssey* above all epics that stands, by reason of its plot, at the head of a great succession.

As in the *Iliad*, there is abundant evidence that Homer held the whole content of the *Odyssey* in his mind during composition. One piece of evidence has been mentioned already in another context: Homer's unrelaxed attention to the parallel theme of Agamemnon and his household and his care to complete the theme by causing the suitors' ghosts to bear to Agamemnon in Hades the news of Odysseus's return and of Penelope's successful resistance and fidelity. Another piece is the careful mention in the first book (189-90) of Laertes living aloof on his farm with an old attendant, nursing his grief; a mention to be taken up in the last book by the wonderful description of Laertes in his orchard, quoted earlier. Again, just as Thetis is introduced in the first and last books of the *Iliad*, so an assembly is summoned in the first and last books of the *Odyssey*. The people do the wrong thing in both, but in different ways. In the first, they fail to speak up in support of Telemachus through fear of the suitors; in the second they are frivolously weak in supporting Eupeithes, the father of Antinous, in his demand for vengeance, and, far from remaining silent, they burst into an uproar. Homer had the assembly in the first book in his mind till he was near the end of his poem.

In this matter of will-power and the predetermined plan as revealed in the composition of the *Odyssey* it is more apt to express astonished admiration than to present more evidence for the obvious.

4. ILIAD AND ODYSSEY AS GROUP-EXPRESSION

Homer belonged to the extreme east of the Greek world, to the Ionians who inhabited the west coast of Asia Minor or the adjacent islands. Nevertheless, he spoke for the whole Greek race, and his poems were looked on as its Bible. It may even be that his peripheral position favoured his grasping the universal rather than the local Greek characteristics. He may have operated like this: separated from the deeply rooted local cults and prejudices of old Greece, made aware by his foreign neighbours (not far distant from the Asia Minor coast) of the peculiar character of the Greek race, Homer was able to seize the shape of ethical ideas and religious beliefs common to the Greeks and to express it with such charm and power that this expression became acceptable and definitive; a part of total Greek (as against Thessalian or Argive or Theban) life, like the Olympic Games. Whatever of earlier 'heroic' habits or ideas he retained, Homer spoke preponderatingly for the whole Greek world till the influence of developed Greek philosophy really made itself felt; and briefly in the following fashion.

On the religious side Homer favoured the Olympian pantheon at the expense of this or that local cult. Thus his Athena has little connection with Athens; she is the foe of the Trojans and the friend of Achilles and Odysseus. By doing this Homer was generally Greek and not specifically 'heroic' or Ionian. Through its relation to this universally shared group of major deities, the Greek race showed its peculiar, anthropocentric conception of the world. Although it recognised the importance and ubiquity of the gods, their tutelage of its moral order, and the need to propitiate them, it figured them as interested primarily in man. The Greek race thought similarly about an after-life. There was indeed one, with its rewards and penalties, but for its character it depended on memories of life lived on earth, which was assumed to be the centre. Homer in embodying such opinions spoke for a large group of men.[1]

On the ethical side Homer worked on the commonest Greek formula. There were certain very definite rules of life. Revenge was virtuous, but insulting the dead was wicked. Odysseus was right both in killing the suitors, who had wickedly wronged him, and in respecting their bodies. Achilles was justified in sacking the Trojan town of Minya and killing Eëtion, the father of Andromache, and he was right in giving him a burial befitting his rank. Odysseus, far from home, committed no offence in sleeping with Calypso, but Phoenix's father offended against his wife and against morality by bringing a concubine into the house. Euriclea was the trusted housekeeper in the palace at Ithaca. Laertes had bought her, and had brought her up respecting her like his own wife. But he did not sleep with her, fearing his wife's anger.[2] And of course that fear was also a moral feeling, acceptable to the gods. Governing these actions is the idea of temperance, of reason keeping passion within decent bounds. Contrariwise there was a regular pattern of sin. The sinner lacked respect for the gods and for the standards they represented. The gods on their part usually warned prospective sinners, if they were people of importance, as Zeus tells us he warned Aegisthus not to seduce Clytaemnestra or to kill Agamemnon on his return to Mycenae. Sinners who neglected or refused to hear such warnings were possessed by a spirit of mischief, and retribution was bound to follow. All these are commonplaces found equally in Homer and in later Greek writers. They are of course not specifically Greek in themselves, but as blended by Homer they are Greek through and through, and by so blending and expressing them Homer spoke for a great group of men.

Isocrates[3] (whether he actually invented the notion or not) believed the *Iliad* to express the great theme of the superiority of the Greeks

---

[1] J. H. Finley in his *Thucydides* (Cambridge, Mass., 1947) 38-9 has a good passage contrasting Homeric and Jewish habits of thought in seeking explanations of God's acts.

[2] *Odyssey*, i. 429-33.   [3] *Panegyricus*, 159.

over the barbarians; but here he was thinking wishfully, propelled by the feelings of his own day. True, Homer is on the Greek as against the Trojan side and he is partial to the prowess of Greek heroes. Hector cannot be allowed to kill Patroclus unaided, and his glory is divided by three, while Achilles must have sole glory when he kills Hector. But, though some of the Trojan allies may have been a little suspect, the Trojans were Greeks[1] and behaved as such. On the other hand Homer does express two matters, one a fact and the other an ideal, which were destined to figure in later treatments of the very important commonplaces about Greeks and barbarians. The fact is the freedom of the Greek service men. They were volunteers, serving under leaders who had chosen to join in a campaign. When Achilles decided not to fight, his Myrmidons followed his example; and there was no question of compelling either him or them to change their policy.[2] But it is in the *Odyssey* that the free relations between leader and men are best presented; and they are the extreme opposite of the oriental habit of driving men into action with the lash. Odysseus advises his men, but never compels them. Usually they consult together and reach an agreement. But he never goes against the sense of the meeting. He is against landing on the island of the cattle of the sun, but his men insist and he yields. In dividing up spoil, the rule is equality. Achilles, when in anger, thinks this an unfair provision, since he has worked harder than the rest. Odysseus merely gets his share with an occasional honorarium for special trouble and responsibility, as when he gets the ram after the escape from the Cyclops. All this is both typically Greek and the kind of situation that later was habitually contrasted with oriental oppression and favouritism.

The ideal is that of unity, always granted the principle of freedom. This is a master-theme of the Greek historians; and there are indeed hints of it in Homer. Nestor preaches the doctrine in the first book of the *Iliad*, and in the second book Agamemnon says that if only counsels were united, there would be no postponement of disaster for Troy.[3] In the *Odyssey* a few resolute men, working perfectly together, defeat the suitors and their would-be avengers.

However, though Homer may imply the theme of unity against *stasis*, he much more certainly embodies, in the policy of Ithaca, the Greek love of the small intimate state. That state was not indeed a democracy, but its monarchy was mild and there was free discussion; its spirit was akin to that of the democratic age at its best, when the tyrants had been got rid of and the population was still small.

---

[1] We too easily forget that Homer calls the invaders of Troy not Greeks but Achaeans and Danaans.

[2] I do not mean that there was no discipline at all. Odysseus (*Iliad*, xix. 233-7) says that for the coming great battle there must be a complete muster and that it will be the worse for anyone staying behind by the ships.

[3] *Iliad*, ii. 379-80.

Homer's characters fit perfectly into the world of Greek ideas to which they belong, but we do not usually separate them from that world to contemplate their Greek characteristics. But there is one exception. As Aeneas is peculiarly Roman, the embodiment of Roman *pietas*, so Odysseus with his endurance, his flexibility, his resourcefulness, and his wit is peculiarly Greek. And we are the quicker to perceive his Hellenism because Achilles and Hector are not so much Greeks as men.

All these matters are Greek rather than Ionian. In one other matter I believe Homer Ionian rather than Greek. Little affected by the superstitions that beneath the Olympian surface of Greek religion were so powerful in the Greek world, believing in reason controlling passion, and himself so dazzlingly clear-sighted in sifting human motives, Homer shows himself akin to those stirrings of mind that prompted the beginnings of philosophical thought in the Ionian cities of the Asia Minor coast. As Herodotus was later to show kinship with that thought, though not himself a philosopher, so Homer's luminousness shows the state of mind favourable to its future generation. In so doing he represents the disposition not indeed of a great body of men but of a small group influential in inverse proportion to its numbers.

Finally, the *Odyssey* stretches and ramifies beyond the Greek world. The civilisation pictured there belongs so easily and calmly to the whole culture of the Mediterranean, with its closeness to the sea, its strong family sense, its fierce belief in property, its remembrance of injury, its love of vineyard and orchard. The *Odyssey* may look back on the heroic age, but much more it depicts the infancy of one great source of western civilisation.

5. EPILOGUE ON HOMER

It would be wrong to end remarks on Homer by referring to the peaceful side of the *Odyssey*, as if it were the principal matter. Homer is always aware of the two opposing values of honour through strife and the cruel sacking of cities, and of domestic and civil order. He may not be able either to relish that opposition or (save at very rare moments) to break it down. But he accepts or puts up with it, and does not worry. He is utterly a part of his world: there are no competing cultures or ways of life. Consequently he describes his world quite from within, and, doing so, enjoys a kind of certainty which all other great epic poets are denied. He is not primitive, he is linked with the later great succession. But his certainty is unique and it makes him uniquely attractive. Other poets will have other things to offer, but not just that.

CHAPTER III

THE GREEK HISTORIANS

*Est enim historia proxima poetis et quodam modo carmen solutum
et scribitur ad narrandum non ad probandum, totumque opus non ad
actum rei pugnamque praesentem sed ad memoriam posteritatis et
ingenii famam componitur.* (Quintilian)

1. THUCYDIDES

I NAME Thucydides only to say why so great a narrative writer
cannot figure in a book on the epic. The qualities attributed to him
by Dionysius and Quintilian, intensity and awesomeness, would in
themselves help him so to figure. But, if he is intense, he is narrow,
and, if awesome, idiosyncratic. He is more Athenian than he is Greek,
and his theme, though it contains a vast amount of political wisdom
and basic human nature, is more restricted and has less variety of
colour than Herodotus's. Herodotus is the child of centuries of Greek
expansion and the kin of the Greeks everywhere, the voice of everyday
Greek religion and of Greek self-respect. 'If in harmony with a naive
folk-lore,' wrote R. W. Macan, 'Herodotus fills his pages with signs
and wonders, theophanies and special providences, yet, in so doing,
he is undoubtedly reflecting the mind of his age and people more
fully than the philosophic Thucydides,'[1] and then spoke of Herodotus
as representing the great age of Greece's deliverance from the
Persians, 'that proof, once for all, of the dynamic and ethical superiority of European culture.'[2] Thucydides speaks for the new Athenian
introspection and the new spirit of self-distrust and he writes of
civil war.

The result is that Thucydides, however great a writer, lacks the
epic amplitude. His affinities are with tragedy. If a writer presents
many things in their sheer variety and wonder but without going
deeply into their causes, he may be on the side of epic, but deep
pondering on causes, without the variety and the wonder, belongs
elsewhere. J. H. Finley[3] has written excellently on Thucydides's
kinship with contemporary tragedy, and especially with Sophocles,
in his intense search for causes. Whether or not Thucydides worked

[1] In *Cambridge Ancient History*, V. 408.
[2] *Ib.* 410.
[3] *Thucydides*. See especially 81 and 322-5. I favour the more general affinity with
tragedy Finley advances against the schematic affinity advanced by Cornford.

on some predetermined tragic scheme, substituting Athens and her downfall for the tragic hero, is here irrelevant; the only point is that though in some things he was a greater writer than Herodotus, his field of action was different.

2. HERODOTUS

"Ὕψος δὲ καὶ κάλλος καὶ μεγαλοπρέπειαν . . . Ἡρόδοτος ἔχει.
(Dionysius of Halicarnassus)

For someone intending to treat history philosophically the study of Herodotus is sufficient. There he will find everything that has gone into the making of all subsequent world history: the activity, the foolishness, the suffering, and the fate of the human race.

(Schopenhauer)

Herodotus was akin to Homer in more ways than one. He was a native of the Asia Minor coast, and, though citizen of a Dorian city, the vehicle of Ionian culture. Like Homer he used the Ionic dialect, and like him a form of it not tied to any one city but a conflation.[1] Like him he used an early form of syntax, with many main verbs and few periods. But above all Herodotus, as a narrative writer, showed himself to be in the Homeric tradition. It could hardly have been otherwise. He was eminently an artist, and what writers of prose history had preceded him were list-makers; they could not help him. For a supporting tradition he had to turn to the poets; and of these the best was to the point, being both a teller of stories and, as was then thought, the recorder of actual events. Herodotus was born between the two Persian Wars, after Marathon and before Salamis. His ears, from the first, must have been full of talk about them; and when he decided to write their history, he could not have failed to bear in mind the writer of the only other war in the Greek world that could match the Persian Wars in significance. This kinship of Herodotus with Homer was recognised in antiquity. Dionysius of Halicarnassus (late first century B.C.) said that in rivalry with Homer he wished to give variety to his history.[2] A recent historian of Greek literature wrote that the breadth of Herodotus's theme was epic and the treatment no less so.[3] There is therefore a good initial case for considering Herodotus as a writer of prose epic, no more disqualified

[1] A different conflation; Homer using non-Ionic forms, Herodotus pooling different Ionic dialects.
[2] *Letter to Pompey*, 771-2: ' Ἡρόδοτος . . . ποικίλην ἐβουλήθη ποιῆσαι τὴν γραφήν, Ὁμήρου ζηλωτὴς γενόμενος.'
[3] H. J. Rose, *Handbook of Greek Literature*, 2nd ed. (London 1942) 301.

as such for being a historian than Aeschylus as tragedian for writing a tragedy on the second Persian War.[1]

At the outset there is the question of literary skill. Does Herodotus command a style capable of compassing the epic breadth?

In antiquity it became the custom to contrast the two historians, acknowledged superior to all others, Herodotus and Thucydides. Herodotus was considered more varied and charming and graceful, Thucydides narrower but more intense and more powerful. But Herodotus's grace was allowed to be equal to a wide range of subjects. To a modern reader acquainted with even a little Greek the charm of Herodotus's style makes itself quickly felt; as quickly as does the weight of Dante's *terza rima* on a reader who knows only a little Italian. But there is the accompanying danger that such a reader may be content with the quickly won and the obvious, and seek no further. And the danger takes two forms. First, it is hard to allow depth to the pellucid and to convince oneself, as one should, that Herodotus's grace was the result of much labour, of long experiment with prose rhythms, of a technique that weighed every syllable in a manner nearer to verse than to most prose writing. Secondly, we are tempted to read Herodotus for the parts and not for the whole. We get a particularly quick return from his separable details: his anecdotes and his reports of the marvels men told him on his travels. His style was so suited to making these charming that we can easily be blind to the other uses to which he could put it. The risk, in fact, is to treat his history as if it were the Greek equivalent of Mandeville's *Travels*. As that equivalent, as the most enchanting of travel-books, it is hard to give it the chance of rising to the height of its nominal argument: the crucial war between East and West.

It is hard for a reader with no Greek to be just to Herodotus, for he is peculiarly untranslatable. Rawlinson's version runs well and is readable, but his competent Victorian periods are distant from Herodotus's harmonious and elegant and subtle sequences of short sentences. B. R.'s version of the first two books (1584) is in agreeable Elizabethan prose, but is full of mistranslations and is too euphuistic to be near the original's simplicity. The *kind* of English prose nearest to Herodotus is the late medieval narrative prose. The syntax of Mandeville and Malory is not unlike; but Mandeville is a much smaller writer, and Malory's nostalgia and tragic spirit are alien to Herodotus's love of his subject and warmth of treatment. If a union of Malory's genius with Mandeville's geniality could be imagined,

---

[1] Questions about date and order of composition of the different parts of Herodotus's *History* do not concern me. It may or may not be that Herodotus did a lot of rewriting and reshaping when he returned to Athens from Thurii in 430 and that he died of the plague with his book complete but unrevised (see Enoch Powell, *The History of Herodotus*, Cambridge 1939, pp. 85 ff.); but only the book as it is concerns me.

a glimmering of Herodotus's style might appear. But my main point
is that Herodotus's simple prose, like Homer's syntactically simple
verse, is capable of many kinds of effect.

Coming to the question whether Herodotus did indeed produce
many kinds of effect, I am compelled to answer it in a way I do not
usually follow in this book. The *History* of Herodotus is so little known
to the general reader that it is only by giving an account of its scope
that I can hope to convey any sense of its nature, whether of content
or of structure. But before I give this account, there are two points
to be made. First, Herodotus's theme provided in itself a scope ample
enough for epic requirements. He had the world to range over and
from which to draw his illustrations; and his action, the clash of East
and West, was a human action of very high significance and was
transacted by men of very varied and very forceful natures. Secondly,
whatever the quality of the structure, Herodotus in composing his
History made the great choice of risking everything on one great work
and showed a very powerful will in carrying it through. This conclusion of course depends on the quality of Herodotus's style. If,
indeed, his prose is concentrated in the manner of very good verse,
then only a strong will could have sustained it so long.

The first great unit of Herodotus's *History* ends with the hundred
and thirtieth chapter of the first book, when Cyrus by the overthrow
of Croesus, King of Lydia, has become master of the whole of Asia
Minor. What does that unit accomplish and what does it lead us to
expect? The answer to these questions should go a long way towards
settling the problem of structure.

In his beginning Herodotus tells us that his theme is the great
actions of the Greeks and barbarians; and there is nothing in his first
unit that contradicts this profession. Further, he leaves no doubt
where his centre of interest is; and for structural coherence a centre is
essential. His centre is Greece, and he shows the highest artistry in
developing his theme *from* Greece. He could easily have begun from
the Persian side and then recounted the defeat of Croesus and the fall
of Sardis; but Croesus and his Lydians were closer to the Greeks
geographically, Lydia was the first country to bring under its sway
the hitherto free Greek colonies on the Asiatic coast, and Solon the
Athenian was supposed to have visited Croesus. By beginning with
Lydia, which has so many relations with Greece, Herodotus maintains the sense of Greece being still central. And lastly the sobering
words of Solon the Athenian to Croesus about the gods' jealousy of
excessive power and wealth and their proneness to bring down the
greatest men look forward to the culminating event in the Persian
Wars, the Battle of Salamis, won mainly by Athenian steadfastness
and resourcefulness. Unlike Thucydides and like Homer, Herodotus
upsets the strict time sequence. He refuses to interrupt the story of

Croesus's fall, and only when that is known do we hear the early history of Cyrus, his overthrower. That being completed, he adds, in conclusion of his first unit: 'It was after these events that he was wantonly attacked by Croesus and overthrew him, as I related before. And by overthrowing him, he became master of all Asia.' This conclusion is brilliant. Herodotus had told Croesus's overthrow with perfect narrative tact and timing and diversified it with delightful contributory stories. But he postponed comment on its *significance* till he got to his overthrower, Cyrus. This delay both heightens its significance—for the statement of that significance comes suddenly and with all the emphasis of brevity—and places it where it is most due, namely in Cyrus, symbol of the astonishing rise to power of Persian imperialism. From being a fascinating and exemplary human tale about a great king (neighbour to the Greeks), the career of Croesus becomes a turning-point in the affairs of a vast empire; a turning-point as fateful ultimately to the Greeks as to the Persians themselves. Herodotus, whether through Homer's example or by native genius, both shows himself a master of the novelist's art and promises a tight control of his main theme. Could he have continued thus, his epic grasp would have been sure.

The rest of the first book is interesting enough. Herodotus is at the height of his narrative powers in describing Persian customs, the fall of Babylon, and the Persian war with the Massagetae, its fluctuating fortunes, Cyrus's total defeat and death, and finally Tomyris's outrage on his body, but our attention does not spread beyond the business in hand. Any hesitation to believe that Herodotus was deserting his main theme is settled by the second book, which, because Cyrus's son Cambyses was destined to conquer Egypt, concerns the geography and customs of that country. The curiosity of Herodotus the traveller, admirable in itself and highly entertaining in its results, is indulged so freely that the original epic purpose is quite lost. Herodotus never loses his artistry; in itself the description of Egypt is admirable: but he had forgotten the lesson of Hesiod that the half is greater than the whole. The same criticism applies roughly to the next two books, which deal with Persian campaigns in various parts of the world and with the manners of various nations. I say roughly, because the theme of Greece does begin faintly to make itself felt in these books. In the third book we hear of Polycrates, tyrant of Samos, of his wealth and his correspondence with Amasis, King of Egypt. The Spartans, supporting some disaffected Samians, made unsuccessful war on him; and Herodotus makes the significant comment that this was the first expedition into Asia of the Dorians from Sparta.[1] He shows that he still has in mind his main theme of wars between East and West. Polycrates, like other very wealthy and

[1] iii. 50.

fortunate rulers in Herodotus, came to an evil end. He was succeeded by two more tyrants, and Herodotus remarks that the Samians appeared just not to wish to be free,[1] thus insinuating the theme, so dominant later, of Greek freedom and oriental tyranny. After the main business of Polycrates, Herodotus recounts the plot to get rid of Cambyses, now a maniac in his excesses and cruelties, and the choice of Darius as king from among the conspirators, after their plot succeeded. Before this choice Herodotus puts into the mouths of three of the conspirators an extremely Greek debate on the comparative merits of democracy, oligarchy, and monarchy, thus strengthening the Greek theme.

In the fifth book the campaigns of Darius bring him much closer to the Greek world. The Persians enter Thrace, and the Ionians revolt. Herodotus very aptly narrates the early history of Athens and repeats what he ultimately makes clear is one of his main themes: the excellence of political independence and free institutions. These are his comments on Athenian prosperity after the tyrants had been expelled:

> So the Athenians grew in power. And it is clear not from one only but from many instances, that equality before the law is a fine thing. While the Athenians in the times of the tyrants prospered no better in war than the peoples around them, as soon as they were quit of the tyrants they became pre-eminent; which proves that while they were kept under they let themselves be beaten because they were working for a taskmaster, but when they were freed each man was eager to give the best account of himself he could.[2]

The sixth book tells how the Persians suppressed the Ionian Revolt and invaded Greece for the first time. It ends with the Battle of Marathon. Herodotus introduces very clearly another master-theme: the need for the Greeks to unite. His picture of Greek dissension before the invading Persians is very vivid. But the Battle of Marathon is described with no special spirit. Herodotus does indeed hint its significance when he says that the Athenians were the first Greeks to charge the enemy at a run and to face the Medes resolutely, the Medes whose very name had been a terror to the Greeks. In spite of vivid or pertinent details, the sixth book resembles its predecessors in the slowness of its pace.

The change comes in the seventh book with the accession of Xerxes and his preparations for a second invasion of Greece. The spirit of the hundred and thirty opening chapters of the first book reappears; events are set in time with a powerful sense of cause and effect. The hints of large themes, scattered through the earlier books, are resumed and made explicit. It thus happens that Herodotus now not only intensifies and vivifies his narrative of actual events but

[1] iii. 143.　　　[2] v. 78.

universalises them by making them illustrate great moral laws. The changed tone, the new solemnity, appear in the council scene when Xerxes declares his intention to invade Greece and invites comment.[1] That this scene has no historical verity but was Herodotus's invention does not make it weigh less as a part of the book. Xerxes tells his council that he aspires to nothing less than world-dominion, and in highly passionate language. He will make the Persian land co-extensive with God's heaven, for once he has broken the Greeks there will be no more resistance in the world. Mardonius, who had been pushing Xerxes into the Greek campaign, supports him, saying that the Greeks may not even dare to fight. Then, after a silence, for the Persians were too timid to say what they thought, Artabanus, Xerxes's uncle and therefore better able to speak his mind in safety, opposed the expedition. His grounds are familiar but not the less impressive in the context. The gods are jealous of any abnormal power or height; a principle seen in the natural world, where God's lightning strikes the large animals, the highest houses, and the tallest trees, sparing the lowly.[2] And he reproves Xerxes's excess by saying that God allows no one but himself to have high thoughts. The scene is entirely successful in giving cosmic importance to the events to be narrated. Xerxes, though little characterised, is kept from being a merely symbolic figure by thinking over Artabanus's warning and ending in doubt about his plan.

Xerxes, now fixed in our minds as a man both of passionate moods and of reflective power, is capable of presenting the kind of general thought Herodotus wants the reader to have. In pride he scourged the Hellespont for breaking his bridge, and in pride he ascended the citadel of Priam in Troy, thinking of himself as reversing the fate of the king who died at the hand of invaders from Europe. When he reviews his forces, military and naval, at Abydos, he grows reflective[3] and laments that after a hundred years not one of his millions will be alive. Then, still apprehensive about the outcome of his expedition, he asks Artabanus his opinion. Artabanus, now resembling one of the Hebrew prophets in his authority, replies that two of the greatest things are against him, sea and land: the first because it has not harbours enough to offer, the second because it cannot yield food enough for the invaders' hosts.[4] Xerxes, as well he may be, is awed

[1] vii. 8-11.
[2] Cf. Shakespeare, *Measure for Measure*, ii. 2. 141-4:

Mercifull heaven,
Thou rather with thy sharpe and sulpherous bolt
Splits the un-wedgable and gnarled Oke,
Then the soft Mertill.

[3] vii. 44-50.
[4] Also in Aeschylus, *Persians*, 792-4:

αὐτὴ γὰρ ἡ γῆ ξύμμαχος κείνοις πέλει,
κτείνουσα λιμῷ τοὺς ὑπερπόλλους ἄγαν.

by the warning, and, ceasing to speak in character, comments chorically on the reasons why great deeds are attempted at all. Artabanus, he says, may be right, but always to be cautious is never to act. It is better to be bold and incur evil than to be ever fearing what may happen. Great empires can be acquired only by great risks. Here Herodotus shows the great gift, so powerful in creating the epic effect, of being on both sides. He knows that the great expeditions of the oriental conquerors are lamentable displays of human pride and cruelty; and he also knows that without the willingness to accept the risks these great expeditions must incur human nature would be the poorer. Not only is the scene at Abydos great and tragic in itself, it is perfectly timed on the brink of the *History's* culminating enterprise and perfectly sited in the last patch of Asia near the bridge to Europe.

The last piece of staging (on the Persian side) is the conversation between Xerxes and the exiled Spartan King Demaratus, now at his court, and it serves to bring out the contrast, already hinted at, between oriental tyranny and Greek freedom. Demaratus assures Xerxes that the Spartans, however few, will resist the Persians, however many. Xerxes is incredulous and says that if like his troops they had one master, their fear of him might cause them to do desperate things or the whip might urge them to face a superior foe, but left to themselves and their own choice how could they? Demaratus replies that though the Spartans are free from a despot, they are not altogether free, for they are bound by a custom which they fear more than his subjects fear Xerxes; and that custom forbids them to run away in battle, however many the enemy, and requires them to stand firm and either to conquer or to die.

In this way Herodotus prepared for the Battle of Thermopylae, from the Persian side. He now turns to the Greeks. Though Xerxes aimed his expedition against the Athenians in revenge of Marathon, the Greeks knew that he really included them all, and each state had to decide how to act. How the Spartans would act we have learnt from Demaratus; and Herodotus tells us—he says he is forced to tell us although the opinion will not be popular—that the Athenians were in the key-position: without their sea-power Spartan valour would be useless. Then, and the timing is perfect, he introduces Themistocles, the true hero of the war, the man who above all others achieved just that measure of unity among a number of small states necessary to repel the Persians. It is the timing and not any direct statement that tells us that Themistocles is the hero.

From now on Herodotus recounts the different stages of the war. He is not particularly strong in battle-narrative, but in the events and the human motives leading up to the decisive engagements he is masterly. Each move has the separate significance and the logic of a perfect game of chess. Herodotus invests his narrative of world events with the kind of clarity Homer attains in domestic. The seventh book ends with the classic Spartan glory at Thermopylae; classic as Plataea could never be, because the special Spartan talent was surpassing valour against overwhelming odds. But Thermopylae in itself did no more than delay the crisis; and the eighth book begins by re-counting that crisis at Salamis. The issue, Herodotus knows, was not whether the Greeks were a match for the Persians—that had been proved already—but whether they would hold together. And it was the Athenians, and Themistocles especially, who knew this and acted on their knowledge; and they are the heroes of this critical portion of the *History*. Their master-stroke of policy and magnanimity was to allow a Spartan to command the united fleet, though they were far the strongest naval power. And Herodotus praises them for having the salvation of Greece at heart and knowing that it could never be achieved if there were quarrels about the command, for, he says (and he uses the word that has typified Greek political tragedy through the ages, στάσις), civil strife is as much worse than international war as war is than peace.

Herodotus had staged his preliminaries with impeccable tact and emphasis; what of the crisis itself? It was both an event of the first world-significance and one which hung on the trivialities of human temperaments, on the decision of a small group of Greek com-manders deeply perplexed and quite divided about the right course of action. And the right course was followed only because Themis-tocles had the wit to act secretly and send an envoy to the Persians. This happening was perfect material for the author of a heroic poem, proving that history, in spite of Aristotle, could on one occasion at least be as philosophical as poetry. The combined Greek fleet was anchored in the bay of Salamis, and it had become clear that there would be a majority among the commanders for quitting. Themis-tocles knew rightly that if they did, the fleet would disintegrate. The message he sent to the Persians had the artistic advantage of being ironical: it was mainly true, but it was misunderstood. He informed the Persians that the Greeks were preparing flight and that if they wanted to destroy the Greek fleet they must immediately cut it off. Xerxes acted on Themistocles's advice, and thus forced on the Greek commanders a unity they would otherwise have lacked. Herodotus's intense simplicity of style proved equal to his difficult task at this culminating point. Every detail stands out sharp, and yet contributes to a single great end: that of symbolising all the other great balancing points in history, when little things became enormous in deciding which of two scales is to kick the beam. Once again Herodotus is on two sides, or rather is both near and far: near, in being quite sunk in the actuality of his supremely thrilling narrative: far, in mastering a whole philosophy of history. The eighth book ends strongly with the episode of Alexander of Macedon seeking on behalf of Mardonius, now in command of the Persians, to persuade the Athenians to change sides. The Spartans, getting wind of this, in great alarm send envoys to Athens. The Athenians, after rejecting the Persian offer, solemnly rebuke the Spartans for their fears.

The ninth book, dealing with the battles of Plataea and Mycale, shows no slackening of grip. That the preliminaries to the battle of Plataea were, as a matter of history, less exciting and more petty than those to Salamis was a gain, for it spared Herodotus the temptation of trying to contrive a second climax. Instead, he advances the theme of Greek moderation and seemliness contrasted with Persian excess and insolence. The *History* ends with the capture of Sestos by the Athenians: Sestos the chief fortress on the Dardanelles and near the bridge which Xerxes constructed from Asia to Europe. They find the bridge already broken up, while the capture of Sestos made any renewal of invasion unlikely. Xerxes's expedition was indeed ended.

It should have become clear, granted high distinction of execution, that Herodotus succeeds partially as an epic writer. He had a theme, belonging it is true to recent history, but sufficiently momentous and typical, sufficiently apt to call forth strong human feelings, to be universal as well as specific. But after a splendid beginning he allowed his consuming curiosity about the world at large to distract him from his real theme and to establish a new and incompatible centre of interest. The world at large ceased to be background and became a second theme. Herodotus should of course have written two books: the greatest of guide-books, and the epic history of the wars between the Greeks and Persians. Not that the dichotomy is so stark in the actual *History* as this sentence suggests. It takes the reader some time to notice the shift of balance, while Herodotus the truant never quite forgets the business he has forsaken. Nor is the guide-book all loss for the epic. It does add weight; it does establish the amplitude of the writer's brain. But it does so at a quite excessive expense; and in the end the dichotomy, for all its mitigations, has to be admitted.

In claiming parts of Herodotus to be epic, I do not mean to say that they are of Homeric quality. Herodotus has less sense of tragedy and of religion. He knows a great deal about human nature, but he creates no characters whose sufferings or ruminations go beyond the present issues and imply the basic problems of man's destiny. His religion, though sincere, is conventional. His cast of mind is primarily comic, and his criterion is the heart of man at its most observant and reasonable and tolerant, or, to vary the expression, the way of the best possible world. Granted that cast of mind, Herodotus achieves a very high order of originality. His passion of observation is all his own, his tolerance a powerful moral principle. This is his comment on the ignoble part borne by the Argives in the Persian War (the Argives who led Greece against Troy):

> Suppose all men to bring their own evil deeds to a common place, in the hope of exchanging them with their neighbours; when they had had a good look at those lying near them, they would be glad to carry their own back again. So the Argives should not be thought to have acted with exceptional baseness.[1]

Rawlinson thinks these sentences show over-tenderness to a guilty nation.[2] More likely Herodotus had in mind the later crimes of the men who acted best in the Persian Wars, the Athenians; and meant that tolerance in judging sins must go with the knowledge that no nation can be morally self-satisfied.

This primarily comic temper does not mean that Herodotus was not serious or that he thereby lacked epic breadth or that he could not cope with his great general themes. It is not by possessing the comic temper but by not possessing the tragic in addition that he falls short of Homer. Here it may be helpful to think of Chaucer. Chaucer, indeed, could never have taken the ultimate risk of putting everything in one great venture. But his most mature verse, that of the least conventional of the *Canterbury Tales*, of the *Miller's* or *Nun's Priest's Tales*, resembles Herodotus's prose in its comic temper. The essentially comic way in which Chaucer recounts the murder story in the *Nun's Priest's Tale* is close to Herodotus's way of recounting the more violent tales in his *History*, while Chaucer's treatment of the marvellous in the *Squire's Tale*, so cool and so fresh, reminds us of Herodotus in Egypt. But the resemblance must not be pressed too far. As Chaucer was not good at finishing things and lacked the epic staying power, so he avoids the more tremendous political themes. Though beginning from the comic side, Herodotus in coping with the great events of the Persian War reaches an epic eminence where merely to have arrived is enough and where the route followed is irrelevant.

Last, does Herodotus speak for a large body of men? Very emphatically yes. But he looks back rather than forward. Writing when the sophists in Athens were revolutionising (or making explicit an already revolutionary) thought, Herodotus interprets an earlier and simpler and highly extroverted world. This world is much like Homer's: generally Greek and not confined to this or that city. The notion that Herodotus wrote as a Periclean Athenian with a partisan bias in favour of the Athenian share in the Persian War has no warrant from his text as a whole and could only have been conceived by an unfair

---

[1] vii. 152.

[2] G. Rawlinson, translation of Herodotus (London 1860) iv. 129, footnote. Herodotus in his impartial view of the Greek states reminds me of Polydore Vergil's view of the Hundred Years War in his *English History*.

concentration on selected parts.[1] Herodotus is the authentic voice of the Greek world in its expansive phase: in its phase as coloniser and pioneer explorer of external nature. As Wells says, he is 'the crown of the intellectual greatness of the Asiatic-Greek sea-board, driven by Persian conquest into exile, and developed in new fields, and on new lines by the enterprising life of the Greek world in the West'.[2] And Wells sees that Herodotus is not only a historian but that he includes all knowledge and that in so doing he 'continues the old tradition of Ionia, where the Philosophers took all knowledge for their province.'[3]

To call Herodotus archaic because he looked back would not be fair. The great critical and introspective trend which began in the second half of the fifth century, and of which the sophists were the worse and Socrates the better representatives, was a local Athenian trend and took years to make itself generally felt. To have come under its influence would have been to forgo all possibility of epic breadth. Though the Greek world for which Herodotus spoke was actually past its prime, it was to persist in some of its parts for many years to come and it was the only world offering an adequate scope to a Greek writer of the highest aspirations.

3. XENOPHON

Some have greatness thrust upon 'em.
(Shakespeare, *Twelfth Night*)

i. GENERAL

Xenophon figures in a book on the epic through two accidents. The first was that once in his life, like the sea-captain in Conrad's *Typhoon*, he was carried by the accidental tide of events into a state of exceptional peril. This awoke faculties which would otherwise have lain dormant, and for once made him write above himself. The second was that the Renaissance insisted on taking for epic one of his works which for us today has little claim to that distinction. Xenophon therefore figures in this book under both the conceptions of the epic set forth in my opening chapter.

As a literary figure Xenophon does not rank high in the modern

[1] See the excellent treatment of this theme by Henry Wells, *Studies in Herodotus* (Oxford 1923) 154 ff. Wells points out that Herodotus's literary references are pre-Periclean and that if he had wanted to flatter Athens he would have praised Periclean architecture. As it is, he praises non-Athenian buildings. I find the above book the most enlightening on Herodotus of those I have read. There is an original and suggestive comparison between Herodotus's *History* and the *Odyssey* in Mark Van Doren, *The Noble Voice*, 47-8.
[2] *Op cit.* 184.   [3] *Ib.* 188.

world,[1] mainly because his Greek, having been found suitable for beginners in the language, has thereby seemed the less worth serious adult attention. Antiquity thought otherwise and put him, if below Herodotus and Thucydides, at least among the great Classics. Cicero said that the Muses spoke through his lips; Quintilian praised his easy charm, easy but not to be imitated by any labour; Dionysius of Halicarnassus called him the successor of Herodotus, possessing equal grace and charm and inferior only in stateliness. Plainly we shall be going against the verdict of antiquity if we do not take Xenophon as a great artist.

Xenophon was younger than Thucydides by a generation and thus missed the influence of Pericles and the tragic experience of seeing the Periclean imperialism degenerate into demagogic tyranny. Bred in the decadence of Athenian democracy, Xenophon turned his hopes to the disciplined oligarchy of Sparta and by enlarging his sympathies beyond the bounds of his city became, like Herodotus, rather a Greek than a member of a Greek state. As a historian he succeeded Herodotus in having as a main theme the conflict between Greek and barbarian; only he adopted it for other reasons, reasons common at that time. Many of his contemporaries hoped to find in a new Greco-Persian war the unity and the stability that the Greek states had failed to find within themselves. They turned their eyes abroad, as Shakespeare's Henry IV dreamt of a Crusade to heal the wounds of civil war. The classic formulation of the Greek dream was the *Panegyricus* of Isocrates written in 380 B.C.; and the irony was that the dream came true only at the expense of Greek liberty, lost when the house of Macedon conquered Greece as a preliminary to its invasion of Asia.

Now these were great world events. Xenophon not only was susceptible to the general states of mind that animated them; he contributed largely to one of the events that created those very states of mind: the nearly successful attempt by Cyrus to win the Persian crown by the aid of Greek mercenaries. Xenophon shared prominently in extricating the Greeks from a position of the greatest danger. He thus stood in a double relation to his material, being both a part of it and its critic. More writers stand in such a double relation than is always realised: Dante, Camoens, Sidney, Milton. But none of these figured so prominently on the active side as Xenophon.

Superficially Xenophon was an ordinary Greek gentleman: pious in a conventional way, with current patriotic prejudices, and with the tastes of a squire. As such he was well suited to take in and then to give out the common thoughts of his age; which would include drawing from the events in which he acted the conclusions most other

[1] I hope Rex Warner's excellent introduction to his translation of the *Anabasis* in the Penguin Classics (1949) may turn popular opinion the other way.

people would draw: the conclusions which helped to lead to Iso-crates's *Panegyricus* and ultimately to Macedonian ambitions. But there was an original side to Xenophon's character. He had curiosity and a mind critical though not philosophical. He was Socrates's pupil and biographer. And Socrates brought out the reflective side of his nature and caused him to formulate for himself certain principles of action. Alexander Grant sums these up as follows:[1]

> A man should train his body by hunting and similar exercises, and his mind by debate and discussion; he should be very sober and temperate; very god-fearing, especially in the matter of seeking signs and omens; very just and truthful; he should possess, or acquire, the art of influencing and ruling other men, and he should use that art for beneficent ends. . . . It was a simple doctrine, com-pounded of the Spartan ideas of education with some of the intellectual and moral ideas of Socrates.

The last sentence indicates rightly that though Xenophon's thought was plain it was enriched by having two origins. He had not just inherited but he had reflected, and chosen from more than one place. He preferred the Spartan form of education; but he owed to Athens the flexibility of mind that enabled him to acquire the preference. Another example of flexibility was his gift of seeing things on a large scale.

Athens before her fall was in schism not only with Greece but within herself: a prey to paltry motives. Turning away from Athens, Xenophon turned away not only from democracy but from the small-scale life of the Greek city-state. Although convinced that a Greek was worth several Persians, he admired the large ambitions and the extensive powers of Cyrus. In the last book of the *Education of Cyrus*, which deals with peace-time government, there is a passage on in-dustry which shows that Xenophon had given thought to the question of large and small units of organisation. He favours more specialisation in the crafts and he perceives that there can be more of it in a big town than in a village.[2] This bit of economics is prophetic of the big-city civilisation of the Hellenistic age. There are similar sentiments in Xenophon's *Anabasis*: critical not at all in a conventional way.

I conclude that Xenophon was a man of some richness of character, but like Walter Scott only too apt to be cried down by those who exclude a flair for average humanity from the qualities that can contribute to such richness. Xenophon's scope was large enough to give him an initial case for qualifying as an epic writer. But I must add at once that his mind lacked the fervour and energy necessary to

[1] *Xenophon* (Edinburgh 1871) 176-7.
[2] The sentiment itself may be derivative, but it gathers meaning when joined to Xenophon's admiration, shown elsewhere, for large-scale things or activities.

give that large scope an epic distinction, except on one occasion, Cyrus's expedition against Artaxerxes; and to his account of that expedition, known as the *Anabasis*, I now turn.

ii. THE ANABASIS

Ma se nella materia [istorica] ch' egli s' ha proposta alcuni avvenimenti si troveranno che così siano succeduti come appunto dovrebbono esser succeduti, può il Poeta, sì fatti come sono, senza alterazione imitarli. (Tasso)

How accidental was Xenophon's implication in great events plain from his own frank account in the *Anabasis*.[1] He happened to the personal friend of Proxenus, one of the Greek generals, and invited to accompany him as a volunteer without specified duties. He was far from choosing the part of hero deliberately; and it was only when the Greek army was in the height of peril that the latent strength in his character was forced to the light. The keen and lively observer became also a leader and was forced into new and uninvited states of feeling. The Greek squire became also the mental voyager; and his true story joins with a few others in transcending or universalising fact through the very intensity of the bare record. Though so different in temperament, Xenophon near Babylon resembles the young Wordsworth in Cumberland or Doughty in Arabia Deserta.

Not that this unusual state of feeling, communicated by an uncommon clarity of account, every touch telling, is kept up throughout. The epic, if it exists, ends with the fourth book when the Greeks reach the sea at Trebizond, the first friendly city, the place where earlier, at the height of their danger, they vowed sacrifice to Zeus the Saviour if they came safely through. There is plenty of interest afterwards, but the Greeks' true Odyssey was over, and the course of events lost the accidental artistry that had marked it up to that point.

But Xenophon bettered by his own skill the accidental artistry of history. Whether consciously or unconsciously he led up to the critical place, the terrible predicament of the Greeks when their commander and other officers were treacherously killed, with accomplished art. He begins quietly enough with the muster at Sardis, the march, the Greek reinforcements picked up on the way, the review with its mimic charge of the Greek phalanx that frightened the Asiatic onlookers out of their wits, the growing apprehension about their goal. All these he recounts sparely and vividly, and out of it there emerge certain characters—Cyrus with his charm and brilliance and Clearchus the dour but respected Spartan commander —and the theme of Greek superiority over Persian. The account of the decisive battle at Cunaxa, where Cyrus lost his life, is masterly,

[1] iii. 1. 4 ff.

but Xenophon is more artist than historian in making it less significant than the Greeks' subsequent troubles. He uses the natural pause in the action after the battle to give an explicit account of Cyrus's character, hints of which he had scattered before. Here the first book ends.

From now on the theme is the plight of the Greeks, deprived of their employer and protector and surrounded by alien enemies in the Mesopotamian fenlands a thousand miles from home. It is now that the realistic details take on their exceptional clarity and carry a meaning so much greater than their bare selves, as when the Greeks on the day after the battle, having no provisions or fuel, killed the baggage animals and cooked them at a fire made from the arrows of the enemy deserters and from the wicker shields of the Egyptians.[1] The great disaster came when Tissaphernes, the Persian general, in an interview outwitted Clearchus, by convincing him he really believed their interests to be one, and persuaded him to sponsor a meeting of high officers on both sides. At the meeting the Greeks were massacred, but Nicarchus the Arcadian, though wounded in the stomach, escaped. Holding his guts in his hand, he managed to reach the Greek camp and told the story. There is a pause in the action, for the Greeks now know how they stand with the Persians; and Xenophon uses the pause to describe the characters of the murdered generals. So ends the second book.

The third book opens with a superb description of Greek despondency in the evening, just after they have heard of the disaster: a description like some of Robinson Crusoe's reflections on his own plight barricaded on his island by the ocean. Thinking on their present lack of friends, their distance from home, the rivers and mountains barring their way, the Greeks

> were in a state of deep despondency. Only a few tasted food that evening, and a few lit fires. Many of them did not parade by the arms that night, but took their rest just where each man happened to be, and could not sleep because of their misery and their longing for their home lands and parents and wives and children, which they thought that they would never see again. In this state of mind they all took their rest.[2]

And this is the setting for Xenophon's own entry, decently introduced in the third person, with the astonishing story of his dream of a thunderbolt falling on his father's house and setting it on fire and his instant decision, on waking, to act. Rousing the captains formerly under the command of Proxenus, his own friend and one of the murdered generals, and convincing them of the need for instant action,

[1] ii. 1. 6-7.
[2] iii. 1. 2-3. Rex Warner's translation, 97.

he was elected their leader and proceeded to call a meeting of all the surviving generals and captains. This was at midnight, and by dawn the position had been transformed. New officers, including Xenophon in place of Proxenus, had been elected to fill the gap, and it had been resolved to assemble the whole army to a council of war. This great council is the culminating point of the narrative.[1] Xenophon (and he tells us he had put on his best suit of armour as fittest for the victory or the death he was soon expecting) by right of nature took the lead. His first words, about the sins of perjurors and the help of heaven in bringing those opposing them to safety, were interrupted by a happy omen, which brought the army to its knees in an access of piety. Xenophon saluted the omen as from Zeus and proposed a vow of sacrifice to him when they reached a friendly country. And they all took the vow and sang the paean. After this community of religious fervour, a return of courage and plans of action followed naturally. Xenophon roused the men's spirits with pious claims that their perjured foes could never stand up against their own god-fearing selves and with the doctrine of Greek superiority over the Persians, the doctrine founded on the belief in liberty—'you were born in free cities and worship no man as master but only the gods'—and exemplified by the victories at Marathon, Salamis, and Plataea.

The rest of the story concerns the working of the plans. It is sufficiently exciting to be worthy of the great scene in which the plans were made and it exhibits a sufficient variety of human passions to claim epic amplitude. It verges on the tragic in recounting the Greeks' sufferings among the snows of Armenia and it culminates in the scene when they first catch sight of the Black Sea and embrace one another, weeping, in their transport of joy and relief.

I do not wish to make too much of the first four books of the *Anabasis* as epic. There can be no question of a man exercising his will to the utmost over many years on a single comprehensive theme. Xenophon does indeed control his material, but to do so did not tax him to the extreme. Nor was he capable on his own unaided resources of achieving anything near a tragic intensity. But if luck eked out those resources and helped to produce better results than he, as it were, deserved, we are not obliged to deny to those results the merits they do in fact possess. And this luck includes more than what has already been mentioned, Xenophon's accidental implication in great events. It includes his literary antecedents. Homer's theme was a war in a (relatively) far country, followed by a return. It is not for nothing that Xenophon, haranguing the assembled army, mentioned the lotus-eaters; accident had made the Greeks re-enact the Homeric themes. Herodotus in his *History* had, in epic manner, described the very country in which they were fighting; and the theme of Greek

[1] iii. 2. 1 ff.

XENOPHON

against barbarian, which they acted in the flesh, he had exploited with his pen. And like the Greeks at Troy and at Salamis, the Ten Thousand were drawn from the whole Greek mainland. The epic context was there ready to be fitted into; and it added to Xenophon's narrative just that element of dignity it most required.

iii. THE CYROPEDIA

For Xenophon, *who did imitate so excellently as to give us . . . the portraiture of a just Empire under the name of* Cyrus, *. . . made therein an absolute heroicall Poem.* (Sidney)

The title of this work of Xenophon, the *Cyropedia* or *Education of Cyrus*, is a misnomer, for the subject is not only Cyrus's education but his military and political and social history and finally his death. It is, as Sidney saw, the picture of a just rule (according to Greek conceptions) exemplified in the person of the first Cyrus, the conqueror of Lydia and Assyria, the subject of the first book of Herodotus. It has little show of being historical and has been called the first European novel.

The contrast between the *Anabasis* and the *Cyropedia* is extreme: in the first, real, recent deeds, differentiated characters, and morality implicated with action; in the second, remote and stereotyped deeds, flat types of character, and a discreet schematised morality largely conveyed through set dialogue or disputation. In the *Anabasis* action was varied, hazardous, and full of unexpected turns; in the *Cyropedia* the hero achieves a monotonous success, there is no hazard because he is too virtuous for the gods to allow him to fail, and he advances in glory with an even and predictable rhythm. In no work more than in the *Cyropedia* does the reader know exactly where he is, whether he wishes to be there or not.

From this it follows that the *Cyropedia* cannot come anywhere near the epic as here defined. It lacks both amplitude and intensity. Yet it contains other qualities necessary for the epic effect, whose presence may retrospectively make us more confident about the claims made for the *Anabasis*. First, Xenophon exercised considerable will-power in shaping the *Cyropedia*. As now divided, it consists of eight books, and Xenophon worked up steadily to Cyrus's culminating victory over the Assyrians in the seventh book and devoted the last book to the way he applied to peaceful organisation the power he won in war, till, full of honour and virtue, he died. The various episodes in the earlier books are nicely proportioned and subordinated to the main theme. Xenophon shows that he has great architectonic power. The style, highly finished and sustained throughout in this finish, also testifies to his having put forth a powerful effort of will. Secondly, Xenophon spoke for a large number of men, for Greek morality at

57

large. Making no pretence of ethnic verisimilitude, putting his hero well in the past and warning his readers that the Persians are now degenerate and quite other than they were in Cyrus's day, he uses his characters to set forth the complete moral framework of his own Greece. It is too little known how much of Aristotle's ethics was already there not merely in men's hearts but in the pages of Xenophon. Cyrus himself illustrates quite as well as Aristotle's μεγαλόψυχος the Greek ideal of the superior man: pious, hardy, a good friend, a fierce enemy, apt to reward, ever vigilant. And the book as a whole illustrates two matters most characteristic of the classical world and most difficult for us today to sympathise with: omens and 'benefits'. To judge from the writers, a large part of civil life consisted in noticing the flights of birds and the entrails of victims and in trying to get in first with presents to your friends. To us the part of Xenophon's morality that most lives has to do with army discipline and etiquette. He obviously speaks from his heart and from the school of his own experience. His principles are those of discipline and *noblesse oblige.* The higher a man's rank, the more is exacted from him: officers must be able to do all that the men can, and more besides. A commander will know his subordinates well and give them personal orders. He will have an eye to detail. Cyrus before his greatest battle told the lancers not to forget the whetstone for their lances for 'he who sharpens his spear sharpens his soul at the same time'. And after the battle Cyrus was especially generous to the Egyptians, who had put up the toughest resistance. There is a lot in common between the *Cyropedia* and the *Field Service Pocket Book.*

The *Cyropedia,* then, though quite un-epic in itself, helps to give body to the first four books of the *Anabasis.*

Why was it that the Renaissance reader felt so much more warmly about the *Cyropedia* than we do? Any attempt to answer this question fundamentally must wait till later in this book. All I can say here is that it was popular by belonging to a whole class of ancient moral works which the men of the Renaissance found fascinating and from which they constantly quoted: for instance, the *Lives* and *Moral Essays* of Plutarch, Cicero *De Officiis* and *De Amicitia,* and Seneca's moral writings. The *Cyropedia,* with its narrative form, its well-shaped plot, its incidental story of Abradatas and Panthea (the first prose short story in western literature), its success in satisfying expectations of what classical literature should concern, was nicely fitted to please. For whatever reason, the Renaissance had a vast appetite for moral commonplaces; and Xenophon supplied them clearly and elegantly. When Croesus, captured by Cyrus at Sardis, gives a moral sermon on the need for a man to know himself, he was thrilling to the Elizabethans, while making us yawn. And when Cyrus, having captured Babylon, speaks at length on the importance of continuing in valour

XENOPHON

—'to have been once brave men is not sufficient; it is harder to hold what you have gained than to gain it'—the Elizabethans did not, as we do, require the rhetoric of Ulysses to Achilles in *Troilus and Cressida* to make the sentiment exciting. Lastly, the *Cyropedia* is full of worldly wisdom and political sagacity; it contains as well as more generous sentiments much of the milder lore of Machiavelli. We know how Machiavelli at once attracted and repelled. The politics of the *Cyropedia*, having the attraction of Machiavelli without the repulsion, must have had an irresistible charm.

It is therefore no wonder that the Renaissance liked Xenophon; how they came to treat him as an epic writer will be explained later in this book.

CHAPTER IV

BETWEEN XENOPHON AND
VIRGIL

1. GREECE

*E siccome ne' piccoli corpi può ben essere eleganza e leggiadria, ma
beltà e perfezione non mai, così anco i piccoli poemi Epici vaghi ed
eleganti possono essere ma non belli e perfetti; perchè nella bellezza
e perfezione, oltre la proporzione, vi è la grandezza necessaria.*

(Tasso)

XENOPHON belonged to the classical as against the Hellenistic
age of the Greek world, albeit to its decadence. Though he was
disgusted with his native city, though he had visions of larger political
organisations than the Greek and of Greek union against Persia, he
retained the habits of thought characteristic of the world of small
city-states in which he was bred, witness his readiness to record in his
Hellenica the petty wars among the Greeks in the early fourth century.
Coming about midway between Homer and Augustus, he was nearer
Homer. But he lived not long before the conquests of Philip and
Alexander destroyed the Greek city-state as an effective unit and
introduced into the western world notions of large political organisations hitherto dominant only in the East. From this great political
change grew changes in the position of the individual. In Homer and
Pindar and Attic literature you feel that more than a few people
count for much: yet without any cheapening of personality; for within
the many states that composed Greece there was scope for the really
distinguished characters to find a large fulfilment; there was relatively
little wastage of high personal potentiality. Thus placed, men were
little thwarted, and naturally turned their eyes outwards: to the
physical universe and to the constitution of the state. As always, the
germs of a new habit of mind showed themselves when the old habit
was still strong, for Socrates turned his eyes from the macrocosm
inwards to the microcosm of man at a time when the man he studied
was still largely an active political animal. When with Alexander the
political unit grew larger and the citizens' responsibility dwindled,
the status of a very few men was inflated at the expense of a relatively
larger number. The dictator became a superman, and the citizen lost
most of his public capacity. Philosophy adapted itself to the changed
conditions, and Epicurus, using the inward-pointing interest initiated

by Socrates, substituted for the conception of man fulfilled through every side of himself, private, social and political, the conception of the inner paradise attainable in spite of a thwarting and capricious outer policy. In compensation for political barrenness men studied more minutely the areas of life still allowed them: nature, the details of social pyschology, the elegances of a now more lavish way of living, the masterpieces of earlier ages.

The Hellenistic age still produced epics; and of these one has survived, the *Argonautica* of Apollonius Rhodius, dating from about 200 B.C. It is short, amounting to less than 7000 lines, and is divided into four books. I mention it only to say that it has no claim to epic quality as defined in this book but that it reflects the age it belongs to and in so doing reaches forward to Virgil in a way earlier Greek literature cannot do. Apollonius's poem tells of Jason's success in winning the golden fleece and Medea. The story is a romance whose very remoteness from political reality implies the world of warring dictators which was its melancholy background. It has plenty of human touches but no command of male character. The one living character is a woman, Medea. Over the whole is an air of delicate refinement; and what we remember most are the prettily described scenes: the Argonauts telling one another tales; all the gods watching them set forth, with Chiron the Centaur going down to the shore to wave them off; Aphrodite seeking Eros and finding him playing dice with Ganymede. Like the painting of the Hellenistic age, Apollonius's poetry was the work of a sensitive and sophisticated professional done for the amusement of a coarser set of patrons: it was not like the art of earlier Greece, the work of one citizen written to interpret the feelings of other citizens. Insofar as Virgil was an extremely sensitive man writing for a patron of coarser fabric, he was in the Hellenistic tradition. But that was not the chief thing; for Virgil was a Roman poet first and only in a minor degree an adapter of Greek modes to Latin uses.

2. ROME

One way for the ordinary reader today (for he has not been brought up on the ancient Classics) to catch the relationship between Greece and Rome is to consider the United States of America in its latest phase of realising its immense wealth and political strength and at the same time the superior refinement of a minority of Europeans. Then consider the present interest of the French in America and their admiration for its abounding strength and energy and for the cruder exuberance of some of its most characteristic fiction; and you will find an analogy with Polybius and other Greek writers who felt a warm admiration for those Roman qualities the Greeks in general so greatly lacked. Consider finally the natures of narrative in the United States of, say, the half-century 1890-1940 and in Rome. The true American form was the documentary novel, whether of Dreiser or Dos Passos, bent on describing what had not been described before, interested in the sheer phenomenon rather than in the shape of presentation. Not that knowledge of Europe or imitations of French austerities and elegances were lacking; but the central native strain used them in only a minor way. The narrative poetry of the Latins resembled the American novel in being documentary and annalistic. It had indeed begun with Livius Andronicus translating the *Odyssey* into a native metre in the last half of the third century B.C. But subsequent writers did not follow the elegant pattern of Homer. Naevius, coming a little after Livius, had fought in the First Punic War and wrote a poem on it, traditionally accorded the epic label. But he dropped the selective method of Homer and took up the chronicle method we habitually associate with the medieval chronicle and its successors. Ennius, the patriarch of Latin poetry, followed Naevius in the next century with his *Annals*, which narrated in the imported hexameter verse Roman history from the foundation of Rome to the latest event. It was the author's death and not any plan that brought the poem to a close. But Ennius, however primitive his architectonics, succeeded in exploiting nobly the possibilities of the Latin language as a weighty and sonorous poetic medium, and became the great early Roman Classic, central to Latin literature and not to be ignored by his successors. One of the books of his *Annals* had concerned an unimportant campaign of one of his patrons, M. Fulvius Nobilior, in Ambracia; and this book is thought to have been the model for any attempts at Latin epic between Ennius and Virgil.[1] Virgil, then, as an aspirant to historical epic poetry, found behind him a powerful and ineluctable tradition of chronicle narrative, usually recounting recent events in honour of some man who had distinguished himself in them. And here was something very different from Apollonius Rhodius.

The reader may well ask at this point: if the Hellenistic epic was no epic at all but an escape from intolerable politics into prettiness, if Virgil like Apollonius lived under a dictatorship, and hence could be expected to choose the pretty rather than the solemn, and if the tradition of the Latin epic was too uncivilised to be to the taste of one so naturally fastidious, why did Virgil choose the epic at all? The answer is first that Virgil was naturally ambitious, that he felt within him the urge to high efforts, hence to one of the major literary forms, and secondly that the dictatorship under which he lived was only one

[1] See R. M. Henry, *Virgil and the Roman Epic* (Manchester 1938) 8. I am indebted to this admirable essay in what I say about Virgil's relation to his Roman predecessors.

of a number of relevant political facts, and that the sum of these facts was not actually unpropitious to a great political poem. Virgil's personal ambitions can be treated more aptly when I get on to his poetry, and I pass to those political matters which we have to bear in mind if we are to understand how the *Aeneid*, a portent in view of the fewness of achieved epics, came to be made.

What some of these political facts were was recognised as long ago as Dryden; and the passage in the *Dedication of the Aeneis* where he describes them is, the unhistorical character of Dryden's age considered, one of the most astonishing pieces of criticism ever written. Dryden is puzzled because, while the political moral of the *Iliad* is the need for national unity against an external foe, that of the *Aeneid* is acquiescence in the rule of a semi-divine dictator, on the face of it a much less noble matter. And he proceeds to point out that in the circumstances the dictatorship of Augustus was a fine affair, worthy of the poet's allegiance. The gist of Dryden's demonstration is by now quite commonplace historically, but it is brilliantly set forth and livingly related to the temper of the *Aeneid*. He says that we must perceive that Virgil was writing his poem

> when the old form of government was subverted, and a new one just established by Octavius Caesar. . . . The Commonwealth had received a deadly wound in the former civil wars betwixt Marius and Sylla. The commons, while the first prevailed, had almost shaken off the yoke of the nobility; and Marius and Cinna, like the captains of the mob, under the specious pretence of the public good, and of doing justice on the oppressors of their liberty, revenged themselves, without form of law, on their private enemies. Sylla, in his turn, proscribed the heads of the adverse party: he too had nothing but liberty and reformation in his mouth. . . . Sylla, to be sure, meant no more good to the Roman people than Marius before him, whatever he declared; but sacrificed the lives, and took the estates, of all his enemies, to gratify those who brought him into power. Such was the reformation of the government by both parties. The Senate and the Commons were the two bases on which it stood; and the two champions of either faction each destroyed the foundations of the other side; so the fabric, of consequence, must fall betwixt them, and tyranny must be built upon their ruins.[1]

Dryden then goes on to describe the vain attempts that followed to preserve or restore the Republic. But though at times it might 'look with a florid countenance' without, all the while it 'was wasting in the vitals'. The battle of Philippi 'gave the decisive stroke against

---

[1] *Essays*, ed. W. P. Ker (Oxford 1900) ii. 168 ff., whence the other quotations are also taken. In this long historical section Dryden appears to be original. He may get a hint or two from Segrais's introduction to his translation of the *Aeneid* (Paris 1668), but not more.

liberty, and not long after, the Commonwealth turned into a Monarchy by the conduct and good fortune of Augustus'. Having finished his historical survey, Dryden sums up Virgil's position as follows:

> Virgil having maturely weighed the condition of the times in which he lived; that an entire liberty was not to be retrieved; that the present settlement had the prospect of a long continuance in the same family, or those adopted into it; that he held his paternal estate from the bounty of the conqueror, by whom he was likewise enriched, esteemed and cherished; that this conqueror, though of a bad kind, was the very best of it; that the arts of peace flourished under him; that all men might be happy if they would be quiet; that, now he was in possession of the whole, yet he shared a great part of his authority with the Senate; that he would be chosen into the ancient offices of the Commonwealth, and ruled by the power which he derived from them; and prorogued his government from time to time, still, as it were, threatening to dismiss himself from public cares, which he exercised more for the common good than for any delight he took in greatness; these things, I say, being considered by the poet, he concluded it to be the interest of his country to be so governed; to infuse an awful respect into the people towards such a prince; by that respect to confirm their obedience to him, and by that obedience to make them happy. This was the moral of his divine poem; honest in the poet; honourable to the Emperor, whom he derives from a divine extraction; and reflecting part of that honour on the Roman people, whom he derives also from the Trojans; and not only profitable, but necessary, to the present age, and likely to be such to their posterity.

Dryden's account, granted some liberty of conjecture concerning the way Virgil's mind worked, could not be bettered as far as it goes, but, naturally, it does not go far enough. There are other reasons why Virgil should have felt about Rome and Augustus in a way a Hellenistic poet could not feel about the fragment of Alexander's kingdom to which he belonged and about its ruler. Even if Alexander's empire symbolised some vague feeling of general Greek superiority to the neighbouring East, that feeling soon evaporated with the break-up of that empire and the infiltration of oriental ideas into it. But when Rome subdued Carthage and emerged the stronger for the conflict, there arose the notion that the Roman dominion was not just one more transitory assemblage of political units but a permanent, coherent thing with a meaning of its own. Further, as well as the notion of Rome was the fact of Italy as both a geographical and a spiritual unit. Italy had on the whole been loyal to Rome in her struggle against Carthage, and Italy was willing to accept the notion of Rome's conquering and organising and ultimately pacifying

mission. Rome, however, was not immediately willing to make Italy
an equal partner in the mission, and she delayed in granting the
Italian boroughs the rights of Roman citizenship. This delay precipitated civil war near the beginning of the first century B.C. and at the
very time when the Republic was beginning to break down, as Dryden
described. Though defeated in the war, the provinces got what they
demanded over the whole of Italy south of the Po. It remained for
Julius Caesar to give Roman citizenship to dwellers between the Po
and the Alps, of which district Virgil was a native. Now though the
Italian provincials supported the idea of Rome's mission, they were
not sentimental about the Roman republican constitution in the way
the Romans themselves were. Dilatory in granting them citizenship,
the Roman republic did not stand unequivocally for the principle of
political liberty. And as for Virgil's countrymen, it was the first
Roman dictator who had emancipated them. From all this it follows
that to Virgil's natural gratitude to Augustus for rescuing Italy from
a prolonged and intolerable period of civil war was added a readiness
to consider a dictator a man from whom more and not less personal
liberty could be expected.[1]

It is my belief that the greatest rendering of an English political
theme in English, and great enough to be called epic were it in narrative form, is the sequence of Shakespeare's history plays from the
reign of Richard II to the accession of Henry VII. Something of
Virgil's feeling for Augustus and Rome may be gathered by considering Shakespeare's feeling for the Tudors and England. If the
Tudors were more despotic monarchs than their medieval predecessors, that despotism was thought of as a small liability compared
with their immense services in rescuing the land from civil war. If
Virgil called Augustus a god, he was expressing in the language of his
day sentiments closely akin to what Shakespeare expressed in Richmond's wonderful speech at the end of *Richard III*, a speech in which
the individual voice of Shakespeare is merged in the common voice
of the whole land:

> *England hath long beene mad, and scarr'd her selfe;*
> *The Brother blindely shed the Brothers blood;*
> *The Father rashly slaughtered his owne Sonne;*
> *The Sonne, compell'd, beene Butcher to the Sire;*
> *All this divided Yorke and Lancaster,*
> *Divided in their dire Division.*
> *O now, let* Richmond *and* Elizabeth,
> *The true Succeeders of each Royall House,*
> *By Gods faire ordinance, conjoyne together:*
> *And let thy Heires* (God, *if thy Will be so*)

[1] For this paragraph I have drawn on T. R. Glover, *Studies in Virgil* (London 1904),
especially Chapter V.

Enrich the time to come, with Smooth-fac'd Peace,
With smiling Plenty, and faire Prosperous dayes.
Abate the edge of Traitors, Gracious Lord,
That would reduce these bloody dayes againe,
And make poore England weepe in Streames of Blood;
Let them not live to taste this Lands increase,
That would with Treason, wound this faire Lands peace.
Now Civill wounds are stopp'd, Peace lives agen;
That she may long live heere, God say, Amen.

If we bear this English analogy in mind along with the political positions of Virgil's day we may understand how he had at hand a political theme worthy of epic treatment, thereby securing spiritual independence from the prestige of contemporary Greek tradition.

CHAPTER V

VIRGIL

La venue même du Christ n'a rien qui étonne quand on a lu Virgile.
(Sainte-Beuve)

1. INTRODUCTORY

VIRGIL[1] was endowed by nature with the highest poetic gifts; he commanded words in a way able to stir men's hearts to their depths. But this is not the opinion of all. In particular, a powerful body of nineteenth-century readers questioned his essential poetical credentials and found him elegant and derivative, lacking the full native force of authentic genius.

It is difficult to know current opinion. For one thing there is so much less of it than there was fifty, let alone a hundred years ago. It is no longer a matter of living controversy whether Virgil erred in making his Aeneas so unyielding to Dido. My impression is that among the surviving readers of Virgil his status has recovered its pre-Romantic eminence and that an attempt like Mark Van Doren's[2] to label him a pretty and not a great poet is an exceptional prolongation of nineteenth-century myopia.

Nevertheless, it may be well, before I point out how Virgil fulfils the various other requirements for the epic, to recall some items from the great weight of testimony to Virgil's supremacy as a master of words that has accumulated through the ages since his death. Dryden, who spent three years in translating the *Aeneid* (and who wished he could spend four more), spoke of his difficulty as translator in matching the richness of Virgil's language, 'for Virgil, above all poets, had a stock, which I may call almost inexhaustible, of figurative, elegant, and sounding words'. He also asserts the absolute rightness of the order of Virgil's words, which 'must be read in order as they lie: the least breath discomposes them: and somewhat of their divinity is lost'. And he rises to a passionate enthusiasm, unique (as far as I remember) in his criticism, when he speaks of Virgil's highest flights:

If I cannot copy his harmonious numbers, how shall I imitate

---

[1] I wish to acknowledge a general debt to two long books on Virgil: T. R. Glover, *Studies in Virgil*, and E. K. Rand, *The Magical Art of Virgil* (Cambridge, Mass., 1931). I found C. M. Bowra's section on Virgil in *From Virgil to Milton* (London 1945) most valuable for what it says on the characters, their significance and development. I wish to record my admiration for C. S. Lewis's short chapter on Virgil in his *Preface to Paradise Lost* and my substantial agreement with its sentiments.

[2] In *The Noble Voice.*

his noble flights, where his thoughts and words are equally sublime? . . . What modern language, or what poet, can express the majestic beauty of this one verse, amongst a thousand others?

> *aude, hospes, contemnere opes, et te quoque dignum*
> *finge deo. . . .*

For my part, I am lost in the admiration of it: I contemn the world when I think on it, and myself when I translate it.[1]

More weighty still is Dante's testimony to Virgil as his master, the poet from whom he derived the high style that has done him honour. The great distinction of Dante's style is the separate weight which each word adds to his sentences. To read him is like watching a shop-man add the last potatoes or apples to the bag he is weighing. Every addition gives the indicator a separate jerk forward till the proper quantity is reached. This is not the way Virgil usually works, but he does so at times, and often enough to confirm the literal truth of Dante's tribute. These are the words Hector's ghost speaks to Aeneas in his sleep, telling him to leave the doomed city of Troy:

> *heu! fuge, nate dea, teque his (ait) eripe flammis.*
> *hostis habet muros; ruit alto a culmine Troia.*
> *sat patriae Priamoque datum.*

Here the words fall with the highest degree of apparent naturalness and yet with a weight of individual emphasis no poetry has excelled. They serve at once to demonstrate whence Dante derived the peculiar excellence of his style and to confute any notion of Virgil as a mainly pretty poet. Finally, for a modern testimony from an expert in poetical technique I quote T. S. Eliot's:

> As for maturity of style, I do not think that any poet has ever developed a greater command of the complex structure, both of sense and sound, without losing the resource of direct, brief and startling simplicity when the occasion required it.[2]

And in the same essay Eliot speaks of how Virgil by this very command exhausted the possibilities of the Latin language in its classical form. Virgil has indeed that supreme stylistic gift of using to the full just those points of diction and of idiom in which a language excels, thus fulfilling the great artistic law of best expressing the universal through the particular. He used the immense weight of the Latin tongue, for instance, both to make simple statements emphatic (as in the words of Hector's ghost to Aeneas) and to make solemn and serene his own

---

[1] *Dedication of the Aeneis*: see *Essays of John Dryden*, ed. W. P. Ker, ii. 233. The passage Dryden quotes ('Dare, my guest, to despise riches, and fashion yourself into worthiness of heaven') comes from Evander's speech to Aeneas (viii. 364) as they are about to enter his humble palace, where Hercules had been his guest.
[2] *What is a Classic?* (London 1944) 22.

delicate perception of human sentiment and power of natural description.

These desultory remarks on Virgil's use of words may serve a little to establish that in his fundamental poetic endowment he was equal to the epic form. I go on to the *Aeneid* and the question how far in it Virgil succeeded in seizing the epic possibilities which, I argued in my last chapter, the age of Augustus presented.

2. THE AENEID

The distinction of a poet—the dignity and humanity of his thought —can be measured by nothing, perhaps, so well as by the diameter of the world in which he lives; if he is supreme, his vision, like Dante's, always stretches to the stars. And Virgil, a supreme poet sometimes unjustly belittled, shows us the same thing in another form; his landscape is the Roman universe, his theme the sacred springs of Roman greatness in piety, constancy, and law. He has not written a line in forgetfulness that he was a Roman; he loves country life and its labours because he sees in it the origin and bulwark of civic greatness; he honours tradition because it gives perspective and momentum to the history that ensues; he invokes the gods, because they are symbols of the physical and moral forces by which Rome struggled to dominion. (George Santayana)

Virgil aimed high, and from the beginning of his poetical career. In his epilogue to the *Georgics* he said that he wrote this poem while Augustus was making his triumphal progress through the East after Actium, and added that he is the same poet who in youthful boldness —*audax iuventa*—wrote his *Eclogues*. Early in the *Georgics* he used the same word, *audax*, of the poem he is now engaged on. In the opening lines of the third book he described, through the allegory of a temple, the poem he *will* write on the triumphs of Augustus, plainly a very ambitious affair. And when he came to begin the *Aeneid* he sent a letter to Augustus saying that the matter was so great that it appeared to him almost an aberration of mind to have undertaken it. We know from contemporary witnesses and from his biographers that Virgil was naturally modest, and I believe Glover was right in saying that to him 'poetry was something like the "burden" of a Hebrew prophet'.[1] He was in his shyness and modesty alarmed at the great things that insisted on finding utterance through him. And those great things are there from the beginning: in the 'prophetic' fourth *Eclogue* and in the interludes in the agricultural theme of the *Georgics*.

Now the passage in the *Georgics* where Virgil proposed to celebrate

---

[1] *Op. cit.* 63.

the triumphs of Augustus is powerful and exalted: he seems well content to pour his prophetic rapture into this theme. But when he came to the point he made the *Aeneid* a very different affair from what he had promised. He does indeed celebrate Augustus's triumphs, but only through anticipatory reference to events in the distant future: they are a subsidiary affair. His audacity is now not merely that of a high theme but of a revolutionary method. Substituting for Augustus a hero from the remotest mythical past, Virgil also broke abruptly (as far as his main design went) with both Hellenistic and Roman epic precedent and went right back to Homer. His mythical narrative was far too seriously symbolic to resemble Apollonius Rhodius's elegant romance, while his tightly constructed and selective plot was the very contrary of Ennius's chronicle-method. The obvious analogy is with Milton's abandoning his more narrowly patriotic Arthuriad, a poem which would have been in the Renaissance mode, for *Paradise Lost*, which reverts to the older medieval themes of world-history and the fight of Heaven and Hell for the soul of Everyman. Further, both poets compensated the traditions they had abandoned as models for the main theme by following them clearly, at times lavishly, in the details. The episode of Camilla in the eleventh *Aeneid* is as pretty a piece of Hellenistic fancy as you could wish for, serving to diversify stretches of warfare that taxed Virgil's ingenuity to animate, while he pays his tribute to the great Ennius by working many of his lines into the texture of the *Aeneid*. Just so Milton endows his Adam (albeit essentially Everyman) with all the dignity of a Renaissance courtier and casts his medieval theme into the most correct contemporary neo-classic form. It is well to try to picture the literary state of affairs *before* a classic was written. Inevitably we tend to regard the classic as a norm and by it to judge not only what came after but what went before. We thus miss those things in the classic which were novel and brilliantly original in their day. We assume that Virgil's reversion to Homer and Milton's use of blank verse for the narrative were the most natural things in the world; actually they were in their day very daring innovations.

In saying that Virgil did not neglect these secondary traditions I was in fact leading to my next topic, his range and diversity. I can bring these out by comparing them with their Homeric counterparts. Virgil imitated Homer partly no doubt to indicate the scope of his ambition but also because Homer by his selective method had given weight and meaning to his great theme. Homer in the *Iliad* gave his version of the whole Trojan War; Virgil through the adventures of Aeneas the outline of a whole pattern of culture. He also imitated Homer in a great many details. But the differences of temper are very great indeed, and show up all the more through the similarities of structure.

The largest difference between the two poets has to do with concentration and diffusion, with simple and ambivalent states of mind, with a vertical shadowless light and a more horizontal variegating one. Or, to resort to another metaphor, Virgil lived in more places of the mind than Homer did. Homer inhabited an island in itself beautiful but containing fearful cliff and chasm as well as stream and meadow; an island explored from end to end and self-sufficient, even if one or two of the more imaginative inhabitants had inklings of other places across the sea. Virgil inhabited a continent less compact and harmonious than the Homeric island, but larger and surrounded by places only shallowly explored.

The same difference is especially evident in the poets' sense of time. Homer lives more intensely in the present than any great poet. There is indeed that mythical past in which his characters are supposed to live, a past when men were on a larger scale physically and mentally than the degenerate contemporaries, and there was a ghostly life after death. But both states are vague and anyhow draw what reality they have from the present. Virgil, in turning his panegyric of Augustus into a poem on Rome, merged the present into a process of evolution and stands nearer to Burke than he does to Homer.

> Our political system is placed in a just correspondence and symmetry with the order of the world, and with the mode of existence decreed to a permanent body composed of transitory parts; wherein, by a disposition of a stupendous wisdom, moulding together the great mysterious incorporation of the human race, the whole, at one time, is never old, or middle-aged, or young, but, in a condition of unchangeable constancy, moves on through the varied tenour of perpetual decay, renovation, and progression.

That is Burke talking primarily of the British political system but also stating a general principle of organic political growth. From Virgil such a developed scientific principle could not be deduced legitimately; but his picture of the Roman dominion painfully born out of the ruin of Troy, gradually fostered through many trials and misfortunes to the golden age of Augustus and ratified by Jove's promise of eternal rule—*imperium sine fine dedi*—is closer in its time-sense to the modern world of Burke than to the antique world of Homer.

Not that Virgil cannot concentrate on the immediate event and the concrete particular. For instance he describes, through the mouth of Aeneas, the details of the sack of Troy from the closest range. Aeneas's ancestral home, set in trees and a little away from Troy's centre, is not Trojan but the house of a great Roman patrician family; and when, roused from sleep, he looks out from the roof-top, he sees, not just fire, but Deiphobus's house fall in and the flames spreading to Ucalegon's next door and an inlet of the sea reflecting the flames.

And we are with Aeneas in Troy, concentrated solely on the present happening. But, whereas Homer, except where he is frankly distanced and romantic and fabulous, sees events in a uniformly brilliant light, on the spot before us, Virgil constantly varies the distance and in this variety creates a varying scale of time. Thus, if, for purposes of immediate narrative effect, Virgil may animate and modernise the region of Troy where Aeneas first sees the fire, Troy is also the city of an immemorial past, symbolic as well as real. Such it becomes in the terrifying passage where Venus (like Michael in the eleventh book of *Paradise Lost*) purges Aeneas's sight and shows him Neptune, Juno, Minerva, and finally Jove himself urging on the Greeks to destroy it. Since Virgil great literature has abounded in such spatial changes, whether of time or of the reader's position; and our very familiarity with them may make us too little curious of asking in what poet they first appear, to whom the innovation (in the western tradition) is due. If we are curious, I believe that we shall agree to assign the innovation to Virgil more than to any one poet. But there is another danger; and that is of assuming a break between classical and modern; of assuming that Virgil is bound to go with earlier classical literature and not with that of the Christian tradition. It is such an assumption that prompted the lamentable and ridiculous habit, common in the nineteenth century, of judging Virgil by Homeric standards. If you judge Virgil by Homer, he largely fails in the sense of present life; if you judge Homer by Virgil, he comes out over-simplified and impoverished.

Let me transfer the comparison of the *Iliad* and the *Aeneid* to the matter of war; where the *Aeneid* has often been blamed for its inferior treatment. The blame is partly justified because in places Virgil was unwise enough to treat battles in the antique Homeric way with single fights and purely individual prowess. Luckily in the single fight that most mattered, that between Aeneas and Turnus at the end of the poem, he evaded comparison with Homer by handing things over to the gods and casting over the duel an air of mystery. But there are stretches of straightforward hand-to-hand fighting between persons; and here, in spite of conscientious and often in themselves successful efforts to embellish, Virgil is out of his element and dully imitative, where Homer is vital. I cannot myself share the common admiration for the episode of Nisus and Euryalus in Book Nine. It lacks the military reality of the *Iliad* and it is strained and extravagant in sentiment. It is kindest to overlook its intention of competing with Homer and to associate it with the episode of Camilla as a piece of Alexandrian prettiness inserted to diversify the amount of fighting which Virgil felt obliged to include out of respect for Homeric precedent. But there are other military elements which are not in Homer and by whose measure he would fail. There is no strategy in

Homer. Agamemnon's job is to ensure that everyone fights as well as possible; he does not direct the war. But Aeneas is a real general; and his Italian campaign is both interesting in itself and expresses the interest the Romans and Latins had in a developed art of war. Aeneas landed at the mouth of the Tiber and at once fortified a camp. In fact, he set up a bridge-head. He then tried for a peaceful settlement with the local rulers. The settlement broke down and he went with a small number of followers to procure allies. First they go in two ships up the Tiber to the site of future Rome, where they get a little help from the Arcadians settled there and learn that a large section of Etruscans are on the brink of revolt and are only awaiting a leader. Aeneas sends back the two ships, keeps a handful of men and borrows horses to take him to the disaffected Etruscans, whose head-quarters are on the coast. He gains his new allies and with them sets out by sea to relieve the camp, which he had ordered his men to hold without risking a battle in the open. The camp has just and only just held out when Aeneas relieves it. When he does so there is a great battle in the country near by which the Trojans and their allies finally win. After a pause for burying the dead, Aeneas passes to the offensive and invades the country towards the capital, beneath the walls of which the last battle takes place. Thus, whatever some of the details, the main outlines of the war are interesting, convincing, and complicated in a way quite beyond Homer's reach.

Along with a different interest in war there is a different feeling about it. Homer thought war terrible and in a way hated it, but he didn't doubt it, for it just was life. The idea of war to end war was outside his ken. But by the irony of history the greatest of all military races had produced it: partly because they believed so passionately in law and order and partly because civil war on and off for some seventy years had altered the Roman disposition to it. The *Aeneid* speaks fully for its age in these things. Aeneas himself has no liking for war and always tries to fulfil fate's exacting demands by peaceful means. He can show fierce anger in battle, but it is a very different feeling from the simple battle-excitement of Homer's warriors—the eager trembling of the men in ambush for instance—and far more complex. It contains a feverish eagerness to be done with the hateful thing, and rage against the enemy either for breaking treaties or for being stupid in resisting, after resistance is plainly hopeless. It is, however, Virgil's account of the fall of Troy that most reflects the sordid horrors of the wars that had preceded the peace of Augustus. The fighting itself is not war but massacre, while the scientific treachery of Sinon is sinister beyond anything in Homer. In the perfection of all its details it deceives all the Trojans, clever and simple alike; and Aeneas's comment on it makes it a terrible thing: something diabolical, not to be defeated by ordinary humanity.

talibus insidiis periurique arte Sinonis
credita res, captique dolis lacrimisque coactis
quos neque Tydides nec Larissaeus Achilles,
non anni domuere decem, non mille carinae.[1]

The feeling resembles Milton's when he comments on the success of
Satan, disguised as a stripling cherub, in deceiving Uriel, regent of
the sun and the keenest sighted of all heaven's host.

So spake the false dissembler unperceivd;
For neither Man nor Angel can discern
Hypocrisie, the only evil that walks
Invisible, except to God alone,
By his permissive will, through Heav'n and Earth:
And oft though wisdom wake, suspicion sleeps
At wisdoms Gate, and to simplicite
Resigns her charge, while goodness thinks no ill
Where no ill seems.[2]

The result of such deception, when discovered, is exaggerated suspicion as sinister as the thing it springs from; and suspicion is the
curse and the terror of all periods of civil war. Sinon re-creates the
conditions of civil war with surpassing force.

More directly the Fury sent by Juno to stir up the Latins and
Rutulians to break up the original truce (Book Seven) expresses
Virgil's hatred and horror of that civil war whose indefinite protrac-
tion must to all men of good will have seemed to have something
uncanny and devilish in it. Juno in sending her confesses to devilish
and destructive motives:

flectere si nequeo superos Acheronta movebo.[3]

And if she cannot prevent the Trojans from getting a footing in Italy
and mingling with its inhabitants, she can make the process futile by
joint destruction:

at licet amborum populos exscindere regum.[4]

And the description that follows of the Fury throwing one of her
snake-locks at Amata, wife of Latinus, combines Virgil's peculiar
power of arousing terror and the spirit of an epoch when terror was
everywhere rife. The snake glides over Amata's body, turns itself into
her golden necklace and the hanging end of the fillet that ties her
hair. It is the identification of the infernal snake with the ordinary

[1] ii. 195-8. 'Such was the crafty art of perjured Sinon that his story gained belief.
And we, whom neither Diomede nor Achilles subdued nor ten years' war nor a
thousand ships, were vanquished by his cunning and his pretended tears.'
[2] *Paradise Lost*, iii. 681-9.
[3] 312. 'If I cannot sway the gods above I will rouse Hell.'
[4] 316. 'At least I may destroy the subjects of both kings.'

THE AENEID

personal objects that is so terrifying, for it reflects the morbid state of
mind when nothing is what it seems, when the man who seemed so
simple and whom you have trusted without question may really be
a spy and an enemy. From corrupting single persons, the Fury goes
to stir up mass suspicion and panic. And here again Virgil differs
from Homer, for though the spirit of Homer's armies may wax and
wane, there is no sense, as there is in Virgil, of mass-movements over
a wide area of country and among whole populations, soldiers and
civilians alike.

The business of war is thus vastly more complicated in Virgil than
in Homer. For instance, Actium could present itself not only as a
glorious victory for the Emperor but as a battle that ended a series of
wars worse than itself. War in fact was for Virgil not just an accepted
activity that raised man to the height of his activities though involving
horrible things, but something so fraught with evil that men could
conceive, even if they did not put in action, a positive revolt against it.

Virgil's horror of war is the negative side of his dearest moral
principle: his belief in the ordered life. I go on to describe this belief.
In doing so, though continuing incidentally the Homeric comparison,
I shall concentrate more on Virgil; on the range of mind this belief
implies and on its kinship with the group-mind of Italy.

The emotional roots of Virgil's feeling for order are in his agricultural origin. The Greeks never were and are not now a purely
agricultural people. They are also shepherds and sailors. The Italians
are farmers and, though farmers may make the best soldiers, they
believe at bottom in a steady way of life that follows the rhythms of
the seasons and their appropriate tasks. Virgil's feeling for order is
profound and it speaks both for Italy and for all agricultural societies.
It also extends beyond its agricultural origin, so as to include the
Roman beliefs in law and in the Roman mission for imposing law on
the lawless. Very properly these different beliefs are blended in the
Aeneid. They are so fundamental to the poem and so ubiquitous that
it is hard to know what illustrations to choose.

For the sheer homing instinct, for the yearning after the settled life
on the land, Aeneas's words to Helenus, Priam's son settled on the
west coast of Greece, will suffice, for they typify Aeneas's feelings
throughout:

> *vivite felices, quibus est fortuna peracta*
> *iam sua; nos alia ex aliis in fata vocamur.*
> *vobis parta quies; nullum maris aequor arandum,*
> *arva neque Ausoniae semper cedentia retro*
> *quaerenda.*[1]

[1] iii. 493-7. 'Live and be happy, you whose destiny has been worked out; we are
called from one fate into another. You have won your rest: you need plough no
fields of ocean, nor seek the plains of Italy ever vanishing.'

The words about ploughing the sea are no mere figure of speech. *Ploughing* is nostalgic: it is the fields of Italy not the sea they should be ploughing. But Virgil can speak more subtly and indirectly about order. Right at the beginning of the poem he insinuates the theme. Seeing the Trojan fleet on the way to Italy, Juno rouses herself to action and visits Aeolus in his cave, where he keeps the winds:

> *hic vasto rex Aeolus antro*
> *luctantis ventos tempestatesque sonoras*
> *imperio premit ac vinclis et carcere frenat.*
> *illi indignantes magno cum murmure montis*
> *circum claustra fremunt; celsa sedet Aeolus arce*
> *sceptra tenens, mollitque animos et temperat iras;*
> *ni faciat, maria ac terras caelumque profundum*
> *quippe ferant rapidi secum verrantque per auras.*[1]

This passage is symbolic as well as a piece of mythological description. The winds, chafing at their bonds and eager to bring back chaos if allowed, have little to do with the quaint episode in the *Odyssey* of Aeolus giving to Odysseus the winds sealed in skins to help him on his journey; rather they have the meaning Lear found in the storm into which his daughters drove him: while Aeolus's action in being over-persuaded by Juno to indulge the winds' lust for destruction beyond the proper bounds was a piece of insubordination in the celestial hierarchy, duly castigated later on by Neptune. Finally, when Neptune calms the waves he is compared to a great statesman quelling a mob in a great nation, *magno in populo*. The theme of order and disorder is thus set forth in the natural world, among the gods, and in humanity. Coming as it does at the very outset of the poem, it shows itself a master-theme. Simply as a storm, and no more, the storm that throws Odysseus on to Phaeacia is superior to Virgil's; it has the certainty of unmixed reality. But it lacks the richness of Virgil's symbolism. Virgil's account of Aeolus's winds revolting and then after doing some mischief being controlled symbolises what he hopes is a general human truth. The richness consists not only in symbolism being added to description but in the division of Virgil's mind between fear and hope: fear lest chaos may indeed prevail, hope that in the last resort it will not.

Having in this passage applied the theme of order and chaos to humanity at large, Virgil immediately after turns to his individual human actors. Aeneas lands in Africa with the crews of the seven

---

[1] i. 52-9. 'Here in his huge cave Aeolus, their king, controls by his rule the struggling winds and loud storms and curbs them with prison bonds. They, in resentment, roar at the barriers making the mountain moan deeply. In his high citadel Aeolus sits sceptre in hand, and eases their temper and mitigates their wrath; otherwise, they would surely carry with them in violent flight seas, land and heaven's vault and whirl them through the air.'

ships which alone appear to have escaped the storm, shoots seven
stags to fit the seven ships and divides the wine that remained in the
ships, thus keeping the proprieties in spite of shipwreck. Then he
cheers his men with splendidly courageous words. But he is far from
cheerful within and acts as he does through sheer will-power:

> *talia voce refert curisque ingentibus aeger*
> *spem voltu simulat, premit altum corde dolorem.*[1]

Thus the conflict between order and confusion rages in Aeneas's
microcosm too, with order finally victorious.

What Virgil here expresses through a single mind he expresses
again through the way in which the Trojans and their chief enemies,
Turnus and his Rutulians, wage war. There had been a skirmish in
Book Seven, but the real fighting first begins in Book Nine with
Turnus's attack on the Trojan camp while Aeneas was away looking
for allies. When the Trojans see the dust rising from the approaching
enemy they man the defences; and the way Virgil describes this is
highly significant:

> *ingenti clamore per omnis*
> *condunt se Teucri portas et moenia complent.*
> *namque ita discedens praeceperat optimus armis*
> *Aeneas, si qua interea fortuna fuisset,*
> *neu struere auderent aciem neu credere campo;*
> *castra modo et tutos servarent aggere muros.*
> *ergo, etsi conferre manum pudor iraque monstrat,*
> *obiciunt portas tamen et praecepta facessunt,*
> *armatique cavis expectant turribus hostem.*[2]

With the natural, instinctive, and primitive part of themselves the
Trojans wanted to go out and fight. But Aeneas, like a good general,
gave his orders before he left; and the Trojans, disciplined and
trusting their leader, used their will-power and obeyed him. In fact,
they showed themselves civilised. When the siege is set, the Trojans
are hard put to it to keep the enemy out. The final episode in the
day's fighting is of Turnus penetrating into the Trojan camp through
one of the gates and then being shut in. He begins killing the Trojans,
and then Virgil makes his comment:

> *diffugiunt versi trepida formidine Troes.*
> *et si continuo victorem ea cura subisset*

---

[1] i. 208-9. 'Such were his words, and although sick with huge misery he feigns
hope in his aspect, he keeps down his heart's profound grief.'

[2] ix. 38-46. 'With a great shout the Trojans seek cover through every entrance
and man the walls. For these were the orders that Aeneas, best of generals, had issued
as he left: that, if any emergency should arise, they should not presume to prepare
for a pitched battle nor try their chance in the open; no, they must do no more than
hold the camp and rely on the secure defences of their walls. Therefore, though
shame and anger prompt them to join open battle, they bar the gates according to
his orders and standing to arms await the enemy under cover of the towers.'

rumpere claustra manu sociosque immittere portis,
ultimus ille dies bello gentique fuisset;
sed furor ardentem caedisque insana cupido
egit in adversos.[1]

Turnus is thus the very opposite of the Trojans, for his instinctive passions quite master him. Finally the Trojans rally, and the book ends with one of the most wonderful things in the poem, the description of Turnus, exhausted, driven back by the concerted weight of Trojan numbers and saving his life only by jumping into the river that bounded the camp on one side and swimming across. The description is closely imitated from the *Iliad*,[2] where Ajax, at the height of the Trojans' fortune, tries in vain to keep them from the Greek ships and is forced back by numbers. Homer's description, simply as one of a great fighter losing finely against odds, could not be bettered. Virgil's description not only equals Homer's in immediate vividness but presses home the symbolic meaning already conveyed by the two passages just discussed. The Trojans stand for rational unity and civilised mutual aid and in the end they overwhelm the gigantic but undisciplined prowess of Turnus. The true parallel with Virgil is Milton's picture at the end of Book Four of *Paradise Lost* showing Gabriel's watch in Eden (composed of angels of humble rank) hemming in Satan and for all his superiority of rank and stature forcing him to fly. It is the same symbolism enlarged into Christian terms.

What is so impressive about Virgil's faith in order is that it includes so much. It ranges from the proper performance of a village ritual to the civilising power of Rome's legal institutions. It includes both the abstract reverence for order analogous to that expounded in the *Laws of Ecclesiastical Polity* and every concrete manifestation of it. Nowhere does Virgil's epic span show itself better than in the varied manifestations of this faith.

So far I have written of Virgil's sense of the complexity of existence as shown in his treatment of time, and of war, and of the principle of order and discipline both military and civil. I pass on to its vaguer and more metaphysical manifestations. Homer presented the contrasts comprised in a single world, with incomparable force. He approximated the extreme peril of Hector in war and the Trojan women bringing the washing to the spring in time of peace, and in doing so he exploited the emotional possibilities of poetry to the extreme. But both matters are steeped alike in what has been happily called the vertical light of Homer's scene; they give not the least hint

[1] ix. 755-61. 'Turned to flight in great fear the Trojans scatter. And if at once Turnus in his victory had had the sense to break the bolt and let his fellows in at the gates, this would have been the last day for war and Trojan nation alike. But wild mad lust of slaughter drove him impetuously against those in front of him.'
[2] xvi. 102 ff.

THE AENEID

of belonging to different worlds of existence. If they had given it they would have lost their proper power. Virgil, on the contrary, is without a rival in the subtle suggestion of different worlds of existence. He was not necessarily better endowed than other great poets with such a power, but living at a time of religious and philosophical eclecticism he was not committed to any rigid dogmatism that might curtail the exploratory freedom of his sensibility. It was in the consciousness of this freedom that he mingled a mild rebuke with his superb tribute to Lucretius in the *Georgics*:

> *felix qui potuit rerum cognoscere causas*
> *atque metus omnis et inexorabile fatum*
> *subiecit pedibus strepitumque Acherontis avari.*
> *fortunatus et ille deos qui novit agrestis,*
> *Panaque Silvanumque senem Nymphasque sorores.*[1]

If Lucretius (to whom he is pointing in the first sentence) succeeded in suppressing the fear of death in his Epicurean philosophy, it was at the price of sterilising certain parts of his mind; in this case the part that values the traditional rural pieties.

It is in some of his theophanies or divine metamorphoses that Virgil most clearly indicates his sense of different worlds. Venus, early in the *Aeneid*, declaring herself to her son and then eluding him, surely goes beyond a mere piece of mythological contrivance:

> *dixit, et avertens rosea cervice refulsit,*
> *ambrosiaeque comae divinum vertice odorem*
> *spiravere, pedes vestis defluxit ad imos;*
> *et vera incessu patuit dea. ille ubi matrem*
> *agnovit, tali fugientem est voce secutus:*
> *quid natum toties, crudelis tu quoque, falsis*
> *ludis imaginibus? cur dextrae iungere dextram*
> *non datur ac veras audire et reddere voces?*[2]

Here definition is impossible, as it is undesirable; but that Virgil intended some reference to a world of appearance and a world of superior truth is not to be denied. Again, later in the same book Virgil seems to posit some difference between the world of business and the world of art, rather as Keats does in his *Ode on a Grecian Urn*. When, after their long sufferings, Aeneas and his men arrive at Dido's

[1] ii. 490-4. 'Happy is the man who could learn the reason of things and who spurned all fears and inexorable fate and the noise of greedy Acheron. Blessed too is that man who knows the country gods, Pan and old Silvanus and the sister Nymphs.'

[2] *Aeneid*, i. 402-9. 'She ended and turning away she flushed over her rosy neck, and her immortal hair breathed forth a divine fragrance from her head; her robe dropped flowing to her feet and by her gait she was revealed a true goddess. He, recognising his mother, followed her thus with his voice as she escaped: "Are you, too, cruel to me, although your son? Why do you mock him so often with deluding appearances? Why am I not allowed to lock hand in hand and to hear your own voice and answer in mine?"'

palace at Carthage, they see sculptured on the temple of Juno pictures
of the Trojan War, including Priam. Aeneas is moved to tears and
says to Achates:

> *quae regio in terris nostri non plena laboris?*
> *en Priamus! sunt hic etiam sua praemia laudi,*
> *sunt lacrimae rerum et mentem mortalia tangunt.*
> *solve metus; feret haec aliquam tibi fama salutem.*[1]

The famous third line is popularly taken from its context and misunderstood in a general sense, which is that life is a melancholy affair
for men. In the whole context *hic* is the important word. *Here,* in the
work of art, in the different realm of the artist, merit, however unfortunate, is recognised; *here* there is sympathy and pity for the
affairs of men.

But though Virgil can indicate better worlds than the obvious one
that confronts us, he can indicate (and with the highest power and
majesty) another world of terror. I have already given two examples.
All unknown to mortals till Venus purged Aeneas's sight, the greatest
gods had been fighting with the Greeks to destroy the city of Troy.
Unknown to Amata, the gold necklace she wore was one of Allecto's
snakes curled round her neck. There are other examples of a Fury's
metamorphosis. After infecting Amata with her venom, Allecto turns
into an old priestess and as such appears to Turnus in his sleep.
Turnus, with characteristic insolence, mocks her forebodings, whereupon Allecto appears in her true form and strikes him with panic.
But Virgil keeps his crowning terror to the end of the poem. When
Aeneas and Turnus are due to face each other in final fight, Jupiter,
as he does at turning-points of history, and as he did when Troy
actually fell, intervenes and takes charge. He has at his bidding two
Furies, who attend on his throne. One of these he sends to warn off
the nymph Juturna, and to baffle Turnus so that he may beyond all
doubt fall at the hand of Aeneas. As the monster approaches the
battle-field she shrinks herself into the shape of a small bird of the
kind that haunts tombs or deserted houses and utters her ill-omened
note. In this shape she flies to and fro shrieking in front of Turnus's
face. His limbs grow numb with dread. Juturna, with the higher
perceptions of an immortal, recognises the fiend and knows herself
beaten. She exclaims

> *iam iam linquo acies: ne me terrete timentem,*
> *obscenae volucres. alarum verbera nosco*
> *letalemque sonum.*[2]

---

[1] *Ib.* 460-3. 'What tract of land is not full of our toil? Behold Priam! Here too
merit has its reward; here are tears for the realities of life, and mortal doings touch the
mind. Dismiss your fears. The fame revealed here will bring you some comfort.'

[2] xii. 875-7. 'I haste to leave the battle. I fear enough; do not terrify me, you birds
of ill omen. I recognise the beating of your wings and their mortal sound.'

The imagination that shrunk the great Fury into the form of a little bird commands a sense of unknown and frightening realms of being surpassed by no other poet.

The types of mental experience just discussed are on the borders of religious experience, or, if you prefer, are the material out of which more definite religious experience grows. I mentioned the religious eclecticism of Virgil's day, and I now add that Virgil shared it and succeeded in putting it to his own poetic uses. If you abstract his religious beliefs from their poetic context, you find an apparently ill-assorted and contradictory array of primitive superstitions, evolved pagan theology, and highly sophisticated ethics. In their context they melt into the pervading spirituality of the poem and enrich without any suspicion of conflict. One reason for this is that all Virgil's religious entities are ambivalent, presenting more than one side from which to make connections. Virgil introduces many primitive deities: household gods and the spirits of trees and rivers. In so doing he expresses his own sympathy both with the simple pieties of an agricultural people and with Augustus's coolly political attempt to foster them in Italy. It is in the eighth book of the *Aeneid* that Virgil most exquisitely mingles the primitive and the political. Aeneas, greatly perplexed at the failure of his peaceful overtures, goes late to sleep and is comforted by the quiet vision of the very genius of the place, the God of the river Tiber.

> huic deus ipse loci fluvio Tiberinus amoeno
> populeas inter senior se attollere frondes
> visus (eum tenuis glauco velabat amictu
> carbasus et crinis umbrosa tegebat harundo).[1]

And the god assures Aeneas that he has found his home at last and fixity for his household deities. Virgil has taken us into the basic realm of simple Italian religion. Then Aeneas goes to the site of Rome and finds Evander sacrificing to Hercules. Evander lives in great simplicity, and Hercules, whom he had known in the flesh, is primitive in another way, a hero-god. Later Evander speaks of the land's first inhabitants, the Fauns and Nymphs and the race of wild men, sprung from oaks and other trees. To these Saturn gave laws and instituted a golden age. Then Evander shows Aeneas round the site of Rome-to-be, and Virgil makes Evander's sight-seeing tour the means of giving the primitive features hitherto described their ambivalence. The Capitol is a rocky wooded hill, and Evander says that it is a holy place and that the rustics are in awe of it; but by calling it the Capitol Virgil associates the rustic superstition with the cult of

---

[1] 31-4. 'Before him the very god of the place, old Tiber with his pleasant stream, seemed to rear himself from among his poplars. Grey drapery of thin lawn wrapped him round, and shady reeds covered his hair.'

Jupiter, who later had his great temple there, and with the whole apparatus of Roman justice and rule. At the same time he wishes us to remember here that Augustus tried to refound the might of Rome on the solidity of rustic piety. Then, host and guest, passing the Forum, now a pasture-ground for oxen, reach Evander's house, which occupied the site of Augustus's palace, and Evander ushers Aeneas in with these most pregnant words:

> haec (inquit) limina victor
> Alcides subiit, haec illum regia cepit.
> aude, hospes, contemnere opes et te quoque dignum
> finge deo, rebusque veni non asper egenis.[1]

The *precise* allegory of these lines we shall never unravel, but we do know that Augustus was reckoned a hero-god like Hercules and that he lived in great simplicity. In some sense Hercules shadows him, as Evander's lowly palace shadows the simple life of Augustus, while Evander's last two lines would be appropriate in Augustus's own mouth as he brought in a guest. But precise allegory does not matter compared with the general multiplicity of meaning.

There has been much discussion about Jupiter and that Fate which is so prominent in the *Aeneid*. Are they identical, or is Fate something more fundamental, whose decrees Jupiter must carry out? I doubt if Virgil wanted his readers to answer the question, for uncertainty may suit his poetic purposes best. On the other hand he surely wishes us to associate in some sort not only Jupiter and Fate but the spirit animating all life of which Virgil writes in the sixth book:

> principio caelum ac terras camposque liquentis
> lucentemque globum lunae Titaniaque astra
> spiritus intus alit totamque infusa per artus
> mens agitat molem et magno se corpore miscet.[2]

It is this spirit and this mind that are the first causes of the great events in history and in particular the rise of Roman dominion. The fall of Troy was one of these events, and Troy was both forfeit to the Fates and had her fall promoted by Jupiter, even though, as one of the pagan pantheon, he had a partiality for her. Plainly in view of such overlapping (which poetically is perfectly acceptable) we should refrain from schematising the provinces of the highest powers Virgil introduces. Or take the most prominent of all the council scenes in heaven, that at the beginning of Book Ten before the battle that

---

[1] viii. 362-5. 'Under this lintel, he said, Hercules passed; this palace received him. Have the courage, my guest, to despise wealth; more, fashion yourself to be worthy of this god and do not think harshly of our straitened state as you visit us.'

[2] 724-7. 'In the beginning a spirit nourished from within the sky and land and watery plains and the round moon and the sun, and a soul infused into their parts stirred the whole mass and permeated the vast body.'

decided the issue of the war. Here Jupiter complains that he had forbidden war in Italy and his decree had been broken. Why not restore the treaty? Whereupon Venus and Juno make passionate speeches, Venus temperamental and despairing, Juno violent and intransigent. And the other gods are divided in feeling. Jupiter then accepts the war as inevitable and utters some very weighty but oracularly ambiguous words:

> quae cuique est fortuna hodie, quam quisque secat spem,
> Tros Rutulusve fuat, nullo discrimine habebo,
> seu fatis Italum castra obsidione tenentur
> sive errore malo Troiae monitisque sinistris.
> nec Rutulos solvo. sua cuique exorsa laborem
> fortunamque ferent. rex Iuppiter omnibus idem;
> fata viam invenient.[1]

The general sense is plain: the time is not quite ripe for a decision; things have got to work themselves out. But who is responsible for working them out? Does Jupiter, feeling that the matter is now beyond him, give over and refer it to the controlling Spirit and Mind, or is he Fate itself, ironically feigning ignorance and withholding the knowledge of the future he surely possesses? I think it would be wrong to attempt to answer such a question. It is the *sense* of fate that matters, and doubt as to the precise way of its workings is more an advantage than not. When, as the book proceeds, in a battle unweighted by divine intervention, Fate declares for the Trojans, Jupiter becomes the traditional father of the family of gods and provokes Juno (*compellat ultro*) with ironical words, telling her—what is now so plainly untrue—that the Trojans owe everything to Venus and nothing to their own toughness in this victory. Juno knows she is beaten, whereupon Jupiter gives her leave to postpone the fatal hour by withdrawing Turnus from battle. Once again we should accept the double function of a Jupiter who certainly derives from Homer's Zeus and who at the same time is either Fate itself or one who knows Fate's workings. That we feel no sense of incongruity as we read is a tribute to Virgil's poetical power.

In sum the multiplicity of the different manifestations of the numinous in the *Aeneid* works powerfully in securing for the poem the variety necessary for the true epic effect.

In composing the *Aeneid* Virgil kept a single heart and a steady mind in a way that fully validates the poem's range. Nevertheless, in one particular of plotting he falls short of Homer and Milton: namely

---

[1] x. 107-13. 'What the fortune of each is today, whatever hope each pursues (whether he be Trojan or Rutulian) I shall be impartial about; whether it be the Italian destiny that holds them besieged in their camp or the sins of Troy and a misleading prophecy. Nor do I exempt the Rutulians from this same principle. The ventures of each shall bring their own toil and destiny. Jupiter is the same to all alike. Fate will find its way.'

in the turning-point of his whole design. The plots of both *Iliad* and *Odyssey* lead with successful logic to the deciding events: the deaths of Hector and of the suitors. And Homer rises as he should when he describes those events. The plot of *Paradise Lost* leads with successful logic to the apparent climax of the Fall of man in Book Nine and to the real climax of the human pair's regeneration in Book Ten. And these two books are worthy of their crucial position. In the *Aeneid* the war which is to decide the fate of Rome and to unite Trojan with Italian reaches its turning-point in Book Ten, when Aeneas relieves the Trojan camp and in the ensuing battle proves himself and his men the favourites of Fate. After that it is a question not of what the end will be but merely of how long it will be delayed and in what form it will come about. But Virgil, in spite of his pregnant council scene in heaven at the beginning, fails in the ensuing battle to rise to the height of his argument. It is possible that if he had lived he would have revised drastically Books Nine to Eleven, where the bulk of the fighting occurs. As they stand they constitute a culminating unit, but in them Virgil most imitates Homer in things which were inimitable, the heroic hand-to-hand battle scenes; and by such imitation inevitably writes below himself. (It is only in the last book, in the duel between Aeneas and Turnus, that Virgil invests his heroes with an air of allegory and remoteness and, free from Homeric comparisons, triumphs in his own way.) They are therefore the weakest part of the whole poem.

Apart from this weakness of execution there is nothing wrong with Virgil's design, which is inferior in its general outline to that of none of the first epics. He follows Homer's selective method; and just as the *Iliad* by a judiciously simplified action pictures the whole Trojan War and then a whole way of life, so the *Aeneid* by an ancient and essentially simple myth pictures the history of Rome and the ethos of Italy. There is of course the difference that Homer pictured a way of life unconsciously and Virgil consciously, but it does not extend to the shape of the picture.

Where Homer and Virgil most differ is in their treatment of character; and this difference has its bearing on their poems' structure. There is nothing symbolic about Homer's characters: none of them sums up in his own person any of the values Homer believed in. Achilles is the first fighter in the war, but he does not represent the value of valour. Diomede or Glaucus are just as much fighters though less eminent as such. Hector through his home at Troy may have more to do with the value of the peaceful order than the Greek chiefs, but Achilles also has to do with it when he thinks or speaks of his father and the peaceful life which, good in itself, he has renounced. But Virgil's main agents are symbols as well as persons and as such belong more closely to the plot than Homer's. Homer's characters act the plot, and out of their combined actions emerge the fundamental ideas of his two epics. Virgil's characters may do the same up to a point, but they simultaneously embody either in themselves or through their mutual relations the same ideas that the plot conveys.

The plot of the *Aeneid* has to do with destruction and rebirth, disintegration and synthesis, or however you prefer to put it. We need not be too curious about the precise significance of Troy, but it was a great city ruled by great men and it was an old city with a tradition of good living. It represents a civilisation more evolved than either Dido's nascent state of Carthage or the more rustic conditions of Latium so beautifully described in the seventh book. But Aeneas escaped from Troy with a large following and he carried, in the shape of his household gods, the spirit of the place with him, a spirit destined, as he learnt in various ways, to a new embodiment. Before Aeneas and the Trojans can achieve their new destiny they have to be tried in various ways. They have to learn and to endure and finally to fight. But the fight is other and better than the old fight over Troy, for it leads not to destruction but to reconciliation and union. Blended with the tough rusticity of native Italy, the more evolved Trojan civilisation turns into something new and lasting.

In speaking of the symbolic side of the main actors I wish neither to deny nor to dwell on their weight and beauty as characters. Enough has been written on the human tragedies of Dido and Turnus. All I am concerned with here is how the symbolic side of the main characters reinforces the trend of the plot.

Dido, on her symbolic as against her human side, stands for the unrestrained sensibility condemned by the Stoics and the implacable spirit of historical Carthage. And these qualities, lack of restraint and implacability, are just those which Aeneas must shun if he is to found Rome. At first sight Dido may seem too good a woman and too pitiful a figure to symbolise Carthage; Virgil may seem to sacrifice symbolic truth to the more human requirements of tragedy. But not necessarily; for Virgil, even if he approved of Roman resolution to tame her, may well have distrusted the conventional, rather melodramatic, denigrations of Carthage, such as Livy presents, and have felt pity for her heroic, though futile and desperate, resistance in the final siege in the Third Punic War. The flames of Dido's pyre are surely too the final conflagration of Carthage, just as Aeneas's previous resistance to the fury of her pleas is also that of Fabius Maximus and the other heroes of resisting Rome in the Second War.

Turnus, modelled (as Aeneas is not) on the fiercer of Homer's Greek warriors, represents an antique and barbaric energy, in some ways fine and an essential ingredient in a race of conquerors, but, when unmitigated, destined to give way because of its stupidity and lack of adaptability. Readers who dislike Aeneas have tended to be sentimental about Turnus, praising his warmth and forthrightness, which they find more attractive than Aeneas's temperance and rigid self-restraint. Virgil designed him as a mixed character and wished to divide our sympathies. However much he makes us admire Turnus's energy and his uncomplaining recognition of impending death, he makes us ever bear in mind his gratuitous pride and brutality when he meets Pallas:

> *solus ego in Pallanta feror, soli mihi Pallas*
> *debetur; cuperem ipse parens spectator adesset.*[1]

Turnus, therefore, represents not only a temper which a conquering civilisation must embody but one which it must reject.

Aeneas himself is more complicated, both in the ingredients of his character and in his power to develop, and as such has an additional structural importance in the poem. As a Trojan he stands for a temper more civilised and less fierce than that of Dido and Turnus, for that side of the mind which must mitigate and blend with the fiercer side, so that a conqueror may become a maker of peace and order as well as a winner of battles. But, as an individual, he does actually command both types of mind represented by Trojans and Latin allies. In fight he is capable of the primitive fury necessary for victory, even if he hates war in itself. He does in fact symbolise the spirit of Rome, as Virgil conceived it. Whether or not he stands for Augustus too, matters much less. Anyhow, Aeneas embodies the theme which the poem's action itself sets forth and in so doing greatly reinforces the structure.

But Aeneas does not succeed in symbolising Rome immediately; for in the first part of the poem he conducts in his own bosom the same battle which in the second half the fighting nations conduct on the fields of Italy. Since Bowra has described this in detail, I can here be brief. The gist of the matter is that until Aeneas has visited the underworld, his character is not settled. In the siege of Troy he is thoughtlessly passionate and fails to heed the warning of Hector's ghost that the time for helping Troy is over and that rational flight is the only sane course. At Carthage his mistake, his weakness, was not that he left Dido but that he ever allowed himself to get so strongly involved. It may not have been noted that in the wanderings before the arrival at Carthage, described in the third book, it is his father Anchises who often takes the initiative. Aeneas has not yet found himself. His resistance to Dido's entreaties (like Milton's Samson to Dalila's) marks the true formation of his character, which is confirmed by his visit to his father in the underworld. In the second part of the poem his character does not change, though his personality may shift away from realism to a vast allegorical vagueness.

[1] x. 442-3. 'Alone I advance against Pallas; to me alone is Pallas forfeit; I could only wish his father were here to watch.'

THE AENEID

This duplication of the main action in the mind of Aeneas seems to me a wonderful stroke of structural genius. But it makes one's demands on the second half of the poem all the more exacting and shows up the more Virgil's comparative failure to touch the heights in Book Ten.

To the question whether the *Aeneid* fulfils the epic condition of speaking for a large group antiquity gave the answer; for it hailed the poem immediately as its own authentic voice. And if in the nineteenth century men valued it less, they did so not because it failed to speak for a large group but because that group, the Roman group, was out of favour while the Greek was in. As the poem of Rome and of Italy it has not been seriously challenged. But the peculiar greatness of the *Aeneid* (and in this it surpasses all epics except the *Divine Comedy*) is that it also speaks for a whole change of human temper in the western world. Though cast in the form of the old heroic epic, the *Aeneid* is distant from the characteristic, unmitigated humanism of the Greek world before Alexander. The human race in the western world, or at least the part of it that was in the front of development and dictated the temper of the period, grew out of its stage of early manhood—one could even say undergraduate stage—into the advantages and disadvantages of middle age. Just as in the growing man the time-sense suddenly asserts itself and induces the reflection that if he chooses this he must reject that, so in the race the attention is taken from a timeless interest in the immediate happening, and its mind suffers divisions. Life then presents itself less simply, and religion begins to draw away from simple acts of propitiation firmly connected with present living, and to rough out a realm of its own. The sense of multiple worlds is created. For a quarter of a millennium before the age of Augustus this process had been gathering speed, and then Virgil embodied it in his poem—along with so much that he inherited from established modes of thought. I fancy that *Faust* is the aptest recent analogy. Goethe fully inherited the theological mode of thought that goes back to the Middle Ages, but he was about the same distance from Copernicus and Descartes and the scientific revolution of the seventeenth century as Virgil was from Epicurus and the introverts, and he was acutely aware of their legacy also. More than any modern work of imagination *Faust* shadows a turning-point in history, doing justice to both hither and hence roads. Virgil does justice to two primitive simple-minded matters, the fierce heroic spirit and the narrow self-confidence of Rome that inspired her great conquests. He does equal justice to new and different ways of feeling, to introspection, heart-searching, pity for one's enemy, doubt of the value of worldly success; and in so doing he looks forward to succeeding ages, when, however eruptive were the forces of barbarism, the leaders of thought held other powers than the worldly the true arbiters of what things are worth.

CHAPTER VI

THE ROMAN HISTORIANS

*The Roman History furnishes more examples of virtue and magna-
nimity, or greatness of mind, than any other.*

(Lord Chesterfield, letter to his son aged 8)

NO Roman historian is clearly epic, but Livy celebrates the glory
of Rome at such length, with such energy, and with such singleness of mind over a long period—he took forty years over his work—
that he at least has an initial case to be considered as such. And if
Livy is considered, so must Rome's other foremost historian, Tacitus,
however briefly.

Certainly Livy's sustained energy of style might well serve the epic
purpose. Philemon Holland, having translated him, has a right to
be heard on the topic, and his testimony is eloquent:

> The farther he proceedeth into a world, as it were, of matter, the
> more copious still he floweth; and with such varietie, as that he
> never iterateth one thing twice; but at every change of new affaires,
> returneth alwaies fresh and gay, furnished with new devices, in-
> ventions, and phrases: much like a second *Antaeus*, gathering
> greater strength and more forces stil at every turn: or after the
> maner of a little rill, which issuing from a small source, is maintained
> with fresh springs and new riverets; and hasting toward the vast
> ocean, carrieth a deeper channell and broader streame.[1]

But the wealth of stylistic resource cannot make up for a defect—as
far as the epic goes—in Livy's relation to his subject. The defect will
best appear through comparisons with Xenophon and Virgil.
Xenophon was within his subject in a very conspicuous and unusual
way. Not only did he see it in imagination from within, but he was
the chief actor in the doings he described. But Virgil too was within
his subject. The Rome he described was for him a living organism
of which he was a part, and, whatever the precise shape of his belief
in Rome's concrete political future, he believed also that the gods
who had guided Rome were spiritual forces greater than Rome,
itself the supreme symbol of their will, and he felt himself to be within
the scope of those forces. Livy, acutely aware of the immensity of his
subject, the history of Rome from the beginning to 9 B.C., was yet
outside it. His material was given to him, whole; and he is the highly
accomplished and vivacious journalist writing it up and presenting it

[1] Preface to translation of Livy's Roman History, 1600.

88

as a grand spectacle of events and characters and as the finest repertory, in the world, of moral examples. While Virgil succeeded in
creating the sense of growth, Livy took stock of things that had quite
ceased to develop.

This relation of Livy to his theme is both made explicit in his
preface and could without the preface be deduced from the hard
brilliance of wit with which he attacks his narrative. In his preface he
speaks of the old Roman spirit, preserved indeed longer than that of
any other empire, as quite passed away. The final passing was
precipitate, and now Rome is beset with vices which she has not
the ability either to put up with or to remedy. It is just not the same
Rome, and all she can now do is to turn her eyes back on her great
past, where she can find incomparable displays of pure religion and
examples of noble deeds. In the history itself Livy is the showman,
not the mixer, *spectator haud particeps*, and he fits the show with the
aptest possible external lineaments. With Livy we are already in the
waning spirit of the ancient world, the spirit so eloquently expressed
in the treatise *On the Sublime*, where there is corruption all around but
consolation in the semi-divine figures of the great writers, majestic
with the majesty of the great rivers, the Rhine, the Danube, or the
Ocean stream itself. Not that Livy himself shares the melancholy and
reflective temperament of the author of *On the Sublime*. He has his
chosen task and he attacks it cheerfully enough, content to enjoy it
without moping over the decadence of his surroundings. And the last
sentences of his preface, which follow his account of Rome's moral
ruin, speak for his own prevailing habit of mind:

> sed querelae, ne tum quidem gratae futurae quum forsitan et
> necessariae erunt, ab initio certe tantae ordiendae rei absint. cum
> bonis potius ominibus votisque ac precationibus deorum dearumque,
> si ut poetis nobis quoque mos est, libentius inciperemus ut orsis
> tanti operis successus prosperos darent.[1]

Of Herodotus and Xenophon I said that their claims to epic
achievement were partial, much of Herodotus being guide-book
matter and only half of the *Anabasis* achieving a formal dignity. Livy
was far ampler than his Greek predecessors, and there is an initial
chance that within the bulk of his annals sections may stand out and
achieve an artistic unity denied to the whole work. If there is such a
section it will be that on the Second Punic War, which the Romans
recognised as the principal crisis in their history. And Livy, as he
comes to it, leaves us in no doubt of the gravity of his theme. Books

---

[1] 'But complaints, which are not likely to be acceptable even when perhaps they
are inevitable, should certainly be spared at the beginning of so great an enterprise
as this. Rather, if we historians share the practice of poets, we should be more glad
to begin with happy auguries and assurances and with prayers to the heavenly
powers that they may give a prosperous issue to the initiation of so great a work.'

Twenty-one to Thirty are given to this war, and Livy opens them as follows:

> In parte operis mei licet mihi praefari quod in principio summae totius professi plerique sunt rerum scriptores: bellum maxime omnium memorabile quae unquam gesta sint me scripturum, quod Hannibale duce Carthaginienses cum populo Romano gessere. nam neque validiores opibus ullae inter se civitates gentesque contulerunt arma neque his ipsis tantum unquam virium aut roboris fuit; et haud ignotas belli artes inter se sed expertas primo Punico conserebant bello; et adeo varia belli fortuna ancepsque Mars fuit ut propius periculum fuerint qui vicerunt.[1]

Here Livy certainly recognises the solemn significance of the theme he is about to enter on, but his tone is elegantly detached. He is ironical at the expense of Thucydides, who had written so solemnly of the magnitude of the war between Athens and Sparta, so minute an affair compared with the clashes of the Roman and Punic empires, and he ends with a conceit about the Battle of Cannae, which brought Rome closer to annihilation than Scipio's African victories near the end of the war brought Carthage.

In recounting the great events of the war and Rome's supreme peril Livy does a sort of justice to his great theme. He simplifies and intensifies the character of Hannibal, making him embody all the toughness, cunning, and ferocity the Romans attributed to their enemy. He makes the Carthaginian attack on Saguntum, the act that began the long struggle, a symbolic piece of lawlessness. And he imitates Herodotus and his Artabanus by making Hanno a wise and virtuous statesman who warns his countrymen against an impious war. In the Carthaginian assembly Hanno said that the siege of Saguntum was an offence against the gods and that Carthage itself was doomed unless the gods were respected. And Livy pauses impressively in his narrative after Saguntum falls to the Carthaginians. Coming to the war in Italy itself, Livy puts Roman piety greatly to the fore. Fabius, appointed Dictator after the Roman defeat at Lake Trasimene, censures Flaminius the Roman commander more for his neglect of the gods than for his rash strategy, and persuades the Senate to consult the Sibylline Books. And Fabius in his subsequent steadfastness becomes a kind of symbol of Rome's essential qualities.

[1] 'I may be allowed to apply to a portion of my work the preface which most historians apply to their complete works: that I am about to describe the most memorable of wars ever waged, namely that which the Carthaginians, with Hannibal as general, waged with the Roman people. No other states or people have joined battle with larger resources, and certainly other states fell short in strength and resolution. In this war too there was not ignorance but mutual knowledge of each other's military skill, derived from the first war. Further the fortune of the fight was so fluctuating and the favour of the war god so uncertain that it was the conquerors who experienced the greatest danger.'

Livy rises to his greatest height when he describes Roman resolution after the disaster of Cannae. He largely lets events speak for themselves, only adding that 'we know of no other nation whose spirit would not have been quite crushed by such a huge load of disasters'. And the twenty-second book, which had described the major Roman defeats, ends with recording the defection of various Roman allies to Carthage—the aftermath of Cannae—and the yet unbroken spirit of Rome:

> Nec tamen hae clades defectionesque sociorum moverunt ut pacis unquam mentio apud Romanos fieret, neque ante consulis Romam adventum nec postquam is rediit renovavitque memoriam acceptae cladis. quo in tempore ipso adeo magno animo civitas fuit ut consuli ex tanta clade, cuius ipse causa maxima fuisset, redeunti et obviam itum frequenter ab omnibus ordinibus sit et gratiae actae quod de republica non desperasset: cui, si Carthaginiensium ductor fuisset, nihil recusandum supplicii foret.[1]

The Carthaginians were in the habit of crucifying their unsuccessful generals; and it is of this that Livy was thinking in his last sentence. In this high place he writes simply and without conceits and does really convey a deep respect for Roman restraint and resolution.

Thus in the last pages of the twenty-second book Livy does identify himself with his subject. For the moment Roman virtue has prolonged itself to Livy's own day and included the writer within it, so that he writes above himself. But such an outburst is the exception. Even in his books on the Second Punic War he is more akin to the *Cyropedia* or Plutarch's *Lives* and to that appetite for moral examples that was so puzzlingly powerful in the Renaissance. It is a case of 'See this example of Roman fortitude!' and 'How typical an act of Punic treachery!' not a case of these qualities being naturally distilled from the context.

When I said in my introductory chapter that the epic voiced the nature of a large group of people I meant that those people belonged to the writer's own contemporary world; that he spoke as part of that world, not that he described the nature of an earlier group from a distance. If this meaning is correct, Livy can touch an epic quality for only a brief time in the course of his immense history. Not that Livy is not interested in the Rome, no longer his, which he looks back on. But his interest is of a kind that does not preclude his using his

---

[1] 'But these disasters and revolts did not provoke the Romans to the least whisper of peace; neither before the arrival of the consul (Varro) at Rome nor after he returned and revived the memory of the disaster they had sustained. And at this very time the temper of the state was so high that when Varro returned from this great defeat (for which he was mainly responsible) there was a great concourse of people of all ranks to meet him and a vote of thanks was passed for his not despairing of the Republic. If he had been a Carthaginian general he could not have escaped the extremity of punishment.'

material not only as a thing valuable or wonderful in itself but as a means of displaying the virtuosity of his rhetoric. And such mixed ways of feeling do not allow the authentic epic seriousness. Nor, apparently, does Livy lack personal opinions. We can learn from his pages that he was conservative in politics, disliked agitators, admired Roman political solidarity in the era of the Second Punic War, despised Greek garrulity and ineffectiveness in action, and was influenced by current Stoicism.[1] But such knowledge comes mostly from the chance remarks he drops; and his opinions do not pervade and give a compelling shape to the mass of events he narrates.

Though Tacitus may be single minded in a way Livy is not, he is remoter from the epic. Livy had a theme which admitted of a mainly approving temper, Tacitus deals mainly with deeds he can only condemn. He is more reflective than Livy, and the opening of his *Histories* is more philosophical than anything of his predecessor. But reflection forces him to conclude that the period of Roman history from the death of Nero on, which is the theme of the *Histories*, was tragic and terrible, though marked by some noble examples. Tacitus has standards of truth and Stoic virtue, but the world around him fails when judged by those standards, and he attacks it in a spirit of reprimand or satire. Now, though the epic may admit satire, its spirit cannot be predominantly satirical, for it thereby loses its breadth and variety. Tacitus's historical writing may be better literature than the *Mirror for Magistrates*, but its moral character is not so different, and there is the common theme of the gods' immediate punishment of sin. Indeed, Tacitus states at the beginning of his *Histories* that in the epoch under review the gods sought to punish, not to protect, the Roman state. Tacitus intended to extend his historical theme to the ages of Nerva and Trajan, when men could say what they pleased with some freedom. But it is unlikely that even so he would have found reason to alter his critical and satirical spirit. What interested him were the failings and vices of Rome's rulers; he shows no sign of being aware of what was really great in the Rome of his day, the provinces of her empire.[2] More than Livy, Tacitus is outside the scope of the epic spirit.

And if these two Roman historians fall outside it, there is no need to consider the others.

[1] See M. L. W. Laistner, *The Greater Roman Historians*, University of California Press (1947) 89-90.
[2] *Ib.* 131.

CHAPTER VII

LATIN EPIC AFTER VIRGIL

And kis the steppes where-as thou seest pace
Virgile, Ovyde, Omer, Lucan, and Stace.
(Chaucer, *Troilus and Criseyde*)

1. INTRODUCTORY

VIRGIL gave a great impetus to the writing of epics in Latin, but he did not thereby assure that the results would equal their pretensions. Indeed, none of these poems comes anywhere near satisfying the requirements I have postulated. Yet two of them demand inclusion for their subsequent reputation and influence: they did indeed help to build up that neo-classic myth of the epic form which is part of the subject of this book.

In selecting as his masters in narrative the five poets that head this chapter, Chaucer was speaking for his age. It is these five ancients (with Horace, not a narrative poet, added) whom Dante in one place or another encounters in the *Divine Comedy*. Homer and Virgil I have written of already. Ovid was never looked on as an epic poet, and comes into the theme only through Lucan's possible debt to the versification of the *Metamorphoses*. Lucan and Statius were the two post-Virgilian epic poets who, known and greatly read through the Middle Ages, became part of the regular epic canon of the neo-classic age.

The two poets were close contemporaries, Lucan being born in A.D. 39 and Statius a year later; but Lucan died young (A.D. 65) leaving Statius to survive him thirty-one years; and Statius, less precocious, wrote his epics later in life. In style and temperament they are very different, but they are united in a common difference from Virgil: they lack his faith. Virgil believed both in Rome's mission and in some mode of being other than the earthly. Lucan in his political pessimism, Statius in his abstention from politics, equally abandon the high political confidence of Virgil. Lucan's avowed and paraded Stoicism, Statius's academic display of divine mythology, are equally distant from the profound Virgilian spirituality. Like Livy they are centred in Rome and have no joy or faith in the achievements of Roman administration in the provinces, no vision of any way of life that can replace the static despairs of the present. A third difference from Virgil is that their poems (I omit Statius's *Achilleis*, of which he wrote only a book and a half) have no obvious hero.

They are nominally heroic poems and they abound in violent and audacious acts, but the things the main characters do mean no more than those the other characters do; they lack all cumulative effect. There is thus little weight of persons, and even if one or two of Lucan's characters suggest that they are allegories of different sides of human nature, they are not attractive and striking as such. The confidence in human dignity and pathos, pre-eminent in Homer and still powerful in Virgil, has disappeared, leaving the heroic form hollow and meaningless.

For all these lapses from Virgil, Lucan and Statius are not negligible poets, though not epic, and, in their different ways, they are original.

2. LUCAN

Tho saugh I on a piler by
Of yren wroght ful sternely
The grete poete, daun Lucan,
And on his shuldres bar up than
·As highe as that I mighte see
The fame of Julius and Pompee.

(Chaucer, *House of Fame*)

Lucan taken in parts excellent: altogidder, naught.

(Jonson, *Conversations with Drummond*)

The great defect of the Pharsalia *is an unhappy laboriousness that strains itself to be first-rate for a moment, and leaves the poem second-rate for ever.* (W. E. Heitland)

The correct title of Lucan's unfinished poem in ten books on the wars between Caesar and Pompey is *De Bello Civili*, 'On the Civil War', but its traditional title is the *Pharsalia*, from the chief battle in that war, described in the seventh book. I use the customary though incorrect title. We know from his life that Lucan was an exceptionally brilliant and precocious youth and we may infer from his poem that he had much vitality and was very highly strung. The violent, sensation-loving, but disillusioned age in which he lived joined with his own neurotic energy to make him strain himself to be startling and clever. He succeeded eminently in being both, yet this success did not exclude some genuine feeling. He professes admiration for the liberties of Republican Rome and for the stoical virtues of the old Romans and a hatred of the cruelties of the civil wars. And he does so with such exaggerated exhibitionism that we tend to doubt his professions. But the feelings are there, however disguised; and he reminds me of that kind of old English inn which, though substantially genuine, ends, at the hand of its restorer, by looking almost more bogus than the out-and-out fake. On the whole, feeling comes out better when Lucan is short and epigrammatic than when he exaggerates at length. His descriptions of the horrors of slaughter, of witchcraft in Thessaly, of snakes in the Libyan desert, excessively drawn out, can only bore not move us. But this briefer description of Cato's stoical habits, stylised and hard and impenetrable as it is, does breathe a genuine admiration:

> *Hi mores, haec duri immota Catonis*
> *secta fuit: servare modum finemque tenere*
> *naturamque sequi patriaeque impendere vitam*
> *nec sibi sed toti genitum se credere mundo.*
> *huic epulae vicisse famem; magnique penates*
> *submovisse hiemem tecto; pretiosaque vestis*
> *hirtam membra super Romani more Quiritis*
> *induxisse togam; Venerisque hic unicus usus*
> *progenies; urbi pater est urbique maritus,*
> *iustitiae cultor, rigidi servator honesti,*
> *in commune bonus; nullosque Catonis in actus*
> *subrepsit partemque tulit sibi nata voluptas.*[1]

At the end of the sixth book, before the culminating battle of Pharsalus, Pompey consulted a witch, who brought back a man from the dead to report on the fortune of the fight. This spirit describes the sorrow of the virtuous Roman dead and the glee of the wicked in Hades at the progress of civil war and how Pluto is preparing a place in Tartarus for the general who shall win the wicked conflict. And the bitterness with which Lucan describes those he thinks his country's enemies is sincere and mordant.

> *Abruptis Catilina minax fractisque catenis*
> *exultat, Mariique truces nudique Cethegi.*
> *vidi ego laetantes, popularia nomina, Drusos,*
> *legibus immodicos ausosque ingentia Gracchos.*
> *aeternis chalybum nodis et carcere Ditis*
> *constrictae plausere manus camposque piorum*

---

[1] ii. 380-91. 'This was the moral habit, this the unswerving discipline of austere Cato: to keep the mean and to hold to a limit and to follow nature and to pay his life to his country and to think himself born not for his own benefit but for that of the whole world. A feast for him was to have tamed hunger; his great mansion to have removed the cold of winter from beneath his roof; his costly robe the rough cloak thrown round his frame in the manner of the ordinary Roman citizen; he never indulged in love but to get offspring; he gave himself to his city like a father and a husband, following justice, observing strict integrity, mindful of the general good. Self-indulgence never insinuated itself into Cato's acts nor had any share in them.' In 387 I follow Bentley and Housman in reading *unicus* for *maximus*.

> *poscit turba nocens. regni possessor inertis*
> *pallentes aperit sedes abruptaque saxa*
> *asperat et duram vinclis adamanta paratque*
> *poenam victori.*[1]

The conceit of Pluto preparing punishment for the triumphing general is at once devilishly clever and genuinely felt.

Lucan shows the young man's desire to shock and hence to attract attention by his unconventional sentiments. In the tenth book of the *Pharsalia* he defies convention by his contempt for Alexander and his conquests, calling him madman and pirate and scourge of mankind. But his refusal to be dazzled by Alexander's brilliance may be genuine enough in itself. At the beginning of the second book he defies the whole pagan apparatus for learning the future—so large a part of ancient life—by blaming the gods for allowing such learning at all. And the lines in which he does this will illustrate not only this typical mixture of exhibitionism and sincerity but that command of tight and weighty and striking sententiousness which is his chief attraction. He has spoken of the omens that point to the approaching civil war and he goes on:

> *Cur hanc tibi, rector Olympi,*
> *sollicitis visum mortalibus addere curam,*
> *noscant venturas ut dira per omina clades?*
> *sit subitum quodcumque paras; sit caeca futuri*
> *mens hominum fati; liceat sperare timenti.*[2]

Not that Lucan is really a rebel against his age. On the contrary, he can be the classic exponent of the Stoicism that was so typical of it and which counted for so much in the Christian ages, especially that of the Renaissance. When Cato was in Africa (as described in the ninth book of the *Pharsalia*) he had the chance of consulting the oracle of Ammon, but he refused it on the plea that he has a better oracle within himself, a better judge of right and wrong. And he goes on to expound his inmost creed.

> *Haeremus cuncti superis temploque tacente*
> *nil facimus non sponte dei; nec vocibus ullis*
> *numen eget, dixitque semel nascentibus auctor*

[1] vi. 793-802. 'Baleful Catiline, his chains burst into fragments, gloats; so does cruel Marius and bare-armed Cethegus. I saw Drusus, traditional demagogue and violent legislator, rejoicing; the Gracchi too, excessively daring spirits. Ghosts, imprisoned in Hell and fettered with eternal steel clapped their hands; and the mob of the guilty demands to be given the fields of the blest. The king of the lifeless realm opens his dim dwelling; he sharpens the spiky rocks and makes ready the hard adamantine chains to punish the coming conqueror.'

[2] ii. 6-8, 14-15. 'Why, ruler of Olympus, has it seemed good to you to add this care to harassed mankind: that they should know through omens their coming disasters? Whatever you devise let it come suddenly; make the mind of men blind to its coming fate; allow frightened man to hope.'

quidquid scire licet. sterilesne elegit harenas
ut caneret paucis mersitque hoc pulvere verum;
estque dei sedes nisi terra et pontus et aer
et caelum et virtus? superos quid quaerimus ultra?
Iuppiter est quodcumque vides, quodcumque moveris.
sortilegis egeant dubii semperque futuris
casibus ancipites: me non oracula certum
sed mors certa facit. pavido fortique cadendum est:
hoc satis est dixisse Iovem.[1]

This is the sort of writing in which Lucan excels; and it is indeed something that he was able thus to exploit the peculiar lapidary terseness of the Latin tongue. Further, however wearisome he grows through his excesses and exaggerations, he does exhibit his proper virtues throughout the length of the *Pharsalia* and does thereby evince a power of will that might have satisfied one epic requirement. But when the best has been said of him, his poetical talent was narrow. He has genuine feelings and a brilliant intellect, and these he translates into the superb, already existing, medium of the Latin hexameter. What he fails to do is to modify that medium, to turn it into something fresh in the very act of feeling and thinking. The first poets create their own music; the secondary use what they find ready. And Lucan was secondary. Even in his finest epigrammatic passages the music, however genuinely Latin, is not very distinctively his own. And if Lucan is not of the first order of poets, he fails in the first epic requirement. Since he fails in this, it would be profitless to spend time on asking whether he succeeds or fails in others.

Lucan's place in the history of the epic is a different matter from his success as a writer of it; and to that place I now turn.

Lucan figures as largely as he does in the history of the epic partly because he was bold or wise enough to depart from the precedent of Virgil. True, he echoes Virgil in many lines and phrases,[2] but this is a minor matter compared with his independence in prosody and in theme. His hexameter, hard and unyielding and with very few elisions, is remote from Virgil's. It may derive from Ovid's as used in the *Metamorphoses* in its lack of elisions, but it has none of Ovid's bright movement. It keeps the prosodic conventions made by the Augustan

[1] ix. 573-84. 'We all cleave to heaven and though the shrine is silent we do nothing but by the will of god; nor does the spirit lack expression, for the Creator once and for all told to man at his birth what it is lawful to know. Could he have chosen these barren sands whence to speak just to a few? and has god any home but land and sea and air and sky and goodness? why do we seek gods beyond? Jupiter is everything you see, every motion of your heart. Let those want soothsayers who are vacillating in themselves and ever worried over coming disasters: for me it is not oracles that make me sure but the sureness of death. Coward and brave man alike must fall: that Jove has decreed this, is sufficient.'
[2] See W. E. Heitland, introduction to C. E. Haskins's edition of the *Pharsalia* (London 1887) cviii-cxxvi.

poets and thus differs greatly from Ennius and Lucretius, but in its heaviness it does reflect the intense Latinity of those two poets and represents a verse movement that would naturally characterise an ordinary educated Latin practitioner. Virgil and Ovid are the wizards who by their magic get more music out of the language than it naturally yields; Lucan does not go beyond what it can naturally command, thus winning a certain kind of solidity and a wise independence from poets beyond his powers and not in any fruitful way imitable. It was this independence of Virgil that made it possible for later writers to consider him an alternative model.

Lucan's theme corresponds to his prosody. He goes behind Virgil to an older Latin mode, but he keeps certain Augustan conventions that corrected the old use. In choosing recent history as his epic theme he followed the tradition of Ennius, but in restricting his subject to a single historical action, the civil war between Caesar and Pompey, he forsook the old annalistic method and copied the Virgilian compression. Again, he forsook Virgilian precedent by cutting out all divine actors and all scenes in the pagan heaven. This is an important matter in the development of the epic because it helped to approximate the epic form to the literal historical event, to reinforce the kinship between poetry and history that was established by Herodotus and perhaps a little confirmed by Livy. It is a kinship which lasted till Gibbon. Apart from helping this approximation, the *Pharsalia* represented a new fusion of history and poetry which, because the poem continued to be read and admired, became a recognised literary form, a new and legitimate variety of the epic.

That this should have happened, when Lucan in modern opinion is so undoubtedly outside the first order of poets, may arouse surprise. That surprise I cannot in reason try to mitigate, for I share it. The best I can do is to end my remarks on Lucan by pointing out how dear, in actual fact, he was to many generations of writers.

I have already mentioned the tributes of Dante and Chaucer. Two medieval Latin epics, Walter of Chatillon's on Alexander and Gunther's on Frederic Barbarossa, were modelled on him; a third, Joseph of Exeter's on the Trojan War, imitates him along with Statius.[1] It was from Lucan that the medieval romances on Caesar drew some of their material. Much Elizabethan writing on the horrors of civil war goes back to Lucan.

Here are a few specific debts. Lucan tells how, when Pompey was dead and buried, his soul mounted into the high heaven; thence it saw how dim was earth's daylight and he laughed at the indignity done to his body. Just so Chaucer makes the soul of his Troilus mount

[1] For the vogue of Lucan see J. E. Sandys, *History of Classical Scholarship* (Cambridge 1903) i. 515, 530, 617; F. J. E. Raby, *History of Secular Latin Poetry in the Middle Ages* (Oxford 1934) i. 34-6.

and laugh at the petty tragedies of earth. When Caesar reached the Rubicon, a personification of his country appeared to him and reproved him; Camoens made a personification of the Portuguese people question the wisdom of Vasco da Gama's Indian expedition about to set off from Lisbon; Daniel made an allegorical figure of England reprove Bolingbroke when he landed illegally from his exile. Tasso's grizzly magical wood outside Jerusalem imitates Lucan's similar wood outside Marseilles. T. W. Baldwin[1] thinks that Shakespeare knew something of Lucan, who was studied in the top form of grammar schools, and there is a passage in *Julius Caesar* which is probably imitated from the beginning of the *Pharsalia*. Much more striking are the gloom and the rhetoric which in Shakespeare's earliest history plays make one think of Lucan. There is not the least certainty in the matter, but in the way he expresses his detestation of civil war Shakespeare might easily owe Lucan a lot. The snakes into which Milton turns his devils in the tenth book of *Paradise Lost* owe something to the snakes that infest Lucan's Libyan desert. Early in his poem Lucan said that fate forbids all greatness and prosperity to last and he pictures how chaos will one day resume its ancient sway; Pope improved on Lucan's picture at the end of the *Dunciad*. Lucan's Pompey dies meanly in a distant land; so does Johnson's Charles XII in the *Vanity of Human Wishes*. There is no genuine organic structure about the *Pharsalia*, but Lucan took care to iterate his theme of civil war and to mark the stages of its progress. Gibbon, who I believe regarded his *Decline and Fall* as an epic, may have been encouraged by Lucan to mark, as he so nobly and emphatically does, the different stages of the Roman downfall.

The list of debts could be multiplied, but I have cited enough to show that Lucan did indeed become an authentic part of the great tradition of western Europe.

3. STATIUS

Al mio ardor fur seme le faville
che mi scaldar della divina fiamma
onde sono allumati più di mille:
dell' Eneida dico, la qual mamma
fummi e fummi nutrice poetando;
senz' essa non fermai peso di dramma.

(Dante)

These words of Statius in Dante's Purgatory are partly true. He imitates the *Aeneid* openly in the way he writes and he acknowledges his debt at the end of his *Thebaid*. Without the suasion of a major

[1] *William Shakespeare's Small Latine and Lesse Greeke* (Urbana 1944) ii. 549 ff.

poet to attempt a poem in a major poetic form he would surely have been content to write well in the less august. As it is, he aimed high and, so he tells us at the end of the poem, spent ten years on the *Thebaid*. The *Thebaid* was associated with the *Aeneid* by the sixth century at least, for Fulgentius gave to them both an allegorical meaning. And by this association the reputation of Statius as an epic poet was greatly enhanced throughout the Middle Ages. But Statius's words in the *Purgatorio* are true only in part, for, however closely he imitated Virgil, he was a poet in his own right, and a better one than Lucan.

It would be vain to look for organic unity in Statius's long epic in twelve books on the matter of Thebes. He showed staying power in carrying his theme through to the end, in taking great trouble over detail throughout, and in imposing on his essentially inorganic material a semblance of unity. Event genuinely follows, even if it does not grow out of, event; and the last book, in which the just king, Theseus, interposes and restores peace and amity, is a gallant, if hopeless, effort to give meaning to the welter of horror and carnage that has gone before. Such an effort to impose unity shows a tender conscience at least and is better than no effort at all. Statius is also helped to a semblance of unity by the sheer quality of the Virgilian hexameter, of which he is a skilful practitioner. He is in something of the position of a secondary Elizabethan playwright or an Augustan translator in the tradition of Pope's *Homer*: helped by the luck of his inherited medium to something which, unaided, he could not have attained.

The case is different when we take the poem's parts. Here Statius can hold his own in his fashion and can create in the true poetic way, with substance and style simultaneously and inseparably conceived. Solider, more sensitive, but with less of the energy of neurosis than Lucan, we can picture him pegging away faithfully and conscientiously at his epic yet frequently caught up for short stretches by his imagination and passing from competence into poetry. I say 'conscientiously', for his erudition in ancient mythology, provided in apparently unnecessary profusion and tedious to the modern reader, was required by his age and argues conscientiousness, not display. The same is true of his horrors. When, for instance, he makes Jupiter accuse Eteocles and Polynices of having stamped on Oedipus's extruded eyes, he is more likely to have consulted the tastes of his age than pleased himself. On the other hand there are times when convention breaks into life or melodrama assumes a genuine, lurid grandeur. I give some illustrations of both kinds of success.

Statius recounts in the first book how when Oedipus, self-blinded at news of his crime, abandoned his throne to his two sons Eteocles and Polynices, they decided to reign a year each by turns, the idle one living in exile: a bad plan, says Statius, and unlikely to work beyond the first year. And he suddenly adds that Thebes was then a poor and primitive city. There was no mechanism of luxury.

> *sed nuda potestas*
> *armavit fratres; pugna est de paupere regno.*[1]

This sudden particularisation of Thebes, this contrast between the poor setting and the abundant passions, show that the poet has done more than repeat his given material and has got inside his theme. As expected, the brothers quarrel and Eteocles succeeds in driving his brother out. Polynices flees for refuge to Argos. As he approaches, night falls and a storm arises with every proper circumstance of melodramatic violence. Statius contrives the whole thing splendidly and is plainly greatly interested, but when he comes to describe Polynices in the storm he rises through a single touch to poetic excellence:

> *Ille tamen modo saxa iugis fugientia ruptis*
> *miratur, modo nubigenas e montibus amnes*
> *aure pavens, passimque insano turbine raptas*
> *pastorum pecorumque domos: non segnius amens*
> *incertusque viae per nigra silentia vastum*
> *haurit iter; pulsat metus undique et undique frater.*[2]

The sudden mention of the brother strikes our imagination. Nature's uproar and his brother's hate unite to drive Polynices on; and by this union mere natural description has become symbolic, and human passions have acquired size and terror.

Here is an example of Statius animating what might have been conventional description by sudden touches of realistic detail. At the beginning of the seventh (one of the best) books Jupiter is angry that the war against Thebes has been delayed so long. He sends Mercury to find Mars in Thrace and rouse him to action. Statius describes the Temple of Mars there (and his description inspired Boccaccio and Chaucer to copy him in their poems on the story of Palamon and Arcite). Mars, roused, sends an allegorical figure of Panic to incite the Argive army to action. Panic's success is recounted with the conventional descriptive violence. It is the details slipped into the

---

[1] i. 150-1. 'But it was a primitive dominion that provoked the brothers to arms; the fight was over a poor throne.'

[2] i. 364-9. 'But he is astonished, now by the rocks falling from the torn ridges, now, as he listens to them in terror, by the rivers the clouds have created on the hills; on all sides he sees the homes of shepherds and of flocks whirled away by the mad wind. He does not check his speed but distracted and uncertain of his road consumes his way through the black dead of night; fear from every side, his brother from every side drive him on.'

account of the Argives arming that turn strong melodrama into poetry:

> *arma, arma insani sua quisque ignotaque nullo*
> *more rapit, mutant galeas alienaque cogunt*
> *ad iuga cornipedes; ferus omni in pectore saevit*
> *mortis amor caedisque, nihil flagrantibus obstat:*
> *praecipitant redimuntque moras. sic litora vento*
> *incipiente fremunt, fugitur cum portus; ubique*
> *vela fluunt, laxi iactantur ubique rudentes.*[1]

The picture of the men putting on the wrong helmets in their hurry and the horses' heads into the wrong collars at once makes the description solid. But the hurry of the ships, long idle in port, to catch the breeze has the note of genuine personal observation (Statius was a native of Naples) and retrospectively animates and makes credible the heightened stuff that has gone before.

Even in the more lyrical passages, for which Statius is justly and principally admired, he works by the sudden turn, the unexpected imaginative stroke. In the tenth book of the *Thebaid* Statius describes the abode of Sleep, and in many ways it is just what you would expect from a Latin poet working in the conventional way. Sleep lives in the west, in a cave deep in the hill; and the cave is guarded by a still, thick wood, star-proof. Various allegorical figures of Quiet and Oblivion and so on attend. Statius manages the conventional stuff with great skill and force, and we should not complain if he did no more. But he does do more, and in these lines:

> *non hic pelagi, licet omnia clament*
> *litora, non ullus caeli fragor; ipse profundis*
> *vallibus effugiens speluncae proximus amnis*
> *saxa inter scopulosque tacet: nigrantia circum*
> *armenta, omne solo recubat pecus; et nova marcent*
> *gramina terrarumque inclinat spiritus herbas.*[2]

All has been motionless in the description, and into this immobility Statius suddenly inserts the river, silent indeed like everything else, but hurrying along though masked by rocks and crags. The surprise of this hurrying river, the contrast not only between itself and the

---

[1] vii. 135-41. 'To arms, to arms they fly madly, each seizing indiscriminately his own or another's. They get the wrong helmets and clap the wrong harness on the horses. In every heart rages the fierce lust of death and slaughter. In their mad enthusiasm there is no stopping them. They plunge forward to make up for their delay. So, as a wind springs up, the shore breaks into sound, when all over the harbour the sailors hurry to leave: sails are flapping, and the ropes are thrown about all over the decks.'

[2] x. 94-9. 'Here there is no roar of sea, nor of sky, though every shore is sounding; the very river, speeding away down the deep valley near the cave is silent within the rocks and cliffs. Round about are black cattle, the whole herd couches on the ground; and the new-grown grass droops, and an exhalation makes the plants bend.'

STATIUS

other motionless things but between its own speed and its own
silence, are both surprising in themselves and suggest with psychological accuracy the mental currents that are only overlaid not
immobilised by sleep.

Probably the most famous and the most influential passage in
Statius is his account of the altar of Mercy—*Clementia*—in Athens. It
occurs in the twelfth book, itself famous for providing the setting for
the story of Palamon and Arcite in Boccaccio, Chaucer, and the *Two
Noble Kinsmen*. Here, after the Theban war, when Creon, now King
of Thebes, refuses to grant burial to the bodies of his enemies, the
Argive women come as suppliants to Athens to obtain the help of
Theseus. Both Athens and Theseus are symbolical: Athens of civilisation, Theseus of the governor who upholds the laws of nature and of
nations. In this righteous city of Athens is an altar,[1] lowly and served
with modest rites, but never without its votaries, who offer it tears
instead of incense. And this is the altar of Mercy. There is no cult-
image, for Mercy's real home is the human heart. The altar is
thronged by the needy—*ignotae tantum felicibus arae*: to the fortunate
only is it unknown. The description is exquisite in itself, but once
more there is the sudden turn: the switch over from the shrine itself
and its earnest votaries to the ignorance of the fortunate, from the
descriptive to the psychological.

There are other virtues in Statius. He can, for instance, exploit the
aptitude of the Latin tongue to be short and weighty with success,
owing perhaps something to Lucan. Early in the poem, at the first
council of the gods, he says of Jupiter

Grave et immutabile sanctis
pondus adest verbis et vocem fata sequuntur,[2]

words which Milton had at the back of his mind when he made God
the Father say, like Lucan so emphatically at the end of a line, 'and
what I will is Fate'. But his main distinction as a poet is what I have
called psychological, for it is here that he is truly original. C. S. Lewis[3]
s observed how much more emphatic are the deified abstractions
of Statius—*Pietas, Pavor*, etc.—than his Olympian gods. Something
of the kind holds good for humanity. Though Statius works hard at
his characters and tries to define them and keep them distinct, he
fails to make us remember them. In the reading we may note that
Tydeus is of a consistently violent spirit and that he may have joined
with Homer's Achilles in prompting Tasso's Rinaldo, but after reading he fades from our minds. But this does not mean that Statius lacks
psychological power. On the contrary, he has a rich and interesting

[1] xii. 481-96.
[2] i. 212-13. 'A solemn and changeless gravity marks his holy words, and Fate
bows to his voice.'
[3] *The Allegory of Love* (Oxford 1936) 49-56.

mind, but he expresses it not in the traditional objective manner through the actors but, like our own Romantics, through the quick and subtle turns he gives to his descriptions.

In this Statius was an innovator, and Dante's claim that he was a covert Christian (surely based ultimately on the account of Mercy described above) is not as far-fetched as it sounds. Not that he shows any signs of sharing Virgil's religious temperament; but he was not imprisoned in the outworn creed of the ancient world. There was a spring of new feeling in his mind, which, coexisting with those things he had inherited, suggests in a small way that complication or conflict of feeling that was to distinguish the medieval mind so sharply from the Homeric and classical Greek and the early Roman.

In the formal history of the epic Statius counts for less than Lucan. Following Virgilian precedent he did not create any new epic form. Less of a school-book than Virgil or Lucan, his *Thebaid* must have reached a smaller audience in Renaissance and neo-classic England. But many of the great poets loved him and copied him. I have mentioned Chaucer and the authors of the *Two Noble Kinsmen* among the English; and it is worth adding Spenser, who copied the brawl that arose when Britomart in stormy weather tried to join the company in the pig-sty outside Malbecco's house from Statius's account in the *Thebaid* of Tydeus and Polynices arriving in stormy weather together at the house of Adrastus and proceeding to box. Finally, it is quite fitting that the forthright vigour of Marlowe should have coped with a book of Lucan and the keen delicacy of Pope with a book of Statius, as material for translation.

CHAPTER VIII

THE GREEK ROMANCE

IT was about the time of Statius, apparently, that a new literary form fashioned itself from old materials. There are romantic improbabilities in the *Odyssey*; Euripides's *Ion* contains the motive of the long-lost child, destined to become the stock of romantic comedy; Xenophon in the *Cyropedia* had turned biography into hagiography; in the Hellenistic age it was fashionable to narrate wild adventures under a thin disguise of history. It was from elements of this kind that the Greek romance, as a regular literary form, was created in the first century A.D. Naturally, the kind was nearer in some things to its own day than to the older writings that may ultimately have supplied its elements. It quite lacks the true characterisation of Homer and Euripides and is nearer to Lucan and Statius in its love for conventionally rhetorical speeches. The following summary[1] of the plot of *Chaereas and Callirrhoe* by Chariton will serve well enough to show the characteristic substance of this literary kind: Callirrhoe is the daughter of the famous Syracusan statesman Hermocrates; she and Chaereas fall in love with each other at first sight, are married, and then, by a misunderstanding, quarrel violently; he strikes her, she faints and is supposed dead, but revives in her tomb, is carried off by robbers and sold as a slave; and then follows a series of adventures in which, after showing unheard-of constancy to her husband, she is happily reunited to him in the last of the eight books.

The love of improbable and exciting incidents and the sentimental treatment of constancy and chastity have their counterparts in other literature of the early Christian epoch. J. Bidez wrote in the *Cambridge Ancient History*[2] of the age of Septimius Severus and Julia Domna (*c*. A.D. 200):

> Everywhere in this age, even among the least educated sections of the population, tales were invented and wonders sought out. Among the Christians, too, edification was sought in the recital of adventures: travels of the Evangelists in the remotest countries, acts of the apostles (Andrew, John or Thomas) and even of the earliest evangelists, the life of Joseph the carpenter, stories of the childhood of Jesus, or Conversions or Confessions such as those of Cyprian of Antioch. . . . In the third century delight in romantic fiction left its mark even on works of the most profound theological speculation.

[1] Taken from H. J. Rose, *A Handbook of Greek Literature*, 415.
[2] xii. (Cambridge 1939) 616-17.

The Greek romance, then, has at least the interest of being more than a weary and academic rehash of old and outworn modes of feeling. It is part of a new, if often crude and simple-minded, appetite for the remote and the improbable. And if I say *new*, I mean that now, for the first time, a perennial appetite, hitherto confined to the humbler regions of oral folk-traditions, broke into that of polite letters and established itself as the staple, not as an occasional ornament, of an important polite literary form. We are indeed well on our way now to the Middle Ages.

No Greek romance has any claim to be epic in the more serious sense of the word, but one of them made an unusual bid for the moral and the solemn: the *Aethiopica* or *Aethiopian History* of Heliodorus. The plot is of the usual kind: a pair of lovers, one a princess lost in infancy, are separated, captured by pirates, tested for their chastity, condemned to death and so on, till their final reunion. There are a perfectly upright king and a wicked and lustful princess among the characters. And it is the steady and deliberate insistence on the courage and chastity of Theagenes and Chariclea, the justice of Hydaspes, and the wickedness of Arsace that make the *Aethiopica* a studiedly moral as well as a diverting story. Bidez[1] conjectures that it is of the same kind as the tendentious and fabulous history of the philosopher Apollonius of Tyana (who lived in the first century A.D.) written by Philostratus for Julia Domna as a piece of pagan hagiography in opposition to the Christian. Anyhow the *Aethiopica* was conspicuous among Greek romances for its serious tone; and, even more important for its destined influence, its action began in the middle, with the earlier portions narrated, on the pattern of the *Odyssey* and the *Aeneid*. Whether in so framing his plot Heliodorus made epic claims for his romance, we do not know: all that matters is that in the Renaissance men made that claim for him and elevated the Heliodoran romance into one of the recognised epic forms.

The *Aethiopica* was not the only Greek romance well known to the Elizabethans. There were two others, the story of *Leucippe and Clitophon* by Achilles Tatius, a follower of Heliodorus, and *Daphnis and Chloe*, a pastoral romance by Longus. But though *Leucippe and Clitophon* lent a character to Sidney's *Arcadia*, it was the *Aethiopica* alone of Greek romances that came into the history of the epic. And its companion as prototype of the prose epic was not any other Greek romance but the *Cyropedia* of Xenophon, which, though lacking the correct epic construction, made up by an even fuller repertory of virtues in the main character and an even more blatant morality.

I said above that with the Greek romance we were well on the way to the Middle Ages. That is in a sense true, but it must not be forgotten that, packed with incident as these stories are, they are shorter

[1] *Op. cit.* 614.

and better constructed than *Huon of Bordeaux* or *Amadis of Gaul* or any other typical romance in the library of Don Quixote. Supplying the kind of wonder found in this still adored medieval kind but disposed in a far more civilised and classical shape, the most moral and correctly shaped of them imposed itself on readers of the sixteenth and seventeenth centuries as something much more august than in fact it was.

CHAPTER IX

WHERE HAVE WE GOT TO?

*Is it not strange, that Desire should so many yeeres out-live per-
formance?*

(Shakespeare, *The Second Part of Henry the Fourth*)

I HAVE written of the classical epic very much from my own
ground, trying to see it in some sort of shape from a long distance.
It is worth while, as a corrective, saying a little about how the ancients
had come to regard their own epics at the point at which this book
has arrived.

I have so far omitted classical criticism as irrelevant. Criticism is
interesting and instructive mainly as it moulds or explains contemporary production. If there was any such criticism when Homer was
writing, it has perished; and the *Iliad* and the *Odyssey* long antedate
anything that was said about them. Attic criticism, naturally enough,
deals mostly with the developing art of the drama; here was possible
the interplay of theory and practice. And Aristotle's last chapter in
the *Poetics* is more a comparison of the epic with the dramatic form
than a treatment of the epic as such. But, though so indirect a piece
of criticism, it is unique in classical antiquity in dealing with the epic
form at all, and I cannot omit comment on it.

Aristotle's main point is that the tragic is better than the epic form.
He is not at his best in making it, indeed he writes like a partisan;
but that is less to the point here than the isolation of his sentiments.
Whatever Aristotle said, Homer's prestige in antiquity extended
irrefragably from the poems themselves to the form in which they
were written. Throughout antiquity to attempt the epic remained
the noblest of all literary ventures. Besides making his main point,
Aristotle implied that the general principles governing tragedy
applied to the epic also. There were differences; for instance, the epic
being so long, admitted more episodes. But it did also conform to its
own kind of unity of action. Aristotle recognised the principle dividing
an organised heroic poem and a picaresque romance. And that is his
first importance as a critic of the epic.

Most people were unlike Aristotle in the way they took Homer;
they read him for the parts, not for the whole. Homer having succeeded in different ways, this piecemeal reading could be of different
kinds. It could be moral, Homer encouraging men (and especially
the young) to be brave and good comrades: or educational, Homer
being a good exercise in the language for the schoolboy; or recreational, Homer being grand to listen to when recited at a festival.

But, in the matter of literary criticism, the most important piecemeal reading had to do with rhetoric. Such reading applies, of course, not to Homer alone but to all the reputedly great authors of Greece. Speech-craft, in an age when the skill of attack and defence in the law-courts was an essential part of every free man's equipment, was the main element in education. And it was thought that the great writers, in verse as well as in prose, were the masters of rhetoric and the means of imparting the art to the young. This rhetorical way of taking literature persisted throughout classical antiquity; and long after the conditions that first engendered it and gave it some sense had ceased to exist. Now rhetorical training paid the greatest heed to detail; and it was in a piecemeal way that the rhetoricians took the poets. They went to them for separable felicities and elegances of expression, or even for mere examples of recognised figures of speech.

The result of this was that Homer, as well as being judged as a whole by Aristotle (and we do not know by how many others), was regarded by a very much larger number as the supreme repository of wisdom and morality and the supreme poetical illustration of the entire rhetorical repertory. Even so sensitive a critic as Longinus, whose criticism was literary rather than rhetorical and who had so delicate a perception of how Homer gets his wonderful effects, showed the cramping influence of rhetoric in that he treated him piecemeal, under the pre-existing headings of passion, phantasia, and so on.

With such different ways of taking Homer it is most improbable that there was any clear idea of epic requirements. Instead there was the immense prestige of Homer, and consequently of the long heroic narrative, and of its vehicle, the hexameter verse. Ennius was probably greatly in earnest when he imitated Homer. He adopted Homer's verse and his high political theme, but he plainly did not include in the epic requirements a respect for organic form.

Whether Virgil was influenced by critical theory in making the *Aeneid* a unity, or whether he owed that unity solely to his native artistic conscience, we shall never know. But in the age of Augustus Horace at least revived or reiterated the organic notion of Aristotle. Whatever Virgil's motives, he had much the same effect as Homer. He added vast prestige to the heroic subject and to the hexameter verse, the *carmen heroicum* as it came to be called. And the Latin rhetoricians fastened on him too as a mine of morality and rhetorical instances.

The prestige with which Homer and Virgil together invested the epic lasted without interruption to the end of the eighteenth century; and it is the matter that most gives unity to the movement in literature of which I am writing. Its immediate effect was unfortunate and might well have brought the epic form into disrepute. Ovid, it is true, coming very soon after Virgil, wisely shunned the straight epic and for his longest work chose a series of loosely connected tales, thus giving scope to his undoubted if not very profound narrative gift; while to satisfy his rhetorical proclivities he caused the tragic heroines of antiquity to churn up their souls in fantastic epistles to their faithless lovers. Later poets were less wise and yielded to the fashionable pressure of the heroic form. Many Silver Latin poets chose that form for experiences that could better have been expressed in another. But for all the failures, the glamour continued to hang about the epic-heroic notion: and to celebrate the doings of great men in hexameter verse was the highest aim a poet could have. One really striking instance of the way the notion lasted must suffice. It is from the encyclopedist, Isidore of Seville. Isidore's date is round the end of the sixth century A.D., and he is early enough to retain a lingering contact with the ancient world. But his encyclopedias were the most popular of all such writings throughout the Middle Ages, and he thus looks right forward. In his *Etymologiae*[1] he discusses various types of verses and says that the Latin hexameter, the *heroicum carmen*, gets its heroic name

> quod eo virorum fortium res et facta narrantur (nam heroes appellantur viri quasi aerei et coelo digni propter sapientiam et fortitudinem); quod metrum auctoritate caetera metra praecedit.[2]

And Isidore proceeds to give the metre its current Christian justification by saying that it antedates Homer, being used in Hebrew by Moses in the Book of Deuteronomy and by the author of the Book of Job, Moses' contemporary.

Finally, something quite different got attached to Homer, of limited importance in classical antiquity but the ancestor of something of vast importance in the Middle Ages. As the Greek world matured, so certain primitive features in Homer became awkward. Taking all Homer so seriously, men could not relegate the immoral vagaries of some of the gods to local comic relief: they had either to repudiate them or to explain them away. Plato took the more honest but less wise course of repudiating them. General educated opinion chose to interpret them allegorically. We must not imagine that such interpretations meant a great deal critically. In classical antiquity no poet composed on a basis of allegory. Even for the Silver Latin writers, when a shift of motive might not be surprising, the driving forces were the heroic notion and rhetoric, and in no degree allegory. For all its future scope allegory remained a way of explaining works of literature pre-existing and founded on another basis; it had not become a creative force.

[1] I. 39. 9-11.
[2] 'because in it the affairs and deeds of brave men are recounted (for the name of hero is given to men almost heavenly and worthy of the skies because of their wisdom and courage). And this metre in its status has precedence of all other metres.'

Part Two

Medieval

CHAPTER I

THE OUTSKIRTS

1. PREFACE

IF I were writing a book in the more accepted way on the epic as heroic poem, it would now be my task to trace the fitful history of the poem on great men from the decline of the heroic tradition in Statius to its faint reawakening in Petrarch's *Africa*. But, on my conception of the epic, the main tradition leaves the heroic form altogether and finds a new life in a quite other one. The 'accepted unconscious metaphysic' of the time, which Abercrombie rightly insists must be the ground of the epic, was in the Middle Ages no longer heroic human action but an ideal of holiness; and, disregarding the now established conventions of the epic—its hero, its economical structure, its entry into the action near the end—we must seek the true epic where we can find it, where the age's metaphysic comes out most truly and most powerfully. This will not be in the regular narrative about distinguished persons; and part of my task in this chapter will consist in explaining why I am leaving out so much that, in a book on the epic of this size, the reader might easily expect to find included or even dwelt on.

2. THE END OF THE CLASSICAL HEROIC TRADITION

> Apollo *from his shrine*
> *Can no more divine*
> *With hollow shreik the steep of* Delphos *leaving.*
>
> (Milton)

To see the exhaustion of the Graeco-Roman humanist tradition at the time of Statius and after, one had best look at the statuary. About the Roman copies of early Greek heroic sculpture and that queer archaistic original work of the time of Hadrian there is an air of hollowness betokening that the old confidence in mere human life as the central concern has broken down. This is, of course, an extreme statement and it should not be taken to mean that there were not pagans who passed their lives contentedly enough. If the sculptors failed to recapture the general humanistic confidence in their copies from the Greek, they had a feeling for the individual and could make a good portrait. The pagan country life depicted by Pater in *Marius the Epicurean* may have more truth in it than his detractors care to allow. Nevertheless, the centre of the pagan way of life was doomed, and the perceptive pagans knew it, consciously or unconsciously. The preponderance of energy had gone elsewhere, just as in the course of nineteenth-century England it transferred itself from agriculture to industry. Now without the old humanistic confidence the old, classical type of heroic poem could not exist. But, it may be retorted, once Christianity had won its victory, why should not the heroic poem have been grafted on to the new vigorous stock? Christianity had its heroes, and if Milton some fourteen centuries later thought a Christian theme

> *Not less but more Heroic then the wrath*
> *Of stern* Achilles *on his Foe pursu'd*
> *Thrice Fugitive about* Troy *wall,*

is it not strange that Christians should not have celebrated their first definitive triumphs in heroic verse?[1] During the third century Latin superseded Greek as the liturgical language in the west; through the Latin versions of the Scriptures culminating in the Vulgate (completed A.D. 405) it showed itself a medium adapted to living uses. Further, by the time of the Vulgate the first of what can be called the heroic ages of the Church, that of the persecutions, was distant enough to become suitable epic material. The distinctive Christian hero, the martyr, took on a typical character favourable to literary treatment. To quote Raby:

> The new conception of the martyr, which was to dominate the whole middle ages, was the creation of the post-Constantinian Church. The persecution of Diocletian, so wide and far-reaching in its effects, made a profound impression on the Christian imagination. It became the type after which all persecutions were imaged; the whole pre-Constantinian epoch was envisaged in its light. . . . The intensity of the persecution and the sufferings of the victim were exaggerated. . . . The calm demeanour of the historical martyr . . . gives place to a new conception. . . . The martyr has become the aggressive soldier of the faith. Fearless, uncompromising, proud and violent, he is always master of the situation.[2]

Why is it that literature did not take advantage of this new active spirit?

This is a less futile question than might first appear, because this spirit did find expression, possibly in architecture, and certainly in the art of mosaic. The reasons for the failure of literature to seize its

---

[1] In this section I am indebted to F. J. E. Raby, *History of Christian Latin Poetry* (Oxford 1927) and *History of Secular Latin Poetry in the Middle Ages*.
[2] *History of Christian Latin Poetry*, 51.

chance are not quite simple; for they belong partly to the medium of literature, partly to the facts of history.

In prose and verse alike, though more conspicuously in verse, literary Latin failed to alter itself in any way comparable to the spiritual change found in Christianity. The new rhetoric of Fronto and Apuleius may have introduced something of the vernacular into prose along with its archaisms; Tertullian may have written more like an African than a Roman; the Vulgate may have gone a long way towards the popular tongue: but Christianity never had her own schools of rhetoric where she might have evolved a new and individual idiom; she grudgingly tolerated, and then used, those that existed. The result was that Latin prose, in spite of the Vulgate, did not break from its Ciceronian ideal nor Latin verse from the domination of Virgil, at the time, towards the end of the fourth century, when Christian epic writing might have been possible. There was thus no new form, comparable to the church-architecture that developed from the basilica or to early Christian mosaic, which was capable of dealing with the new things that could have been said. Augustine has been called 'the greatest poet of the early church', and rightly. And if in his youth he had not only wept over the sorrows of Dido and Aeneas but had inherited a new Latin poetic medium associated with the new religion, he might well have thought better of some kinds of literature and have become the great creative writer of early Christianity. As it was, there was only one possible medium for heroic verse, and it was dead for present use. I do not think that this mention of Augustine along with the epic, though superficially startling and improbable, is idle, or that we need minimise his affinity to Virgil. Virgil had both believed in Rome and had added a new spiritual dimension to the epic. He had knit politics and religion, and the gods had expressed themselves, he believed, *per civitatem hominum*. Augustine too, was not untouched by the grandeur of Rome and her empire; and, had events allowed, might have been glad to set forth the workings of another religion through an earthly polity.

But Augustine brings in the second reason why Christian heroic poetry was impossible. It was the capture of the great earthly city, Rome, by Alaric in 410 that impelled him to write of the other, heavenly, city in a work which made him one of the world's most influential authors. If he had contemplated an epic on the earthly triumph of the Christian faith over its enemies, how could he have persevered with it when Rome was captured by the infidel? And such was the recurrent pattern of events. Fate had always another barbarian invasion up its sleeve whenever Christian Rome appeared to be regaining stability. True, the age of Justinian achieved the mosaics of Ravenna, but it was not long before the Lombard invasions put an end to his triumph in the west.

Although conditions, as just described, made the Christian heroic poem impossible, it is worth recording a few samples of the Latin epic in the tradition of Virgil, Lucan, and Statius, for that tradition, ineffective in itself, did yet persist throughout the Middle Ages, and, reinforced by the new learning, helped to shape the genuine epic revival of the Renaissance and neo-classic ages. In the reign of Constantine, Juvencus, a Spaniard and a priest, wrote a Christian epic on the story of the Gospels in the manner of Virgil. 'He was, so far as we know, the first of the Latins to attempt to provide for educated Christian readers a substitute for the perilous beauties of the classical poets.'[1] Round the middle of the fourth century several distinguished men of letters were born: St Ambrose, St Jerome, Prudentius, St Augustine, Claudian, only the last being a pagan. They all reached mature manhood when the Roman Empire seemed to be recovering under the strong rule of Theodosius the Great (382-95) and when the age of persecution had been distanced and stylised in the way I have described before. Jerome and Augustine are known by their prose; but Ambrose was poet as well as prose-writer. While Ambrose stands at the head of the great mode of medieval hymn-writing and in his way worthily interprets his age, Prudentius and Claudian hold to the dead classical tradition, including epicising narrative in their repertory. Prudentius's *Psychomachia*, or battle of the Virtues and Vices for the soul, is a small-scale epic with the traditional trimmings. Vastly influential in subject, the first fully developed allegory in the medieval manner, it is crude and debased as poetry. Claudian, an Asian, wrote competent and polished narratives about the campaigns of Stilicho, guardian of the young Emperor Honorius the son of Theodosius, and a great general. He archaises with a truly amazing brilliance, but he had lost his battle before he began. More remarkable is another work on recent history. It is the *Johannis* of Corippus of the mid-sixth century. John, the hero of the poem, was a commander in Africa, after Justinian's general, Belisarius, had subdued the African kingdom of the Vandals. John led a successful expedition against the Moors; and Corippus made this expedition the subject of a long epic. He is a fervent Christian and he issues from the same breeding-ground that produced the finest mosaics at Ravenna. His method is scrupulously antique and dead. He used the proper epic devices, including the catalogue of fighters and the narrative of events that happened before the poem's action begins. Christopher Dawson considers Corippus the last genuine representative of the classical tradition in Latin poetry. In so long and so unnatural a literary phenomenon as the classicising epic between Statius and Petrarch it is difficult enough to draw the line between genuinely traditional and artificially imitative. But Corippus ante-

---

[1] Raby, *op. cit.* 17.

dates the Carolingian revival, and there is no harm in ending with him our samples of classicising heroic verse in this section.

A single example of another kind of narrative verse in Latin hexameters must suffice to introduce another topic. Venantius Fortunatus, who managed to spend a tranquil middle age at Poitiers, towards the end of the sixth century, when things generally were the reverse of tranquil, is best known as a great writer of hymns and especially of *Vexilla regis prodeunt*, 'The royal banners forward go.' But he also wrote a life of St Martin in hexameters. It has no literary merit, and it serves to remind us not only that it was futile to prolong the classical epic metre but that the Lives of the Saints generally do not come into the epic scope. With the emphasis now on holiness it is surprising that this should be the case; but it seems as if the reaction against humanism was so strong that the highest seriousness had first to consider abstract things and only then descend to human beings—even the most saintly. It is not the highest seriousness but the romantic and the miraculous that attached themselves to the great mode of hagiography.

Now such an attachment is absolutely and consistently typical. In the Christian Middle Ages, the world that sprang in the west from classical antiquity and the Christian religion, writers never lavished their full powers, their total seriousness, on the topics that in the natural way should have appealed to them. On the literary side they never, except along with much else, made the most of their saints and, granted some exceptions, they blurred and complicated and weakened the powerful intensity of the native epic which the Teutonic converts brought into Christendom with them and which, like the martyr myths of Diocletian's persecutions, offered such apparently obvious help to the main stream of European literature.

3. TEUTONIC PERIPHERY

> *But in another Countrey, as he said,*
> *Bore a bright golden flowre, but not in* this *soyl.*
>
> (Milton, *Comus*)

When the Goths broke into the now largely Christian Roman Empire and Rome retaliated by converting them to the new religion and enlisting them on her side against their heathen kin or the Hun or the Saracen, the epic did not take the obvious tidy course we should expect it to take. If the Romans had been unable to christianise the heroic poem, surely the converted Goths with their more primitive vigour should have been able to do so. A. W. Schlegel, lecturing at

Vienna in 1808 on the drama, drew a picture of converted Germany which certainly suggests that so it should have fallen out:

> After Christianity, the character of Europe has, since the commencement of the Middle Ages, been chiefly influenced by the Germanic race of northern conquerors, who infused new life and vigour into a degenerate people. The stern nature of the North drives man back within himself; and what is lost in the free sportive development of the senses, must, in noble dispositions, be compensated by earnestness of mind. Hence the honest cordiality with which Christianity was welcomed by all the Teutonic tribes, so that among no other race of men has it penetrated more deeply into the inner man, displayed more powerful effects, or become more interwoven with all human feelings and sensibilities. The rough, but honest heroism of the northern conquerors, by its admixture with the sentiments of Christianity, gave rise to chivalry.[1]

Well, if the blend of Teutonism and Christianity produced chivalry, it should have produced heroic poems to match.

Now there are true epic elements in some of the heroic verse and prose that issued from out of the Teutonic invaders and their descendants, in both Teutonic and Romance languages: elements that raise a few pieces of this literature above any heroic writing in western Europe since Virgil. But in the main such elements were retrospective, interpreting a barbarian way of life and drawing their vitality from it. When they joined with the Christian element, they either suffered a loss of vitality or they remained in juxtaposition, unfused. There is one conspicuous exception to this general rule.

Why should the Teutonic conquerors have found it so hard to animate the new religion with their own unimpaired vitality? H. V. Routh[2] asserts that the gap between the Christian doctrine of original sin and the unabashed self-confidence of the barbarian hero was too wide to be bridged. But one could retort that Christian doctrine did not eliminate the hero but changed his character from warrior to martyr. About the time when the unknown poet wrote *Beowulf*, Bede near the beginning of his *Ecclesiastical History* described in lavish terms the martyrdom of St Alban. And the Anglo-Saxon poems on Judith and St Andrew are surviving examples of what must have been a common literary form: the heroic episode on a Jewish or Christian theme. The earliest English poets dreamt at least they could extract poetry from a mixture of new theme and old form. But Routh, though he may be wrong in making original sin the principal obstacle, is right in asserting that a gap of some sort existed.

---

[1] A. W. Schlegel, *Dramatic Art and Literature*, translated by John Black (London 1861) 25.
[2] *God, Man and Epic Poetry* (Cambridge 1927) ii. 91 ff.

One gap is that between what the Teutonic peoples thought of, or would have liked to think of, their own traditional literary forms and what the captive ancient world thought of them. For all their success as conquerors the Romans had not been proof against Greek self-confidence in matters of culture. In the same way the Goths, aware of the superiority of Roman culture long before they became the aggressors, were little likely to stick out for the excellence of their native lays (which the Emperor Julian likened to the harsh cawings of birds) when they settled within the old bounds of the Roman Empire. If their poets continued to compose in the old way, they did so with the chilly knowledge that their Latin neighbours despised their efforts as being in a class not to be thought of along with Virgil and Lucan and Statius and Claudian. Ekkehart's *Waltharius*, written presumably in the monastery of St Gall in the middle of the tenth century, looks, for all its late date, like a forlorn effort to close the gap of which I am speaking. This poem recounts in some fifteen hundred hexameters the story of Walther of Aquitaine and Hildegund the Burgundian princess, whom Attila carried home as hostages. It was a well-known Germanic story; and two fragments of it survive in the old English *Waldhere*. Ekkehart presumably knew a German version and tried to make it respectable by putting it into Latin hexameters, Virgilian in aspiration but wooden in fact.

But the matter of literary form is only a detail in a general state of affairs which W. P. Ker has described in a few masterly pages in *Epic and Romance*.[1] This state of affairs was that the peoples of western Europe experienced the impact of the Roman culture and religion before they had had time to bring their own to maturity. They had their own mythology,

> but they were not left to themselves, in this labour of bringing mythology within bounds; even before they had fairly escaped from barbarism, before they had made a fair beginning of civilisation and of reflective literature on their own account, they were drawn within the Empire, into Christendom. Before their imaginations had fully wakened out of the primeval dream, the cosmogonies and theogonies, gross and monstrous, of their national infancy, they were asked to have an opinion about the classical mythology, as represented by the Latin poets; they were made acquainted with the miracles of the lives of saints. More than all this, even, their minds were charmed away from the labour of epic invention, by the spell of the preacher. . . . The fascination of religious symbolism crept over minds that had hardly yet begun to see and understand things as they are.

Nor was it a question of literature only, it was a question of the

[1] London (1922) 45-9. I owe much to this book in parts of this section.

primitive Teutonic forms of society. These did not have a chance of realising themselves. Out of the great conquests emerged not a new Germania but the Holy Roman Empire.

The result of all this was that in general there were not sufficient clarity and certainty about life to make the most serious literature possible. But there were the exceptional cases either when the old Teutonic strain kept itself undaunted by the new and more sophisticated strains long enough to mature, or when by a happy miracle the old came to satisfactory terms with the new. It is the first of these two cases that applies to the present section on the Teutonic periphery. The second takes us to France and must wait till another section.

And here I must insert a reminder that I use the word *epic* in an unusual way; more specially that I do not equate it with *heroic*. It is very difficult not to fall into the habit of equating them, partly because we tend to derive our ideas of epic from the poems of Homer, which happen to be heroic as well as epic, and not from the *Divine Comedy*, which is epic without being heroic; and partly because there lingers in our mind the idea that only the primitive is truly epic, and in primitive times it is mainly the heroic strain that has sufficient seriousness to have an initial chance of qualifying as epic. Thus we are apt to assume that *Maldon* is epic in a way that the *Faerie Queene* is not. What I wish to insist on here is that the heroic episode is not an epic, any more than a fable of La Fontaine is a comedy. Such insistence is necessary when so authoritative a writer as W. P. Ker in so fine a book as *Epic and Romance* shows himself hazy on the relations of the heroic and the epic. He talks of an epic age, by which he means one of a certain degree of social primitiveness, but goes on to postulate for the epic poem things which need have nothing to do with the primitive: the sense of dignity and the energy belonging to a great age of history and the power of dealing simply and directly with the great human passions and of creating great characters. Surely this is to pursue two incompatible methods of procedure, when the only rational method is to choose between them. Either, if you will, equate *epic* with *heroic* and relegate the epic to those pieces of narrative literature that succeed in dealing with the heroic age (after the manner of Bowra's *Heroic Poetry*); or sever the connection and base epic on requirements not exclusively heroic. It is because I follow the second method that I refuse to take it for granted that *Beowulf* is an epic but apply to it the same tests as I apply to *Piers Plowman* or the *Pilgrim's Progress*.

The common reader, if he tries to find his way through the history of the Dark Ages, sees this epoch in terms of the decline and fall of the Roman Empire or of the rise of the Christian Church, but not of the triumph of Germania. He would not dream of accompanying Alaric on his conquests; he remains centred in the Roman provinces Alaric overran. He therefore has to make an effort of adjustment when he is told (and very rightly told) that the period from the fourth to the sixth centuries A.D. was from the Teutonic point of view one of glory and expansion. Through the great movements of Teutonic peoples tribes ceased to think in tribal terms, and the great achievement of one part of the people became the public property of the rest. It was to these centuries of victory and change and expansion that the more ambitious forms of later Teutonic literature turned for their subject-matter. However changed from their historical selves, Theodoric and Attila are two of the great recurrent characters in Teutonic narrative; and the great invading groups of Goths, Franks, Burgundians, and the rest are presented in juxtaposition. But though these centuries might from the Teutonic side have offered to their poets the great subject of primitive and unspoiled valour and simplicity triumphing over sophisticated and corrupt luxury, the conditions described above made it impossible for the conquerors to use their opportunity. The nearer the centre of Christendom and of the old culture the invaders found themselves, the more hampered were they in expressing the sense of their great achievements. On the Continent the Teutonic consciousness, as such, failed to mature; and what flowering there was belonged to the periphery.

From what remains of Old English narrative poetry it seems that a principal part of its strength lay from beginning to end in what can be called the heroic episode. *Beowulf*, *Waldhere*, the *Fight at Finnesburh*, *Judith*, *Andreas*, and the *Battle of Maldon* ranging from the early eighth to the eleventh centuries, can all be put in that category. Whether *Beowulf* breaks out of it into that of the epic is not likely to cease to be a matter of dispute. The answer does not depend ultimately on the facts of quality or cultural affinities. It seems agreed that *Beowulf* is very good in its way. And it does not make a fundamental difference how much Christianity and sophistication you see in it. Even if the author was a monk who had read Virgil and had modelled Beowulf's reminiscences on Aeneas's (as an extreme view would make him), it remains true that what gives the poem its character is its picture of early Teutonic life and morality. Even if Hrothgar and Beowulf have some share in the Christian virtue of patience, we should not dream of going to *Beowulf* rather than elsewhere to find a classic expression of that virtue. In emphasis the Christian patience pictured in *Beowulf* counts for little compared with a tradition of daring and of endurance that long antedated the arrival of Christianity among the Anglo-Saxons. It may be that eighth-century England showed an astonishing mixture of English and Mediterranean and that we should not forget that *Beowulf* and Bede's *Ecclesiastical History* are near each other in date. But once again it is not to *Beowulf* that we go to become greatly aware of that mixture. Primarily *Beowulf* depicts the old Teutonic world, and the present question is whether it does so broadly enough and at the same time dramatically enough to reach to epic height.

Intensity of a sort no one can deny to *Beowulf*. The descriptions of Beowulf's journey to Heorot, the watchman's challenge to him and his company when they land, and of the journeys to and from the mere are brief and clear and exciting. Beowulf's own courage is cool and powerful to a degree, as when he tells Hrothgar before the fight with Grendel that he will need no burial if he loses, for Grendel will gnaw his bleeding body as he carries it to his lair. But one has only to think of the *Odyssey* on the one hand and of the Icelandic Sagas on the other to see that the world of *Beowulf* is comparatively narrow, that the poem does not truly fulfil the epic function of conveying the sense of what it was like to be alive at the time the author wrote. There are no touches of ordinary feeling or of homely quotidian life to supplement the grim exercises of heroic will-power or princely bounty: nothing like the sudden picture of the labourer returning home with the mist rising behind him which Milton inserted in the last lines of *Paradise Lost*. The true epic amplitude is not here. The characters are powerful and adequate to the comparative narrowness of the world they inhabit. But there is no inner conflict, and they do nothing to widen by their own richness the setting in which they are placed. However evolved and sophisticated the art of *Beowulf* may be, that sophistication does not include the motivation of the actors.[1]

It would be vain to prolong the discussion of *Beowulf* if only because the poem does in fact lie mostly outside the epic tradition which is the subject of this book—a consideration which overrides the question whether or not *Beowulf* is a true epic. I say 'mostly' because *Beowulf* may have been one of the channels through which the alliterative metre was conducted underground till its emergence in the fourteenth century and its use by Langland in a poem which I believe has some claim to the epic status. To attach anything but the metre of *Piers Plowman* to an Old English tradition would be perilous in the extreme. The importance of English culture in the eighth century and of its influence on world history may have been immense, and people today should probably be much more alive to it than they are. But to give it due weight in its own day is no excuse for exaggerating its permanent influence in England. The culture that Alcuin took with him to France may have been a fundamental inspiration to Europe; but that did not prevent its being pretty well wiped out in England by the Norse invaders. Later, Alfred may have regained touch with Christian

[1] For the basic nature of *Beowulf* see J. R. R. Tolkien's British Academy Lecture for 1936, *Beowulf, the Monsters and the Critics*. Tolkien considers it not epic, 'not even a magnified lay', but elegiac rather, 'an heroic-elegiac poem . . . one of the most moving ever written' (33).

learning, but what for instance did his translation of Boethius mean to Chaucer and his age? Nothing whatever. The tradition was broken again, and Chaucer looked not to early England but to the Continent for cultural nourishment; and when he translated Boethius he did so from the Latin original, as if Alfred's translation had never existed. This is not to deny that continuity of English prose that R. W. Chambers argued for so well, but it is to insist that the mere existence of strong Continental cultures in England before the Conquest is no proof that the Continental cultures that existed in England afterwards were derived from them. An immense change took place in Europe in the twelfth century and it was the new culture arising from it which set going the English literary tradition that has persisted in spite of so many changes to our day. It is through Europe and not through early England that the true English epic tradition runs.

If *Beowulf* is but slenderly connected with the English works I consider epic and hence is not an integral part of my theme, it would appear that there is even less reason to write of the Icelandic Sagas, whose isolation, their surpassing merits considered, is one of the most astonishing things in literary history. But, having begun to generalise on the Teutonic epic, I can hardly omit the literary kind in which it finds its best embodiment. A second reason for including the Sagas is that they serve to ratify my contentions that prose may be an epic medium and that epic and history are akin. The great Icelandic prose stories belong to the twelfth and thirteenth centuries and they draw their subject-matter from the days of Norse movement and expansion in the tenth and eleventh centuries. 'The heroic age of the ancient Germans', wrote W. P. Ker,[1] 'culminates and ends in Iceland in the thirteenth century.' At the time when the Goths and other Teutonic tribes were on the move, the northern ones stayed at home. They were thus the least exposed to the disturbing effects of a more mature culture and had the longest leisure to perfect their own way of life. Of the colonisers of Iceland these two statements are true in a specially strong degree. By leaving the mainland they removed themselves still further from Mediterranean influence and they had some two centuries more time than their kin to work out their own purely Nordic institutions. They came from the most daring element in an already daring people and they left Europe (like the Pilgrim Fathers) to escape what they thought political tyranny and to found a state after their own heart. That state had its laws, but the great families took the law into their own hands when it suited them. Superficially Icelandic life in the great age presents an appalling picture of feuds and violent revenges. But this does not mean that the other things in

[1] *Op. cit.* 57. For an excellent account of the literary characteristics of the Icelandic Sagas see Dorothy M. Hoare, *The Works of Morris and Yeats in relation to early Saga Literature* (Cambridge 1937) chap. 1.

life were not transacted with relish. In the history of Sturla, founder of one of the great Icelandic houses, it is told how on a winter night in Sturla's house at Hvamm there was dancing which lasted till late. The air was still and from time to time a man would look out and listen for the sound of an enemy. That gives us the lawless state of the land; yet there is no need to doubt the hilarity of the dancers. Little as the Icelandic way of life is to our taste today, those whose it was believed in it and found it satisfying; and by the time Iceland came into line with the rest of Europe, it had of itself ceased to satisfy, having worked itself out. There was no question of another and more mature culture cutting short a different growth.

It was in the difficult matter of mythology, referred to above, that the Saga writers conspicuously triumphed. Independent, secure from the bewilderment of classical mythology and Christian hagiology, they tamed or eliminated 'the cosmogonies and theogonies, gross and monstrous, of their national infancy' in a way beyond the powers of the author of *Beowulf* and as successfully as Homer in the *Odyssey*. The characters of the Sagas have traffic with one another, not with dragons: and superstitions exist within the characters' mind; they do not objectify themselves into monstrous mythological appearances. The drama of real life has asserted itself without the least sacrifice of the authentic Nordic genius.

To discuss the Sagas in any detail, to answer, for instance, the question whether that of Njal is or is not an epic, would be inappropriate in this book; for the Sagas have no contact with the epic tradition I am concerned with. On the other hand it helps to understand the epic generally to point out that the Icelandic Sagas are what you can call an 'epic area'. Whether or not any one Saga is an achieved epic, the epic ingredients are all there for the writers to make use of; and these writers, taken together, exhibit them all piecemeal, whether or not any one succeeds in combining them into a single organism. The number of human beings who made up the Icelandic polity may have been small, but they covered between them a large part of the human spirit. It is a whole world the Sagas represent. And though they represent that world so coolly and with such apparent critical externality they are far from failing to penetrate the depths of men's hearts. W. P. Ker has made the point so well that it is pointless to use other words than his:

> The charge of superficiality or externality falls away to nothing in the mind of anyone who knows by what slight touches of imagination a character may be brought home to an audience, if the character is there to begin with. It is not by elaborate, continuous analysis, but by a gesture here and a sentence there, that characters are expressed. The Sagas give the look of things and persons at the critical moments, getting as close as they can, by all

devices, to the vividness of things as they appear, as they happen; brief and reserved in their phrasing, but the reverse of abstract or limited in their regard for the different modes and aspects of life, impartial in their acknowledgement of the claims of individual character, and unhesitating in their rejection of conventional ideals, of the conventional romantic hero as well as the conventional righteous man. The Sagas are more solid and more philosophical than any romance or legend.[1]

In their power to evoke the sense of total life the Saga-writers resemble Homer. Just as Homer let in a large side of life into the *Iliad* when he mentioned the Greek storekeepers and sailors, so do the Saga-writers by their small touches. Here is a passage from *Njal* where children suddenly come in. The situation is that Unna had persuaded her father Mord to promote a divorce from her husband Hrut. The divorce went through; but Mord failed to get the dowry back from Hrut, because Hrut refused to surrender it without ordeal by battle, and this Mord would not face, to the great loss of his reputation. Hrut and his brother Hauskuld are guests at the homestead of Lund.

> There had been much rain that day, and the men got wet, so long-fires were made down the length of the hall. Thiostolf, the master of the house, sat between Hauskuld and Hrut, and two boys, of whom Thiostolf had the rearing, were playing on the floor, and a girl was playing with them. They were great chatterboxes, for they were too young to know better. So one of them said—

> 'Now, I will be Mord, and summon you to lose your wife because you have not been a good husband to her.'

Then the other answered—

> 'I will be Hrut, and I call on you to give up all claim to your goods, if you dare not fight with me.'

> This they said several times, and all the household burst out laughing.[2]

For all the simplicity of style, and indeed because of the strength this simplicity betokens, the clashes of character and the perplexities into which the persons of living drama must fall are wonderfully rendered. In *Laxdale* Gudrun loves Kjartan most, yet she must plot his death when he is married to Hrefna. When her husband Bolli returns with the news that he has done the killing, she says that he has done a good work; while she was spinning twelve ells of yarn, he had killed Kjartan. And the thought which pleases her most is that 'Hrefna will not go laughing to her bed tonight.' Gudrun is the kin

---

[1] *Op. cit.* 245.
[2] G. W. Dasent's translation in one volume (London, no date) 16-17.

of Clytaemnestra. We are far from the simple and dreamlike motivation of *Beowulf*.

Lastly the Sagas render incomparably the sense of what life was like as lived in Iceland. The reader finds himself in it, on the spot, without a trace of romantic distancing.

I wish to make my point about an epic area, because here the Iceland of the eleventh and twelfth centuries offers so apt an analogy with the England of Elizabeth. There was no clear and undoubted epic in that age; yet Elizabethan England was an 'epic area' and it produced three major manifestations, although not fully achieved, of the epic spirit. Both ages had that self-confidence without which genuine epic writing is impossible.

The Icelandic Sagas concern real people of some two centuries before, and we need not doubt that Homer wrote of real people too. But the Sagas are closer to the people they deal with and contain a higher proportion of true fact. It is thus natural that Icelandic history, of which Sturla's account of his own family is the most eminent example, should be closer in method to the Sagas than Herodotus is to Homer. W. P. Ker aptly compares the relation of the Sagas to early Icelandic history with that of Fielding's novels to the *Voyage to Lisbon*: the method of the one kind was prolonged into the other. Anyhow, there are epic elements in Icelandic history. I must not dwell on them, but I may be allowed to note them in order to justify my including a few selected pieces of historical writing in the epic category.

4. THE SONG OF ROLAND

I come now to the magnificent exception to the general rule that the old heroic strain of the north and the new religious strain of the converted south never came to satisfactory terms. Like most English readers I first became acquainted with the text of *Roland* through Arnold's quotation in the *Study of Poetry*, the first essay in the second volume of *Essays in Criticism*. Arnold complains that certain poems receive excessive praise through being judged not only on their poetic merit but on their historical importance. And he cites *Roland* as an example. He says:

> Let us try the *Chanson de Roland* at its best. Roland, mortally wounded, lays himself down under a pine-tree, with his face turned towards Spain and the enemy—

> '*De plusurs choses à remembrer li prist,*
> *De tantes teres cume li bers cunquist,*

De dulce France, des humes de sun lign,
De Carlemagne sun seignor ki l'nurrit.'[1]

That is primitive work with an undeniable poetic quality of its
own. It deserves such praise, and such praise is sufficient for it.

And Arnold goes on to quote two lines of Homer, which he says belong
to another and immeasurably higher order of poetry. I was more grate-
ful to Arnold for introducing me to the French lines than convinced
that he had said the right things about them. They seemed to be good
enough poetry to make any question of primitiveness irrelevant; and
to stand up pretty well to the Homeric touchstone. Here was terseness, resonance, and controlled feeling. And further acquaintance
with the poem confirmed the impression.

We now know that *Roland*, whether it dates from the eleventh or
twelfth century, whether or not the song of Roland sung by Taillefer
at Hastings was the same as that preserved in the Bodleian manuscript, is not primitive in its art but comes towards the end of a
literary movement. If it is inferior to Homer it is so for other reasons
than callowness. It is, for instance, on a much smaller scale—about
4000 lines—and if it succeeds, its success is a smaller affair. But
though the movement of its lines is more abrupt than that of the roll
of the Homeric hexameter, it is suited to the smaller scale of the poem.
And what these facts mean is that *Roland* is a poem which exists in
its own right as achieved poetry and can be judged on its own merits,
unhampered by any Homeric comparison. What, then, are the claims
of *Roland* to be an epic?

It is, first of all, well and coherently plotted: simple in its lines yet
complex enough to allow the characters to develop. As in Shakespeare, there are doings on whose motivation one must not dwell.
For instance, it is quite taken for granted that Roland's position as
commander of the rear-guard when the French army cross the
Pyrenees northward is one of extreme and certain peril. This is difficult to account for, because Charles was crossing the Pyrenees only
because Ganelon had persuaded him that Marsilie, the king of the
Saracens, had genuinely come to terms. But there is never any vague
plotting where the motives of the principal persons are concerned.
The source of Roland's tragedy is his recommending to Charles that
Ganelon should undertake the perilous task of envoy to the Saracens
(who had murdered the two envoys sent before). And the poet hints
at earlier hostility between Roland and Ganelon when he tells us that
Ganelon was Roland's step-father. From Ganelon's resentment at
Roland's act springs his treachery, and from his treachery the various

[1] 'Then began he to call many things to remembrance,—all the lands which his
valour conquered, and pleasant France, and the men of his lineage, and Charlemagne his liege lord who nourished him.' (Arnold's translation.)

doings of Christian and Saracen that lead to Roland's death. The poem is fully rounded off by the account of Ganelon's punishment when Charles finally returns to Aix. The proportions, too, are just. The poet never dwells on an incident too long; and if he dwells longest on Roland's dying it is because that is the culmination of the poem. As far as he goes, he shows a strong controlling will; but the poem is not long enough to put the poet's will to the supreme test a full-scale epic provides.

Within the four thousand lines there is considerable variety. Like Homer and any other poets who belong to an age of artistic sophistication growing out of a more primitive one, the author of *Roland* had to come to terms with a legacy of crude barbarism and fantasy. He does so in a manner that is intermediate between those of *Beowulf* and the Sagas. There is no killing of monsters on the one hand nor the consistently cool realism of the Sagas on the other. There is a good deal of fantastic exaggeration; but the poet keeps it from interfering with the crucial development of the characters. Charlemagne, with his two hundred years of age and yet with the bodily vigour sufficient to kill in duel the paynim admiral, is a fabulous figure, but he serves to heighten by contrast, rather than to confound, the credible characters of Roland, Oliver, Archbishop Turpin, and Ganelon. The numbers of paynims that the first three of these kill at Roncesvalles are fabulous, but we are not worried, nor diverted from the prime human business, since they are answered by other fabulous items in the setting. When the battle reached its height there was wind and earthquake through the length and breadth of France. Then there was darkness at noon.

> *Cuntre midi tenebres i ad granz,*
> *N'i ad clartet se li ciels nen i fent.*
> *Hum ne le veit ki mult ne s'espaent;*
> *Dient plusur: 'C'est li definemenz,*
> *La fin de l'siècle ki nus est en present.'*
> *Il ne le sevent ne dient veir nient:*
> *C'est la dulur pur la mort de Rollant.*[1]

What takes the sting out of the fantasy, what reduces it to its proper proportion and makes it do its proper work as picturesque contrast is the evidence that the poet is after all close to his central human subject. Charles may be a fabulous figure, but Roland's lovely words describing what a warrior must be prepared to suffer for his lord come right out of the real France of the first crusading epoch:

---

[1] Ed. L. Gautier (Tours 1880) 1431-7. 'At noon there is great darkness. There is no light save where the sky is rent. No man sees it but is in great terror. Many say: "It is finished; it is the end of our age which is now upon us." They neither know the truth nor speak it: it is sorrow for the death of Roland.'

Pur sun seignur deit hum suffrir granz mals
E endurer e forz freiz e granz calz;
Si'n deit hum perdre de l'sanc e de la carn.[1]

Further, though there is nothing so intimately realistic as the children playing at being Mord and Hrut in *Njalsaga*, there are a few touches which have enormous value in reassuring us that the author of *Roland* was close to his own world. When Charles suspects Ganelon of treachery he arrests him and puts him in the custody of the cooks, who hate and insult him. This mention of the 'Q' department of the army, slipped in so coolly and suddenly, recalls Homer's mention of the storekeepers in the *Iliad*. The Archbishop, who had seemed nothing but a fighter, at the height of the battle reminds us that there are other kinds of clerics. Speaking of the true knight, he says:

En bataille deit estre forz e fiers,
O altrement ne valt quatre deniers;
Monies deit estre en un de cez mustiers,
Si preierat tuz jurz pur noz peechiez.[2]

There is a wonderful description of the sad and exhausted French army asleep after the rout of the Saracens who have killed Roland. Victory was so complete and exhaustion and grief so great that they do not trouble to post sentinels.

Par tuz les prez or se dorment li Franc:
N'i ad cheval ki poisset estre en estant;
Ki herbe voelt il la prent en gisant.
Mult ad apris ki bien conoist ahan.[3]

The realistic touch of the horses too tired to crop the grass standing again reminds of Homer. Sometimes realism and symbolism and the fantastic are blended. One of the great moments of the poem is when the first army of ordinary Saracens, whom Roland and his men have routed, are replaced by blackamoors. Nothing could be less realistic than this replacement. Where could they have found room to advance with an army of dead heaped up round the few surviving Frenchmen? But their colour serves superbly to shadow the coming death of Roland and to suggest that they are a worse type of paynim than that already dealt with. And they are described realistically.

---

[1] 1117-9. 'For his lord a man should suffer great harms and bear both hard frost and great heat. A man should lose both blood and flesh.'

[2] 1879-83. 'In battle he should be stout and proud; otherwise he is not worth fourpence. He should be a monk in one of those monasteries where he will pray all his days for our sins.'

[3] 2521-4. 'Over all the fields now sleep the French. There is no horse that can keep on its legs; any one that wants to graze does so lying. A man who really knows sorrow has learnt much.'

They are

> *la cuntredite gent*
> *Ki plus sunt neir que nen est arrement*
> *Ne n'unt de blanc ne mais que sul les denz.*[1]

In sum the blackamoors create, in a small space, a wonderful sense of diversity.

Another way in which *Roland* does much in a small place is through the sudden turn of thought or action in a single line. The passage just quoted about the weary French ended abruptly with the single gnomic line about the discipline of sorrow. Near the beginning of the poem there is the longish episode of Ganelon, on his perilous embassy to the Saracen king, Marsilie, finally agreeing to betray Roland. Marsilie praises him and promises him ten mules loaded with the finest gold of Arabia: 'only be certain Roland is in command of the rear-guard. If I can catch him in the narrow defiles, he will fight a mortal battle.' At which

> *Guenes respunt: 'Mei est vis que trop targe.'*
> *Pois est muntez, entret en sun veiage.*[2]

That is the right kind of abruptness: it administers a shock and leaves us guessing. Are we to think that Ganelon left in a hurry through self-disgust, or fear? Or are his motives irrelevant, the poet merely wanting to close the episode? There is no answer; yet the point is that we should be stirred to ask the questions. Most sublime of all is Roland's sudden call to re-enter into battle after his tragic self-reproaches at having caused the death of so many French lords:

> *Baruns Franceis, pur mei vus vei murir.*
> *Jo ne vus pois tenser ne guarantir;*
> *Aït vus Deus, ki unkes ne mentit!*
> *Olivier frere, vus ne dei jo faillir;*
> *De doel murrai s'altre ne m'i ocit.*
> *Sire cumpainz, alum i referir.*[3]

It is the switch from self-reproach to action coming *within* the speech that is so gloriously surprising. Consider the difference if the poet had put it outside the speech, saying, 'And then Roland and Oliver returned together to the battle.'

Roland's speech points to what is perhaps the main virtue of the

---

[1] 1932-4. 'The cursed people who are blacker than ink and who have nothing white about them but their teeth.'

[2] 659-60. 'Ganelon answered: "I think I tarry too long." So he mounted and began his journey.'

[3] 1863-8. 'It is my fault, barons, that I see you die. I cannot defend or safeguard you. Help you God, who is never false! Brother Oliver, my duty is never to fail you. I shall die of grief, if no one kills me here. Sir comrade, come: let us return to smite the paynims again.'

poem: its successful tragic drama. The speech itself is highly dramatic and reminds me of a culminating place in Shakespeare's *King John*, where Falconbridge, deeply perplexed at the death of Arthur and half suspicious of the king, abruptly decides on action and leaves to deal with the king's 'thousand businesses'. But it is only a part of a larger process of motivation which makes Roland satisfy (in a way that may be unique in medieval narrative verse) Aristotle's requirements for the tragic hero. Roland is the pattern of brave knighthood, but his fault is that his ardour is excessive. His friend Oliver says so when Roland volunteers for the dangerous mission of envoy to the Saracen: he would not make a good envoy because too impetuous. When Charles refuses to send Roland or Oliver or the Archbishop and asks for the nomination of a man from his own district, Roland unguardedly nominates his step-father, Ganelon. When later the French retire from Spain and Charles asks who is to command the rear-guard through the Pyrenees, Ganelon retaliates by nominating Roland. There is much propriety, if nothing conspicuously tragic, in Roland's incurring the price of his own impetuosity. It is when his pride involves others that the real tragedy comes in. The rear-guard Roland commands consists of twenty thousand men and includes all the first knights of France. As they hold the narrows they see a much greater force of Saracens approaching. Oliver implores Roland to sound his horn to recall Charles and the main army. Roland refuses because he will lose glory by so doing. Oliver accepts Roland's decision, though he knows it wrong, with complete loyalty. Later, Roland repents and, all too late, proposes to blow his horn; but now Oliver, as befits the slower and more reflective man, wants to abide by the earlier decision. Nevertheless, Roland has his way. He blows so fiercely that he bursts his brain. When he sees the dead French lords laid out he bitterly repents his rashness. Later, Oliver, near death and not knowing what he does, strikes Roland with his sword; and Roland forgives him. Roland dies last of all the French. The lines of the friends' characters are simple but perfectly true to basic human nature. And there is the entirely adequate irony that if Roland had blown his horn earlier he would not only have saved his fellows but spared bursting his own brain. Here is the true spirit of tragedy.

Lastly, *Roland* does indeed speak for a large body of people. As I shall seek to show, the essential subject of medieval epic was the Christian one of the earthly pilgrimage leading to salvation and a higher life. Such a conception accorded ill with the vigorous self-assertiveness of a heroic age. In the main the Christian world suppressed this self-assertiveness before evolving a humanism of its own. But before the great intellectual and humanist movements of the thirteenth century there did exist, and in northern France especially, a compromise between the violent worldliness of the heroic age and the Christian awareness of another life. The excessive individualism of heroic society was mitigated by high notions of feudal loyalty, while the spiritual integrity on which Christian notions of salvation had at their best been founded was coarsened and simplified into crude visions of a Paradise to be attained by a technical and quite unspiritual fidelity. Thus modified, the primitive and the Christian were able temporarily to coalesce. This coalition was a genuine affair that satisfied men's hearts and enabled them to look round and to arrange some of the things that pressed upon their minds. They could take some stock of the great events that had filled recent centuries. Some of the results were the earliest crusading impulse, the strong, plain, yet neat vigour of Norman architecture, and the *Song of Roland*.

The facts of history are in *Roland* excessively distorted, and yet the poem does in its queer exaggerated way faithfully express the sort of feeling that lingered in men's minds after the tremendous conflicts of Châlons and Tours. The two hundred years of Charlemagne and the immense horde of negroes who are needed for the deaths of the three last French champions are faithful correlatives of a historical epoch that, probably in its day self-blind to its own crucial importance, took on for later ages an overmastering air of the fabulous.

I quoted above three lines of one of Roland's speeches about a vassal's duty to his lord. There is another which repeats the sentiment and adds something else; in so doing it represents a whole way of thinking:

> *Bien devum ci ester pur nostre rei.*
> *Pur sun seignur deit hum suffrir destreiz,*
> *E endurer e granz calz e granz freiz;*
> *Si'n deit hum perdre e de l'quir e de l'peil.*
> *Or guart cascuns que granz colps i empleit,*
> *Male cançun ja cantée n'en seit.*
> *Paien unt tort e chrestien unt dreit.*
> *Malvaise essample n'en sera ja de mei.*[1]

There you have the traces of the old unmitigated heroic self-assertion; but softened by the belief that courage should be put to the public service, and given a new turn by a simple uncompromising piety. Nor can I find (with Arnold) that the expression of these great general sentiments is unworthy of them. In their sublime emphasis the last two lines are fit to be compared with Milton's Satan when, reviewing the possibility of submitting to God, he says,

> *That Glory never shall his wrath or might*
> *Extort from me.*

[1] 1009-16. 'It is indeed our duty to stand here for our king. For his lord a man should suffer pain and bear great heat and great cold. A man should lose both skin and hair. Let each man see to it that he deals great blows that an ill song be never sung about him. Paynims are wrong and Christians are right. A bad example shall never come from *me*.'

Roland's simple-minded piety in the penultimate line is developed by Archbishop Turpin in his speech to Roland and his men before the battle. The battle is inevitable; the Saracens are upon us; Christianity must be defended; you must fight to the death;

> *Clamez vos culpes, si preiez Deu mercit.*
> *Asoldrai vus pur vos anmes guarir:*
> *Se vuz murez esterez seint martir;*
> *Sièges avrez el' greignur Pareïs.*[1]

If for the faithful their own religious problems are simple, so too are their religious dealings with the infidel. When near the end of the poem Charles captures Saragossa he sees to it that his soldiers enter all the mosques and synagogues. There they break up all the idols. Charles, says the poet, really does believe in God and wishes to serve him. The bishops bless the water and the captive infidels are brought to the baptistery. If any one of them resists Charles's will he is hanged, put to the sword, or burnt. More than a hundred thousand are baptised and become 'veir chrestien', true Christians. Only the Saracen queen is kept back to be converted later by gentler means.

In spite of its rather short length and largely in view of its very pregnant simplicities, I think that *Roland* should take its place among the epics.

I have to admit that there is no direct connection between *Roland* and the English epic; and it may be objected that I should not have allowed it more space than I did the Icelandic Sagas. Yet there is a difference. The Sagas came to a dead end; they had no European progeny: *Roland*, as well as being a Romanesque epic, led to the Gothic romance. It is full of those fabulous elements which, held here in decent subordination, were destined to become the principal affair in the narrative mode that followed. *Roland* is thus a part of European literature in a way that the Sagas are not; and as such it may have had an ultimate if vague and untraceable influence on *Arcadia* and the *Faerie Queene*.

I have spent space enough on the epic or epicising works that are peripheral to the main epic area in England, and it is now time to revert to the central theme.

---

[1] 1132–52. 'Cry out your sins and ask God for mercy. I shall absolve you to heal your souls. If you die you will be holy martyrs; you will have places in the higher Paradise.'

CHAPTER II

THE MEDIEVAL BACKGROUND

1. ALLEGORY AND THE CHANGED
WORLD PICTURE

Now I a fourfold vision see,
And a fourfold vision is given to me;
'Tis fourfold in my supreme delight
And threefold in soft Beulah's night
And twofold Always. May God us keep
From Single vision. (Blake)

Even allegory, which would seem to require constant reference to a
preconceived design, cannot be written in cold blood.

(Michael Roberts)

NOW that I am back on the main road of my inquiry I must ask the reader, if he can, to recollect my introductory remarks on Virgil. In the intervening sections there may have been hints of the great transition in the history of the epic from the heroic to the allegorical, but they bulked small compared with other matters and they contribute little to what Virgil in his prophetic genius did in fact adumbrate. I will try to refresh the reader's memory by repeating in different words some of the earlier statements that led my theme to its new stage, adding new matter as I go.

However closely medieval allegory became tied up with rhetoric, however mathematical and mechanical was the medieval theory of multiple meanings, the allegorical form was not a mere accretion but the index of a whole new way of thought. That way is sharply opposed to the heroic way shown whether in Homer or in the Icelandic Sagas. There is something anti-humanist in it; and its rise corresponds to the change that came over art in the early Christian centuries: the change from a decadent realism to an abstraction and a spirituality it is easy to perceive, however difficult to define. The Greek world generally from Homer to Theocritus made the present life the single fixed standard. There were terrifying supernatural happenings, but they were interpreted by their effect on the life of every day and usually accounted for by human negligence or error. There was no impulse to vary the criterion and to judge the life of every day by the supposed standards of another order of existence. The change came partly from within the Greek world, partly from farther east. Greek philosophy, turning with Socrates from external nature to the mind of man and with Epicurus from social to individual man, helped to divide the mind within itself. C. S. Lewis, in his fine chapter on allegory in the *Allegory of Love* (a chapter that deals with some of the substance of this section at much greater length and in rather different ways), notes how the idea of the mental fight as the very substance of the moral life characterises pagan and Christian thought alike in the first century A.D.,[1] in contrast to Aristotle's conception of the virtuous man acting rightly by immediate free choice. And once the old Greek unity of mind was dissolved, men were open to the different and sometimes more spiritual forms of religion that were waiting in the East to assert themselves. The allegorical form has something to do with these changes. The old heroic form presented individuals whole and indivisible, and increased the weight of individuality by separating one man cleanly from another. If a feeling is presented, it is as A's feeling or B's feeling, never as feeling in itself. The allegorical form, while admitting exceptional detail, does divest the pictured human being of those differentiating marks that give him most force as such, does assert the opinion that life is not confined to a single dominant province: that of the individual. And by this assertion it allows credibility to other provinces: to those of the angels or of the abstract qualities such as Loyalty, or the Cardinal Virtues, or the Seven Sins. Let me add that in neither the humanist nor the allegorical modes are the greatest writers confined to the usual limits of their ages. Aeschylus and Sophocles achieve spirituality from the humanist side, Dante and Langland realism from the allegorical. But we must not pretend that they set out from anywhere near the same place.

My present point is this. We must seek the epic in those concerns that an age takes most seriously and in the literary forms that embody those concerns. In one age the concerns had been the individual at his highest or most intense or most assertive; and they had been presented, quite naturally, through heroic action: in the next they became the struggles of mankind to reach certainty in a world that had become complex and bewildering; and they were presented in a species of vision that need have little immediate relation to ordinary life or contain little concrete action. What forms the vision tended to take I will speak of later, for these can be understood best through looking a little at the history of allegory, to which I now turn.

Earlier in this book I distinguished between allegorical interpretation of non-allegorical works and works truly pursuing an allegorical method. The Greeks subjected Homer to allegorical interpretation when they came to find the actions of his gods awkward, but they did not produce much allegorical writing. Some indeed, like most

[1] 60.

races, they did produce. Homer himself in the speech of Phoenix in the ninth book of the *Iliad* (mentioned in my chapter on Homer) personifies men's prayers, making them the daughters of Zeus; and the *Pinax* of Cebes, a contemporary of Plato, is a kind of allegorical chart (resembling the Victorian evangelical posters of the broad and narrow ways) of Virtue on her hill of difficulty and the means of reaching her. But these are exceptional; and the first great landmark is Virgil himself. I have pointed out how Aeneas is both a distinct individual and the personification of a trend of civilisation and how Virgil's Jupiter is both the Homeric father of the gods and the Mind of the Greek philosophers. Virgil himself is both the political poet, the poet of Roman imperialism, and the man who intended to retire from active life and end his days in studying philosophy. Thus he represents the greater complexity of life that had come into existence since the break-up of the old Greek world. And he represents it better than later authors like Statius and Prudentius who technically are closer to the allegorical habit of the Middle Ages. While confirming the importance C. S. Lewis gives to these two poets in the history of allegory, I cannot help thinking that the more general suasion of Virgil's spirituality counted, among the poets, most strongly of all in the process of shifting the emphasis from great men to wandering mankind. On the other hand, Lewis's remarks about Seneca's moral writings and their suggestiveness are enlightening. He notes how Seneca in describing the moral struggle that is central to life puts it in terms now of warfare, now of a lawsuit, now of a journey.[1] And he asserts that it is the journey that makes the best subject for allegory:

> While it is true that the *bellum intestinum* is the root of all allegory, it is no less true that only the crudest allegory will represent it by a pitched battle. . . . Seneca, with his imagery of life as a journey, was nearer to the mark than Prudentius; for Seneca outlined the theme of the *Pilgrim's Progress*, and the *Pilgrim's Progress* is a better book than the *Holy War*. It is not hard to see why this should be so. The journey has its ups and downs, its pleasant resting-places enjoyed for a night and then abandoned, its unexpected meetings, its rumours of dangers ahead, and, above all, the sense of its goal. . . . Now this represents far more truly than any combat in a *champ clos* the perennial strangeness, the adventurousness, and the sinuous forward movement of the inner life.[2]

While it was Prudentius who in his *Psychomachia* represented the moral struggle in terms of an allegorical warfare, it was Virgil in the *Aeneid* who, subjected to a distortion violent indeed but not altogether

[1] 63 ff.
[2] 68-9. While agreeing that the pilgrimage is initially a richer theme than a siege, I disagree about Bunyan. The *Holy War* is different from the *Pilgrim's Progress*, but not necessarily worse. See my chapter on Bunyan.

unjustified, came pre-eminently to represent for the Middle Ages the earthly pilgrimage of the human soul to eternal life.

The idea of allegorising Virgil was as pagan in its origin as Christian but it ended as a characteristic Christian habit.[1] Already in the fourth century the *Fourth Eclogue* was interpreted as foretelling the birth of Christ; but for purposes of the epic the most important document is of the sixth century, the *De Continentia Vergiliana* of Fabius Planciades Fulgentius. This book subjects the *Aeneid* to a very thorough process of allegorising, making it represent the journey of man from birth (the shipwreck in the first book) to his final triumph over the Vices. Fulgentius was very popular in the Middle Ages; and John of Salisbury in the twelfth century does not hesitate to make Aeneas stand for the human soul. I said that Fulgentius's distortion was not entirely unjustified; and indeed it rests on elements which were there, however faintly, in the very beginnings of the western epic. The wanderings of Odysseus are not primarily a moral test; they happen because Poseidon was offended. And the character of Odysseus was settled before ever he embarked on them. At the same time they represent, however faintly, an ordeal; an impression which gains strength by the undoubted testing of Telemachus and his successful transition from adolescence to manhood. Thus the theme of the mental voyage is present, albeit in an embryonic state, in the *Odyssey*, a statement that the very existence of the stock phrase, *soul-Odyssey*, confirms. Virgil drew the idea of his hero's wanderings from Homer, and, though the progress of Aeneas's mind from partial to complete self-mastery is not the main theme, it is undoubtedly there and supplies a considerable ground of truth for the elaborate distortions of Fulgentius. That he was in part if only in small part right, is one reason why Fulgentius deserves our attention. There is another and a more important. He really spoke for his age and gave it what it had to have. However much the stiffer clerics disapproved of Virgil, the Middle Ages adored him and, adoring, they were compelled to remake him in the image of their own most compelling fictions. The *Aeneid* was the supreme poem, and men had to impose on it the theme that lay nearest their hearts: the salvation of the human soul on its earthly pilgrimage. Or one can put it the other way round and say that the *De Continentia Vergiliana* of Fulgentius is the classic proof that the soul's pilgrimage was the central subject of medieval epic.

2. THE NATURE AND IMPLICATIONS OF ALLEGORY

At this point I had better do something to define my terms. In earlier chapters I did not scruple to use *symbol* and *symbolism* not in

---

[1] For this paragraph I have drawn on D. Comparetti, *Vergil in the Middle Ages*, tr. E. F. M. Benecke (London 1895) 100-17.

any precise sense but as rather more emphatic forms of *represent* and *representation*. And in the present chapter I have not so far tried to give to *allegory* and *allegorical* any closer meanings than those fluid and approximate ones that may serve well enough in a general context. But there are reasons at this point for being more definite. First, there were peculiar components in medieval allegory. Secondly, there still lurks in men's minds a prejudice against allegory as an inferior literary device, as something mechanical and a little frivolous: a prejudice due partly to lingering notions of the Middle Ages as barbaric and partly to the vogue of 'Symbolist' poetry, which has been assumed to have a distant if opposed relationship to allegory and to be immeasurably superior to it. Having the medieval allegory as my present subject, I ought to mention its peculiarities. Believing it to be the literary vehicle of the age's most serious ideas, I ought to seek to allay current prejudice against it as a serious form. I take the second obligation first.

In general critical parlance *symbolism* is most often used to denote an organic mode of composition as against the mechanical mode of *allegory*. Baudelaire wrote a poem on the resemblance of the poet to an albatross. If he had written allegorically, it is supposed, he would have gone to work somewhat as follows: I want to describe the poet; what can I compare him to? of course, it must be to something with wings; eagles and swans are stale; for a change, what about an albatross? but he did not write like that; he conceived the poet-albatross relation by a single inseparable act of the mind; the albatross is a symbol. Now such a use of the word *symbol* is feeble because it is too general, describing a principle that applies to all good poetry: a principle better described by the more general and less hieratic word *organic*. Only a narrower use of the word *symbol* serves a purpose; and such a narrowing is to be found in the idea of permanence commonly associated with symbolism. I say 'commonly associated', because it would be possible, for instance, to adopt the Greek letter *phi* as the symbol for an artichoke, using it in a piece of writing once only and explaining the use in a footnote. But this would be a less common practice than using x as the permanent symbol of an indefinite number. To pass to literature, if Baudelaire had used the poet-albatross comparison frequently he might, by thus fixing it in our minds, have turned his albatross into a symbol. Further, symbols become most emphatic, most truly themselves, when their permanence is due not only to repetition but to fundamental congruence. When readers, as they sometimes do, call Blake's 'O Rose, thou art Sick!' a symbolist poem, they have more reason than if they do the same to Baudelaire's poem on the albatross, because the equation of the blooming of roses with that of love does appear to present a permanent congruence to the human mind. Their pink and white may suggest the human body, and their glowing but changing bloom, ardent mortality. But if such a narrowing of the notion of symbolism is insisted on, as I think it should be, it is plain at once that it enters into only a small proportion of poetry, however effectively it does so. Most of the comparisons used in poetry, however passionately conceived and compelling, do not exist permanently but are absorbed at once into the contexts where they occur. It follows, therefore, that symbolism is too confined or specialised an affair to be a general poetic mode at all. Hence it does not compete with allegory, which can be sustained indefinitely, and we are free to deal with allegory alone.

Doing so, we may begin by asking whether allegory does necessarily imply a largely mechanical and hence inferior operation. First, we should beware of taking too literally what the medieval writers said about their own poetical methods. Most writers on rhetoric, classical medieval and Renaissance alike, assume that poets make a poem as a conscientious housewife makes a pudding, by following the successive directions of a recipe. And the poets may have thought they worked that way. But we know that the best of them did not; and the right way to understand the allegorical method is to examine it in practice and not through the theories on which it was supposed to be based.[1] Two examples will suffice for my purpose: one showing the method at its simplest, the other sticking to the strictest allegorical convention yet showing the possible complications within it.

The first is Gilbert's song *The Magnet and the Churn* from *Patience*.

> A Magnet hung in a hardware shop,
> And all around was a loving crop
> Of scissors and needles, nails and knives,
> Offering love for all their lives;
> But for iron the Magnet felt no whim,
> Though he charmed iron, it charmed not him,
> From needles and nails and knives he'd turn,
> For he'd set his love on a Silver Churn!
>
> His most aesthetic,
> Very magnetic
> Fancy took this turn—
> 'If I can wheedle
> A knife or needle,
> Why not a Silver Churn?'
>
> And Iron and Steel expressed surprise,
> The needles opened their well-drilled eyes,
> The pen-knives felt 'shut up' no doubt,
> The scissors declared themselves 'cut out',

---

[1] I think that C. S. Lewis (*Allegory of Love*, 44-8) defines allegory with a rigidity that may indeed be supported by medieval theorists but which does not square with the best medieval practice or with some of his remarks later in the book.

The kettles they boiled with rage, 'tis said,
While every nail went off its head,
And hither and thither began to roam,
Till a hammer came up—and drove it home,
While this magnetic
Peripatetic
Lover he lived to learn,
By no endeavour
Can Magnet ever
Attract a Silver Churn!

Gilbert's song is a very simple translation of a dramatic situation into other terms. Bunthorne, the aesthetic sham, attracts the chorus of well-bred girls but not the milkmaid, Patience, whom he prefers. In the allegory Bunthorne becomes a magnet, the girls all sorts of iron-mongery, Patience in accord with her occupation a churn and in accord with her insusceptibility to magnetic attraction a silver one; and Bunthorne has to recognise that he is powerless to attract her. There are also correspondences of detail between one side of the allegory and the other through the double meanings of words. Kettles can boil literally and jealous young women metaphorically. I call Gilbert's song simple because, though there may be additional emphasis, there are no new elements of meaning in the terms into which the given situation is translated. The hardware shop does its bare allegorical job. It is not even a realistic shop, for you do not find a silver churn in one. Of course, it is unfair and inept to subject Gilbert's airy little piece to so solemn an analysis; but as simple allegory it does indeed illustrate my point.

The second illustration is Spenser's description of the House of Alma in the ninth canto of the second book of the *Faerie Queene*, one of the most obvious and mathematically precise of his allegories. Nothing better illustrates our prejudice against anything like a sustained allegory than the almost unvaried assumption that this episode *must* be dull; indeed, it is reckoned the classic example of Spenser at his worst. Most readers enter on it with so fixed an antipathy that they do not give it a chance. Given one, it is far from nugatory. *Alma* is the poetical word in Italian for the soul, and the House of Alma is the human body, where the soul lodges. The context is that Arthur and Guyon, who stand for heavenly grace and temperance respect-ively, having dispersed the unruly passions that were assailing the soul are admitted into the soul's fortified house and shown round it. So Spenser's House of Alma stands for the human body properly regulated by theological and ethical wisdom. The translation of the parts of the body into terms of a medieval castle is as precise and obvious as the translation in Gilbert's lyric. Here is the description of the passage leading to the stomach, of the stomach itself, of the lungs, and of the process of digestion, put in terms of the kitchen.[1]

> It was a vaut ybuilt for great dispence,
> With many raunges reard along the wall,
> And one great chimney, whose long tonnell thence
> The smoke forth threw: And in the midst of all
> There placed was a caudron wide and tall
> Upon a mightie fornace, burning whott,
> More whott then Aetn', or flaming Mongiball:
> For day and night it brent, ne ceased not,
> So long as any thing it in the caudron gott.
>
> But to delay the heat, least by mischaunce
> It might breake out and set the whole on fyre,
> There added was by goodly ordinaunce
> An huge great payre of bellowes, which did styre
> Continually, and cooling breath inspyre.
> About the caudron many Cookes accoyld
> With hookes and ladles, as need did requyre;
> The whyles the viaundes in the vessel boyld,
> They did about their business sweat, and sorely toyld.

This is a different picture from Gilbert's of the hardware shop, for it is coherent and we believe in it in its own right apart from the allegory. And when we believe in it we have to pull ourselves up and remember what the picture of the castle kitchen and the cauldron represents. And when we remember, we look on the parts of the body in a new way. Spenser was perfectly at home with the human body as an external presentation of glamour or disgust, witness Britomart unarming and letting her hair fall to her feet as she removes her helmet or Duessa stripped naked; he knows it as presented to the senses. But he knows that it is a strange aggregation of parts, considered in its different functions; and this the artificiality and abruptness of the House of Alma express to perfection. Or take the description of one of the three parts of the brain, the memory. This is lodged in an old room at the back of the castle keep (the head).

> And therein sat an Old old Man, halfe blind,
> And all decrepit in his feeble corse,
> Yet lively vigour rested in his mind,
> And recompenst them with a better scorse:
> Weake body well is chang'd for minds redoubled forse.
>
> The yeares of Nestor nothing were to his,
> Ne yet Methusalem, though longest liv'd;
> For he remembred both their infancis:
> Ne wonder then if that he were depriv'd

[1] Stanzas 30-1.

Of native strength now that he them surviv'd.
His chamber was all hang'd about with rolls
And old records from auncient times deriv'd:
Some made in books, some in long parchment scrolls,
That were all worm-eaten and full of canker holes.

Amidst them all he in a chair was sett,
Tossing and turning them withouten end;
But, for he was unable them to fett,
A little Boy did on him still attend
To reach whenever he for ought did send:
And oft, when thinges were lost, or laid amis,
That Boy them sought and unto him did lend;
Therefore he Anamnestes cleped is,
And that Old Man Eumnestes, by their propertis.

This charming picture of the small boy fetching books for the half-
blind or short-sighted old scholar in a Cathedral or College library
goes right beyond the strict requirements of simple allegorical substitution and creates a different stratum of meaning. A method that
in Gilbert was a mere matter of rather greater emphasis has become
a complex way of regarding experience.

The conclusion to be drawn from these passages is that all but the
simplest allegory (I mean when it has any literary value) tends to
grow complicated and that we should think of it not as a cool rhetorical substitution but as allied to the medieval impulse to stratify
existence, not, like the classical Greeks, choosing a fixed position and
approximating everything to it, but recognising several positions and
passing to and fro between them.

Having thus defended the method of allegory and suggested its use
in the age when it was dominant, I can revert to Virgil as he was and
as he was made to be. For all its anticipatory spirituality, the *Aeneid*
is in the main a political poem, it concerns man's kingdom on earth.
Fulgentius made it principally man's quest for a home in heaven.
And in so doing he did represent the dominant trend of thought for
many centuries. In spite of the great conquerors and their ambitions,
Charlemagne, Barbarossa, William, and the others, what must have
been a small minority of men, I suppose most of them clerics, did
succeed in keeping the prestige of spiritual things above that of
political, with the result that, though much was written in praise of
great men, none of it has that unconscious assurance that is necessary
for giving it a chance of entering the highest category of letters. Much
less was written on the spiritual pilgrimage, but what there was began
with the initial possibility of greatness.

In speaking of allegory as a literary device suitable to a general
shift from the political to the spiritual I do not wish to minimise its

schematism and its consequent aptness to a side of the Middle Ages that accompanied their otherworldliness: a mathematical passion for correspondences. That passion can be perceived, literally at a glance, by looking at an early Italian rendering of the Last Judgement and comparing it with, say, the Olympia or Parthenon pediments. In the Greek works there is balance indeed but admitting of a very sinuous variety, in the early Italian rendering there are the most detailed balance and correspondence between the two halves of the composition. The greater spirituality of the medieval work co-exists with a far more precise and detailed and rigid scheme.

Having written in my *Elizabethan World Picture* on the system of correspondences created and elaborated in the Middle Ages, I do not wish to repeat myself here. What I can do is to mention it, insist on its importance, and illustrate it briefly.

However earnestly the most serious thought of the Middle Ages looked to God in heaven, it insisted on seeing God's imprint in earthly creation too. In fact, one great way of seeing God was to study his visible works. So studied, creation presented a wonderful and complicated picture of order. Every item in it had to be given a significant place; and, so placed, not only did it form an indispensable part of the kind of creation to which it belonged, but it corresponded to another item in a different kind. The king was not only a necessary item in the order of the state, he corresponded to the sun in heaven, to the oak among the trees, and the diamond among stones.

This hierarchical idea is so paramount in the serious thought of the Middle Ages that no true medieval epic can fail to be permeated by it. Because the works of Dante, Deguileville, and Langland are so permeated, they stand the better chance of being indeed epic.

Finally, we must not be surprised at the kind of correspondences the Middle Ages enjoyed and apparently took seriously. Here are two typical examples. First, the wood out of which the cross of Christ was made was said to be ultimately derived from the tree of life in Paradise. Second, Dante in his *De Monarchia*, to establish the right of Rome to dominion over the three continents that then made up the world, argues that Aeneas's three wives, Creusa, Dido and Lavinia, correspond to these continents; Creusa being daughter of Priam, king of a city in Asia Minor, Dido being queen of Carthage, an African city, Lavinia being a princess from the noblest region of Europe. It is vain to be astonished and disgusted that the great mind of Dante could stoop to such trivialities; we should instead measure and wonder at the strength of the impulse that persuaded the great mind of Dante to obey it.

The portion of the medieval habit of seeking correspondences within a pervading atmosphere of spirituality that most concerns the literary critic is the system of multiple meanings. In its origin it had nothing to do with literary creation, but, like the first allegorising of Homer, with the interpretation of what was already there. It must surely have owed something to pagan allegory and was first applied to the Bible. Origen distinguished three parallel meanings there, and his distinction or something like it extended right through the Middle Ages. By the twelfth century at least, what had been a principle of interpretation had become one of composition, for Alain de Lille in the preface to his *Anticlaudianus*, a theological poem, claimed that this must be read in three senses: literal, moral, and allegorical. Sometimes a fourth sense was added, the anagogical. Dante claims four senses for his *Divine Comedy*; and probably the best known exposition of what these senses are comes in Dante's letter to Can Grande, in which he explains his aims in the poem. Dante takes for illustration the verse of Scripture, 'when Israel came out of Egypt and the house of Jacob from a people of strange speech, Judaea became his sanctification, Israel his power.' The literal sense, he explains, is simply the departure of the Jews from Egypt; the allegorical sense, which also concerns some sort of event, is the redemption of man by Christ; the moral sense is the soul's conversion from sin to a state of grace; the anagogical (or celestial) sense is the passing of the redeemed soul from the bondage of earth to the glory of Paradise.[1]

It must not be conceived that the medieval poet thought himself under the perpetual obligation of introducing as many as three or four senses into the whole of his work. Indeed, what appears to aim at a very hampering rigidity may actually result in the elusive and ambiguous and iridescent. If all three or four senses are not maintained throughout but come and go, there must be a transfer from complex to simpler scales of allegory and back again; and such acts of transfer will themselves express the habit of mind, the contrary of the ancient Greek, that refuses to stick to one fixed humanistic centre of reference and varies its abode from earth to heaven. This habit of mind lasted, though in less spiritual form, to Spenser, whose *Faerie Queene* constantly varies in the amount of attention the allegorical meaning requires. And such a variation is a source not of weakness but, by taxing the reader's adaptability, of strength.

Finally, I wish to correct some possible false impressions these last pages may have given. First, I do not wish to imply that medieval allegorical writing was *usually* subtle and spiritualised. Within the mode there was the widest choice, and it could satisfy the prosaic and the imaginative temperament with equal success. What concerns me now is that it *could* embody men's highest thoughts in the Middle Ages, and that through one of its characteristic varieties, that of the soul's pilgrimage, it did so as no other mode could do.

[1] For a lucid exposition of the four meanings in the Middle Ages see Nevill Coghill, *Visions from Piers Plowman* (London 1949) 137-9.

Secondly, I may have seemed to simplify overmuch. I may for instance have seemed to suggest that for the Middle Ages Virgil was mainly a great poet with a hidden spiritual meaning. This is far from the whole truth, for Virgil was other things too: the celebrator of great men, the incomparable sage, a magician, a saint, and one of the great repositories of rhetorical practice. But while to some he was almost a god, to others he was a dangerous seduction from the sacred to the secular. Virgil, then, as taken by the Middle Ages, illustrates the extreme confusion of literary ideas at the time. Last, I may have given the impression that allegory was a dominant literary *form*, and that too would be wrong. Allegory was not a form but a rhetorical method, favoured in different degrees at different times and by different writers. We are apt to speak of the *Faerie Queene* and the *Pilgrim's Progress* as 'allegories', as if the allegory was a literary form like the novel. And the reader may well have fallen into this way of thought if he has found me speaking of allegory supplanting the heroic poem. Instead, allegory was a method, used in only a minority of verse-writing (at least in the age before Langland), attributed wrongly to certain classical writers, and destined, because of its aptness to the age's 'unconscious metaphysic', to serve some of the highest literature.

3. CRITICAL IDEAS

I referred near the end of the last section to the confusion of medieval critical ideas on the nature of literature. Out of it emerge two that may have some bearing on the epic as understood in this book.

First, although the status of great men may have declined, it was generally agreed that they deserved a memorial and that it was the task of literature to supply one. Bede in his preface to his life of St Cuthbert spoke of it as a memorial to his devotion to him. John of Salisbury (twelfth century) said that the chief use of literature was to eternise great men.[1] Thomas of Cabham (who died in 1313) said in his *Penitential* that though some minstrels were to be condemned, there were others who sang the deeds of princes to the accompaniment of their instruments, and these were to be tolerated.[2] Barbour began his *Bruce* with some lines on the value of true records of great men. Dante took Virgil's account of the doings of Aeneas as true. We today do not, and we justify Virgil on other grounds; but Dante's opinion (which was not exceptional) would help to give authority to

---

[1] See J. W. H. Atkins, *English Literary Criticism: the Medieval Phase* (Cambridge 1943) 67.
[2] Quoted by E. K. Chambers, *The Medieval Stage* (Oxford 1903) ii. 262.

the kind of literature that recounted the true deeds of great men. And this authority, other things being equal, might have helped to create in writers a state of mind favourable to an epic seriousness when they chose to write historical poems. And they did actually choose to write such poems in an unbroken succession through the Middle Ages. Most were in Latin, and these are described in Raby's book on secular Latin poetry in the Middle Ages. The most distinguished English practitioner was Joseph of Exeter (twelfth century), who wrote a lost *Antiocheis* celebrating the deeds of Richard I and an account in six books of the Trojan War, taking his material from Dares Phrygius and his verse and rhetoric from Lucan.[1] Writing in the Latin hexameter at a time when Latin verse was truly alive only in the forms it acquired from the pressure of living forces from outside it, the rhymed forms, lyric and other, Joseph of Exeter and the rest of the classicisers could not produce works of the highest quality. Their importance is mostly historical, that of maintaining a tradition of narrative which was to find more vital embodiments in the Renaissance.

The other idea was that of the poet as prophet. Of this there is an excellent account at the beginning of Karl Vossler's *Poetische Theorien in der italienischen Frührenaissance*.[2] It was an idea held by a minority and it was fiercely attacked. In the age of Dante its great champion was Alberto Mussato. Mussato insisted that poetry was the twin or even the mother of philosophy, a divine art. Its material was boundless. The poet may use ancient precedent, and his scope will be widest in theology. Mussato is also active in finding allegorical explanations of pagan writing. This idea of the poet as prophet had a real bearing on epic practice. It helped Dante to be as ambitious as he was, to recognise his high mission as poet and to include theology in his material, in fact to achieve the amplitude necessary for the epic poet. Whether the same idea filtered through to Langland I dare not conjecture. But if he wrote poetry on the theory of four parallel meanings and if, like other advanced thinkers of his time, he was puzzled by the problem of what happened to the virtuous heathen after death, is it impossible that the notion of the inspired poet-theologian penetrated to him likewise? If it did, it co-existed with more modest ideas about the poet's function.

4. DANTE

I must explain why I have so little to say about Dante when I said so much about Homer. Both poets are the head of different kinds of

---

[1] See J. F. E. Raby, *History of Secular Latin Poetry in the Middle Ages*, ii. 132-7.
[2] Berlin 1900. He of course includes in this book the other idea about celebrating great men.

epic and as such would call for equal treatment. But whereas Homer
led on to Virgil and Virgil to a great European form of poetry, Dante
created no school. The epic attempts of Petrarch and Boccaccio were
not after his fashion. The English medieval poet who owed most to
him, Chaucer, was not an epic writer and valued him more as a learned
man and the master of much substance than as a poet. The English
medieval poet who most resembles him in substance and method,
Langland, may have heard of him but shows no signs of having read
him. If Dante and Langland both faced the problem of the righteous
heathen and their fate, they derived their knowledge of the problem
independently. Nor did Dante affect the course of the later English
epic. From the Renaissance on he could not, as a model, compete
with the classical epic writers. Milton read and admired him, but
Paradise Lost would have been much the same if he had never done
so. It was not till after the time-period covered by this book that the
poets began to draw direct inspiration from the *Divine Comedy*.
Shelley's *Triumph of Life* and Keats's revised *Hyperion* do indeed show
a fundamental debt to it, but they are fragments and they come after
the great tradition of English verse epic had expired. Dante scarcely
counts as an influence on the English epic.

There are other reasons why I should say little about Dante. There
is more agreement about his quality than about Homer's and Virgil's.
Many people continue the belief that the Homeric poems are com-
posite; and many continue the nineteenth-century habit of degrading
Virgil from the highest rank. No one seeks to find more than one
author for the *Divine Comedy* or thinks it inferior poetry. Where there
is no controversy, there is less reason to intervene. In the reaction
against the long dominance of the Greek and Latin Classics the
modern reader has tended to cloak them with the dust of a now hated
scholarship and to think of them as more jejune and less human than
the classics of other times and races. It is therefore wholesome to try
to speak of them as literature like other literature. Dante has not
suffered in the same way, and there is no reason to persuade the
modern reader to put aside prejudice and to give him the chance
to which all literature is entitled.

But though I should be wrong to write of Dante at length, it is
fitting at this point to repeat the commonplace that Dante was the
great poet of the Middle Ages and to say that this greatness was of the
epic kind, in the way I use the word. Dante's span in the *Divine
Comedy* equals that of any other poet. He ranged from the homely
human passions to the highest religious emotion. He included theology
and the whole medieval world picture. He sustained his will-power
with a completeness surpassed by none. And though his structure
resembles that of a great picture of Fra Angelico and not that of one
by Titian, it is complete in every way. Probably no poem of com-

parable length is so elaborately interlocked. The *Divine Comedy* has never been questioned as the voice of its age and of Italy. Its subject is the great contemporary one; the pilgrimage of the human soul: not indeed through a realistically conceived journey but from a mental Hell through a mental Purgatory to a mental Paradise.[1] But this unquestioned choric character must not blind us to the high originality of the poem. Dante took much from the age's great poetic master, Virgil; and yet, except for the formal epic simile, he refrained from imitating him. He nourished himself on Virgil's spirit while transmuting it and making it his own. He broke with tradition by using his own language and not Latin for a very serious poem; and yet the seriousness he commanded was largely that of his age. Dante possessed every attribute of the epic poet in the fullest measure that appears humanly possible.

5. ENGLAND BEFORE LANGLAND

In England it was the language that first governed the possibilities of epic writing. The age of Henry II, with the building of the abbeys in the north, with John of Salisbury's humanist influence, and with the free interchange of insular and continental culture, might in itself have been propitious to major literary forms; but the requisite language did not exist. English was no longer an effective literary language; Latin and French were too artificial and limited to speak for a whole people. Besides the language there was the general European trend of narrative away from heroic austerity to the fervid prettiness of romance: for before the middle of the twelfth century Geoffrey of Monmouth had written his *Historia Britonum* and thus brought into Europe the lore of Arthur and his knights; and, to quote W. P. Ker,

> from within and without, from the resources of native mythology and superstition and from the fascination of Welsh and Arabian stories, there came the temptation to forget the study of character, and to part with an inheritance of tragic fables, for the sake of vanities, wonders, and splendours among which character and the tragic motives lost their pre-eminent interest and their old authority over poets and audience.[2]

In the thirteenth century English as a literary language began to revive but, whether in the alliterative form of Layamon's *Brut* or in the imported form of short rhymed couplets in *King Horn*, narrative verse never rose to dignity. The best verse, that of the *Owl and the Nightingale*, is argumentative. *Brut*, dealing with early British legend

---

[1] See H. O. Taylor, *The Medieval Mind* (4th ed. London 1925) ii. 579: 'The *Commedia* is the pilgrimage of the soul after all wisdom.'

[2] *Epic and Romance*, 34.

shading off into history and deriving ultimately from Geoffrey of Monmouth, has its importance as the earliest versified form of some of the substance of the *Faerie Queene* and of what would have been the substance of Milton's never written *Arthuriad*. Early in the four-teenth century come the competent but uninspiring couplets of *Cursor Mundi*, dealing chroniclewise with Bible history, a narrative counter-part of the cycles of Miracle Plays. It has its importance historically as a better than average specimen of a type of literature that found its finest expression in the last two books of *Paradise Lost*.

About the time of *Cursor Mundi* Dante finished the *Divine Comedy*, a little after which the *Roman de la Rose* was completed in France and Deguileville wrote his long poem on the pilgrimage of human life. For all the vogue of the romance, the allegorical method was now at its height in Europe. We should remember this when we come to the second half of the fourteenth century, the earliest age in England since the Conquest when linguistic conditions made epic possible. English now became the language of all classes and was capable of the epic function of voicing the mood of a multitude.

It is truly astonishing that at this time of national energy and drawing together there should have been two literary methods in poetry, that the old alliterative form should have chosen to reappear from underground just as French sophistication worked its strongest influence on English versification and poetic content through Chaucer and Gower. If there had been two levels of expression, a courtly and a humble, a *Herrenstil* and a *Bauernstil* as the Germans say, one deriving from the Norman aristocracy and their sustained contact with French and the other from the English peasant population, the thing would not be so surprising. But *Pearl* and *Sir Gawayne and the Grene Knight* are as sophisticated and elegant in form and content as Chaucer's *Book of the Duchess*, which is roughly contemporary.

One thing we should conclude from the surprising duality is that the period was greatly alive: an 'epic area', whether or not it did in fact produce a true epic. It happened that its chief poet, Chaucer, although he was ambitious and used long literary forms, had not the epic cast of mind but was primarily a comic writer. His greatest single unit, *Troilus and Criseyde*, is a comedy not merely through its humorous details and its studiedly social setting but through its steady refusal to allow the pathos, of which it contains a good deal, to be ambitious of becoming tragedy. The *Canterbury Tales*, though many of them may be well adjusted to the characters of their tellers, would never, even if Chaucer had lived to complete and revise them, have had an effective structural unity; they never could have competed with *Troilus and Criseyde* in this matter. They would in fact have remained a series of tales but loosely connected. The longest of them, the *Knight's Tale*, though less obviously comic than *Troilus and Criseyde*, never attempts to leave the less serious area of romance for the more serious one of epic. It is perfect, but its emotional scope is strictly confined. There is no case for including Chaucer within the scope of this book.

There is another reason why Chaucer is not epic. He is not primarily a religious poet, and though by the end of the fourteenth century the Middle Ages were growing old, the times were still those of religion; and only a religious subject could answer their 'unconscious metaphysic'. If there was a core of ideas capable of animating an epic it could only be that religious one of which such divers things as the sermons, the Miracle Plays, a narrative like *Cursor Mundi*, and the decoration of the churches were all manifestations. It is also possible that the late fourteenth century was more propitious to an English religious epic than any time since the Conquest. Only a very few historians can have a clear idea of how deeply or superficially Christian ideas penetrated the mass of the Englishmen relatively at different periods of the Middle Ages. Most people think of an age of faith extending over centuries and dominated by a uniformly powerful and effective Church. But even if we are not historians, a little reflection and common sense should prove such a way of thinking wrong and should tell us that the Church's civilising influence in the Middle Ages must have been a gradual process and that the extent of its sway was much less in the year 1100 than it had become by the year 1300. In the age of Chaucer, for all the abuses, the preaching, the art, the drama, and the literature were all bent to the same end of instruction in the supposed facts of Christian history and of moral exhortation, revealing the immense weight of theological sway and proclaiming themselves as sides of a single core of dominant ideas. The legend of the Harrowing of Hell was referred to by the preachers, represented in paint and stained glass in the churches, and acted in the religious dramatic cycles. It also forms one of the culminating episodes in Langland's *Piers Plowman* and in so doing it should instruct us that this poem is in part a narrative rendering of this very core of ideas to which I have been referring. As such it issues out of the centre of its age and stands an initial chance of being a true epic.

CHAPTER III

LANGLAND

*Qu'on le mette aussi loin de Dante qu'on voudra, il est le seul poète
du siècle dont l'épopée mystique mérite d'être nommée après celle de
l'illustre Florentin.*

(J. J. Jusserand)

PIERS PLOWMAN[1] is puzzling like no major work included in
this book. I am not thinking of authorship, for I have no doubts
that William Langland wrote all of it except the few lines added to
the earliest version by John But. It is the text that is the trouble.
Langland kept at his long poem all his life, as Wordsworth kept at the
Prelude; yet with different results. The original *Prelude* is complete,
and we can read it with the other poems of his greatest years. We can
also read the final version as something equally complete but rather
different; and we need not worry much about the stages between first
and last versions. But there are three versions of *Piers Plowman* (known
as A-text, B-text, and C-text) and, while none of them is satisfactory
without the others, it is impossible to devise a satisfactory conflation.
The poem consists of an allegorical vision of the world, and in
particular England, situated between Heaven and Hell, and of the
quest for the three different spiritual states of Do-wel Do-bet and
Do-best. The A-text, dating round 1370, while showing that Langland
had the total plan in mind, breaks off in the middle of the section on
Do-bet.[2] The B-text, dating perhaps round 1376, amplifies the A-text
and finishes the poem. The C-text, of uncertain date, is a revision
of the B-text. It is a little longer, and though it adds indispensable
new matter it omits or weakens some of the most precious things in
its original. Yet many of its small changes are for the better. Most
readers, if they had to choose between the three texts, would choose
B, but in doing so they give up some of the best things in the poem.
I will give a few examples.

The A-text is more vivid, vehement, and concise than B: the work
of a younger man. When Langland revised and completed it he was
more mature and comprehensive; but he sometimes did ill to meddle
with his first draft. An example is the description of Lady Meed's
proposed marriage to Falsehood. (Meed is bribery, or the power of

---

[1] I pay tribute to the writings of R. W. Chambers, Nevill Coghill, and H. W.
Wells on Langland. Detailed references below. E. T. Donaldson's *Piers Plowman:
the C-Text and its Poet*, New Haven 1949, is valuable not only as a special study but
as gathering up and assessing much previous criticism.
[2] For questions of dating see Donaldson, *op. cit.* 18-19.

money.) In the A-text the marriage-deed is short and emphatic and a perfect parody of the marriage-service:

> *Hit witen and witnessen that woneth uppon eorthe,*
> *That I, Favvell, feffe Fals to that maiden, Meede,*
> *To be present in Pruyde, for pore or for riche.*
> *With the erldom of Envye ever for to laste*
> *With all the lordschupe of lengthe and of brede,*
> *With the kingdom of Covertise I croune hem togedere,*
> *With the isle of Usure. And Avarice the false,*
> *Glotonye and grete othus ich yive hem, i-feere*
> *With alle delytes and lustes, the Devel for to serve*
> *In al the servyce of Slouthe. I sese hem togedere*
> *To habben and to holden and al heere heyres after*
> *With the purtinaunce of Purgatorie into the pyre of Helle,*
> *Yeldynge for this thing at the yeres ende*
> *Heere soules to Sathanas to senden into pyne*
> *Ther to wonen with Wrong whil God is in Hevene.*[1]

The B-text expands these fourteen lines to thirty-two, padding out the simple enumeration of the Sins and their domains with the kind of detail with which the poem already abounded. Thus Gluttony is not just coupled briefly with 'great oaths' but is found drinking and quarrelling in taverns and eating on fast-days.[2] The simple and ironic majesty of the sins' dominion and the parody of the marriage-service are ruined in the later version.

The C-text sometimes does violence to the B-text. For instance it takes some of the beauty out of the famous opening lines. And it cuts out the exquisite reference to illuminated books, found in the B-text only. Repentance tells Avarice that if he were a friar he would not take a penny from him, for the best book in the house:

> *Ne have a peny to my pittaunce of thyne, bi my soule hale,*
> *For the best booke in owre hous, theighe brent golde were the leves.*[3]

But the C-text improves on B in many details as well as adding some striking and indispensable passages. One would expect Langland as

[1] ii. 60-74. 'Know and witness it, all that live on earth, that I, Flattery, pledge Falsehood to the maiden, Meed; so as to be conspicuous in Pride, for rich or poor. With the earldom of Envy in perpetuity and through its length and breadth, with the kingdom of Covetousness and with the island of Usury, I crown them equally. And Avarice the false, Gluttony and great oaths I give them, together with all lustful joys, so as to serve the Devil in the whole service of Sloth. I take all these together for their endowment, to have and to hold, they and all their heirs after, along with the furnishings of Purgatory into the torment of Hell; yielding in return, at the year's end, their souls to Satan for him to send into torment, there to dwell with Wrong, while God is in Heaven.'

[2] ii. 92-100.

[3] v. 270-1. 'Nor have a penny of yours to my portion, by my salvation, for the best book in our house, no, though its leaves were of burnished gold.'

he grew older to behave as Wordsworth did in the *Prelude*: prefer more smoothness and more generalisation. Thus in the boat-stealing episode Wordsworth cut out the earlier information that the boat's home was the shore of Patterdale. Now though Langland in the C-text is commonly held to fulfil this sort of expectation by his habit of moralising the specific effect of his earlier version,[1] in some places he does the opposite and to the benefit of the poem. In an early passage he makes the Holy Church call the dreamer by his own name *Will* instead of *son* of the B-text. In Passus iv 140 the king threatens to imprison Lady Meed in Corfe Castle. This sudden mention of a particular place within the allegory is very effective; it is absent from the B-text. At the beginning of Passus v of the B-text Langland, after awakening, dreams again and sees the field full of people for the second time. This is how he introduces the sermon which Reason preached to them:

> And thanne saw I moche more than I bifore tolde,
> For I say the felde ful of folke that I bifore of seyde,
> And how Resoun gan arrayen hym alle the reume to preche;
> And with a crosse afor the kynge comsed thus to techen.[2]

And this is the corresponding passage in the C-text:

> Thenne mette me moche more than Ich byfore tolde
> Of the mater that Ich mette fyrst on Malverne Hulles.
> Ich sauh the feld ful of folk fram ende to other,
> And Reson revested ryght as a Pope,
> And Conscience his crocer byfore the kynge stande.[3]

This is distinctly more vivid and particular. Langland specifies the Malvern Hills, adds to Reason's vague preparations the vestments of a Pope, and makes Conscience his crosier-bearer where before the position of the cross was quite vague. His artist's eye has grown keener with age. It is just before this passage that Langland made the most striking and valuable addition to the C-text: the piece of auto-biography describing how he lives with his wife, Kit, in Cornhill and how Reason met him and challenged him to justify his manner of life, about which we learn something. The passage is in itself very moving, in the same way as Keats's conversation with Moneta in the revised *Hyperion*; but it is also very apt to its context, confirming the impression given by the C-text that Langland revised his poem not only as a moralist but as an artist. Aristotle said that ornament should come at the pauses of the action and he has not been contradicted.

---

[1] See E. T. Donaldson, *op. cit.* chap. iii. and especially 50 ff.
[2] v. 9-12. 'And I saw much more than I told of before, for I saw the field full of people that I spoke of before and how Reason began to prepare himself to preach to the whole realm; and with a cross before the king he began thus to teach.'
[3] vi. 109-13.

Langland follows the principle and inserts his piece of autobiography at a most decided resting-place, when the king has Lady Meed in safe keeping and has dismissed all his corrupt officers, and when the dreamer has waked up.

I have said so much on this topic to try to show how difficult it is for the ordinary reader to get a fair view of Langland and hence to judge whether he really earns the high title of epic writer. H. W. Wells has produced a reasonable conflation of the texts in modern English; Nevill Coghill has produced a good shortened version in modern English and has introduced many people to Langland through broadcasts of that version: and so far, so good. But modern English and attempts to reproduce Langland's alliterative metres can never go really well together; and quite as much as for Chaucer the reader must go to the original to grasp and assess the poetry. And when he does so he encounters not only a language and a metre more difficult than Chaucer's but the bewilderment of three versions each in some ways better than either of the other two. Not a great many of the class in whose hands the judgement of literature rests in the end, the intelligent amateur, are likely to stay the course and get a total view. Let us hope that when the labours now proceeding to clean up the difficult problems of the text have been concluded, a man who is both a scholar and a linguist and is blessed with the finest literary perception may make as good a conflation of the three texts as is humanly possible—no conflation can ever approach anywhere near perfection—print it without modernising words but with some standardising of spelling, and publish it for the use of the intelligent amateur reader. Only then can Langland find his place and his level in the literature of England.

2

The first question that meets us when we begin to examine the claims of *Piers Plowman* to be epic is the fundamental one of whether Langland was poet enough to command one of the great literary forms. That he could write sweetly or pointedly for a short stretch is generally admitted; but for prolonged expression does his alliterative metre incline towards the prosodic weakness of Blake's longer prophetic books or towards the strength of *Paradise Lost*?

The first obvious fact about Langland's metrics is that he was gifted in a very high degree with the natural power of enriching sense through sound. When the dreamer, near the end of the poem, witnesses the descent of the Holy Spirit at Pentecost, he says:

> *I wondered what that was and wagged Conscience,*
> *And was afered of the lyghte, for in fyres lyknesse*
> Spiritus Paraclitus *over-spradde hem alle.*[1]

[1] B xix. 199-201.

Here the first line is staccato, expressing tension and expectation, with a slightly stronger emphasis on *wagged*, expressive of the physical nudge the dreamer gave Conscience. The second line has a less regularly staccato rhythm, expressing in its brokenness the flickering of the heavenly light. The third line issues into solemn breadth and serenity and tells us of the spirit's all-embracing, pervasive power. The materials of the lines are the simplest; there is no imagery, only direct statement: but the sound of the verse first fits and then enriches the sense so wonderfully that the final effect is masterly and majestic. Two lines earlier in the same passus show similar mastery: they speak of the Nativity:

> *For alle the angeles of hevene at his burth kneled,*
> *And all the witte of the worlde was in tho thre kynges.*[1]

Here the first halves of both lines express, through their sound, expansion, the second halves contraction: the universe contrasted with the confinement of the inn-yard at Bethlehem. But in the first line the *a*'s and *l*'s convey height, as befits heaven; in the second the *w*'s convey breadth, as befits the earth. Again and again Langland crowds a wealth of feeling into a single line through his instinctive command of verbal music. Imaginative in B xii. 4 bids the dreamer think on his end and how many of his years are fled and how few remain,

> *And how fele fernyeres are faren, and so fewe to come.*

The thick crowded rhythm of the first part of the line and the weak, thin rhythm of the second part are perfectly expressive of the bare prose sense and animate it immensely.

The alliterative metre is peculiarly apt to proverbial utterance (indeed, there are few of the proverbs now current that lack alliteration); and Langland is master of the short gnomic statement.

> *Al is noght good to the gost that the gut asketh.*[2]

> *Moni chapeleyns ben chast, but Charite is aweye.*
> *Ye have no more merit in Mass ne in houres*
> *Then Malkyn of hire maidenhed that no mon desyreth.*[3]

It would be superfluous to illustrate further a gift that no one is likely to deny Langland. But it is allied to a deeper kind of sententiousness: a kind of prophetic terseness and finality. It is the sententiousness of Milton's attack on the clergy in *Lycidas*; and again and again Langland reminds me of that Miltonic passage. Milton gains one of his

---

[1] 77-8.
[2] C ii. 34. 'All things that the belly demands are not good for the spirit.'
[3] A i. 164, 157-8. 'Many chaplains are chaste but lack charity. You have, without charity, no more credit from your Masses and offices than an old maid from her virginity which no man covets.'

most tremendous effects there by the bare weight of simple statement in the words, *and nothing sed*, coming at the end of a line:

> *Besides what the grim Woolf with privy paw*
> *Daily devours apace, and nothing sed.*

Langland is master of such final effects, as in:

> *Eremytes on an hep with hokede staves*
> *Wenten to Walsyngham, and hure wenches after,*[1]

or,

> *Persones and parshe prestes playnede to the bisshop*
> *That hure parshens ben poore sitthe the pestelence tyme,*
> *To have licence and leve in Londone to dwelle,*
> *And synge ther for symonye, for selver ys swete,*[2]

and with a less denunciatory and more humorous but still grim turn these lines about what happens to Anger in the better sort of monastery, if he tells tales,

> *And if I telle any tales, thei taken hem togyderes*
> *And do me faste Frydayes to bred and to water;*
> *And am chalenged in the chapitelhous as I a childe were,*
> *And baleised on the bare ars, and no breche bitwene.*[3]

Langland is like Blake in his natural power over the music and emphasis of words. He can evoke a picture and give weight to a sentiment with great speed and with the minimum of waste. But can he extend this power to the longer unit? The answer is that he certainly *can*, though this must not be taken to mean that he always *does*. To illustrate I take a passage not from the culminating episodes dealing with Christ's history and the subsequent founding of the Church, episodes where Langland writes most freely and rapturously, but from one of the finer homiletic passages. It is a part of the rebuke which Imaginative (that is, memory and reflection) administers to the dreamer for having too hastily condemned learning. His argument is that if you do not define the province of learning correctly but make too great claims for it of course you will find it defective. The passage to be quoted[4] refers to learning's limits: there are things in the world that learning can never understand and which are open to Nature (Kynde) alone.

---

[1] C i. 51-2.   [2] *Ib.* 83-4.   [3] B v. 172-5.

[4] B xii. 217-35. 'And so I tell you, who pursue the *why*'s of things and have argued with Reason, as if in rebuke of her, you who wish to know about the forest flowers and their fair colours and where they got those colours from so clear and bright, and about the mating of birds and beasts—why some nest low and others high you would like to know—and you study the stones and the stars, and how every beast or bird has so vigorous an understanding; all these things neither learning nor natural intelligence can ever explain; but Nature himself can explain and no creature else. Nature is the magpie's protector and whispers in his ear to build and breed where the thorn is thickest. And Nature prompted the peacock to tread its mate thus and

And so I sey by the, that sekest after the whyes
And aresondest Resoun a rebukyng as it were
And of the floures in the fryth and of her feire hewes,
Whereof thei cacche her coloures so clere and so brighte
And willest of briddes and of bestes and of hire bredyng to knowe,
Why somme be alowe and somme alofte thi lykyng it were;
And of the stones and of the sterres thow studyest, as I leve,
How evere beste or brydde hath so breme wittes—
Clergye ne kynde witte ne knewe nevere the cause;
Ac Kynde knoweth the cause hymselve and no creature elles.
He is the pyes patroun and putteth it in hire ere
That there the thorne is thikkest to buylden and brede.
And Kynde kenned the pecock to cauken in swich a kynde
And kenned Adam to knowe his pryve membres
And taughte hym and Eve to hylien hem with leves.
Lewed men many tymes maistres thei apposen
Why Adam ne hiled nought first his mouth that eet the apple
Rather than his lykam alow, lowed axen thus clerkes.
Kynde knoweth whi he dede so, ac no clerke elles.

There you again have Langland's characteristic virtues, but in a large setting. There is the lovely, proverbial, alliterative emphasis of *He is the pyes patroun*, followed by a stealthy rhythm perfectly adapted to the sense of Nature communicating a secret. And there is the voice of the seer in the final simplicity of the four last words. But the whole is a masterly piece of unbroken rhetoric. The voice is sustained through the enumeration of all the things the dreamer had wished to know and it drops with the sober information, given in a single slow line, that such knowledge is beyond learning or man's natural understanding. But the drop lasts only one line, being caught up by the triumphant emphasis of *Ac* Kynde *knoweth the cause*, followed by the exquisite beauty of the lesson nature can teach. And the passage expires in the lines about the foolish scholars and, to change the metaphor, is fixed and bonded by the sober certainty of the last line. A poet commanding such rhetoric has an initial right to aspire to the epic. Not of course that Langland had the least notion of such an aspiration: he knew nothing about the epic form, and any motives of which he was aware were doctrinal not aesthetic.

3

There is one epic quality which no one would deny Langland: that of speaking for a great body of people. It may well be that he was not

thus, and prompted Adam to know his secret parts and taught him and Eve to hide them with leaves. Ignorant men often question their masters why Adam did not sooner hide his mouth that ate the apple than his lower body: that's what these ignorant scholars ask. Nature knows why he did so but no scholar else.'

personally a sociable man; but that did not prevent him speaking with the voice that thousands recognised as *their* voice. He may have been very much more pious than most of his readers; but that piety of which he may have had more was *their* piety. He had the keenest eye for the things around him; but the things he saw were what his fellows saw, however much more clearly he focussed them. Apparently he did not become a part of literature till after his death; he wrote not for a literary circle but for the people at large. And though he knew the customs that prevailed in sermon-writing, he did not share the polite notions of poetry-writing as an exercise of rhetoric. He wrote consciously to teach, unconsciously to ease his mind of its burden. The result was that the people at large read him widely, the polite writers of the age ignored him, and later ages grouped him with Chaucer, Gower, and Lydgate as the earliest English Classics. The fate of his poem was thus much like that of Bunyan's *Pilgrim's Progress* except that it was luckier in being born in an England unsevered by a great religious feud. But Langland, though as English as a man could be, speaks also for his age. His poem illustrates to perfection the violences and the extremes of sentiment which Huizinga in his *Waning of the Middle Ages*[1] has so convincingly demonstrated as typical of all western Europe. Or take a single point. There is a famous passage where Imaginative argues with the dreamer about the vanity of his spending his time verse-making when he could be saying his psalter:

> *And thow medlest the with makynges and myghtest go sey thi sauter*
> *And bidde for hem that yiveth the bred, for there are bokes ynowe*
> *To tell men what dowel is, dobet and dobest bothe,*
> *And prechoures to preve what it is.*[2]

And Langland replies with the well-known plea that occasional recreation may fit a man for more serious things. Such a debate between the call of poetry and the call of religion is central to the whole age. Langland talking to Imaginative is like Petrarch talking to Augustine in his *Secretum*.

It is easy to pass from Langland's success in speaking for many men to the variety of his substance. And here again I believe him to fulfil any possible epic requirement. In some ways he is more varied, or presents sharper contrasts, than Chaucer himself. *Piers Plowman*, however much of England he puts into it, is in substance a religious poem. The books behind it are the Vulgate, some of the Fathers, the proverbs of Cato, all the common property of western Europe. The allegory, the different layers of meaning, belong no more to London

[1] London 1927.
[2] B xii. 16-19. 'And meddle with writing poetry while you might say your psalter and pray for those who give you bread. For there are books enough telling men what Do-wel is, and Do-bet and Do-best too, and preachers to prove it.'

than to Paris, Warsaw, Bologna, or Fulda. But this common European material[1] is put into the purely English alliterative metre which, going right behind the Norman Conquest, managed to survive in the west and north of the country. It is a vivid, a spicy contrast; and its successful creation resembles another masterly thing in literature, Henryson's successful bending and suppling of the strong obstinate northern dialect to the dulcet requirements of Cressid's lament in the *Testament of Cressid*. Not that we must think of the alliterative metre as something mean or unaristocratic. On the contrary, as R. W. Chambers[2] points out, this metre was the vehicle of poems that delighted the gentry of England in the west and in the north. Its character is regional, not proletarian. The mention of the west, or rather West Midlands, of which Langland was native, suggests another contrast betokening variety. Though born in the district of Malvern and writing in the local alliterative metre, he spent most of his life in London and many of his descriptions are of the London scene. Chaucer wrote in the speech and prosody of the East Midlands and describes mainly what he found there; and though he may have been more European than Langland, he does not unite as Langland does the two great regions of the Severn and the Thames watersheds, regions which in the fourteenth century were more separated and individual than we now find easy to imagine.

It is not only regions of England that Langland brings together, but all ranks of society. It was what Chaucer did in the Prologue to the *Canterbury Tales*, but Langland includes more of the wreckage of society and he is didactic where Chaucer is, or at least appears, descriptive only. Langland does not hesitate to speak plainly about kings, as in the fable of the cat and the rats, and in his picture of the king seeking to wed Meed and Conscience. And he gives the sense of life in the highest places in two passages to which I have already referred: the attempted wedding of Meed to False and the sermon preached by Reason before the king, with Conscience holding his crosier. Lower in the social scale, but like Chaucer's monk within the gentry, is Religion pictured as a worldly cleric:

> *Ac now is Religioun a ryder, a rowmer bi stretes,*
> *A leder of lovedayes and a londe-bygger,*
> *A priker on a palfrey from manere to manere,*

[1] R. W. Chambers in *Man's Unconquerable Mind* (London 1939) 91 sees in *Piers Plowman* a continuance of the spirit of Anglo-Saxon endurance shown in *Beowulf* and hypothetically prolonged after the Conquest, in the Kossovo manner, in the district of which Langland was native. Is this not wishful thinking? The theme of endurance is one of the commonest in literature. Langland had *Job* at hand and he may well have known of the trials of endurance the courtly lover had to undergo. Endurance is a main theme of the *Aeneid*, which Langland may well have known by hearsay. [2] *Ib.* 100.

An heep of houndes at his ers as he a lorde were.
And but if his knave knele that shall his cuppe brynge,
He loureth on hym and axeth hym: who taughte hym curteisye?[1]

There is abundance of low life. The most ebullient description, in the classic manner of the Low Countries, is that of Glutton's performance at the tavern and, afterwards, in the setting of the Seven Deadly Sins. His description of downright poverty has no fellow in English poetry, Blake's *London* in *Songs of Experience* coming nearest to it in spirit but lacking the detail. He speaks of the women in the cottages squeezed almost dry of money by paying the rent, scarcely able to provide pap enough to still the cries of their children, having to rise at night in winter to rock the cradle and to work,

That reuthe is to rede othere in ryme shewe
The wo of these women that wonyeth in cotes,
And of meny other men that muche wo suffren
Bothe a-fyngrede and a-furst, to turne the fayre outwarde
And beth abasshed for to begge.[2]

But most characteristic of all the passages in Langland about the different classes of society are those that treat them together. Langland was of gentle birth on his father's side and he was brought up in a part of the country which still maintained its antique feudal character. He was anything but a leveller and believed in a strictly hierarchical society, but he held the accompanying belief that ennobled the hierarchical theory: that no grade in the hierarchy, however lowly, was less necessary than any other to make up the whole. The great jig-saw puzzle of life was incomplete if the humblest piece was lacking. These passages are so important in illustrating not only Langland's range but his creed that I must mention several. In Reason's long discourse on Charity in B xv all sorts of men are included, while in these lines kings, clerics, knights, and poor men are deliberately approximated:

Edmonde and Edwarde eyther were kinges
And seyntes ysette fro Charite hem folwed.
I have seyne Charity also singen and reden,
Ryden, and rennen in ragged wedes.[3]

---

[1] B x. 306-11. 'But now Religion is mounted and frequents the highroads; he takes the chair at arbitration-courts and buys land; he spurs from manor to manor on his palfrey, with a pack of hounds at his arse as if he were a lord. And if the servant who brings his drink fails to kneel to him, he glowers at him and asks: who taught him manners?'

[2] C x. 82. 'So that it is piteous either to read about, or to express in verse, the misery of these women who live in cottages, and that of many other folk who suffer much misery, both from hunger and thirst, so as to present a decent appearance, and are too modest to beg.'

[3] 217-20. 'Edmund and Edward were both kings, and held saints, for Charity followed. I have also seen Charity sing and read, ride, and run in ragged clothing.'

In the first section of the poem Reason's speech to the whole people has a tremendous effect. The Seven Sins confess and are taken in hand by Repentance. In fact, we have a picture of a vast medieval revivalist meeting. The multitude on the wave of their enthusiasm set out on a pilgrimage to Truth. Only Piers Plowman can show them the way and he says he has first to 'plough his half-acre by the highway': in other words, there are first of all urgent practical reforms that must be put through. At this point a gentlewoman wearing a wimple asks what the women are to do meanwhile. Piers answers that some must sew sacks to contain the wheat, and, turning to the gentlewoman,

> And ye, lovely ladyes with youre longe fyngres,
> That ye han silke and sendal to sowe, whan tyme is,
> Chesibles for chapelleynes cherches to honoure.[1]

And he tells the middle-class wives and widows to spin wool and flax and help clothe the naked. All classes of women must be active in plying their needles, but the materials they sew must suit their social degree. To illustrate the different degrees in Paradise Langland takes the act of dining in the hall of a gentleman's house.

> Right as sum man yeve me mete and sette me amydde the flore,
> Ich have mete more than ynough ac nought so moche worship
> As tho that seten atte syde table or with the sovereignes of the halle,
> But sitte as a begger bordelees by myself on the grounde.[2]

Here, though the beggar has the lowliest place, he is part of the community of the hall and he has all the food he can eat. More explicit still is the attack on lords and ladies who do not eat in hall but in private.

> Elyng is the halle uche daye in the wyke
> There the lorde ne the lady liketh noughte to sytte.
> Now hath uche riche a reule to eten by hymselve
> In a pryve parloure for pore mennes sake
> Or in a chambre with a chymneye and leve the chief halle,
> That was made for meles men to eten inne;
> And all to spare to spille that spende shal another.[3]

[1] B vi. 10-12. 'And you, lovely ladies with your long fingers, see that you have silk and sendal to sew, as the time offers, chasubles for chaplains for the honouring of churches.'
[2] B xii. 198-201. 'As if someone gave me food and seated me on the floor: I have more than enough food but not so much honour as those that sit at a side-table or as the principal guests in the hall; I sit as a beggar without a seat, apart, on the ground.'
[3] B x. 94-100. 'Unhappy is the hall, every day in the week if it happens, where neither lord nor lady pleases to sit. Now every rich man makes it a rule to eat alone in a private parlour, on account of the poor men (whom they wish to avoid), or in a room with a chimney, and forsake the great hall, which was made for men to eat their meals in; and all to avoid spending what another shall spend in his turn.'

The great hall is at once the preserver of rank and the means of uniting all classes of society; and the lord who eats apart breaks the social bond.

But if Langland showed great variety in picturing human society, this was not his main theme. His true reach is apparent only when we see this society in another and wider setting. Langland's pictures of the life around him and his hierarchical but organic conception of society are subordinated to larger religious motives. The religious theme of his poem is personal salvation, and the religious complexion is that of the unmitigated Christian doctrine of self-sacrifice and love as found in the Gospels and in the life of St Francis. Although Langland mentions and quotes St Paul and the four great Fathers and is perfectly orthodox dogmatically, and though he seeks God in the mirror of nature in the correct manner, it is the imitation of Christ that counts for most, and the law of Charity is greater than any formulated rule. Charity was found supremely in Christ,

> *And in a freres frokke he was yfounde ones,*
> *Ac it is ferre agoo in Seynt Fraunceys tyme.*[1]

The law of Charity is also powerfully vindicated in one of the most original passages in *Piers Plowman*: the consideration of the righteous heathen and their possible salvation.[2] This consideration comes at the end of Passus x and in Passus xi and xii in the B-text, and it represents both a struggle in Langland's mind and a shift of position. Admitting that the doctors of the Church have consigned Aristotle to Hell, for all his wisdom and uprightness, while the dying thief and Mary Magdalen for all their unholy lives were saved, he passionately embraces the saying of Augustine that simpletons storm the sky, while we wise men are sunk in Hell, thus side-tracking the heathendom of Aristotle and accepting his damnation as belonging to the case, common to baptised and unbaptised alike, of mere learning without simple faith being insufficient for salvation. But Aristotle could not, for Langland, be permanently settled thus; and in the sequel the matter of the virtuous pagans comes up again. First, Trajan interposes, the virtuous pagan who was undoubtedly saved at the instance of Pope Gregory. Yet Langland will not have it that it was the Pope's prayers that brought salvation; Trajan's own love and loyalty were the cause. Finally, at the end of Passus xii Langland goes further (through the mouth of Imaginative) and seeks to extend Trajan's salvation to an indefinite number of virtuous heathen. To his earlier acceptance of Aristotle's damnation, now repented of, he retorts that we do not *know* whether he was saved or not: Scripture tells us nothing. But he

---

[1] B xv. 225-6. 'And Charity was found once in a friar's habit, but that was long ago in St Francis' time.'

[2] For this topic see principally R. W. Chambers, *op. cit.* 142-9.

hopes that God is good enough to save Aristotle and the other good heathen who have taught us so much. And he finds hope in there being two other ways of baptism than by water: namely by blood and by fire. And these, he would have us think, may extend to places beyond the reach of orthodox formulations. The whole discussion shows Langland right beyond the common thought of his day, and in so doing adds yet another element to his variety.

But most plainly of all the rule of Charity is shown in the culminating episodes of *Piers Plowman*. Passus xvi had described Faith through the person of Abraham. Passus xvii goes on to Hope in the person of Moses. But Charity is figured not by any Old Testament figure but by the Good Samaritan, who turns out to be Christ himself on his way to Jerusalem to put his charity to the supreme test on the cross and to its supreme fulfilment towards mankind in haling out Adam and Eve, the cause of his own passion, from Hell.

These culminating episodes, however important and solemn in content and pre-eminent poetically, are yet subordinated to the main theme of salvation through a pilgrimage. But before entering on that theme, I must point out that these episodes, together with a part of the next Passus (xix) do make up a heroic poem, a *Christiad*. (Earlier in this book I said that the shift of emphasis from one world to more than one had made heroic poetry impossible as the most serious type. I omitted to say that the one possible heroic poem in which a writer could feel full confidence was a *Christiad*. Langland by including his *Christiad* in his larger allegory gave his poem a weight that contributes to the epic effect.) One of Langland's habitual pieces of technique is to sow the seeds of a new motive well in advance; and he uses it in his treatment of Jesus. In Passus xvi, arising out of a reference to Adam and the forbidden fruit and the Devil's success in making his hoard of men in Hell, comes a short account of the life of Jesus ending with Good Friday, when for mankind's sake he 'jousted in Jerusalem'[1] and on the cross won the battle against death and the Devil. The notion of Christ as the jousting Knight, striking though as old as the old English *Dream of the Rood*, anticipates a later episode. Then Langland drops this theme, to interpose other matter, before returning to it. He manipulates his return as follows. His ruling theme in this part of the poem has been different trinities, and he chooses another entry into the life of Christ, through the Pauline trinity of Faith, Hope, and Charity. After Faith and Hope have been described, a man on a mule, a Samaritan, on the way from Jericho to a tournament in Jerusalem,[2] overtakes them. The Samaritan is Charity and as such has nothing to do with the heroic world of the tournament; but the seed has been sown in these two passages for the transformation of the Samaritan, who is Charity, into Jesus, who in Piers's

[1] B xvi. 163.   [2] B xvii. 51.

armour, or the human body, will win his heroic victory. And the Passion is described in terms of a fight. When darkness descended and there was an earthquake, dead bodies rose and one said that Life and Death were in this darkness in a struggle, and that mankind will not know the issue till daybreak on Sunday. Thereafter Christ is the heroic conqueror. The gates of Hell cannot resist him; and, when, after the harrowing of Hell, the dreamer awakes and sleeps again, his first vision is of Christ in his armour, blood-smeared but the conqueror. And Conscience explains that Jesus, Knight and King, is now Christ, the Conqueror, the invading monarch who can free men held captive. So much for the incidental *Christiad*.

I come now to Langland's main theme, that of salvation and of the earthly pilgrimage, and I cannot maintain that it is strikingly obvious. On the contrary, we tend to forget it (if we have ever noticed it) for long stretches. Langland knew the plain motive of the pilgrim's progress well enough, for Piers Plowman himself at his first appearance sketches it out for the benefit of the great multitude, fresh from the exhortations of Reason and Repentance and anxious to set forth on their pilgrimage.[1] But immediately after, Piers cut short this general pilgrimage with the assertion that he cannot act as guide till he has ploughed his half-acre; and it is never resumed. Langland, indeed, does not care for simple, sustained allegory. He prefers to push an allegory to a certain length, to achieve some kind of approximation and then suddenly to drop it and to substitute something which, though different, may yet end in working in the same direction. Thus though the multitude with their desire to find Truth through a pilgrimage fade away, their place is soon taken by the dreamer who 'roamed about all a summer season to seek Do-wel'. This kaleidoscopic use of allegory has something to do with the cast of Langland's mind. Jusserand perceived it when he used the metaphor of clouds, although he went wrong in implying through it a confusion of mind of which Langland was not in fact guilty:

> Par moments les nuages, les brouillards, les abstractions remplissent la scène; on est aveuglé, on étouffe; et tout à coup la nuée se déchire, le vent l'emporte, et nous voyons, nets comme si nous y étions, une rue de Londres au xive siècle.[2]

Jusserand, who in this passage does admirable justice to Langland's realism, should have distanced his clouds and seen them not from within but as a pageant in the sky. That pageant presents definite shapes, but these keep moving and one melts into another. Though Langland had at times the keenest eye for things presented simply to the senses and could give them the solidest embodiment, at others he

---

[1] B v. 570 ff.
[2] J. J. Jusserand, *L'Épopée Mystique de William Langland* (Paris 1893) 5.

felt only their insubstantiality and that only the divine was firm. It is because of this sense of insubstantiality that it suits him to keep his allegory perpetually on the move, or to make Piers appear and disappear so suddenly.

But though there is no one overriding allegorical pilgrimage, the motive exists in three main forms as well as in details like Piers Plowman's sketch of the pilgrim's way, just referred to. There is the quest of the dreamer for salvation, there is the progress from Do-wel through Do-bet to Do-best, and there is the progress of Christ to the status of victorious king. By their combined force these themes do indeed make the pilgrimage the dominant concern of the poem. In his characteristic manner Langland inserts the notion of the dreamer's pilgrimage in an alien context and long before he develops it. When early in the poem he meets Holy Church the dreamer beseeches her to tell him how he may save his soul.[1] After that he pursues his search for the means of salvation, questioning this and that allegorical figure with imperfect satisfaction. By the middle of the poem he is still in doubt. In Passus xi he questions not only the salvation of the virtuous heathen but his own:

> *And in a were gan I wex and with myself to dispute*
> *Whether I were chosen or nought chosen.*[2]

It may be perilous to seek an end to the dreamer's pilgrimage. Langland may well have dropped it before completion and passed on to the other two themes of progress. But he may have meant us to take great note of the passage in Passus xvii where the dreamer runs after the Good Samaritan (who has completed his deed of mercy and is riding to Jerusalem in company of Faith and Hope) and offers to serve him. The Good Samaritan accepts his offer and says he will prove a friend to him in need.[3] And his certainty of salvation is proclaimed in the most wonderful and violent turn of the whole poem: his awakening from his vision of the Four Daughters of God dancing to celebrate the harrowing of Hell, and calling to his family to kiss the cross:

> *Tyl the daye dawed this damaiseles daunced*
> *That men rongen to the resurrexioun; and right with that I waked,*
> *And called Kit my wife and Kalote my daughter:*
> *'Ariseth and reverenceth goddes resurrexioun,*
> *And crepeth to the crosse on knees and kisseth it for a juwel.*

---

[1] A i. 82. Note that this motive occurs in the earliest text as well as in the other two. Langland intended from the first that his main theme should be salvation, however much social invective be included.

[2] B xi. 111-12. 'And I began to grow in doubt and to question myself whether I were chosen or not chosen.'

[3] B xvii. 83-6.

For goddes blissed body it bar for owre bot,
And it afereth the fende, for such is the myghte
May no grysly gost glyde there it shadweth.'[1]

But though these words may ratify the dreamer's salvation, his own case, after he has been accepted as the Good Samaritan's servant, is in a way merged into the case of Christ's other servants. His, like theirs, depends on the issue of the 'jousting in Jerusalem'. And this brings us to another of the three main pilgrimages: that of Jesus from an embodiment of Charity to the Conqueror. Of it I have said enough earlier in this chapter, except of the reason why Langland chose to make the harrowing of Hell the central event of Christ's career and the climax of the whole poem. Deriving from the apocryphal Gospel of Nicodemus, the story of Christ's irruption into Hell between his burial and resurrection to hale out Adam and Eve from the Devil's clutches should never have been allowed to fall out of Christian mythology, for it brings the story of the Fall and the redemption back to the place where it began: in Adam and Eve. In Langland's day it ranked with the canonical stories and he might have used it for his climax for no more reason than that he was thrilled by it. But I think he chose it because it was the most concrete expression, in the whole Christian story, of human salvation. The cross expressed the struggle which made salvation possible, but it was a struggle in which ordinary humanity had no part. The harrowing of Hell presented the first example of human salvation itself. It was thus peculiarly fitted to catch up and bring to fulfilment the theme of human salvation that had been fitfully presented through the dreamer. It may be significant that at the end of the poem, when the pilgrimage motive recurs, it is Conscience not the dreamer who is the pilgrim. The dreamer, though never in this life released from the quest for personal salvation, now knows the conditions of its attainment. So Langland turns to the Christian commonwealth, that has been betrayed from within; and it is not just one man but a general figure, an allegory of Conscience, who leaves the home country of the commonwealth to find Piers Plowman where he may.

The progress of Do-wel through Do-bet to Do-best has been described well enough in other books to make long comment superfluous. Do-wel is the active life, the life of the good layman; Do-bet is the contemplative life, the life of the man of a religious order; Do-best is the life of the highest human responsibility made possible by the union of activity and contemplation, the life of the Bishop. It was

[1] B xviii. 424-end. 'Till the day dawned these damsels danced, when men rang to celebrate the Resurrection; and straitway with that I waked, and called Kit my wife and Calote my daughter. "Get up and do reverence to God's resurrection and creep to the cross and kiss it as a precious thing. For it carried God's blessed body for our salvation; and it scares the Devil; for so strong is it that no frightful phantom may glide where it casts its shadow."'

common at one time to contrast this scale unfavourably with that of
Dante, who in his Paradise places the great saints of contemplation
highest of all and above the most virtuous rulers; and Langland was
suspected of being after all the practical Englishman at bottom, prone
to compromise. One of the most valuable aids to understanding *Piers
Plowman* was the discovery by H. W. Wells[1] that Langland in placing
the mixed life above the other two was following excellent medieval
precedent, including that of Thomas Aquinas. R. W. Chambers[2]
pointed out that Langland's contemporary, Walter Hilton, was
familiar with the notion. And after all, if we need more precedent, is
there not Plato himself? In the myth of the cave in the *Republic* the
exceptional men who have turned from the shadows and seen the fire
that cast them on the wall of the cave return to instruct their fellows
concerning their vision. Granted then that Langland's scale is not
something merely personal or provincial, it can reinforce the general
theme of life being a pilgrimage towards a definite goal.

Finally, before I leave the allegory, I must point out that Langland's method of allowing one allegorical significance to melt into
another did not preclude his using the medieval convention of three
or four layers of meaning. Exactly how far one can detect this use
will never be decided; and to *try* to detect it is perilous in the extreme,
because ingenuity will nearly always crown the trial with success and
end by achieving absurdity. But those who know the poem best agree
that these significances are to be found to some extent. Nevill Coghill
believes that certain of the main themes can be schematised under
the four senses or meanings. I refer the reader to his discussion[3] and
reproduce his scheme below. The italicised words refer to the four
senses.

Literalis	*Allegoricus*	*Moralis*	*Anagogicus*
Piers the Farmer	Laity	Do-wel	God the Father
Piers the Teacher	Clergy	Do-bet	God the Son
Piers Barn-Builder	Episcopate	Do-best	God the Holy Ghost

4

So far I have said nothing of what Langland makes of the sum of
the admirable details I have touched on. The epic ingredients are
there for certain, but what of their organisation?

[1] In *Publications of the Modern Language Association of America*, 1929, article on the
Construction of Piers Plowman.
[2] *Op. cit.* 104-5.
[3] *The Pardon of Piers Plowman*, Sir Israel Gollancz Memorial Lecture (1945) 51-5.

First, Langland had the courage to make the great choice of risking everything on one long poem and the staying power to keep at it for many years on end. He had the heroic cast of mind. But did his heroism extend beyond mere dogged aggregation of details to a total conception which moulded and modified those details till they became inseparable? Did he patch together predetermined items, or did the items remain fluid and susceptible of modification during the whole course of composition? The answer cannot be simple *yes* or *no*; it has to be much more complicated.

First, the reader who insists on reading with an eye to the whole and refuses to confine his interest to whatever detail he is now concerned with must admit that there is a great deal of repetition. This repeated material is mainly homiletic: the stuff of the medieval sermon.[1] Those who know Langland best are apt to grow interested in him for reasons other than literary (which is legitimate enough) and to allow that interest to weaken their critical insight (which is quite another matter). They can be too tolerant of Langland's repetitions and irrelevant moralising. But at least one of the specialists, Nevill Coghill, recognised these shortcomings by the drastic cuts he made in his abbreviated translation for the modern reader.[2] The plain fact is that Langland was moralist and preacher as well as poet, and that certain topics, bribery and corruption, ecclesiastical sloth, the sufferings of the poor, and the virtues of poverty, roused him to such a reforming passion that he spoke of them out of season as well as in. Let me give a short and simple example first. The discourse of Imaginative in B xii is one of the most varied and beautiful things in the poem. In it occurs the passage about Nature's way with the animals ('He is the pyes patroun'), so certain and yet so obscure to human understanding: the passage I chose to illustrate Langland's power of sustaining his poetry. Immediately after the magpie and Adam and Eve and Nature's prompting of them through the instincts comes more about the peacock. And instead of driving home his point and using the peacock as another instance of Nature's prompting, Langland uses him as an allegorical invective against the evils of wealth, an invective which is both perfectly inept in the context and the substance of which we have heard a dozen times before. Even in the last passus, which on the whole is greatly to the point and where irrelevance is peculiarly disastrous, he inserts a separable and inorganic invective against degenerate friars. The effect of so much repetition is to destroy the illusion of art and temporarily to reduce the poem to a political pamphlet. When Langland dwells too insistently on the sufferings of the poor, I feel like the man who reviewed

[1] See G. R. Owst, *Literature and Pulpit in Medieval England* (Cambridge 1933) *passim*.
[2] *Visions from Piers Plowman*.

the *Lyrical Ballads* for the *Monthly Review*. Of Goody Blake he wrote, 'She should have been relieved out of the *two millions* annually allowed by the State to the poor of this country.'

Such homiletic accretions, however annoying, are not necessarily fatal. I am reminded of Langland's own fable of the man in the boat in a rough sea. He may reel and stumble, yet if he can somehow control the rudder he may make his journey. But there is one much more serious structural flaw: one which amounts to a prolonged abandonment of the rudder and the danger of complete disaster. The poem is divided into four sections: the Vision (Prologue and i-vii), Do-wel (viii-xiv), Do-bet (xv-xviii), and Do-best (xix and xx), all these numbers referring to the B-text. The transition from the Vision, which mainly concerns contemporary England, to Do-wel, which concerns the active life in general, occurs in Passus vii, where Piers, now busy with ploughing his half-acre, is granted a pardon for himself and his helpers. The meaning of this pardon, of its sudden challenging by the priest, and of Piers's destroying it, is much in dispute; but it is generally clear that the pardon does not reach far enough and that some more inclusive principles must be sought for. The dreamer is not satisfied and in the next passus sets out in search of Do-wel, Do-bet, and Do-best; and in that order. But such a pilgrimage is structurally shocking because most of the poem has already concerned Do-wel, the practical life. Langland thus sets out on a pilgrimage to a place where he has already arrived. Nor do I think it helps the structure to draw, as H. W. Wells does,[1] a distinction between the two places. He holds that the Vision concerns one department of active life, secular government, while Do-wel concerns another department of it, church government and its theological side generally. Technically Wells may be right; but in actual fact the overlap of the two departments is such that in reading we fail to separate them. The Vision is full of clerical life, and both sections are full of a general life that eludes classification. How much on the same lines they run appears from the accounts of the Seven Deadly Sins which occur towards the end of both sections. In the Vision the Sins confess in response to Reason's sermon; in Do-bet they appear as the spots on the coat of Haukyn, the active man. But the treatment is identical. That is, in the B-text. In his final version Langland transferred the second set of descriptions and embodied them in the first set, thus betraying that he perceived the redundance. It may have been this same fear of redundance that prompted him to cut out Haukyn's repentance (the Seven Sins having repented in the Vision), to the great detriment of the poem.

But when the worst is said, *Piers Plowman* is after all nobly planned. Even if Langland repeats himself, he never quite loses sight of his

---

[1] *Loc. cit.* See also Donaldson, *op. cit.* 158 ff.

goal, and the turning-points of the plot are usually magnificent. The appearances of Piers himself, of the priest who questions the pardon, and of Imaginative are thrilling in their suddenness, and force on us the sense of something most significant in the poem's progress. And we must not minimise Langland's power of enlightening us later about things that at first sight appear irrelevant. In Passus xi the remarks of Imaginative on Nature, splendid in themselves, come in abruptly. But in the end we see their point. He draws two lessons from the operations of Nature: one that unlike man Nature is ruled by Reason, the other that the operations of Nature are beyond man's ken. The dreamer then turns to Reason personified and asks why he treats man so ill. Reason retorts that such inquiries are futile and illustrate the very lack of reason to which man is prone. The dispositions of Nature are none of his business, but 'suffrance is a sovereign virtue'; and by suffrance is meant not mere subjection to pain but self-control and patience. Reason's rebuke, arising easily out of the context, touches the dreamer, who had shown himself impatient in his judgements, and when he awakes he now realises that 'to see much and suffer more is Do-wel'; and this marks a stage in his spiritual pilgrimage. When Do-wel gives way to Do-bet, the plotting becomes masterly, and there is much less irrelevant matter. The progression from Faith and Hope to Charity, who becomes the Good Samaritan, who becomes Jesus on his way to joust in Piers's armour in Jerusalem and, having won, to free Adam and Eve from Hell, is entirely convincing; technically a most brilliant contrivance. Not less masterly is the building of the barn (the foundation of the church) in the Do-best section. It catches up the imagery of the Plowman and the ploughing of the half-acre. It also introduces, through the notion of the Bishop as the embodiment of Do-best, the practical life once more. And having done thus much, Langland with perfect propriety introduces echoes of the beginning of his poem to make it end, as it began, in the life of the present. Apart from some homiletic irrelevance, the last passus is perfectly plotted, and it ends, as in the circumstances of the time— the great schism and the many ecclesiastical abuses—it was bound to end, in sorrow but not despair. Though driven out of what should be his home, Conscience has yet the strength to set out on another pilgrimage to find Piers Plowman. It is the same end as that of *Paradise Lost* or of a typical Charlie Chaplin film, and there is no fault to be found with it.

In spite then of numerous small and one very large fault in plotting, *Piers Plowman* does yet emerge as the contrivance of no small mind. Curiously enough, the major work so far discussed most like it in point of plot is the *History* of Herodotus. What travel for its own sake was to Herodotus, the desire to denounce certain evils of the time was to Langland. Both proclivities diverted them from their main theme. Yet through all their truancies they never quite forget their goal, and they make recoveries of a magnificence that forces us to pardon most previous lapses.

5

I conclude, therefore, that *Piers Plowman* emerges as the undoubted, if imperfect, English epic of the Middle Ages. The only literary phenomenon that could at all match it would be a complete cycle of Miracle Plays, which might stand to its age a little as Shakespeare's History Plays do to the Elizabethan. But *Piers Plowman* contains more areas of the mind, and in any case I am not meddling with the drama.

Taking *Piers Plowman* as the medieval epic, we can see that to a large extent it set the pattern for all the subsequent English works (history and translations apart) that can claim the status of epic. It is of course not a case of direct influence. Langland worked out his own method for himself, and the others in reaching similar effects worked out *their* method without any debt to Langland. But this independence does not make the similarities less worthy of note; and they consist in all these authors' combining a public theme, whether political or religious, with the individual, tragic theme of personal salvation. In Langland the public theme is powerful at the opening, but it is never lost in the greater theme of personal salvation and it re-emerges at the end with the thought of the corruption of official Christianity. In the first two books of the *Faerie Queene* Spenser makes the theme of personal salvation the chief one, but the public theme is there too. In the fifth book there are the same themes but with the emphasis reversed. Sidney, too, combines public and private in *Arcadia*, the latter emerging with special plainness when Pamela and Philoclea are tested in prison. Milton does the same in *Paradise Lost*, though the actual references to contemporary public life may be a subordinate feature of the whole. Into the *Pilgrim's Progress* there enters the theme of the England Bunyan knew besides the more obvious one of personal salvation. Shakespeare's Histories, which I hold to express, as a sequence, something of the epic spirit, are rather different. Their theme is mainly public, and they had to be supplemented not from within themselves but by the Tragedies, for the expression of personal salvation or integrity.

In sum, however different in technique from these other books, *Piers Plowman* is their kin, and we shall understand each the better for dwelling on the kinship of them all.

CHAPTER IV

THE FIFTEENTH CENTURY

1. LYDGATE

Gray left notes on Lydgate, the only extant fragment of his projected History of English poetry. It was a sound instinct that led him to make sure of Lydgate first.

(W. L. Renwick and Harold Orton)

LYDGATE was younger than Chaucer by a generation and he was at once more archaic and more modern than his master. Powerless to imitate Chaucer's innovations, he was content to give unoriginal versions of things Chaucer had either passed by or abandoned or improved on. Instead of taking Chaucer's *Troilus and Criseyde* as his example on account of its shapely plot and its living characters, he went back to the vast traditional version of the Troy legends. But some of his theories of what poetry should aim at are akin to Petrarch and Boccaccio, not to his English predecessor, and look forward in a new way to the Renaissance. Lydgate therefore will figure in two sections of this book: in the present section as working in the now archaic medieval tradition; in the next section as looking forward to the sixteenth century in England.

To his own age Lydgate was a great poet and to the Tudor age he was a classic along with Chaucer and Gower. In more modern ages, when the poetic and the learned were more sharply separated, he could not keep such a status. But he remains a massive figure and quite central to the English literary tradition.[1] His output was large and he exploited nearly all the major literary types of contemporary English poetry. He was well versed in foreign learning, having probably been to the universities of Paris and Padua as well as Oxford. He must have had an exceptionally swift and assimilative intelligence to have seized on and adapted so large a bulk of the literature that was genuinely congenial to his contemporaries. But his effort was not so much poetical as what Arnold would have called critical. Through a competent, agreeable, but not often poetically exciting verse he made known to his countrymen much of the genuine cultural fare of contemporary western Europe. It was not his fault that no man came after him capable of profiting by this 'critical' effort, of making great

---

[1] A fact not sufficiently recognised. On Lydgate W. F. Schirmer is conspicuously sound. See, for instance, his *Das Ende des Mittelalters in England* in *Kleine Schriften* (Tübingen 1950) 24-39, and finally his comprehensive work *Lydgate: ein Kulturbild aus dem 15. Jahrhundert* (Tübingen 1952).

poetry out of the learned material he supplied. Since Lydgate included in his poems a work having as its subject the essential epic one of that time, and since that work points to two much greater works in the later English epic tradition, I must say a little about him in spite of his usual poetical mediocrity.

I said above that the *Divine Comedy* and *Piers Plowman* were both allegorical pilgrimages; but they were not very obviously so. It was in France that the pilgrimage motive was made explicit. The original medieval allegory had been moral, and its original subject had been more a battle than a pilgrimage. The great French allegorical poem, the *Romance of the Rose*, both popularised the mode of allegory and affected its course. Its obvious innovation was to turn allegory from a religious to an erotic theme. But it ended by giving new stimulus and a new turn to that very religious tradition with which it had broken.[1] It was not that the plot of the *Romance of the Rose* gave any special encouragement to the pilgrimage notion. The lover does indeed make a kind of journey into the recesses of love's enclosed garden; but he is closer to the knight who forces his way into the fortress. It is rather the variety within the plot—the many allegorical characters and the abundant criticism of contemporary life—that gave a new turn to the allegorical mode. The new variety stirred men's minds, and not only to praise and imitate the poem but to attack it. In C. S. Lewis's words,

> Personifications and themes from the culprit work were naturally borrowed by the works that reproved it: they appeared in order to be rebuked, but they appeared. And thus insensibly a new kind of allegory arises. To set Virtue and Venus in action within a single poem is also to transcend the narrowness both of the strictly homiletic and the strictly erotic allegory, and to come a step nearer to a free allegorical treatment of life in general. . . . If the hero is to be subjected to the appeals both of the false gods and the true, some sort of visionary geography at once becomes necessary, and some amount of journeying.

As well as the *Romance of the Rose*, the chivalric romances popular in early fourteenth-century France encouraged writers of any kind of narrative to adopt a serpentine plot; more specifically they encouraged a writer if he included 'Some amount of journeying' in his plot to prolong and complicate it. A French work that embodies these innovations is Deguileville's *Pelerinage de la Vie Humaine*; and it was one of the Continental classics translated or adapted by Lydgate.

Deguileville was born in 1294, entered monastic life in 1316, wrote his first version of the *Pelerinage* in 1330, and the second (that used by Lydgate) in 1355. He says his poem was inspired by the *Roman de la*

---

[1] See the important pages of C. S. Lewis, *The Allegory of Love*, 259-60.

Rose, and he was just old enough to have met in his youth Jean de Meun, the second author of that work. But if he admired and imitated the *Roman,* he is forward in correcting it. *His* Venus is no beautiful woman, but an old hag riding on a sow. For his metre Deguileville used the octosyllabic couplet; Lydgate in his *Pilgrimage* retained it, but ran to rather greater length, 24,832 lines in all.

Lydgate's *Pilgrimage* is so central to its age and contains so precisely the stuff out of which an epic would have been compounded, had there then been a sufficiently great poet of epic capacity and in-clination, and is so interesting in its anticipations, that I will give a brief description of it. Lydgate tells us that he began it in 1426 but not when he finished it. The poem begins with the usual dream. In his vision the dreamer sees the heavenly Jerusalem, which he knows must be his goal, and at the other end of the way leading to it, Babylon. And he wishes to be a pilgrim. But the journey cannot begin for nine months; and he has to wait in the prison of the womb. (It will be remembered that according to medieval interpretation Aeneas's shipwreck signified the birth of the pilgrim soul.) Released from the womb, he sets forth, but lacks equipment for his journey. He meets Gracedieu, the daughter of a great emperor, and one of the principal characters of the poem; and we may remember that in the *Faerie Queene* Prince Arthur in his most important significance stands for heavenly grace. Gracedieu sets out to take the pilgrim to her house (the Church). It hangs between earth and heaven and can be reached only through a river. The pilgrim is frightened, and Gracedieu tells him that it is only a little river and not like the great flood he must pass at the end of his pilgrimage. And this little river will wash off the filth of his nine months' imprisonment. The baby-pilgrim dis-claims uncleanness and has to be instructed in the doctrine of Original Sin. In her homily on the subject Gracedieu makes the upsetting of order the main part of the Fall. As man failed in his obligation to the sovereignty of a higher being, so things once subordinate within his mind and in the natural world revolt; and we may remember that Milton prolonged this conception of the Fall in *Paradise Lost.* Finally Gracedieu convinces the pilgrim that baptism is necessary, and an advocate sponsors him.

So far the theme of the pilgrimage has progressed sufficiently to secure the requisite plot-interest, but with the entry of Reason in line 1500 plot gives way to homily for several thousands of lines. An immense debate ensues between Nature and Gracedieu about their proper realms. There are indeed lively passages as when, Reason having reported the matter, Nature complains that Transubstantia-tion is an invasion of her proper rule of things under the moon and goes on to describe the sway of Gracedieu above the moon. There is a touch of comedy when Nature says that having no interest in things above the moon she does not care if Gracedieu turns Venus into an ugly horned beast and Mercury into a snail. Nature then describes her own seasons with considerable feeling. Gracedieu replies that Nature is her servant and holds all her possessions in lease from her, who has power over the whole universe. But though this whole passage is lively it does nothing to forward the plot; and the subsequent description of the pilgrim's equipment, though nominally part of the plot, is extended to prodigious length. Finally the pilgrim gets scrip, staff, and armour. But he has no armour on his legs, that these may be free to carry him when he flees, as later he must, from Venus and Cupid. (Even so a later pilgrim, Télémaque, fled with his Mentor from Calypso's island to escape the passion that was destroying him.)

It is not till after the ten thousandth line that the pilgrim sets out on his true pilgrimage, but there is ample space left for him to encounter adventures. And these are of a kind that are familiar to many readers from the first, second, and fifth books of the *Faerie Queene* and from the *Pilgrim's Progress*. The pilgrim meets several allegorical personages, as Rude Entertainment, Youth, a Net-maker representing toil of different kinds, Idleness who reads romances. He takes several false paths and repents of straying from the true way. He meets the Seven Deadly Sins. Tribulation captures him, and he uses St Bernard's prayer to the Virgin. He enters a wood, where he finds errors, such as Necromancy and Heresy. Then his journey is through the sea, and, as he swims, his legs are clogged by the weeds of riches. He samples Fortune's wheel, from which he is finally thrown. Then the pilgrimage, as in Spenser, takes the pilgrim to islands. Idolatry inhabits one of these, and there is a marsh on it. Finally, when he is in great trouble, a ship with a cross and a white dove on the mast comes to save him. In the ship is Gracedieu. The pilgrim does a mild penance and is put on board the ship Religion. He may choose one of the orders and live in a castle frequented by various virtuous abstractions. But in some of these castles there are abuses. Then Age and Sickness warn him of approaching death, and the poem ends.

It cannot be known how far Lydgate was read at the end of the sixteenth century in England. Though many people may not have troubled to test the commonplace that he was one of the few English classics before Elizabeth, it is unlikely that the more inquiring spirits did not do so. I am convinced that in *Troilus and Cressida* Shakespeare showed a live knowledge of Lydgate's *Troy Book*.[1] It is quite likely that Spenser read, among other of Lydgate's poems, the version of Deguileville's *Pelerinage*. That version is indeed a likely enough origin of some of the medieval things in the *Faerie Queene*, though not necessarily the sole origin. With Bunyan the case is different. He is not

[1] See my *Shakespeare's Problem Plays* (London 1950) 38 ff.

likely to have met a copy of the *Pilgrimage*, but it is worth recording that Aldis Wright thought he had access to a condensed version of it in prose.

2. MALORY

At first sight it is ridiculous to include Lydgate in a book on the epic and then to mention Malory only to say that he is not relevant. Malory's prose is so much finer an instrument than Lydgate's verse and he himself understood violent action so much better than Lydgate that he appears to have far the stronger claim for inclusion. The point however is not Malory's literary excellence but of what kind that excellence is. Lydgate could not begin to claim epic status, yet some of the things he dealt in had true epic potentiality. Malory is a great artist, but his quality is not epic at all but tragic. His case is in fact precisely that of Thucydides as described above (pp. 40-1).

Malory was more than a generation younger than Lydgate and yet he is less touched by the literary happenings in Italy that promoted the Renaissance. He is thus at the very tail-end of a tradition. Not that this is fatal to great literature. Milton, writing around the time of the Restoration, looks to the old humanist not to the new scientific way of thinking and, though fully aware of Copernicus and his followers, can present a Ptolemaic universe with conviction. Malory's chivalric world is not ineffective because by then antique and outmoded. It is indeed highly effective, but only in expressing an individual vision. Set *Morte Darthur* alongside *Piers Plowman* and you will see how little group-feeling Malory possesses. He creates no picture of general life; he almost makes us forget that there are other classes in the world than the knightly. Even his notion of chivalry is less true to his age than is, for instance, Spenser's to the Elizabethan. Spenser's knights are in themselves ridiculously archaic, and yet their quests have a true affinity with the adventurous spirit of the time. Malory's notion of chivalry is nostalgic and not expressive of the actual England of the Wars of the Roses. That is, in the main; for it may be that something of contemporary gloom has got into the account of Arthur's final battle.

This conclusion, that Malory's bent was not towards epic, applies to Caxton's version of Malory (till recently the only version) as well as to the one that has superseded it. But it has been strengthened by W. F. Oakshott's discovery of a new manuscript of Malory in the Library of Winchester College and Eugène Vinaver's edition of Malory based upon it. Vinaver has made the most important demonstration that what Caxton in his edition called *Morte Darthur* was not a consecutive narrative at all but a series of romances constituting Malory's collected works. Previously it had been natural to think of *Morte Darthur* as one thinks of *Piers Plowman*, a single great work on which the author spent his working life. Now we know there can be no question of Malory's applying his will at a single great stretch. There is, Vinaver tells us, great variety among the different romances. Some are very close to their originals, others are free rehandling with much added matter. And Malory grew freer as he went on. At one extreme is his earliest section, the romance of Arthur and the Emperor Lucius, stiff in style and close to its original, the English alliterative *Morte Arthure*; at the other extreme are the romances that follow the episode of the Grail, recounting the story of Elaine of Astolat, the jealousy of Guinevere, Launcelot's accidental killing of Gareth and Gaherys with his consequent breach with Gawain, their brother, the breach between Arthur and Launcelot, and the final battle.

It is then in the stories following the Grail episode that Malory is most himself. There if anywhere we shall discover his true bent. And that bent is towards the basic human passions, those that have least to do with time and that are as apt to the ages of Homer or of Queen Victoria as to the fifteenth century. Guinevere's jealousy makes one naturally think of Anna Karenina, Launcelot's bounty to his friends when banished from England and the Round Table, of Shakespeare's Antony in *Antony and Cleopatra*. Further, it is the passionate cadence of the speeches that now counts for more than any narrative or description. And that cadence, though produced through English of the fifteenth century, belongs to all human passion.

'Fy on hym!' seyde the quene [to Sir Bors about Sir Launcelot]. 'Yet for all his pryde and bobbaunce, there ye proved youreselff better man than he.'

'Nay, Madam, sey ye nevermore so, for he bete me and my felowys, and myght have slayne us and he had wolde.'

'Fy on hym!' seyde the quene. 'For I harde Sir Gawayne say before my lorde Arthure that hit were mervayle to telle the grete love that ys betwene the Fayre Maydyn of Astolat and hym.'

There is also in these last episodes a strong sense of the logic of destiny. The turning-point in Launcelot's career was his killing accidentally two of Sir Gawain's kin, Sir Gareth and Sir Gaherys; and it is significant that Malory specifies Sir Gareth in a way his French original does not. Gareth was especially dear both to Launcelot himself and to his rival Gawain; and his killing meant an irremediable feud between Gawain and Launcelot. But though Launcelot killed Gareth and Gaherys accidentally, it was through his adultery with Guinevere that the occasion arose for the accident to happen. And it was from this accident that the breach between Launcelot and Arthur became such that it could never be healed. And this breach brought with it the ruin of the Round Table and the death of Arthur. Both the timeless passions and the logic of destiny are the marks of tragedy; and the last of Malory's series of romances are tragedy of a magnificence which perhaps has not generally been sufficiently recognised.

But if I have compared Malory's power of depicting the human passions with that shown in *Anna Karenina* and *Antony and Cleopatra* I can only point to contrasts if the comparison is extended to other things. The setting of *Anna Karenina* is all Russia, of *Antony and Cleopatra* the East and the West of the ancient Roman world. Shakespeare and Tolstoi combine tragic narrowness and timelessness with epic breadth and the sense of varied life. Malory is more akin to Webster in his tragic capacities than to Shakespeare. His genius does not extend to epic.

3. EPILOGUE TO THE MIDDLE AGES

To end the English medieval epic with the fifteenth century looks like a large error. Parts of the *Faerie Queene* prolong the tradition; in forsaking Arthur for Adam as his hero, Milton went behind the Renaissance mode to the medieval; the *Pilgrim's Progress* and the *Holy War* are entirely in the tradition. Nevertheless, to include the *Faerie Queene* in this part would be wrong, because by Spenser's time the basis of the most serious sort of narrative had changed. Langland wrote of the quest for holiness; Spenser wrote to fashion a gentleman. The Middle Ages interpreted the *Aeneid* as if it had the same theme as *Piers Plowman*; Sidney spoke for his age when he said that 'if the Poet doe his part a-right he will show you ... in Aeneas ... each thing to be followed'. And though there is much medievalism in Spenser and though some Elizabethans still interpreted the *Aeneid* allegorically, the basis of the epic had changed. As for Bunyan, he should in a way be included in this chapter. Yet to treat him before Calvin would be just as absurd as to include him in the Renaissance or neo-classic age. Wherever you put him you go wrong; and I prefer to follow the chronology.

It is difficult to say when the basis of the English epic changed as just described; but I think the turn of the centuries corresponded pretty closely with this other turn. Anyhow, if in the age of Henry VIII there had been a poet of epic stature desiring to excel in the epic mode, I think he would have chosen as his subject not the pilgrimage or the spiritual war but the fashioning of a gentleman or the education of the prince. But this does not mean that there was not a long prolongation of medieval themes and habits of thought into the sixteenth and seventeenth centuries; and in my section on the Renaissance I shall perforce include a great deal that appears out of place. And all I can say is that to divide up my subject into its old divisions, as I do, is not a good but only the least unsatisfactory method of working.

Part Three

The Renaissance

CHAPTER I

THE FOURTEENTH CENTURY
IN ITALY

1. PRELIMINARY

I MUST here ask the reader to recall what I said about the plan of this book in the first pages. It was to pursue concurrently two different objects. The first was to describe how the theory that dominated the strict, formal epic in England was born and developed. The second was to define the epic not by outward form but by inward spirit and to describe the background and the nature of those works in English literature which, the drama and the novel excepted, fulfilled this definition. So far this book has concerned the second object almost entirely. True, I mentioned Xenophon's *Cyropedia* and Heliodorus's *Aethiopica*, works which have mainly to do with my first object: but only briefly, there being indeed no occasion to talk at length of the theory of the formal epic; for that theory, though nominally of classical origin, was actually the product of the Renaissance and would have presented a most odd appearance to antiquity. Now it is in the fourteenth century that the theory of the formal epic has its first genuine if faint beginning. Having finished with the English medieval epic, I must now go back to that faint beginning and say how I think epic theory progressed up to the time of Spenser and Sidney. In so doing I shall indeed have to say something on how certain works do or do not fulfil the true epic function as I have defined it; but my main concern will be with the theme I have hitherto mainly neglected.

When I said that Renaissance epic theory would look odd to antiquity I did not mean that there was no relation between the serious long poems of the two ages, or that their ideas about the long poem were totally at variance. The Renaissance and neo-classic epic resembled the heroic poem of antiquity and differed from medieval epic in taking up its main position in this and not another world; in putting more weight on action and less on contemplation, more on the councils of human rulers and politicians and less on the timeless decrees of heaven. A second bridge was Aristotle, the classical critic who conceived of the epic in a way that was congenial to modern Europe. In his *Poetics* he described the epic not as a heroic story or as something written in a particular metre but as a mode of imitation parallel to and comparable with tragedy. He treated epic as a form, as something with its own natural laws and aptitudes. But Aristotle was exceptional, and Horace represented current classical opinion more truly when in his *Ars Poetica* he confined his theorising on the epic to saying that Homer demonstrated the proper metre in which to describe the deeds of kings and generals and cruel war.[1] The following quotation sums up the state of things in antiquity fairly enough:

> Throughout antiquity a wide range of poems was commonly regarded as 'epic'. Generally speaking, hexameter poems were called 'epics', whether they were heroic in character (as the *Iliad*, *Odyssey*, the Cyclic Epics, the *Argonautica*, *Aeneid*, *Pharsalia*, *Thebaid*), or didactic (Hesiod, Empedocles, or Lucretius), or commemorative of religious mysteries (Orphic poems, *Theogony* of Hesiod). To be sure, Aristotle had protested against grouping Homer and Empedocles under one head and had provided the basis for distinguishing types according to method of imitation: but the formal view that the metre determined the type of the poem dominated ancient criticism as a whole.[2]

Such a state of things was different indeed from the one that prevailed in the full Renaissance in Europe; and this difference dwarfs the resemblances between the classical and Renaissance conceptions.

I will now try to describe what the mature neo-classic conception of the epic was, so that the reader may see to what end the development I shall later recount was tending. I have already said a little on this topic at the very beginning; but something more detailed is now required.

The epic was one of a number of literary forms, all of which had ideal existences. Each form had its own distinct nature, and to that nature certain qualities (of length, language, metre for instance) were appropriate according to the great principle of decorum. Whether or not these ideal existences were inferred from the actual literary examples does not matter. The ideal existences were there, and the actual works of art were embodiments of them, more or less successful. The epic form was the highest of all, and its successful embodiments were few. Not every critic would assign to the epic exactly the same qualities, but here are the most important. The epic must be a heroic narrative (though not necessarily in verse) and it must be ample in scope. The narrative must be in the highest degree exemplary, and to the highest persons. It must present noble acts meriting and requiring imitation: and it might include acts leading to disaster and teaching, not what to imitate, but what to avoid; but since these were primarily the subject of tragedy, they were suitable only for secondary inclusion in the epic. The noble acts presented for imitation must be apt to the

[1] 73-4.
[2] C. M. Gayley and B. P. Kurtz, *Methods and Material of Literary Criticism: Lyric, Epic, and Allied Forms of Poetry* (Boston 1920) 515-16.

ruling classes and particularly to the prince himself, for the chief
practical aim of high literature was to educate a prince or to fashion
a gentleman, But the moral lesson did not necessarily cease with
presenting this or that act for imitation or avoidance. Great truths,
human or divine, could make themselves felt through the tenor of
the narrative. Recent events, and the morality governing them, could
be implied through happenings in a near or remote or fabulous past.
Since the greatest embodiments of the epic idea belonged to antiquity,
it was first advisable, and it ended by becoming essential, to use the
formal conventions of Homer and Virgil, though you need not go to
antiquity for your plot. But though your form had to be classical, it
was less the ancient world than your own country that you glorified
by a successful imitation of this sort. And this patriotic virtue did not
depend on the language used. It ennobled your country just as much
to use Latin for your epic as to use your own vernacular. But since in
practice the vernacular produced the best results, it became the
favoured medium.

Such was the nature of the epic as conceived of in the mature
Renaissance. My next task is to say how opinion began to set in its
direction.

2. PETRARCH AND BOCCACCIO

i. PRELIMINARY

Though the Renaissance may have been distant from classical
antiquity in its notion of the epic, the Middle Ages were more distant
still, for they quite upset the conventions of the literary forms common
to the other two ages. In classical and neo-classical criticism alike
there was such a thing as heroic narrative, and tragedy and comedy
were kinds of drama. But Dante called his long narrative a comedy
because the action moved from woe to joy; and a fourteenth-century
manuscript in Paris, repeating the common definition of tragedy as
the misfortune of eminent persons, cites the heroic narrative poems
of Lucan and Statius as tragedies.[1] Nevertheless (as mentioned above
p. 146), in their practice medieval writers did show a fitful allegiance
to the conventions of the classical heroic poem, thus maintaining a
kind of continuity between classical and neo-classic ages. They sometimes wrote Latin poems to celebrate great men; they occasionally
employed the conventions that were the peculiar mark of the classical
epic. For instance, the convention of the council of the gods, found
in Homer, Virgil, Statius, and Claudian, did not quite perish in the

---

[1] I owe this reference to R. W. Babcock, *The Medieval Setting of the Monk's Tale*
in *Publications of the Modern Languages Association*, 1931, pp. 205-13.

Middle Ages but served as a kind of bridge, faintly significant, from Claudian to Tasso.[1] Such allegiance to the classical epic proves that a reverence for classical models lingered faintly on and that the neo-classic movement of the Renaissance had something positive to take off from.

But the most evident piece of classicism occurs not in a classiciser writing in Latin but in the most centrally medieval author using his mother tongue, Dante. No epic convention is more striking or more the exclusive property of the epic than the formal simile or the type of image most expanded and least like the abbreviated method of metaphor.

> As from some rocky cleft the shepherd sees
> Clust'ring in heaps on heaps the driving bees,
> Rolling, and black'ning, swarms succeeding swarms,
> With deeper murmurs and more hoarse alarms;
> Dusky they spread, a close embody'd crowd,
> And o'er the vale descends the living cloud.
> So, from the tents and ships, a length'ning train
> Spreads all the beach, and wide o'ershades the plain.

This is Pope's version of the first of Homer's formal similes in the *Iliad*, a comparison of the Greeks pouring out of their tents to a swarm of bees; and it was the type of an abiding practice in the classical epic. Its use is to slow down the speed, to insist on a pause, and to give a ceremonious touch beyond the usual reach of simple metaphor. Dante was the first medieval poet to revive it, and in so doing he anticipated the more obvious beginnings of neo-classicism in Petrarch and Boccaccio.[2] The true historical importance of this act of Dante was that he both borrowed from the ancients and put his loan to his own use. To write an *Antiocheis* in Latin hexameters is one thing; to make the traditional epic simile serve your own purpose in a vernacular poem is another. Dante's formal similes are immensely valuable in giving ceremony and colour to his pared-down and austere poetic style; and they represent the principle of all legitimate neo-classicism, the putting of an old habit to a new and living use. Further, when you come to think of it, Dante's use of the vernacular was itself a piece of neo-classicism. It was not the habit of fifth- and fourth-century Athens to write long poems in the Persian or other foreign tongue, nor of the best Latins to use Greek for their long poems. The vernacular was itself a classical use. Dante in daring to treat a great theological theme in Italian, however unorthodox by medieval standards, was only doing in his way what the greatest ancients had done in

[1] See Mason Hammond, *Concilia Deorum from Homer through Milton* in *Studies in Philology*, 1933, pp. 1-16.

[2] For this topic see W. P. Ker, *Essays on Medieval Literature* (London 1905), the first essay, called *Historical Notes on the Similes of Dante*.

theirs.[1] Once more in his patriotism Dante looks forward. His use of
the vernacular is part of his passion for an Italy whose subsequent
failure to keep pace with other European countries in the process of
national crystallisation would have broken his heart. But that passion,
though abortive in its particular form, was truly prophetic of one of
the great distinguishing marks of the Renaissance epic.

Dante's anticipations are all of this or that detail. It is in Petrarch
and Boccaccio that the fundamentals of the epic form begin to change.
Begin to change rather than *change*; for Petrarch and Boccaccio share
fully in the contradictions that mark the temper of their day, contradictions that have been so well described in J. Huizinga's *Waning of
the Middle Ages*. Huizinga describes the highly emotional tone of the
fourteenth and fifteenth centuries, the mixture of crude reality and
refined fantasy, the extremes of cruelty and pity, of perfidy and
fidelity, of sin and sainthood. Even so, though Petrarch and Boccaccio
may begin a new way of regarding antiquity and a new orientation
of the epic, they balance every novelty with a continuation of medieval ways of thought. Spiritually Petrarch's mind, as revealed in his
Secretum and as could be inferred from elsewhere, owes equal allegiance
to Augustine and to Cicero. The two must somehow inhabit the same
brain, and if they come to blows the battle must be drawn. Boccaccio,
the passionate advocate of the classical form of the epic as revived by
Petrarch, is quite medieval in his love of allegory and prolonged and
popularised medieval habits of thought in his moralisings of history.
The reader therefore must not expect any clean and tidy treatment
in the present section.

In one thing Petrarch was more remote than Dante from the
typical Renaissance form of the epic. Though not indebted to him,
Petrarch began his poetical career by following the example set by
Dante (and others in the thirteenth century) of writing in Italian;
and when in 1341 he was crowned in Rome with the poetic laurel, it
was on account of his Italian poems, his sonnets to Laura and his
Trionfi. But from then on he turned against his mother tongue,
reversed his practice, and wrote nothing but Latin. This did not mean
that he cared for Italy less than Dante. On the contrary, he fully
maintained the patriotic object of poetry; only he thought that this
object could be better served through the more universal medium.
But the medium of Latin was desirable not only because it was more
widely understood than Italian[2] but because the writing of it in a

---

[1] Boccaccio perceived this. In his Life of Dante he said that Dante was the first
to exalt and bring into use the vernacular among the Italians as Homer did among
the Greeks or Virgil among the Latins. (See *The Early Lives of Dante*, trans. P. H.
Wicksteed, London 1904, p. 39.)

[2] E.g. Humphrey, Duke of Gloucester did not read Italian. He read Boccaccio's
Carbaccio in a Latin, and his *Decameron* in a French translation. See R. Weiss, *Humanism in England during the Fifteenth Century* (Oxford 1941) 64.

'pure', that is a would-be Ciceronian or Virgilian, form promoted that regard for classical antiquity which Petrarch did indeed think most desirable. Petrarch's Ciceronian prose style is not to the point here, but his heroic poem in Latin, imitated in part from Virgil, his *Africa*, is important in the history of the epic though much less so in that of literature. But before I write of *Africa* I must point out how well his Italian poems and this would-be epic, taken together, illustrate the confusion of this age's literary currents. The sonnets to Laura, in that they were in Italian, carry on the practice of writing in the vernacular that was destined to mark the best Renaissance literature; yet their imagery is old-fashioned and medieval, the old stock-in-trade of the Provençal love-poets. *Africa* is in the very forefront of literary progress in being the first of a great succession of neo-classic epics, but it is retrograde in using Latin as its vehicle. The *Divine Comedy* had been less medieval than Petrarch's Italian poems through its epic imagery, at once neo-classic and realistic; compared with Petrarch's *Africa* it had been more advanced in the tongue it used, and in form centrally medieval where *Africa* had been startlingly modern.

ii. PETRARCH'S AFRICA AND DE VIRIS ILLUSTRIBUS

Petrarch finished his *Africa* in 1341 after he had received the crown of poetry in Rome. It thus follows immediately on his Italian verse and initiates the extraordinary change from Italian to Latin as the language of serious literature that marked the age in Italy; a change so compelling that it had the support of the most brilliant of the wielders of the vernacular, Boccaccio. *Africa* is a heroic poem on the African campaigns of the elder Scipio in the Second Punic War, written in strict imitation of the Latin epic, except that it contains nine and not twelve books. The time of the action itself is short, but past events are narrated and future foretold. The poem includes epic similes, the appearance of Scipio's father in a dream, and a love episode on the model of Dido. There are no councils of the gods, but Scipio's soul is rapt to heaven and converses with Jupiter. Petrarch composed his poem with cool deliberateness: witness a passage near the beginning where he sets forth some of his ideas on epic writing and explains why he chose this theme and not another.

> *Namque solent, similis quos cura fatigat,*
> *Longius isse retro: tenet hos millesimus annus*
> *Solicitos: pudet hac alios consistere meta;*
> *Nullus ad etatem propriam respexit, ut erret*
> *Musa parum notos nullo prohibente per annos*
> *Liberior: Troiamque adeo canit ille ruentem,*

PETRARCH AND BOCCACCIO

Ille refert Thebas iuvenemque occultat Achillem,
Ille autem Emathiam Romanis ossibus implet.[1]

Petrarch takes the reader into his confidence here with prosaic definiteness. He has chosen a theme from the distant past partly because he must copy the chief Latin poets and partly because it is safer and less likely to provoke interference to do so. And he considers his chief Latin models to be Virgil's *Aeneid*, the *Thebaid* and the scarcely begun *Achilleis* of Statius, and Lucan's *Pharsalia*. Later, with equal gravity he explains why out of the three Punic Wars he has chosen the second for his theme.

Ter gravibus certatum odiis et sanguine multo;
At captum primo profligatumque secundo
Est bellum, si vera notes: nam tertia nudus
Prelia finis habet modico confecta labore.[2]

What are we to make of this poem which presents the aspect of a singularly cold-blooded imitation of an august Roman model? I will try to answer the question on the criteria first of intrinsic merit and second of the history of the epic.

As poetry *Africa* is almost unknown, and if heard of or sampled usually regarded as dead. Taken in bulk this painful imitation of the Latin epic, closest perhaps in style to Lucan but thick with borrowings from Virgil, with its huge rhetorical speeches, is certainly a failure. It lacks the high and steady distinction of style that is the prerequisite of any true epic. But Petrarch was a true poet and even in the very artificial medium of a tongue that was not only not the vernacular but not the habitual Latin of his day he can at times create poetry. And though what poetry he does achieve does nothing to give *Africa* the epic quality, I like to be just to the poem even at the price of irrelevance. In spite of his resolution to deal with past events, he does once or twice comment on the affairs of his own day; and when he does, his verse takes on a new and authentic poetical tone. In the second book Jupiter warns the soul of Scipio of the future of Rome, how it will decay, not through the action of any one conqueror, but by its own internal corruption; and when he does so, the feeling of the verse

[1] Petrarch, *Africa*, ed. R. Festa (Florence 1926) i. 45-52. 'For those who have undertaken the same hard task habitually go far into the past for their themes; some occupy themselves with events a thousand years old, others are ashamed to halt there; none has concerned himself with his own age for he can write more freely and with less fear of opposition if he ranges through less known centuries. Thus one poet sings the fall of Troy, a second tells of Thebes and of the youthful Achilles in retirement, and a third fills Thessaly with the bones of Roman soldiers.' The three poets he refers to are Virgil, Statius, and Lucan.

[2] *Ib.* 109-12. 'They fought thrice with heavy hate and much bloodshed. But, on a correct view, the war was begun on the first occasion and nearly completed on the second. On the third occasion the issue exacted but moderate efforts and had a simple end.'

rises, and we are reminded of Petrarch's sonnets on Rome, for instance the 138th, 'Fontana di dolore'.

> *Non victa sub hoste*
> *Roma ruet, nullique data est ea gloria genti,*
> *Nulli tantus honor populo. Vincetur at annis*
> *Rimosoque situ paulatim fessa senescet*
> *Et per frusta cadet. Nulla unquam, nulla vacabit*
> *Civilique odio et bellis furialibus etas.*
> *Tempus adhuc veniet cum vix Romanus in urbe*
> *Civis erit verus, sed terras lecta per omnes*
> *Fex hominum.*[1]

The moral and elegiac note of this passage is sincere and moving. Near the end Petrarch addresses his own poem and deplores the unhappy age in which it has been created. He hopes it may survive into a better. And the same moving sincerity is evident in his description of the sad kind of world he inhabits and his resolution to put up with it nevertheless.

> *Non licet ire retro. Nos cuncta novissima seros*
> *Et ferus adverso prospexit Iupiter axe.*
> *Utendum sorte est et sidera nostra sequenda,*
> *Qua ducunt, ne forte trahant. Mihi degere vitam*
> *Impositum varia rerum turbante procella.*
> *At tibi fortassis, si—quod mens sperat et optat—*
> *Es post me victura diu, meliora supersunt*
> *Secula: non omnes veniet Letheus in annos*
> *Iste sopor. Poterunt discussis forte tenebris*
> *Ad priscum purumque iubar remeare nepotes.*[2]

These lines show Petrarch's Latin poetry at its height, but they also introduce the topic of what *Africa* stands for in the history of the epic. For him his darling poem—and he valued it above all the rest—has something prophetic about it. It looks back indeed to the great days of Rome, but it looks forward from an evil present to a better future

---

[1] ii. 299-307. 'It is not through the victory of an enemy that Rome will collapse; no nation can claim that glory. Time will overcome her and she will grow old and weary in a kind of dry rot and she will disintegrate piecemeal. No age, no, none, shall be free from civil hate and raging battles. Moreover, the time shall come when there shall be scarcely a genuine Roman citizen in the town but only the dregs of humanity drawn from every region.'

[2] ix. 448-57. 'There is no putting the clock back. We, the late-comers, must endure every new and strange experience. A harsh god has viewed us from a hostile sky. We must use our allotted scope; we must follow the lead of our stars or they will drag us in their wake. I am compelled to pass my life in a shifting storm of events that rages around. But you, my book, if, as my heart hopes and desires, you are destined long to survive me, a happier age perhaps awaits. The stifling dullness of to-day will not invade all epochs. It is possible perhaps that the shadows may disperse and that our descendants may return to the pure and primitive fountain of light.'

PETRARCH AND BOCCACCIO

and to a future better just because it will realise what can be learned from Rome's great past. Petrarch, in fact, considered his *Africa* not only an isolated achievement, a piece of defiant neo-classicism in a decadent age, but a type of subsequent regeneration. Quite apart therefore from any value that it might have as a poem it vindicated itself as demonstrating a new sense of civilisation.

It was on this ground that Petrarch took his own poem with such extravagant seriousness and Boccaccio loaded it with such extravagant praise. Of which extravagances here are some examples. In the ninth and last book Scipio and the poet Ennius (who wrote of the Punic Wars in his *Annales*) have a long conversation about poetry. After some interesting talk (to which I shall refer later) on the poet's task, Ennius grows confidential and recounts how during the recent war Homer, the constant object of his study, appeared to him in vision and showed him the unborn soul of Franciscus (that is Francesco Petrarca) destined in his poem called *Africa* to record the great deeds, just accomplished, of Scipio himself.

> *Ille diu profugas revocabit carmine Musas*
> *Tempus in extremum, veteresque Elicone Sorores*
> *Restituet, vario quamvis agitante tumultu.*[1]

Africa is thus something quite other than its medieval antecedents, and through it the world's great age is to begin anew. Boccaccio's references to *Africa* accord precisely with this sentiment. In 1350 he was deputed by the Florentines to invite Petrarch to accept a chair in the newly founded university of Florence. One of his arguments to induce Petrarch to accept is that *Africa* may thereby become the inspiration of a new school of poetry.[2] In his poem *Pro Africa Petrarchae*, written soon after Petrarch's death to urge that *Africa*, never published, should not be allowed to perish, Boccaccio speaks of it as 'renewing the glory of Italy and Latin poetry'.[3] In his Life of Petrarch Boccaccio singled out *Africa* as the crown of all the poetry he wrote at Vaucluse, a work composed 'by divine rather than human genius'.[4] A few pages later[5] he calls Petrarch 'that glorious poet', who composed a number of works most worthy of being kept in memory. Worthiest of all was the *Africa*, written in the heroic metre and with a wealth of rhetorical skill. This poem, though not yet published, has been seen by many and is considered to be in the vein of Homer.

There is then no doubt of the very high value that Petrarch himself and his contemporaries put on *Africa*; it was a great event in the

[1] ix. 229-31. 'He shall recall through his verse the long exiled Muses into the earth's latest age and he will restore these ancient sisters on their mount of Helicon, for all the varied tumult that rages round.'
[2] F. Corazzini, *Le Lettere edite ed inedite di Boccaccio* (Florence 1877) 393-4.
[3] See *Francisci Petrarchae Poemata Minora* (Milan 1834) iii. appendices 52.
[4] Domenico Rossetti, *Petrarca, Giul. Celso, ed Boccaccio* (Trieste 1828) 319.
[5] 323.

THE ENGLISH EPIC AND ITS BACKGROUND

history of civilisation itself. I turn now to its more restricted importance in the history of the epic.

The principal importance of *Africa* here is that it marks a complete
transfer of the centre of importance from the allegory to the heroic
poem, from the theme of the soul's pilgrimage towards its heavenly
home to that of the politics of this world. There is much politics in
the *Divine Comedy*, but it is peripheral; there may be much religious
lore in *Africa*, but it is peripheral too. The soul's pilgrimage is central
to the *Divine Comedy*; a political and cultural conception of Rome is
central to *Africa*. So drastic a shift was an anticipation rather than a
true sign of the times, even in Italy. There is nothing in Boccaccio
that reverses so uncompromisingly the habits of the Middle Ages. And
when one looks outside Italy for a comparison one is forced to the
surprising realisation that *Piers Plowman*, the central event of the
English medieval epic, is younger than *Africa* by about half a century.
Africa was isolated, yet, as Petrarch hoped, it was genuinely prophetic; it does indeed look beyond the intervening continuation of
medieval things to Vida, Camoens, and Tasso.

But as well as being prophetically important in the history of the
epic itself *Africa* does contribute to the history of the epic idea. Karl
Vossler indeed makes much of this contribution, asserting that the
poem implies the emergence of the epic as a literary kind, presumably
in something like our modern sense.[1] But of this I can see no evidence.
It was not till the *Poetics* of Aristotle was rediscovered, translated into
Latin, and finally taken real notice of, that people began to conceive
of the literary kinds at all. Petrarch did not think he was writing an
epic; he thought he was imitating the great Latin poets, Virgil,
Statius and Lucan, just as in his letters he thought he was imitating
Cicero. Where he does contribute to the development of the neo-
classic idea of the epic is in having certain conceptions about how
you imitated the Latin poets and about the importance of doing so.
If you revert to the passage I quoted on pages 186-7 above to illustrate
Petrarch's deliberateness, you will see that he there implied first the
supremacy of the best Latin heroic poems, next that the most serious
work a poet could undertake was to imitate them. Petrarch also held
that such a work was not only serious but a credit to your country,
though it remained for Boccaccio to make this point with the strongest
emphasis. He also postulated certain qualities in any poems written
on the model of these great poems; and the passage in the last book
of *Africa* where he does so is sufficiently interesting to demand quoting
entire.

> *Scripturum iecisse prius firmissima veri*
> *Fundamenta decet, quibus inde innixus amena*
> *Et varia sub nube potest abscondere sese,*

---

[1] *Poetische Theorien in der italienischen Frührenaissance*, 56-8.

PETRARCH AND BOCCACCIO

Lectori longum cumulans placidumque laborem,
Quesitu asperior quo sit sententia, verum
Dulcior inventu. Quicquid labor historiarum est
Quicquid virtutum cultus documentaque vite,
Nature studium quicquid, licuisse poetis
Crede: sub ignoto tamen ut celentur amictu,
Nuda alibi, et tenui frustrentur lumina velo,
Interdumque palam veniant, fugiantque vicissim.
Qui fingit quodcumque refert, non ille poete
Nomine censendus, nec vatis honore, sed uno
Nomine mendacis.[1]

The most serious poem then will imitate the ancients, it will be founded on truth but will use fiction to embroider and enhance it, and it will include many things in its subject matter. These requirements are truly prophetic; for instance the *Faerie Queene*, constructed deliberately on literary theory, fulfils them all. But, though prophetic, Petrarch's remarks state no theory of the literary forms.

The other work of Petrarch's that has a bearing on the history of the epic is his series of biographies in Latin prose, the *De Viris Illustribus*. It was written about the same time as *Africa* and, except for one or two Greeks, it consists of lives of the ancient Romans from Romulus to Caesar. The life of Caesar is far the longest and almost a book in itself. The *De Viris* is important for the way it treats history; and, history and epic being often related, it is important for the epic too. In his preface Petrarch claims that he is writing history and he makes it plain that his conception of history is different from the characteristic medieval conception of mere chronicling. Echoing Livy's preface to his history of Rome, he makes morality through the example, good or bad, the sole reason for his historical theme. Thus moralised history could regain the status it had in antiquity and hold a position not far from the veiled truth of poetry. Herodotus had derived from Homer, Ennius had written annals, and Lucan had gone behind Virgilian fictions to copy Ennius. Petrarch's repetition of Livy's sentiments facilitated the themes of Camoens's *Lusiad* and Daniel's *Civil Wars*.

Petrarch's *De Viris Illustribus* has also a most important bearing on

[1] ix. 92-105. 'It is proper that the aspiring writer should first have laid the most solid foundations of truth. Relying on these he can then conceal his meaning beneath a pleasant and varied veil of fiction, thus piling up for the reader the need of a long and quiet process of labour, by which the meaning though harder in the search becomes sweeter in the finding. Whatever is comprised in the toil of the historian, in the pursuit of the virtues, in the lessons of life, in the study of nature, all this, believe me, is the legitimate material of the poet. But see to it that things elsewhere obvious should in poetry be hidden by a cloak, that they should deceive the reader's eyes by their thin covering; at times let them come into the open, only to vanish once more. He who makes up all he tells must not be awarded the name of poet nor the honour of the bard but he must be branded with the title of liar alone.'

the Renaissance conception of the epic as providing the highest examples of virtue for the prince or the courtier to imitate. But since it was Boccaccio who did most to popularise and disseminate this idea, I postpone my treatment of it to the next section.

iii. BOCCACCIO

If Petrarch balanced his extravagant claims for *Africa* by the doubts expressed in his *Secretum* concerning the spiritual safety of leading a life of letters, Boccaccio after a youth and early middle age given to vernacular verse and prose experienced some kind of religious conversion that caused a panic in his mind about the life he had hitherto led. It was Petrarch himself, the master he never ceased to look up to, who wrote him a letter of comfort that restored him to sanity. He had already imitated Petrarch by ceasing to write in the vernacular, and after his conversion he wrote long didactic works in Latin prose. One of these was the *Genealogia*, which includes the most important piece of literary criticism transitional from Middle Ages to Renaissance.[1] The bulk of the *Genealogia* is a large handbook of classical mythology, resembling the handbook of Conti that was composed and much used in the later Renaissance. This bulk is appropriate as introducing Boccaccio's final portion, on poetry, because the accumulation of mythology was specifically intended to help the poet in his subject matter and rhetorical ornamentation. And very serious subject matter Boccaccio thought classical mythology to be, because it had multiple meaning after the familiar medieval manner. Multiple meaning had first been applied to Scripture, and Dante had expounded the four meanings of a scriptural passsage in his letter to Can Grande. Boccaccio with equal seriousness expounds the four meanings of the Greek myth of Perseus killing the Gorgon. There is the literal meaning and then in addition the three hidden meanings; the moral meaning is the wise man's triumph over vice; the allegorical is the pious man's scorn of worldly delight; and the anagogical is Christ's victory over Satan and ascension. By making this claim for a Greek myth Boccaccio shows himself the transitional figure he is. The doctrine of the four meanings is a medieval inheritance; the passionate promotion of Greek mythology has the accent of the Renaissance. And what applies to this detail of Boccaccio's treatise on poetry applies to the whole. As Osgood points out, Boccaccio says nothing original about poetry; he defends it on grounds already familiar in medieval writers; yet there is an assurance about his utterance of old arguments that is new and looks forward to those defences of poetry which are so fine a part of Renaissance criticism. In reading Boccaccio we are often reminded of Sidney.

[1] The last two books (xiv. and xv.) have been translated by Charles G. Osgood (Princeton 1930) with a valuable introduction, to which I am indebted.

The most important passage for the criticism of the epic concerns the *Aeneid* and especially the episode of Dido.[1] Here too the sentiments are not original, but they are of very recent borrowing and echo Ennius's words in *Africa*, quoted above, on the poet's duty. Boccaccio gives various reasons for justifying the Dido episode. First, through the portion of it that narrates earlier history, Virgil imitates the practice of Homer, his predecessor. Such imitation is good both because it is imitation and because the practice imitated is a right one. Poets are not like historians (Lucan, many think, was too much of one) and should begin their narrative in the middle or towards the end. Secondly, Virgil had a veiled purpose: through the Dido story he shows 'with what passions human frailty is infested, and the strength with which a steady man subdues them'. Thirdly, by praising Aeneas Virgil seeks to extol the *gens Julia*. Lastly, through the symbolism of Rome and Carthage he exalts the name of Rome. Here, very clearly, are the qualities Petrarch required in the most serious and ambitious poetry: the copying of a great model, a veiled as well as a literal sense, a subject largely political. No more than Petrarch does Boccaccio treat the epic as literary form; indeed, it is scarcely yet a heroic poem, for he makes out Aeneas more a repertory of virtues than a character. Nevertheless, he later calls Petrarch's *Africa* a divine poem written in heroic verse and recounting the great exploits of the first Scipio Africanus. Boccaccio's references to the formal epic entirely confirm the assumptions or assertions of Petrarch as described in my last section.

To revert to Boccaccio's general critical tone, one of the finest passages and also the most prophetic of full Renaissance criticism comes near the end of the *Genealogia*. It describes the different aptitudes of mankind; how nature intended this man for a lawyer, that for a farmer. And ordinarily we should follow nature's intention. He believes that God intended him for a poet and he adds a charming piece of autobiography about his own struggles to escape being put to business. The passage is effective because it puts the poet and poetry into a larger context, into the context of the Chain of Being, where every diversity of existence has its proper and necessary place. That the poet and poetry are important parts of the Chain is their complete and sufficient justification and renders them immune from any attack by medieval puritanism. This assurance is in the true spirit of the Renaissance and very different from the heart-searching of Langland about his own justification as poet. And without this assurance men could never have dared to raise the noblest of the literary forms, the epic, to such a pinnacle among the possible achievements of man.

Boccaccio also reinforced Petrarch's belief in the patriotic virtue of

---

[1] Osgood, *op. cit.* 67-9.

great poetry, and especially in his Latin letter to Pizzinghe.[1] Here he says that Italy is being made illustrious by its new poets and especially by the *Divine Comedy* and *Africa* (Boccaccio never allowed Petrarch's contempt for the vernacular to influence his judgement of Dante). He hopes that God has decided to be merciful to Italy's good name by inspiring Italian hearts with the spirit of antiquity and making them ambitious to excel not in cunning or violence but, through their poetry, in the fame they will acquire after their death throughout distant ages.

Such is the nature of Boccaccio's explicit criticism, and I have upset the time order in speaking of it before his original works in Italian and the criticism implicit in them because it naturally follows on and confirms the assertions of Petrarch. W. P. Ker thinks that his criticism counts for little in the history of literature and that his original works count for much. He finds him little troubled about rhetorical principles and uninformative about his art beyond explaining his allegorical theories. In his lectures on Dante, he points out, Boccaccio brings in Virgil, but in so doing speaks of him as a magician and says nothing about the idea of the heroic poem:

> but while he neglected the theory of poetical composition he was making discoveries and inventions in literary form, and establishing literary principles in a practical way. He has no criticism in him, but he does more than the work of criticism by the example he sets.[2]

While thinking that Ker misses the importance of Boccaccio's *Genealogia* I agree with him generally in thinking Boccaccio important for the examples he sets in his original works; and some of these works have a bearing on the epic. These are three: the *Filocolo*, the *Teseida*, and the *Ameto*. They were all composed in the 1340's and before Boccaccio met Petrarch; and of them the *Teseida* is by far the most important, the other two having no more than an accidental relevance. That relevance is briefly the following. The *Filocolo* is a long and complicated romance about the loves of Biancofiore and Florio and it derives from the French romance of *Floire et Blanceflor*. Whether by accident or whether because the French original went back to a lost Greek romance, Boccaccio's story is quite in the vein of Heliodorus's *Aethiopica*, and in so doing is at the head of the long series of prose stories, of which *Arcadia* is the most prominent English example, aspiring in the full Renaissance and neo-classic ages to the status of epic. The *Ameto* is a pastoral romance with verses scattered in it and thus sets the model for this practice in Montemaior and Sidney.

The *Teseida*[3] differs greatly from these other two, being in verse and having most features of the epic form. It tells the stories of Theseus and Hippolyta, of Palamon, Arcite, and Emilia in a classical

---

[1] Corazzini, *op. cit.* 193-4.   [2] *Essays in Medieval Literature*, 70.
[3] Ed S. Battaglia, Florence 1938.

not a medieval manner. There is no dream-introduction, and the poet invokes the Muses, introduces classical mythology, and follows Dante's lead in using the formal epic simile. But there is no narrative of past events and no council of the gods. It is long, in twelve books; and Chaucer greatly abbreviated it in his *Knight's Tale*. The *Teseida* has a special importance as being the first would-be epic on the classical model written in the vernacular; it is an example of what much later was the dominant epic form and is thus prophetic in one way the Latin of *Africa* is not. W. P. Ker goes further and says:

> *Paradise Lost* is one of the successors of Boccaccio's *Teseide*. *Paradise Lost* was written with the same kind of ambition, to show that the epic form of the ancients could be reproduced, and filled afresh, by a modern imagination using a modern tongue.[1]

I think Ker goes much too far. There is no evidence that Boccaccio had any conception of the epic form or that he took his poem very seriously. The *Teseida* is less severely neo-classic than *Africa*, and he never mentions the two poems together. He probably grouped it with other romances, while thinking that his classicising made it pleasantly and even startlingly different. It is only part of the plot that comes from a classical source, namely Statius; the source of the Palamon and Arcite story is unknown, but is certainly medieval and not classical. And when in this supposed classicising epic Boccaccio calls Theseus 'magnifico barone' he is not departing from the spirit of his work. If the *Teseida* stands at the head of the classicising epics in the vernacular it does so rather by accident than by any intention of the author. Like the *Filocolo* and the *Ameto* it is there, half accidentally anticipating a common use of many years later but exercising no influence and founding no school; in the history of the epic much less important than *Africa*.

It is not easy for us to realise that the works of Petrarch and Boccaccio which have stood the test of time and which exercised the greatest influence a hundred and fifty years after their day were not those that had the highest repute in their authors' lifetimes. It was not till the sixteenth century that the sonnets to Laura and the *Decameron* came into their own. Petrarch's Latin pastorals and pseudo-Ciceronian letters were more highly regarded than his sonnets, and Boccaccio's moralisings in Latin prose than his *Decameron*. There was in fact something premature about much of their work, including their would-be epics. Europe was not yet ready to confirm Petrarch's effort to make an imitation of a classical epic the most serious thing a poet could undertake. When Chaucer rehandled Boccaccio's *Teseida* he (quite rightly) removed much of the classicising, the excess of rhetoric and much of the pomp, and put the clock back by making

[1] *Op. cit.* 68.

it entirely medieval. But Boccaccio's Latin moralisings were in a different category from all the works I have just mentioned. They really spoke for their age and they were *immediate* influences as these other works were not. Since they have their place in the history of the epic I must include them in this book.

Willard Farnham in his *Medieval Heritage of Elizabethan Tragedy*[1] found that Boccaccio's *De Casibus Virorum Illustrium* was of prime importance in the history of tragedy: and I welcome this finding as making more probable the conclusion, independently reached, that this work was important for the history of the epic also. The *De Casibus* was Boccaccio's first book after his religious conversion and his renunciation of profane literature in the vernacular for moral prose in Latin. It recounts the falls of many eminent people throughout history, beginning with Adam and coming right up to date in the French King John who was captured by Edward III of England. In general, it is in the tone of the medieval works preaching the contempt of the world, but Boccaccio was the first writer to express the old sentiment not through the homily but through an elaborate series of biographies. Further, he treats the old material with a new humanist vitality and at times gets away from the pessimism of the 'contempt' literature with its despair of earthly conditions to a state of mind that admits of some connection between man's acts and his fate in this world. It may have been this new turn given to the old and familiar literature that made *De Casibus* extremely popular when it was published and very influential for years after.

But though the *De Casibus* was outstanding in its popularity and influence it should not be separated from Boccaccio's own *De Claris Mulieribus* and the work that suggested the second, if not both, of these, Petrarch's *De Viris Illustribus*. All three works are portents of certain fundamental changes in the thought of western Europe. They are all biographies and they all show how about this time biography began to take on a different character. (I must here remind the reader that they are all serious narratives and as such may have some bearing on another form of serious narrative, the epic.) In his note of explanation to his *De Claris Mulieribus* addressed *Altevillae Comitissae* Boccaccio explains that, except for Eve, he writes about pagan women because these have been less written of than saints; and this mention of hagiography points aptly enough to the nature of medieval biography. Dorothy Everett in her article, *A Characterization of the English Medieval Romances*, commenting on Saintsbury's idea that the legends or lives of the saints gave its origin to the romance, said that the two modes were different: 'the legend is written with didactic intent, the romance chiefly to give pleasure'.[2] Of course, the lives of the saints

---

[1] Berkeley 1936.
[2] *Essays and Studies of the English Association*, 1929, p. 113.

were meant to instruct but in actual fact they were mainly recreational. Bede in the preface of his life of St Cuthbert addressed *ad Joannem Presbyterum* said he undertook the work to commemorate his own devotion and to lighten John's journey: *ad memoriam meae devotionis vel ad tuae peregrinationis levamentum*. He thus had no doubt about the recreational side of biography being legitimate. In most of the legends themselves a modern is struck by a note of what can only appear as frivolity. The marvels are presented with an airy levity out of keeping with the nominal holiness of the matter. Though the medieval mind would have noticed no incongruity, it would have admitted to gaining great entertainment from such narrative. And anything like heavy and earnest didacticism is generally absent from the legends. Indeed, Bede's remark to John is true of most medieval biography, whether secular or sacred. It served to record events worthy to be remembered, and to entertain. In so doing it did of course instruct, but the tone of the works themselves shows that this was not the chief thing. The first lines of Barbour's *Bruce*, in which the author speaks of his own narrative work, give us the state of affairs. Barbour begins with the recreational notion. Even fabulous stories are delightful, but true stories (like that of Bruce) much more so. And when stories are true they are also instructive. Further, brave deeds, like those of Bruce, are worthy of record so that their memory may be perpetuated.

At first sight it is strange that in the age of faith the legends of the saints should have received such light treatment. But there were a great many saints, and they were individuals; and in an age when an ideal of holiness was more important than the individual, however good, it was not natural to accord great solemnity or severe didactic emphasis to this or that saint. It was more natural to record and to amuse.

If such was the typical medieval state of affairs, it will be evident how great a change was shown in Petrarch's grim, selective statement in his preface to *De Viris Illustribus*:

> Apud me nisi ea requiruntur quae ad virtutes vel virtutum contraria trahi possunt: hic enim, nisi fallor, fructuosus historicorum finis est, illa persequi quae vel sectanda legentibus, vel fugienda sunt.[1]

Mere record is not to be tolerated; pleasure does not enter in. Severe didacticism is now the rule. And the lives themselves of the illustrious Romans Petrarch recounts are long and scholarly and instructive in a manner alien to medieval practice. In this new kind of

---

[1] Ed. L. Razzolini (Bologna 1874) 6. 'In my book only those things are to be found that can bear on the virtues or their contraries: for this, I believe, is the profitable aim of historians, to seek out those things which the reader should either embrace or avoid.'

didacticism Petrarch was much in advance of his age; but he does also truly interpret a great change of conditions that was taking place at the time.

This change was partly religious and partly political. The dominance of an ideal of holiness over the homage to the great individual could only continue when effectively backed by the Church. When the Church began to weaken, and particularly when the Popes lived at Avignon, the balance began to shift the other way. And when it did begin to shift, some of the awe that had invested the spiritual ideal began to be transferred to the individual. There has always been great men, good and bad. But now they counted for more. Through the same processes the different nations of Europe began to count for more, and Europe itself, that is the area that accepted the Roman Catholic religion, counted for less. Politically, the fourteenth and fifteenth centuries were ages of pessimism. The papacy failed to abbreviate the long and exhausting wars between England and France. The Italy of Petrarch and Boccaccio was distracted by feuds and civil war, and Rome itself was half deserted and wholly corrupt. The character of the individual ruler appeared to count more than ever before in the gamble of whether a country was to be happy or wretched. When Petrarch wrote the lives of the eminent Romans, he had these new conditions in his mind. Roman history, he thought, provided an unsurpassed repertory of great men, good and bad; and if the princes or dictators of Italy could model themselves on the good Romans and learn what to avoid from the warning of the bad, the state of the land could be really bettered. Petrarch, it must be remembered, was hopeful of what the dictatorship of Rienzi could do for Rome, and he supported him. By moralising biography in the *De Viris Illustribus* Petrarch thought he was serving his country and advancing the general political good of mankind.

Boccaccio's two works did the same kind of thing but by less abrupt and more traditional means. Petrarch goes straight to antiquity: Boccaccio, as pointed out above, introduced the traditional motives of the medieval works *de contemptu mundi* into the composition of biography; at the same time he insinuated a conception of human responsibility absent from them. I say 'insinuated' because it is only in some stories that Boccaccio goes beyond the mere impact of fortune on any great man and relates that impact to the mind or acts of the victim. But these exceptional stories, in giving a more reasonable appearance to the events of this world, show man as more of a resident and less of a passenger on earth and mark a true change of centre: a change favourable to substituting the story of a hero for the pilgrimage as the epic theme. To give examples: Boccaccio made Agamemnon a good man who did not deserve his sufferings, but adds that if he had lacked ambition and been content with poverty he would have escaped. Hannibal was not the mere victim of fortune in a capricious world; he was partly responsible for his own decline because he failed to ride to Rome and take it when, after the battle of Cannae, he had the chance.[1] Boccaccio's innovation was not that the introduced human cause and effect into unfortunate events; his gropings are feeble things compared with Dante's achieved sense of human responsibility. It is that by shifting the centre from which human events are seen he gave to the causes of those events a different value. Dante and Langland show the liveliest sense of human responsibility, but for them the ultimate human goal and home are heaven: Boccaccio has a fainter sense of human responsibility, but he combines it with the beginnings of a new orientation of man.

But Boccaccio's *De Casibus* and his *De Claris Mulieribus* also derive from (and very significantly modify) another medieval practice, the *exemplum*. The medieval *exemplum* was a story, usually quite short, serving to illustrate a moral in a longer work, whether homiletic or narrative. In a homiletic work like Gower's *Confessio Amantis* the moral comes first, and the story illustrates the moral; in biography an incident is seized on as exemplary, and a moral is added. In Barbour's *Bruce*, when Bruce was in his worst plight on the island of Arran, his hostess there prophesied a happy issue. Bruce was encouraged but did not altogether put faith in her words; whereupon Barbour inserts a little homily upon the virtues and vices of prognostication. Such a moral homily is not organic but decorative; and in general the *exemplum* was not independent but illustrative and subsidiary. The main point about Chaucer's *Monk's Tale* is that the Monk, nettled by the Host's impertinent request for a risky tale, does not give a tale at all but brings out of his clerical cold storage a great string of *exempla* which should never have been strung together at all but which should have served severally to illustrate morals already stated in the abstract. Now in his *De Casibus* Boccaccio did just what Chaucer's Monk did: he made the *exemplum* into an independent tale. But what for Chaucer was a joke was for Boccaccio serious, and an act destined to have an immense influence. The change from the medieval form of biography, till now dominant, to Boccaccio's form of the independent moral example is indeed great. In the first the subject was a man who did things worthy of record, diverting, and capable of illustrating incidental items of morality. In Boccaccio's biography the man or woman begins to be himself the embodiment of certain virtues and vices in such a way that he serves *in his own right* as a great example, a highly significant object-lesson, a figure of solemn and inspiring didacticism.

I was careful to say that Boccaccio *began* this process, because his narrative method is not consistent. Sometimes he narrates without

[1] For the importance of these and other stories see Farnham, *op. cit.*, 90-101.

comment, as if the mere story was self-justified. But there are quite enough men who explicitly embody a moral to make Boccaccio's intention plain. Thus in the first book of the *De Casibus* Adam and Eve embody the vice of disobedience, and Nimrod that of pride; and we are shown their reward. Theseus embodied excessive and sudden credulity; he ought to have been more suspicious about Phaedra and Hippolytus. And in the prefaces to both works under review he leaves no doubt about his didactic intent. He says in the preface to the *De Casibus* that he recognises the insensibility and the viciousness of men and wishes to correct them. But such insensibility is beyond the reach of straight argument and elegantly narrated history, and can only be reached by the awful example. In the preface to *De Claris Mulieribus* he tells the Countess that these lives are presented to her so that the example of these noble women may incite her already noble mind to higher nobility.

These two works of Boccaccio do really mark the beginnings of conceptions that came to dominate the tragic and the epic forms of the Renaissance. Tragedy, whatever else it was, was a concrete demonstration that evil motives brought ruin: and the line of its descent was destined to be from Boccaccio through Lydgate, the *Mirror for Magistrates* and *Gorboduc* into the main body of Elizabethan drama. Neo-classic epic was, on one side, a narrative showing exemplary men in action, and that side descends from Petrarch's *De Viris Illustribus* and the two works of Boccaccio that derive from it. The line of descent is not so clear as for tragedy, as will appear in the next section; but there is no doubt that, by whatever devious means, Boccaccio's words to the Countess look right forward to Sidney when he says, 'If the Poet doe his part a-right, he will shew you in *Cyrus, Aeneas, Ulisses*, each thing to be followed.'

CHAPTER II

THE FIFTEENTH CENTURY
IN ENGLAND

For while the tired waves, vainly breaking,
Seem here no painful inch to gain, . . .   (Clough)

A
T first sight it would seem that in a book which ranges over so
wide an area and which can have little space for detail, there
would be no sufficient reason for including fifteenth-century England
in the section on the Renaissance. R. Weiss in his *Humanism in
England during the Fifteenth Century*, while finding a growth in humanism between 1418, when Poggio visited England, and 1485, the year
of Henry VII's accession, shows how spasmodic the movement was;
confined to a very few exceptional persons. And usually the men who
patronised foreign scholars or read Petrarch and Boccaccio were
unaware of the change of standards for which these stood. The poetry
of the fifteenth century in England seemed to have forgotten Chaucer's
elegance and terseness and to have reverted to the worst kind of
medieval prolixity. In particular, Chaucer's most famous successor,
Lydgate, seems quite to have let his master down. And yet Lydgate
not only prolonged the typical medieval epic theme of the soul's
pilgrimage, as described above, but was the channel, in a way
Chaucer never was, of the innovations in the ideas governing the
serious narrative brought in by Petrarch and Boccaccio.

Lydgate was about thirty years younger than Chaucer. He lived
through the deposition and murder of Richard II, the civil wars
under Henry IV, the victories of Henry V, the dynastic rivalries
during Henry VI's minority, and the loss of English possessions in
France. All these events confirmed the convictions about politics
(including the importance given to the prince's personal character)
that had impelled Petrarch and Boccaccio to colour biography in the
way they did. It was therefore with an assurance created by the
events he had himself witnessed that Lydgate translated Boccaccio's *De
Casibus Virorum Illustrium*. He did this not directly but through the
French version of De Premierfait. This version he put into over 36,000
lines, mainly of rime royal, under the title of the *Fall of Princes*.
Lydgate's own preface to his translation shows that he sympathised
with Boccaccio's conception of the exemplary tale. He speaks at
length of Boccaccio's advice to princes not to trust fortune but to take
warning from those who have fallen and thus learn the virtues of

wisdom and moderation. But he also gives his translation a contemporary turn by referring to one of the great politicians of his age, Humphrey, Duke of Gloucester, Regent during Henry VI's absence in France. Humphrey is a scholar as well as a knight; he eschews idleness, hates heretics and knows the lesson, taught by the examples in Boccaccio's book, of avoiding confidence in fortune. To give examples to princes in general Humphrey, Lydgate tells us, had ordered him to translate Boccaccio's book. Lydgate wrote his poem between 1431 and 1438. Nine years after he finished it fortune showed its irony by allowing Duke Humphrey, who according to Lydgate had learnt the lesson taught by Boccaccio, to fall from office and be murdered. Thus he was not only the man who prompted Lydgate to introduce Boccaccio's book into England but in the next century became the subject of one of the 'tragedies' in the *Mirror for Magistrates*, itself a continuation of Lydgate's *Fall of Princes*.

Lydgate's *Troy Book*, begun in 1412 at the request of Prince Henry, and notoriously medieval in its treatment of the Troy legend, is a shapeless and ingenuous affair compared with Chaucer's *Troilus and Criseyde*; but though fundamentally less serious it may, through the Prologue, show a touch of the new and grimmer ethical temper that was to mark the neo-classic epic. Lydgate there says that the Prince ordered the work

> By-cause he hath Ioye and gret deynte
> To rede in bokys of antiquite,
> To fyn only, vertu for to sew
> Be example of hem.[1]

The poem itself is romantic and recreational in the medieval manner, but here Lydgate insists on its being above all exemplary.

Lastly, Lydgate is strong in both prefaces on the notion of glorifying your country by writing in the vernacular. He praises Chaucer's services in ennobling his tongue and suggests that Prince Henry wanted Lydgate to turn Guido delle Colonne's Latin version of the Troy story into English for the credit of the language.

Towards the end of the century Caxton's prefaces and epilogues[2] to the books he published intensify the notion of the narrative as having as its chief use the examples it provides for the use of prince or ruler. Indeed, he goes out of his way to impose the notion on works to which it does not in the least apply. When in the Epilogue to *Godefroy of Bologne*[3] (1481) Caxton says that the book was translated out of the French 'to the end that every Christian man may be the better encouraged to enterprise war for the defence of Christendom

[1] Ed. H. Bergen (London 1906) i. lines 79-82.
[2] These have been collected by W. J. B. Crotch for the Early English Text Society: *The Prologues and Epilogues of William Caxton* (London 1928).
[3] 48.

and to recover the city of Jerusalem', he does not surprise us: but when he drags into the Prologue to the *Mirrour of the World*[1] (1481, a short medieval encyclopaedia) the idea of educating the noble through the example, then indeed he does surprise us and reveals himself as almost obsessed by it. In his Prologue to the *Canterbury Tales*[2] he praises the poets and historians who have recorded the lives of saints and the doings of great men and then says Chaucer should be especially praised. As a general description of the subject of the *Canterbury Tales* the 'lives of saints and the doings of great men' is inept and misleading to a degree. Yet Caxton must have it so. We have thus the curious and for my present purpose interesting happening of an editor publishing the old medieval matter, still the staple reading of the educated public, and imposing on it new and inappropriate critical ideas. And the very inappropriateness shows how powerful the ideas were. Another proof of this power is the number of times Caxton iterates them. To enumerate and illustrate would be wearisome, and the reader who wishes for more details must go to the Prologues and Epilogues themselves.

One of the Prologues, that to the *Four Sonnes of Aymon* (1489), gives another piece of modernity. Caxton there[3] quotes Aristotle's *Metaphysics* to the effect that all men naturally desire knowledge and especially to learn new things. This desire has been satisfied by philosophy, poetry, history, and chronicles. Here is an idea that dominated the Renaissance: that man's special function in the order of creation was to learn and that serious poetry resembled philosophy and history in conveying knowledge. The mention of this Renaissance tendency not to draw any clear line between the two narrative forms of epic and history naturally leads to my next section.

[1] 50. [2] 90-1. [3] 106.

CHAPTER III

HISTORY IN THE RENAISSANCE

*Hoc illud est praecipue in cognitione rerum salubre ac frugiferum,
omnis te exempli documenta in illustri posita monumento intueri: inde
tibi tuaeque reipublicae quod imitere capias; inde foedum inceptu,
foedum exitu, quod vites.*

(Livy, Preface to his History of Rome)

THE gist of these words of Livy is that as one of its principal uses
history serves to put in a powerful light the exhibition of different
kinds of events teaching us and our polity what to imitate and what
to avoid. I have put them at the head of this section for two reasons:
first because Livy was the chief model for the new kind of history that
arose in the Renaissance, secondly because they indicate the turn
this kind of history took; the turn, already noted, away from mere
chronicling or unmoulded truth to something where truth can be
admitted only on certain terms and in a limited measure and in a
prescribed shape. Livy's rhetorical form, his journalistic insistence on
writing events up, his moralising of events, and his strictly Roman
point of view, all helped to shape the usual type of Renaissance
history.[1] In history as in other matters Petrarch and Boccaccio were
the innovators. Petrarch,[2] though he wrote no consecutive history,
was a great innovator in going straight to the classical sources, and
using them alone; and in his self-reliance. He was not employed to
write history, he was not influenced by the Church in writing it: he
'was an independent layman and treated history according to his
personal conception'. That conception was moral and political, and I
touched on it in dealing with *Africa*: it is that Italy might be regenerate through imitating classical and especially Roman antiquity.
Boccaccio[3] followed Petrarch in admiring Livy (he translated Livy's
fourth decade) and in moralising history in his own way; also in a
personal conception of history. But that conception was different,
coming out not in idealised portraits of illustrious Romans but in the
unpretentious realism of his life of Dante, a work that stands at the
head of the many lives of the artists in the Renaissance. The first
regular history in the new manner belongs to two generations after
Petrarch and Boccaccio; it is Bruni's[4] twelve books (in Latin) of
Florentine history. Bruni's life extended from 1369 to 1444; the first

---

[1] In the following pages I am indebted to Eduard Fueter, *Geschichte der neueren
Historiographie* (Munich and Berlin 1911 and Munich 1936). References are to the
French translation by Jeanmaire (Paris 1914).
[2] Fueter, 1-6.   [3] *Ib.* 6-10.   [4] *Ib.* 19-26.

book of his history was published in 1416 and the last not till after his death. After Bruni there is much writing of his kind of history in Italy and elsewhere in Europe.

What matters for my present purpose in the new trend of history are the things that approximate it to other types of narrative literature. When there is close approximation there is the chance that some history may rise to the status of epic. Now the new type of history did share some of the qualities that I have described in my last section. It usually concerned a particular city and was little influenced by the Church, thus answering to the rising spirit of nationalism. It could also be used to glorify a princely patron. But above all it dramatised events and imitated the rhetorical methods of the Roman historians to do this. Wishing to dramatise, it chose to record only those events that seemed best to serve that purpose; and these were political crises, wars, and revolutions. It thus came about that the subjects of heroic narrative and of history tended to draw together, as they had done at certain times in classical antiquity. Petrarch indeed had insisted that poetry must contain a big element of fiction; and it was one of the commonplaces of Renaissance criticism to compare the poet and the historian and to represent the historian as tied to fact in a way the poet was not. But such comparisons did not alter the actual approximation of the two during the Renaissance. And though Lucan was sometimes censured as too historical a poet, he was admitted as one of the chief writers of heroic verse and he was always there as a possible model.

The exemplary character of history, illustrated by the quotation from Livy's preface, was yet another thing it shared with other forms of literature. But here we have to distinguish two kinds of example. There is first the kind of which I have been writing in this part of my book: the moral and religious kind. History according to this kind provides personal object-lessons of what to copy and what to avoid. It shows great men getting the reward of their virtuous efforts by achievement and fame; it shows bad or mistaken men punished by heaven or reaping the harvest of their own errors. But as time went on history became exemplary in a second way, more scientific and less moral. It was thought that the practical politician could, through studying the issue of affairs in the past, find out the truly repaying course in the present. Such a study was more like the study of the earlier performances of race-horses or the examination papers of the last ten years with an eye to policy in the coming race or examination than like the simpler moral exemplary theory. An eminent specimen of it is Machiavelli's commentary on Livy's Roman history. It is of course only the first kind of exemplary end that history and epic had in common in the Renaissance.

Though Livy was the dominant classical historian in the beginning, other forces came to be added. Bruni translated some of Plutarch's *Lives* into Latin, and from then on Plutarch was the great model for historical biography. One of the early humanists, Filelfo (1398-1481), translated Xenophon's *Cyropedia* into Latin,[1] thus making available to a wide audience a piece of writing perfectly suited to neo-classic taste. I have described this work above (pp. 57-9) and need only point to a few things in it that connect with the theme of the present section. The Renaissance mistook this highly idealised and falsified biography for true history, and for the kind of history which they valued: history moulded into a form that pleased as rhetoric and drama and that presented edifying moral examples. Here was something the remotest possible from medieval chronicling; and that it quite lacked the touches of real life and genuine humanity which could enliven the formlessness of that chronicling did not worry the Renaissance reader. The *Cyropedia* provided so much that was new and delightful to him that he was quite uncritical of what to us are its all too obvious deficiencies.

It must not be thought that the English historians generally followed the lead of the Italian humanists any more than the dramatists of the English Renaissance kept the neo-classic rules. Nevertheless, you cannot understand the indefinitenesses of the different forms of English Renaissance literature unless you are aware of the definitenesses that prevailed elsewhere and constantly threatened to prevail in England. The new methods of writing history were known and to some extent practised in England, but medieval methods continued and largely prevailed till the age of Clarendon. Since medieval methods continued so long, it is surprising how early England came in touch with humanist historians. In the reign of Henry VI an Italian, Titus Livius de Frulovisiis or Tito Livio da Forlì, also known as Frulovisi, came to England to join the household of the great English patron of the new learning, Humphrey, Duke of Gloucester. While attached to Humphrey he composed the two first neo-classic works to be written in England, the Latin comedies *Eugenius* and *Peregrinatio*.[2] But Humphrey also commissioned him to write the official biography of his brother, Henry V.[3] Such a commission, designed to bring credit on a royal or princely house, was typical of one side of Renaissance history. Tito Livio resembles Petrarch and differs from medieval chroniclers in the way he isolates a single king from the ceaseless flux of events as normally recorded. But Tito Livio had no influence on the writing of history in England in the fifteenth century. Even John Whethamstede, Abbot of St Albans, a classical

---

[1] See J. E. Sandys, *History of Classical Scholarship*, ii. 55.
[2] See R. Weiss, *Humanism in England during the Fifteenth Century*, 42.
[3] See the *First English Life of Henry V*, ed. C. L. Kingsford (Oxford 1911), and E. M. W. Tillyard, *Shakespeare's History Plays*, 27.

scholar and in touch with Italian humanism, wrote history in the old way. 'His conception of history under the form of encyclopedia, and biography as a collection of anecdotes, is typically medieval.'[1]

Another Italian was to make a greater impression on the writing of English history, but since he belongs to the sixteenth century I hold him over till the next section.

[1] Weiss, *op. cit.* 37.

CHAPTER IV

THE SIXTEENTH CENTURY IN ENGLAND BEFORE SPENSER

To these Heroycall Works of Homer *in Greeke and the heavenly verse of* Virgils Aeneidos *in Latin though wee have no English worke aunswerable in respect of the glorious ornaments of gallant handling, yet our auncient Chroniclers and reporters of our Countrey affayres come most neere them.*

(William Webbe, *Of English Poetry*)

WITH so strong a trend of thought towards politics England had no chance of producing an epic during its worst period of political unrest, the Wars of the Roses, nor in the early days of the Tudors before that house was firmly established. But the first two Tudors were strong kings and they increased their strength by dramatising their own position in English history. This drama, with the history of England immediately before them arranged in a striking outline, was propitious to epic composition. Part of this drama, though taken for granted in the sixteenth century, was forgotten and has only recently been rediscovered. It is probably still so little known as to make a short account of it advisable at this point.[1] Not too happy about his title to the crown, Henry VII fostered two historical notions that became great national themes. The first was that the union of the two houses of York and Lancaster through his marriage with the York heiress was the providential and happy ending of an organic piece of history. The Wars of the Roses could thus be seen not as mere unrelated evil but as evil arising from certain causes and evil out of which good was destined to spring. The second was that through his Welsh ancestry Henry VII had a claim to the throne unconnected either with his Lancastrian descent or his Yorkist marriage. Not only did he claim through his ancestor Owen Tudor, husband of Henry V's widow, direct descent from Cadwallader, last of the British kings, but he encouraged the old Welsh superstition that Arthur was not dead but would return again, with the suggestion that he and his heirs were Arthur incarnate. Had Henry VII's claim

---

[1] The rediscovery of the Tudor claims to revive the old line of British kings is due most to E. A. Greenlaw. See the first two chapters of his *Studies in Spenser's Historical Allegory* (Baltimore 1932). See also A. E. Parsons, *The Trojan Legend in England*, in *Modern Language Review*, 1929, pp. 253-64, and C. B. Millican, *Spenser and the Table Round* (Cambridge, Mass., 1932) 9-25. I have given an account of what I call the Tudor myth in my *Shakespeare's History Plays*, 29-32.

to be *Arthurus redivivus* been confined to himself as a temporary and perhaps a rather desperate expedient to strengthen his claim to the throne, it would have amounted to little. But it showed great persistence and had a strong hold on the imaginations of men. Henry sought to extend the fiction by naming his eldest son Arthur; but the death of this prince did not prevent the other Tudors making the Arthurian claim. In the ancient legends the return of Arthur was to bring back the age of gold; and the age of Elizabeth was sedulously called golden not in mere unrelated praise but to imply that the golden age, as prophesied, had indeed come in.

I can now speak of the second Italian historian who lived at the English court and was employed by an English king. In 1501 an Italian scholar, Polydorus Vergilius of Urbino, came to England as sub-collector of Peter's Pence for the Pope. Polydore was the friend of Erasmus and had a recommendation to Henry VII. Henry near the end of his life asked Polydore to write a complete English history, and Henry VIII encouraged him in this work. Polydore enjoyed various ecclesiastical offices in England and spent most of his life there. He reported his history nearly finished in 1517, but it was not printed till 1534. In 1555 he finally closed it with the events of 1538. Polydore's history[1] was written in Latin, was popular, and was soon translated into English as far as the death of Richard III. Most of the translation is still in manuscript, but portions, including the important period from Henry VI to Richard III, were published in the nineteenth century by the Camden Society. Polydore is not a chronicler but a historian writing in conscious imitation of Livy and Tacitus. When he came to the reign of Henry V he made a hero of him and wrote him up in the manner of Tacitus's *Agricola* and Plutarch's *Lives* and in full accord with the contemporary vogue of the example. Generally Polydore is critical in spirit in a manner alien to medieval chronicling. He tightens his story by tracing cause and effect. This is most evident in the stretch of history from Richard II to Henry VII, the stretch which the Tudors were most concerned to see in a shape convenient to themselves. Polydore saw it in a solemn moral light; it showed the justice of God punishing and working out the effects of a crime till prosperity was re-established in the Tudor monarchy. Polydore points to the ancestral curse brought on the English crown by the usurpation of Henry IV and the death of Richard II and sets alongside it the hope in the line of Tudor. Owen Tudor is called 'a gentleman of Wales, adorned with wonderful gifts of body and mind, who derived his pedigree from Cadwallader, the last king of Britons'. Henry VI, restored to his throne, on seeing the future Henry VII then aged nine, is made to say, 'This truly, this is he unto whom both

---

[1] For a longer account than I can give here see my *Shakespeare's History Plays*, 32-8. For a general study of Polydore Vergil see Denys Hay's book, Oxford 1952.

we and our adversaries must yield and give over our dominion.'
Henry VII's exile in Brittany as Earl of Richmond and the various
hazards he there experienced are told fully and with an emphasis that
suggests throughout the guidance of God. Polydore in fact put into
his history most of the elements of the Tudor political myth, making
this an available theme for contemporary writers.

If political conditions under Henry VII were still too uncertain to
allow of epic writing with a political subject, they changed under
Henry VIII with his strong rule and firm tenure of the throne. But
there was no poet of sufficient genius to use the opportunity. It would
seem therefore that in this book I ought to omit this period altogether.
Nevertheless, I believe that it will help the continuity of the process
I am trying to describe if I conjecture the kind of poem that would
have come into being had there been a poet or poets of epic stature
and proclivity.

Much of course would have depended on whether the poet lived
early or late in Henry VIII's reign. Naturally, medievalism was
stronger in the earlier part. But the options were there throughout.
For the conservative majority Lydgate was the living poetical model.
Hawes acknowledged him as his master, and his *Pastime of Pleasure*,
belonging to the first year of Henry VIII's reign, 1509, is entirely
medieval in method. It is an allegory, and its subject is the pilgrimage
of the soul of the active, not the contemplative, man. Hawes did not
have enough poetry in him to begin to approach epic quality; but if
a greater poet than Hawes had reached his prime early in the age
of Henry VIII it is possible that he would have chosen, as Hawes did,
the subject of the soul's pilgrimage.

But it is Wyatt and Surrey and not Hawes and Barclay whom we
incline to think typical of the age; and we may ask what kind of an
epic a greater poet than either of these two but with their background
would have written. It is of course possible that there existed no metre
at this time capable of epic dignity, but the very great do surprising
things in shaping their literary tools and we need not rule out the
possibility of epic on technical grounds. Anyhow, as far as substance
goes, the various changes from medieval habits had by this time gone
far enough in England for it to be clear that a greater Wyatt would
not have continued in the medieval mode or imitated Hawes's
Pastime of Pleasure. What then would he have done? Whether he
chose to write in Latin or in English, he would have chosen an active,
princely hero and have presented him in heroic action as a model to
the contemporary ruler. That he would have used Polydore Vergil
and the Tudor myth, as just described, for his theme I doubt, though
we must remember that Camoens in his *Lusiad* was to do something
analogous. The Wars of the Roses, however suited to the quasi-heroic
chronicle, were too recent and too painful for poetic treatment. They

might indeed have figured indirectly, through prophecy, like much of Spenser's historical matter, but they would not have been the main subject. We shall get a better notion of our hypothetical epic by considering not Polydore Vergil but two other prose works of the age of Wyatt and Surrey.

In 1529 Antonio de Guevara, Bishop of Guadix in Spain, published a book called *Marco Aurelio*. It is a kind of romance on the life of the Roman Emperor, Marcus Aurelius. Making use of certain matters of fact, it is not history but an exemplary tale. It uses fact and fiction exactly as Xenophon had used them in the *Cyropedia*, on which Guevara almost certainly modelled his work. Guevara had been at the court of Charles V and he fashioned Marcus Aurelius into the perfect ruler expressly as a pattern for his own master. Guevara's romance about Marcus Aurelius was sometimes called the *Golden Book*. In 1535 Lord Berners, translator of Froissart's Chronicles, published a translation of it under the title of the *Golden Book of Marcus Aurelius*.[1] Guevara expanded his book in a second edition, calling it *Libro del Emperador Marco Aurelio con el Relox de Principes*. In 1557 Sir Thomas North, who later translated Plutarch's *Lives*, published a translation of this second edition under the title of the *Dial of Princes*. Both translations were popular, going into several editions.

Sir Thomas Elyot, author of the *Governour*, was at the court of Charles V along with Guevara; and the two may well have talked of literary matters. Be that as it may, in 1530, the year after Guevara published his book, Elyot was accumulating the substance of a book called the *Image of Governance*, published in 1540.[2] The full title of Elyot's book is *The Image of Governance, compiled of the actes and sentences notable of the moste noble Emperour Alexander Severus*. With perfectly open falsehood Elyot says the book was 'late translated out of Greke into Englyshe'. Elyot did to Alexander Severus what Xenophon did to Cyrus and Guevara to Marcus Aurelius: on an exiguous ground of biographical fact he created an exemplary romance. Elyot's action in writing the *Image of Governance* is in exact keeping with the sentiments of the *Governour*. There he recommends that in their education young noblemen should go straight from their Greek study in Aesop to Homer and Virgil themselves. And his chief reason is that these children will thereby absorb political and military wisdom 'with the worthy commendation and laude of noble princis: where with the reders shall be so all inflamed, that they most fervently shall desire and coveite, by the imitation of their vertues, to acquire semblable

---

[1] Not to be confused with the *Meditations* of Marcus Aurelius. These are the Emperor's own devotional notes, written in Greek. In the Temple Classics they are misnamed the *Golden Book of Marcus Aurelius* on the cover.

[2] See H. H. S. Croft's edition of Elyot's *Governour* (London 1880) i. cxlvii.

glorie'. Elyot also recommends history and especially Xenophon's *Cyropedia* and Quintus Curtius's life of Alexander, for here are abundant examples of what to follow and what to shun.[1]

If a member of the circle that dominated letters in the second half of Henry VIII's reign had written an epic poem, I do not doubt that it would have been secular and political, not religious, and that it would have dealt in a highly moral manner with the heroic deeds of a great prince with the avowed aim of serving as an example to the king himself or to the ruling class in general. The morality would have been drawn largely from Xenophon, Plutarch, Cicero, and Seneca; but the three moral romances I have mentioned, the *Cyropedia* of Xenophon, Guevara's *Golden Book of Marcus Aurelius*, and Elyot's *Image of Governance*, might all have been influential as objectifications of the commonplace classical morality and have helped not only to supply matter to the epic but to frame it. There would doubtless have been a strong religious element, which would have to be more obvious if the hero chosen was a Christian. Next, the epic would have been tinged with the growing nationalism of the day; and this makes it probable that the language used would have been English. Leland, the antiquary, praised Wyatt for improving the English tongue from its early rudeness; Surrey in his elegy on Wyatt spoke of Wyatt's 'lively brain',

> *where that some work of fame*
> *Was daily wrought to turn to Britain's gain.*

The hypothetical epic would have performed the same patriotic function. In view of the Tudors' British ancestry the hero chosen would probably have come from the early mythology of Britain as created by Geoffrey of Monmouth. Wyatt himself may give a hint of this in his nostalgic and patriotic poem beginning 'Tagus, fare well', written when he was returning from his diplomatic post in Spain. There he calls London, for which he is bound, 'the town which Brutus sought by drems'. Brutus, the leader of the mythical Trojans who colonised Britain, might well have been the poem's exemplary hero.

I do not wish these conjectures to be taken at all literally; but they may serve to show the sort of shape an English epic of the years 1530 to 1550 might have taken.

When it comes to achievement in the reign of Henry VIII the only work with the slightest epic tinge is historical. Edward Hall,[2] the historian, was writing at the same time as Wyatt and Surrey and died in 1547. It is unfortunate that his version of English history from Richard II to Henry VIII is commonly known as Hall's *Chronicle*.

---

[1] Everyman Edition (London 1907) 36-7 and 44-5.
[2] For a fuller treatment see my *Shakespeare's History Plays*, 40-50.

Nothing could be more misleading, for Hall's history is less like a chronicle than anything that went before in England, and the word *chronicle* does not occur in his long and explicit title. Hall called his work *The Union of the two noble and illustre Families of Lancaster and York*; and what he did was not to chronicle events but to put in a solemn and dramatic form that stretch of English history which Polydore had made rather more significant than the rest: the stretch that had led from the prosperity of Edward III through the Wars of the Roses back to prosperity under the Tudors. True to the new proclivity to motivate history, Hall makes one event spring out of another. Anxious to see history not as a shapeless flux but as a pattern, he matches the perfection of Henry V by the monstrosity of Richard III. Inevitably there is a good deal of the sheer recording of events, but Hall is ever the artist seeking to dramatise them and to see them as a pattern. That pattern is strictly the one that the Tudors sought to impose, what I have called the Tudor drama or myth. Hall consistently supported Henry VIII and was a strong Protestant. And thus he represented the opinions of many men. He did the same in seeing in history a great repertory of moral examples, for imitation and avoidance, and in advancing the doctrine that the sins of a first generation are apt to be punished in the third. He was a nationalist, according to the dominant trend of his age.

In writing of Herodotus and Xenophon I pleaded that history could indeed approximate to epic. Hall is like Herodotus in having a large general theme and in treating it dramatically. His style, though inflated by the use of synonyms and equivalent phrases common in this age ('as the course of water astricted and letted will flow and burst out in continuance of time'), has plenty of colour and energy. He is positive, knowing what he thinks and feels; and such certainty on the political side would in a greater man of letters have been a powerful means to the epic effect. But Hall's span of human nature is much less than that of Herodotus, as is the range of his style. He may be a little way on the epic road, and that is something, but he is far from arriving. His chief epic interest is prophetic. One of the main manifestations of the epic spirit in the age of Elizabeth was Shakespeare's History Plays. Hall's history is right behind them. It is from Hall that Shakespeare got the happy picture of Edward III's seven sons, the high point of prosperity from which there was so steep a decline, and the picture at the battle of Towton of son fighting father, as well as the general shape of history from Richard II to Henry VII. And if, as I believe, Shakespeare read Hall at a very early age, Hall must have the credit of being a formative influence of our greatest poet.

CHAPTER V

ITALY: EARLY SIXTEENTH CENTURY

1. INTRODUCTORY

AS, having dealt with Malory and Caxton, I had to go back in time to Petrarch and Boccaccio, so now I have to go back to Italian authors who antedate my last topic, the later years of Henry VIII. The influence of those authors, too, was felt in England only after a lapse of many years.

There is an admirable account in the first pages of W. L. Renwick's *Edmund Spenser*[1] of the literary situation in Italy round the turn of the fifteenth and sixteenth centuries. Following the lead of Petrarch and Boccaccio in their defection from the vernacular, the fifteenth century was the century of the Latinists, the imitators. That is, in literature, for the painters dealt with the Classics in the right way, putting them to their own uses. There had indeed been some distinguished writing in Italian. For instance, Politian had written social verse in Italian as well as translated five books of the *Iliad* into Latin; and Boiardo, as well as his romance, wrote a *canzoniere* in Italian following the lead of Petrarch.[2] But still the correct thing was to imitate the ancients in Latin. At the end of the fifteenth century came a change of temper:

> To a scholar of the time of Petrarch it was a high endeavour to attempt the re-creation of the Virgilian epic and the Ciceronian dialogue; he could feel the inspiration of belonging to the mighty company of the ancients. By the sixteenth century the thing had been done about as well as might be.[3]

Such a realisation could only serve to moderate enthusiasm for Latin pastiche, and there was a swing over in favour of the vernacular. But the belief in imitation was still strong, and one joint result of these two impulses was that Petrarch's Italian lyrics and Boccaccio's Italian prose narrative were revived and copied. Here were native classics, and by copying them you satisfied at once the longing to write in the vernacular and the critical obligation to imitate. But these matters do

---

[1] London 1925.
[2] See D. Pettoello, *An Outline of Italian Civilization* (London 1932) 233. Pettoello thinks that there was more original poetry in the fifteenth century in Italy than is usually supposed.
[3] Renwick, *op. cit.* 11.

not concern this book; and the relevant event here is that about the turn of the century Ariosto decided against the advice of Bembo to forsake Latin, in which he had first excelled, as the language for his ambitious poem. It is a famous decision, partly through Milton's reference to it in the autobiographical passage in *Reason of Church Government*. Milton there says that a main motive of his aiming at a great poem was the honour and instruction of his country:

> For which cause, and not only for that I knew it would be hard to arrive at the second rank among the Latines, I apply'd my selfe to that resolution which *Ariosto* follow'd against the perswasions of *Bembo*, to fix all the industry and art I could unite to the adorning of my native tongue.

The actual incident Milton refers to is told in Giovanni Battista Pigna's life of Ariosto.[1] Bembo, the eminent classical scholar and believer in the virtue of copying the ancients, was at Ferrara in the years 1498-1500. Ariosto also was there at this time and was making his plans for a great work. Part of his plans was to write in Italian, and Pigna then says:

> Da questa impresa volendo il Bembo levarlo, con dirgli che egli piu atto era allo scrivere Latino che al Volgare; e che maggiore in quello che in questo si scoprirebbe; dissagli all' incontro l'Ariosto che piu tosto volea essere uno de primi tra scrittori Thoscani, che appena il secondo tra Latini: soggiungendogli che ben egli sentiva à che piu il suo genio il piegasse.[2]

Ariosto's decision was of capital importance in the history of narrative verse. His *Orlando Furioso* was overwhelmingly popular, and though men continued to write and to enjoy narrative verse in Latin, the main channel of creative energy was thereafter the vernacular.

By the time Ariosto began his great poem, that is about 1503, France had invaded Italy, and the patriotic motives that had animated Petrarch and Boccaccio had become irrelevant there. But outside Italy the victory of the vernacular in the country that led the fashion in literary taste could unite its influence with the desire to glorify your country by noble or correct literary works. I noted such a union in writing of Wyatt: in France it was to be a dominant matter in the work of the Pléiade. But this is a principle that goes beyond my subject, and I must revert to Ariosto for something central to the

---

[1] Pigna's life was published in his *I Romanzi* (Vinegia 1554), and the incident in question is told pp. 74-5 of this book.
[2] 'When Bembo wanted to deflect him from this plan by telling him that he was better suited to write in Latin than in the vulgar tongue and that he would show himself greater in the former than in the latter, Arisoto retorted by saying that he would rather be one of the first among the Tuscan writers than barely in the second class among the Latins, adding that he was clear in his mind whither his own genius inclined him.'

history of the English epic: the form into which he cast his narrative. But to speak of this I must speak also of Ariosto in general.

2. BOIARDO AND ARIOSTO

Peravventura chi l'Innamorato *e* 'l Furioso *come un solo poema consideasse gli potria parere la sua lunghezza soverchia, anzi che nò, e non atta ad essere contenuta in una semplice memoria.* (Tasso)

Ariosto . . . *the artfull woofe of his ingenious though unmeaning fables.* (Rynolds, *Mythomystes*)

Whatever the merits of Boiardo's *Orlando Innamorato* and Ariosto's *Orlando Furioso*, whether or not they come within the epic category, they were a novelty in narrative verse, they were very popular, and they ended by altering the course of the English epic. Ariosto's poem supplanted Boiardo's in popularity; but it was also a continuation of it, and the two should be considered together. Both poets were attached to the court of Ferrara where society was quasi-feudal and in this different from the urban middle-class society of Florence, hitherto the dominant literary centre. At the court of Ferrara traditional ideas of chivalry either survived or were affected; and here it was possible, even natural, to continue the form of the French romance.

Boiardo himself was a noble and bred to the practices of chivalry. He was also a man of the Renaissance who wrote Latin poems and translated Herodotus and Xenophon. Thus in rehandling medieval material he was bound to fashion it afresh. For the theme of his great narrative poem he chose the matter of France, the Charlemagne cycle: the war between Christian and infidel and the love of the great hero Orlando (or Roland) for Angelica. In some ways his poem is still medieval. He continues the convention of imploring the barons in the hall, where the poet is supposed to be reciting, to hear him in silence. The gorgeousness of some of the scenes, for instance Charlemagne's tournament in i. 2. 35 ff., recalls medieval rather than later splendour and ceremony. Further, Boiardo does up to a point believe in the chivalric world he describes. Strangely enough he does in some things make us think of his contemporary, Malory. Both have some faith in that chivalric world which was passing; the chief characters in their books, Launcelot and Orlando, are perfect types of chivalry but with the one defect of amorousness; both authors have a keen eye to character. But there the likeness ends. Malory embodies the Grail legends and is religious in a deeper way than Boiardo could be. And the theme of *Timor mortis conturbat me*, so powerful in fifteenth-century England, is little evident in Italian Ferrara. In compensation Boiardo is highly civilised. He had of course Boccaccio's *Teseida* to go back to for the sophisticated use of romantic material and he profited by this example. But the kind of control Boiardo exercises springs from a steadier and more considered study of the Classics than Boccaccio's. He keeps a tight hold over motivation. In the first canto Malagise could have killed the sleeping Angelica and prevented all the trouble she subsequently caused, but he yielded to lust. Rinaldo's unthinking impetuosity is contrasted with Orlando's self-consciousness. The chivalric scenes are untouched by the gloom that was ever ready to cloud them in the North; they have, J. A. Symonds[1] said, the light and joy of the pictures of Gozzoli and Piero di Cosimo. Above all, Boiardo aimed at fashioning a single poem out of the abundance of the old romances. How well he would have succeeded in this aim we cannot know, for he died in 1494, having finished only a fragment of his poem.

Ariosto chose to continue both the fable and the idiom of Boiardo. But events as well as the inevitable difference of character prevented any very close continuation. In the words of Symonds,

> When Ariosto repieced the broken thread, the spirit of the times was changed. Servitude, adulation, irony, and the meridian splendour of Renaissance art had succeeded to independence, frankness, enthusiasm and the poetry of natural enjoyment.

Not that Boiardo's theme did not suit Ariosto. He did not believe in chivalry, but he saw the possibilities in a chivalric subject. Here was hallowed material, but by this time vulnerable enough to enable a man to stand away from it and treat it in the comic spirit. Ariosto in fact had to hand the same sort of material as Euripides had in the legends of the Greek gods and heroes, or Lemaître in the Bible and the Classics. Gifted with rare vitality and inventiveness, he chose to multiply and complicate his themes. A greater artist in language than Boiardo and the genuine mouthpiece of his age, he supplanted his master in the hearts of his compatriots.

Whether or not Ariosto's *Orlando Furioso* is a true epic will never cease to be disputed. And if by epic you simply mean a long and very fine narrative poem, you cannot exclude it. On my own definition I think it falls outside the category, as I found *Troilus and Criseyde* and *Don Quixote* to do. It has immense variety and covers many sides of human nature. But it lacks the tragic element; and above all the kind of will-power it displays is consecutive and cumulative rather than organic. Ariosto had energy and staying power. He was a tireless improver of what he had written. But he settled one thing at a time, even if he did return and improve later. Had he worked otherwise, had he adopted a higher standard of interlocking, had he refused to

---

[1] *Italian Literature* (London 1881) i. 462-3.

fix the form of any part of his poem till he had reached the very end, he could never have run to so prodigious a length. Working as he did, he achieved something that both astonished and delighted but that was different from the achievement of Virgil, or Dante, or Milton. If we want kindred achievement we shall find it in two works which the *Orlando Furioso* actually helped to inspire, *Don Quixote* and Byron's *Don Juan*. 'The *Orlando Furioso* has neither the primitive and robust spirit of the *Chanson de Roland*, nor the severe depth of the *Divine Comedy*; it is no real epic like the *Iliad*, it has not the national background of the *Aeneid*, nor the symbolic pageantry of the *Faerie Queene*'[1]: but it gave Ariosto's contemporaries exactly what they wanted. They did not want unadulterated classical imitation, but they did want something that embodied the new critical spirit which had grown up with the new awareness of the Classics. Ariosto, continuing in his mother-tongue the old medieval legends chosen by Boiardo, gave them a new turn by telling them in a manner more elegantly critical than Boiardo's and in an intonation that commanded every shade of variety from sober earnest to wild burlesque. Renwick has written well of the great innovation wrought by Boiardo first, and then to a greater degree by Ariosto:

> True medieval romance died a natural death with the feudal society whose ideals and interests it expressed, but while Malory was writing the last romance in England, Boiardo was writing the first in Italy, and he and Ariosto gave it a new lease of life amid new conditions, just as Petrarch did to the Provençal love-song. While in the North Romance was being degraded in chapbooks and street ballads, they rescued it from the ballad-mongers and raised it to a new status. To Ariosto it was a new form, neither constrained by its old social function nor contaminated by the memory of old conflicts; to the North it was an old-fashioned and well-worn thing, to him fresh and full of opportunities for an enterprising artist.[2]

It matters little for my present purpose whether or not the *Orlando Furioso* was a true epic; what does matter is that its first publication in 1516 was an event of capital importance in the history of every kind of narrative verse in western Europe. Here was something new, immensely popular, and impossible for the most rigid classicist to ignore.[3]

So far I have spoken of Ariosto's innovations in using the vernacular for the most ambitious kind of poem, the long narrative, and giving a new turn to the material of medieval France. But he made others. First, he quite ignored the severe moral tone and the doctrine of the

---

[1] D. Pettoello, *op. cit.* 291.

[2] Renwick, *op. cit.* 21.

[3] Criticism of Boiardo and Ariosto I have found helpful is in J. A. Symonds, *Italian Literature*, i. and ii., and C. S. Lewis, *The Allegory of Love*.

'example' that had characterised the most influential writings of Petrarch and Boccaccio and their successors. Ariosto's characters are people and not object-lessons, whatever later writers in the Renaissance said about them. And secondly Ariosto broke with the simple or severe plotting of the *Teseida* and of *Africa* and substituted a great ramification of stories. Having been disciplined in the Classics and having gained his first poetic fame through his classical verse, he was in a strong position to meet the classical purists, as a modern artist who produces abstract work can defend himself best if he can point to a preliminary discipline in a more realistic style. Further, Ariosto had an exceptionally clear head and was perfectly at home in his own ramifications. He could not be accused of mere medieval rambling. Thus he was able to establish the multiple plot, the method of having several stories going at the same time, as an approved method in serious narrative verse. And this is his principal importance for the history of the English epic. He conditioned the form of one of the great English narratives, the *Faerie Queene*. Without Ariosto Spenser would have written a totally different poem.

3. VIDA

Loud o're the rest Cremona's *Trump doth sound.* (Milton)

In spite of the popularity of the *Orlando Furioso*, neither the theory nor the practice of the strict classical epic was abolished. The propriety of Ariosto's poem was strongly assailed, and, though it was generally granted that his form of the narrative was to be allowed as a second option, the pressure of critical opinion was on the side of a classical strictness. The result was that the next vernacular narratives of the first order in the Latin countries, the *Lusiad* of Camoens and the *Jerusalem Delivered* of Tasso, were cast in strict Virgilian form. And not only that: the example of the Latin epic set by Petrarch in his *Africa* continued to be followed, and with greater success. There was a parallel activity in the Latin drama; and Vida and Buchanan were considered poets of the first rank in their own age. Buchanan did not write an epic, but the *Christiad* of Vida, influential throughout Europe, must figure in any book on the subject.

Marco Girolamo Vida (1480-1546) was born at Cremona: a fact that explains the reference of the line that heads this chapter. He was a cleric and ultimately a bishop. In 1513 Pope Leo X ordered him to write a poem on the life of Christ. Believing, as he later told the world in his *Art of Poetry*, that Virgil was the supreme poet and that to imitate Virgil was the highest poetic task, he put the story of the Gospels into the metre of the Latin hexameter and into the strictest classical form. The action begins near the end of Christ's ministry. The story of creation is told through the scenes that adorned the temple in Jerusalem. After the capture of Jesus in Holy Week, Joseph, husband of Mary, and John visit Pilate and talk with him. Joseph uses the occasion to narrate the events leading to the Nativity and some of Christ's subsequent history. John then becomes the speaker. He proceeds to talk theology to Pilate, expounding the doctrine of the Trinity and the fall of man, and then takes up the story of Christ's life where Joseph left it. Past events having been narrated up to where the principal action began, this action is resumed; and the rest of the poem concerns events from Judas's suicide to Pentecost. Vida supplemented the canonical gospels with the *Gospel of Nicodemus* and included the Harrowing of Hell with Christ leading away with him Adam and the prophets.

And it is not only the verse and the plotting that are in the rigid classical convention. Christ is called *pulcherrimus heros*; and the entry into Jerusalem on Palm Sunday with the boys and girls skipping in front resembles a Bacchic procession in the classical style or a picture by Alma-Tadema. The Devils are used as supernatural machinery, precisely like the Gods in Homer and Virgil: an act of strict propriety because in orthodox doctrine they were identified. Mary, like Catullus's bride, is the loveliest of girls, desired by many. When Satan thinks that Pilate may release Jesus he sends two allegorical figures, Fear and Sloth, to prevent him. And these are Virgilian, not medieval, personifications.

Though the *Christiad* contains nothing poetically equal to the best things in Petrarch's *Africa*, it is far more readable as verse. It is an efficient piece of work carried through with persistent and scrupulous care. It represents a considerable and praiseworthy effort of the will. And it gains weight in embodying a great store of orthodoxy, where *Africa* sought to embody an uncertain personal aspiration. But when the best has been said, Vida fails to get anywhere near the epic effect, because, in spite of the superimposed unity of the classical epic form, he composed his episodes piecemeal. They are strung together and are never fused. Vida's true talent was descriptive; and we get the most out of him if we remember that he was the contemporary of the great painters of the high Renaissance in Italy. It was a correct instinct that prompted Pope, in describing that epoch, to say:

> With sweeter notes each rising Temple rung;
> A Raphael painted, and a Vida sung.

Here is a passage which illustrates Vida's pictorial power. It comes from the second book and is a minstrel's account of the Israelites crossing the Red Sea.

Nempe Pharetoniis cantu deducit ab oris
Isacidum genus, arrepta maris aequora virga
Ut profugum dux findat, aquasque impune per altas
Ut sine navigiis ierint pelagique profunda
Sicco calcarint pede. Namque induruit humor
Aridus, et liquidas late est via secta per undas.
A tergo toto ex Aegypto curribus hostes
Quadrijugis vecti instabant fulgentibus armis.
Jamque pios canit emenso pelago alta tenere
Littora, littoreisque metu se condere sylvis.
Nulla mora est: iterum telo tellure recussa
Divino redeunt in se maria ecce refusa,
Quae media ingenti dirimebat semita tractu.
Inde hostes ruere et salsis in fluctibus arma,
Armaque quadrupedesque et corpora mersa virorum
Aspiceres magis atque magis subsidere in undis.[1]

There is considerable pictorial skill in the presentation of the Israelites, still terrified, hiding in the woods that bordered the sea.

What concerns me most was that Vida was really read, and over a
wide area. And his vogue continued through the eighteenth century,
when the *Christiad* was twice translated. (Among the subscribers to
J. Cranwell's Latin text with his verse translation, published in 1768,
there is 'William Cowper, Esq.') Vida was in fact read by the main
English poets for some two hundred and fifty years. And this vogue
does something to explain why Milton at one time toyed with the
idea of writing his epic in Latin.

Some ten years after the *Christiad* Vida wrote his *Ars Poetica*, second
in the succession from Horace's *Ars Poetica*, through Boileau's *Art
Poétique* to Pope's *Essay in Criticism*. Pope hailed this poem along with
the *Christiad* as immortal; and it is a commonplace of the history of
criticism that Vida expressed there in classic form the rigorous
Renaissance doctrine of the need for serious poets to compose in
strict imitation of the ancients, among whom Virgil was supreme.
What matters here is that in the 1520's there should be no sign of the

---

[1] Ed. Edward Owen, Oxford, 1725, ii. 610-25. 'The minstrel described in his song
the retreat of the Israelites from the coast of Egypt; how seizing his wand the
fugitives' leader divided the levels of the sea, how they went safe through the deep
waters without shipping and trod the ocean floor with dry foot. For the barren
moisture hardened, and a way was cut deep through the transparent waves. Behind
them the enemy, gathered from all Egypt, borne in four-horsed chariots, pressed on
them in shining arms. And now the minstrel sings that the faithful have crossed the
sea and attain the shore; in their terror they hide in the woods near the shore.
Immediately the earth heaves at the bidding of the divine instrument; and behold,
the seas, which the path was even now dividing with a huge furrow, have poured
back. Then could you see the foe and their arms rolled in the salt flood; arms and
beasts and the drowned bodies of men overwhelmed ever more and more by the
waves.'

epic as a literary form in this severely classicising piece of criticism. All Vida says is that after divine poetry there is none superior to the kind that records the deeds of heroes and that the priestess at Delphi gave her oracular answers in the heroic metre, that is the hexameter.[1] Later, he puts Homer at the head of the Greek poets. The pre-Virgilian poets in Rome were rude, but Virgil is prince not only of Latin but of all poets:

> *Unus hic ingenio praestanti gentis Achivae*
> *Divinos vates longe superavit, et arte,*
> *Aureus, immortale sonans; stupet ipsa pavetque*
> *Quamvis ingentem miretur Graecia Homerum.*[2]

The greatness of Virgil is a far more important matter than any dignity the epic form might have in itself. As a critic, therefore, Vida looks back to Petrarch rather than forward to the developed neo-classicists. But his *Ars Poetica* leads naturally to my next section and the beginning of the orthodox theory of the epic poem.

4. THE CRITICS

Nearly all, if not all, of the rules that ultimately formed the neo-classic canon of correctness in criticism, a canon that had its head-quarters in France after the foundation of the French Academy in 1637, can be found stated or implied in the Italian critics of the Renaissance. And this generalisation holds good for the epic. But there was no single Italian academy to codify in the French manner; and in Italy there were plenty of options and alternatives. Because of these options Italian practice and theory could genuinely promote epic practice in unmethodical Elizabethan England. English practice is anything but tidy; and I shall give a truer picture of its Italianate background if I select, without any rigid order, some of the Italian critics' most relevant doings or statements.

What differentiated the criticism of the mature Italian Renaissance from its antecedent was the irruption of Aristotle's *Poetics* into the critical consciousness of the age. This work had been virtually un-known during the Middle Ages and early Renaissance. Its vogue began when it was translated into Latin in 1498 and was included in the Aldine edition of the Greek orators in 1508. These publications 'had considerable influence on dramatic literature, but scarcely any immediate influence on literary criticism'.[3] Another Latin translation

---

[1] i. 33-8.

[2] i. 170-3. 'Virgil alone by his outstanding genius and artistry far surpassed the divine poets of the Greek race, golden, uttering immortal sounds; Greece herself is amazed and terrified, although she admires gigantic Homer.'

[3] J. E. Spingarn, *A History of Literary Criticism in the Renaissance* (sixth impression, New York 1924) 17.

appeared in 1536, and the first Italian translation in 1549. In 1548 Robertelli produced the first critical edition with a Latin translation and a commentary. And it was about this time that the influence of the *Poetics* on Renaissance criticism really made itself felt.

The principal change that Aristotle's *Poetics* caused in the history of the epic was to shift the emphasis from the practitioners to the kind. Vida had thought of the epic or heroic poem in terms of certain writers, the greatest of whom was Virgil. If you wrote a heroic poem yourself you copied Virgil. But Aristotle wrote of epopoeia, tragedy, and comedy as literary forms with their own distinguishing natures. It is true that he argued inductively and reached the form through the example; and it is probable that if he had been shown new examples he would have modified his description of the forms to suit them. But he had the philosopher's preference for the fixed general principle covering all the relevant details. Though he reached his fixed position inductively, he preferred to think principally of the proper abstract form of the epic and next of this or that epic poem. I doubt if you can credit any one Italian critic with introducing this Aristotelian way of thinking; but certainly it began in Italy around the middle of the sixteenth century. Without saying anything or much about the epic form, critics then begin to assume that there is such a thing. Later they try to be precise about the form and to go far beyond Aristotle in codifying its rules. Along with this concern about the details of the epic form grows a reverence for the abstracted form itself, apart from its manifestations. Not that the authority of the *Iliad* and the *Aeneid* diminished, but this authority consisted not only in their being great poems but in their being the most nearly perfect embodiments of the abstract idea. This last position belongs to the neo-classic age.

I go on now to a few samples of the Italian criticism belonging to the years when Aristotle first made himself felt. In this criticism there is a great deal of repetition and some of it consists in summaries or paraphrase or expansion of Aristotle himself. Here I try to point to a few passages that have a real bearing on epic practice or on the history of epic theory.

Giovan Giorgio Trissino (1478-1550) was both poet and critic. He is a pivotal figure. He wrote a *Poetica* in six books, publishing the first four in 1529 and writing the last two between 1548 and his death in 1550. In the interval between 1529 and 1548 he was engaged on an epic in Italian blank verse called *La Italia Liberata da Gotti*. This epic spends twenty-seven books on the conquest of Italy by Justinian up to the capture of Ravenna. Its importance belongs to the history of criticism rather than that of literature. Poetically it did not succeed, but it is what W. P. Ker, as I think wrongly, called Boccaccio's *Teseida*, the first poem in a vernacular to attempt to embody correctly

the epic form of classical antiquity. It was also an unsuccessful reply
to the romance forms of Boiardo's and Ariosto's poems, as Tasso's
Jerusalem Delivered was to be the successful one. Trissino appears indeed
to be jealous of Ariosto. He rarely mentions him in his criticism and
then usually to find fault; and in his constant praise of the earlier
Italian poets he gives the impression of wishing to divert interest from
Ariosto to the masterpieces of Dante and Petrarch. Tasso was probably thinking of Trissino's ambitions and jealousy when he contrasted the fates of the *Orlando Furioso* and the *Italia Liberata*: the first
read and re-read by people of all ages and both sexes, known by men
of different tongues, giving pleasure to all, praised by all, never
staling in its reputation; the other, though copied religiously from
Homer and faithful to the rules of Aristotle, mentioned by few, read
by scarcely any, valued by none, silent in the theatre of the world,
to be found buried in the libraries and in the book-shelves of one or
two of the learned.

Tasso was right to say that Trissino went to both Homer and
Aristotle, thereby indicating his pivotal position. The first four books
of Trissino's *Poetica*, published before he began his epic, are
linguistic and prosodic and rhetorical. They owe much to Dante's
De Vulgari Eloquio and are largely reminiscent of medieval rhetoric. At the end of the fourth book Trissino gives notice that he
intends to write on tragedy, comedy, and epic. But he did not do so,
apparently, for years, turning his attention to writing poetry. Nevertheless, it is probable that the substance of his later remarks on the
epic was present in his mind while he was writing his *Italia Liberata*
and that it was somewhere about the time he published the first
books of the *Poetica* (1529) that he began to take serious notice of
Aristotle. I conjecture that he wrote his epic partly on the principles
of his contemporary Vida, whose *Art of Poetry* was published in 1527,
and partly by the rules of Aristotle's *Poetics*. True, for Vida's imitation
of Virgil he substitutes that of Homer, Homer being the origin and
fountain of all poetry.[1] But in one way he looks on his epic (on which
he spent twenty years and for which he had the most ambitious hopes,
dedicating it to the Emperor Charles V himself) as the re-creation,
through imitation, of the best that antiquity could produce. But, in
observing the rules of Aristotle, he must have had some inkling of the
idea of the epic as a form, even though his remarks on the epic in the
sixth book of his *Poetica* are on this or that detail. He thus looks both
back to Vida and forward to the new Italian criticism.

The most interesting part of Trissino's remarks on the epic is not
the sixth book of his *Poetica*, where he treats it at some length, but

---

[1] 'Si può dire che Omero sia stato il principio e quasi il fonte di tutta la Poesia',
and he adds that no one has touched Homer since his day. (*Opere*, Verona 1729,
ii. 93.)

the short introduction to his *Italia Liberata*,[1] addressed to Charles V. This tells us shortly and vividly the kind of thing the serious epic tried to be at that time. Heroic verse aims at preserving for posterity the record of heroic deeds. The great deeds of Justinian have not been celebrated, and Trissino will attempt to do so. But he will conform to the laws of poetry and to Homer's example and confine his poem to *one* of Justinian's great actions. He will also follow the precepts Aristotle advances for tragedy, for these apply to the epic also. The peculiar epic quality is largeness, of which Homer, though his action was simple, was absolute master, and Trissino has tried to attain it. He claims that his poem is the first in Italian to be modelled on Homer. He has adorned it 'di varie digressioni e di altre ingegnose et allegoriche ficzioni'. Charles V is a second Justinian in his great deeds. Trissino hopes that his poem will encourage other poets to celebrate those deeds as they deserve. All these sentiments would have found the approval of their age. Trissino had all the ingredients of a great epic writer of the Renaissance except poetical genius.

One or two of the observations in his *Poetica* deserve mention as early if not the first statements of important commonplaces. The marvellous is of peculiar importance in the epic. Though it should be found in tragedy too, it matters more in the inferior vividness of the non-dramatic form.[2] Trissino repeats Aristotle's principle that unity in a work of art must not consist merely in events happening to a single person; and he cites as offending against Aristotle's rules the *Achilleis* of Statius, the *Filocolo* of Boccaccio, and *Amadis of Gaul*. These two last, he adds, are poems though not in verse. Here is an early statement of a common Renaissance doctrine that you could have an epic in prose. Finally, Trissino is like Milton in making the unpopular plea that the continuity of blank verse suits the epic better than the interruption of rhyme. He attacks the stanza form that was used for romances from Boccaccio to Ariosto.

Trissino is not a great critic any more than a great poet, but he is important as an early neo-Aristotelian and as an uncompromising believer in using the vernacular for a close imitation of the Classics. In spite of Ariosto's success and his own failure, the majority of future successes in the epic were through the form he favoured.

Trissino had managed almost to ignore Boiardo and Ariosto in spite of their great popularity. Some of the livest Italian criticism concerns their status as poets: was the loose form they chose justified in view of Aristotle's rules? And this criticism is not only alive but illustrates the happy diversity of Italian critical ideas before the rigidities of the neo-classic age: a diversity which can make us under-

[1] This can be found either in the original edition of the poem, Rome 1547, or in the first volume of Trissino's works 1729.
[2] *Opere*, ii. 115.

stand that Spenser's *Faerie Queene* and Daniel's *Civil Wars* had as good warrant in certain critical quarters as Tasso's *Jerusalem* itself. It was shortly after Trissino's death, in 1554, that one of the most intelligent and flexible Italian critics, Cinthio, published an essay on the above topic, entitled *Discorso intorno al comporre de i Romanzi*. Giambattista Giraldi Cinthio (1504-73), known sometimes as Cinthio, sometimes as Giraldi-Cinthio, was also author of the *Hecatomithi*, to which the plots of Shakespeare's *Measure for Measure* and *Othello* ultimately go back, and, as himself a reteller of old tales, he was sympathetic to Boiardo and Ariosto. Unlike Trissino he recognised that the two *Orlando's* had been justified by their success and he knew that they had to be fitted in. This justification, which is the main aim of *I Romanzi*, is the occasion of some interesting observations on the epic generally.

First, Cinthio takes it quite for granted that the epic is a form with certain features proper to it. He follows Aristotle in thinking the fable of prime importance, but he maintains that Aristotle's *Poetics* does not cover all the legitimate types of it. Cinthio believes that though Aristotle's type of fable confined to a single action is a perfectly good type, there is another and equally legitimate type with more than one main action. And this was the type practised by Boiardo and Ariosto. There is a third type, the account of all the actions of a single man. Aristotle mentions this but condemns it because the unity of the hero does not constitute the organic unity of the poem. Cinthio thinks that all three types of epic are legitimate and he enunciates a liberal principle that does him the greatest credit and marks him off from the more doctrinaire trend of the century. He wrote,

> Le leggi date da Aristotele non si stendeno senon alle Poesie che sono di una sola attione; e tutte le compositioni Poetiche che contengono fatti di Heroi non sono chiuse tra i termini c'ha messo Aristotele a Poeti che scrivono Poema di una sola attione.[1]

Aristotle is valid as far as he goes, but he does not go everywhere, and in particular he does not go as far as the *Orlando's* of Boiardo and Ariosto. And what Cinthio claims for these two holds good for Spenser also.

Such is Cinthio's main thesis. In his detailed comment on the epic whose unity is that of the hero he illustrates his principle of legitimate diversity with special force and in a way that illustrates admirably the wide range of the Renaissance epic. It is indeed true that Aristotle condemned this kind of epic, but subsequent writers showed that the poem that described a great man's life from cradle to grave could be

---

[1] *Discorso intorno al comporre de i Romanzi* (Vinegia 1554) 22. 'The laws given by Aristotle extend only to poems with a single action; and not all poems containing the deeds of heroes are contained within the limits which Aristotle has set to poets who write poems with a single action.'

successful. These were Xenophon in his life of Cyrus, Statius in his *Achilleis* and Silius Italicus in his account of the life of Hannibal in his *Punica*. There are, too, the lives of Themistocles, Coriolanus, Romulus, and Theseus which we read and enjoy in the prose of Plutarch: is it less profitable to read them in the proper ornaments of verse? There is nothing wrong in the mere fact of beginning a hero's life with the cradle:

> If in the cradle the hero gives sign of his greatness, from the cradle should begin the events of his life. And if someone should tell me that Virgil did not treat Aeneas thus nor Homer Achilles in the *Iliad* and Ulysses in the *Odyssey*, I can reply with propriety that both these poets aimed at not poems of one sole action and to the poem that follows the style and form of history.[1]

Cinthio goes on to disagree with Aristotle concerning the possibility of putting all the events of a man's life into a single poem. Aristotle said this could not be done; but Cinthio insists that there are ways of abbreviating. You can select the important things for detailed treatment and dispose quickly of the less important. How much a poet can succeed in crowding into a poem Ovid demonstrates in his *Metamorphoses*, where he begins with creation itself and treats 'con maravigliosa catena tanta varietà di cose'.

The whole passage renders admirably the Renaissance vitality and love of variety and the fluid and accommodating notions men had of the epic before the neo-classic age. Ariosto's immense romance, Xenophon's *Cyropedia*, Silius Italicus's unreadable, correctly classical pastiche, qualify along with the *Iliad* and the *Aeneid*, while Plutarch's *Lives* are near doing so. Cinthio ends his section by saying that you cannot lay down a single rule. But the poet should first decide in which of the three epic varieties he intends to write. If he chooses the variety with the single action, he should follow ancient example and Aristotle's rules. Only—and he must have had Trissino's recent failure in mind—there is so far no good Italian poem on these lines.

Cinthio is an inspiring critic with his eye genuinely on literary creation; and his temper is much like that of the Elizabethan age in England.

A second critic who defended the verse romances is Giovanni Battista Pigna, one of the early biographers of Ariosto. His *I Romanzi* was published in the same year as Cinthio's essay on the romances, 1554. He includes Boiardo and Ariosto in the epic category and insists that the epic must treat of the most marvellous things.[2] In a later essay, *Gli Heroici*, prefixed to some verses in honour of one of the Este family, Pigna insists on the need of a basis of fact in the epic, thus

---

[1] *Ib.* 20-1.   [2] G. B. Pigna, *I Romanzi*, 15.

approximating it to history. The type of fact is the heroic action of a great noble; and it is not reasonable that such action should not be made manifest to the world. The epic poet seeks perfection and should heighten the heroic theme he has chosen, to his utmost ability.[1] To show forth the great virtues of a prince, the time of action must not be less than a month; while the reversals of tragedy can be transacted in a single day.[2]

The critics so far mentioned were less influential than the two critics who wrote long and systematic treatises on poetry, Antonio Sebastiano Minturno and Julius Caesar Scaliger. These were the authoritative handbooks of the age and were read and heeded outside Italy. Minturno wrote two treatises, one in Latin, *De Poeta* (1559), the other in Italian, the *Arte Poetica* (1563). A great deal of his criticism concerns the drama, but there is a section on the epic in his later treatise. There are also some important sentences about the epic in the earlier treatise. So far I have said nothing about how the epic, in spite of Aristotle's preference for tragedy and of the Renaissance reverence for Aristotle, came to be regarded as the supreme literary form. Exactly what the process was may be impossible to say. Trissino is doubtful which form, epic or tragedy, is superior. But Cinthio and Pigna, adoring the romances and adding them to the epic repertory, incline to exalt the epic. Moreover, they do not regard Aristotle as infallible. Added to this there is the steady belief that Homer and Virgil are in a class apart as poets. Anyhow, in the authoritative treatises of Minturno and Scaliger the epic is the supreme form. In his *De Poeta* Minturno asserts the supremacy of Homer and Virgil.[3] In another place he talks of the status of heroic poetry. This he does not equate with epic. Epic is a large term, including much that is neither dramatic nor lyric. There are three kinds of it. First, the kind which is not poetical in subject and is poetry on account of the verse alone; of which the poems of Lucretius and Empedocles are examples. Second, heroic poetry. Third, pastoral. Heroic is divine and in the poetic canon by a long way the most noble. It includes in its great variety both other kinds of epic; indeed, every literary kind has its origin in the heroic. Tragedy and comedy derive from Homer.[4] Minturno's treatment of narrative comes in the first book of the *Arte Poetica*. He discusses the status of the verse romance, and though he praises Ariosto he thinks the form he uses defective.[5] Minturno is thus more rigid than Cinthio, who thought the Ariostan form not defective but simply different from the Aristotelian.

Julius Caesar Scaliger, gifted with great learning, a zest for the literature of most ages, and great self-confidence, was the nearest

---

[1] Pigna, *Gli Heroici* (Venice 1561) 11.   [2] *Ib.* 14.
[3] *De Poeta* (Venice 1559) i. 5.   [4] *Ib.* ii. 105.
[5] Minturno, *Arte Poetica* (Venice 1563) 32.

approach to a literary dictator of the age. There is not a great deal about the epic form in his long *Poetices Libri Septem*[1]; but there is one chapter (iii. 95) both to the point and very influential. The chapter heads those that concern the different forms of poetry. And Scaliger makes it do this because he believes epic not only the supreme form but the form from which all the other forms take their rules. His words are important because of their philosophical, almost esoteric, tone. Here perhaps is a beginning of the almost mystical notion of the epic form that existed in the neo-classic age.

> Dicebamus supra omni in re unum quippiam esse rectum ac primum quod aliorum norma sit ita ut ad id caetera omnia referantur. Tota igitur in Poesi, Epica ratio illa, qua Heroum genus vita gesta describuntur, princeps esse videtur: ad cuius rationem reliquae Poeseos partes dirigantur. Quae partes, propterea quod variae, ut in primo libro indicavimus, existant: ita superiora praecepta universalia ex Epica maiestate mutuabimur ut secundum cuiusque aliarum idearum naturas aptentur argumenta rerum. Post igitur communes leges privilegia specierum instituamus ab ipsis Heroicis sumpto initio.[2]

That this crabbed piece of Latin foreshadows the mystical notion of the epic is the more likely because it occurs in the book Scaliger calls the Idea of Poetry. And he is thinking of the Platonic ideas, wishing to describe the various ideal parts of poetry to which this or that poem strives to approximate. I think too that Scaliger looks on the heroic poem as head of one of the many hierarchies that compose human life. His first chapter of all deals with the importance of speech in general; and I think we should bear in mind throughout Scaliger's book the total human setting. The heroic poem would be to the other forms of poetry what the king is to the rest of a polity and the sun to the rest of the heavens. Such considerations help us to understand what the epic meant to the neo-classic age.

In the same chapter there occurs a passage that reinforces the existing notion of verse not being essential to the epic. Speaking of the need of the epic poet not to divulge all the early history of a hero at the beginning, he cites Heliodorus as a correct writer:

---

[1] Published posthumously in 1561; written by 1558, the year of Scaliger's death.

[2] The passage begins the chapter mentioned in the text. 'We said above that in every affair there is one correct and basic thing that is the measure of the rest so that to it all other things are referred. Thus throughout all poetry that epic mode in which the origin, life, and deeds of heroes are described, seems to be the chief; by whose principle the other parts of poetry should be regulated. And since, as we showed in the first book, these parts exist in multiplicity we shall borrow the controlling universal laws from the epic dignity and apply them to the different divisions of our subject, but according to the special character of all the forms other than the epic. It is therefore after these universal laws, taking the principles of the heroic poem as the basis, that we should lay down the privileges of the varieties.'

Hunc disponendi rationem splendidissimam habes in Aethiopica
historia Heliodori. Quem librum epico Poetae censeo accura-
tissime legendum ac quasi pro optimo sibi proponendum.[1]

This sentence, from the most influential Italian critic, probably
encouraged Sidney to rewrite *Arcadia* on the model of Heliodorus.

Of all the writings on the epic in the Italian Renaissance the finest
is Torquato Tasso's *Discorsi dell' Arte Poetica*. Though published later,
they were composed not later than 1561, the year when Scaliger's
Poetics appeared. Tasso is often thought of as the product of the
new rigidity of mind displayed by the Counter-Reformation in
religion and by the hardening of critical dogma into the neo-classic
rules. But this early piece of his writing retains the more liberal spirit
of Cinthio and Pigna even if it differs from their findings. It also
expresses, better than any other piece of writing I know, the kind of
thing enlightened men of the late Renaissance and neo-classic ages
expected the epic to be. It is less relevant to Spenser than is Cinthio
and it looks forward to Milton, and especially Milton when he was
contemplating an Arthuriad and enlarged on his literary plans in
Reason of Church Government. Tasso is indeed a bridge between the
Renaissance and the neo-classic age. I will summarise some of the
main assertions of Tasso's essay.[2]

Tasso divides his subject into three, the matter, the form, and the
adornment of the epic poem. The matter must be 'by its own nature
capable of every perfection'. But for both epic and tragedy it must
also be founded on historical fact. Like most of his contemporaries
Tasso thought that this basis in fact facilitated aesthetic acceptance.
Novelty there must be, but of treatment not of matter. The marvellous
is necessary to the epic; Hebrew and Christian marvels are credible
where other marvels are not: therefore a Hebrew or Christian subject
is preferable. The object of the epic is to create the pattern of a
perfect knight; and here too a Hebrew or Christian subject has an
obvious advantage. Better choose a period not too old and not too
new. Arthur and Charlemagne are eminently suited to being epic
heroes. Pity and terror, essential to tragedy, are accidental in epic.
Epic action must be splendid; it must consist of the adventures of
men of exalted martial virtue, of deeds of courtesy, generosity, piety,
and religion. An epic character must represent the height of a special
virtue; as Aeneas represents *pietas*, Achilles courage, Ulysses prudence,
Amadigi loyalty, and Bradamante constancy. (Here Tasso is entirely
elevant to the structure of the *Faerie Queene* and resembles Cinthio

[1] 'This method of construction you have at hand in the most splendid form in the
Ethiopian History of Heliodorus. I believe that the epic poet should read this book
with all care and set it before himself as the best possible model.'
[2] I use for this essay the fifth volume of Tasso's works, Venice 1735. The essay
begins on p. 489 of this volume.

and Pigna in the way he includes the romances.) Tasso grants the status of epic, though not of the highest kind, to Boccaccio's *Il Filocolo* and Heliodorus's *Ethiopian History*. Both Virgil and Trissino used matter of suitable nobility.

The second discourse, though nominally treating of what the poets made of the material selected, is not at all sharply divided from the first. Tasso resumes the question, put in the first discourse, of how much matter an epic may include. And in so doing he tries to define the position of Boiardo and Ariosto. This attempt is the most original matter of detail in Tasso's essay. Seeing that drama had certain natural physical limits affecting the number of words in a play, he sought to discover a natural limit to the size of an epic. Such a limit he believes to exist and he finds it in the extent of a man's powers of memory: in other words, a man of average memory should be able to retain in his head, while reading, all the details of an epic. 'La memoria commune degli uomini è dritta estimatrice della misura conveniente del poema'. This is surely a sound principle, if you postulate unity in an epic. And Tasso proceeds naturally to the old question of the single and the multiple plot. And the question brings with it the status of the romance. Considered as one poem (as by plot-connection they are), the *Orlando's* of Boiardo and Ariosto form too long a series of events to be grasped by the ordinary memory. He admires Ariosto immensely, but his admiration will not persuade him to the position that a multiple is as good as a single plot or that you can reduce the *Orlando Furioso* to the laws of Aristotle. In a picture, however large, unity is the principle; and it should extend to poetry. A poem with multiple actions is not one poem but several poems. It is legitimate to exploit this kind but not to pretend that it is as good as the unified kind demanded by Aristotle. Tasso ends this section with a splendid comparison of the true epic to the diversity in unity of God's creation. It is a comparison that not only expresses Tasso's own high idea of epic possibility but connects, as in a smaller way Scaliger had done, poetry with the workings of the whole universe. I quote it at length to illustrate the status to which epic poetry had arrived after the middle of the sixteenth century.

Io[1] per me e necessaria nel poema eroico la (*sc.* unità) stimo e possibile a consequire, perocchè, siccome in questo mirabile magis-

[1] 'For myself I consider unity in the heroic poem both necessary and possible to obtain, for, as in this wonderful masterpiece of God called the world the sky appears scattered over and divided by so great a variety of stars and, to descend then step by step, the air and the sea appear full of birds and fishes and the earth harbours so many beasts wild and tame, the earth where are found brooks and springs and lakes and meadows and plains and woods and mountains, here fruits and flowers there ice and snow, here dwellings and tillage there wildernesses and terrors, yet for all this the world is one though folding into its bosom so many different things, its form and essence are one, and one the fashion in which its parts

terio di Dio che mondo si chiama il cielo si vede sparso o distinto
di tanta varietà di stelle, e, discendendo poi giuso di mano in mano,
l'aria et il mare pieni di uccelli e di pesci, e la terra albergatrice di
tanti animali così feroci come mansueti, nella quale e ruscelli e
fonti e laghi e prati e campagne e selve e monti si trovano, e quì
frutti e fiori là ghiacci e nevi, quì abitazioni e culture là solitudini
ed orrori, con tutto ciò uno è il mondo che tante e sì diverse cose nel
suo grembo rinchiude, una la forma e l'essenza sua, uno il modo dal
quale sono le sue parti con discorde concordia insieme congiunte
e collegate, e non mancando nulla in lui, nulla però vi è di soverchio
o di non necessario. Così parimente giudico che da eccellente
Poeta, (il quale non per altro divino è detto se non perchè al
supremo artefice nelle sue operazioni assomigliandosi della sua
divinità viene a partecipare) un poema formar si possa nel quale
quasi in un piccolo mondo quì si leggano ordinanze d'eserciti, quì
battaglie terrestri e navali, quì espugnazioni di città scaramucce e
duelli, quì giostre, quì descrizioni di fame e di sete, quì tempeste,
quì incendi, quì prodigi. Là si trovino concili celesti ed infernali,
là si vedano sedizioni, là discordie, là errori, là venture, là incanti,
là opere di crudeltà di audacia di cortesia di generosità, là avvenimenti d'amore or felici or infelici or lieti or compassionevoli; ma
che nondimeno uno sia il poema che tanta varietà di materie
contenga; una la forma e la favola sua; e che tutte queste cose siano
di maniera composte che l'una l'altra riguardi, l'una all'altra
corrisponda, l'una dall'altra o necessariamente o verisimilmente
dependa, sicchè una sola parte o tolta via o mutata di sito il tutto
ruini.

The third discourse of Tasso deals with adornment or style. It
matters less to this book than the other two and amplifies the thesis
that to the exalted matter of epic an exalted style must correspond.

I do not know of any writing on the epic better than Tasso's
Discorsi dell' Arte Poetica. His principle of diversity in unity gets to the
heart of epic requirements; and his principle of memory conditioning

are joined and knit together with a kind of discordant harmony; and though nothing
is lacking to it, nothing is there either superfluous or not necessary. So likewise I
assert that the sublime poet (called divine for no other reason than that he models
himself in his works on the supreme artificer and arrives at sharing thus his divinity)
can indeed shape a poem in which as in a microcosm there are brought together
here the marshalling of armies, battles by land and sea, captures of cities, skirmishes
and duels, tourneys, descriptions of hunger and thirst, tempests, fires, prodigies.
Let there be found there heavenly and infernal councils, revolutions, strifes, errors,
misfortunes, enchantments, deeds of cruelty of daring of courtesy of generosity,
love-adventures prosperous and unfortunate, happy or pitiful but only so that the
poem which shall include such a variety of substance should nevertheless be one;
the form and the fable one; and that all things should be put together so that one
thing refers to another, one corresponds to another, one either by necessity or probability depend on another, so that the removal of a single part or its transference
should ruin the whole.'

length is not only original but simple and convincing. Tasso was a severe moralist but he advances no crude didacticism. The greatness of heroic poetry is that it duplicates the divine act of creation not that it conveys this or that moral. And though his Christian hero is to be an example of virtue, Tasso spares us the solemn and relentless iteration of the example notion that marks the criticism of northern Europe. In this he resembles other Italian critics. Less touched by the changes of heart that precipitated the Reformation, nurtured on Ariosto instead of Lydgate, they could thrive on a little more light and a little less gloom.

CHAPTER VI

FRANCE

IF we are to understand Spenser we must take the French critics and poets into account as well as the Italian. It is indeed possible that the greater laxity of French ideas of the epic together with the failure of Ronsard's grandiose attempt to match the *Aeneid* may have helped to persuade Spenser to use the loose Ariostan form and to shun the poem with the single hero.

The French poets and critics of the mid-sixteenth century had no regard for their own narrative tradition of earlier days. The *Song of Roland* had to wait till the nineteenth century to come into its own. Instead, they looked to Italy and in particular to recent Italian successes in the vernacular. They thought that the way to poetic success was to combine a profound knowledge of the Classics and respect for classical precedent with the exploitation of your own tongue. There was nothing wrong with the French language; only you must use it to imitate the most civilised literary forms. These were, for instance, the classical pastoral, the Petrarchian sonnet, the elegy, and above all the long poem. This linguistic patriotism appears in an acute form in Henri Estienne, *De la Précellence du Langage François*. This work was not published till 1579, but Estienne was born in 1528 and represents faithfully the temper of the literary movement in France that was centred in the Pléiade. He maintained not only that the French language was capable of any task, however high or difficult, but that it was better in itself than the Italian language. The classic text for the capacity of French is Du Bellay's *Déffence et Illustration de la Langue Françoise*, but unlike Estienne's work it contains a chapter on the long poem that demands special mention.

Du Bellay's *Déffence* was written as early as 1549, and this chapter (ii. 5) is notable among other things for exalting Ariosto to epic stature before Giraldi Cinthio and Pigna published their defences of the Romance in 1554. Ariosto, Du Bellay thinks, has through his great poem exalted his language to the eminence to which Homer and Virgil by their great poems had brought theirs. And now it is the turn of some Frenchman to do the same for the French tongue, choosing for his hero Launcelot or Tristram or another of the medieval knights. Spenser was certainly aware of these French aspirations when he began on the *Faerie Queene* and he may well have heeded Du Bellay's accompanying exaltation of the *Orlando Furioso*, believing that the great thing was to excel in a long poem and not necessarily in the

long poem with the single hero. Granted this vaguer notion of the
long poem and the absence of any feeling such as I have noted in
Tasso about the epic as a form, Du Bellay takes the task of writing a
long poem with the greatest seriousness. The attempt to write such a
poem was hazardous and only too likely to fail. Only a man exceptionally endowed had a chance of success: he must have natural
genius, be learned in all arts and sciences (above all in natural
sciences and mathematics), he must be thoroughly versed in the
Classics, he must know men and manners, he must be of middle
condition so as to escape both the public duties of the ruler and the
handicaps of poverty, and he must have achieved tranquillity of
mind by a combination of high, courageous spirit with foresight and
self-control. Even if he was vague about the epic as a literary form,
Du Bellay was clear about the difficulty and the dignity of the long
poem.

In 1555 Jacques Peletier du Mans,[1] himself something of a poet,
published his *Art Poétique*, a longish prose essay in the full Renaissance
style. He has much the same conception of the epic as Du Bellay.
It is an immense affair, 'une mer, une forme et image de l'univers',
and all other forms derive from it.[2] It is a matter of national importance that an epic should be written in this or that tongue, such a
poem being 'de tel compte et de tel honneur qu'une langue n'est pas
pour passer en célébrité vers les siècles sinon qu'elle ait traité le sujet
héroique'. Again here is something most apt to Spenser: the patriotic
notion of the epic and the requirement of vastness and variety.
Peletier finds fault with Ariosto, while admitting him among the
writers of epic.[3] He grants that the romances provide good epic
material—adventures of knights, love, journeys, enchantments,
battles—as Ariosto has shown.[4]

Not all French critics were as catholic in their conception of the
epic as Du Bellay and Peletier. If these two correspond to Cinthio
and Pigna, Ronsard and Vauquelin de la Fresnaye are more like in
sentiment to Minturno and Scaliger. They share the patriotic sentiment of the other two Frenchmen, and Vanquelin is as emphatic on
the subject of epic vastness and variety as Peletier; but they recom-
mend only Homer and Virgil and other classical writers as the best
models. Ariosto is not the poet to be copied. Ronsard's main criticism
is his *Abrégé de l'Art Poétique* (1565) and his introductions to his epic,
the *Franciade* (1572 and 1587). Much of his criticism has to do with
language, and some of this kind must have suited Spenser. He favours
in the *Abrégé* a judicious use of archaic and dialect words and of

---

[1] For Peletier see especially E. Egger, *L'Hellénisme en France* (Paris 1869) i. 396.
[2] Ed. A. Boulanger (Paris 1930) 194. Peletier was a spelling reformer and his own
spelling is peculiar. I prefer to modernise.
[3] *Ib.* 103. [4] *Ib.* 201.

technical terms. It is in the first preface to the *Franciade* (1572) that Ronsard objects to Ariosto. This objection is part of a wider argument about the poet and the historian. Ronsard's version of the perennial attempt in the Renaissance to approximate or distinguish the two is that though both epic poet and historian have the same material—princes, wars, politics—their conception of truth is different. The province of the historian is *le vrai*, that of the poet *le vraisemblable*. And for the latter fiction is necessary. But there is fiction and fiction:

> Le Poëte qui escrit les choses comme elles sont ne merite tant que celuy qui les feint et se recule le plus qu'il luy est possible de l'historien: non toutefois pour feindre une Poesie fantastique comme celle de l'Arioste, de laquelle les membres sont aucunement beaux mais le corps est tellement contrefaict et monstrueux qu'il ressemble mieux aux resveries d'un malade de fievre continue qu'aux inventions d'un homme bien sain.[1]

Ronsard is emphatic about the exemplary function of heroic poetry. He recounts how King Charles, interested in his poem, refused to allow him to select for treatment a few among his sixty predecessors but insisted on all being included 'à fin que la bonté des bons et la malice des mauvais luy fussent comme un example domestique pour le retirer du vice et le pousser à la vertue'.[2] Speaking for himself, Ronsard tells the reader that he culls blooms from any classical authority and mentions Homer, Virgil, and Apollonius Rhodius. He follows Minturno in thinking a year the proper span of the imagined time of the epic.

Vauquelin began his verse *Art Poétique* in 1574 and took many years over it. He does homage to Vida and Minturno as well as to Aristotle and Horace, thus identifying himself with those who were critical of Ariosto. He repeats Ronsard and Minturno in his rule for the imagined time of an epic and echoes Peletier when he says that the epic, that form of the utmost variety, is the parent of all other literary forms.

For all their concern with the epic the Pléiade failed to produce a successful one from among themselves. The great effort was Ronsard's *Franciade*: the French counterpart in some ways of Trissino's *Italia Liberata* in Italy and of Cowley's *Davideis* in England. But it has its resemblances to the *Faerie Queene* also. It resembles the *Davideis* in being a fragment of four books; it resembles *Italia Liberata* and the *Davideis* in being constructed on strict classical lines with much of the action narrated retrospectively or foreseen through prophecy; it resembles the *Faerie Queene* in its patriotic subject and the amount of history it contains. The story of Francus and his nephew Francion,

---

[1] *Oeuvres Complètes*, ed. H. Vaganay (Paris 1923) vi. 525.
[2] *Ib.* 526.

the Trojan founders of the French kingdom and of Paris, is a French parallel to the legends of Geoffrey of Monmouth about British history, with Francus corresponding to Brutus, the Trojan founder of London. Ronsard's fiction is that Francus (a corruption of the Greek φερέ-εγχος=*carry-spear*) was really Astyanax, son of Hector; the Astyanax who perished at Troy being a phantom created by Zeus. The full plot would have concerned a Trojan migration through Europe to found the French kingdom. As it is, most of the action takes place in Crete; but it is there (Book Four) that a prophetic account is given of the French kings up to Pepin. Spenser can hardly not have had Ronsard in mind when he gave his own prophetic account of British history from Brutus to Elizabeth. The *Franciade* never begins to be an epic because the poetic style lacks weight. The metre is not the usual Alexandrine but the ten-syllable couplet. It is clear and unemphatic. The poem has a portion of romantic and idyllic charm and bears some resemblance to the *Argonautica* of Apollonius Rhodius. It has a place in the history of the epic but not among true epic writings.

CHAPTER VII

PORTUGAL

1. GENERAL

THE last two sections have been concerned mainly with critical ideas; and in the natural sequence I should go from Italian and French critical ideas to those of England and thence to the original English works that were or pretended to be epic. Portuguese criticism of the sixteenth century, if there was any, did not reach England; and to step aside to Portugal is to interrupt the course of my narrative. But this I do because of Camoens's neo-classic epic on Vasco da Gama's voyage to India. The *Lusiad* demands inclusion in this book through its relation to Milton; and it demands it here and not later for two reasons. First, it responds to a phase of critical thought I have described in the last two sections. Secondly, its mere existence with its strict classicising may have influenced the turn epic took in England and strengthened whatever trends towards neo-classicism existed there in the years after its publication in 1572. It is true that the Elizabethans showed no signs of reading it. And yet it may well be that a few of them talked of this remarkable poem that succeeded in casting a recent event into strict Virgilian form, even if their talk was not recorded. Anyhow I ought to comment on the *Lusiad* before dealing with the *Faerie Queene* and *Arcadia*, even at the price of interrupting my remarks on the theories of the epic in the sixteenth century.

2. CAMOENS[1]

> *Sometimes committed to* Sea's *rolling Towr's,*
> *Sometimes to bloody dangers* Marteale!
> *Thus I (like desperate Canacee of old)*
> *My* Pen *in this, my* Sword *in that hand hold.*

Os Lusiadas, or the *Sons of Lusus*,[2] the epic of Camoens celebrating

---

[1] I refuse to yield to the deplorable habit, now on the increase, of abandoning the traditional anglicised forms of proper names and substituting the foreign. *Camoens* is the traditional English form of the Portuguese *Camões*, and it is misguided pedantry to depart from it. Those who do so usually lack the conviction of their own pedantry and continue to talk of Lisbon instead of *Lisboa*. It is heartening to read the following entry in the catalogue of the Cambridge University Library: 'Camões (Luis de). *See* Camoens (Luis de).'

[2] The traditional English title of Camoens's epic is the *Lusiad*, meaning the epic of Lusus. It is incorrect, for the epic is not about Lusus, the eponymous hero of Lusitania or Portugal, but about his supposed descendants. Because of this incorrectness, the epic has more recently been called the *Lusiads*. But this is neither traditional nor obvious; and I prefer either the traditional name, the *Lusiad*, or the more

the Portuguese nation through the voyage of Vasco da Gama, has had a fitful vogue in England. Few English-speakers have read it, since its publication in 1572, in the original; and of the translations only that of Mickle in the heroic couplet (1775) was genuinely popular, and this popularity did not survive the anti-Augustan movement of the nineteenth century. There have been many individual readers of the translations by Fanshawe, Burton, and others; but they have never formed a coherent body. Further, Fanshawe's, the earliest translation, was not published till 1655. Camoens therefore has fared poorly in England, and his reputation has not matched his deserts. It is to be hoped that this state of things will change; and in that hope it may be worth saying something about the English versions on which most English-speakers will have to depend. First, none of the nineteenth- or twentieth-century versions can compete with the two classic versions of Fanshawe and Mickle, for, whatever their virtues, they are individual and isolated, unbacked by a solid tradition, and fundamentally uncertain of themselves. Fanshawe, writing in the eight-line, Ariostan, stanza of his original, can rely on the still-living tradition of Spenser; Mickle, writing in the heroic couplet, relies without question on the great translations of Pope. Fanshawe's reliance is less serene, for he is unconsciously forced to improve on Spenser's liquid simplicity of speech by inserting abundantly the fashionable conceits of his age. Nevertheless, he writes living verse. When it comes to fidelity to the original, both translators have their merits and their defects. Fanshawe translates stanza by stanza and alters the order of Camoens's sentences hardly at all. Where he takes liberties is in inserting small quips, for which there is no warrant in the original. Southey,[1] who wrote of Fanshawe's *Lusiad* with discrimination, instances the couplet,

> *Neptune disclosed new isles which he did play*
> *About, and with his billows danced the hay.*

In the Portuguese, Neptune merely encompasses and washes the islands; there is nothing there about dancing the hay. Mickle, explicitly forswearing a literal verbal rendering, takes greater liberties and makes more serious additions. For instance, towards the end of Book One the Portuguese ships fire their cannon at the treacherous Moors on the Mozambique shores. In the description occur the lines,

> *Unnumber'd sea-fowl rising from the shore,*
> *Beat round in whirls at every cannon's roar.*[2]

obvious *Sons of Lusus*. It was partly with an eye to the *Lusiad*, now popularised by Mickle's translation, that Peter Pindar in 1785 called his mock-heroic poem the *Lousiad*: a confirmation of the traditional validity of the incorrect name of Camoens's epic.

[1] *Quarterly Review*, xxvii. 1-39.
[2] The *Lusiad*, translated by William Julius Mickle. Second Edition (Oxford 1778) 34.

It is a graphic touch, but it is absent from the Portuguese original. Further, Mickle does not hesitate to alter the order of Camoens's sentiments and to translate paragraph by paragraph, not sentence by sentence, after the manner of Pope. But fidelity can be to other things than detail; and it remains to consider the larger qualities of the two translations. At his height Fanshawe is a better poet than Mickle, but he is lazier and more uneven. He can rise in the great passages, where his interest kindles, beyond anything within Mickle's reach. Here are two stanzas from the ninth book, part of the description of Venus's miraculous island:

> *Three goodly* Mountains *with a graceful pride*
> *Thrust their majestick* Heads *into the Ayre*
> (*With green imbroydred* Hangings *beautify'de*)
> *In this gay* Isle *delicious, fresh, and faire.*
> *From their three* Tops *three crystal* Springs *did glide,*
> *Lacing the Liv'ry their rich* Margents *ware,*
> > *Jumping on* Pebbles *while their* Crystals *brake:*
> > *Such* Musick *never* Water-works *did make.*
>
> *In a pure* Valley *which those* Hills *divides,*
> *As by appointment the three* Currents *meet,*
> *Shaping a* Table *with proportion'd sides,*
> *Broad, and beyond imagination, sweet.*
> *A* Frenge *of* Trees *hangs over it, and prides*
> *It self in so cleer* Glass *it self to greet.*
> > Now *prancks its* locks *therein, and* now *retires;*
> > Now *looks again, and its own form admires.*[1]

But in the less lyrical or less impassioned passages, and especially where Camoens compresses the facts of Portuguese history into a narrow space, Fanshawe can be graceless and obscure, untrue to the limpidity of his original. It is here that Mickle scores. He saw this limpidity of Camoens and resolved at any cost to be readable. Granted no initial distaste for eighteenth-century poetic idiom, Mickle succeeds in giving a poetic colouring to the whole of his translation. One can read it at a stretch with pleasure as one cannot read Fanshawe; and in this sustained legibility it is the most faithful to its original of all the English translations. However much better Fanshawe may be in certain parts, Mickle for all his liberties is the best translator for a sustained rendering of the poem as a whole.

Since Camoens first enters English literature and the English epic

---

[1] ix. 54-5. Fanshawe's translation, which I use for most quotations from Camoens. This is now available in J. D. M. Ford's edition (Cambridge, Mass., 1940). The recent verse translation by Leonard Bacon (New York 1950) is too flat poetically to compete with Fanshawe and Mickle. There is a recent prose translation by W. C. Atkinson in the Penguin Classics (1952) but the *Lusiad* more than most narratives loses its flavour in prose.

through Milton, I had better say something of the relation between the two poets. Milton was so great a lover of travel-books that we must be cautious of thinking that every coincidence of *Paradise Lost* and the *Lusiad* implies a debt. Take the simile in *Paradise Lost*, ii. 636-42,

> As when farr off at Sea a Fleet descri'd
> Hangs in the Clouds, by Aequinoctial Winds
> Close sailing from Bengala, or the Iles
> Of Ternate and Tidore, whence Merchants bring
> Thir spicie Drugs: they on the trading Flood
> Through the wide Ethiopian to the Cape
> Ply stemming nightly toward the Pole.

It might easily be thought that Milton, writing here of Portuguese fleets rounding the Cape with cargoes of spices, had in mind part of a stanza of Camoens:

> Through all these Orientall Seas, behold
> Sown infinite of Isles that have no name.
> Tidore see! Ternate, whence are roll'd
> (Holding black Night a Torch) thick Plumes of Fame.
> See Trees of burning Cloves, that shall be sold
> For Lusians blood.[1]

By itself this setting together of Tidore and Ternate, two of the spice islands in the Moluccas, by Camoens and Milton proves no connection, for Purchas too set them together. But when we find other, less doubtful connections, we may take it that here too Milton had his eye on the poet as well as on Purchas. For in Book Eleven of *Paradise Lost* (399-400) Milton wrote

> Mombaza, and Quiloa, and Melind,
> And Sofala,

and though Purchas writes of these places it is difficult to believe that Milton did not have in his mind the line of Camoens,

> De Quiloa, de Mombaça, e de Sofala.

Moreover, Melinde, like the other towns the scenes of Portuguese adventures on the east cost of Africa, has a very prominent place in the *Sons of Lusus*. Far more important than these details is Milton's general debt to Camoens (noted by Mickle in his translation and recently by Bowra[2]) in the last two books of his epic. After Gama and his men have left India, near the end of the poem, Venus causes them to land on her miraculous island and there to wed the sea-nymphs.

[1] x. 132.
[2] C. M. Bowra, *From Virgil to Milton*, 238. He also notes the resemblance between Camoens's single line and Milton's line.

After the wedding Thetis, their queen, leads Gama up to the top of a mountain to her palace, where they are later joined by the others. To the assembled company a Muse or Siren narrates the future fate of the Portuguese kingdom and describes the nature of the universe. It is from this final episode in the *Sons of Lusus* that Milton derived the disposition of Books Eleven and Twelve of *Paradise Lost*. There Michael takes Adam up onto the top of a mountain and instructs him, partly by vision partly by word of mouth, in the future history of man. Camoens was not the only object of imitation here but he was the principal one.

I come now to the question whether the *Lusiad* fits in with any of the phases of critical thought I have described in this section. It is initially probable that any poem so academically correct should do so, and I think Bowra[1] is probably right in making Vida's *Art of Poetry* with its doctrine of imitating Virgil the critical background of Camoens. Camoens was at the University of Coimbra around the year 1540. The place was flourishing and was well aware of the trend of Italian humanism. But the developed theorisings of the Italian critics had not yet begun, and the epic was thought of as the imitation of this or that classical model not as the realisation of the idea of the epic form. At Coimbra Camoens received a thorough training in Latin and read the Italian classics, Petrarch, Boiardo, and Ariosto.[2] It is almost certain that he formed his literary tastes and critical ideas during his university days, for his life thereafter was active not studious and could not have given him the chance to consider new critical ideas. He thus belongs in critical temper to an early stage of the Renaissance. The *Lusiad* is the successful counterpart of Trissino's *Italia Liberata*. That anything so fresh, so living, so completely itself could have been composed in the spirit of Vida's apparently barren and hampering injunctions, is at first sight one of the miracles of literature. It is a similar miracle that an epic that imitates Virgil very closely should be so different from the *Aeneid* that in reading we grow conscious of the imitation only by a determined exercise of the will. When we consider longer, we should see that Virgil's rigorous form was ideally suited to checking and making effective the immensely powerful sense of present actuality that inspired Camoens to write. Had he imitated the form as well as the stanza of Boiardo and Ariosto, his intensity would have been lost, his confined energy would have evaporated; the simplicity of his language would have lost its pregnancy.

Camoens's sense of present actuality was at once personal and national. Unable to live in Lisbon without getting into trouble, he

[1] *Op. cit.* 89.
[2] See J. D. M. Ford, introduction to his edition of *Os Lusiadas* (Cambridge, Mass., 1946) 6 ff.

fought the Moors in Africa and spent seventeen years of varied adventure in the Far East. And not only did he share but he believed in the perilous action through which the Portuguese Empire was founded and confirmed. No weakness at home or abuse abroad upset his simple faith in Portugal's mission of extending Latin culture and imposing the Christian faith on heathen and Mohammedan. Portuguese history had a peculiar cogency because, like that of Rome, it showed an unexpected, an almost incredible growth from a small beginning, and that growth had scarcely faltered. The great European countries, France, England, Germany, Italy, had nothing comparable to show in their development. Not only had Portugal a single growth, it had a single enemy, Islam, an enemy that gave continuity and apparent reason to the close domestic struggles for independence from the Moor in the Iberian peninsula and the distant struggles with Arabic fleets for the Far Eastern trade routes. There was too a different continuity in these struggles, for they prolonged those Crusades which the larger nations, better equipped for the venture, had weakly abandoned. In this new form of crusading the Portuguese, though so few, were the first to stir. It was Henry the Navigator, son of John I of Portugal and grandson of John of Gaunt, who, realising that the Moor could be defeated only by sea, sought to improve the existing methods of navigation and learnt by the middle of the fifteenth century the art of crossing the great stretches of ocean by sail alone. Moreover, he too illustrates the way the new Portuguese adventures grow out of medieval contact with the East, for he read and pondered on a copy of Marco Polo's Asiatic travels, procured in Venice, and may thereby have inspired the Portuguese with the ambition of reaching by sea the scenes of those travels. Anyhow, Portuguese exploration of the west African coast was the first stage in the opening up of the globe, and Diaz rounded the Cape of Good Hope six years before Columbus discovered America. The whole trend, therefore, of Portuguese history was that of simple, progressive, and understandable action, a trend unfavourable to critical rumination but calculated to develop the grand simplicities of character.

Now Virgil has his own grandeur, but he does not see things simply; and it should be obvious that Camoens, however strictly he imitated Virgil's form, could never be like him. In his closeness to action he is more like Herodotus in his last books, though Herodotus is spectator not participant; and in his simple view of the enemy he resembles the author of the *Song of Roland*: *Paien unt tort e chrestien unt dreit*. But it is idle to talk of resemblances without a greater emphasis on Camoens's uniqueness. There is no writer of epic really like him and he represents one large phase of man's history like no other poet.

I will use Camoens's closeness to action as the starting-point from which to describe the nature of his epic. From several of his statements it is plain that he set a high value on the literal truth of his story, as when Gama, about to tell the King of Melinde the geography of Europe and the history of Portugal, says that he is animated by the knowledge that he will tell no lies. Not only does Camoens take the less popular side in the current critical dispute whether unaltered history could be the theme of epic, but he shows an emotional reverence for the actual event which among the great poets can perhaps be matched only in Wordsworth. When it came to the point Wordsworth could not feel so keenly about an imagined theme as about the things, big and small but yet wonderful, that had befallen himself; and plans for an objective epic had to give way to autobiography. Camoens, the man of action and less self-centred than Wordsworth, must have for his theme the actual happening, though he is less tied to the literal truth of every detail and is content to forget his own small share in events and to merge them in the great actions of his country's heroes.

When he treats the events themselves he does so with a surprising, indeed an exaggerated economy. Following Homer in choosing a single episode to represent a great complex of events, he gives the plain story of Vasco da Gama's voyage to India; a voyage of the highest historical significance, diversified indeed by the accidents that beset any long ocean voyage at that time, but not in itself conspicuously tragic or eventful. The Portuguese risked destruction through Arab treachery but they escaped it, they suffered from scurvy but not so seriously as to be forced to abandon the expedition. Gama was held prisoner by the Indian king in Calicut, but he was released before very long and was able to make the journey home. The most violent and the most tragic and the most romantic events— the capture of Lisbon from the Moors, the murder of Inez de Castro, the story of the Twelve of Portugal who defended the honour of twelve Englishwomen—are all recounted in the less immediate form of narration. About the main narrative there is a matter-of-factness which I believe represents the natural instinct of the true man of action to speak quietly of the events in which he has been concerned.

But this matter-of-factness, fundamental and impressive though it is, cannot be considered apart from the rampant ornamentation with which it is combined; for it is precisely the interplay of the two elements that does most to give the *Lusiad* its unique character. When I speak of ornamentation I include two easily distinguishable matters: first the ornamentation accompanying the elaborate classical form into which the literal facts of history are cast, and second the episodes (above all the visit of Bacchus to the palace of Neptune, Adamastor, and the landing of the sailors on the magic island of Venus) that

Camoens is at pains to add. The first forms a constant check to the matter-of-fact of history; the second are of the nature of special interventions.

Camoens was not only a Virgilian but a thorough-going believer in the complicated mechanism proper to most classical epic. For a recent historical subject he had the powerful precedent of Lucan; but he corrects Lucan by reverting to the Homeric and Virgilian practice of bringing in the gods. He follows Virgil in making Venus the protectress of his hero, but differs from him in making Bacchus not Juno the hostile divinity. In so doing he copied Statius while being able to claim the added propriety of Bacchus having journeyed to India in triumph. He had read Homer in a Latin translation and may have owed some details to him. Anyhow he gloried in being in debt to the Classics and uses that debt persistently and without stint to enrich his narrative. His extraordinary achievement is to work the enrichment without any sacrifice of his sense of truth. A good example occurs in the second book. Gama has been deceived by the King of Mombasa and attempts to sail into the harbour, where treachery awaits him. To recount how Gama was saved from the trap Camoens has recourse to some Virgilian mechanism. Venus, powerful in the sea because born of it, collects the nymphs, the daughters of Nereus, and speeds them to divert Gama's ships from their intention.

> *Now through the* ocean *in great haste they* flunder,
> *Raising the white foam with their silver* Tayles.
> *Cloto with bosom breaks the waves in sunder,*
> *And, with more fury then of custom, sayles;*
> *Nise runs up an end, Nerine* (younger)
> *Leaps o're them; frizled with her touching Scales,*
> > *The crooked* Billows (yielding) *make a lane*
> > *For the feard Nymphs to post it through the* Maine.
>
> *Upon a Triton's back, with kindled Face,*
> *The beauteous Erycina*[1] *furious rode.*
> *He, to whose fortune fell so great a grace,*
> *Feels not the Rider, proud of his fair load.*
> *Now were they almost come upon the place*
> *Where a stiff gale the* warlike Navy *blow'd.*
> > *Here they devide, and in an instant cast*
> > *Themselves about the* Ships *advancing fast.*[2]

The nymphs oppose their bosoms to the ships, Venus, as is only proper, choosing the flagship for her own attention. The ships are held up and forced back. In their violent efforts to go forward the sailors raise a cry. The treacherous Moorish pilots, fearing their

---

[1] Venus.   [2] ii. 20-1.

treachery has been discovered, take alarm and jump overboard. A rock is discovered ahead; the flagship drops anchor to avoid it and the other ships do likewise. Da Gama, witnessing all these events, recognises and hails a miracle, and heads the fleet away from Mombasa. Camoens's verse records the actual incident as told by Orosius, with the slight difference that in Orosius the flagship cast anchor before the Moors jumped overboard. Truth and fantasy are in the closest proximity: a proximity enriched by the poet's introducing through two similes another form of actuality. He compares the Moors jumping overboard to startled frogs jumping from land into a pond; and he makes this stanza follow the heightened description of the nymphs coming to hold up the ships:

> As to their Store-House when the Houswife Ants,
> Carrying th'unequal Burthens plac't with slight
> To their small shoulders (lest cold Winter's wants
> Surprize them helpless) exercise their might;
> This tugs, that shoves, one runs, another pants;
> Strength far above their size, they All unite:
>   So toyl the Nymphs, to snatch and to defend
>   The men of Lusus from a dismal end.

If classical fantasy enriches literal truth, a simile like this prevents fantasy getting out of hand and looking silly.

Of the great episodes that of Venus's island is the most important because, though an episode, it is structurally essential. In the historical event the climax is Gama's dealings with the Indian king at Calicut: on them depends the fulfilment of his great mission. Now these dealings were crossed by complicated intrigue. The Arab traders were naturally jealous of the Portuguese and tried to influence the king and his advisers. Gama was heroically willing to sacrifice his own life to the fleet's safety; but he was not called on to do so. Instead he was able to buy his liberty after being kept a prisoner some days. Camoens refuses to compromise but sticks to historical truth, although it fails to yield a sufficient culmination of the great voyage that had preceded it. Instead he adjusts the balance by yet another display of fantasy and actually sites the poetical climax in Venus's allegorical island where the sailors disembark soon after they have begun the return journey, their exploratory mission accomplished. On the island, a place of a more riotous beauty than Ariosto or Milton ever pictured, nymphs, prompted by Venus, are in ambush to draw the sailors to the fulfilment of the most voluptuous delights. By itself the episode is wild, extravagant, ridiculous, rotten-ripe; but in its context perfection, and the rotten-ripeness is, as the French use the phrase to describe the kind of grape that goes to make *Château d'Yquem, la pourriture noble*. And the reason is that all this excess is steadied and justified by the faithful historical truth, so sober and damped-down and unmelodramatic, that has gone before.

The mixture of hard fact and of high fantasy was not a new thing, and writers after Camoens were to exploit it. Dante before and Spenser after him were prominent exploiters. But their methods are different. In them the framework itself is monstrous or romantic, and hard fact is inserted into it. Camoens works the other way round. His framework is hard fact and he uses fantasy to remove the hardness without destroying the reality. And that is his great originality. And it shows that Camoens's mind, though in some of its lines simple, was capacious as well.

That Camoens was an original poet and that he wrote a heroic poem according to strict classical precedent is beyond doubt. There is still the question whether he did indeed succeed in writing what, according to the standards I am using, was a true epic.

To begin with, did Camoens display the true epic variety? His poem is shorter than most epics, containing less than 9000 lines; and there is an apparent sameness about some of the material. Moors (by which Camoens means Mohammedans in general as well as the Moorish race) are little differentiated in their treachery (the friendly Melindians apart). The deeds of the great men of Portugal are narrated in a little varied tone of formal rhetoric. The plot itself is thin compared with those of the *Odyssey* or the *Aeneid*. Yet, elsewhere, apparent thinness is due not to any congenital poverty of mind or invention but to an austere economy. For so marine a plot there are fewer details of seafaring and of adventure than you would expect. But what details there are—the wonder at the new constellations, the waterspout, the sudden storm raised by Neptune at the request of Bacchus—are so convincing that they vouch for all the other details that Camoens could have produced, had he wished. They show that the variety is there all the time. And similarly for other parts of the subject-matter. But the most convincing proof of Camoens's rich mind and capacity for variety is the wonderful description of the fleet leaving Lisbon, at the end of Book Four. The crews are all eager to set sail, yet they dare not face the reproaches of their families, who grudge their departure.

> *Wee (not so much as lifting once our Eyes*
> *On* Wife *or* Mother, *though our* Soules *it grinds,*
> *Whereby in vain laments to* Sympathize,
> *Or change the purpose of our* fixed *minds)*
> *T'embarque our selves, conceiv'd it was most wise,*
> *Without those* Farewells *to which custom binds:*
> > *Which (though it bee* Love's *most indeering way)*
> > *Galls more both* Those *that goe* and Those *that stay.*[1]

[1] iv. 93.

And then, as they leave, an 'old man of venerable look' from among the crowd on shore denounces the whole expedition, the foolish ambition that inspires it, the hypocritical show of religious zeal by which it is justified. Once again Camoens is stating the fact. The old man represents the very strong body of Portuguese opinion at home that disapproved of the current policy of colonial expansion. But this is not the end of the matter. The old man speaks so splendidly and with such heartfelt conviction that we know the author has identified himself with him. In fact Camoens, the man of action, the warm supporter of Portugal's colonial greatness, is also the critic of the dearest articles of his belief. He is great enough to see both sides at once. In doing it Camoens reminds me most of all of Homer, the Homer who could on the one hand deplore the sacking of cities and on the other believe that only through the act of war could man attain his full stature.

Where Camoens is indeed defective is in his handling of character. Here he lacks intimacy and flexibility. Gama is a fine commander, but he has neither the humanity of Achilles nor the symbolic power of Aeneas. The gods are conventionally motivated. The enemy characters are uninteresting. I do not think that Camoens was insensitive to character, but the life of adventure if much prolonged, though bringing with it certain advantages, does not quicken interest in the light and shade of human personality.

In the sustained application of the conscious will Camoens is second to none. He spent anything up to twenty years on his epic; and the resolution that made him confine the products of so wealthy an imagination to less than 9000 lines was immense. He selects and compresses with the greatest rigour. This economy combines with his respect for the actual fact to validate the lushness of his fantasy.

Portugal recognised the *Lusiad* as its own special poem as quickly as Rome recognised the *Aeneid*. And in some ways it is specifically Portuguese. For instance, one of Camoens's recurrent themes is the small size of Portugal and the wonder that so few men can achieve so much. But the *Lusiad* speaks for more than a single small nation. It is the one worthy poetic record of the expansive spirit of the whole of western Europe, a record which is valid for happenings as widely separated in time as Henry the Navigator's inventions and Dutch voyages in the seventeenth century. This choric quality combined with the rich variety of Camoens's matter and the strength of will with which he controlled it makes the *Lusiad* one of the few true epics that Europe has created.

The better the poetry, the more difficult it is to see the poem as a typical product of its age. And such is the case with the *Lusiad*. But, tracing as I do the history of the epic as well as speaking of epic poems, I must make the effort to point to the *Lusiad* as a work illustrating the trend of the epic in its own age. As a poem bringing honour to its home-country by exploiting a heroic theme in the vernacular and in the correct classical form, it is the successful Portuguese counterpart of the unsuccessful attempts by Trissino and Ronsard in Italy and France. Its theme is purely of the Renaissance and constitutes an utter break with the Middle Ages. Venus may be an allegory of divine love, Bacchus may represent the supposed jealousy and excesses of the East, but Gama is a successful and conscientious and loyal commander and in no sense whatever an allegory of the human soul. And his action is military and political and not religious. This is not to say that Camoens was not very pious, but he was not pious in the medieval way. Again, morality, in the Renaissance manner, has drawn to itself some of the passion that in the Middle Ages belonged to religion. The true commander and the true servant of the king must be a man of the sternest and most self-sacrificing moral integrity; and some of Camoens's finest stanzas have this as their theme. For instance, at the end of the seventh canto, that is before the culminating episodes at Calicut, occur these stanzas:

> *Nor think, O* Nymphs, *I'l waste your pretious* Fame
> *On* Him *who to his* King *and* Countrey's weal
> *Prefers his* private interest (*The same*
> *Will from the* Throne, *yea from the* Altar, *steale*)
> *No, no* Ambitious Man *shall hide his shame*
> *Under my* leaves, *who mounts that he may deal*
> > *More largely to his* Lusts, *and exercise*
> > *His* Office *not, but his* impieties,
>
> *No man That stalks with* popularity,
> *Thereby to catch the* Prey *he hath design'd,*
> *Who, with an erring* Vulgar *to comply,*
> *Changeth as oft as Protheus, or the* Wind.
> *Nor (Muses) fear, that ever sing will I*
> *Whom, with grave* Face, *grave* case, *grave* pace, *I find*
> > (*To please the* King, *in the new* Place *he's in*)
> > *Fleece the poor* People *to the very skin.*
>
> Those (*and those Worthies* onely) *will* I *sing,*
> *Who their dear lives have ventur'd and laid down,*
> *First for their God, and after for their King;*
> *To be repaid in* use *in due renown.*
> *Help me Apollo, and the* Muses' *Ring,*
> *With doubled* Rage *their Lawrell'd heads to crown,*
> > *Whilst (almost tyr'd) I here take breath a while,*
> > *So with fresh* Spirits *to renew my Toyle.*

And lastly Camoens shows himself thoroughly imbued with the current notion of the epic as providing examples for the ruler to follow. In his opening stanzas he presents the heroic deeds of the Portuguese to King Sebastian, then still young, the present ruler, and incites him to imitate and better them. And the whole poem is a fervent plea that the Portuguese of his own day may be worthy of their great ancestors.

CHAPTER VIII

THE ELIZABETHAN AGE: GENERAL

I

BY 1590, the year when works with a serious claim to be epic first appeared, England was aware of most of the critical theories I have been describing. But that does not mean that she held them as Italy and France did or that she did not include other theories in her repertory of critical beliefs. What is immediately clear through comparing the English and the Continental critics is how much less precise and exacting the English are. There is, for instance, nothing to correspond to the clear-cut critical issue concerning the nature of the epic; in Italy between Cinthio and Pigna on the one side and Minturno and Scaliger on the other, in France between Du Bellay and Peletier on the one side and Ronsard and Vauquelin de la Fresnaye on the other. Through this lack of precision, English critical theories on the epic are not easy to describe. However, I must try to do so.

First, however lax in their judgements of actual poems, the English critics were agreed on the superiority of epic to all other literary forms and on its supreme didactic virtue as presenting deeds for imitation. William Webbe was true to general opinion when in his *Discourse of English Poetrie* (1586) he wrote thus:

> After these was *Homer*, who as it were in one summe compre-
> hended all knowledge, wisedome, learning, and pollicie that was
> incident to the capacity of man. . . . For so did that worthy Poet
> frame those his two workes, that in reading the first, that is his
> *Iliads*, by declaring and setting forth so lively the Grecians assembly
> against Troy, together with their prowesse and fortitude against
> their foes, a Prince shall learne not onely courage and valiantnesse,
> but discretion also and pollicie to encounter with his enemies, yea
> a perfect forme of wyse consultations with his Captaines and
> exhortations to the people, with other infinite commodities.
> Agayne, in the other part, wherein are described the manifold and
> daungerous adventures of *Ulisses*, may a man learn many noble
> vertues; and also learne to escape and avoyde the subtyll practises
> and perrilous entrappinges of naughty persons; and not onely this,
> but in what sort also he may deale to knowe and perceive the

affections of those which be neere unto him, and most familiar with him, the better to put them in trust with his matters of waight and importaunce.[1]

And later Webbe speaks of

that princelie part of Poetrie, wherein are displayed the noble actes and valiant exploits of puissaunt Captaines, expert souldiers, wise men, with the famous reportes of auncient times, such as are the Heroycall workes of *Homer* in Greeke and the heavenly verse of *Virgils Aeneidos* in Latine: which workes, comprehending as it were the summe and grounde of all Poetrie, are verilie and incomparably the best of all other.[2]

Harington was even more explicit when in the preface to his translation of Ariosto (1591) he talked of the chief of all sorts of poetry 'which by all mens consent is the Heroicall'.[3]

But if the Elizabethan critics agreed on the supremacy of the epic and of its special didactic function in teaching the prince or fashioning a gentleman by the example, they could be lenient in what works they admitted to the epic category. Spenser in his letter to Raleigh prefixed to the *Faerie Queene* puts without the least question Ariosto along with Homer, Virgil, and Tasso as an authentic writer of epic. Harington, in the section after the passage just referred to, argues that Ariosto matches Virgil so closely that he belongs to the same class. And when he speaks of Ariosto having been 'disliked by some (though by few of any wit or judgement)' he is likely to refer to his Italian and not to any English censurers. Sidney included Xenophon's *Cyropedia* and Heliodorus's *Ethiopian History* in the epic. But none of these inclusions lacked Continental authority; and what is really surprising is that William Webbe should include in the class of heroic poems Christopher Ocland's *Anglorum Praelia*,[4] a simple and pedestrian poem in Latin hexameters about some of the English victories over the Scots and French, designed for school use; that Puttenham should call that dreary medieval verse-chronicler Hardyng 'a Poet Epick or Historicall'[5]; and that Meres should not be the only critic to admire another dreary verse-chronicler, Warner. Meres spoke of Warner's 'absolute *Albion's Englande*',[6] adding that he had heard the best wits of both our universities term him our English Homer. Such inclusions show the Elizabethans little heedful of the organisation of an epic, a fact that leads to my next observation.

In spite of a universal classical education, Elizabethan criticism

[1] Gregory Smith, *Elizabethan Critical Essays* (Oxford 1904) i. 234-5.
[2] *Ib.* 255.
[3] *Ib.* ii. 211.
[4] Published in 1582. For Webbe reference see Gregory Smith, *op. cit.* i. 239.
[5] *Ib.* ii. 64.   [6] In *Palladis Tamia, ib.* ii. 317.

was anything but rigid in demanding from the epic a strict imitation of classical models.[1] The classicising impulses behind the *Franciade* and the *Lusiad* hardly exist in England. We may be pretty sure that Daniel, one of the age's chief classicisers, was glad in composing his *Civil Wars* to have the precedent of Lucan for the nature of his theme and his straightforward treatment of it (he speaks of 'my Homer-Lucan' just before referring to this work near the end of his *Defence of Ryme*); yet when he comments on his *Civil Wars* in the epistle dedicatory to his second edition (1609) it is not any classical imitation he stresses but the nature of his political theme:

> And, whereas this Argument was long since undertaken (in a time which was not as well secur'd of the future, as God be blessed now it is) with a purpose to shewe the deformities of Civile Dissension, and the miserable events of Rebellions, Conspiracies, and bloody Revengements, which followed (as in a circle) upon that breach of the due course of Succession, by the Usurpation of Hen. 4; and thereby to make the blessings of Peace, and the happinesse of an established Government in a direct Line the better to appeare: I trust I shall doo a gratefull worke to my Countrie, to continue the same, unto the glorious Union of Hen. 7: from whence is descended our present Happinesse.[2]

And if Daniel slurs over classical precedent, how much more are other Elizabethans likely to do so. But though writers felt no obligation to follow the precepts of Vida and the precedents of him and of Camoens, they owed spasmodic debts to the Classics and they acknowledged the literary kinds. To begin a narrative in the middle of the action was an added grace, as it was to work in specific references. Spenser must have felt good (quite apart from the superb success of his act) by the mere fact of working into his poem a translation of Lucretius's opening lines. Meres, the second-rate, derivative, and hence representative author of *Palladis Tamia*, was speaking for his age when he wrote:

> As there are eight famous and chief languages; so there are eight notable several kindes of Poets. Heroicke, Lyricke, Tragicke, Comicke, Satiricke, Iambicke, Elegiacke, and Pastoral.[3]

But, having admitted the epic as the chief of the literary modes, they cared little about any rules governing the mode or any strict classical

---

[1] The exception to this statement is the attempt to impose on English a quantitative or classical instead of a native form of verse. This attempt does not especially concern epic, and it was bound to fail. In these ways it differs from any possible attempt to impose classical epic plotting and machinery on the English epic. There was nothing in the nature of things to prevent an English *Lusiad*.

[2] Ed. Grosart (Blackburn 1885-96) ii. 6.

[3] Gregory Smith, *op. cit.* ii. 319.

precedent; and they seem rather to have thought that the way to succeed in the epic was to command the right kind of subject, witness the quotation from Daniel.

Along with a tempered allegiance to the Classics goes a tolerance of medieval literature that differentiates the late Elizabethan age from that of Wyatt and Surrey. This remarkable act of compromise, performed unconsciously and not on any set theory, found magnificent expression in Daniel's *Defence of Ryme*, when he said that 'all our understandings are not to be built by the square of *Greece* and *Italie*' and that it was a sign of 'arrogant ignorance to hold this or that nation Barbarous, these or those times grosse'.[1]

Not only did medievalism linger on in the sixteenth century in England; but one important part of medieval literature, the romance, enjoyed something of a new vogue in the Elizabethan age. The hostility to the medieval romance, natural in the early years of the Reformation and typified by Ascham's attack on *Morte Darthur* in his preface to *Toxophilus* and in the *Scholemaster*, dwindled with the growing ecclesiastical stability of Elizabeth's reign. Ascham had attacked Chaucer as well as Malory, but he did not prevent later opinion considering Chaucer the father of English poetry. 'To Ascham the meeting of Chaucer and Virgil meant conflict—to Spenser, reconciliation.'[2] The most classicising of all the Elizabethan critics, Sidney, wrote in his *Defence of Poesie*,

> *Chaucer*, undoubtedly, did excellently in his *Troylus* and *Cresseid*; of whom, truly, I know not whether to mervaile more, either that he in that mistie time could see so clearely, or that wee in this cleare age walke so stumblingly after him.

Chaucer, Gower, Langland, and Lydgate became the recognised early English classics, and it was perfectly correct to make use of their works. Some of the more popular romances, like *Amadis of Gaul*, were reprinted late in the Elizabethan age. These happenings, along with the vogue of Ariosto's *Orlando Furioso*, whose translation by Harington was published in 1591, ensured that medieval and especially romance material was available for even the most serious epic writers: a fact that explains many things in the *Faerie Queene* and *Arcadia*.

But if the Elizabethans did not require from their epic writers a close imitation of Homer and Virgil and if they were tolerant of a degree of medievalism unthinkable on the Continent, they were like the citizens of other countries in wanting their poets to compete with their fellows whether ancient or modern. Writers vary in the degree in which they think the English epic poets succeeded in this competi-

---

[1] *Poems and a Defence of Ryme*, ed. A. C. Sprague (Cambridge, Mass., 1930) 139. English edition, London 1951.
[2] W. L. Renwick, *Edmund Spenser*, 37.

tion. Webbe, in a passage I shall refer to again, thinks there is nothing in English to compare with Homer and Virgil, though there is hope of better things on account of the improvement in English rhetoric effected by Lyly in *Euphues*. Daniel in his *Musophilus* (1599), that beautiful verse dialogue on the status of learning in England, is pessimistic about the position of literature (and particularly of the two chief epic writers) not only in the world but in England itself:

> *Is this the walke of all your wide renowne,*
> *This little point, this scarce discerned Ile,*
> *Thrust from the world, with whom our speech unknown*
> *Made never any traffike of our stile?*
>
> *Poore narrow limits for so mightie paines,*
> *That cannot promise any forraine vent:*
> *And yet if here to all your wondrous vaines*
> *Were generally knowne, it might content:*
> *But lo how many reads not, or disdaines*
> *The labors of the chiefe and excellent.*
>
> *How many thousands never heard the name*
> *Of* Sydney, *or of* Spencer, *or their bookes?*[1]

This is Philocosmus, the practical man, speaking; and that he is referring to the epic works of the two poets is plain because later he says the heroic is the only kind of poetry he has a use for. To this pessimistic estimate of the low estate of English poetry Musophilus, the poetry-lover, has no direct answer. All he can retort is that, though the present position is bad, there is hope for the future. There is nothing wrong with our language, and in the end the patience of the North may better the 'hotter spirits' of the Continent:

> *And who in time knowes whither we may vent*
> *The treasure of our tongue, to what strange shores*
> *This gaine of our best glorie shal be sent,*
> *T'inrich unknowing Nations with our stores?*
> *What worlds in th'yet unformed Occident*
> *May come refin'd with th'accents that are ours?*[2]

For optimism about the status of English poetry compared with that of the Classics we can go to Meres and his own ridiculous parallels between the ancients and the English: parallels preceded by the claim that the English poets would excel if they had proper patronage:

As the Greeke and Latine Poets have wonne immortall credit to their native speech, beeing encouraged and graced by liberall

---

[1] Sprague's edition, 426-9, 434-41.   [2] 957-62.

patrones and bountifull Benefactors: so our famous and learned Lawreat masters of England would entitle our English to far greater admired excellency if either the Emperor Augustus, or Octavia his sister, or noble Maecenas were alive to rewarde and countenance them.[1]

And Gabriel Harvey, writing against Nash, includes in his ecstatic encomium of contemporary English achievements a comparison of the heroic adventures of Pyrocles and Musidorus in Sidney's *Arcadia* with similar adventures in Homer and Virgil.

I come now to the characteristic which, though belonging to the common nationalist urge in western Europe, most marks off the Elizabethan epic from that of other countries. It is well known that the serious historical play on recent history, usually called the Chronicle Play, is a form of drama found in England alone. Similarly, the English epic was historical as it was nowhere else. On the Continent there was constant discussion and much difference of opinion about the relations between epic and history, with the preponderant opinion that the two must be kept decently separated. But the Elizabethan critics made no firm distinction at all. Spenser called Homer and Virgil 'the antique poets historicall'. Before Spenser, Puttenham in his *Arte of English Poesie* had certain chapters showing how fluid he made the above distinction. He begins by making the basis not only of epic but of tragedy historical (book 1, chapter 15), tragedy being a literary form designed to reprehend the vices of great historical personages. And he opens his next chapter by saying:

> But as the bad and illawdable parts of all estates and degrees were taxed by the Poets . . . and those of great Princes by Tragedie in especial . . . to th'intent that such exemplifying of their blames and adversities, now being dead, might worke for a secret reprehension to others that were alive, living in the same or like abuses: so was it great reason that all good and vertuous persons should for their well doings be rewarded with commendation, and the great Princes above all others with honors and praises, being for many respects of greater moment to have them good and vertuous than any inferior sort of men.

And when in chapter 19 Puttenham comes to describe the poetry that celebrates great men, he calls it 'historicall poesie' and gives it both the highest status and a very wide definition.

> The Poesie historicall is of all other next the divine most honorable and worthy . . . no one thing in the world with more delectation reviving our spirits then to behold as it were in a glasse the lively image of our deare forefathers.

[1] Gregory Smith, *op. cit.* ii. 312-13.

But, says Puttenham, not all historical truth makes for profit or pleasure; and fiction may be admitted if it is exemplary in the correct way. Indeed, it is legitimate to range from the wholly truthful to the wholly fictitious.

And this may be apparent to us not onely by the Poeticall histories but also by those that be written in prose: for as *Homer* wrate a fabulous or mixt report of the siege of Troy and another of *Ulisses* errors or wandrings, so did *Musaeus* compile a true treatise of the life and loves of *Leander* and *Hero*, both of them *Heroick*, and to none ill edification. Also, as Theucidides wrate a worthy and veritable historie of the warres betwixt the *Athenians* and the *Peloponeses*, so did *Zenophon*, a most grave Philosopher and well trained courtier and counsellour, make another (but fained and untrue) of the childhood of *Cyrus*, king of *Persia*; nevertheless both to one effect, that is for example and good information of the posteritie.

These passages from Puttenham, as his most recent editors, Miss Willcock and Miss Walker, have shown, date in the 1560's. But he saw fit to publish them in 1589 and could not have thought them superannuated. Not only do they show a vague and comprehensive conception of the epic, but a conception of tragedy that has in view not classical or Senecan examples but the narratives of the *Mirror for Magistrates* and those of Lydgate which the *Mirror* continues. In sum Puttenham illustrates the fluidity and frequent archaism of Elizabethan theories of literature as well as the optional approximation of history and epic. In mentioning Thucydides as a 'poet historical', Puttenham did not add any English historians. He could have done this without causing surprise. Webbe after his words about the 'princelie part of Poetrie' and the supremacy of Homer and Virgil, referred to above, adds these:

To these, though we have no English worke aunswerable in respect of the glorious ornaments and gallant handling, yet our auncient Chroniclers and reporters of our Country affayres come most neere them: and no doubt, if such regarde of our English speeche and curious handling of our verse had beene long since thought uppon, and from time to time been pollished and bettered by men of learning, judgement, and authority, it would ere this have matched them in all respects.

There, indeed, is the complete equating of epic and history.

In writing this about the importance of history in the Elizabethan epic, I do not mean that there was no foreign counterpart or that the Elizabethan epic was compelled to deal with modern history. The *Lusiad* dealt with recent history, the *Franciade* was patriotic much as the *Faerie Queene* was. *Arcadia* did not deal with English history except allegorically, though its political theory is very much up to date. What I do mean is that the critics in approximating history and epic were reflecting a political state of affairs unique in England and bound to colour in one way or another any serious narrative.

But patriotism was not confined to history; it extended to geography, and the Elizabethans looked on certain geographical poems as epic. It was symptomatic of this that Harrison's geographical account of England formed the first part of Holinshed's *Chronicle*. In an interesting article Lewis F. Ball[1] gives an account of this queer backwater of Elizabethan literature, the geographical epic. He mentions several works where local topography is made patriotic and is blended with history. The two chief examples of the geographical epic proper are Thomas Churchyard's unfinished *Worthines of Wales* (1587) and Drayton's *Poly-Olbion*. Drayton's long poem belongs to the reign of James I; but both poets refer to the Welsh ancestry of the Tudors and thus to what I earlier called the Tudor myth. Addressing Queen Elizabeth in his introduction, Churchyard said:

> Thus, gracious lady, under your princely favour I have undertaken to set forth a work in the honour of Wales, where your Highness' ancestors took name, and where your Majesty is as much loved and feared as in any place in your Highness' dominion.

It is strange to us that Drayton's long leisurely poem should ever have been called epic. But William Drummond considered it the only epic England had to be proud of. William Slatyer, author of the *History of Great Britanie to this present Raigne* (1621), William Browne, and Wither all look on it as epic. Historical and patriotic it certainly is, blending England extended through time with England extended in space and referring to the second of two claims made by James I to be descended from the ancient British kings. The first rested on his plain descent from Margaret Tudor, daughter of Henry VII. The second was more complicated. The story was that when Fleance, son of Banquo, escaped the ambush set by Macbeth, he took refuge in Wales. There he married Nesta, daughter of Griffith ap Llewelin, the last of the native Welsh kings. They had a son, Walter, who returned to Scotland and became Lord High Steward and the ancestor of the Scottish lines of kings extending to James I. It was from this office that he and his descendants derived the royal name of *Stuart*.[2] Thus the geographical poem was also patriotic and satisfied the current conditions for qualifying as epic.

---

[1] *English Literary History*, i. 63-89.
[2] See R. Florence Brinkley, *Arthurian Legend in the Seventeenth Century* (Baltimore 1932) 16-17.

2

Although the Elizabethans give the impression of being easy-going in their requirements for the epic, and although they passed some judgements that we simply cannot understand, they did achieve a remarkable unanimity on the question of what the real masterpieces were (a unanimity we should do well to respect); for it must be asserted with all possible emphasis that the *Faerie Queene* and *Arcadia* were for the Elizabethans not only the chief epics of the age, but its masterpieces in the whole of their literature. They were the works to be proud of and to put up as worthy competitors in a literary contest extending to all ages and all nations. They were, though so new, England's chief classics. It has been already noted how Philocosmus in Daniel's *Musophilus* bracketed Spenser and Sidney as the only two poets of the age worth mentioning. Again, in his preface to *Cleopatra* (1594) Daniel patriotically wishes that English poetry, by which he understands the *Faerie Queene* and *Arcadia*, may invade decadent Italy. Gabriel Harvey in 1593 put Sidney and Spenser side by side in the place of honour among recent writers:

> Is not the Prose of *Sir Philip Sidney* in his Sweet Arcadia the embrodery of finest *Art* and daintiest *Witt*? Or is not the Verse of M. *Spencer* in his brave Faery Queene the Virginall of the divinest Muses and gentlest Graces? Both delicate Writers, always gallant, often brave, continually delectable, sometimes admirable. What sweeter taste of Suada then the Prose of the One; or what pleasanter relish of the Muses than the Verse of the Other?[1]

That Spenser held so high a position a modern may allow without effort, but that Sidney was bracketed with him he may find hard to believe. So I add a little more evidence. Richard Carew in his *Excellency of the English Tongue*, dated by Gregory Smith possibly 1595-6, asking the question, 'Will you have all in all for prose and verse?' answers, 'Take the miracle of our age Sir Philip Sydney.'[2] Early in the next century George Hakewill called *Arcadia* in its 'inventive parts' equal to the best ancients. And (probably in the 1630's) Sir William Alexander in his *Anacrisis, or, A Censure of some Poets ancient and modern*, wrote:

> The *Arcadia* of S. P. *Sidney* is the most excellent Work that, in my Judgment, hath been written in any Language that I understand ... wanting no Virtue whereof a Humane Mind could be capable.[3]

[1] Gregory Smith, *op. cit.* ii. 282.
[2] *Ib.* ii. 293.
[3] J. E. Spingarn, *Critical Essays of the Seventeenth Century* (Oxford 1908) i. 187.

It was not indeed till towards the end of the seventeenth century that the then traditional yoking of the *Faerie Queene* and *Arcadia* as the two masterpieces of Elizabethan literature was abandoned.

3

Though, as presented through its own self-conception, Elizabethan epic is a confused and complicated affair, judged, not by contemporary standards, but in the light of other ages it becomes clearer.

First, it should be evident that, apart from any achievement, the Elizabethan age was one of epic potentiality: what I have called an 'epic area.' And the physical metaphor is helpful. Just as there exist volcanic areas with the minor manifestations of geysers and so on as well as areas with an authentic volcano, so you can have a literary area favourable to the epic yet lacking a major manifestation. In the Elizabethan age national sentiment, the feeling of proper pride that the old divisions had been overcome and that England was at last true to herself, the feeling of having acquired standards of civilisation comparable to the Continental and of showing at least the promise of becoming a world-power of the stature of Spain and Portugal, was sufficiently diffused through the whole country and through the different classes of society to make it possible for an epic writer to speak for a large body of men. Corresponding to this consciousness of having grown more civilised was an enrichment of the language and a greater skill in the artifices of rhetoric.

Coming to the use the Elizabethans made of these epic potentialities, I should say that they produced three important but imperfect epic attempts: Shakespeare's History Plays, Spenser's *Faerie Queene*, and Sidney's *Arcadia*. Daniel's *Civil Wars* comes into the picture, but only in a smaller way.

By Shakespeare's History Plays I mean the cycle of eight plays, based on Hall's work, dealing with English history from the reign of Richard II to the Battle of Bosworth. They cannot figure in this book, both because I exclude dramatic forms of the epic spirit and because I have already dealt with their epic character, in my book on Shakespeare's History Plays.[1] It must suffice to say that these plays do express, uneconomically and fitfully it must be granted, but in the end better than any other works, the temper of Elizabethan England. In the present context the most important thing to remember is that in expressing this temper they are closely akin to the other two great epic attempts. They may present a higher proportion of purely historical matter; but Shakespeare differed from the other writers of historical plays in being far more philosophical. He was always aware of the world order that was the background of all history and he saw

---

[1] See especially pp. 241-4, 262-3, 298-304.

history not as a series of unrelated events but as a pattern. This philo-sophical temper unites him to Spenser and Sidney far more than his greater abundance of historical detail distinguishes him from them. Nor must we overlook the amount of political matter in the *Faerie Queene* and *Arcadia*. The gentleman whom Spenser wished to fashion was also one of his country's rulers; and the ethical virtues which he was to acquire would find their highest expression in political or military action. *Arcadia* is primarily concerned with how to fashion perfect specimens of the ruling class, the love interest, however important and bulky, being secondary.

As the medieval epic had been primarily religious, so the Renais-sance epic was primarily social and political. The three great Eliza-bethan manifestations of the epic spirit are all perfectly representative of their age in Europe. For epic perfection none of them can compete with *Paradise Lost*, but taken together they constitute the most substantial body of epicising works in the whole of English literature.[1]

[1] I have been brief on the historical background of the Elizabethan epic, because I have dealt with it at length in my *Shakespeare's History Plays*. What is valid for Shakespeare is equally valid for Spenser and Sidney.

CHAPTER IX

SPENSER

Spenser could have planned an heroic design on the exact classic model. . . . But the charms of fairy *prevailed. And if any think, he was seduced by Ariosto into this choice, they should consider that it could be only for the sake of his subject; for the genius and character of these poets was widely different. Under this idea then of a Gothic, not classical poem, the Faery Queen is to be read and criticized.*

(Hurd, *Letters on Chivalry*, 1762)

THOUGH much Elizabethan criticism was amateurish and easy going, that on which Spenser and Sidney based their epic attempts was the reverse. As Renwick has shown, Spenser wrote in the full consciousness of a formidable array of inherited literary conventions, while Sidney's *Defence of Poesie* is the work of a professional, fully informed of what was going on in men's minds in western Europe. It cannot be proved that Spenser knew all the criticism of the epic that I have referred to in this section of my book, but it cannot be doubted that in some form or another he knew all the main ideas and that he reflected on them. He knew that the epic should be patriotic and exemplary. He knew that some allegiance was owed to classical precedent. But he knew too that there was good academic authority for the epic with more than one hero and that Ariosto was widely accepted as a legitimate epic writer. Above all I am sure he knew the doctrine, found in both Italian and French criticism, that the epic form was like the sea, or nature itself, in its immense variety. The deliberateness with which he worked is proved by his correspondence with Gabriel Harvey, E. K.'s introduction and notes to the *Shepheardes Calender*, and the letter of explanation written to Raleigh and published with the original appearance of the first three books of the *Faerie Queene* in 1590. Finally, there is evidence that he deliberately adopted the epic poet's career according to the precedent of Virgil and the rules of Vida. Spenser cast his first big effort at poetry in the form of the pastoral; and at the beginning of the *Faerie Queene* he both referred to this act and challenged comparison with the same development in Virgil with the lines,

> *Lo! I, the man whose Muse whylome did maske,*
> *As time her taught, in lowly shepherds weeds,*
> *Am now enforst, a farre unfitter taske,*
> *For trumpets sterne to change my oaten reeds,*

lines which imitate Virgil's opening the *Aeneid* with

> *Ille ego, qui quondam gracili modulatus avena*
> *carmen . . .*

In Spenser, then, we have to do with a poet who chose to compete with the chief epic poets, ancient and modern (these, as we learn from the prefatory letter to Raleigh, were Homer, Virgil, Ariosto, and Tasso), and who knew precisely the rules of the competition. And this is something that needs saying roundly, because Spenser is still widely thought of as an exquisite inconsequent.

Spenser was open not only to the critical theories of western Europe but to the toleration of some medieval literature that marked off his own age from that of Ascham. He was perfectly cool and unabashed in using the material of the romances, whether he got it in the sophisticated version of Ariosto or went straight to Malory and *Huon of Bordeaux*. He also acknowledged Chaucer as one of his chief masters. And, perhaps most important of all, he did not shrink from using among others the medieval epic theme of the spiritual pilgrimage. In doing so he betrayed no sense of guilt in departing from a strictly martial or political theme, just as he betrayed none in having several heroes. Indeed, in having a different hero in each book and Prince Arthur as the general hero of the whole poem he may have thought that he was combining the merits of both kinds, and thereby outdoing Ariosto, as he told Gabriel Harvey he was ambitious of doing. As for the obligation to imitate the classical epic, he was careful to stress in his letter to Raleigh his beginning the action in the middle; he was assiduous in shaping his moral lessons on the patttern of Aristotle; and he inoculated his epic with big doses of imitation of Virgil and Lucretius. In his epic intentions he was far from the shy dreamer he is sometimes pictured, and gloried in the very wealth of correct things that he was at pains to display. He must have thought of his poetry largely in terms of fulfilment; fulfilment of debts to predecessors classical, Continental, and English; of the current theories of the epic; and of the potentiality of his native language. He felt himself right in the centre of things, and his age enthusiastically corroborated his feeling. We should bear this self-estimate in mind rather than the drift of nineteenth-century criticism of Spenser when we try to penetrate the still largely obscure world of his stupendous poem.

Certain scholars, in particular Janet Spens[1] and Jsoephine W. Bennett,[2] have sought to stratify the *Faerie Queene*. In view of Sidney's having rewritten *Arcadia* on a more classicising model and of the various signs of patchwork, there is some probability in such theories.

[1] *Spenser's Faerie Queene* (London 1934).
[2] *The Evolution of 'The Faerie Queene'* (Chicago 1942).

Miss Spens's idea that Spenser's original plan was a poem in eight books of eight cantos, the first seven dealing with the Seven Deadly Sins and the last with Arthur's successful quest for the Faerie Queene, or Gloriana, or Heavenly Beauty, is very attractive. But my concern here is only with the poem as it is; and, whatever were the stages by which it came to take its present form, it shows the signs, in spite of dead ends and inconsistencies, of much labour having gone to the shaping. Spenser may have planned something other than this at the beginning; but he believed in what he had done by the end. My only business is to try to answer the question whether, as it stands, the *Faerie Queene* fulfils the conditions of the epic as I conceive of them.

The first question is whether the language and the verse are equal to the epic scope and dignity. Spenser's detractors might well say that his language is too diffuse and his stanza too monotonous to be thus equal. The answer—and the same answer applies to several adverse criticisms of Spenser—is that you cannot begin by putting the matter in so general terms. Spenser's language is sometimes diffuse, his stanza may become monotonous in certain stretches; but only sometimes and only in certain stretches: and the right way to deal with Spenser is not to accept generalisations but simply to be ready for anything. If you read Spenser with an eye constantly watching for instances of diffuseness and redundance, you will find plenty of those things. But you will thereby miss more important things than you catch.

Take first the diction. The real point is whether this gets there, whether it does in fact make its impression, whether it convinces. And if it does, as I believe it to do for the unprejudiced reader, one may then add that it works, more often than not, by a kind of enveloping method. Apart from the archaic words (which one can get used to very quickly), Spenser's vocabulary is remarkably plain and innocent; and because of its innocence we easily let it through. Even so, it does not always make its effect at once, but if it fails then it returns to reinforce its intention; and through its very redundance it ends by persuading. The process resembles the incoming tide on a stretch of level sand. At one time a single wave will establish the tide's progress; at another the tide seems to pause, and wave after wave is needed to gain the same amount of ground. Reading Spenser is like watching this process. Kenelm Digby described better than anyone else the general nature of Spenser's language in *A Discourse concerning Edmund Spenser*:

> Spencer in what he saith hath a way of expression peculiar to him selfe; he bringeth downe the highest and deepest misteries that are contained in human learning, to an easy and gentle form of delivery: which sheweth he is Master of what he treateth of; he can

SPENSER

wield it as he pleaseth; And this he hath done so cunningly, that if one heed him not with great attention, rare and wonderfull conceptions will unperceived slide by him that readeth his workes, and he will thinke he hath mett with nothing but familiar and easy discourses. But let one dwell a while upon them and he shall feel a strange fulnesse and roundnesse in all he saith.[1]

Here are two stanzas, quite simple and representative, that achieve, through Spenser's peculiar method, exactly the desired fullness of effect. They describe Phaedria bringing Guyon to her island. Guyon did not want to land, but Phaedria had been courteous and he did not like to offend her, although he had come to see that she was empty-headed.

> *Yet still she followed her former style,*
> *And said, and did, all that mote him delight,*
> *Till they arrived in that pleasant Ile,*
> *Where sleeping late she left her other Knight.*
> *But, whenas Guyon of that land had sight,*
> *He wist himselfe amisse, and angry said;*
> *'Ah! Dame, perdy ye have not doen me right,*
> *Thus to mislead mee, whiles I you obaid:*
> *Me litle needed from my right way to have straid.'*

> *'Faire Sir,' quoth she, 'be not displeased at all;*
> *Who fares on sea may not commaund his way,*
> *Ne wind and weather at his pleasure call:*
> *The sea is wide, and easy for to stray;*
> *The wind unstable, and doth never stay.*
> *But here a while ye may in safety rest,*
> *Till season serve new passage to assay:*
> *Better safe port then be in seas distrest.'*
> *Therewith she laught, and did her earnest end in jest.*[2]

If you look close you may find some repetitions, not strictly necessary, as you will find a very high standard of rhyming and a plain aptitude of diction. But if you simply open yourself to the effect the poet seeks to set up, you find that you have apprehended certain things with a maximum of ease and the minimum of fuss: a further detail in the narrative, the restrained annoyance of Guyon, the more ample excuses of Phaedria and her silliness in laughing (simply and without the least satirical intent) after rising to a perfectly respectable platitude. Spenser's ease reminds me of Homer's transparency, Homer who with his rudimentary syntax can succeed in expressing thoughts of a complication you would think it quite incapable of.

The same principle holds good for Spenser's stanza. The thought

---

[1] In H. S. Davies, *The Poets and their Critics* (Pelican Books 1943) 38.
[2] ii. 6. 22-3.

of it and the fact of it are two very different things. If you think about it, you are forced to perceive that there are four *b*-rhymes and that the last line is an Alexandrine. These two features—the first calculated over a long period to make a high standard of rhyming impossible, the second to make each stanza self-contained—ought in the nature of things to tell on the technique and ruin the narrative interest. Yet if you take the stanza as Spenser presents it to you and not as you think it ought to be, you find that his technique in no way deteriorates and that you do want to go on from one stanza to another. Having found this, you may read with a less prejudiced eye and see, for instance, the variety of rhythm he imposes on his Alexandrines, a variety that makes it ridiculous to generalise on the effect a final Alexandrine must have.

My conclusion is that though Spenser's diction and metre ought in theory to be unequal to the high exactions of the epic, they are in fact capable of so much that it is vain to set them up as initial bars to his competing with Virgil or Milton.

I come now to the question whether Spenser sees life in the varied way which is essential to the epic effect. That he is ample in a sense is obvious from the length of his poem; but is this amplitude of the right kind? The answer will depend on the terms on which we judge amplitude. Are they our terms or his terms? In our terms we take for granted that the following matters for instance are included: close observation of the details of human conduct and of the working of the human mind, a sense of humour, an eye for odd juxtapositions, a feeling for natural phenomena in apparent objectivity. It is unnecessary to add to the list, for it will soon be plain that Spenser will satisfy our terms—at least in any obvious and immediate sense—less than Homer or Milton, let alone any of the few novelists who have touched epic quality. But if you are content with Spenser's own terms, if, as I said you had to be in the matter of diction and prosody, you are prepared for anything, then you find an uncommon variety, though in things which we too readily think are incapable of it. Take human nature. Spenser is less rich than Homer in exposing its variety through the kind of human action that the majority has agreed to consider central or normal: the kind conducted in the 'vertical light' of the Homeric world. Spenser was not ignorant of this kind or incapable of presenting it; but his variety consists not in different presentations within it but in the differences of the kinds themselves. He presents human beings not only or even principally in plain traffic with one another, but also as dead instruments of a moral idea, or as intensely feeling receptacles of an obsession, or as actors in a show seen from a distance. In the same way, though he rarely calls up the actual object when he describes nature, he can present her under an uncommon variety of guises.

And here I must make a distinction: that between Spenser's naturally varied mind and the varied subject matter he deliberately set himself, in accordance with contemporary critical theory, to introduce into the epic. It is of his varied mind I have been speaking and shall go on to speak, for this is the thing that most counts, that gives life to a varied subject matter, and the lack of which no variety of subject matter can compensate. It has nothing to do with Spenser's deliberate choice of great themes, Platonic, Aristotelian, or political, as fitting his exalted task. The variety of these will be apparent in a later section, that which treats of structure of the *Faerie Queene*; and I need not say anything about it here.

One way to perceive the amplitude of Spenser's mind is to read some of his best critics and then to read the *Faerie Queene* itself. However true the criticism, one is first struck by the great proportion of the poem to which it does not apply. There is no need to go further than Hazlitt's classic account of the Spenserian music in his *English Poets*; it tells the truth as far as it goes, but it does not go beyond a few of the purpler patches.

The best I can do here is to collect a few examples of Spenserian variety and hope they will carry their own conviction.

Spenser is often praised for his incantatory power, but it is usually assumed that he shows this power only in his long, almost hypnotising descriptions, like that of the Bower of Bliss. But it may start up anywhere: in a single line,

> *And wrapt in fetters of a golden tress,*

which suggests the elegant incantation of Pope; or in a single stanza, as in this description of Blandina in vi. 6. 42:

> *Yet were her words and looks but false and fayned,*
> *To some hid end to make more easie way,*
> *Or to allure such fondlings whom she trayned*
> *Into her trap unto their owne decay:*
> *Thereto, when needed, she could weepe and pray,*
> *And when she listed she could fawne and flatter;*
> *Now smyling smoothly like to sommers day,*
> *Now glooming sadly, so to cloke her matter;*
> *Yet were her words but wynd, and all her tears but water.*

Spenser is often blamed for the deadness of his landscapes. J. W. Mackail, for instance, remarked that no wild life patters through his forests. And it is true enough that those forests do not usually recall the actual forests of our own experience. At their dimmest they are just literary conventions, things borrowed from the writers of romance generally, a mere signal (like the warning light switched on in a broadcasting studio to indicate that reception is now alive) that the poem is proceeding and that something may happen; and as such they do a positive job of work. Or they can take their share in recording mental experience. But every now and then Spenser relates his subjective forests to concrete experience and with the most startling effect, as in these three lines from vi. 4. 17:

> *Now whenas Calepine was woxen strong,*
> *Upon a day he cast abrode to wend,*
> *To take the ayre and heare the thrushes song.*

In the usual Spenserian forest there is no air, and most Spenserian birds are unspecified and artificial: as on Phaedria's enchanted island,

> *No tree, whose branches did not bravely spring;*
> *No braunch, whereon a fine bird did not sitt;*
> *No bird, but did her shrill notes sweetly sing;*
> *No song, but did containe a lovely ditt.*
> *Trees, braunches, birds, and songs, were framed fitt*
> *For to allure fraile mind to careless ease.*

But the air Calepine breathed has the concrete sweetness of air breathed by a real convalescent, and the thrush is an actual bird, whose actuality is not compromised by any moral or allegorical commitment. Spenser has a liking for caves, and most of them are like Shelley's in representing directly states of the human mind. But the cave-dwelling of the brigands who raided the pastoral countryside where Pastorella and her parents lived is an entirely different place.

> *Their dwelling in a little island was,*
> *Coverd with shrubby woods, in which no way*
> *Appeard for people in nor out to pas,*
> *Nor any footing fynde for overgrowen gras.*

> *For underneath the ground their way was made*
> *Through hollow caves, that no man mote discover*
> *For the thicke shrubs, which did them alwaies shade*
> *From view of living wight and coverd over;*
> *But Darknesse dred and daily Night did hover*
> *Through all the inner parts, wherein they dwelt;*
> *Ne lightned was with window, nor with lover,*
> *But with continuall candle light, which delt*
> *A doubtful sense of things, not so well seene as felt.*[1]

This cave is unlike that, for instance, of Mammon, for it answers to a physical cave not to a state of the human mind. The island, the shrubs, the grass betokening no habitation, the candle, are all actual in a way contrary to Spenser's usual practice. And they are so

[1] vi. 10. 41-2.

vividly actual that it is plain that if he wished he could have exploited this method of writing.

As with nature, so with a proportion of the action in the *Faerie Queene*, for instance with some of the battles and the love-making. At their lowest these can mean no more than 'the action is proceeding according to the rules', with the hope of better things to come.

> *Thus long they trac'd and traverst to and fro,*

writes Spenser; and we are comfortably assured that matters are proceeding according to the precedent of Malory. Again, he writes,

> *This day, as he and I together roade*
> *Upon our way to which we weren bent,*
> *We chaunst to come foreby a covert glade*
> *Within a wood, whereas a Ladie gent*
> *Sate with a Knight in joyous jolliment*
> *Of their franke loves, free from all gealous spyes.*[1]

There is nothing here to startle: the 'covert glade' and the 'joyous jolliment' remind us that Spenser is writing in one kind of tradition and they have just the import of a conventional opening of a game of chess. A game has to be opened, and the dull correctness of the opening does not prevent the stir of life later on. Nor have we long to wait, for the lady who has spoken these lines proceeds with

> *Faire was the Ladie sure, that mote content*
> *An hart not carried with too curious eyes,*
> *And unto him did shew all lovely courtesyes.*

In other words the second woman (for whom she has been jilted) was good-looking enough, if you didn't look too closely. The speaker has certainly come to life, even if in the 'lovely courtesyes' she relapses into the conventional. But when he pleases Spenser can give us violent action, and love-making of a very different kind. Shortly after the above account he describes how a brutal knight, charmed by the beauty of the lady just referred to, turns against his own lady and maltreats her:

> *Then, as it were t'avenge his wrath on mee,*
> *When forward we should fare, he flat refused*
> *To take me up (as this young man did see)*
> *Upon his steed, for no just cause accused,*
> *But forst to trot on foot, and foule misused,*
> *Pounching me with the butt-end of his speare.*[2]

The enforced trot of the lady and the butt-end of the spear correspond very closely indeed to such action and such an object in actual life.

---

[1] vi. 2. 16. [2] vi. 2. 22.

Or take the love-making of Scudamour and Amoret, when they meet at last after many adventures. The passage comes at the end of the third book in the original publication of the first three books in 1590; it was omitted when the six books were published.

> Lightly he clipt her twixt his armes twaine,
> And streightly did embrace her body bright,
> Her body, late the prison of sad paine,
> Now the sweet lodge of love and dear delight:
> But the faire lady, overcommen quite
> Of huge affection did in pleasure melt,
> And in sweet ravishment pourd out her spright.
> No word they spake, nor earthly thing they felt,
> But like two senceless stocks in long embracements dwelt.
>
> Had ye them seene, ye would have surely thought
> That they had been that faire hermaphrodite,
> Which that rich Roman of white marble wrought,
> And in his costly bath caused to be site.
> So seemd those two, as growne together quite;
> That Britomart, halfe envying their blesse,
> Was much empassiond in her gentle sprite,
> And to her selfe oft wisht like happinesse:
> In vaine she wisht that fate nould let her yet possesse.
>
> Thus doe those lovers with sweet countervayle
> Each other of loves bitter fruit despoile.
> But now my teme begins to faint and fayle,
> All woxen weary of their journall toyle;
> Therefore I will their sweatie yokes assoyle
> At this same furrowes end, till a new day:
> And ye, fair swayns, after your long turmoyle,
> Now cease your worke, and at your pleasure play;
> Now cease your work; to-morrow is an holy day.

For the powerful but sane sensuality of sex I know nothing to equal these lines in English literature. They make Donne's *Exstasie* look academic in comparison. And the criticism of sensuality through the phrase 'loves bitter fruit' is both sudden and brilliant. But Spenser shows us where he thought his norm should lie when he brings his book to an end in the traditional comparison of the poet to the ploughman.

What I have been illustrating in my paragraphs on Spenser's treatment of nature and action in the *Faerie Queene* is his power to range between a conventional or emblematical deadness to the acutest actuality. Before going on to his use of allegory, which contains a rather different kind of variety, I wish to illustrate the same power in larger units. It is rarely that Spenser is dramatic, that he approximates the doings of his people to what happens in the usual traffic of life. But we should see and ponder on his power to do this, if we are to get the measure of his variety. The most elaborate example is the story of Malbecco and Hellenore, and her seduction by Paridell. But this is complicated by the substitution of allegory for realism at the end in a way that does not suit my present purpose. And the most unmixed stretch of dramatic writing in the *Faerie Queene*, the stretch where the characters are least allegorical and most themselves, is the episode in the fifth book (5. 26 to 6. 18) of Artegall imprisoned by the Amazon Radigund and his rescue by Britomart. Allegorically Artegall stands for justice, Radigund for unnatural domination by womankind, and Britomart for chastity. But in this passage Artegall is just an honourable knight in captivity, Radigund an ambitious woman who falls in love with her captive, and Britomart, already betrothed to Artegall and deeply in love with him, a strong-minded, single-hearted, and passionately jealous girl.

The episode begins in imitation of the Dido episode in the *Aeneid*. Radigund is forced to admit she is in love with her captive, who, she recognises, is in her power not because he is the weaker but through mistaken chivalry. As Dido reluctantly confessed her love to Anna, so does Radigund to 'her nearest handmayd, whom she most did trust', Clarinda. She engages Clarinda to pay Artegall frequent visits and to woo him for her by hints and the hope of better treatment and final liberty. Before long Clarinda too falls in love with Artegall and proceeds to make trouble between him and her mistress and to ingratiate herself with him. She tells Radigund that Artegall scorns her offers of kindness; she tells Artegall that Radigund has given orders for his harsher treatment, but that she, Clarinda, of her good-will is taking the risk of disobeying them and of procuring him greater comforts. The relations between the three are purely human and dramatic (Clarinda has not even a nominal allegorical significance) and the verse goes forward with an easy, stealthy movement, un-obtrusive and directing the reader to the actual story. Radigund's confession to Clarinda illustrates the drama well enough.

> 'Clarin,' sayd she, 'thou seest yond Fayry Knight,
> Whom not my valour, but his owne brave mind
> Subjected hath to my unequall might!
> What right is it, that he should thraldome find
> For lending life to me a wretch unkind,
> That for such good him recompense with ill!
> Therefore I cast how I may him unbind,
> And by his freedome get his free goodwill;
> Yet so, as bound to me he may continue still:

> '*Bound unto me; but not with such hard bands*
> *Of strong compulsion and streight violence,*
> *As now in miserable state he stands;*
> *But with sweet love and sure benevolence.*'

The repetition of 'bound unto me' at the beginning of the second stanza is wonderfully successful in bridging the two stanzas and giving the sense of a flow of conversation. Meanwhile Talus, Artegall's squire, carries to Britomart, already in agonies of apprehension, the news of his master's captivity. When she learns that this is to a woman, her jealousy leaps to the bitterest conclusion and she will not allow Talus to complete his story, but goes to her room to vent her grief and rage in solitude.

> *And then she in her wrathfull will did cast*
> *How to revenge that blot of honour blent,*
> *To fight with him, and goodly die her last:*
> *And then againe she did herselfe torment,*
> *Inflicting on herselfe his punishment.*
> *Awhile she walkt and chauft; awhile she threw*
> *Herselfe uppon her bed, and did lament:*
> *Yet did she not lament with loude alew,*
> *As women wont, but with deepe sighes and ingulfs few.*

> *Like as a wayward childe, whose sounder sleepe*
> *Is broken with some fearfull dreames affright,*
> *With froward will doth set himselfe to weepe,*
> *Ne can be stild for all his nurses might,*
> *But kicks, and squals, and shriekes for fell despight;*
> *Now scratching her, and her loose locks misusing,*
> *Now seeking darkenesse, and now seeking light,*
> *Then craving sucke, and then the sucke refusing:*
> *Such was this Ladies fit in her Loves fond accusing.*

When she calms down somewhat she hears the rest of Talus's story, whereupon she loses no time in setting out to be revenged on Radigund.

> *So forth she rode uppon her ready way,*
> *To seeke her Knight, as Talus her did guide:*
> *Sadly she rode, and never word did say*
> *Nor good nor bad, ne ever lookt aside,*
> *But still right downe; and in her thought did hide*
> *The felnesse of her heart.*

Before she arrives to deal with Radigund she has adventures of the more usual Spenserian type, but when she does arrive she kills Radigund with a dispatch true to her character in the episode I have been describing.

I have spent so long on Spenser's power to evoke the feeling of actual life not because he should be judged primarily on this power but because it adds to his variety, to his reach in a certain direction; while the other things he can do are made more secure by this different type of competence. Nor is it irrelevant to take Spenser's essay on Ireland into account. It reveals a man of lucid intellect and keen practical ability. Such gifts help to validate the obviously powerful metaphysical vein in him. However, though one should value Spenser's dramatic gift when it shows itself (and I do not agree with Janet Spens's notion that as a rule it does so 'only when the poet's inspiration is running low'[1]) and the penetrating lucidity of his essay on Ireland, one should do so only in the context of his more usual and predominant gifts. As a rule Spenser is not dramatic, and his position as narrator is not close to, or identified with, that of his actors. He is a visionary, in the sense of seeing things from a certain distance, and as a show not an actual happening. And he is a visionary as much when he recounts action as when he describes places like Mammon's cave and the Bower of Bliss. Spenser's success as an epic poet will depend largely on the nature and the power of these visions which give his work its prevailing character.

To describe the significance of Spenser's visions is difficult, probably impossible. It is easier to say what they are not; and I can at the outset repudiate Hazlitt's insistence on their narcotic quality and Emile Legouis's on their primary kinship in form and effect to Elizabethan pageantry. When it comes to accounts of their positive significance, I must pay my tribute to Janet Spens's effort to explain, as the bravest and least unsatisfactory I know. Some of Jung's accounts of different forms of art may also be helpful.

In trying to understand Spenser's visions we should first decide whether his special methods denote special states of mind or whether he uses them to say roughly what the others say. For it is possible to reach comparable results through opposite means: for instance, to arouse the sense of wonder through realistic as well as through romantic means. First, it is best to notice how very different his means are from those of his predecessors in the epic; how widely he departs from them for all his assumption of pious imitation. His romantic method is flagrantly different from that of Homer and Virgil and Camoens; his debts of plot to Ariosto only serve to bring out his opposition to the authentic Ariostan temperament. If anything is un-Spenserian it is Ariosto's hard external brilliance. Superficially Spenser's visions may bear some resemblance to Langland's. But Langland's bent was dramatic and religious, and if he had been born in Spenser's day he would not have chosen to write in Spenser's manner. Further, it is instructive that Spenser succeeded in the dramatic method and yet refused to make it his norm. His preponderating genius must have

[1] *Op. cit.* 68.

been powerfully in another direction. I conclude therefore that Spenser's peculiarity of method was also one of mind.

Whatever the exceptions, it is safe to say that now and for many years past English readers consider that in the larger literary forms the normal method of conveying states of mind is through dramatic action and descriptions of nature which are not evidently symbolic. They derive their norm from classical narrative and drama, from parts of Chaucer, from Shakespeare, from parts of Milton, and from some nineteenth-century nature-poetry. They are also convinced that the general state of mind is more naturally conveyed through the particular detail. The general state of mind which the author is interested in and which he wishes to convey is broken down and parcelled out into a number of easily assimilable details, to be re-assembled as a generalisation in the minds of the readers. And the details are most easily assimilable if they consist of human action or natural objects. Wordsworth, wanting to convey a certain kind of awe, translates it into a description of a wild landscape on the Simplon Pass; and the English reader thinks this is a very natural and proper method. That he is able to include in his own response to Wordsworth's poetry his own recollections of similar scenes is for him a legitimate advantage. Shakespeare, wanting to convey a general sentiment concerning duty, breaks it into a number of pieces and embodies them in the characters that transact the rejection of Falstaff in the closing scenes of *Henry IV, Part 2*. But though this is the popular (and not on that account inferior) method it is not the only one, and it was not Spenser's. Janet Spens describes another method, Spenser's, as follows:

> Spenser, though he loved the world of sense, thought it almost accidental. The true life of man lies not in this temporal and material realm of mutability, but in the invisible world of mind. The soul's dealings with abstractions and values is the measure of its true character: the real tissue even of our secular existence is not the visible world but our reactions to it . . . it is this inner life that is Spenser's Land of Faerie.[1]

That is how Spenser, according to Miss Spens, saw his material. In another passage she indicates how he shaped it:

> He never deals so much with the sensuous fact as with the mental translation of the fact—with the use which the soul's faculty makes of the impact and stir of the physical sensation; and he is more excited by the infinitely various web which man has woven to adorn and clothe the physical universe than by the simple physical facts themselves. He cared more for the artificial than for nature, because in the artefact the sensuous element is more visibly held in solution by the concept.[2]

[1] *Op. cit.* 117-18.   [2] *Ib.* 70.

When Spenser, then, is most himself, he translates his general feelings about life not into the forms of men and nature that remind us of the real world but into dehumanised or monstrous figures and into physical objects that correspond but vaguely to the objects we see and touch. If this method succeeds, it should have the advantage of great directness. There is no translating the feeling into and back from the world of men and of tangible objects. But, in compensation, the dead and artificial conceptions into which the poet translates his feelings so directly must be very apt and striking to do their work; and the risk of signifying nothing is greater than in the more naturalistic method.

I will illustrate from an episode from the Pastorella incident in Book Six of the *Faerie Queene*. While Calidore, the book's hero, was living the life of a shepherd and courting Pastorella, he wandered off one day alone and came on 'a place, whose plesaunce did appere to passe all others on the earth'. This was a hill, set in the open country girt with high trees, and crowned with a spacious plot of flat ground, a perfect dancing-place. Hearing the sound of a pipe and yet fearing to appear in the open, he kept within the covert of the wood and looked to see what was going on. What he saw was the dance of 'an hundred naked Maidens lilly white' in a ring, three other ladies within this ring, and in the very centre a single girl. All these are dancing to the music of Colin Clout. It is a rapturous description, and the vision ends thus:

> Much wondred Calidore at this straunge sight,
> Whose like before his eye had never seene;
> And standing long astonished in spright,
> And rapt with pleasaunce, wist not what to weene;
> Whether it were the traine of Beauties Queene,
> Or Nymphes, or Faeries, or enchaunted show,
> With which his eyes mote have deluded beene.
> Therefore, resolving what it was to know,
> Out of the wood he rose, and toward them did go.
>
> But, soone as he appeared to their vew,
> They vanisht all away out of his sight,
> And cleane were gone, which way he never knew;
> All save the Shepherd, who, for fell despight
> Of that displeasure, broke his bag-pipe quight,
> And made great mone for that unhappy tune:
> But Calidore, though no lesse sory wight
> For that mishap, yet seeing him to mourne,
> Drew neare, that he the truth of all by him mote learne.

In the conversation that follows we learn that the maidens were Graces, the three dancers the three chief Graces, and the single girl

275

Colin Clout's betrothed. We know already that Colin Clout is Spenser himself. The general feeling the poet seeks to convey is the rapture and the elusiveness of poetic inspiration. The episode itself is intensely alive but is concerned neither with living characters nor with events that could occur in actual life. Nor is it primarily allegorical. It is the vision and its disappearance that matter, not the identification of the dancers with the Graces. And the vision is a wonderfully successful and direct agent of a general feeling, a feeling that has to do with the act of writing poetry. How successful we may the better realise if we meditate on what some recent writers, even respectable ones, have made of their objectifications of the artistic temperament. For another direct rendering of general feeling I refer the reader to Miss Spens's comment on the Cave of Mammon.[1]

Yet, though there are a number of other episodes in the *Faerie Queene* comparable to the Dance of the Graces and the Cave of Mammon, and though these pre-eminent episodes (partly through their poetical pre-eminence and partly because they appear superficially to be detachable from their context) are the most admired parts of the poem, they are not the rule and do not in themselves reveal the full variety of Spenser's poetical method. If we are to get that, we must turn to Spenser's allegories and learn to take into account even the dullest and most purely emblematical of them. Rosemary Freeman in her *English Emblem Books*[2] has an excellent account of the emblematical method generally and of Spenser's use of it, though I think she underestimates the effectiveness of this method when it leads to or is combined with others. She distinguishes the emblematical spirit, which belongs to the Renaissance, from the medieval allegorical spirit. 'For the mediaeval man the whole world had been symbolic, and all the details of experience had formed part of one unified allegorical conception of the meaning of life.' But by the Elizabethan age this total conception had broken up, and only fragments of the old allegorical way of thinking remained.

A much greater freedom of presentation was possible when a unified allegorical picture of the world existed. The personified figures of the later Middle Ages were often accorded a treatment far more realistic than that which the Elizabethans were able to provide. They could move and act because their place in the symbolised world was assured. . . . The Elizabethan symbol is isolated, and, partly perhaps for that reason, is treated statically and quite unrealistically. . . . The emblem writers, however familiar their material might be, never wearied of explaining its significance: over and over again the points of likeness between the picture and what it stands for are elaborated. They are not taken for granted

[1] *Op. cit.* 123-6.   [2] London 1948. See especially 19-22 and 110-13.

276

and made a part of the living human being as they are by Dunbar or by Skelton in the *Bouge of Court* or by Chaucer in his list of personifications in the *Knight's Tale*. Instead, the details are laboriously enumerated and attached to a figure that is, and remains, lifeless.[1]

This passage describes the detached quality of emblematical allegory very justly. And that some of Spenser's allegory is of this kind is undoubted. As good an example as any is the canto (ii. 4) in which Guyon and the Palmer find a handsome stripling being grievously beaten by a madman whom an old hag with hair growing only on the fore part of her head eggs on to even more outrage. Guyon plucks the madman off the stripling and tries to quell him, but in vain. Then the Palmer tells Guyon that before he can succeed he must deal with the hag. The madman is Furor, and the hag Occasion. Not till Occasion has been eliminated can Furor be quelled. Guyon seizes Occasion by the forelock and throws her to the ground. But even so she goes on with her abuse. Finally Guyon fastens an iron lock on her tongue and, when she continues to incite Furor by gesture alone, binds her hands to a stake. In this passage the forelock, the iron lock on the tongue, the bonds on the hands are all added to the circumstances of the story from without, they do not grow from within it; and they certainly deprive it of life. And it is appropriate here to recall that Occasion was a common figure in the Emblem Books; and that Spenser's presentation of her here reminds us of them.

But to isolate instances of this kind in Spenser and then to contrast them with the more lifelike allegorical figures of Bunyan (a common practice) is artificial and unjust. It is true that the lock on Occasion's tongue is most dehumanising, but it is also true that before this process she had transcended the narrow scope of the Emblem Books. She is indeed a formidable figure, impossible to contemplate with complete allegorical coldness:

> *And, ever as she went, her toung did walke*
> *In fowle reproch and termes of vile despight,*
> *Provoking him, by her outrageous talke,*
> *To heape more vengeance on that wretched wight:*
> *Sometimes she raught him stones, wherwith to smite;*
> *Sometimes her staffe, though it her one leg were,*
> *Withouten which she could not goe upright.*

It is precisely the mixture of such a living picture of the hag with the subsequent allegorical deadness of the iron lock on her mouth that makes Spenser so strange and varied and interesting and that makes a comparison with Bunyan beside the point. To see this strangeness

[1] 20-1.

in its acutest form turn to the end of the long, realistic episode of Malbecco, Hellenore, and Paridell (end of iii. 10). Old Malbecco, having failed to get back his young wife, who is now living among the Satyrs, and having been robbed of his money, goes wild and rushes over hill and valley. So doing he loses his human shape and substance and when he flings himself over a cliff he is too light and airy to take harm. He lands on a rocky ledge and finds a cave:

> Into the same he creepes, and thenceforth there
> Resolv'd to build his baleful mansion
> In drery darkenes and continuall feare
> Of that rocks fall, which ever and anon
> Threates with huge ruine him to fall upon,
> That he dare never sleepe, but that one eye
> Still ope he keepes for that occasion;
> Ne ever rests he in tranquillity.
> The roring billowes beat his bowre so boystrously.

> Ne ever is he wont on ought to feed
> But todes and frogs, his pasture poysonous,
> Which in his cold complexion doe breed
> A filthy blood, or humour rancorous,
> Matter of doubt and dread suspitious,
> That doth with curelesse care consume the hart,
> Corrupts the stomacke with gall vitious,
> Cross-cuts the liver with internall smart,
> And doth transfixe the soule with deathes eternall dart.

> Yet can he never dye, but dying lives,
> And doth himselfe with sorrow new sustaine,
> That death and life attonce unto him gives,
> And painefull pleasure turnes to pleasing paine.
> There dwels he ever, miserable swaine,
> Hatefull both to himselfe and every wight;
> Where he, through privy griefe and horrour vaine,
> Is woxen so deform'd that he has quight
> Forgot he was a man, and Gelosy is hight.

What is so astonishing is that this allegory crowns a powerful, realistic episode. It is no case of Malbecco turning from a living to a dead figure, as with Occasion; he is translated from one life into another of a very different kind. I admit that you could construct out of the cricumstances of Spenser's account an adequate, dead emblem of Jealousy; but the passage itself is full of passion and is far from inviting such a construction. Malbecco's transformation, though cast into allegorical form, is rather the direct rendering of Spenser's general horror of the workings of jealousy: a horror he puts into a different kind of direct statement, a purely homiletic one, in the first stanza of the next canto.

> O hatefull hellish Snake! what Furie furst
> Brought thee from balefull house of Proserpine
> Where in her bosome shee thee long had nurst,
> And fostred up with bitter milke of tine,
> Fowle Gealosy! that turnest love divine
> To joylesse dread, and mak'st the loving hart
> With hatefull thoughts to languish and to pine,
> And feed itselfe with selfe-consuming smart,
> Of all the passions in the mind thou vilest art.

In final illustration of Spenser's varied use of allegory I choose a political one. It is different from anything I have cited so far because it is a simple equivalence, with no startling changes of position, and yet strongly felt. It comes in the eighth canto of the fifth book, the battle between Arthur and the Soudan. The Soudan rides in a high chariot, and Arthur is quite unable to approach him. Seeing that he can do nothing by the ordinary means of battle, Arthur, for the only time in the poem, takes the covering off his miraculous shield. The brilliance of it dazzles the Soudan's horses, and they bolt in terror.

> Such was the furie of these head-strong steeds,
> Soone as the Infants sunlike shield they saw,
> That all obedience both to words and deeds
> They quite forgot, and scornd all former law:
> Through woods, and rocks, and mountaines did they draw
> The yron charet, and the wheeles did teare,
> And tost the Paynim without feare or awe;
> From side to side they tost him here and there,
> Crying to them in vaine that nould his crying heare.[1]

The whole description of the fight is one of the most energetic and elaborate and brilliant in the poem. The allegory, clearly political in its context, is of the defeat of the Spanish Armada. The light English vessels could not in ordinary open fight match the Spanish galleons. For the English to win, it was popularly thought, the direct intervention of heaven was necessary; and it came in the form of weather that scattered the Spanish ships. The runaway horses are the allegorical equivalent of the ships out of control. The allegory is so easy and direct that if it fulfilled the natural expectation of a modern, it could not fail to be dull. In actual fact it is thrilling.

Another source of variety may be certain traces of the four medieval layers of meaning. I doubt whether there is any organisation of them

---

[1] *Faerie Queene*, v. 8. 41.

comparable to what there seems to have been in *Piers Plowman*. Here again a medieval generality has broken down and only the fragments remain. But Spenser would not have been averse to using such fragments if they served his turn. For instance, in the dazzling account of Mercilla in the ninth canto of the fifth book there are at least three meanings, possibly a fourth. She is a character in the story; she is, as her name denotes, an allegory of Mercy, here in a high place and joined with justice; she is Queen Elizabeth; and she may well be a form of the Platonic Good. In the episode of Mammon's Cave there is a passage where the meanings multiply. Mammon says to Guyon:

> God of the world and worldlings I me call,
> Great Mammon, greatest god below the skye,
> That of my plenty poure out unto all,
> And unto none my graces do envye:
> Riches, renowme, and principality,
> Honour, estate, and all this worldes good,
> For which men swinck and sweat incessantly,
> Fro me do flow into an ample flood,
> And in the hollow earth have their eternall brood.

> Wherefore if me thou deigne to serve and sew,
> At thy command lo all these mountains bee.[1]

Here as well as the literal and moral meaning there is a third of the Devil tempting Christ in the wilderness.

In describing these different kinds of variety I hope I have made it plain that they do not occur in any mechanical pattern, but, as I said early in this chapter, you must in reading Spenser be ready for anything. There may or may not be large general drifts and great unifying ideas, but this doubt makes no difference to the endless variety of detail and of method and the need to read alertly. Spenser's syntax is not difficult and his expanded style makes for easy reading in one sense. But any alertness that is saved in one department is required to cope with the shifts of allegorical method, the shifts from the symbolic to the realistic and back. The true requisite for the reader of Spenser is a kind of sustained tact, a tact of knowing when to press the allegory, when to abandon it, and when to allow it to count for not too much without losing sight of it altogether. The need for such a tact should be the complete antidote to any somnolence that the so-called dreaminess of the Spenserian stanza has been supposed to induce.

So far I have dealt with Spenser's variety mainly in the place where it is least looked for, that is in the allegory. In his large subject-matter variety is usually admitted. Religion, Platonic idealism, Aristotelian

[1] ii. 7. 8-9.

ethics, political doctrine, and patriotism admittedly enter his poem. I shall not deal with these as testifying to Spenser's variety, though I shall have to refer to them incidentally when I go on, as I now do, to questions of structure and control.

Spenser's first aim in writing the *Faerie Queene* was, I believe, to fulfil the requirement of universality, the requirement stated so nobly in a passage I quoted from Tasso and in Peletier's comparison of the epic to a sea. And in actuality the *Faerie Queene*, far from being the placid lake, the Killarney or Lugano in repose, so often pictured, does attain to the grandeur of a sea, varying from calm to tempest and including in the shores that bound it not only idyllic bays but terrifying cliffs and the occasional discharge of sewage. Constituted thus, it can hardly remain within the dimension recommended by Tasso, the dimension that can be grasped by the average human memory. Even in its incompleteness the ordinary man cannot retain the whole in his mind. In choosing to compete with Ariosto Spenser relinquished all claim to the kind of unity attained by the best epics in the classical mode. He could only compose stage by stage; there could not be the kind of interlocking found in the *Odyssey* and *Paradise Lost*. However, though by writing at such length he forwent one kind of structural unity and of mental control, he may have achieved others of a different kind.

First, although he wrote other good verse, he did make the great sacrifice incumbent on the true epic poet: that of risking nearly everything on the great poem. He gave the best years of his life to the *Faerie Queene*; and, whatever the calls on his time when he served his government in Ireland, we can be sure of the singleness of heart with which he followed his poetic calling. And such singleness could be assured only by an intense exercise of the will. Secondly, even if he wrote too much to be able to keep the whole poem in solution, so that the beginning of the poem was not complete till the end, there is every sign that he took immense pains to arrange the parts. Thirdly, there is always the chance that in the course of a very long poem certain large trends or ruling ideas may show themselves and be the effective substitute for more rigorous unifying bonds. The first point will be generally granted, and I need say no more about it. But the arrangement of the parts of the *Faerie Queene* and the question whether any large ideas emerge from it and rule it are still very much open to discussion.

The parts of the *Faerie Queene* are very different in themselves and have different origins; and one may easily infer that they should not be associated any more closely than the separate plays of a dramatist. That is going too far, but any structural connection or pervading quality had best be arrived at through admitting and reflecting on the independent character and virtue of the parts.

THE ENGLISH EPIC AND ITS BACKGROUND

In his edition in 1715 Hughes remarked that the first book of the *Faerie Queene* was almost a separate poem; and, whether or not you go as far as that, you must admit that it has very important differences from all the other books and that it achieves a self-sufficiency not found elsewhere. For one thing it owes very little to Ariosto, for another 'the supporting imagery comes from the romances and the Bible, with scarcely a draught on Spenser's large accumulations of classical lore'.[1] It is indeed a purely religious book, a version of the medieval theme of the soul's pilgrimage. Woodhouse, in the important article just mentioned in the footnote, shows how Book One is unique in being set in the region of Grace, the region of revealed religion, whereas the other books, though there may be interventions from the region of Grace, are all set in the region of Nature. How predominantly Book One sets forth the theme of the pilgrimage may not be sufficiently recognised. C. S. Lewis summarised the book as follows: 'Una's parents, who represent *homo*, or even, if you like, Adam and Eve, after long exclusion from their native land (which is of course Eden) by the Devil, are restored to it by Holiness (Red Cross) whom Truth (Una) brings to their aid.'[2] This theme certainly exists, but the Red Cross Knight as well as Holiness is also the human soul, or Everyman, endowed with natural virtue and frailty, achieving something, falling, rescued by Divine Grace, and by the aid of Truth subduing the Devil and perfecting itself in Holiness. This second allegorical significance of the Red Cross Knight is plain not only from the trend of the story but from Spenser's letter to Raleigh. Spenser there narrates how the Knight's adventure began. At the annual feast of the Fairy Queen he presented himself as 'a tall clownish younge man' and it is only when he is equipped in the spiritual armour of St Paul that he looks like a knight. He is in fact natural man who can contend with the world's evil only by divine aid. In the poem he is not at all a consistent symbol of holiness: he is rather natural man, fallible, and erratic in his use of the divine armour; but not ineducable and in the end perfected. At the beginning he is able to defeat straightforward, palpable error, sustained by the instinct of truth that was his birthright. He also defeats Sansfoy or straightforward atheism or paganism, but, separated from Una, he is deceived by specious imitations of truth, including the Catholic Church. Then he is tempted by the Seven Deadly Sins and inhabits for a time the House of Pride. He defeats Sansjoy, perhaps melancholy, but is wounded by him: the pressure of the worldly life is beginning to tell. However, he has the strength of mind to leave the House of Pride, only to fall

---

[1] A. S. P. Woodhouse, *Nature and Grace in the Faerie Queene*, in *English Literary History*, xvi. 208. I am indebted to this interesting article in parts of the following pages.
[2] *The Allegory of Love*, 334.

victim to another kind of pride symbolised by the giant Orgoglio. This is not the crude kind of worldly pride he has escaped, but some sort of spiritual pride, probably the belief in human self-sufficiency. From this there is no natural escape; and he is saved only by the infusion of heavenly Grace, typified by Prince Arthur. It is significant that when captured by Orgoglio he was without his spiritual armour. The whole trend of the book so far is that natural man may go a certain way on his own resources but in course of time must come to grief. The rest of the book narrates the Red Cross Knight's re-generation. But this cannot take place till he is rescued from despair, into which he has fallen, through perceiving his failure. He passes through a species of purgatory and then is instructed by Faith, Hope, and Charity in the house of Celia, or heavenly virtue, till in the end he has a vision of the New Jerusalem: the pilgrimage through hell, purgatory, to a glimpse of heaven is complete. Regenerate and per-fected, he kills the diabolic dragon after a three days' battle that duplicates the three days of Christ's death and resurrection; and his perfection in true religion is typified by his marriage to Una in the last canto.

The first book of the *Faerie Queene* is the best shaped and most coherent of them all; and if it could have been split off and made an independent poem it would have been read more widely than it is as the part of a larger whole and have enchanced Spenser's reputation as a popular poet. Its very restrictions make it readable. And it is indeed tempting for those who wish that Spenser was more read to advertise this book as a little epic in itself, the culminating expression in English verse of the great medieval theme, matched in prose by Bunyan's *Pilgrim's Progress*. But to do so would be to do something Spenser never intended. Doubtless he meant to prolong the tradition of Deguileville through Lydgate or its equivalent; doubtless he meant to keep fairly clear of the Classics and Ariosto and be medieval and scriptural in accordance with his theme: but he also meant the qualities of this first book to be elements in a vast series of contrasts.

The second book of the *Faerie Queene* is both a parallel and a con-trast to the first. In plot it is parallel. Guyon, although he hardly stands for Everyman in addition to his allegorical meaning of temper-ance, does perform a quest that traverses the same stages as the Red Cross Knight's pilgrimages. He is initially successful, surviving difficult ordeals; he weakens and is the victim of enemies; he is rescued by Prince Arthur; and he succeeds in the main object of his quest. Where the plot differs is in the absence of penance and educa-tion after failure; and the difference points to a larger contrast. Guyon's action is ethical not religious; he acts in the realm of Nature not of Grace. It is true that heaven intervenes to rescue him. But

Arthur, although heaven's emissary in the rescue, is not heavenly Grace as in the first book but the prime ethical quality of magnanimity.[1] His intervention restores Guyon's ethical balance, and no penance or further education is needed. Another difference in Book Two is that a solemn historical theme enters the poem. Arthur takes on yet another part as the ancestor of British kings, including the Tudors. He is also the instrument of an ending different from that of the first book. In both the last cantos of the first book the Red Cross Knight was protagonist. But in the second book Spenser stages a superbly varied ending by making Arthur victorious in a terrible and monstrous struggle with Maleger,[2] and Guyon in the mainly passive struggle to resist the specious glamour of the Bower of Bliss.

Books Three and Four, although they nominally concern two different ethical qualities, chastity and friendship, form, together with a couple of cantos in Book Five, a single unit. There are certain links between this unit and the previous book. Spenser continues the solemn historical theme. As C. S. Lewis has shown, he is at pains to contrast the specious and barren sensuality of the Bower of Bliss with the true and productive sensuality of the Garden of Adonis in Book Three. There is more borrowing from Ariosto in Book Two than in Book One, and this makes a bridge to the predominantly Ariostan organisation of the great central unit. Here indeed is a really fundamental change. To borrow episodes from Ariosto is one thing, but to adopt a predominantly Ariostan scheme is another. Quite abandoning the medieval scheme of the pilgrimage, Spenser in his central unit adopts Ariosto's plan of keeping a number of stories going at the same time. It is a plan which can suit a brain of uncommon fertility; and, alien as Ariosto's mind was in most ways, Spenser had the fertility of invention necessary to make the Ariostan plan succeed. This central unit is Spenser's most brilliant effort. Within it are the maximum of his realism and his wildest romance, like the capture of Florimel by Proteus and her residence in his submarine palace; or the enchanting contrasted picture of the two sisters, the fierce Belphoebe and the pattern of affectionate femininity, Amoret. Pictorially, the colours are more broken and brighter than in the rest of the poem. There is more excitement and dazzlement than coherence, but a reasonably close reading will show that there is a single theme that overrides and binds together the less powerfully felt allegorical themes of chastity and friendship. It is that of love in all its parts and with all its accompaniments. It is love ranging from the bestial and incestuous

---

[1] See Woodhouse, *loc. cit.* 204-6.

[2] See again Woodhouse, 221-2. His idea that Maleger, only to be quelled by water, stands for original sin is most illuminating. Arthur, here an ethical quality, cannot quell it by his own power: only the water of baptism will work. This hint of the purely religious realm makes for continuity with the first book within a context that mainly provides a contrast.

to the most pure and spiritual; from the most tranquil fruition to the cruellest tortures of jealousy. It is a vast theme and quite different from what has gone before.

The fifth book is one of the least read, largely because it contains none of the great scenes of pageantry which are the chief attraction for most readers of Spenser. In the place where pageantry could have been introduced most aptly, the description of the temple of Isis, he is brief and restrained. Nevertheless, this book is in some ways the most important of all, for it deals with the supreme civil virtue, justice, and with his sovereign lady not only as the perfection of regal womanhood but as the dispenser of that supreme virtue. In his magnificent exordium on justice in general Spenser calls it the 'most sacred vertue of all the rest' and compares it, in the grand Elizabethan hierarchical manner, with God himself among the heavenly powers and the prince among mankind. Having so august a subject, the fifth should be a culminating book of the poem as totally planned and the culminating book of the poem as we have it.

In structure Spenser reverted to that of Books One and Two, making his hero, Artegall, first succeed, then commit the crime of sparing the wicked Radigund because of her beauty when she is at his mercy, an act leading to his enslavement, and only when found by Britomart succeed in his original quest of freeing Ierna from Grantorto (in other words establishing the reign of justice in Ireland). The allegorical world of the part of the second canto that has to do with the toll-exacting giant and his daughter Munera (who is the same as Langland's Lady Mead) goes back to the medieval strain of the first book. While the third canto, dealing in the main with the marriage of Marinel and Florimel, left over from the book before, ties up various threads that have hung loose from as far back as Book Two. Thus the fifth book serves to sum up the past as well as to set forth the new theme of justice. In pursuing this theme (apart from the splendid episode of Artegall's set-back and rescue by Britomart) Spenser gives several examples of justice in action through the agency of Artegall and his squire, the iron man Talus, and then issues into a prolonged exposition of contemporary politics through the just acts of Artegall, Arthur, and the Queen herself. This is the climax of the book and occupies the last five cantos. It contains some of Spenser's grandest writing but deteriorates near the end.

There is considerable novelty in the sixth book. Its general structure is peculiar. Calidore, the chief character, disappears for five of the middle cantos, and his place is taken by several other characters, chiefly Calepine. More important, the book is less violent, more subdued, and more inward than the others. In the opening stanzas Spenser says that Courtesy, the quality which the book presents, grows 'on a lowly stalke' and that 'Vertues seat is deepe within the mynd'. Humble people figure in the book: savages good and bad, shepherds, pirates. The proud Mirabella, who caused many lovers to suffer through her callous discourtesy, was low-born. Her foil, the generous but meek Pastorella, though in fact of gentle birth, lives, her origin unknown, a shepherdess. Further, it is the contemplative as much as the active virtues that flourish in this setting. In the sixth canto a hermit seeks to cure Timias and Serena of the wounds inflicted on them by the Blatant Beast and he tells them that there is no outward salve; only inner purity can help. The same is true for Mirabella when penitent; heaven cannot help her till she helps herself. Beginning the book in an undifferentiated allegorical way, Spenser slides delicately and quietly into the idyllic and thereby achieves something new. Allied to the idyllic is the mystical; and the book's climax is the account of the Graces in a remote pastoral spot dancing to the music of Colin Clout. The sixth stands in relation to the other books of the *Faerie Queene* somewhat as Shakespeare's last plays do to the rest. Like Shakespeare, Spenser chose a new model to motivate, in part, his new mood. I have written already of Heliodorus's Greek prose romance, the *Ethiopian History*, being a possible model for the Renaissance epic. This work together with two other Greek romances, *Clitophon and Leucippe* of Achilles Tatius and *Daphnis and Chloe* of Longus, were popular in Elizabethan England. They had all been translated into Latin and French by 1569; and the two of Heliodorus and Longus into English by 1587.[1] It is to the Greek romances that Spenser went to motivate the Pastorella episode, which is the climax of the sixth book.

The question that presents itself from this account of the different parts of the *Faerie Queene* is whether it reveals any rational structure. And the answer is that it shows Spenser carefully planning his bigger effects. The simultaneous similarity and dissimilarity between Books One and Two is very pleasing. But the similarity has continued long enough to demand a fundamental change, which is forthcoming in Books Three and Four. Book Five makes a climax with its heavy weight of political allegory, to which the delicacy of the next book is the perfect antidote. There are more links between the different books than is often realised; and, though there may be little close interlocking and many loose ends, Spenser could remember what had gone before. The episode in the fifth book of Arthur uncovering his shield refers straight back to the first book. Thus, quite apart from any structural unity created by the scheme of the twelve moral virtues of Aristotle set forth in the letter to Raleigh and supposedly followed in the text (a unity which if it exists I do not find at all satisfying), there are signs that Spenser did have a plan when he arranged the parts of the poem as he did.

[1] See S. L. Wolff, *The Greek Romances in Elizabethan Prose Fiction* (New York 1912).

Whether he had a conscious plan is another question; and I incline to think that he worked with a kind of unconscious tact. Setting out on an enormous scheme of twelve books on twelve ethical virtues to be followed perhaps by twelve more on the political, he may in the course of composition have acquired fairly soon the secret knowledge that he would never go through with his plan. He must have recognised that one allegorised quality was apt to impinge on another and that he was making his ethical scheme too political to allow, without redundance, his proposed sequel; in fact, that his great plan was not really working. From this recognition would come the secret resolution to substitute another and less rigid organisation. Unable to present a great serried phalanx of allegorised ethical virtues, perfectly equipped, individual, and yet chained into one engine of war, he substituted a less palpable and more insinuating fitness. The different sections might have to possess a large measure of independence, but not so much as need make them sovereign states. They would be in the position of component parts of a loose though genuine federation. In the act of reading, or, to continue the metaphor, in exploring the component parts, we are not particularly aware of the federal union; but later in reviewing the parts together we change our vision and perceive a fitness of sequence. The diversity in unity of the first two books is attractive in itself. There is a different attraction and a pleasing contrast in the complex unity of the next two books. Books One and Two are juxtaposed and counterpointed; Books Three and Four are intertwined. The fifth and culminating book is simple and heavily weighted with moral commonplace and living political fact and doctrine. It contains in its second canto Spenser's most declared and weighty statement of the great doctrine of degree and in its second half the crucial contemporary themes of Mary Queen of Scots and the Spanish Armada. It recalls the first two books by its plot structure; it points to the third and fourth through the acute contrast which its stern simplicity insists on. The delicacy of the sixth book befits the quiet ending which, more often than not, a very long work prefers to employ.

Besides this unconscious structural tact there are two large motives that help to hold the six books of the *Faerie Queene* together.

Although attempts to extract detailed political and personal significances from large tracts of the *Faerie Queene* are both unconvincing and excessively boring, there are some clear political references and there is a recurrent political fervour, bordering on the religious. And this fervour is one of the things that gives to the poem, in spite of the elusive, shifting quality of the allegory, so assured a tone. Although the old allegorical unity of the Middle Ages had broken up, the old assurance of an ordered universe, arranged on a hierarchical plan, still persisted in outline. That plan was less theological and more political than the medieval, and it may have owed its survival and certainly owed its peculiar nature to the political success of the Tudors. Through being head of the English Church as well as secular monarch Elizabeth held a position in the hierarchical order different from that held by a medieval prince: a position almost magical if successfully held and open to peculiar execration if unsuccessfully. Elizabeth emerged as the successful maintainer of order in an England still acutely aware of the earlier chaos of the Wars of the Roses and came to be looked on not merely as the successful maintainer of order in the practical sense but as the supreme English symbol of that Order which is the theme of the first book of Hooker's *Laws of Ecclesiastical Polity*. This state of affairs is perfectly typified by Sir John Davies's *Orchestra*, which, having as its theme the ordered universe seen under the likeness of the dance, brings it to a close in Queen Elizabeth and her court. Spenser shared the current belief and he used what I have called the Tudor myth, the fiction that the Tudors were descended from the old British kings and fulfilled the prophecy of a reincarnation of Arthur, as one of his means of expression. His version of the British stories that go back to Geoffrey of Monmouth concerning the Trojans in Britain and its early kings, and of the fantastic genealogies of Berosus,[1] contained in the tenth canto of the second book and the third canto of the third, are integral parts of the poem and are told with an energy which our natural distaste for potted history in verse usually causes us to miss. They culminate in covert references to the Tudor myth and the reign of Elizabeth. Spenser treats the Britons as the true possessors of the land and the Saxons as usurpers, punished for their crime by the Danish and Norman invasions.

> *Tho, when the terme is full accomplishid,*
> *There shall a sparke of fire, which hath longwhile*
> *Bene in his ashes raked up and hid,*
> *Bee freshly kindled in the fruitful Ile*
> *Of Mona, where it lurked in exile;*
> *Which shall breake forth into bright burning flame,*
> *And reach into the house that beares the stile*
> *Of royall majesty and soveraine name.*
> *So shall the Briton blood their crowne again reclame.*

> *Thenceforth eternall union shall be made*
> *Betweene the nations different afore,*
> *And sacred Peace shall lovingly persuade*
> *The warlike minds to learne her goodly lore,*
> *And civile armes to exercise no more:*

[1] See Isabel E. Rathbone, *The Meaning of Spenser's Fairyland* (New York 1937) 79-93.

SPENSER

Then shall a Royall Virgin raine, which shall
Stretch forth her white rod over the Belgicke shore,
And the great Castle smite so sore withall,
That it shall make him shake, and shortly learn to fall.[1]

Here the spark is Arthur, typifying the old line of British kings, awaiting resurrection in the remoteness of Anglesey, to be rekindled through the Tudor dynasty. This dynasty will both heal civil war and reconcile the Britons and the Saxons. (This bringing together of the Wars of the Roses and the opposition between Welsh and Saxon is not without all foundation, for the Welsh welcomed the Earl of Richmond when he landed from Brittany and supported him in the Battle of Bosworth.) The final references to Elizabeth, the Low Countries, and Spain are obvious and they are developed in the great political section of the fifth book. We must remember further that the action of the *Faerie Queene* is supposed to be transacted at a certain period of history, namely the reign of Uther, Arthur's father, and that Arthur is still prince not king. Arthur therefore is, in one of his parts, the historical Arthur. And as such his quest for Gloriana has a political as well as a moral and mystical meaning. It means what the Tudor myth meant: Arthur's reincarnation in the house of Tudor and now specifically in Elizabeth. How powerfully Spenser felt about Queen Elizabeth as a symbol of the world-order appears not only from the eloquent and prophetic tone of the above two stanzas but from the rapturous tone of his description of her whether in the form of the apparation that haunted Arthur, or Belphoebe, or Mercilla. They are a genuine tribute not to a remarkable person but to a great symbolic figure.

The Tudors and their ancestry were not the only means by which Spenser conveyed his feelings for a political order duplicating a world-order. There is also a very impressive episode conveying them directly. It is in v. 2 and it tells of Artegall disposing of an egalitarian giant. This giant considers the present arrangement of the world unfair and proposes to weigh all things in his scales and then confiscate all surpluses and make up all deficiences. He is the professed enemy of all 'degree' or hierarchical system. Artegall argues with much fervour that it is beyond earthly wit to weigh the ingredients of the world and of life and that anyhow God himself has ordained inequalities, and that 'all creatures must obey the voice of the most hie'.

They live, they die, like as he doth ordaine,
Ne ever any asketh reason why.
The hils doe not the lowly dales disdaine;
The dales doe not the lofty hils envy.

[1] iii. 3. 48-9.

He maketh Kings to sit in soverainty;
He maketh subjects to their powre obay;
He pulleth downe, he setteth up on hy,
He gives to this, from that he takes away:
For all we have is his: what he list doe, he may.[1]

These political themes are important in the *Faerie Queene* and exert a beneficial, steadying influence; they help to bind the poem together. They are also symptomatic of a larger and genuinely pervasive way of feeling, which I must try to describe.

Some sentences in Spenser's letters and his tract on Ireland show that he had a shrewd and even hard practical sense. Nevertheless, what really distinguishes his mind is a certain faculty of vision. I do not think that this faculty was like Blake's, that of seeing something other in an object and keeping both elements apart ('With my inward Eye 'tis an old Man grey; with my outward, a Thistle across my way'). It is rather that he could apprehend an abstract world with an uncommon intensity and thereby lend to certain things actually experienced a corresponding brilliance. His description of Arthur's vision of the *Faerie Queene*, symbolising so much else, must surely as its ground recount a personal experience. Arthur tells his own story:

Forwearied with my sportes, I did alight
From loftie steed, and down to sleepe me layd:
The verdant gras my couch did goodly dight,
And pillow was my helmett fayre displayd:
Whiles every sence the humour sweet embayd,
And slombring soft my hart did steale away,
Me seemed by my side a royall Mayd
Her daintie limbes full softly down did lay;
So fayre a creature yet saw never sunny day.

Most goodly glee and lovely blandishment
She to me made, and badd me love her deare;
For dearly sure her love was to me bent,
As, when just time expired, should appeare.
But, whether dreames delude, or true it were,
Was never hart so ravisht with delight,
Ne living man like wordes did ever heare,
As she to me delivered all that night;
And at her parting said, She Queene of Faeries hight.

When I awoke, and found her place devoyd,
And nought but pressed gras where she had lyen,
I sorrowed all so much as earst I joyd,
And washed all her place with watry eyen.

[1] v. 2. 41-2.

SPENSER

From that day forth I lov'd that face divyne;
From that day forth I cast in carefull mynd,
To seek her out with labor and long tyne,
And never vowd to rest till her I fynd.
Nyne monethes I seek in vain, yet ni'll that vow unbynd.[1]

It is the same kind of experience that Shelley described in his *Hymn to Intellectual Beauty*, in the vision in *Alastor*, and in the personal passage in *Adonais*, where he describes himself as having gazed on nature's naked loveliness Actaeonlike. But Spenser had a steadier and more disillusioned view of humanity than Shelley and he inherited and shared with his fellows an organised world-picture denied to Shelley. He was thus better equipped with the means of balancing his mental transport. The unexpected inrush of actuality in the mention of the 'pressed gras' shows in itself how well he could check a realm of vision by a realm of fact. But the vision is none the less powerful and it represents a species of feeling that held his mind. It would be possible to apply various unsatisfactory words to that feeling, and it may find best expression not in any phases of today but in the words of a contemporary, Spenser's friend Sidney, in his *Defence of Poesie*. Sidney here tries to explain the nature of poetic creation.

> Neyther let it be deemed too sawcie a comparison to ballance the highest poynt of mans wit with the efficacie of Nature: but rather give right honor to the heavenly Maker of that maker; who having made man to his owne likenes, set him beyond and over all the workes of that second nature; which in nothing hee sheweth so much as in Poetrie; when, with the force of a divine breath, he bringeth forth things far surpassing her dooings, with no small argument to the incredulous of that first accursed fall of *Adam*: sith our erected wit maketh us know what perfection is, and yet our infected will keepeth us from reaching unto it. But these arguments will by fewe be understood, and by fewer granted.

I have no doubt that among the few who understood and the fewer who granted this doctrine was Spenser. In whatever terms you put this 'perfection' of Sidney's, Christian or Plotinian, Spenser had apprehended it and felt the gap between what he had apprehended and what actually was on earth, an actuality about which he had no illusions. It is his sense of the two sides of this gap that animates his poetry, that casts such a glow over his greatest descriptions, that makes him feel so acutely about earthly mutability. His finest pageantry, whatever its connection with the brilliant externals of

---

[1] i. 9. 13-15. That these stanzas have as 'source' Chaucer's burlesque *Sir Thopas* means nothing here. Spenser writes with complete seriousness and at the height of his powers.

Elizabethan life, in its essentials says something like this: here is some experience, or something imagined, extremely good or, if not good, heightened above the pitch of average living; here is what normal life ought, but fails, to give. It should be easy now to see where Spenser's feeling for order, cosmic and political, comes in. Acutely alive to the gap between the glimpsed perfection and the actual world, he is deeply concerned with fostering whatever in the world was not unworthy of what he had glimpsed. One of these things was the political order established by the Tudors.

Spenser's visionary power serves both to control and to colour his poem. It motivates not only the great descriptions but the shifts in the degrees of allegorical meaning and those from the imaginary to the actual, it differentiates Spenser's from all other epics, and it provides a sustained unity of tone that quite saves the poem from incoherence.

It thus turns out that although the *Faerie Queene* cannot pretend to the close and unrelenting concatenation of the *Aeneid* and *Paradise Lost* and must forgo the peculiar thrill and pleasure that such concatenation gives, it does possess more than one partial substitute. Spenser had the sheer drive of will to carry through, without deterioration of quality, a very long poem. He had a mind that commanded certain steady modes of thought and feeling and imparted these consistently to his theme. And finally he organised his six books into a genuine if loose totality.

Finally, has the *Faerie Queene* a choric character, does it speak for a large body of people? In its own day it did. The Elizabethans had no doubt that it was their great poem. Its amplitude, its blend of medievalism, Protestantism, and Plotinian idealism hit off their taste perfectly. From the Augustan age on it has never lacked readers, and a high class of readers, but it has never got home to the big heart of the reading public (and I do not intend this phrase in a pejorative sense). Spenser in fact has been something of an oddity. It is not that people cannot understand the things Spenser saw. The gap between the best man can imagine and the actual world is something of which we are all aware in some degree and whose vigorous exploitation in poetry we can enjoy. People can easily recognise and enjoy Spenser's excursions into the actual world. What they find odd is the way round he sees things. Ordinary people will put up with and admire large measures of the extraordinary if it is reached from an ordinary beginning. They want their heroes first to have their home among them and then to set out on their lonely expeditions and strange adventures. On this condition they will surrender their attention to their heroes' reports. Shakespeare, perfectly at home in normal humanity, quite fulfils it, Milton pretty well. But Spenser, though aware of what goes on in the city, has his home apart outside the

city-walls. His habitual vision is rather strange, and the basic strangeness is not altered by fairly frequent excursions into the quotidian.
He is hardly one of us, however much he is to be admired. Thus, he
does not altogether fulfil the choric function of the true epic. But we
must not forget that in his own day he did and that the time may
come when he will be not only a great but a popular poet. And when
he is he will resume an epic status not indeed perfect but, in its
imperfection, attained by very few.

CHAPTER X

SIDNEY

Gallant Gentlemen, you that honor Vertue and would enkindle a noble courage in your mindes to every excellent purpose, if Homer be not at hand, you may read his furious Iliads and cunning Odysses in the brave adventures of Pyrocles and Musidorus.

(Gabriel Harvey)

The vain amatorious Poem of Sr Philip Sidneys Arcadia; *A book in that kind full of worth and witt, but among religious thoughts and duties not worthy to be nam'd.* (Milton)

His end in his Arcadian Romanties was not vanishing pleasure alone, but morall Images and Examples (as directing threds) to guide every man through the confused Labyrinth *of his own desires and life.*

(Fulke Greville, *The Life of the renowned Sir Philip Sidney*)

The Countess of Pembroke's Arcadia, *which is spun with great labour out of the author's brains, and hangs like a huge cobweb over the face of Nature.* (Hazlitt)

The Images which lie before our feet (though by some accounted the only natural) are least natural for the high Sydnean love to express its fancies by. (Lamb)

S. P. Sidney had ane intention to have transferr'd all his Arcadia to the stories of King Arthure.

(Jonson, *Conversations with Drummond*)

THE above extracts, taken together, should give some hint of the confusion of ideas with which Sidney's *Arcadia* has been beset. Milton called it vain and amatorious after having used it four times in his commonplace book as providing examples of political wisdom. Hazlitt thought it supremely laboured and unnatural; Lamb retorted that the Arcadian extravagance was for Sidney nature itself. In recent years, scholarly opinion, deriving mainly from a fine essay by Greenlaw,[1] has reverted to the general Elizabethan opinion, typified by the passage from Fulke Greville, that *Arcadia*, for all its complication of romantic incident, is in its outline a serious didactic work, Sidney's attempt at the prose epic as he described it in his *Defence of Poesie*. But, however active the scholars have been since 1913 in finding

[1] E. A. Greenlaw, *Sidney's 'Arcadia' as an Example of Elizabethan Allegory* in *Kittredge Anniversary Papers* (Boston 1913) 327-37.

things out about *Arcadia* and re-assessing its value, their findings have not been checked by the ultimate arbiter of taste, the intelligent amateur reader. *Arcadia*, in fact, is not generally read, at least in bulk; and I believe mainly for the simple and sufficient reason that there is no really readable modern edition. The standard edition, that by Feuillerat in the Cambridge English Classics, with its crowded print and faithfully archaic punctuation and abbreviations, is well calculated to depress the amateur. It is indeed a sad reflection, illustrating the growing gap between the scholar and the common reader (a gap even more conspicuous in America than in Great Britain), that there has been a great output of scholarship, published and unpublished, on *Arcadia* in recent years but no provision of a text to enable this output to serve any widely human use. The result is that we do not yet really know where we are with *Arcadia*.

It is also possible we never shall know, because of its incompleteness and of its different versions. (Incidentally, it is noteworthy, and especially for the natural inference that the epic is extremely difficult to achieve, that none of the four chief attempts at the epic between Langland and Milton, the *Faerie Queene*, *Arcadia*, the *Civil Wars*, and the *Davideis*, was finished.) Sidney died at the age of thirty-two and compressed much study and much action into his short life. Poetry for him was a most important part of the total activities of the properly balanced aristocrat, but it could not be allowed to encroach too far on the social and political activities. An aristocrat of the governing class like Sidney could apply himself vehemently to literature for certain periods; he could hardly maintain a steady and prolonged application to it while still an active servant of the Queen. Whether, if he had lived, Sidney could or would have contrived to give more of himself to literature we cannot tell. I had better describe the different versions and say to what version or portion of *Arcadia* one should look if one is considering it as an epic.

Between the years 1577 and 1581[1] Sidney wrote his first version of *Arcadia*. It was addressed to the ladies in the circle of his sister, the Countess of Pembroke, and it circulated in manuscript. But it was not printed, was superseded by the revised, posthumously printed version, and for some three hundred years was forgotten. In 1907 two manuscript copies came to light, to be joined shortly by others; and in 1926 Feuillerat published the first printed edition. The *Old Arcadia*, as it is now usually called, is a novel in five books with long interpolations of poetry and of incidental narrative at the end of the first four. It has a firm political backbone, but its main substance is amorous adventure and intrigue. It concerns the foolish and blameworthy acts

---

[1] See R. W. Zandvoort, *Sidney's Arcadia, a Comparison between the two Versions* (Amsterdam 1929) 5-6. The book is valuable not only for comparing the versions of *Arcadia* but for discussing earlier criticisms of the novel.

of Basilius, King of Arcadia. Basilius, though a good king, was over-curious to pry into the future. He consulted an oracle and, acting on an ambiguous reply, handed over his rule to a deputy and retired with his wife Gynecia and his daughters, Pamela and Philoclea, to a rustic retreat. Meanwhile Musidorus, Prince of Thessalia, and Pyrocles, Prince of Macedonia, visit the Peloponnese privately and pass though Arcadia. Pyrocles, happening to see the portrait of Philoclea, falls in love with it. To gain access to the privacy of Basilius's household he disguises himself as an Amazon. Musidorus, having decided not to desert his friend in his madness, sees Pamela and falls in love with her. He disguises himself as a shepherd. The bulk of the book deals with the courtships of the two princes, greatly complicated by the infatuation of Basilius and Gynecia, both in love with the Amazon, and Gynecia suspecting the disguise. Meanwhile the state of Arcadia falls into political unrest. The various tangles, political and amorous, are straightened out by Euarchus, King of Macedonia and father of Pyrocles, then happening to visit Arcadia. It falls to his lot to try the princes for the suspected murder of Basilius and for attempting to marry without due parental consent. But Basilius had been temporarily drugged not murdered; and the end is happy.

Old Arcadia (and if the old, still more the new) is not a pastoral, contrary to the still current assumption. There are shepherds in it, but that is because Basilius has retired to the country. The king's chief herdsman is called Dametas, but he is a genuine herdsman and unlike his aged namesake in *Lycidas*, who, in the genuine pastoral convention of the Renaissance, stands for one of the Cambridge dons. The political structure is clear and simple. Basilius, the king, once efficient but grown foolish and culpably negligent, is contrasted with Euarchus, the perfect ruler. Euarchus did not seek war but was a fierce fighter when attacked. In restoring the state of *Arcadia* he shows perfect impartiality and disregard of personal feeling, for he condemns his own son and nephew to death when the evidence is apparently against them. Musidorus and Pyrocles are perfect kings in the making. Nevertheless, the chief substance of the *Old Arcadia* concerns friendship and love, ethics not politics. Musidorus and Pyrocles fulfil the Renaissance code of bosom friends, and the game of love is played with all the ceremony of extreme sensibility and high rhetoric and with all the complications and cross-purposes that the age held dear. The telling is straightforward apart from the narratives within the eclogues; and the plot progresses evenly to its various climaxes and to their solutions. In its kind it is a harmonious and well-proportioned composition; but that kind is the romantic novel not the epic.

Old Arcadia, then, was harmonious in its own way. Nevertheless, when Sidney found that he had more to say and enlarged his ambitions, he did not take a new theme but chose to recast his first version. He died in 1586; and in 1590 the fragment of his revision was published. In recasting, Sidney altered the narrative method and added much new matter. His revision breaks off in the middle of some of this new matter, but he had reached the point in the main story (which he preserved) where the princes have succeeded or nearly succeeded in their courtship. In 1593 Sidney's sister, the Countess of Pembroke, issued an expanded version of the 1590 volume. With certain differences, not to the point here, this new version consists of the 1590 volume together with the rest of the story according to *Old Arcadia*. The Countess did not venture to complete the material added in the 1590 version but was content to leave a gap and to resume the plot of *Old Arcadia* at the point in it where Sidney had arrived in his revision. The 1593 version, though it became the accepted one, both adds nothing worth considering to the fragmentary revision of 1590 and lacks Sidney's own warrant, and I cannot take it into account. When I refer to *Arcadia* and consider it as an epic, it is the unfinished 1590 version I mean.

Structurally the old *Arcadia* had been straightforward in the romance manner. The new *Arcadia* is constructed on the classical model of Heliodorus, with the action beginning in the middle and previous action narrated. It also has resemblances with Xenophon's *Cyropedia*.[1] There can be no doubt that Sidney was glancing at his revised *Arcadia* when he wrote about the prose-poem in general in his *Defence of Poesie*:

> The greatest part of Poets have apparelled their poeticall inventions in that numbrous kinde of writing which is called verse: indeed but apparelled, verse being but an ornament and no cause to Poetry; sith there have beene many most excellent Poets that never versified, and now swarme many versifiers that neede never aunswere to the name of Poets. For *Xenophon*, who did imitate so excellently as to give us *effigiem iusti imperii*, the portraiture of a just Empire, under the name of *Cyrus*, made therein an absolute heroicall Poem. So did *Heliodorus* in his sugred invention of that picture of love in *Theagines* and *Cariclea*. And yet both these writ in Prose: which I speak to shew, that it is not riming and versing that maketh a Poet, no more then a long gowne maketh an Advocate; who though he pleaded in armor should be an Advocate and no Souldier. But it is that fayning notable images of vertues, vices, or what els, with that delightfull teaching, which must be the right describing note to know a Poet by.

The new *Arcadia* corresponds to this passage not only through its imitating the *Cyropedia* and the *Ethiopica* but in its heightened didactic tone, its far more emphatic 'fayning notable images' of virtues and

---

[1] See Greenlaw, *op. cit.* 331.

vices. The truth of this becomes evident if we consider the main additions.

To go into this matter of additions in any detail would take far too long, for Sidney added many new motives. But his principal additions are two: much more ample information about the earlier deeds of Musidorus and Pyrocles and the very long and important episode of Cecropia, sister-in-law to Basilius, inciting her son Amphialus to wrest the throne of Arcadia from his uncle. The first addition serves to make the new *Arcadia* relatively more martial and political and less erotic than the old. The second not only has the same effect but serves to alter the whole balance and tone of the novel. I must explain briefly how it does this. In *Old Arcadia* no major character was a villain; by adding the villainous Cecropia to the major characters Sidney almost added a new dimension to his novel. Cecropia is boundlessly ambitious and quite ruthless and unscrupulous. She dominates her son Amphialus and distorts his naturally good character a long way (but not quite irredeemably) to evil. We hear of her evil nature first through the adventure of the lion and the bear. In *Old Arcadia* these beasts had broken into Basilius's country quiet, to be killed by the two princes. They served, through the princely valour that went to their killing, to promote the course of true love; Pamela and Philoclea naturally warming towards their protectors. We are not told how the beasts got there. In the revised *Arcadia* we have the same episode but with the added information that Cecropia had them let loose from her menagerie in the hope that they would harm Basilius and his family. Later she succeeds by a stratagem in capturing Pamela, Philoclea, and Zelmane (as Pyrocles called himself in his Amazonian disguise) and holds them prisoner in her castle. Cecropia subjects the captive princesses to torture both physical and mental and persuades Amphialus, in love with Philoclea, to force his suit on her. Zelmane is nearly driven to suicide by the exhibition of the pretended execution of Philoclea. Cecropia is an atheist of the Lucretian school and she tries to argue Pamela out of her religion. The theme of a supreme test of character and of martyrdom is added to *Arcadia* through this episode. Naturally the Arcadians rouse themselves to deal with Cecropia's crimes, and there result battles more closely and lengthily described than any in *Old Arcadia*. This testing of character and these battles not only give *Arcadia* a new and different type of seriousness but structurally they constitute the climax. They turn *Arcadia* into a different kind of novel, one dealing principally with the ultimate problems of man's destiny and in its scope competent to be an epic. The question whether these very serious additions blend with the predominantly erotic character of the first version must wait till I consider the success of the structure. All I seek to assert now is that the ingredients of the revised *Arcadia* admit of the epic dignity.

Having made that assertion I can leave *Old Arcadia* and ask whether the *Arcadia* of 1590, as far as it goes, realises the epic potentialities of its ingredients.

At the outset we are confronted with the style, for according to some of its critics it could certainly not be the vehicle of the most serious kind of feelings. The popular conception of the style is of the high fantastic, and Hazlitt gave the most brilliant as well as the most hostile account of it at the end of his sixth lecture on the *Literature of the Age of Elizabeth*. Recent writers on *Arcadia* do not regard Hazlitt's attack as important; at any rate they mostly ignore it. But Hazlitt says things about *Arcadia* that have enough truth in them to make it perilous not to heed them. What Hazlitt cannot abide and what no reader can ignore is a persistence in amplifying the plain sense of a thing. Sidney, says Hazlitt,

> never lets a casual observation pass without perplexing it with an endless running commentary, he never states a feeling without so many *circumambages*, without so many interlineations and paren-thetical remarks on all that can be said for it, and anticipations of all that can be said against it, and he never mentions a fact without giving so many circumstances and conjuring up so many things that it is like or not like, that you lose the main clue of the story in its infinite ramifications and intersections.

Hazlitt will not even have it that Sidney's habit of amplification springs from poetic vitality; on the contrary it shows only a low poetic vitality in subservience to an irrelevantly high intellectual one.

> The quaint and pedantic style here objected to was not, however, the natural growth of untutored fancy, but an artificial excrescence transferred from logic and rhetoric to poetry. It was not owing to the excess of imagination, but to the want of it, that is, to the pre-dominance of the mere understanding or dialectic faculty over the imaginative and the sensitive. . . . Imagination consists in enriching one idea by another, which has the same feeling or set of associa-tions belonging to it in a higher or more striking degree; the quaint or scholastic style consists in comparing one thing to another by the mere process of abstraction, and the more forced and naked the comparison, the less of harmony or congruity there is in it, the more wire-drawn and ambiguous the link of generalisation by which objects are brought together, the greater is the triumph of the false and fanciful style.

Hazlitt's attack, so reminiscent of Johnson's on the Metaphysicals, whether justified or not, goes, again like Johnson's, to the heart of the matter. There are many stretches of the *Arcadia* where every sentiment is qualified in some way or another; and Sidney did exert his dialectical faculty extensively in composing them. In fact, he wrote a great deal of prose in a style that anticipated the Metaphysical style in verse. Of such a style, whether in prose or verse, we are now rightly more tolerant. But there are certain natural limits to its use. In Donne it graces the individual *Songs and Sonettes* better than it does the sustained length of the *Anniversaries*. In reading certain parts of *Arcadia* and the *Anniversaries* alike the reader not excessively prejudiced in favour of the Metaphysical style is forced to exclaim to himself something like, 'the damned fellow can't keep off it', or 'if only he would spare us for a few minutes'. The wit browbeats the reader and ends by dulling his faculties. Here is a passage containing samples of the kind of writing in *Arcadia* I am thinking of:

> Then fell she to so pitifull a declaration of the insupportablenes of her desires, that *Dorus* eares (not able to shew what woundes that discourse gave unto them) procured his eyes with teares to give testimonie, how much they suffered for her suffering: till passion (a most cumbersome guest to itselfe) made *Zelmane* (the sooner to shake it off) earnestly intreate *Dorus*, that he also (with like freedom of discourse) would bestow a Mappe of his little worlde, upon her; that she might see, whether it were troubled with such unhabitable climes of colde despaires, and hot rages, as hers was. And so walking under a fewe Palme trees, (which being loving in their own nature, seemed to give their shadow the willinger, because they held discourse of love) *Dorus* thus entred to the description of his fortune.
>
> Alas (said he) deare Cosin, that it hath pleased the high powers to throwe us to such an estate, as the onely entercourse of our true friendshippe, must be a bartring of miseries. For my parte, I must confesse indeede, that from a huge darkenes of sorrowes, I am crept (I cannot say to a lightsomnes, but) to a certain dawning, or rather, peeping out of some possibilitie of comfort: But woe is me, so far from the marke of my desires, that I rather thinke it such a light, as comes through a small hole to a dungeon, that the miserable caitife may the better remember the light, of which he is deprived: or like a scholler, who is onely come to that degree of knowledge, to finde him selfe utterly ignorant.[1]

The first paragraph of this passage is typical of what maddened Hazlitt: who would have complained that instead of mentioning the palms and allowing them to do their own work Sidney must needs complicate the effect and hold up the action by attributing to them gratuitously a kind of life they do not in fact possess; that instead of asking plainly for a summary of Dorus's state of mind—the real point —Zelmane drags in the commonplace of the great world of nature

---

[1] *Arcadia, 1590*, ed. Feuillerat (Cambridge 1912) 152-3. Subsequent references to the revised *Arcadia* will be to the pages of this edition.

and the little world of man and frigidly puts human feelings in terms of physical geography, of arctic ice and desert heat. Now in one sense Hazlitt was wrong in attacking such a loading of the plain action. He failed to see that Sidney wanted to write like this, that his emotions dictated these intellectual parentheses. He failed also to see that to any Elizabethan it was natural to introduce the symbolism of the palm and to go beyond its mere physical, vegetable self; and that Sidney delighted to compare microcosm to macrocosm because he was greatly aware that God's creation was, for all its diversity, yet of a piece. Lamb, in fact, knew better than Hazlitt when he said that for a Sidney it was natural to be unnatural. But in another sense Hazlitt was right; for there is a limit to the amount of this paren-thetical writing the ordinary reader can endure on end. It is no use justifying the parts of a long passage if they offend when taken to-gether. And there are stretches in *Arcadia* that weary. But I must add the immediate qualification that their number is far smaller than Hazlitt and his school imagine. That the school of Hazlitt still flourishes is clear from T. S. Eliot's statement that 'the *Arcadia* is a monument of dulness'.[1] And the only way I can account for such flourishing is to suppose that an immediate dislike for such para-graphs as I have been discussing clouds the reader's vision and persuades him to see all the rest of *Arcadia* (except for a few habitually anthologised passages) in the same guise. This process of obfuscation can be illustrated by turning to the second paragraph of the extract under discussion. Here there is more imagery and less circumlocution. When in the first paragraph Dorus's ears pass on to his eyes the job of showing sympathy with Zelmane's grief, Sidney is indeed in the region of rhetoric, of preconceived decorum, of manners not of feeling. But when in the next paragraph Dorus tries to define the 'huge darknes' of his sorrows and feels his way from one comparison to another, Sidney has stopped being rhetorical and is seeking to de-scribe as well as he can the motions of a human heart. Now it would not be difficult for a reader, hating the literary climate of the first paragraph, to read the second so slackly as not to see the change, to consider the progression from a 'lightsomnes' to 'a certain dawning' and then to a 'peeping out' to be mere rhetorical amplification, when it is actually a search for ever more and more precision. Having missed the greater naturalness and directness of the second paragraph, such a reader must miss another thing: the contrast between the two para-graphs; the first resembling a stilted recitative, the second a freely melodic air.

This last observation brings me to the principal thing I have to say about the style of *Arcadia*. In spite of some stretches where the rhetorically parenthetical style is sustained too long for the reader's

[1] *The Use of Poetry and the Use of Criticism* (London 1933) 51.

comfort, Sidney in his revised *Arcadia* showed a variety and a contrast of styles with which, popularly, he has never been credited. Further, this variety is much greater and more evident in the new than in the old *Arcadia*; corresponding with the maturer power of Sidney's mind.

The first few pages of the revised *Arcadia*, which are new writing, furnish an evident example of contrasted styles: an example particularly significant too, because here, if anywhere, in his revision, Sidney would have sought to establish his tone and demonstrate his method. *Arcadia* opens with the two shepherds, Strephon and Claius, haunting the coast of Laconia at the spot whence their adored mistress, Urania, embarked for the island of Cythera. These two are a superior sort of shepherd and they lack all jealousy in their hopeless common passion for Urania. Urania is a mysterious figure, just mentioned in *Old Arcadia* as being 'thought a Shepherdes Daughter, but in deede of farr greater byrthe'. In the new *Arcadia* on a later page she is the subject of one of the most thrilling short passages Sidney ever composed, itself an instance of a style far removed from the ample and parenthetical. Among the descriptions of the pictures carried in triumph by Phalanthus after his defeat of the champions who fought for the different subjects of these pictures occurs the following:

> It was of a young mayd, which sate pulling out a thorne out of a Lambs foote, with her looke so attentive uppon it, as if that little foote coulde have been the circle of her thoughts; her apparell so poore, as it had nothing but the inside to adorne it; a shephooke lying by her with a bottle upon it. But with al that povertie, beauty plaid the prince, and commanded as many harts as the greatest Queene there did. Her beautie and her estate made her quicklie to be known to be the faire shepheardesse, *Urania*.[1]

Whether Strephon and Claius represent actual people or symbolise a contemplative kind of man I do not know; but plainly Urania is not named so for nothing and represents something heavenly towards which a chosen few aspire. After referring to the other shepherds and their ordinary shepherdish occupations, Strephon says:

> Ah you base minded wretches, are your thoughts so deeply bemired in the trade of ordinary worldlings, as for respect of gaine some paultry wooll may yeeld you, to let so much time passe without knowing perfectly her estate, especially in so troublesome a season? to leave that shore unsaluted, from whence you may see to the Island where she dwelleth? to leave those steps unkissed wherein *Urania* printed the farewell of all beautie?[2]

However, the present point is not the precise meaning of the two shepherds' adoration of Urania; it is the style in which they couch it.

[1] 104.   [2] 6.

And this is one of high and strained rapture, built up with elaborate artifice. It is as fully intended as the suddenness with which Sidney in this passage interrupts it with a very different theme expressed in a very different style:

> But in deede as wee can better consider the sunnes beautie, by marking how he guildes these waters and mountaines then by looking upon his owne face, too glorious for our weake eyes: so it may be our conceits (not able to beare her sun-stayning excellencie) will better way it by her workes upon some meaner subject employed. And alas, who can better witnesse that then we, whose experience is grounded upon feeling? hath not the onely love of her made us (being silly ignorant shepheards) raise up our thoughts above the ordinary levell of the worlde, so as great clearkes do not disdaine our conference? hath not the desire to seeme worthie in her eyes made us when others were sleeping, to sit vewing the course of heavens? when other were running at base, to runne over learned writings? when other marke their sheepe, we to marke ourselves? hath not shee throwne reason upon our desires, and, as it were given eyes unto *Cupid*? hath in any, but in her, love-fellowship maintained friendship betweene rivals, and beautie taught the beholders chastitie? He was going on with his praises, but *Strephon* bad him stay, and looke: and so they both perceaved a thing which floted drawing nearer and nearer to the banke; but rather by the favourable working of the Sea, then by any selfe industrie. They doubted a while what it should be; till it was cast up even hard before them: at which time they fully saw that it was a man.[1]

And there follows the vivid account of the burning ship and the blood-stained sea. One of the most sympathetic critics of *Arcadia* says that it begins with the shipwreck, thus having failed to remember that it begins with a contrast, both of substance and of style, between the idea of man's 'erected wit' and the pitiful spectacle of what in crude fact man has made of man. And if a sympathetic critic can thus go wrong, is it surprising if ordinary readers still assume that Sidney uses a style of unvarying ornateness through which to tell an unprofound though complicated and improbable set of tales?

Here is a second example of deliberate stylistic contrast. To while away the time in their country retreat Basilius and his company tell one another stories. They draw lots, and it falls out that the sluttish Mopsa, daughter of Dametas the king's herdsman, tells her story before Pamela tells hers. Mopsa's story is a beautifully ludicrous version of common folk-lore and romance matter. It begins like this:

> And so being her time to speak (wiping her mouth, as there was good cause) she thus tumbled into her matter. In time past (sayd

[1] 7-8.

she) there was a King, the mightiest man in all his country, that had by his wife, the fairest daughter that ever did eat pappe. Now this King did keepe a great house, that every body might come and take their meat freely. So one day, as his daughter was sitting in her window, playing upon a harpe, as sweete as any Rose; and combing her heade with a comb all of precious stones, there came in a Knight into the court, upon a goodly horse, one haire of gold, and the other of silver; *and so* the Knight casting up his eyes to the window, did fall into such love with her, that he grew not worth the bread he eate; till many a sorry day going over his head, with Dayly Diligence and Grisly Grones, he won her affection, so that they agreed to run away togither. *And so in May, when all true hartes rejoyce*, they stole out of the Castel, without staying so much as for their breakfast.[1]

After some more in the same style,

> Now good *Mopsa* (said the sweete *Philoclea*) I pray thee at my request keepe this tale, till my marriage day, and I promise thee that the best gowne I weare that day shal be thine.

Mopsa accepts the bargain and refrains, leaving the field to Pamela and her tale of Plangus. This tale, dealing with the machinations of Plangus's wicked step-mother, resembles Mopsa's in springing from the stock of immemorial folk-lore. Through this resemblance the exquisite art of the telling is made to contrast the more sharply with Mopsa's ridiculous ineptitude.

I give a final example of Sidney's variety of style; and from a different and more tragic context. The culminating scenes of the revised *Arcadia* are those that describe the imprisonment of Pamela, Philoclea, and Pyrocles (still disguised as the Amazon Zelmane) and the cruelty Cecropia uses towards them. Cecropia's maltreatment of Philoclea culminated in physical violence, which is thus described:

> At length, abhominable rage carried her to absolute tyrannies, so that taking with her certaine olde women (of wicked dispositions, and apt for envie-sake to be cruel to youth and beautie) with a countenance impoysoned with malice, flew to the sweet *Philoclea*, as if so many Kites should come about a white Dove, and matching violent gestures with mischievous threatnings, she having a rod in her hand (like a fury that should carry wood to the burning of *Dianas* temple) fel to scourge that most beautifull body; Love in vaine holding the Shield of Beautie against her blind cruelty. The Sun drew clouds up to hide his face from so pitiful a sight; and the very stone wals did yeeld drops of sweate for agonie of such a mischiefe: each senselesse thing had sense of pittie; onely they that had sense, were senseles.[2]

[1] 241.   [2] 470-1.

This is a high point of the book; and many readers may think it ruined by the intrusion of Diana's temple, the comparison of beauty to a shield, and the imparting to the sun and the stone walls the feelings of persons. They might also think that Sidney thus elaborated through sheer cold-blooded habit. They would be wrong. Sidney feels keenly but he remembers contemporary decorum and that a queen must not scourge a princess in the style a cook boxes the ears of a scullery-maid. And that his elaboration is not cold-bloodedly habitual but intended is made evident by the simplicity of a passage that comes very soon after. When the scourging is over and Philoclea is once more in her solitary confinement, Sidney describes the feelings of her and of her lover, Pyrocles, captive also and separated from her. Although Pyrocles did not yet know of Philoclea's scourging, yet his measure of grief was full because he was powerless to help:

> for well he knew the confidence *Philoclea* had in him, and well he knew *Philoclea* had cause to have confidence: and all troden under foot by the wheele of senselesse Fortune. Yet if there be that imperious power in the soule, as it can deliver knowledge to another without bodilie organs: so vehement were the workings of their spirites, as one mette with other; though themselves perceaved it not, but only thought it to be the doubling of their owne loving fancies. And that was the onely worldly thing, whereon *Philoclea* rested her minde, that she knewe she should die beloved of *Pyrocles*, and should die rather than be false to *Pyrocles*.[1]

This high speculation on the telepathy of souls and the dignity of Philoclea's single-hearted love were so far from any possibility of being vulgar that Sidney can safely put them into simple language. And in its simplicity the passage is both moving and deliberately contrasted with the mannered account of the scourging itself.

To sum up my argument so far, I have sought to show by examples that in his revised *Arcadia* Sidney commands a style of considerable range, a range that admits the possibility of the work attaining to the rank of epic.

I come now to the nature of *Arcadia* as a whole. Like Spenser, Sidney had current critical theory in mind when he wrote *Arcadia*, however little the reader is aware of such a remembrance. His claim that a poem need not be in verse and that Xenophon wrote a prose epic had been made already by Trissino and Cinthio.[2] Scaliger and Tasso had approximated the *Ethiopian History* to the epic. When

[1] 472.
[2] C. M. Dowlin, *Sidney and other Men's Thought* in *Review of English Studies*, 1944, pp. 257-71, claims originality for Sidney's notion of the prose-epic, which goes beyond Scaliger's pronouncement about Heliodorus (see pp. 229-30 above). It may well be that Sidney gave weight and vogue to a number of current notions, even if he did not create them.

Sidney revised *Arcadia* on the model of Xenophon and Heliodorus he knew, and meant others to know, that he followed the critical lead of western Europe. Trissino and other Italians had demanded the marvellous; and Sidney in recounting the amazing feats of valour performed by Pyrocles and Musidorus, the shipwrecks, the disguise of Pyrocles as an Amazon (destined to be the subject of a king's and a queen's infatuate love), the drugging of Basilius and his supposed death, and the accident of Euarchus having to condemn his own son to death sought not merely to delight his readers but to fulfil the epic obligation to astonish. Tasso thought the epic amplitude should not exceed what the average human memory could deal with; and Sidney's revised *Arcadia*, though it defeats the average modern memory, would have just been within the power of the better-exercised Elizabethan. Tasso thought too that the characters should represent a single quality of mind; and it would be easy to see, for instance, in Basilius foolish curiosity, in Cecropia pride, in Pyrocles courtesy, in Philoclea sweetness of disposition, and so on. K. O. Myrick[1] has written on Sidney's knowledge of the Italian critics, and it may well be that he was especially aware of Minturno. But one must not forget that debts of English writers to Italian critics may derive just as well from a kind of common pool of their ideas known through talk and detached from any particular critic. Sidney may have contributed to that pool himself, but he may also have drawn from it notions the contributors of which are unknown. The main point is that Sidney was aware of the gist of Italian theories of the epic and that he revised his *Arcadia* in the light of that awareness. And the most important single conclusion from the drift of this paragraph is to confirm the evidence of the *Defence of Poesie* that Sidney meant his new *Arcadia* to be a heroic poem.

Like Spenser, Sidney classicised: only more effectively and more extensively. Spenser claimed to have begun his action in the middle but intended to postpone any account of the beginning so long that the effect of his act would have lacked force. Sidney too begins at a far advanced stage of his story, but he does not wait too long before informing us of the past history of Basilius, Euarchus, and the two princes by related narrative. Much of the fighting is medieval, but the great battle between the forces of Basilius and Amphialus is predominantly Virgilian. The same kind of thing is true of the characters. Euarchus, the two princes, and two princesses are, humanly speaking, perfect. They do not conform to Aristotle's definition of the tragic hero. Cecropia, on the other hand, is un-Aristotelian in her complete badness. But Sidney makes Basilius and Amphialus Aristotelian. Basilius was a good king but corrupted by a foolish curiosity about the future: a curiosity that led him to deplorable acts and much trouble

---

[1] *Sir Philip Sidney as a Literary Craftsman* (Cambridge, Mass., 1935) 150 ff.

in compensation. Amphialus was naturally noble but he had the failing of being too much under his mother's influence. He becomes greatly but not irretrievably corrupted. It looks as if in revising *Arcadia* Sidney wished to cross the medieval unmitigatedness of most of his characters by Aristotelian elements. The resultant mixture of medieval and classical elements has a strange air today but caused no surprise to the Elizabethans.

In another way, too, Sidney is more modern and less medieval than Spenser. Though there may be incidental references to actual persons, though for instance Philisides and Myra may be Sidney and Penelope Devereux, there is no large allegory dominating the book.[1] The characters are firmly attached to the story; none of them even begins to turn into a personification of a quality. Spenser's Malbecco, once a jealous old man, ceased to be human and became Jealousy, living in a cave on a cliff. There is nothing in the least like this in *Arcadia*; and if, as said above, Basilius, for instance, can be made to stand for foolish curiosity, this happens not in the reading but by a process of deduction after having read. Again, *Arcadia* is like the *Lusiad* and unlike the *Faerie Queene* in having nothing to do with the theme of the soul's pilgrimage. Some of the characters may be educated by experience; but no one of them stands for Everyman, and the experiences are not arranged in the pattern of partial success, failure, repentance, regeneration, and triumph. Pamela and Philoclea are indeed tested in prison and through the test perfected; but they do not have to retrace their steps to the true road they had forsaken. They have never left that road and merely proceed further along it.

But in one principal matter the *Faerie Queene* and *Arcadia* are alike: they are both concerned with the fashioning of a gentleman. Indeed, whatever the difference between the two in their actuality, their authors had the same intentions. Spenser said his aim was 'to fashion a gentleman or noble person in vertuous and gentle discipline' and he divided his discipline into the ethical and the political. Sidney's aim was the same, but in what he completed of *Arcadia* he included that political education which Spenser said he might one day demonstrate in action through his Arthur after he had succeeded to the throne.

It is important to be clear on this main aim of *Arcadia*, for usually it has been missed. In the first paragraph of this chapter I mentioned the recent change of opinion on the book's nature. For some two hundred years opinion, with some notable exceptions, thought of *Arcadia* as remote and fantastic, as presenting a world of make-believe, once enjoyed as an entertaining refuge from the realities of ordinary life. Scholars have denied this opinion and have especially stressed

---

[1] I agree with Myrick here against Greenlaw. See Myrick, *op. cit.* 236-42. I have found some of the best observations on Sidney in this book.

the work's political seriousness. But if you do so too earnestly, you risk falling into another error. And for this error there are reasons. For one thing, Fulke Greville is very emphatic about the politics of *Arcadia*, and he, as Sidney's intimate friend, possesses authority. Greville spoke of *Arcadia* as an absolute repertory of every kind of political example.[1] For another, the *Old Arcadia*, though more romantically erotic than the new, is, where it is serious, relatively more political. There, the main theme, apart from the love-making, is the political disaster of Basilius's retirement, the consequent insurrection, the ultimate chaos, and the final intervention of Euarchus. The political chaos is indeed the climax of the plot; and the contrast between Basilius, the king in name but not in deed, and Euarchus, the perfect ruler, not seeking war but tested in wars not of his own choosing, is the grand contrast that gives reason to the whole book. Some scholars write as if the same was true of the revised *Arcadia*; but they are wrong. It is too easy to include in the revised *Arcadia* the portions of the old attached to it by the Countess of Pembroke for the 1593 edition. But Sidney might have altered these drastically, including the end with its main stress on the unflinching political justice of Euarchus. Anyhow, in the authentic *Arcadia* Sidney did alter the main stress of seriousness from politics to ethics and religion, and I cannot conceive that he would not have carried this process through. In the revised *Arcadia* the culminating episodes concern Pamela and Philoclea in prison and the perfecting of their characters through their display of Christian patience and fortitude in unjust persecution. When the revised version breaks off, Pyrocles and Musidorus have not yet reached the degree of perfection to which their betrothed princesses have arrived. Musidorus was impatient in his courtship and attempted to kiss Pamela before that stage had been reached, incurring her indignant censure. Pyrocles attempted suicide in captivity, when he thought he saw Philoclea's execution. It is probable that if Sidney had carried through his revision he would have made the patience of Musidorus and Pyrocles under the mistaken sentence of Euarchus match the patience of Pamela and Philoclea when in captivity to Cecropia. In *Old Arcadia* it is the ethical theme of friendship that is most prominent at this place, each prince begging for his own death in place of the other's. Not that Sidney need have removed this theme in revising; but I believe he would have introduced a more definitely religious tone in accordance with the powerfully religious tone of the culminating episode of Pamela and Philoclea in prison. Only when the two princes had cleansed themselves of worldly desires and even transcended their passionate friendship would they be worthy husbands of the two female 'confessors.' Through such a cleansing they would be the dominant figures of the

---

[1] *Life of Sir Philip Sidney*, chap. 2. Ed. Nowell Smith (Oxford 1907) 12-16.

last scene; Euarchus, still important, would become relatively less so; and the purely political contrast between Basilius and Euarchus would be subordinated to the theme of educating two princes and two princesses in the virtues—ethical, political, and religious— appropriate to their sex and rank. And the example of this educational process would be the supreme justification of the book and the means of raising it to the epic height.

This interpretation of the ground of *Arcadia* seems to me undoubted. It also approximates Sidney to Spenser. Like Spenser, Sidney passed from pagan ethics to Christian; from the realm of Nature to the realm of Grace. And in so doing he fulfilled what his contemporaries would undoubtedly have considered the duty of the most serious kind of poet. It is here that we should remember that Greville spoke not only of the political didacticism of *Arcadia* but (in the words quoted as one of the captions of this chapter) of its comprehensive moral virtue. Such virtue could not but include the ethics of the Christian religion.

As Sidney makes the education of the four princely young people his central theme, so he carefully arranges them in a pattern. Musidorus, the elder prince, is a more purely masculine character than Pyrocles, the younger. Pamela, the elder princess, has more male pride and resolution in her than her entirely feminine younger sister, Philoclea. (Surely Goldsmith modelled his account of Olivia and Sophia at the beginning of the *Vicar of Wakefield* on the corresponding account of Pamela and Philoclea in *Arcadia*.) As J. F. Danby[1] noticed, Pamela combines woman-and-man, and Pyrocles man-and-woman. But Sidney does not pair these two. It is the more purely masculine Musidorus who is set to cope with the more powerful woman, Pamela; and the more sensitive Pyrocles to understand and manage the more feminine woman, Philoclea. Danby points out that Pyrocles's disguise as an Amazon is not a mere piece of romantic ornament but expresses a symbolic truth: the genuinely feminine element in Pyrocles. And he claims, I think rightly, that this symbolic significance disinfects, as it were, the queer complication of events—the infatuation of Basilius and Gynecia—this disguise occasions. Certainly, this disguise is the nearest approach to the Spenserian habit of making characters shift along the scale from realism to abstraction. Anyhow, it warns us to be chary of approximating the conditions governing the acts it occasions, to those of ordinary life. If we do so approximate them, the double infatuation of the king and queen, the one old the other no longer young, is both ridiculously improbable and slightly disgusting. Kept in the more abstract realm dictated by the emblematic nature of the disguise, it qualifies as a series of moral examples of what to

[1] J. F. Danby, *Poets on Fortune's Hill* (London 1952) 50 ff. The section of this volume on *Arcadia* is the best modern appreciation of it I know.

avoid. To revert to the treatment of the four main characters, Danby puts the education which they undergo in terms of Sidney's pronouncement in the *Defence of Poesie* that Homer's Ulysses exemplified the virtues of patience and magnanimity. And these terms suggest aptly enough that combination of the active, Aristotelian, virtues with the Christian virtues of patience and humility which the Christian humanism of the Renaissance postulated. This double process of education proceeds briefly as follows. Musidorus and Pyrocles are intensely active men, whether in war or in peaceful government. And one of the principal themes of the book is the contrast between this activity and the fugitive and cloistered life of Basilius. In the revised *Arcadia* Sidney inserted quite near the beginning a long new episode, that of the war between the Helots and the Lacedemonians. It occurs immediately after the account of Basilius's retirement and it contains a duel between the two princes, each unknown to the other and now the principal fighters on opposite sides, and an account of their masterly statesmanship in settling the war, once they recognise each other. Having thus proved themselves in magnanimity, they fall victims to the discipline of love, a passion uniting the provinces of action and contemplation, and they end by having to submit in Christian humility to the prospect of abandoning the fruits of all their virtuous active elements. Pamela and Philoclea have less scope in action; yet they make themselves felt as great ladies, condemning the course their father has chosen and ready to take their part, when called to do so, in the exacting life of head of a great married establishment. The great lady of Tudor times was in her way as much a governor as her husband. Their ordeal and their Christian conduct in prison have already been mentioned.

In making the education of the princes and princesses the central theme of *Arcadia* I have no wish to minimise the amount of political doctrine it contains, or the zest with which Sidney writes of politics. Out of many possible illustrations of this zest I choose a passage from the end of Musidorus's account of the state into which the kingdom of Macedonia had fallen, through misgovernment, when his uncle Euarchus came to the throne:

> Hence grew a very dissolution of all estates, while the great men (by the nature of ambition never satisfied) grew factious among themselves: and the underlings, glad indeede to be underlings to them they hated lest, to preserve them from such they hated most. Men of vertue suppressed, lest their shining should discover the others filthines; and at length vertue itself almost forgotten, when it had no hopefull end whereunto to be directed; olde men long nusled in corruption, scorning them that would seeke reformation; yong men very fault-finding; but very faultie; and so to new-

SIDNEY

fanglenes both of manners, apparrell, and each thing els, by the
custome of self-guiltie evill, glad to change though oft for a worse;
merchandise abused, and so townes decayed for want of just and
naturall libertie; offices, even of judging soules, sold; publique
defences neglected; and in summe, (lest too long I trouble you) all
awrie, and (which wried it to the most wrie course of all) witte
abused, rather to faine reason why it should be amisse, then how it
should be amended.[1]

But Sidney's zest for politics was not just vague and general; it was
founded on detailed knowledge and conviction. Greenlaw has
written well on this topic.[2] He points out, for instance, how well
diversified are some of the bad political characters and how well
grounded in Machiavelli are some of their acts. There is Plexirtus,
bastard son of the King of Paphlagonia and brother of Leonatus
(corresponding to Edmund, Gloucester, and Edgar in *King Lear*),
who usurps the throne, uses foreign mercenaries to keep it, blinds his
father, and seeks to murder his brother. By carefully hiding his faults
he gets the service of good men. And he ends as the completely bad
ruler, the cunning Machiavellian tyrant. Then there is Clinias, the
plotting coward, once an actor and hence a master of insincere
oratory, the venal tool of wicked employers. And then there is
Amphialus, a more important and a more complicated figure. He is
not radically bad but accepts the results of his mother's plotting.
Acting on this he holds the rightful heirs to the throne of Arcadia,
to which he aspires, in captivity. He then foments rebellion and in
particular gathers the various malcontents of the realm around him.
In his strategy he follows the advice of Machiavelli, paying especial
attention to his citadel, his supplies, and the kind of men he has near
him. In choosing these men he is careful to turn their vices to his own
advantage. In arranging tournaments he is careful to preserve the
outward appearance of courtesy, but he actually uses them to
advertise his own powers and to establish his own influence: in
accordance with the principles laid down in the twenty-first chapter
of the *Prince*.

The mention of these three characters from outside the range of
Basilius's household prompts my next observation. Although the
education of the four princely young people with the important
though subordinate theme of the contrast between Basilius and
Euarchus constitutes a powerful central theme and although the
main structural lines may be classical, there is a vast wealth of subordinate detail. To describe this adequately is impossible in a small
space; and the most I can do is to present a few samples.

[1] 186.
[2] *Loc. cit.* 334-7. As said above, I do not follow him in the details of the political
allegory he postulates.

For all the classicising there is a great amount of detail derived from the medieval romance. Sidney may copy Virgil in the big battle scene between the forces of Amphialus and Basilius he inserted in the revised *Arcadia*, but much of the fighting and the jousting is in the style of the medieval romances, for instance the duel already mentioned between Musidorus and Pyrocles unknown to each other, Phalantus's beauty challenge, and Amphialus's reputation for being 'the best knight in the world'. Or take this sentence:

> And so went they, making one place succeed to an other, in like uncertaintie to their search, manie times encountring strange adventures, worthy to be registered in the roulles of fame.

The evident desire here to amplify, to swell the lake of adventure into a sea, is characteristically medieval and quite different from the classical desire to omit everything that does not promote the business in hand.[1]

But in spite of much remote medievalising, close observation of nature, human and animal, is constantly breaking in. Sidney is not a whit behind contemporary drama in this respect. When near the beginning Musidorus, weak from the shipwreck and dulled with grief at his loss of Pyrocles, walks with the shepherds to Arcadia, at first he cannot listen, but gradually their talk penetrates his consciousness. When Basilius and Gynecia are both in love with Pyrocles in his Amazon disguise, Gynecia one night, while Basilius slept, gave vent to her grief:

> More she would have said but that *Basilius* (awaked with the noise) tooke her in his armes, and began to comfort her; the goodman thinking, it was all for a jealous love of him: which humor if she would a little have maintained, perchance it might have weakned his new conceavd fancies. But he finding her answeres wandring from the purpose, left her to her selfe.[2]

That is nature indeed. Or take this description of a spaniel hunting duck:

> There the Princesses determining to bath themselves, though it was so priviledged a place, upon paine of death, as no bodie durst presume to come thither, yet for the more surety, they looked round about, and could see nothing but a water spaniell, who came downe the river, shewing that he hunted for a duck, and with a snuffling grace, disdaining that his smelling force coulde not as well prevaile thorow the water, as thorow the aire; and therefore

---

[1] For Sidney's debt to medieval romance see Zandvoort, *op. cit.* 189 ff.; M. S. Goldman, *Sir Philip Sidney and his Arcadia* (Illinois Studies in Language and Literature, xvii. 1934-5) 14, 192.

[2] 252.

wayting with his eye, to see whether he could espie the duckes
getting up again: but then a little below them failing of his purpose,
he got out of the river, and shaking off the water (as great men do
their friends, now he had no further cause to use it) inweeded
himselfe so, as the Ladies lost the further marking his sportfulnesse.[1]

There is no doubt here of the reality of the animal.

'Separate your selfe a little (if it be possible) from your selfe, and
let your owne mind looke upon your owne proceedings', said Musidorus to Pyrocles, rebuking him for having assumed the disguise of
an Amazon; and Sidney himself had the faculty of self-criticism.
Having it, he is naturally able to see things in a comical as well as in
a serious light. Some of his comedy falls flat today; some gets home.
Basilius, old but in love with Zelmane, is at times truly ludicrous, as
when he sings her a sonnet,

> which being done he looked verie curiously upon himselfe, some-
> times fetching a little skippe, as if he had said, his strength had not
> yet forsaken him.[2]

The romance of Phalantus and Artesia ends in comedy. Theirs was an
adolescent, exhibitionist passion. Phalantus had been touring Greece
upholding his beauty-challenge on behalf of Artesia in tournaments.
He prospered until beaten by the ill-apparelled knight, who was
Pyrocles disguised.

> But the victorie being by the judges given, and the trumpets
> witnessed to the ill apparelled Knight; *Phalantus* digrace was in-
> grieved in lieu of comforte by *Artesia*; who telling him she never
> lookt for other, bad him seeke some other mistresse. He excusing
> himselfe, and turning over the fault to Fortune, Then let that be
> your ill Fortune too (saide she) that you have lost me. Nay truely
> Madame (saide *Phalantus*) it shall not be so: for I thinke the losse
> of such a Mistresse will proove a great gaine: and so concluded;
> to the sporte of *Basilius*, to see young folkes love, that came in maskt
> with so great pompe, goe out with so little constancie.[3]

The satisfaction of Basilius, doomed from the beginning both as
elderly lover and as lover of a girl who is really a man, adds irony to
straightforward comedy.

Such are some of the strains of *Arcadia*, and there are others. Sidney
had a brilliantly varied mind, and it is not on the side of variety that
any weaknesses as an epic writer are likely to be found.

In the matter of structure we have to distinguish between what
Sidney did accomplish and what he could have accomplished. Sidney
had a massively powerful as well as a brilliantly active brain and a

[1] 216-17.   [2] 149.   [3] III.

will capable of the highest efforts. If he had dedicated brain and will exclusively or even principally to literature he could have carried through the structure of a serious long work with full success. Even with the partial attention he gave to literature he accomplished a good deal in his fragmentary revised *Arcadia*. He had a firm conception of his main scheme, the education of four princely persons, and he had all his details firmly in mind.[1] And, in view of the number and diversity of the details, this was a great feat. But he did not achieve the further structural feat of keeping all the details in suspension and not finally settled till the very end, so that every addition and subtraction of detail was made with reference to its influence on all the rest. Sidney does indeed suffer from a lack of moderation in his structure. He is a bountiful writer and he does not sufficiently heed the effect of his bounty on the aims he most has in view. And that effect, though certainly not to obliterate, is partly to blur those aims. Sidney did not make his supremely difficult task of structure any easier by revising old work instead of writing something quite new. He begins brilliantly, as I have already indicated, by two large contrasts; those between the high Platonic passions of the two shepherds and the ugly actuality of the shipwreck, and between the politically irresponsible retirement of Basilius and the martial prowess and political sagacity of Musidorus and Pyrocles in the part they take in the war between the Lacedemonians and the Helots. Most of this is new writing. But as soon as Sidney begins incorporating large portions of *Old Arcadia*, his grasp becomes less comprehensive and more confined to whatever detail he has in hand. Ben Jonson in his talks with Drummond recorded the legend that Sidney intended to turn his *Arcadia* into an Arthuriad. He had better have done so. To amalgamate old and new material into an organic whole was more difficult than to write a new work. Anyhow, this is certain: if Sidney had lived and had found the leisure to bend all his powers to the epic task, he could quite have transcended what of *Arcadia* there now survives.

I come now to the question of *Arcadia*'s choric character. In my chapter on the Elizabethan age in general I wrote of the peculiarly English form the epic was likely to assume at this time. In England, as in no other European country after the collapse of Portugal in the Battle of Alcazar, national sentiment was likely to be a principal subject of epic writing. And it was the subject likely to spread its appeal to the widest extent of the community. Shakespeare in his History Plays best satisfied such a demand. But there was another

---

[1] It is interesting that Greville (*op. cit.* 15) speaks of Amphialus's 'marriage with *Helena*; their successions'. Neither version of *Arcadia* includes this. The revised version breaks off with Queen Helen taking away Amphialus when near death. It looks as if Sidney had told Greville of some of his further intentions. There would have been no loose ends if Sidney had completed his revision.

epic theme appealing to another kind of public. To repeat words I used when writing on Shakespeare,

> it is the idea of education or 'nurture'. The political theme, in the form adopted by Shakespeare, was peculiarly English: a set of generalisations given special vitality through the favoured position in which by good luck England found herself. The idea of education was the great Renaissance motive, applicable equally to Christian and Stoic, Protestant and Catholic, translatable into terms as well of knowing yourself as of losing your life to gain it.[1]

Arcadia is absolutely at one with its age in dealing primarily with this great theme. Its English vogue would not have extended as far down the social scale as Shakespeare's Histories. But for the educated classes it was their book from the start. They hailed it with astonishing rapidity and they were astonishingly faithful in their admiration. Before ever *Arcadia* was printed, in 1588, Abraham Fraunce chose Sidney as one of the seven authors through whom to illustrate the use of rhetorical figures, the others being Homer, Virgil, Tasso, Du Bartas, Boscan, and Garcilasso. His editor has noted that Fraunce habitually gives Sidney the place of honour after Homer and Virgil and that half the quotations are from the prose of *Arcadia*.[2] About eleven years later John Hoskins published his *Directions for Speech and Style*, which his editor[3] says 'remains chiefly as a document witnessing to the charm exerted by the person and writings of Sir Philip Sidney'. In this book it is *Arcadia* that above all provides the model of good writing and of the instructive creation of character. In its substance and its style alike the late Elizabethans found it to speak with their own authentic voice. It was soon translated into other tongues, a diffusion which no play of Shakespeare enjoyed by anywhere near so early a date. A further sign of the hold *Arcadia* had on men's minds is the persistent attempts to complete and continue it. There were six of these in the first half of the seventeenth century, not to speak of the narrative poems deriving from it.

I have not yet committed myself to saying how Sidney ranks among the great literary figures, of what quality is his work when we have finished commenting on his age and on contemporary ideas of the epic, how deeply he moves us. The answer is that, besides impressing us by his commanding intellectual grasp, as shown by the grand basic scheme of *Arcadia*, he can achieve writing of great beauty and intensity, though through means now unfamiliar, and that he can build up characters who have it in them to acquire the kind of proverbial quality that marks one kind of distinguished character-creation. The

[1] E. M. W. Tillyard, *Shakespeare's History Plays*, 145.
[2] The *Arcadian Rhetorike*, ed. Ethel Smeaton (Oxford 1950) xix.
[3] H. H. Hudson (Princeton 1935) xxi.

taste which in recent years would judge a long and ambitious narrative rests unconsciously on works whose highest places consist of dialogue or rumination at moments of intense mental action or development: Andromache saying farewell to Hector; Dido blaming Aeneas; Lady Macbeth goading her husband; Jeanie Deans pleading for her sister's life; Dorothea Casaubon talking on the meaning of marriage; Anna Karenina caught in the transports of jealousy. And such taste is apt to miss intensity reached by other means. Now Sidney in places corresponding to those just mentioned seems to let us down. Instead of allowing his characters to say the words their passion appears to dictate he fills their mouths with rhetoric apparently fabricated on a preconceived code of decorum. In compensation he touches his greatest heights through the isolated display made by this or that character. He had what you could call a heraldic mind and when he writes most intensely he does so in a manner more plastic or pictorial than literary and progressive. I have given one example in the description of the shepherdess Urania pulling the thorn from the lamb's foot. To establish my point I give two more; and it is worth noting that none of the three occurs in the old *Arcadia*. While Musidorus was posing as the shepherd Dorus, in order to secure Pamela's attention, he procured a horse and made her a display of his horsemanship. This is how Pamela, in talk with Philoclea, builds up the picture of him riding:

But oh how well it did with *Dorus*, to see with what a grace he presented him selfe before me on horseback, making majestie wait upon humblenes? how at the first, standing stil with his eies bent upon me, as though his motions were chained to my looke, he so staide till I caused *Mopsa* bid him doo something upon his horse: which no sooner said, but (with a kinde rather of quick gesture, then shew of violence) you might see him come towards me, beating the ground in so due time, as no daunce can observe better measure. If you remember the ship we saw once, when the Sea went hie upon the coast of *Argos*; so went the beast: But he (as if Centaurlike he had bene one peece with the horse) was no more moved, then one is with the going of his own legges: and in effect so did he command him, as his owne limmes, for though he had both spurres and wande, they seemed rather markes of soveraintie, then instruments of punishment; his hand and legge (with most pleasing grace) commanding without threatning, and rather remembring then chastising, at lest if sometimes he did, it was so stolen, as neyther our eyes could discerne it, nor the horse with any chaunce did complaine of it, he ever going so just with the horse, either foorth right, or turning, that it seemed as he borrowed the horses body, so he lent the horse his minde: in the turning one might perceive the bridle-hand somthing gently stir, but indeed so gently, as it rather did distill vertue, then use violence.[1]

That is no mere supererogatory description but the distillation into a single self-sufficient picture of Sidney's passionate belief in the chastening discipline that elevates the natural gifts of both beast and man to the highest reaches of which they are capable. It is eloquence but of very powerful significance, and very moving if properly understood.

And here is the description of Pamela during her supreme testing-time in prison doing embroidery work:

Cecropia threatning in her selfe to run a more ragged race with *Philoclea*, went to her sister *Pamela*: who that day having wearied her selfe with reading, and with the height of her hart disdaining to keepe companie with any of the Gentlewomen appointed to attende her, whome she accounted her jaylours, was woorking uppon a purse certaine Roses and Lillies, as by the finenesse of the worke, one might see she had borrowed her wittes of the sorow that owed them, and lent them wholy to that exercise. For the flowers she had wrought, caried such life in them, that the cunningest painter might have learned of her needle: which with so prety a maner made his careers to and fro through the cloth, as if the needle it selfe would have bene loth to have gone fromward such a mistres, but that it hoped to return thenceward very quickly againe: the cloth loking with many eies upon her, and lovingly embracing the wounds she gave it: the sheares were also at hand to behead the silke, that was growne to short. And if at any time she put her mouth to bite it off, it seemed, that where she had beene long in making of a Rose with her hand, she would in an instant make Roses with her lips; as the Lillies seemed to have their whitenesse, rather of the hande that made them, then of the matter whereof they were made; and that they grew there by the Sunnes of her eyes, and were refreshed by the most in discomfort comfortable ayre, which an unwares sigh might bestow upon them. But the colours for the grounde were so well chosen, neither sullenly darke, nor glaringly lightsome, and so well proportioned, as that, though much cunning were in it, yet it was but to serve for an ornament of the principall woorke; that it was not without marvaile to see, howe a minde which could cast a carelesse semblant uppon the greatest conflictes of Fortune, coulde commaunde it selfe to take care for so small matters. Neither had she neglected the daintie dressing of her selfe: but as it had ben her marriage time to Afflic-tion, she rather semed to remember her owne worthinesse, then the unworthinesse of her husband. For well one might perceyve she

[1] 178-9.

had not rejected the counsaile of a glasse, and that her handes had pleased themselves, in paying the tribute of undeceyving skill, to so high perfections of Nature.[1]

Here most readers would echo Johnson's condemnation of *Lycidas*: that 'it is not to be considered as the effusion of a real passion; for passion runs not after remote allusions and obscure opinions'. And like him they would be wrong. For Sidney has elaborated a passionately felt emblem of fortitude dressing it in the *sprezzatura*, or nonchalance, which in the opinion of Castiglione put the last touch of perfection on the courtier. By concentrating so entirely on her embroidery when her life was in peril, Pamela both manifested a consummate power of will and achieved the height of aristocratic irony by being light-hearted over great things and serious over small. And though in other places Sidney may elaborate for no better reason than bare decorum, he does so here in the very manner of his own Pamela, clothing a tragic feeling in the artifice of fine writing. One may best get the sense of Sidney's picture of Pamela embroidering by imagining the scene painted: the girl dressed in exquisite finery, her attention quite riveted to her work, and some symbol of death drawn faintly in the background.

If people habitually read *Arcadia* they would find certain characters drawn powerfully enough to become as it were proverbial. These do not include the two princes, who, though differentiated up to a point, have both to be such impeccable soldiers and politicians and such faithful friends to each other that they end by lacking great individual emphasis. But Pamela and Philoclea could well become classic examples of two feminine types, not inferior in their way to Rosalind and Celia in *As You Like It*. The other two great characters are Cecropia and her son Amphialus. In Cecropia, born princess of Argos, Sidney created a convincing picture of declared pride and forthright ambition. She has not the least doubt that she had the right to all that she wants; and she uses words that well express her confidence. This is how she describes to Amphialus her state when she married Amphialus's father, then heir presumptive of Arcadia, Basilius having given out his intention of remaining a bachelor:

for else you may be sure the King of *Argos*, nor his daughter would have suffered their Royall bloud to be stained with the base name of subjection. So that I came into this countrie as apparant Princesse thereof, and accordingly was courted, and followed of all the Ladies of this countrie. My porte and pompe did well become a King of *Argos* daughter: in my presence their tongues were turned into eares, and their eares were captive unto my tongue. Their eyes admired my Majestie, and happy was he or she, on whom I would

[1] 402-3.

suffer the beames thereof to fall. Did I goe to church? it seemed the very Gods wayted for me, their devotions not being solemnized till I was ready. Did I walke abroad to see any delight? Nay, my walking was the delight it selfe: for to it was the concourse; one thrusting upon another, who might shewe him selfe most diligent and serviceable towards me: my sleepes were inquired after, and my wakings never unsaluted: the very gate of my house full of principall persons, who were glad, if their presents had receaved a gratefull acceptation. And in this felicitie wert thou borne, the very earth submitting it selfe unto thee to be troden on as by his Prince.

Energy pulses through this speech; and though her lofty pride degenerates into furious spite Cecropia never ceases to be a woman on a grand scale. Amphialus is a truly tragic character, well intentioned but dragged against his will and finally without his knowledge into a position that he abhors. His genuine and honourable love of Philoclea cheats him into misguided agreement with his mother's prompting to court her while in captivity. Sidney presents his consequent plight with great power.

Sidney thus shows himself able to shape comprehensively, to write greatly, and to create great characters. He was a man of epic capacity. On the other hand he died young; and of his short life he put much of the best into action. He could not therefore achieve a true epic; and *Arcadia* is no more than an epicising fragment, successful in part and of great promise. It is not for us to complain that he did not distil all of himself drop by drop into literature. We are lucky enough to know much about his life; and there is every reason why we should think of his life and writings together. So thinking, we shall acknowledge that he did much in each and that the sum leaves no doubt of the great height of human distinction to which he rose.

CHAPTER XI

THE CHRONICLER–POETS

Warner, in his absolute Albion's Englande, *hath most admirably penned the historie of his own country from Noah to his time, that is to the raigne of Queene Elizabeth. I have heard him termd of the best wits of both our Universities our English Homer . . . As Lucan hath mournefully depainted the civil wars of Pompey and Caesar: so hath Daniel the civil wars of Yorke and Lancaster, and Drayton the civil wars of Edward the second and the Barons.*

(Meres, *Palladis Tamia*, 1598)

1. GENERAL

OF the Renaissance chronicler-poets in England Daniel is the only one who has a claim on the poetic side to be included in this book. Yet the class of such poets is of the first importance as showing the temper of the time and where the true epic subject lay in the age of Elizabeth. Writers as cosmopolitan as Spenser and Sidney might make the fashioning of a gentleman and a governor a genuine aim of the most serious poetry; but for the bulk of the English population the aim, though political, was narrower and more local. It was to celebrate the present miracle: the internal peace and the security from outside foes achieved by the Tudors generally and Elizabeth in particular. This miracle was a modern version of what I called the Tudor myth, whose chief exponent was the historian Hall, in the reign of Henry VIII (see pp. 212-13 above). Hall's theme was positive: not the mere bewailing of civil strife, but the joy that the terrible decline from the great age of Edward III with his seven sons into an age of prolonged civil strife should have issued into the strong stable rule of the two first Tudors. But after Henry VIII, first with the peril of a boy-king and next with a queen who invited civil discord by upsetting the religious settlement, there was little encouragement to carry on the positive side of Hall's theme. It was more appropriate to deplore the sins of mankind and the punishment they bring on a nation than to celebrate any national achievement. The chronicle matter, positive and purposeful in Hall, takes tragic form in the *Mirror for Magistrates*, a work originating in the reign of Queen Mary. It took many years of Queen Elizabeth's reign to clear away the doubts that persisted from the two previous ones. And it is quite natural that the *Mirror for Magistrates* kept on being reprinted with additions up to the year 1578 and became finally a huge bulk of stories including the matter of Geoffrey of Monmouth as well as that of the more strictly historical chroniclers. After the execution of Mary Queen of Scots in 1587 and the defeat of the Armada in the next year, it was borne in on the nation that the miracle had happened and that civil war had been averted as well as foreign invasion repulsed. Once more, as in the days of Hall, men could be positive and exult in political achievement. Nevertheless, with the succession in doubt, it was still possible to be pessimistic. Drayton's *Mortimeriados*, his heroic poem on Mortimer and Isabella and the civil war between Edward II and the Barons, first published in 1596, is tragic and tearful in the manner of the *Mirror for Magistrates*. Nor did he alter its character when he enlarged it and published it in 1603 under the title of the *Barons' Wars*. Poetically memorable for its descriptions alone (that for instance of the chamber in Nottingham Castle which Isabella prepared for herself and Mortimer[1]) and here much indebted to Spenser, the poem in its main outline goes straight back to the 'tragedies' of the *Mirror for Magistrates*. It was not till the next reign that Drayton wrote his positive work: his celebration of England through its geography and history in *Poly-Olbion*. Drayton, whose true bent was to the dulcet, the elegiac, and the fanciful, was singularly unsuited to coping with an epic theme. That he tried to do so is strong evidence that a historical theme was genuinely central to the age.

Another piece of evidence is the incredibly uncritical nature of the appetite shown by the Elizabethans for literature dealing with the myths or history of their country. True, this uncriticalness is partly a matter of the reading habits that then prevailed. Jonson in his *Discoveries* wrote, '*Spencer*, in affecting the Ancients writ no Language: Yet I would have him read for his matter'. To us it is inconceivable that anyone who disliked Spenser's manner could have brought himself to read him for his matter. But, even allowing for a general willingness to excuse the manner for the matter, we can only infer that the appetite for English myth and history was uncommonly fierce to enable it to assimilate the lame and dreary versions into which these things were put. The sheer poetic badness of some of the tragedies in the later parts of the *Mirror for Magistrates* is astounding. How, we ask, could readers have borne it? And the answer can only be because of an excessive prejudice in favour of the substance of these tragedies. We may draw the same conclusion from Meres's comment on Warner, printed above as caption to this chapter. It is as astounding that the best wits of Oxford and Cambridge compared Warner to Homer as that readers could enjoy some of the later tragedies of the *Mirror for Magistrates*. Like Drayton's, Warner's genius was the least suited to the heroic. He can be pleasant and gossipy and in

---

[1] *Barons' Wars*, vi. stanzas 30 ff.

a homely way elegant in describing simple scenes, having learnt something of the use of the fourteener, from the *Ovid* of his master, Goulding. But in bulk a modern reader finds this long narrative from Noah to Queen Elizabeth unreadable; without the grimmest exercise of the will he cannot keep his attention fixed: and pleasure is out of the question. Plainly, the best wits of Oxford and Cambridge were excessively prejudiced in favour of Warner's substance.

My conclusion is that, however unepic in themselves, the *Mirror for Magistrates*, the *Barons' Wars*, and *Albions England* represent part at least of the substance that the true epic in the age of Elizabethan was bound to assume in order to achieve the necessary epic choric character.

I mentioned the *Barons' Wars* and *Albions England* together. But in one way they differ. The first deplores civil strife; the second makes civil strife issue into the great age of Elizabeth. It is the second that presents the larger range of act and feeling proper to an Elizabethan epic and that, in so doing, brings me to Daniel, the true successor of Hall.

2. DANIEL

My Homer-Lucan.   (Daniel, *A Defence of Ryme*)

Daniel wrott civill warres and yett hath not a batle in all his Book.   (Ben Jonson, *Conversations with Drummond*)

You must read over these Civil Wars *again. We both know what a* mood *is; and the genial mood will—it shall come for my sober-minded Daniel.*   (Coleridge to Charles Lamb)

In calling his *Civil Wars* 'my Homer-Lucan', Daniel implied a double truth. Spenser wanted to be looked on as the English Virgil, and in some ways he was. But the form of his epic was anything but Virgilian. Poetically Daniel may have less right to invoke comparison with the classical epics but in the matter of form he is their first true imitator in English. And this makes him a landmark in the history of the English epic. Further, he is a sincere classiciser. While the dullness of *Gordubuc* is due partly to its conscientious imitation of Senecan tragedy, any dullness in the *Civil Wars* is unconnected with its neo-classicism. On the contrary, Daniel thrives on his care to construct neatly and economically and to maintain an austere rhetoric. To imitate the classical epic is for him an inspiration. Although as much an Elizabethan as Spenser and Shakespeare, he genuinely looks forward to May and Cowley and to the neo-classic side among all the many sides of Milton, and in doing so he showed himself a poet of uncommon resolution and initiative.

The second truth contained in his Homer-Lucan claim will take longer to set forth. Though the theme of civil war occupies most of the poem's contents, it was not the final theme, while the ethical temper went beyond Lucan's stoical resistance in a world of despair. Through the contrast with the Wars of the Roses Daniel intended to make the peace of the Tudors more striking. The Homeric analogy pointing to this intention is not too obvious, but Daniel may have been thinking of the reconciliation at the end of the *Odyssey*. Anyhow, through mentioning Homer Daniel rightly claims to go beyond Lucan's narrow ethical temper. Unfortunately the claim is not fully verifiable, for Daniel wrote only eight out of his projected twelve books: but he leaves us in no doubt that he would have celebrated the peace of the Tudors. After beginning with the words 'I sing the Civil Wars' and deploring the madness of Englishmen in earlier days, he writes as follows in his third stanza:

> *Yet now what reason have we to complain,*
> *Since hereby came the calm we did enjoy,*
> *The bliss of thee,* Eliza? *Happy gain*
> *For all our losses; when as no other way*
> *The Heav'ns could find, but to unite again*
> *The fatal sever'd families, that they*
> *Might bring forth thee: That in thy peace might grow*
> *That Glory, which few times could ever show.*[1]

At the end of the second book, which deals with Bolingbroke's triumph over Richard II, there occurred in the original edition (1595) a picture of what England's fate might have been had Bolingbroke's genius been given a virtuous outlet. Civil war would have been averted; England would have dominated western Europe; and even now the Earl of Essex might have been leading an expedition against the Turk. Naturally the passage had to be cut after the fall of Essex, but it shows that Daniel while describing the wars of the Roses had his eye all the time on the present too. Near the beginning of Book Six there is the strange and powerful episode where Nemesis, seeing and envying the prosperity of a Europe divided into many small states and afflicted only by small, domestic, quarrels, prompts the invention of printing and artillery. Through the first, seditious doctrines are easily spread; through the second, war becomes more horrible. With these inventions Daniel associates the climax of English civil wars in the breach between York and Lancaster. But Nemesis, who describes these happenings in a speech, ends with the accession of the Tudors. England will in the end recover and be able to look back on her past sorrows as if they were a play.

[1] I use Grosart's edition of Daniel for quotations.

Then when their power, unable to sustaine
And beare it selfe, upon it selfe shall fall,
She may (recovered of her wounds againe)
Sit and behold their parts as tragicall:
For there must come a time, that shall obtaine
Truce for distress; when make-peace Hymen *shall*
Bring the conjoyned adverse powers to bed
And set the Crowne (made one) upon one head.

Out of which blessed union, shall arise
A sacred branch, (with grace and glory blest)
Whose Virtue shall her Land so patronize,
As all our power shall not her dayes molest:
For shee (fair shee) the Minion of the skies,
Shall purchase (of the high'st) to hers such rest,
(Standing betweene the wrath of heaven and them)
As no distresse shall touch her Diadem.

Finally, in his Epistle Dedicatory to his second edition (1609) of the *Civil Wars*, enlarged now from four to eight books, Daniel writes of his plan for the complete poem. It is:

> To show the Deformities of Civil Dissension, and the miserable events of rebellious Conspiracies and bloody Revengements which followed (as in a Circle) upon that Breach of the due Course of Succession by the usurpation of Henry iv; and thereby to make the blessings of peace and the happiness of an established government in a direct line the better to appear. I trust I shall do a grateful work to my country to continue the same unto the glorious Union of Henry vii, from whence is descended our present Happiness.

It is clear therefore that if he had finished his poem Daniel would have celebrated the Tudors as well as presented the Wars of the Roses.

That Daniel discriminated between the methods of Lucan and of Homer in the way I have indicated, making one poet stand for the tragic happenings to be shunned and the other for the deeds to be emulated, appears from a fine and interesting passage at the beginning of the fifth book. He has come to the accession of Henry V, but he has clearly decided not to interrupt the course of England's decline by a full narrative of Henry's victories. So he pictures the ghost of Henry appearing to him and chiding him fiercely for failing to do justice to his deeds and, incidentally, for omitting one half of the epic function. Speaking of the great deeds of himself and his officers, Henry said:

What everlasting matter here is found,
Whence new immortall Iliads *might proceed!*
That those, whose happie graces do abound
In blessed accents, here may have to feed
Good thoughts; on no imaginarie ground
Of hungry shadowes, which no profite breed;
Whence, musick-like, instant delight may growe;
Yet when men all do knowe, they nothing knowe.

And why dost thou, in lamentable verse,
Nothing but blood-shed, treasons, sinne and shame,
The worst of times, th'extreame of ills, rehearse;
To rayse old staynes, and to renew dead blame?
As if the mindes of th'evill and perverse,
Were not farre sooner trained from the same,
By good example of faire vertuous acts,
Then by the shew of foul ungodly facts.

Daniel here confesses that he knows that he has been a Lucan rather than a Homer and that he intends to omit the present excellent chance of fulfilling the prime epic function (according to Renaissance theory) of instructing through the example of heroic deeds. And this confession should strengthen our opinion that Daniel intended to make good his deficiency elsewhere.[1]

I have spent so long over Daniel's intention to praise the Tudor settlement because without it his claim to be Hall's successor and the nearest analogy to the Shakespeare of the Histories would be much less cogent. Granted that intention, Daniel's *Civil Wars* is the most successful rendering in narrative of the theme of Hall, since 1588 once more relevant, if in somewhat different guise, as the true epic theme of the age.

To a modern reader one of the chief interests of Daniel's *Civil Wars* is that its subject matter and its political temper are close to the great cycle of Shakespeare's History Plays. Both poets begin with the prosperity of Edward III with his seven sons; both make the murder of Woodstock a prominent cause of Richard II's misfortunes: both make Bolingbroke's usurpation and disposal of Richard the supreme crime that only the full horrors of civil war could expiate; both make Margaret of Anjou, wife of Henry VI, a dominant character but England's evil genius; both make the death of the Talbots prominent; both make the Battle of Towton the culminating horror of the Wars of the Roses, with Henry watching it from a little hill. Daniel broke off at a point corresponding to the middle of *Henry VI, Part 3*, the

---

[1] He does indeed partially make it good shortly after his confession. Through the rhetorical device of listing all the things about Henry he will not deal with, he does indeed deliver an eloquent panegyric.

point where Warwick, indignant with Edward IV for withdrawing from the French match he had gone to France to negotiate, changed his allegiance to Lancaster from York. There is no doubt that if he had finished his poem Daniel would have treated events up to the Battle of Bosworth much as Shakespeare did.

Common to Shakespeare and Daniel is a solemn political philosophy. It is a philosophy, much like that of Aeschylus, of the visiting of a crime on future generations but with the hope of ultimate expiation, The whole cycle of events from Richard II to Henry VII is a classic and awe-inspiring illustration of the process. Daniel, a more academic poet than Shakespeare, is naturally more definite and explicit; and partly because he supplemented poetry by history. His unfinished *History of England*, extending from where history as against myth begins, and ending with the death of Edward III, is a useful gloss on the *Civil Wars*. In it Daniel claims no originality of matter, but admits that he draws general conclusions from known fact: as he says in his preface *To the Reader*,

> For the Worke it selfe, I can Challenge nothing therein but onely the sowing it together, and the observation of those necessary circumstances, and inferences which the History naturally ministers.[1]

There is no need to read all history for general truths: a sample will serve, because

> We shall finde still the same correspondencies to hold in the actions of men: Vertues and Vices the same, though rising and falling, according to the worth or weaknesse of Governors: the causes of the ruines, and mutations of States to be alike.[2]

And when he comes to the end of his book he writes a paragraph that sets forth not only his philosophic conception of history but the historical position from which the events described in the *Civil Wars* took off:

> Thus have we seene the end of this great *King*: who, how he came to the Crowne, we know, and now how he left it we see: In both are considerations of importance. His stepping over his Fathers head to come to his throne, though it were not his fault, yet had it a punishment, and that in a most high kinde: For, having so plentifull, and so able an Issue Male, he had not yet a sonne of his owne to sit on his Seate; but left the same (worse then he found it) to a Childe of eleven yeares of age, exposed to the Ambition of Uncles, which over weighed him: to a factious and discontented State at home: To broken and distracted inheritances abroad: Himselfe having seene all his great gettings, purchased with so much expence, travaile and blood-shed, rent cleane from

[1] iv. 83.   [2] *Ib*. 86,

him, and nothing remayning, but onely the poore Towne of *Calais*. To show that our Bounds are prescribed us; and a pillar set by him who beares up the Heavens, which we are not to trespasse.[1]

Such was the ordinance of heaven: though Edward III was a fine king in every way with a wife to match and sons of the lucky number of seven, his initial irregularity could not escape divine vigilance, although we may think that it could have been expiated with comparative ease. Unexpiated it led to crimes vastly greater. In the *Civil Wars* Daniel enunciates this same great principle as a prelude to the reign of Henry VI (as Shakespeare had implied it through Henry V's prayer on the eve of Agincourt that God should suspend vengeance for his father's crime). There were various reasons why things should have gone wrong in the reign of Henry VI: but the profoundest reason was

> *the now ripe Wrath (deferd till now)*
> *Of that sure and unfayling* Justicer,
> *That never suffers wrong so long to growe,*
> *And to incorporate with right so farre,*
> *As it might come to seeme the same in showe,*
> *(T'incourage those that evill minded are*
> *By such successe) but that at last he will*
> *Confound the branch, whose root was planted ill.*

> *Else, might the impious say, with grudging spight,*
> *Doth God permit the Great to riot free,*
> *And bless the mightie though they do unright,*
> *As if he did unto their wrongs agree?*
> *And only plague the weake and wretched wight,*
> *For smallest faults, ev'n in the high'st degree?*
> *When he, but using them for others scourge,*
> *Likewise of them at length the world doth purge.*[2]

Whether Daniel would have resembled Shakespeare in making Richard III the scapegoat of the accumulated sins of both parties we cannot say, but the probabilities are that he would. Some expiation he finds in the innocent sufferings of Henry VI; but plainly more is needed before Lancaster and York can be united, and Richard III offered the obvious motive. But it is not the details that matter but the steady and coherent moral that runs through the whole of Daniel's poem and unites him to Shakespeare as to no other contemporary poet.

Daniel then had a great and living theme; the question remains what he made of it. Much more, I think, than is commonly allowed. Readers have praised Daniel for his smaller poems and his *Defence of*

---

[1] *Ib.* 290.   [2] *Civil Wars*, book v. stanzas 49, 50.

Ryme; scarcely anyone has a good word for the *Civil Wars*. Its most distinguished advocate was Coleridge, who wrote a letter to Lamb on it in Lamb's own copy of Daniel. After his exhortation to Lamb to acquire the right mood for the *Civil Wars* (printed in the caption to this section), Coleridge went on:

> Gravely sober on all ordinary affairs, and not easily excited by any, yet there is one on which his blood boils—whenever he speaks of English valour exerted against a foreign enemy. . . . He must not be read piecemeal;—even by leaving off and looking at a stanza by itself, I find the loss. . . . Thousands even of educated men would become more sensible, fitter to be members of parliament, or ministers, by reading Daniel; and even those few who, *quoad intellectum*, only gain refreshment of notions already their own, must become better Englishmen.

I do not think Coleridge right in suggesting that the only subject that fired Daniel was 'English valour exerted against a foreign enemy', for much of his political moralising is impassioned. But he makes one essential point which other writers on Daniel fail to make or deny: 'he must not be read piecemeal'. He did grasp that the *Civil Wars* is a continuity and not a compilation. It is for this reason that it must be seriously considered as an epic.

In a martial poem, such as the *Civil Wars* professes to be, readers naturally expect some kind of pattern to be made out of the fighting. Tasso had constructed his *Jerusalem Delivered* in this way. It was Daniel's failure to do this that is at the bottom of his contemporaries' doubts of his success as an epic writer. He was considered too much of a historian and too little a poet. Ben Jonson went further and complained that there was not a battle in the book. Literally he was wrong—Daniel includes more battles than Shakespeare—but impressionally he was right. The active, heroic side leaves no impression. But this does not mean that there are not impressions, and powerful ones, of another kind. Daniel is a reflective poet, who is above rather than in the battle, and he is powerfully aware of the great processes of which the battles are the expression. And if we follow our author and not our expectations of what a poet writing on an exceptionally active period of history ought to be doing, we shall find that Daniel had some definite and comprehensive things to say.

Now the 'processes' of which I have just spoken are of two different kinds. There are the great processes of history, one could almost say God's processes; and there are the processes of mind through which the actors come to do what they do. It is in these two types of process that Daniel's interest lies.

Of some of God's processes as conceived by Daniel I have just written in course of comparing him with Shakespeare. But Daniel's conception included more than Shakespeare, with his power of presenting action at close quarters, found convenient. In the first place it took more of the world and more of history into its ken. This enlarged vision is found outside the poetry. Take that splendid section of his *Defence of Ryme* where he begins by protesting that 'all our understandings are not to be built by the square of *Greece* and *Italie*'.[1] Whatever the use men have made of them, God distributed potentialities for good or ill evenly to the different ages. It is thus vain to exalt one age to the exclusion of another:

> The distribution of giftes are universall, and all seasons hath them in some sort. We must not thinke, but that there were Scipioes, Caesars, Catoes and Pompeies, borne elsewhere then at *Rome*, the rest of the world hath ever had them in the same degree of nature, though not of state.

Moreover, we must judge the quality of ages not on the narrower ground of articulateness but on the wider ground of successful government:

> It is not the contexture of words, but the effects of Action that gives glory to the times: we finde they had *mercurium in pectore* though not in *lingua*, and in all ages, though they were not Ciceronians, they knew the Art of men, which onely is, *Ars Artium*, the great gift of heaven, and the chiefe grace and glory on earth; they had the learning of Government, and ordring their State, Eloquence inough to shew their judgements.[2]

Through this wider rule of humanity instead of the narrower one of culture Daniel had an unprejudiced view of history rare in his time. It led him to defend the Middle Ages and to allow some qualities to the barbarian conquerors of the Roman Empire. It is a view remarkably commanding and philosophic, in itself propitious to the epic reach. Coming to the providential principle governing actions of men upon this uncommonly capacious stage, Daniel puts the decisive weight on the soundness of the beginning. If the foundations are good, if the core is sound, great results will follow. Contrariwise, if the core is unsound, no amount of added virtue or wisdom will secure them. The Roman Republic was well founded, with the result not only that it achieved great things but that the Roman state lasted in spite of the many abuses that should have caused its ruin. The opposite case has already been illustrated from the *History of England*. Edward III succeeded to the throne of England in a not completely lawful manner; and, though he had every virtue and achieved great things, his prosperity could not last. His achievements were neutralised by the time of his death, and a boy-king was his successor.

[1] A. C. Sprague's edition of *Poems* and *A Defence of Ryme*, 139 ff.   [2] *Ib* 144.

Both this comprehensive vision and this ruling principle of history, set forth in the *Defence of Ryme*, appear in the *Civil Wars*.

In his History Plays Shakespeare related the stretch of English history he chose for his great cycle to the current philosophy of order or 'degree'. He did not relate it (and in the drama why should he?) to any theory of world history. Within this stretch, however, he did, to my thinking, indicate his sense of the differences between the more formal and ceremonious England of the Middle Ages and the England of his own day.[1] Daniel too is aware of the brilliance of medieval England, but unlike Shakespeare he reveals a conception of medieval history far wider than his insular subject strictly demanded, just as he divagated from tragic fact by conjecturing the course of world events had Bolingbroke used his great powers in a righteous cause. (I mentioned this divagation above, but I must add here that it included the notion that Spain would not have become an imperial power but have remained in provincial Castilian tranquillity.) Daniel's conception of medieval history comes in a striking episode at the beginning of the sixth book. The political situation at this point is the beginning of Yorkist action. York for the first time has raised an army. He has taken it to London, halts outside the city on the Kent side, 'and there, intrenched, plants his Artillery'. And the mention of artillery causes him to embark on his episode by pondering on medieval Europe before this dreadful invention:

> *It was a time when fair* Europa *sate*
> *With many goodlie Diadems addrest*
> *And all her parts in florishing estate*
> *Lay beautiful, in order, at their rest:*
> *No swelling member, unproportionate,*
> *Growne out of forme, sought to disturbe the rest:*
> *The less subsisting by the greaters might;*
> *The greater, by the lesser kept upright.*[2]

For greater emphasis Daniel added this footnote:

The principal Part of *Europe*, which contain'd the most flourishing State of *Christendom*, was at this time in the Hands of many several Princes and Commonwealths, which quietly governed the same: For being so many, and none over-great, they were less attemptive to disturb others, and more careful to keep their own, with a mutual Correspondence of Amity. As *Italy* had then many more Principalities and Commonwealths than it hath. *Spain* was divided into many Kingdoms: France consisted of divers Free Princes, Both the Germanies, of many more Governments.

There may have been minor broils, but 'no eruption did in general

---

[1] See the section on *Richard II* in my *Shakespeare's History Plays*.   [2] vi. 28.

Break down their rest with universal sin'. Seeing this prolonged peace, fierce Nemesis, 'Sword-bearer of th'Eternal Providence', who had been busy afflicting the Christians of Asia with the incursions of 'foul impious Barbarism', turns her attention to the West. She calls Pandora to her aid, knowing that mankind can be tricked and made to suffer by the offer of gifts. Her account of the pious and innocent peace of western Europe is remarkable:

> *Devotion (mother of Obedience)*
> *Beares such a hand on their credulitie,*
> *That it abates the spirit of eminence,*
> *And busies them with humble pietie,*
> *For, see what workes, what infinite expence,*
> *What monuments of zeale they edifie;*
> *As if they would, so that no stop were found*
> *Fill all with Temples, make all holy ground.*[1]

Pandora is to break the peace of these simple, pious cathedral-builders by the old temptation of enlarged knowledge; she is indeed Eve tempting Adam, as well as Pandora bearing her box with its fatal gifts to mankind. And the new knowledge is of the two arts of printing and artillery. Both arts, by giving power to base men, upset the soundness of the old hierarchy. Printing is an art,

> *Whereby all quarrels, titles, secrecies,*
> *May unto all be presently made knowne;*
> *Factions prepar'd, parties allur'd to rise;*
> *Seditions under faire pretensions sowne;*
> *Whereby, the vulgar may become so wise,*
> *That (with a self-presumption over-growne)*
> *They may of deepest mysteries debate,*
> *Controule their betters, censure actes of State.*[2]

And artillery is the means of making the confusion wrought by printing more horrible and more extensive,

> *For by this stratagem, they shall confound*
> *All th'antient forme and discipline of Warre:*
> *Alter their Camps, alter their fights, their ground,*
> *Daunt mighty spirits, prowesse and manhood marre:*
> *For, basest cowards from a far shall wound*
> *The most couragious, forc't to fight a farre;*
> *Valour wrapt up in smoake (as in the night)*
> *Shall perish without witnesse, without sight.*[3]

In preparation for the mischief to be spread by the two inventions Nemesis orders Pandora (but without indicating by what means) to

[1] vi. 33.   [2] vi. 38.   [3] vi. 40.

upset the existing balance of large and small states in western Europe
and to make great states swallow up the lesser. Then let her breed
factions in the 'Fairest Land', that is, England. When these things
have been done, printing and artillery will be able to produce a
general chaos.

Obviously we must not inquire too nearly into Daniel's version of
the facts of history. The relevant and remarkable thing is that he sets
the Wars of the Roses into a large context: that of western Europe
and Byzantium at one end and the wars of religion at the other, for
the chaos to which the Wars of the Roses are prelude can only be that
which prevailed in parts of Europe in the sixteenth century.

It is in the course of this enlarged picture of history that Daniel
presents an enlarged picture of God's way with nations: something
that goes beyond the Aeschylean scheme of the Wars of the Roses,
common to himself and Shakespeare. It is that in this world God
cannot allow perpetual prosperity. The Nemesis that upset the simple
life and the virtuous pieties of the earlier Middle Ages was God's
agent. It may be true that the Roman state, founded honestly, was
allowed a long span; but even so there is a tragic and unalterable law
of necessary change. The reason for this (though Daniel does not state
it) would surely have been that the condition of earth must not be
allowed to compete with that of heaven, for that would upset God's
order and scheme. Whether in making Nemesis God's agent Daniel
meant that men would always discover the reasons for their own
decline from prosperity or whether he conceived her as an interposition
of God is not clear, nor need the question be decided. All that matters
here is that Daniel showed a conception of God's processes remarkably
comprehensive for a poet of his day.

I come now to the other 'process' in which Daniel was interested:
that of men's minds on the way to action. It will be recalled that in
the passages quoted from the *Defence of Ryme* Daniel referred to the
unknown Scipios and Caesars of the inarticulate nations and how,
though they were not Ciceronians, they knew 'the Art of men, which
onely is *Ars Artium*'. In his *Civil Wars* he seeks to demonstrate this art
of men by describing less their actions than their motives for action;
and his literary eminence consists mainly in this demonstration.
Indeed, the only way to read Daniel aright is to agree with the spirit
of Ben Jonson's pronouncement that there is not a battle in the book,
and to expect the high places not in the acts themselves but in the
preparation for them. A good example of Daniel's interest and of his
method occurs in the third book[1]: the conspiracy of the Abbot of
Westminster, Surrey, Exeter, and others. He lets us know he sets
store by the episode because he invokes the Muse at its beginning.
Richard II is now a prisoner and the conspirators plan to murder

[1] 26 ff.

Henry IV and restore Richard to the throne. The Abbot invites the likely men to a feast ('For when Men will have fed, th'Blood being warm / Then are they most improvident of Harm') and makes an equivocal speech, feeling his way.

> *This open-close, apparent-dark discourse,*
> *Drew on much speech: and everie man replies:*
> *And every man addes heate: and words enforce,*
> *And urge out wordes. For, when one man espies*
> *Anothers mind like his, then ill breedes worse;*
> *And out breaks all in the'end what closest lies.*

The conspirators become clamorous, and one vows himself ready to kill Henry. Then they plan a concerted scheme to kill him at a masque and take an oath of secrecy. There is, however, one of the band who is more cautious and perceptive, Sir Thomas Blount. He wants the rest to realise what they are in for, and recounts the dangers before and after the deed. He does not want to back out, though he would have preferred open war. He is committed, and the great thing now is success.

> *This sayd, a sad still silence held their mindes,*
> *Upon the fearefull project of their woe;*
> *But that, not long, ere forward Furie findes*
> *Incouraging perswasions on to goe.*
> *We must (sayd they) we will; our honour bindes,*
> *Our safety bids; our fayth must have it so.*
> *We know the worst can come, 'tis thought upon:*
> *We cannot shift; being in, we must goe on.*

Thus far, the scene is clear and forceful, and it corresponds aptly to our notions of human nature. Men do indeed act, we say, on such motives. But the event itself, the betrayal of the conspiracy by Aumerle, is recounted with a flatness that astonishes if we expect the stress to be on the climax of action and not on the preliminaries to it.

> *And on in deed they went; but O! not far;*
> *A fatal stop traverst their headlong course;*
> *Their drift comes knowne, and they discovered are:*
> *For, some of many will be false, of force.*
> Aumarle *became the man, that all did marre,*
> *Whether through indiscretion, chance, or worse;*
> *He makes his peace with offring others blood,*
> *And shewes the King, how all the matter stood.*

And after two or three more weak stanzas the episode closes.

I will give one more out of many possible examples of Daniel's preference for the preliminaries of action over action itself. It comes from the eighth book, at the end of what Daniel completed of his poem. The Earl of Warwick was deeply offended by Edward IV's going back on the French match he went to France to promote. But he concealed his feelings on his return, resolving to retire to his own estates to meditate and then set about revenge. So he goes to Warwick Castle and visits his estates. His confessor guesses what is passing in his mind: and there ensues a debate; the confessor setting forth the advantages of moderate ambition and the ordered life in the sphere allotted by God, and Warwick answering in the vein of Renaissance restlessness. If, says Warwick, he could get free from the sphere in which he is fixed, he would rather wish his palace to be 'that Sheepcot, which in yonder Vale you see / Than any roof of Proudest Majesty'. But honour forbids, for

> *I knowe, that I am fixt unto a Sphere,*
> *That is ordayn'd to move. It is the place*
> *My fate appoints me; and the region where*
> *I must, whatever happens, there, imbrace,*
> *Disturbance, travaile, labor, hope and feare,*
> *Are of that Clime ingendred in that place;*
> *And action best, I see, becomes the Best:*
> *The Starres that have most glorie, have no rest.*

The confessor is of course a fiction, and the poet uses him to express the real conflict in Warwick's mind. And he does express it nobly. Into this conflict, the preliminary to action, action breaks in with the customary frigidity. The Reverend Father would have replied,

> *But that a speedy messenger was sent*
> *To shewe, the Duke of Clarence was hard-by.*
> *And thereupon, Warwicke breaks-off, and went*
> *(With all his Train attending formally)*
> *To intertaine him with fit complement;*
> *As, glad of such an opportunitie*
> *To worke upon, for those high purposes*
> *He had conceiv'd in discontentedness.*

This stanza ends the book and all we have of the *Civil Wars*.

Daniel's philosophy of history and his solemn concern with the motives of great political action are the two things that most give his poem an epic tinge. They are worthily answered by the simple and solid sententiousness of his verse. His metre, the *ottava rima*, was, I should guess, borrowed from Tasso[1] direct rather than from Haring-

---

[1] Daniel, who had visited Italy, knew and borrowed from the *Jerusalem Delivered*. In particular, stanza 107 of Book Six comparing the growing power of York to the swelling Severn is borrowed from *J.L.* ix. 46 with Severn substituted for Po. See A. Castelli, *La Gerusalemme Liberata nella Inghilterra di Spenser* (Milan 1936) 47.

ton's *Orlando Furioso*. He probably thought of it as the proper form for a modern classicising epic, the form hallowed by the two greatest recent practitioners. His style, that middling near-prose style admired by Coleridge, is all his own. It is extremely direct, uses a high proportion of very simple words, is hardly metaphorical at all except through occasional similes, and yet, though often dull, hardly ever lacks dignity. Though not great verse, it has a decided character and could have been evolved only by a severe effort. Its dullness is of the right kind, negative not positive; the index of not having a great deal to say just then without being worried by the deficiency. It is worry that breeds the harmful kind of positive dullness. Daniel knows serenely that he will not be dull for long and is content. At its best his verse rises to a passionate but controlledly passionate eloquence; but its characteristic vein is one of even dignity.

These matters of thought and style give Daniel's poem some share of epic quality. It is of course vain to seek in him the amplitude and variety that mark the great epics. Daniel's mind was not flexible and it shows no humour. What gives most relief from the pervading moral solemnity or stark matter-of-factness is a sense of pity. In describing the misfortunes of Richard II he alters his position of philosophic remoteness and takes his stand near the doomed king. There is an exquisite passage (iii. 64) where Richard from his prison sees the traffic of the ordinary world outside:

> *The Morning of that day, which was his last,*
> *After a weary rest rysing to paine,*
> *Out at a little grate his eyes he cast*
> *Upon those bordering hills, and open Plaine,*
> *And viewes the towne, and sees how people past:*
> *Where others libertie makes him complaine*
> *The more his owne, and grieves his soule the more;*
> *Conferring[1] captive Crownes, with freedome poore.*

Then there is the equally pathetic picture of his queen watching for him from a window as the procession goes through London and thinking she sees him in the place of honour:

> *Thus does false joy delude her wrongfully*
> *(Sweete Lady) in the thing she held so deare.*
> *For, nearer come, she findes she had mistooke;*
> *And him she markt was* Henrie Bullingbrooke.[2]

Daniel showed considerable strength of will in carrying through the *Civil Wars* to the end of the eighth book. It is a surprise, as well as a pity, that he did not write the last third. He may have felt that the emotional strength of his great subject was slipping away after the

---

[1] I.e. 'comparing'.　　　　[2] ii. 71.

death of the last of the Tudors. His architectonic power, corresponding to the power of his will, was not of the greatest: there is no sign
of his keeping the total shape fluid till the very end. He seems to have
composed slowly, piece by piece. But he had a plan, and a well-
shaped one; and he stuck to it with determination. An example of
resolute plotting has occurred already: his subordination of the reign
of Henry V to his theme of civil war. His plan was to present the
beginning, development, and issue of the dynastic curse; and he
refused to be diverted by the brilliant intrusion of Henry V's successes.
He allows himself a panegyric (and a splendid one), but he describes
none of Henry V's triumphs, military or other, in France. That he
has done all this deliberately should be evident from the care and
thoughtfulness of all his work; but he confirms what we should in any
case have inferred by the statement that follows his account of the
death of Henry IV. Instead of turning to the triumphs of Henry V,
he wrote:

> And now, into the Ocean of new toyles;
> Into the stormie Maine (where tempestes growe
> Of greater ruines, and of greater spoyles)
> Set foorth my course (to hasten on my vow)
> Ov'r all the troublous Deepe of these turmoyles,
> And if I may but live t'attaine the shore
> Of my desired end, I wish no more.

The Wars of the Roses themselves are his main theme, and the
preceding troubles lead up to them. And within the Wars Towton
is the culminating horror. The gradual leading up to this culmination
is nobly contrived; it is the more remarkable for having been contrived
in a literary age when copiousness was far commoner than order.

Did Daniel speak for a large body of men? No: he was too academic
and too little concerned with men at large. On the other hand his
high political subject was in itself the age's true epic subject: there he
was absolutely central. And in his treatment of it he did represent a
most important minority. Daniel speaks for the political aristocracy
of England, and most for the statesmen of the Cecil type, the sage and
conscientious servants of the crown. His terribly exacting standards
for the ruling aristocracy found superb expression in his *Epistle to the
Lady Margaret Countesse of Cumberland*, surely as worthy an expression
of the theme of *noblesse oblige* as exists in literature. The *Civil Wars*
should be read in the light of this epistle. Both poems come out of the
heart of that extraordinary governing class of Elizabethan England: a
class which combined high passions with peculiarly exacting con-
sciences; wildnesses with extravagantly humble loyalty. Daniel was
the epic successor of the political side of Sidney's *Arcadia* and he
enjoyed the favour of Fulke Greville, the friend and biographer of

Sidney and the man who has best described the essentially political theme of his friend's masterpiece. He was of course the spectator not the participant of the political life which was his essential subject; and he was thus at a disadvantage compared with a man who was poet and doer equally. But that he watched and wrote of the states of mind that were truly paramount in his age was sufficient cause to make him produce a poem with a partial claim to epic dignity.[1]

[1] There is little encouragement to write on Daniel's *Civil Wars*, because there is no accessible edition. Grosart's was limited and privately printed. The common reader is without the means of enjoying the poem or having an opinion on it. Tannenbaum's recent bibliography of Daniel (most useful in itself) reveals the depressing truth that while money has been spent freely over theses and articles on Daniel none has gone to making available to the common reader the work that he himself most valued. His ghost, if it could speak, would have something to say on the matter. And even his critic may complain when the kind of reader he most minds about hasn't the means of judging whether he is writing sense or nonsense.

CHAPTER XII

THE GREAT TRANSLATIONS

1. GENERAL

POPE'S Homer shows that a translation can achieve high merit as an independent work of art; and in this book I must at least review the great translations of foreign epics on the chance that they may touch epic quality in their own right. I prefer to treat the earlier examples in a separate chapter, for they do not fit into the story of the epic in English very well, while the earliest, Gavin Douglas's *Aeneid*, is exceptionally difficult to classify, belonging as it does both to the Middle Ages and to the early Renaissance.

2. DOUGLAS'S AENEID[1]

That Douglas's *Aeneid* (finished in 1513) is one of the great translations is undoubted; but there may be now the danger of making too much of it. When Ezra Pound calls it better than its original,[2] we need not take him seriously. But when he couples Douglas with Chaucer as the two medieval poets writing in English who matter most and illustrates abundantly,[3] it is time to reflect and ask questions. There are splendid things in the passages Pound quotes, and there are splendid things all through Douglas's *Aeneid*. But what of the whole poem? Many people have read the original *Aeneid* from beginning to end with pleasure. Some people may have read Douglas's *Aeneid* right through with pleasure in his own day. But how many of those who have praised it recently have read and enjoyed the whole? The knottiness of Douglas's language, admirably effective for certain passages and in small doses, does not make for intelligible narrative and wearies the reader after a few hundred lines. Douglas's prosody, admirably expressive in some passages, often collapses into incoherence; leaving the reader doubtful how to read lines, and having no particular point on any reading. One need go no further than one of the passages anthologised by Pound, for illustrations. It comes from the description of the storm at the opening of Book One.

---

[1] I wrote this section before reading Bruce Dearing's article on Douglas's *Aeneid* in *Publications of the Modern Language Association*, 1952, pp. 845-62. Dearing reaches similar conclusions about the political, didactic importance of the translation and its Renaissance affinities.

[2] *How to Read* (London 1931) 45.

[3] *ABC of Reading* (London 1934) 101 ff.

DOUGLAS'S AENEID

> With the cloudis hevynnys son and dayis lycht
> Hid and brest out of the Troianis sycht;
> Derknes as nycht beset the see about,
> The firmament gan rumyllyng rare and rout.
> The skyis oft lychtned with fyry leven;
> And schortlie baith are see and hevyn;
> And every thyng manissis the men to de
> Schewand the dede present before thare E.[1]

There is a good deal of noise and violence here, but it is not especially
appropriate. The wrenched rhythm of 'Hid and brest' at the beginning of line two has no special point. The rumbling alliteration in
the fourth line is crude and poetically elementary. How did Douglas
mean us to read the fourth and fifth lines: do they form a decasyllabic
or octosyllabic couplet? should we accent them thus,

> The skýis óft lýchtned with fýry léven;
> And schórtlie báith are sée and hévyn,[2]

or thus,

> The skýis oft lýchtned with fýry léven,
> And schórtlie báith are sée and hévyn?

The first accentuation supplies an unpleasantly halting and quite
inept rhythm; the second a lilt and a speed out of keeping with the
rest of the passage. I can only agree with Saintsbury's comment[3] on
Douglas's Alexandrines: that they are entirely legitimate if he
intended them as such; but that you cannot be certain that he did.
Douglas's weakness is cruelly conspicuous if you set his lines against
their Latin original:

> Eripiunt subito nubes caelumque diemque
> Teucrorum ex oculis; ponto nox incubat atra.
> intonuere poli et crebris micat ignibus aether,
> praesentemque viris intentant omnia mortem.[4]

Here rhythmically every detail stands out clear and startling; and
with the terrifying clarity in which perilous things are seen by those
who experience them.

[1] 'With the clouds' onset heaven's sun and the light of day were hidden and swept
out of the Trojans' sight. Darkness like night compassed the sea around; the sky
began to rumble with roar and bellow. The heaven kept flashing with fiery lightning; soon sea and sky are confounded; everything threatens to make men die,
showing Death itself before their eyes.'
[2] With the r in schortlie strongly pronounced almost making an extra syllable,
this accentuation is not impossible.
[3] George Saintsbury, A History of English Prosody (London 1906) i. 275.
[4] Aeneid, i. 88-91. 'Suddenly the clouds snatch away sky and daylight from the
Trojans' eyes; black night settles on the sea. The poles of heaven thunder and the
upper air flashes with many fires. Everything threatens the men with instant death.'

Douglas's queer prosodic uncertainty can beset him too even in successful passages. Here is his translation of the two lines with which Virgil ends his fifth book: Aeneas's farewell to Palinurus the steersman, who fell overboard conquered by sleep:

> *O nimium caelo et pelago confise sereno,*
> *nudus in ignota, Palinure, iacebis harena.*

> *Allace! our mekle thow lipnit has,*[1] *quod he,*
> *Into the stabillit heven and calmit see;*
> *Bair and wnerdit, in ane uncouth land,*
> *Palynurus, sall thow ly on the sand.*

The first three lines represent wonderfully the rhythmical effect of the Latin: that of reluctant grief followed by awe. The fourth line trickles away into ineffectiveness, or, to change the metaphor, it is like a weak chin below an emphatic upper face.

In spite of these weaknesses Douglas's *Aeneid* is a very distinguished work, probably the best translation of one of the great epics till Dryden and Pope. It is permeated throughout, even if spasmodically, with passion, and a passion which, different from the Virgilian, gives the work a character. Virgil can deal with quick and violent action surpassingly well, but it is not his special and central concern. Douglas has the keenest sense for close and rapid action. He pictures happenings so vividly that he constantly adds particular strokes that are missing in Virgil. Often when he appears to err by breaking the taut, packed, yet exquisite quality of his original, he compensates by infusing his own special vigour through greater amplitude and circumstantiation. This is Douglas's account of the combined party of Trojans and Arcadians setting out from Evander's settlement on the site of what was to be Rome.[2]

> *The wofull moderis, quakand for cauld dreyd,*
> *Stude on the wall, behaldand quhayr thai yeyd,*
> *And dyd convoy or follow wyth thair sycht*
> *The dusty sop, quhayr so the rak went rycht,*
> *Govand apone thair brycht armour that schayne,*
> *So far as that thair luik mycht thaim attane.*
> *The cumpany all sammyn held array*
> *Throw scroggy bussis furth the nerrest way,*
> *Enarmyt ryding thidder as thai wald;*
> *The bruyt and dyn from thaim upsprang thickfold,*

---

[1] 'Over much hast thou trusted to etc. . . .'
[2] *Aeneid*, viii. 592-6.

DOUGLAS'S AENEID

The horny hovyt horsis wyth foure feyt
Stampand and trotand on the dusty streyt.[1]

These twelve lines represent five of Virgil's. But, though so few, Virgil's lines give an absolutely precise picture and they are very close packed. They describe the mothers watching the company's progress: the dust and the shining of arms, the short-cut through the brambles, the shout as the riders get into the open country, fall into formation, and break into a gallop. Douglas destroys this precise picture with its differentiated stages, but adds many details. The mothers not only watch but watch till the party is out of sight. The bushes the horsemen pass through are not just bushes but 'scroggy' ones. And Douglas's horses do a good deal more than break into a ringing gallop. Further, he shows immense zest in taking us into the thick of the horsemen; the shout of Virgil's riders has been changed into the general din of a confused press of horses and riders, armour and harness. Douglas must always be on the spot; he lives quite in the present. Virgil holds past, present, and future together in his mind. Douglas would have kept far nearer his original if he had translated the *Iliad* instead. But that does not mean that he was any less alive in translating someone more distant from his own temper. It merely means that he had to force things more.

To show how Douglas sustained his ardent spirit to the end I choose a passage from the last scene of the *Aeneid*: part of Juturna's speech when, recognising the Fury sent by Jupiter to baffle her brother Turnus, she knows she is powerless to help him any longer.

> *Quid nunc te tua, Turne, potest germana iuvare?*
> *aut quid iam durae superat mihi? qua tibi lucem*
> *arte morer? talin' possum me opponere monstro?*
> *iam iam linquo acies: ne me terrete timentem,*
> *obscenae volucres; alarum verbera nosco*
> *letalemque sonum, nec fallunt iussa superba*
> *magnanimi Iovis.*[2]

> *Turnus, my best belovyt brother, quod sche.*
> *Quhat may thy sistir help now, wa is me!*
> *Or quhat now restis to me, wrachit wycht?*
> *Thy life prolong quhou may I? Be quhat slycht*
> *May I oppone me to resist or stryve*
> *With sik a monstre? Na, nane wicht alyve.*

[1] Gavin Douglas, *Poetical Works*, ed. John Small (Edinburgh 1874) iii. 193. Sop, *company*; rak, *dust*; govand, *gazing*.
[2] xii. 872-8. 'What can your sister do now to help you, Turnus? or what remains for me in my enforced hard-heartedness? by what art should I extend your life? To such a monster how can I oppose myself? I haste to leave the battle. I fear enough; do not terrify me, you birds of ill omen. I recognise the beating of your wings and their mortal sound. The haughty commands of highhearted Jupiter are plain to me.'

341

> *Now, now, I leif the feild, and gois away.*
> *O ye myschevus foulis, I you pray,*
> *Do me na mair agrys trymland for feyr;*
> *The clapping of your wyngis I knaw and heyr,*
> *And eik the dedly soundis weill on far:*
> *The proud command of mychty Jupiter,*
> *That gydis al thing by his maiestie,*
> *Dois me nocht now astart, for I it se.*

Douglas here mistranslates *durae* of the second line with *wrachit wycht.* Juturna does not complain of her misery but of her enforced hard-heartedness in not continuing to help her brother. But on the whole he rises wonderfully to the magnificence of the original. He conveys Juturna's sudden change from sad reflection to terrified protest that she will no longer try to interfere, shown in *iam iam linquo acies,* with complete success though by very literal means. The shudder of terror Virgil conveys through the powerful stress of *obscenae* Douglas conveys through the equally powerful stress on *trymland.* Douglas is of course diffuse compared with Virgil, but here he is, at the end of his arduous work, competing not too unsuccessfully with one of the highest places of Virgil's writing. And this is a great achievement. Or take Aeneas's farewell words to Helenus, discussed in my chapter on Virgil (p. 75 above), contrasting Helenus's good fortune in being settled and Aeneas's necessity to continue his wanderings. Douglas here succeeds in a different way, namely in accommodating his violent northern dialect to the elegiac beauty of Virgil's lines:

> *To thaim I said: Deir freindis, weill ye be,*
> *Weill mott ye leiff in your felicite,*
> *Quham till the prosper fortoun is brocht to end;*
> *Bot we from werd to werd and chance mon wend.*
> *Your rest is found, you nedis seuch throw na seis,*
> *Nor seik fieldis of Itaile, that ever ws fleis.*[1]

There is real mystery here in the contrast between the smooth contented rhythm of the second line and the halting nostalgic rhythm of the last.

I conclude then that for all its faults Douglas's *Aeneid* has merits enough at least to be considered as touching epic quality.

Coming to Douglas's positive claim to epic quality, we had better first face and admit his limitations; and this we can quickly do through assessing the degree of control he exercised over his material. Douglas's architectonic faculty consisted of unfailing recurrences of *ad hoc* vitality not of a sustained and moulding pressure of the will. That his vitality should not fail to recur is something but not enough

[1] Werd, *fate*; seuch, *plough.*

to make him equal to the total grandeur of his original. It is known that he spent about a year and a half on his work. Now this contains many more lines than its original, being not only more ample than Virgil himself but including the thirteenth book that Mapheus Vegius had recently added. Plainly Douglas did not spend long on his work, its length considered. He may have undertaken it with zest but not with the prolonged discipline the true epic requires. Douglas's *Aeneid* can therefore never be an epic of the first rank; all it can aspire to is the secondary success of being a meritorious long poem having a choric as well as an individual meaning, of being a long poem that still has vitality and that speaks for its age.

I said at the beginning of this section that Douglas's *Aeneid* was particularly difficult to classify. But this difficulty did not mean that it was not typical; it meant rather that it typified transition. The setting of his translation is medieval. For instance, he pictured and we picture the Trojans and Arcadians setting out from Evander's settlement much as Chaucer pictured the medieval knights who took part in the tournament in the *Knight's Tale*. On the other hand Douglas misses Virgil's spirituality and has no share in the genuine medieval trend of making the poem an allegory of the human soul. It is true that in his prologue to Book Six he argues on conventional lines that Virgil can be squared with orthodox Christianity and that, for instance, his underworld is correctly divided into the departments of Hell, Purgatory, and Heaven. But the centre of Douglas's interests is political and ethical in the Renaissance manner. And his prose postscript to Book Six is more truly felt than is the prologue. Here Douglas, now half way through the poem, pauses and says that the second part shows Aeneas a 'Prince indued with al nobyl and princely vertewis': a pattern of excellence.

> He was verteous, sincer, gentill, and liberall: in justice, wysdome, and magnanimitye, a myrroure to all Pryncis, quhais vertewis gif the Pryncis of our dayis wyll follow, they schal not onely be favored of God, bot also weil beloved of all gud men: thare impyr, king-domes, and posteritye schal be the mair durabyll: for it is vertew that ever has promoved commoun welthys, and vyce has ever bene the caus of dystructione of the same, as we rede in all historyis both civil and ecclesiasticall.

Here is the full Renaissance doctrine of the example and the accompanying belief in the didactic importance of history.

It would doubtless be possible to find the same apparent mixture of medieval and Renaissance elements in contemporary England; yet I fancy that the elements themselves had a peculiarly Scottish character. Scotland at that time was at once more barbaric and, through its French affinities, closer to the Continent. Such a combination of qualities was destined to persist; and Walter Scott embodied it in the person of Fergus Mac-Ivor. Douglas himself was in the thick of the turbulent political life of early sixteenth-century Scotland; but when at the end of his days he was an exile in England he became the friend of that cultured cosmopolitan, Polydore Vergil. True in himself and in his own life to this peculiarly Scottish union of interests, he succeeded, consciously or not, in expressing it through his translation of Virgil. His peculiar vitality, the exuberant violence of his vocabulary, and his closeness to action correspond nicely to the fierce political life of Scotland at that time; while his unfailing respect for his original and, his age considered, the remarkably high level of his scholarship correspond to the impact of the superior culture of the Continent. I doubt if any other Scottish poet achieves this union. Douglas does indeed have some claim to speak for his nation.

But here we must distinguish. If Douglas had been conscious of the things he stood for, if he had meditated long on them, and had used Virgil as their vehicle, then he would have been a different and a greater poet, worthy to be compared with his original. When at the end of the *Aeneid* Jupiter and Juno are reconciled through the compromise that the victors shall accept the language of the vanquished, there is a great symbolic meaning. The compromise stands for all those acts of wise concession that made the Roman Empire possible. There is nothing of this kind in Douglas and he probably failed to see it in Virgil. For epic breadth of an order near the Virgilian Scotland had to wait for the first few Waverley Novels, where the themes of England and Scotland, Highland and Lowland are exploited with brilliant success.

Douglas in translating the *Aeneid* wrote a meritorious long poem, in doing which he unconsciously achieved a choric success, conveying something of what it was like to be alive in the Scotland of his time. This success, though it could not make his translation a true epic, did ensure that it contained some epic qualities. And this is no small achievement.

3. HARINGTON'S ARIOSTO

Least of all do I purpose to bestow any long time to argue . . . whether Master Faire *translating* Virgil, *Master* Golding *translating* Ovids Metamorphosis, *and my selfe in this worke that you see, be any more than versifiers, as the same* Ignoto *termeth all translators.*

(John Harington, Preface to his translation of *Orlando Furioso*)

Phaer's *Aeneid* is too uncouth a translation to warrant inclusion here. Golding's *Metamorphoses*, beautiful in its way, is a work which, though long and technically well sustained, does not claim the epic status. Harington's *Orlando Furioso*, though its original has figured but dubiously in this book, is good enough to merit a short mention.

It has not been reprinted since the early seventeenth century: a regrettable omission because it is a tolerably faithful translation and in poetic quality vastly superior to the versions of Rose and Hoole. Rose, like Harington, used the stanza of the original, but with a heavy hand. Hoole's competent eighteenth-century couplets are remote from the Ariostan point and elegance which Harington is surprisingly successful in recapturing. The surprise is all the greater when we reflect that Harington published his translation as early as 1591 and that he was at work on it some years before. And yet, though writing so early, he is sure of himself metrically, and without showing any sign of having had to rely on the new metrical assurance of the *Shepheards Calender*. For a stanza not too far removed from the *ottava rima* to be helpful he had examples in the many rime royal tragedies in the successive instalments of the *Mirror for Magistrates*; but he did not need such help, for his own verse is very much more accomplished; more flexible and less sombre. Harington is indeed master of his craft in a way few Elizabethan translators are. While remaining true to the chief things in his original, he retains just the amount of freedom needed to make his translation sound like a poem in its own right. Take these two stanzas from the beginning of canto twenty-nine, containing Ariosto's comment on a change of mind in one of his bad characters:

> *Oh mynds of men, unconstant and unstable,*
> *As subject unto change, as Westerne wynd,*
> *In all designments fond and variable,*
> *But chiefly those, that love breeds in the mind:*
> *Lo he that late devisd all he was able,*
> *To slaunder and deface all women kynd,*
> *Yet now with them whom he so sore revild,*
> *Ev'n on a sudden, he is reconcild.*

> *Certes (most noble Dames) I am so wroth*
> *With this vile Turke, for this his wicked sin,*
> *For speaking so great sclander and untruth*
> *Of that sweet sex, whose grace I fain would win,*
> *That till such time he shall confess the troth,*
> *And what a damned error he was in:*
> *I shall him make be so in conscience stoung,*
> *As he shall teare his flesh, and byte his toung.*

Harington here conducts his verse as an experienced rider makes a well-trained horse pick its way across country; not just accepting the one tolerable course but choosing as he goes the option that suits him best. There is nothing in the original about the *Vile Turke*, yet the phrase is perfectly true to Ariosto's comic scorn at this point. The last line is a mis-translation, but closes the stanza excellently for all that.

When in his preface Harington defends the bawdy parts of Ariosto, he brings in Chaucer and the 'decorum' that alone 'excuseth and maketh more tolerable' the Miller's and others of Chaucer's tales. And it is likely that Harington went back to Chaucer for help in a comic style to match Ariosto's. Whether or not he looked back in this way, he certainly looked forward, for he succeeded in translating the more comic parts of Ariosto by methods that remind us of Frere and Byron. This is his translation of Ariosto's apology for the host's story of Astolfo at the beginning of the twenty-eighth canto:

> *Peruse it not, or if you do it reed,*
> *Esteeme it not, but as an idle bable;*
> *Regard it not, or if you take some heed,*
> *Believe it not, but as a foolish fable:*
> *But to the matter, thus it was indeed,*
> *When all the guests were cheared at the table:*
> *Neare Rodomont (so was the Pagan named)*
> *Downe sat mine Host, and thus his tale he framed.*

This, whether by accident or not, is near the tone of Chaucer introducing the *Miller's Tale*.

Harington's skill in using double or triple rhymes for various degrees of comedy is like Byron's. I illustrate from the eighth canto. When Ariosto has got Angelica into the plight of being bound and about to be sacrificed, he feigns such sympathy that he really cannot go on with the story but must take up his tale elsewhere. Harington translates Ariosto's final stanza before he shifts his story as follows:

> *Wherfore I must some other matter find,*
> *Untill my muse her sorow may asswage,*
> *For sure no cruell beast were so unkind,*
> *Nor tyger in their greatest wrath and rage,*
> *Nor anie cruell tyrant can we find,*
> *(Although there are good store in ev'ry age)*
> *That could behold or thinke, without compassion,*
> *A Ladie bounden in so vile a fashion.*[1]

The line about there being good store of tyrants is not in the original. But its cool insertion is faithful to Ariosto's tone and leads to the slightly comic effect of the double (or triple) rhyme of the final couplet. In the following stanza, concerning an earlier adventure of Angelica, the triple rhyme is broadly comic. The poet describes a lecherous old hermit:

[1] 8. 59 in Harington representing 8. 67 in Ariosto.

> *Who all the while had in a corner stood,*
> *Hearing her make this piteous plaint and mone,*
> *Proceeding from her sad and mourning moode,*
> *Able to move a heart as hard as stone:*
> *It did the* Senex *fornicator good,*
> *To thinke that he was there with her alone,*
> *Yet so devoutly commeth this old carrion,*
> *As though it had been* Paule *or Saint* Hillarion.[1]

The final couplet, translating

> *E venne a lei, fingendo divozione*
> *Quanta avesse mai Paulo o Ilarione,*

brilliantly renders the comedy of the original even if it exaggerates.

Harington, godson to Queen Elizabeth and entirely accustomed to the court, was well equipped to understand the temper of Ariosto. He is indeed one of the most successful of English translators. But he has not the force of Douglas, and his translation is less of an original poem than Douglas's *Aeneid*. He has a smaller claim to have achieved an epic through translation; quite apart from the different natures of their originals.

4. FAIRFAX'S TASSO

Many besides myself have heard our famous Waller own, that he derived the harmony of his numbers from Godfrey of Bulloign, *which was turned into English by Mr Fairfax.*

(Dryden, *Preface to the Fables*)

Having mentioned Harington's *Orlando* I can hardly not mention its eminent Elizabethan pendant, Fairfax's *Godfrey of Bulloigne* (1600), though in itself less worthy. Fairfax, unlike Harington, has enjoyed modern publication and has had more readers. But his verse, copied from Spenser, is not as strong and distinctive as Harington's: and he gives a greater sense of labour. Fairfax's merit is that he can respond to the finer things in his original: for instance, to the account of the enchanted wood raised by Ismeno and of the Christians' adventures in penetrating it. But for stretches he can be no more than competent, though competence may at any time give way to liveliness. Here, for instance, is a lively stanza (9. 8) following several uninteresting ones; it describes the Fury, Alecto.

> *To him* Alecto *came, and semblant bore*
> *Of one whose age was great, whose lookes were grave,*
> *Whose cheekes were bloodlesse, and whose locks were hore,*
> *Mustachoes strouting long, and chin close shave,*

---

[1] 8. 39 in Harington representing 8. 45 in Ariosto.

A steepled Turbant on her head she wore,
Her garment wide, and by her side, her glave,
Her guilden quiver at her shoulders hong,
And in her hand a bow was, stiffe and strong.

Fairfax is a most meritorious translator, whose verse runs evenly and pleasantly and who can touch poetry in some passages. But his is not the kind of translation that comes within the scope of this book. He is not a forceful writer, and the affinity Waller claimed with him indicates well enough the limits of his talent.

5. CHAPMAN'S HOMER[1]

The ballad-manner—Chapman's manner. . . . To feel that Chapman's measure, though natural, is not Homeric; that, though tolerably rapid, it has not Homer's rapidity; that it has a jogging rapidity rather than a flowing rapidity; and a movement familiar rather than nobly easy, one has only to read half a dozen lines in any part of his version.   (Matthew Arnold *On Translating Homer*)

It is easy to see why Chapman claimed, and his fellows accorded him, praise for his translation of Homer. In an age when literature was judged so largely by didactic value, it was a virtuous deed to translate into however crude a form one of the great works of antiquity. A good knowledge of Greek was uncommon and was the more prized. Chapman's chief claim to have served his fellows well was that he applied his uncommon knowledge of Greek to making the first translation into English of the whole work of one of the world's two greatest poets. To do this at all was prodigious; and if he achieved any competence it was hardly decent to inquire what precise degree of competence this should be. But once it had become common to have enough Greek to translate Homer, the grounds for the reputation of Chapman's version become difficult to understand. That reputation, depressed during the Augustan age, mounted when towards the end of the eighteenth century the Elizabethans came into favour. It was probably helped by current notions of the primitive nature of the Homeric poems and their supposed kinship to Ossian, for instance: notions that fostered the belief that the primitive vigour of the Elizabethans was better fitted to Homer than the elegant sophistication of Pope. Anyhow, Romantic prejudice prompted Keats to write an indiscreet sonnet on Chapman's Homer; a sonnet on the strength of which the book has enjoyed an undeserved reputation that has not yet been exploded.

[1] *Iliad*: translation of fourteen books published 1598, of rest 1610-11. *Odyssey*: 1614-15.

CHAPMAN'S HOMER

Judged as a feat of endurance, Chapman's Homer is indeed a prodigy; judged as a poem, the very things that made it a prodigy destroy its value. Bent beneath his labour, Chapman had no strength left to match poetry with poetry. There is little to distinguish the great from the normal passages. In metrical amenity the fourteeners of the *Iliad* and the heroic couplets of the *Odyssey* are equally lacking. They both move with the same kind of unwieldy effort and are both equally ill adapted to prolonged narrative. This heaviness is the more to be regretted because Chapman in his preface to the *Odyssey* wrote very well of the Homeric limpidity. Disagreeing with Longinus on the inferiority of the *Odyssey* to the *Iliad*, he claimed that Homer's 'divine inspiration doth render vast, illustrious, and of mighty composure' the initially meagre theme of the return of Odysseus. It is unfair to compare the *Odyssey* to the sea,

> Nor can it be compared to any one power to be named in nature, being an entirely well-sorted and digested confluence of all; where the most solid and grave is made as nimble and fluent as the most airy and fiery, the nimble and fluent as firm and well-bounded as the most grave and solid.

Nimbleness and fluency, the qualities Chapman attributes to the *Odyssey*, are precisely those that are missing from his translation.

But my contention that Chapman's Homer cannot begin to be considered as epic writing on account of its deficiencies of style can be verified only by the effect it has on a number of readers. Here is his translation of one of the great things in Homer, Priam's speech in the last book of the *Iliad* begging Achilles to pity him and to restore Hector's body:

> *See in me, O godlike Thetis sonne,*
> *Thy aged father, and perhaps, even now being outrunne*
> *With some of my woes; neighbour foes (thou absent) taking time*
> *To doe him mischiefe; no meane left, to terrifie the crime*
> *Of his oppression; yet he heares thy graces still survive,*
> *And joyes to heare it, hoping still to see thee safe arrive*
> *From ruind Troy: but I (curst man) of all my race shall live*
> *To see none living. Fiftie sonnes the Deities did give,*
> *My hopes to live in; all alive, when neare our trembling shore*
> *The Greeke ships harbord, and one wombe nineteene of those sons bore.*
> *Now Mars a number of their knees hath strengthlesse left, and he*
> *That was (of all) my onely joy, and Troyes sole guard, by thee*
> *(Late fighting for his country) slaine; whose tendered person now*
> *I come to ransome. Infinite is that I offer you,*
> *Myselfe conferring it; exposde alone to all your oddes:*
> *Onely imploring right of armes. Achilles feare the gods,*
> *Pittie an old man like thy sire; different in onely this,*

> *That I am wretcheder; and beare that weight of miseries*
> *That never man did: my curst lips, enforc't to kisse that hand*
> *That slue my children.*

These jerky, clotted fourteeners are unworthy of the intense, pellucid original. And here is the beginning of the twenty-second book of the *Odyssey*, where Odysseus throws off his beggar's disguise and begins his vengeance:

> *The upper rags, that wise* Ulysses *wore,*
> *Cast off; he rusheth to the great Hall dore*
> *With Bow and Quiver full of shafts; which downe*
> *He pour'd before his feet; and thus made known*
> *His true state to the wooers: This strife thus*
> *Hath harmlesse bene decided: Now for us*
> *There rests another marke, more hard to hit,*
> *And such, as never men before hath smit;*
> *Whose full point likewise my hands shall assay,*
> *And try if Phoebus will give me his day.*
> *He said; and off his bitter Arrow thrust*
> *Right at* Antinous; *that strooke him just*
> *As he was lifting up the Bolle; to show*
> *That 'twixt the cup and lip much ill may grow.*
> Death *toucht not at his thoughts at Feast: for who*
> *Would thinke that he alone could perish so*
> *Amongst so many? And he, best of all?*
> *The Arrow in his throate tooke full his fall;*
> *And thrust his head farre through the other side:*
> *Downe fell his cup; downe he; downe all his pride.*

This is a cool and pedestrian rendering of a tremendous climax. Chapman has been as overestimated for his translation of Homer as Pope has been underestimated.

Chapman's failure of style is the more to be regretted because he did, through many small alterations, give Homer a genuine contemporary colour, an act propitious in itself to an epic effect. Coleridge indeed called Chapman's *Odyssey* as truly an original poem as the *Faerie Queene*. Chapman's alterations are the subject of an interesting article by Phyllis B. Bartlett, *The Heroes of Chapman's Homer*.[1] Chapman no longer interpreted Homer allegorically but was chiefly interested in ethics. He expressed his ethical notions through the persons to whose characters he often gives a turn different from the Homeric. He did this above all in the *Odyssey*, where his Ulysses 'has become a moral hero of the Renaissance'.

But, when the best has been said for Chapman's Homer, I do not

---

[1] *Review of English Studies*, 1941, pp. 257-80.

see how it can stand up to Dryden's rough handling in his *Examen Poeticum*:

> The Earl of Mulgrave and Mr Waller, two of the best judges of our age, have assured me, that they could never read over the translation of Chapman without incredible pleasure and extreme transport. This admiration of theirs must needs proceed from the author himself; for the translator has thrown him down as far as harsh numbers, improper English, and a monstrous length of verse could carry him.[1]

6. SYLVESTER'S DU BARTAS[2]

> *And* Silvester *whome from the* French *more weake*
> *Made* Bartas *of his sixe dayes labour speake*
> *In naturall* English.   (Drayton, *Epistle to Reynolds*)

I omitted Du Bartas from my remarks on the French epic of the Renaissance, preferring to deal with him through his English translator, Joshua Sylvester. Sylvester—who demands inclusion through his relation to Milton, Cowley, and Dryden—accentuates just that single quality in Du Bartas that makes one think of him as an epic writer. Thus, in a book dealing with the English epic it is proper to speak of Sylvester first and of Du Bartas, if at all, through him.

Du Bartas's *Semaines* belongs to the class of literature that attracts the foreigner more than the native. Goethe admired it warmly; and the casual English reader finds some of it noble and inspiring. But though it went into thirty editions near its own day, no Frenchman has troubled to edit it in modern times. Saintsbury complained that Du Bartas was 'always unjustly treated in France, probably from a curious tradition of mingled sectarian and literary jealousy'.[3] I doubt this reason and suspect that such jealousy has no more to do with French opinion of the literary merits of Du Bartas than has prudery with English opinion on those of Oscar Wilde. It seems as if there must be some radical defect in the poetic style of Du Bartas.

In subject the *Semaines* combines Old Testament myth and history with the lore of the hexemeral commentators and of the medieval encyclopedias. To an age that loved length and wealth of matter this combination was attractive, but it did not conduce to the tight

---

[1] W. P. Ker, *Essays of John Dryden*, ii. 14.

[2] Sylvester's translations of Du Bartas, *La Première Semaine* and *La Seconde Semaine*, lacking the last three days of the second week, were published at intervals 1592-9: collected edition 1608 (see George Coffin Taylor, *Milton's Use of Du Bartas*, Cambridge, Mass., 1934, p. 7 note 1). His translation of Du Bartas, *Judith*, comes later. That both originals were esteemed in the Elizabethan age is especially clear from the use Abraham Fraunce made of them in his *Arcadian Rhetorike*, for which see above p. 315.

[3] *Short History of French Literature*, 7th edition (Oxford 1917), 183 note.

organisation necessary for the full epic effect. Du Bartas, though he could elsewhere adopt a classical form, chose here to gossip and to expatiate. It has been in fact stupid and to the detriment of Du Bartas's reputation to apply the term *epic* to the *Semaines* at all. And people committed the stupidity only because they looked on *Paradise Lost* as a superior version of it and were thus tempted to give to the inferior work the label that it was agreed fitted the superior. The other work of Du Bartas that concerns me is the *Judith*, a narrative of nearly 3000 lines, cast in classical form, of the apocryphal story of Judith and Holofernes.

The span of Sylvester's life, 1563-1618, is close to that of Shakespeare. His translation of Du Bartas's *Semaines*, the *Divine Weekes and Workes*, was very popular in the first half of the seventeenth century and was the early reading of the three poets most important in the history of the epic in that century, Milton, Cowley, and Dryden, on all of whom it had real, if different, influences. In so doing it has its place in this book. Having to include it, I cannot refrain from protesting against the unfair condemnation which it has received and from pointing out the sort of effect it can in a modest way attain. The *Divine Weekes* has suffered not only from the inept comparison with *Paradise Lost* but from a short passage in Dryden's dedication of the *Spanish Friar*. This passage has persuaded conventional opinion that the whole poem was written in the style of the lines held up to ridicule. Dryden wrote:

> I remember, when I was a boy, I thought inimitable Spenser a mean poet in comparison of Sylvester's *Dubartas*, and was rapt into an ecstasy when I read these lines:
>
> > *Now, when the Winter's keener breath began*
> > *To chrystallize the Baltick Ocean;*
> > *To glaze the Lakes, to bridle up the Floods,*
> > *And periwig with Snow the bald-pate Woods.*
>
> I am much deceived if this be not abominable fustian that is, thoughts and words ill-assorted, and without the least relation to each other.[1]

To see what Sylvester was guilty of in these lines, compare them with their original:

> *Mais soudain que l'Hyver donne une froide bride*
> *Aux fleuves desbordez: que la face il solide*
> *Du Baltique Neptun: qu'il vitre les guerets,*
> *Et que de flots de laine il orne les forests.*[2]

[1] *Essays of John Dryden*, ed. W. P. Ker, i. 247.
[2] References to Sylvester are not easy to give. Early editions of the complete works are more easily obtained than Grosart's limited one. But lines are not numbered. This passage is from 2nd Week, 1st Day, 4th Part, line 184: on p. 104 of the 1633 edition of the complete works.

Certainly this periwigging the bald-pate woods is a vile, gratuitous addition. But Sylvester rarely offends so grossly; and the offence is of the kind we get elsewhere in the century. Sylvester's gratuitous addition is like those found in Fanshawe's *Lusiad* and some of the extravagances of Dryden's own earliest verse. Writing in 1681, Dryden is naturally intolerant of the vices of a now outmoded age; this intolerance leads him to condemn a whole work of which in fact they form but a small part.

I suspect that it is these factors that induced Bonamy Dobrée to dismiss the *Divine Weekes* in the following words:

> To us this is an infinitely dreary fabrication; its matter and its manner are both repugnant to us; and it is turgid, violent, overloaded—and it is intolerably long.[1]

If you begin reading in the expectation of great ruling ideas and an organised form, of course you find the *Divine Weekes* intolerable. But if you know that it is a long didactic poem containing not only an account of the seven days of creation but much myth and history from the Old Testament, a sketch of man's destiny to the end of time, and much fabulous and scientific matter from the medieval encyclopedias, and if you judge it on the details it provides and not as an organised whole, you will find that Sylvester provides a mass of distinctive and entertaining verse: good sound stuff for cut-and-come-again reading. We should associate Sylvester not with Milton, except for details, but with the Elizabethan masters of easy, agreeable, didactic verse, Sir John Davies, Daniel, and Drayton, however much less accomplished he is than these. Granted this association, we should also note important differences and a thoroughly distinctive talent in Sylvester. He took over from his original the vice of pleonasm, and probably not against the grain. But he has in compensation the gift of measured, easy argument; and his verse bustles agreeably in a manner quite its own. In one matter he goes further than his original. Du Bartas was a French Protestant; and his work reflects the solid, thrifty qualities of Protestantism. One of the best sections is 2nd Week, 2nd Day, 3rd Part, dealing with the different races and parts of the world and their traffic. In it Du Bartas shows his interest in trade and enterprise. It was Sylvester's special distinction to intensify and individualise this interest of Du Bartas.

I must now illustrate the qualities I have claimed for Sylvester. Here is an average specimen of his expository skill from near the poem's beginning:

> *The World's a Book in* Folio, *printed all*
> *With God's great Works in letters Capitall:*

[1] In *English Literary History*, iii. 83.

> *Each Creature is a Page; and each Effect*
> *A faire Character, void of all defect.*
> *But, as young Trewants, toying in the Schools,*
> *In steed of learning, learne to play the fools:*
> *We gaze but on the Babies and the Cover,*
> *The gawdy Flowrs, and Edges gilded-over;*
> *And never farther for our Lesson look*
> *Within the Volume of this various Book;*
> *Where learned Nature rudest ones instructs,*
> *That by His wisdom, God the World conducts.*

What distinguishes it from its original is a greater particularity and homeliness of detail. Du Bartas's *grand livre* becomes a *Book in Folio*; and there is nothing in the French about the babies on the book-cover.

> *Le monde est un grand livre, où du souverain maistre*
> *L'admirable artifice on lit en grosse lettre.*
> *Chasque œuvre est une page, et chasque sien effect*
> *Est un beau charactere en tous ses traicts parfait.*
> *Mais, tous tels que l'enfant, qui se paist dans l'eschole*
> *Pour l'estude des arts, d'un estude frivole,*
> *Nostre œil admire tant ses marges peintinez,*
> *Son cuinfleur delizé et ses bors sur-dorez:*
> *Que rien il ne nous chaut d'apprendre la lecture*
> *De ce texte disert, ou la docte Nature*
> *Enseigne aux plus grossiers, qu'une Divinité*
> *Police de ses loix ceste ronde Cité.*

Here is an example of how Sylvester can sustain his argument through a long comparison. The passage comes a little after the first passage and 240 lines from the beginning. It describes God's preliminary plans for creation.

> *Yet did this* Nothing *not at once receive*
> *Matter and Forme: For, as we may perceive*
> *That He, who means to build a warlike Fleet,*
> *Makes first provision of all matter meet,*
> *(As Timber, Iron, Canvase, Cord, and Pitch),*
> *And, when's all ready; then appointeth, which*
> *Which piece for planks, which plank shall line the waste,*
> *The Poup and Prow, which Fir shall make a Mast;*
> *As Art and Use directeth, heedfully*
> *His hand, his tool, his judgement, and his eye:*
> *So God, before This Frame he fashioned,*
> *I wote not what great* Word *he uttered*
> *From sacred mouth.*

354

And this is the original:

> *Et toutes fois ce Rien ne vit ensemblment*
> *Paroistre sa matiere et son riche ornament.*
> *Car comme c'il qui veut équiper des gallees,*
> *Pour se faire seigneur des provinces sallees,*
> *A son œuvre songeant, fais grand amas de bois,*
> *De cordages, de fer, de toiles, et de poix:*
> *Puis quand tout est ensemble, à l'arbre un arbre vouë,*
> *Ce bout d'ais à la poupe, et cet autre à la prouë*
> *Et cet autre au tillac: comme l'art et le soing*
> *Luy guident l'œil, l'esprit, et le fer, et le poing:*
> *Ainsi le tout-puissant, avant que sage il touche*
> *A l'ornement du monde, il iette de sa bouche*
> *Je ne sçay que beau mot.*

Du Bartas, like his translator, is interested in the list of things required for the boat. But Sylvester is more homely still and closer to the shipwright's trade. He drops Du Bartas's elegant circumlocution of 'des provinces sallees' and adds the particularity of the 'fir'. When Sylvester becomes really interested he is bold enough to add to his original. Entirely agreeing with Du Bartas in his interest in matters of trade, as mentioned above, he cannot refrain from interposing his own account of contemporary London.

> *For, as in London (stuft with every sort)*
> *Heer's the Kings Palace, there the Innes of Court:*
> *Heer (to the Thames-ward, all along the Strand)*
> *The stately Houses of the Nobles stand:*
> *Heer dwell rich Merchants; there Artificers:*
> *Heer Silk-men, Mercers, Goldsmiths, Jewellers:*
> *There's a Church-yard furnisht with choyce of books;*
> *Heer stand the Shambles, there the Rowe of Cooks:*
> *Heer wonn Upholsters, Haberdashers, Horners;*
> *There Pothecaries, Grocers, Tailors, Turners.*

> *For costly Toys, silk Stockings, Cambrick, Lawn,*
> *Heer's choicefull Plenty in the curious Pawn:*
> *And all's but an Exchange, where (briefly) no man*
> *Keeps ought as private. Trade makes all things common.*

Sylvester's didactic tone differs from that of the more aristocratic didactic poets like Davies just because it is hearty and middle class. He had been put to trade at the age of thirteen; he was a Puritan, and as such he reminds us of Bunyan and Defoe rather than of his poetic contemporaries. It is this Puritan strain that, in another poem, gives to Sylvester a slight claim to be included in a book on the English epic.

355

THE ENGLISH EPIC AND ITS BACKGROUND

In 1565 Du Bartas published a narrative poem of about 3000 lines on the story of Judith and Holofernes. In 1608 Thomas Hudson published a translation of it into heroic couplets under the title of *The History of Judith*, a translation which came to be included in the works of Sylvester. It is dull metrically, more pompous and less homely and vivid than Sylvester's verse. In 1614 Sylvester also translated *Judith*, calling it *Bethulians* (later *Bethulia's*) *Rescue*. (*Bethulia* was the Hebrew town where Judith lived, besieged by Holofernes.) This translation figured along with Hudson's in Sylvester's collected works. Sylvester did to Du Bartas's *Judith* what he did to parts of the *Semaine*. He easily and gladly accepted the Puritanism of his original, but also anglicised it and made it more homely. Moreover, he had in *Judith* better material to work on, for this poem is in its essence a little Puritan fable while in the *Divine Weekes* the Puritanism is not in the story but in the additions to the story. By domesticating and strengthening Du Bartas's Puritan tone Sylvester was able through his *Bethulians Rescue* to become the voice of an important section of the English population. His art is indeed modest, at times pedestrian; there is no question of his competing with the great epic writers. But he is interested in his story, and its construction is clear and satisfying. Through these virtues Sylvester's choric gift, his gift of voicing the feelings of a big group of men, is able to find in a small way an adequate expression. *Minor epic* sounds like a contradiction in terms; but *Bethulians Rescue* is an example of a very minor one.

Since *Bethulians Rescue* is almost unknown, I had better give a short account of it. There are six books. In Book One we hear how the Jews, at first terrified and scattered by the inroads of Holofernes, decide to resist. It is a simple account but containing some classical similes. In the second book Holofernes, learning that the Jews are to resist, asks the Prince of Ammon who in fact they are. The Prince, here the rather crudely obvious instrument of the classical narrated episode, tells their story from Abraham on. He turns out to be their admirer and warns Holofernes that if they have not broken their covenant with God they are bound to conquer. Furious with the Prince for praising the Jews, Holofernes has him bound hand and foot and left for the Jews to take captive. In both books occurs the moral that God chastens the nations he loves, when they are easy and prosperous, 'by some Stroak severe of just Correction'. Only so can they continue in righteous zeal. The moral, as expressed by Du Bartas, is in keeping with the severity of contemporary Calvinism.

The third book describes how the enemy beleaguer Bethulia and cut off the water supply, reducing the besieged to fearful straits. The people agitate for surrender as better than death by thirst; the rulers are firm, believing that God will rescue them. But they agree to surrender unless help comes within five days. It was through the

Bible-reading habits of one of the inhabitants, the widow Judith, that help was to come.

> But *Judith* (*who the while incessant Showres*
> *From her sad eyes, in signe of sorrow poures*)
> *With mournfull voice now calls upon the Lord;*
> *Anon, her sad Soule comforts in his word:*
> Prayers *were her Stairs, the highest heav'ns to clime;*
> Gods Word, *a Garden, where* (*in needfull time*)
> *Shee found her Simples* (*in Examples pure*)
> The Carefull Passion *of her* Heart *to cure.*
> *There, Judith reading* (*then not casually,*
> *But by God's will, which still works certainly*)
> *Light on the place where the left handed Prince,*
> *Who griev'd for Israels grievous languishments*
> *Under the* Heathen; *to deliver them*
> *Slew* Moab's Eglon, *by a Stratagem.*

At first inspired to follow Ehud's example, she falls into doubt, when a breath of wind opens the Bible at the page recounting the death of Sisera at the hand of Jael. 'This last Example did so fortify the fearfull widow' that she went to the rulers, reproached them for their weak compromise with the people, and got their blessing on her proposed expedition to the enemy camp.

The fourth book describes how Judith adorned herself as alluringly as possible and went over to the enemy. There follows one of the most attractive parts of the poem, an account of Judith's Puritan education. Her father Merari brought her up with extreme care:

> *Or, as som Damsell, having speciall Care*
> *Of som faire Flower, which put outs early-rare*
> *Th'Incarnate Bud, weeds, waters every houre*
> *The fertill Plot that feeds her* Gilli-flower;
> *That, one day blown, it may som Sunday morn*
> *Her lilly Bosom, or her head adorn:*
> *So wise* Merari *did endeavour fair*
> *To form the Manners of his tender Heir.*

His household was a pattern of virtuous order:

> *Their House, for Order so religious,*
> *Seem'd more a Temple than a private House.*
> *There, did no Mayd, with* merry tricks, *intice*
> *The bashfull Stripling to lascivious vice:*
> *There did no drunken Groom sick healths disgorge*
> *Nor against Heav'n blasphemous Oaths re-forge;*

> *There no broad Jesters, no bold common Lyer,*
> *No Gamester, Theef, Rogue, Ruffian, Apple-squire,*
> *Had ever Harbour; but all Servants, there*
> *To their grave Rulers Rules conformed were.*

By the age of twelve Judith was entirely formed in virtue.

> *Shee, ever modest, never us'd to stay*
> *Abroad till midnight at a Mask or Play;*
> *Nor trip from feast to feast, nor Street-webs span*
> *To see, or to be seen of every man.*
> *But rather, knowing that such fond desire*
> *To gaze and to be gaz'd on* (flax and fire)
> *Undid light Dina, and such gadding Dames*
> *A thousand more; their Noble houses shames;*
> *Shee wisely kept at home; where, Morn and Even,*
> *Daily shee call'd upon the God of heaven.*

If she had any leisure she used it to embroider sacred stories and sing psalms to her lute. Though chaste and cold she married Manasses; and the two maintained a perfect puritanical house. Manasses, knowing the corruption of courts, preferred to live quietly at home. He was a keen gardener, full of good works;

> *But, as one day, his Reapers he beheld,*
> *Who, swelting, swift the yellow handfulls feld;*
> *Sol, from his head, caus'd a* Catarrh *descend,*
> *Which shortly after caus'd Manasses End.*

Judith was left affluent but disconsolate. Now three years a widow, her only comfort is to visit the afflicted. The rest of the book describes how Holofernes received her kindly, while she prays God to sustain her.

The fifth book describes Holofernes's immoderate desire for Judith. As a result of it discipline in the army goes to pieces. The poet holds up Holofernes as an awful example of the ravages lust makes on a brave man. His son Bagos acts willingly as pandar, and the poet moralises on the iniquity of pandars and facile ladies of the court. Holofernes entertains Judith in his tent, which is hung with tapestries showing oriental history. He recounts her an episode in Persian history in which he had a part and then, encouraged by Judith (who knew that men like talking of themselves),

> *began*
> *A long Narration how hee playd the man;*
> *Halfe truth, halfe tales: For, 'tis great Souldiers guise*
> *To bombast oft their Own Exploits with Lyes.*

Dinner (and here the sixth and last book begins) interrupts Holofernes's story, and affords the occasion of an attack on gluttony. There are guests at dinner, which turns into a debauch. When they have reeled off to bed, Judith and Holofernes are left alone. Judith consents to go to bed with him, and there follows an account, intentionally comic, of Holofernes, clumsy from drink and lust, fumbling with his clothes:

> Then letting her slide from his arms away
> Hee goes about himselfe to disaray:
> Now he unbuttons, now pulls-off his hose;
> But his heat hinders and his haste foreslowes:
> For (sleep-awake, blind-seeing) while he plyes
> T'untrusse his Points, them (stumbling) faster ties:
> Till, overcome with Rage, and Longing, more,
> He cuts his Knots, and off his Clothes hee tore;
> And then to Bed. Where (as the Crossbowman,
> Who, for his pleasure, watcheth, now and than,
> By some Cross-path some Coney, or some Hare;
> At every Noise, on every side doth stare
> Where stirs a leafe, and levels thitherward
> At the least Wren, or the least Worm that stird
> Neer where hee stands, still in a Hopefull Doubt
> Turning his Body and his Bow about)
> The lustfull Tyrant, if hee hear a Mouse
> Never so little stir about the house,
> Shivering for Joy, he thinks his Mistresse there.

But he has drunk so much that sleep seizes him and he is at Judith's mercy. In spite of fears and doubts, and strengthening herself with the thought that Holofernes is a tyrant not a ruler, she brings herself to kill him. She returns to Jerusalem with his head, and next day the Jews attack and rout a disorganised enemy.

Du Bartas wrote his *Judith* at a time of religious strife in France and he expressed the militant Protestantism of his day. It was in a way a heroic poem. Sylvester is uncertain in translating the heroic parts, but excels in the social parts which Du Bartas added to the heroic. Like other Puritans he could see fun in the weaknesses of the unregenerate and he could enjoy describing their licentiousness. He views the exploits of the great commander, Holofernes, not with an aristocratic eye but critically as a member of the Puritan middle class. In his day that class was asserting itself, and Sylvester drew his strength from the genuine vitality of the assertion. In spite of passages that thoroughly deserve Dryden's condemnation, he did somehow communicate a positive way of thinking.

Sylvester's influence was mainly through his *Divine Weekes*. It is possible that Cowley modelled the realism of his account of Samuel's college in the *Davideis* on Sylvester's realism in *Bethulians Rescue*; but this poem counted for little in comparison with the longer work. And

Sylvester's main influence was metrical. It was not for some time that the seventeenth century decided that the correct metre for the epic was not a stanza but the heroic couplet; but I believe Sylvester helped largely towards that decision. His *Divine Weekes*, Sandys's *Metamorphoses*, and Chapman's *Odyssey* were the three major narratives in the couplet in the early seventeenth century, and the first and third were the more read. Further, Sylvester's verse had qualities that commended it to a later age. It was a mean between the dulcet couplets of the post-Spenserians and the harsh couplets of the satirists. And its aptitude, in spite of the frequent turgidity of expression, to conducting an argument would appeal to the pioneers of the age of reason. Sylvester's *Divine Weekes* was one of the poems that persuaded Cowley to use the couplet for his *Davideis*. Dryden confesses his juvenile admiration for Sylvester, and however much he turned against him, his verse in *Religio Laici* and the *Hind and the Panther*, for all its superiority, does invite faint comparison with Sylvester's more didactic passages. And Dryden's use of the heroic couplet in his *Aeneid*, due to several promptings, may have gone back in part to his early admiration for Sylvester and a consequent assumption that the couplet was the right metre for a long poem on a serious subject.

CHAPTER XIII

THE HISTORIANS

*Besides those fruitfull Ilands that dispersedly are scattered about
the Mayn, like to beautiful pearls that incompasse a Diademe,
the Ile of Great Britaine doth raise it selfe first to our sight.* . . . .
*Being by the Almighty so set in the maine Ocean as that shee is
thereby the High Admirall of the Seas; and in the terrestiall Globe
so seated as that she is worthily reputed both the garden of pleasure
and the Storehouse of Profit.* (Camden)

*God is decreeing to begin some new and great period in his Church.
. . . What does he then but reveal Himself to his servants and, as his
manner is, first to his Englishmen?* (Milton)

IN the fourth chapter of this book I wrote of Hall and of his rendering of the 'Tudor myth'. In the period now under review, the late
Elizabethan and Jacobean, it was the poets not the historians who
most worthily continued his themes. Spenser made poetry of the
Tudors' Welsh ancestry; Shakespeare made great, and Daniel good
poetry out of Hall's Aeschylean treatment of the civil wars and their
happy conclusion. No historian-successor of Hall equalled the achievement even of Daniel. Nevertheless, my story would not be complete
without mentioning some of these.

The most accomplished historian in the period under review was
Bacon. But his *Historie of the Raigne of King Henry the Seventh* was not in
the least epic. Bacon writes as the politician, and he is interested in
the immediate happening and in the immediately relevant motives.
But he does not place the reign of Henry VII in a larger context, nor
seek any principle behind the doings he reports. His artistry is
excellent, but the clarity that results from it makes his remoteness
from epic breadth the more obvious.

Hall's true successor among the Elizabethan historians is, if any,
John Hayward, in his *Life and Raigne of King Henrie IV*. Hayward
includes many of the facts and events that made the stretch of history
from Edward III to Henry VII significant: the seven sons of Edward;
the corruption of Richard II, lamentable yet not leading to undoubted tyranny; Henry IV's guilt in prompting or condoning
Richard's death; the hereditary curse descending from grandfather
to grandson; the idea of Richard III as scapegoat of the curse. He
combines a clear eye for historical events with a philosophical temper

that seeks for the general laws behind them. He recounts certain things splendidly: Henry's victory, when he was merely Earl of Derby, over De Vere, Duke of Ireland; his expedition against Tunis; the great tournament between himself and Mowbray. But Hayward's work is incomplete. There is nothing about the Percies' rebellion; and even to finish the reign he was nominally writing on was not to finish his real theme. No place short of Bosworth could constitute an end, granted the premises on which he wrote. Nevertheless, with Daniel he creates the best counterpart to Shakespeare's history cycle.

But Hall's philosophy of history, though it prevailed in Elizabethan literature, was not the only one. There was another, complementary rather than opposed, that began from a different place. Hall was a strong Protestant, but he did not begin from the side of religion. He was primarily the upholder of the Tudors and of the political order they established after the chaos of civil war. As such, they were of course God's instruments and they were the means of the Reformation in England, but these matters, however important, were secondary in the disposition of Hall's theme. It was possible to see history the other way round: to begin with religion and to make the Reformation, not the House of Tudor, the hero of the myth. The Tudors would of course come in, but they, however important, would be secondary. The formulator of the second myth was John Foxe in his so-called *Book of Martyrs*. William Haller puts the difference between the two versions of history as follows:

> Elizabethan chroniclers presented a view of English history which centered attention on the crown and the achievement of national unity under the crown. The view presented by Foxe centered on the English church in relation to the church at large and hence on England's place in the world, her historic calling and destiny. . . . The two were not commonly regarded as anything but complementary until they were brought into conflict by the Puritan preachers at the outbreak of the revolution in 1640.[1]

Foxe fared differently from Hall in the Elizabethan age, for no poet used his material for great poetry. His own version of it was never bettered. Nevertheless, that material was striking and widely accepted; it had epic potentialities: and it was destined to come for a short period within the scope of England's chief epic poet. So, although the *Book of Martyrs* can hardly be called an epic in its own right, it forms a part of English epic history and claims inclusion in this book.

[1] From *John Foxe and the Puritan Revolution* in the *Seventeenth Century* (Studies by and in honour of Richard Foster Jones, Stanford 1951) 210. In the pages that follow I make free use of this important article.

Foxe's *Book of Martyrs*[1] had a history like that of the *Mirror for Magistrates*. It was first compiled in the reign of Mary and it was enlarged in one edition after another. Further, it resembled the *Mirror* in its exemplary subject, presenting stories of virtuous men as objects of imitation where the *Mirror* presented the falls of ambitious statesmen as objects of what to avoid. But Foxe differed from the authors of the *Mirror* in one great matter: in his successive enlargements he not only added new matter but ended by relating all his matter, old and added, to an overriding scheme of universal history. It is this great scheme that turns Foxe's book into epic material. The first version of the *Book of Martyrs*, written in Latin and published in Basel in 1554, began with Wycliffe and came right up to date, including the persecution of English Protestants by Mary. There were brief accounts of Huss, Jerome of Prague, and Savonarola. The book took its final form in 1583. Something of its new scope can be gathered from the descriptive title. The correct name of Foxe's book in its English version is not the common one but *Actes and Monuments of Matters most speciall and memorable happening in the Church, with an universall Historie of the same*, and there follows this description, 'Wherein is set forth at large, the whole Race and Course of the Church, from the Primitive age to these later times of ours, with the bloody times, horrible troubles, and great Persecutions against the true Martyrs of *Christ*, sought and wrought as well by heathen Emperors, as now lately practised by Romish Prelates, especially in this Realme of *England* and *Scotland*'. Foxe's title-page gives a fair idea of the nature of his book. He did include a vast number of 'acts and monuments'; and he was primarily popular because he could tell a story clearly and enthusiastically. But he did indeed knit these 'acts' into a universal history. As Haller puts it,

> every individual case was charged with the whole meaning of history as he conceived it. The blood of English martyrs of yesterday was shown to be one with the blood of all the martyrs back to Nero. All history was one.[2]

This unity of history was composed briefly as follows. First, the Scriptures had already plotted out the whole course of Christ's Church on earth: the Old Testament had prefigured it; the New Testament had recounted its foundation and first motions in the Gospels and the

[1] Foxe's true worth as a man and as a historian, obscured in the nineteenth century, has been re-established by an excellent recent book, J. K. Mozley, *John Fox and his Book* (London 1940). Foxe, though holding decided opinions, was a man of peace and the practical opponent of the kind of persecution he described. Indeed, it looks as if he were drawn to his subject through seeking to compensate for the revulsion he naturally had from it. His tenderness of heart extended to animals. He was unworldly in his life and a great spiritual counsellor as well as a most industrious writer.

[2] *Loc. cit.* 217.

Acts of the Apostles, and had predicted its future symbolically in *Revelation*. Foxe's task is to narrate the history of the Church as prophesied in *Revelation*. It is the history of Christ at war with Antichrist; and the fortunes of the war fluctuate. Within it there were five periods. The first comprised three hundred years of struggle and persecution, years of virtue. The second comprised a second three hundred years, peaceful as well as virtuous, thanks to Constantine. The third period, extending in England from Egbert to William the Conqueror, was one of decline, the corrupting influence of the Roman clergy beginning to make itself felt. The fourth period, from the Conqueror to Wycliffe, showed Roman tyranny at its height but resisted in England by some of its rulers. The last period was that of the Reformation; and it is here that Foxe's peculiarly English version of Church history is most evident. By the beginning of this period Roman abuses had reached their height and the Popes were indeed the embodiments of Antichrist. Though true religion had always lived on in England in spite of the general decline, Wycliffe began another epoch, that of Reformation. True, these beginnings were fostered most on the Continent, but God showed his special favour towards England by causing the first motion there. Foxe goes on to the sufferings of the Lollards and the Hussites and to other sides of the Reformation abroad. But the bulk of his books concerns Protestant heroism in the reigns of Henry VIII, Edward VI, and Mary. The end concerns the fortunes of Queen Elizabeth. God's hand appeared with especial clarity in her preservation during her time of extreme peril when her sister was queen. The long course of Church history was thus given a strong, contemporary, patriotic turn, and thus duplicated the patriotism inherent in the other, the Tudor, myth. In 1589 Timothy Bright published an abridgement of Foxe's book for the benefit of those too busy or too poor to be able to profit by the original, for 'there is not a booke, under the Scriptures, more necessarie for a Christian to be conversant in'. Bright summed up Foxe's patriotic creed by stating that England was the first kingdom to accept Christianity through its whole extent, and that Constantine, the first Christian emperor, was an Englishman; that Wycliffe was the first divine to defy the Pope, and Henry VIII the first king to forgo allegiance to him. Thus, in Church affairs, England was regularly in the van, God's favoured nation.

The *Book of Martyrs* fulfils some of the requirements of the epic. Its bulk is subordinated to a scheme which, though fantastic by present-day standards, is bold and noble. There is nothing petty in the guise in which Foxe sees history. And he spent the best energies of his life in shaping his book, making it the monument of a powerful will. Further, it was dear to a large section of the population: its choric character was undoubted. But its style does not reach an epic pitch. It is admirable in its way, clear, unpretentious, and forceful, worthy of Latimer and of the other early reformers who worked to make the doctrines of the Church available to the understandings of simple people. But it could not be the instrument of high imaginings and deep passions; it lacks the overtones and the undertones that Bunyan could include in his own form of the simple style. Nor is there variety enough in Foxe's book for the epic amplitude. He can be vivid and dramatic in his stories; but his theme is confined. That theme was very present to his contemporaries and ensured the choric character of his work; but it did not at the same time declare that amplitude of interest that gives the achieved epic one of the means of its survival.

When we consider the great vogue of Foxe's book, it is strange that so little of it found its way into the greater literature. The most famous echo of it is in the epilogue of *Henry IV*, *Part 2*, where Shakespeare says that

> *Falstaffe* shall dye of a sweat, unlesse already he be killed with your hard Opinions. For *Old-Castle* dyed a Martyr, and this is not the man.

Oldcastle was one of the Lollard martyrs in Foxe; and it was necessary for Shakespeare to guard against any confusion between Falstaff (originally named Oldcastle) and the martyr of the same name, not only to avoid giving offence to Oldcastle's kin but not to arouse the resentment of the humbler members of the audience, who loved and revered Foxe's *Book of Martyrs*. But Shakespeare's reference, though in what I think an epic context, is slight; and a truer analogy with Foxe can be found in the prison scenes of *Arcadia*. Timothy Bright dedicated his abridgement to Sir Francis Walsingham, Ambassador at Paris at the time of the St Bartholomew Massacre; and Walsingham had given Sidney and other Englishmen, who happened to be in Paris at that time, asylum in the English Embassy. Into the resistance of Pamela and Philoclea to their persecutor, Cecropia, something of the spirit of Protestant martyrdom has entered. But it is only a detail in Sidney's larger context of the Christian humanism of the Renaissance.

But the influence of Foxe's book did not end with Elizabeth. In 1632 there was yet another edition, including a continuation by a different hand and contrasting the blessings of England with the misfortunes of France. Where France suffered the massacre of the flower of her Protestants, England was miraculously preserved from the Spanish Armada and the Gunpowder Plot. Plainly England was under the special protection of Providence. This faith was one of the things that animated the revolution of 1640. As such, it affected Milton and the plans he had at that time for writing an epic on Arthur.

The last book I must mention here is Raleigh's *History of the World*. Of all the historians of this epoch he had the most capacious mind and was initially best equipped to elevate history to an epic height. He was both scholar and man of action; he was deeply religious while well versed in theological heterodoxy; he repudiated the general political philosophy of Machiavelli only after having recommended some of the details of it. He wielded a grave and sonorous, at times majestic prose. And he had the patience and the will to concentrate on a great work over many years. Nevertheless, the *History of the World* is not epic. Raleigh wrote it in prison under James; and the personal change from active life and great influence to prison, with the national change from a queen who embodied an ideal to a king who was no hero, induced in him a mood of pessimism ill suited to the positive quality of the epic. Yet, though not epic, it has sufficient kinship with other epicising writings to merit a little more than a bare mention.

Raleigh's *History of the World* was never finished, not even reaching the Christian era. But we know from his preface that after dealing with early world history he intended to narrow his scope to English history with only a little of the foreign background added. His scope would thus have been much like that of Warner in *Albions England*. We know something too of how Raleigh would have treated English history, for he reviews a portion of it in his preface. He saw it, in the accepted way, as a great repertory of moral examples ('for the *Sea* of Examples hath no bottom') with the sins of the grandfather visited on the grandson. And these examples were of what to avoid; for there appears in his summary no compensating panegyric of the house of Tudor. On the contrary he gives a solemn list of all the crimes committed by Henry VIII. And the tenor of the work is not to exalt England but to point to the passing of all royal glory. It is true that he can give in Epaminondas the picture of a perfect prince; but his prevalent tone is elegiac not heroic, not the celebration of great deeds but their transience and their pettiness in the light of eternity. Raleigh looks back to the *Mirror for Magistrates* in his pictures of the falls of princes and forward to Thomas Browne in the nobility of his elegiac tone and in his ruminations on death. Though having as his material the common Elizabethan stock, he uses it in a manner the remotest possible from the Protestant manners of Hall and Foxe. Thus the noblest writer of history in the period under review is the remotest from the epic kind.

Part Four

The Neo-Classic Age

CHAPTER I

OVERFLOW FROM THE PAST

1. GENERAL

I HAVE reached the most confused portion of my story: the fortunes of the English epic in the first sixty years of the seventeenth century. Into this period I have already trespassed, but only to speak of works written by writers genuinely formed in the central Elizabethan age and more or less the contemporaries of Spenser and Sidney. The youngest of these, Sylvester, was born in 1563, nine years after Sidney. The men I have to deal with in this chapter are significantly younger, the oldest, Heywood, being born in 1575. They belong substantially to the next century; yet, Milton excepted, they do not share the opinions of Ben Jonson, the dominant literary figure, but continue, anachronistically, earlier modes of writing, some of them going back to the Middle Ages. In their style they do of course reflect their age in part, but they are unaware of much of the new life that was stirring, and they copy their predecessors, adding perhaps some touches of novelty but certainly not modifying them enough to achieve a new direction. One of these anachronisms was Bunyan, but he was a man of genius and he was not only an anachronism. Like Browne he was a Janus-figure, with one face looking back to the Middle Ages, with the other looking forward to the realistic novel of the trading classes. He is too great to be included with such small narrative writers as Heywood and Patrick Hannay and must have a chapter to himself.

If some of the creative writers are anachronisms, so too are some of the critics. Henry Peacham, oblivious or ignorant of Ben Jonson and of the example of Tasso, in his section *Of Poetry* in the *Compleat Gentleman*, repeats the age-old 'example' notion saying that by reading Homer Alexander was 'especially mooved to goe thorow with his conquests'.[1] Henry Reynolds in his *Mythomystes* (of about the same date as Peacham's work) dwells on the high allegorical wisdom of Homer, the supreme poet.[2] Sir William Alexander in *Anacrisis* (also of about the same date) quotes Scaliger on the pre-eminence of the epic and praises *Arcadia* as the great English example of the epic in prose.[3] None of these critics could give a lead or in any way go beyond the older wisdom of Sidney's *Defence*.

---

[1] 1634; reprinted Oxford 1906, p. 81; Spingarn, *Critical Essays of the Seventeenth Century*, i. 119.
[2] Spingarn, *ib.* 157.
[3] *Ib.* 183, 187.

There is a good deal of narrative verse with heroic pretensions, partly accessible in Saintsbury's *Caroline Poets*. It is of limited value poetically, and some of the rather better poems have no genuine epic quality at all. Shakerley Marmion's *Cupid and Psyche* calls itself 'an Epick poem of Cupid and his Mistress'. It is in fact a pleasant little narrative in couplets, reminding one of Marlowe's *Hero and Leander*. Chalkhill's *Thealma and Clearchus* is a tangled, romantic story, told with some vigour and not without merit. But neither begins to take on the kind of seriousness an epic requires, and it would be a waste of time to say more about them. But there are writings with rather more claim to inclusion, either for their pretensions to the epic or for their interest as items in the course of its literary history. These I have chosen according to the best of my judgement; but it has been an arbitrary choice.

2. THE SPENSERIANS

These are the brothers Giles and Phineas Fletcher. Giles, though habitually put first, was the younger, and wrote, while yet a B.A., his *Christs Victorie, and Triumph in Heaven, and Earth, over, and after Death*, published in 1610. Phineas, the elder, wrote some of *The Purple Island, or the Isle of Man* about the same time. It was not printed till 1633 and at the end of the poem James I is referred to as dead. But the author says that his poem was written in his youth; and his brother refers to it at the end of *Christs Victorie*: so it belongs mainly to the beginning of James's reign. The brothers were both country clergymen of the militantly Protestant type, and they show no trace of the divisions that were to afflict the Anglican Church under the Stuarts. Both seem to have thought of their poems as epics of a sort, though they say nothing about theories of the epic. Giles in his address to the reader cites Du Bartas and Spenser as the great modern poets and is plainly indebted to the *Faerie Queene* for his stanza. This is of eight lines with a final alexandrine; identical with Spenser's less the seventh line. Giles dropped Spenser's archaic language, but he attempted a heroic poem on the deeds of Christ after Spenser's model. Phineas Fletcher in his opening stanzas makes his epic intention even clearer. There he mentions earlier poets: the sacred poets of the Bible, Homer, Apollonius Rhodius, Virgil, Ovid, Sannazaro, Du Bartas, Spenser. That is the company to which he aspires. And later in the poem he mentions Virgil, the greatest of all poets, and Spenser, the second. His stanza is of seven lines with final alexandrine, and is that of the *Faerie Queene* with not only the seventh but the eighth line dropped.

Christs Victorie contains four books and something over 2000 lines. The books deal with the debate between Justice and Mercy in heaven over the fall of man, Christ causing Mercy to triumph; Christ's victory over the Tempter in the wilderness; Christ's victory over death on the cross; and finally Christ's Resurrection and Ascension. The poem ends with an ecstatic account of heavenly beatitude, into which is inserted a reference to England's blessed peace under James. Giles Fletcher had a sultry imagination, and some of his descriptions are flamboyant. He is a minor poet in his own right. The point here is that he is quite untouched by the classicising trend of the epic in Europe. He writes as if Vida's *Christiad*, now nearly a hundred years old, had never been written.

The *Purple Island* is longer, running to about 5000 lines. The setting is pastoral. Thirsil (or Phineas Fletcher) has been chosen with his brother as May-lord by the shepherds of Cambridge and is invited to sing a song. He refuses to sing of love and thinks fit to use only divine matter. His subject is man, his body and mind, and his salvation. And the poem proceeds by an allegory similar to that used by Spenser in his House of Alma. But Fletcher uses the figure of an island not of a house. He begins with a brief account of creation, the Fall, and the Redemption: but the bulk of his poem refers to man in his present condition. He goes on to an account of the body's structure, the bones and muscles and flesh. Then come the three parts of the island, governed by the liver, the heart, and the head. Then follow the island's rulers, beginning with the intellect and the will. But the hosts of Hell surround and threaten the island: the flesh, idolatry, covetousness, and so forth. Ten books go to these descriptions. Then Fletcher calls the Spirit to inspire him to a higher theme; and devotes the two last books to the *psychomachia*, the battle of the forces of good and of evil for the soul, the perennial theme going back to Prudentius. At first the Virtues prevail, but the Parthian tactics of the archers of Venus disorganise them badly, and in the end Christ himself intervenes, binds the Dragon, and weds Eclecta, daughter of the Intellect and the Will, the governors of the island. Eclecta[1] is the Church, the company of the Elect, and the marriage is related in accordance with the customary allegorical interpretation of the *Song of Solomon*. Phineas Fletcher is more even and less flamboyant than his brother. He inherits the Spenserian clarity of diction and shows great skill and even some charm in conducting his allegory. He is a better poet than is usually allowed, but not of the stature to figure in a book on the epic for his literary merit alone. His relevant interest is that though later than Spenser he is more consistently in the medieval tradition. His anatomy and psychology are entirely antique, and the last two books are in the pure medieval tradition running from Prudentius

---

[1] Masson in his *Life of Milton*, i. (London 1859) 419, makes *Eclecta* mean *Choice*. This is surely wrong. *Eclecta* means *chosen* in the feminine and refers to the bride chosen by Christ, which is the Church.

into the medieval sermons and Morality Plays. True, Fletcher alters the more usual allegory of town or castle into one of an island, but this is a minor alteration. G. R. Owst[1] quotes a specially apt passage from a sermon by Robert Rypon, a contemporary of Chaucer. He speaks of Man,

> whose body is as it were a town, in which his bodily members are like the houses, his mouth, eyes and ears like the town gates, through which the populace enters and goes out. . . . The lord of this town is the Soul or Intellect, his lady the Will, which, according to Augustine, is queen in the realm of the Soul.

Fletcher followed this medieval tradition in making Intellect and Will the princes of his island; and any differences he introduces are small compared with his fidelity to tradition in pursuing the theme of the Holy War, along with the spiritual pilgrimage a possible epic subject in the Middle Ages. And it is Du Bartas, heir of the medieval encyclopedists, and not Camoens or Tasso, to whom he gives allegiance. His medievalism is more surprising than Bunyan's was later to be, because Fletcher was a University man, learned in the Classics, and presumably aware of what was going on in the literature of western Europe.

Another writer who, though not a direct imitator of Spenser, prolonged medieval themes in narrative verse and prose was Thomas Heywood. In 1609 he published his *Troia Britanica or Great Britaines Troy*, a long ambitious chronicle-poem, purporting to deal with world-history. It is in seventeen books. It begins with creation, and the world's early ages; it is voluble on the legends of the Greeks and Romans; and in the last two books it compresses British history beginning with Brute and the founding of London and continuing through the Saxon and Plantagenet kings. A. M. Clark,[2] Heywood's biographer, thinks that the matter of Troy, which occupies so much of the poem, was taken from the 1607 edition of Caxton's *Recueil of the Histories of Troy*. Anyhow Heywood's matter is entirely medieval and in the line of *Cursor Mundi* and Lydgate's *Troy Book*. His stanza is more recent, being the *ottava rima*, probably borrowed from Harington's translation of Ariosto. The style shows the influence both of this translation and of Spenser. *Troia Britanica* is thus in substance a medieval overflow, in style an Elizabethan one. Later Heywood produced a piece of heroic history in prose that is equally medieval in substance. It is the *Exemplary Lives and memorable Acts of nine the most worthy Women of the World*. These women are three Jews, three Pagans, and three Christians; and they are modelled on the Nine

---

[1] In *Literature and Pulpit in Medieval England*, 29. I quote Owst's translation from the Latin original.
[2] A. M. Clark, *Thomas Heywood* (Oxford 1931) 51.

Worthies of the Middle Ages. In his introduction Heywood talks in the most conventional and traditional way of the value of history as a repertory of examples. Heywood's interest is that he prolongs with unruffled calm the habits of thought of other ages, apparently unaware of the violent cross-currents, so exciting intellectually, of the age in which he lived.

Another narrative poem illustrating the prolongation of an earlier type is Patrick Hannay's *Sheretine and Mariana*,[1] published in 1622. Unlike the poems of the Fletchers and Heywood it has not any epic aspiration, but it is worth a mention because it illustrates the same trend. It recounts the tragic Hungarian story of the two title characters, and it is put in the mouth of Mariana, who caused Sheretine's death through yielding against her desire to the love of another man. Mariana's ghost tells the story, which is in fact simply a very late example of the medieval Mirror, of which the *Mirror for Magistrates* was the conspicuous example in the sixteenth century.

When we meet such prolongations of medievalism in cultured authors we need not be surprised that another kind of medievalism survived even longer among the humble and less literate, providing Bunyan with the substance of his prose epics.

3. THE INFLUENCE OF SIDNEY

Arcadia had no prose successor in English, while the pastoral and heroic romances of France in the seventeenth century were a growth independent of it. But it entered into English narrative poetry of the seventeenth century and it was related to the French romances by being a parallel part of a large European mode of writing. That mode, *Arcadia* apart, has little affinity with the seriousness of the epic till Fénelon's *Télémaque* late in the century. But without the theory of the prose epic on the Heliodoran model *Télémaque* would never have been written, and Fénelon is after Du Bartas the one French writer who seriously affected the course of the epic in England. Thus, in treating of the influence of Sidney, I shall have to include the very different themes of English narrative verse and the theory of the prose epic.

Though *Arcadia* had no prose successor it had a pervasive if usually untraceable influence on English romantic verse. It enters, for instance, into the heroic elements of the plays of Beaumont and Fletcher. But how much those elements are indebted to Spain, how much to Sidney it would be hard to say. Several of the poems mentioned in the first section of this chapter are indebted to *Arcadia*. But the most obvious example of a poem made on the Heliodoran-

[1] Included in G. Saintsbury, *Caroline Poets* (Oxford 1905) vol. i.

Arcadian model is William Chamberlayne's *Pharonnida: a Heroick Poem.* This has the complexity of *Arcadia* without the seriousness, and the fullness of its rhetoric without the clarity. Its debt is obvious at the very beginning, when Argalia and Aphron are shipwrecked and taken to court by Aminander, thus corresponding to Musidorus, Pyrocles, and Kalander respectively. *Pharonnida* was written long after *Arcadia*, in the early years of the Civil War, and thus testifies to the persistence of Sidney's influence. It has no claim to epic dignity. Its plot is tortuous, and its couplets, excessively enjambed, have no dignity; and it owes what reputation it has mainly to Saintsbury's admiration of it, an admiration partly fostered by his interest in the prosody. *Pharonnida* contains striking phrases and some good bits of rhetoric probably inspired by the drama Chamberlayne grew up with. But as a whole it is quite dead.[1]

In spite of *Arcadia* it was not in England that the idea of the prose epic was chiefly fostered. But on the Continent Scaliger's historic approximation of the epic and the prose narrative was greatly influential. In *Don Quixote* Cervantes took up Scaliger's hint and made his claim for the prose epic, whether or not he was thinking of his own work. In 1607, D'Urfé published his pastoral romance *Astrée*. This, going back to Montemaior's *Diana*, has certain stylistic resemblances to *Arcadia*. But it is more purely pastoral, less political, and more concerned with the social elegances than *Arcadia*. It is in fact lacking in just those things that shifted the centre of *Arcadia* from romance to epic. Nevertheless, *Astrée* was regarded by later French writers as a prose epic, and it is thus historically on the direct line between Heliodorus and Fénelon. Another link is the *Argenis* of John Barclay. Barclay was a Scot. But he lived a great deal abroad, and writing in Latin he achieved a great Continental success. His *Argenis* (1621) is a long romance with the scene laid in Sicily. It may owe something to *Arcadia*, especially at the opening when Archombrotus and Poliarchus land in Sicily and after some adventures go to the house of Timoclea. But up till then they had been strangers, and unlike Musidorus and Pyrocles they become rivals in love. *Argenis* resembles *Arcadia* in being political. It is in fact a very much closer political allegory. Sicily is France in the sixteenth century, and there are various precise equivalences. *Argenis* is a good story and closer to life than *Astrée* and the French romance generally. Although it has no claim to the dignity of the epic, it may have helped to keep the romance, always a potentially epic form, from settling entirely into pastoralism and prettiness.

It is with Georges and Madeleine de Scudéry that the rules for the prose epic begin to be formulated. These rules are in place not here

---

[1] For a recent account of *Pharonnida* see A. E. Parsons in *Modern Language Review* 1950, pp. 296-311.

but in my chapter on the apex of neo-classicism. What is in place here is to say that in the preface, *Au Lecteur*, in *Artamène ou le Grand Cyrus*, the authoress says that her models are the immortal Heliodorus and the great D'Urfé, confirming my statement that *Astrée* is one of the links between the *Aethiopica* and *Télémaque*.

4. THE PURITANS

Behold, with the eye of pittie, the great ruines and desolations of thy Church. Heale up the wounds, and make up the breaches thereof in all Nations. . . . Specially we intreat thee (deare father) to set thy selfe against that Anti-christ of Rome. . . . Give us not over into the hands of the cruel Spaniard as our sins have deserved. . . . Blesse our stocke and store, corne and cattel, trades and occupations, and all the works of our hands: for thy blessing only maketh rich.

(Arthur Dent, *A Morning Prayer*)

It might be questioned why I have separated the Puritans from the Spenserians, Giles and Phineas Fletcher, when, as will appear, I find so much common to both. Like the Puritans, the Fletchers were enthusiastically Protestant; like the Fletchers, the Puritans inherited a great deal of medievalism. And of course you cannot, in the early seventeenth century, draw a rigid line between the Puritans and the rest. Nevertheless you can detect the two opposed ecclesiastical tendencies: the one to preserving unity, the other to possible separation. The Fletchers were a part of an inherited Elizabethan culture: a culture that kept its eye on the rest of Europe and was broad and tolerant enough at home to include many different opinions. Their ornate writing was a part of a general European baroque manner; and they accepted the existing hierarchies at home. There is nothing revolutionary about them and they had it in them to compromise. The Puritans were great simplifiers; and the only European ideas that influenced them were those that supported their simplified religion. But what they lost in bulk they gained in clarity and in the emotional force with which they invested their simplifications. Having seen so clearly and so passionately, they were prepared to hold to their opinions at any cost. While it was in its rising, militant phase, while it gave a direct shape to history, puritanism found no undoubted epic voice. Only when it was in retreat, when its spirit was mildly pervasive, when it endured rather than acted, was it embodied worthily in literature. And even that worth was lessened through the accident that the man of genius who embodied it was of humble origin and no education. Nevertheless, in his way Bunyan was an epic writer; and I must say something of the things that led up to him.

One of the achievements of puritanism favourable to epic creation was the invention of its own mythology. I mentioned one part of that mythology in my pages on Foxe's *Book of Martyrs* and I shall revert to it briefly at the end of this section. Foxe's scheme was historical, but the other part of the myth was theological. In the traditional theology two main ways of access to God were through the contemplation of natural things and through the imitation of Christ. The Puritans did not deny these ways but, with Calvin directing their thought, they were more interested in another main matter: the dogma derived from certain chapters of St Paul, especially the eighth of *Romans*. From this they elaborated a drama of salvation. The drama began with God's creating man from nothing and proceeded to man's utter depravity through the disobedience of Adam and his descendants' failure to follow God's will as declared in his law. In this process Satan was of prime importance, since it was he who defeated Adam, the Old Man, in the Garden of Eden. The process was reversed by Christ, the New Man, and principally when he defeated Satan in the Wilderness. Out of depraved humanity God by his grace chose certain favoured people, the rest being left for damnation. Through the victory of Christ the elect became more numerous than under the old dispensation. And there was the prospect of Christ and his Saints triumphing on earth. The holy life was precisely mapped out in the stages of election, vocation, justification, sanctification, glorification. But though elected and called and so on, the Saint was never free from sin. He was a fighting not an innocent soul. And though he was sure of salvation if he persisted in his fight he knew, as Bunyan was later to put it, that there was a gateway to Hell even at the foot of the Heavenly Mountain.

In the substance of this myth there is nothing new, for it all derived from existing theology. The novelty consists in the selection and in the fierce concentration on the items selected. In the same way the images used through which to express the Puritan's spiritual struggle were inherited from the allegory of the Middle Ages. I quote William Haller[1] to describe these images:

> The Puritan imagination saw the life of the spirit as pilgrimage and battle. The images of wayfaring and warfaring which fill the Old Testament had been exploited by that fighting itinerant, Paul, and by generations upon generations of subsequent evangelists. Reaching the pulpits of the seventeenth century by a hundred channels, they there underwent new and peculiarly vigorous development. [The Christian] was a traveler through a strange country and a soldier in battle. He was a traveler who, fleeing from destruc-

---

[1] *The Rise of Puritanism* (New York 1938) 142. I have drawn freely on this book in my account of puritanism.

tion, must adhere through peril and hardship to the way that leads home. He was a soldier who, having been pressed to serve under the banners of the spirit, must enact faithfully his part in the unceasing war of the spiritual against the carnal man.

The main purveyors of these images of pilgrimage and war were the Puritan preachers. Though, says Haller, their sermons did not give a straightforward account of the pilgrim's progress or of Satan's rebellion, they did abound in wayfaring and warfaring imagery. They are, most of them, diffuse and repetitive, and their interest is that they preserve and transmit the mythology; they do not give it an artistic embodiment. They contain the material out of which Bunyan was to construct works of art.

There are also two works, not sermons, that lead in this same direction. Possessing some literary merit and being dramatic or narrative, not homiletic, they deserve mention here. The first is one of the two books which Bunyan tells us his wife brought with her as her entire dowry.

> This woman and I, though we came together as poor as poor might be (not having so much house-hold-stuff as a dish or spoon betwixt us both) yet this she had for her part, *The Plain Man's Path-way to Heaven*, and *The Practice of Piety*, which her father had left her, when he died.

Arthur Dent, author of the *Plain Man's Path-way*, was born near the beginning of Elizabeth's reign and died in 1607. He was Cambridge bred and an Anglican of the extreme Puritan wing. As an Essex clergyman he supported a petition of twenty-seven of his colleagues concerning their refusal to declare that there was nothing in the Prayer Book contrary to the word of God. The book by which he was known was published in 1601 and by 1640 had reached its twenty-fifth edition, with more editions to follow during and after the Commonwealth. It is a handbook of Calvinist theology in the form of a dialogue between Theologus a divine, Philagathus an honest man, Asunetus an ignorant man, and Antilegon a caviller. It points the way to Bunyan not so much because it contains the ideas of wayfaring and warfaring (which it does in a minor way) as because it has a semblance of a plot and is constantly falling into the idiom of allegory; as when Dent enumerates the nine gates of Hell, Infidelity, Presumption of God's mercy, etc. Further, Dent, addressing himself to humble people, commands a clear and easy and emphatic style and was one of the worthy models of Bunyan's masterly idiom. Here is a passage recounting how a single blemish in a public man will mar all his virtues, a passage which in its alert observation was well calculated to encourage the same faculty in Bunyan. After instancing a nobleman and a judge, Dent goes on:

> Furthermore, if a Preacher be a man of great gifts, the common people will say of him: Oh, he is a worthy man indeede, an excellent Scholler, a profound Divine, a singular man in a Pulpit: but yet, for all that, hee hath a shrewd touch which marreth all: he is an exceeding proud man: hee is as proude as *Lucifer*. Hee hath very great gifts indeed: but I warrant you, hee knoweth it well enough. For he carieth his crest very high, and looketh very sternly and disdainefully upon all other men. Hee is unmeasurably puft up with overweening, and thinketh that he toucheth the cloudes with his head. Thus therefore we see how some one sinne doth disgrace a man, that otherwise doth excell. The reason hereof is, because such men are as a Candle, set upon a Candlestick, or rather upon a scaffold, or Mountaine, for all men to behold and looke upon. And sure it is, they have a thousand eyes upon them every day; and that not only gazing upon them, but also prying very narrowly into them, to spie out the least moate: that they may make a mountaine of it. For, as in a cleane white paper one little spot is soone espied: but in a piece of browne paper, twenty great blurs are scant discerned. Even so in Noble-men, Judges, Magistrates, Justices, Preachers, and Professors, the least spot or specke is soone seene into; but amongst the baser sort, and most grosse livers, almost nothing is espied or regarded.[1]

It is most instructive to reflect on the sort of thing that was being written about 1601 in other places, the florid rhetoric that was considered appropriate in a dedication, for instance, and then to look again at the *Plain Man's Path-way to Heaven*. More than one observation comes out of the comparison. For all the starkness of his Calvinism and the proletarian appeal of his style, Dent, living in the Elizabethan age, does not begin to rank as a revolutionary. Somehow the age could safely contain him along with so much else. But the book itself became after his death a main agent of revolution, the very type of what Laud made the fatal error of underestimating. And its revolutionary power was religious. It has become fashionable to make the Puritan revolution social and economic rather. But the twenty-four editions of the *Plain Man's Path-way to Heaven*, a genuinely religious book if ever there was one, between 1601 and 1640 are not to be discounted lightly. I have said that the Renaissance epic differed from the medieval in shifting its centre back from religion to politics, from an abstract conception of holiness to a hero, who, however religious he might be made, was certainly a man. The Puritan temper, at its most intensely religious, harked back to the medieval. The

---

[1] Seventh impression (1605) 202-3.

actual religions may have been sharply different in some things; it was the position of the religions in the total scheme of things that constituted the likeness. Through the writings of Owst, Coulton, and Haller it has come to be recognised that the Puritan preachers are the descendants of the medieval. It is thus to be expected that Dent and Bunyan should have their kinship with Langland rather than with Sidney, that they should prolong the Middle Ages not only through their allegorical tendencies but in the position they give to religion. Dent and Bunyan were shrewd, homely people, but they believed in a world beyond the present with a degree of vividness that the Elizabethans as a whole, pious though they were, did not attain to. Here, emotionally, they are with Langland.

Richard Bernard (1567-1641) was a younger divine than Dent, and his main activities fall after the reign of Elizabeth. He was an extreme Puritan, but unlike some of his associates he remained within the Church of England. He too was Cambridge bred and was known as a scholar through his translation of Terence. In 1626 he published his religious allegory in prose, the *Isle of Man*. This title is identical with the sub-title of Phineas Fletcher's *Purple Island*, and the notion of describing human attributes under the guise of an island is common to both. But Bernard is not learned like Fletcher and addressed his book to a simpler audience. His style has not quite the plain force of Dent's, but it is lucid and unencumbered. The *Isle of Man* (which reached its twelfth edition in 1648) is a true narrative counterpart of the contemporary Puritan sermons and joins with them in leading to the *Pilgrim's Progress* and especially to the *Holy War*. It is thus far closer to Bunyan in its form than is the *Plain Man's Path-way to Heaven*. In the *Path-way* the allegory was at best incidental, and there is hardly any plot. The *Isle of Man* shows the shape a Puritan epic might have taken around 1626 had there been a great writer at that time to do the work.

The *Isle of Man* relates the trial of sin in its different forms. It is incomplete, because Bernard fails to tell us what happens to the island when the sins have been condemned. The story implies election and vocation but not the other stages in the Puritan scheme of the holy life. It is easy to see why Bernard fell thus short. When, after the trial of various bad characters, he comes to Covetousness and Idolatry (now called Papistry), he forgets allegorical narrative for homiletic fervour and upsets the balance by indulging in prolonged denunciation of current evils. After which he closes the book abruptly.

The first part of the *Isle of Man* gives the setting. Bernard uses the metaphor of the island to express the isolation of the individual before God, but mainly substitutes that of the town. In the town of the Soul Sin is the great malefactor.

This Towne is very spacious and large, for besides many *Back-*

sides, *By-lanes*, and *Out-corners*, these are foure great streets: *Sence-street*, *Thought-street*, *Word-streete*, and *Deed-street*; in some of which this lewd companion Sinne, and his Copesmates will be found wandring.[1]

Godly Jealousy is the watchman on the look-out for Sin. And this is where he is most likely to find him:

> The place is a *Common Inne*, an Harlots house called Mistris *Heart*, a receptacle for all Villaines, Whores, and Theeves, and for all dishonest persons whatsoever, none denied house roome or harbour there. . . . But to cover her naughtinesse as much as she may, she hath gotten into her house one called *Old man*, corrupted by her deceitfull lusts, to become her husband, when indeed shee is his own daughter, and so live they in incest together, and keep rout and ryot night and day. If any honest Traveller (a good and godly motion) happen sometimes to fall in there unawares, he is straight way denied entertainment. Her answer is by and by, that her lodgings are taken up for other manner of men, there is no roome for any such troublesome guests as these bee: none can be merry for them, where they come hindering all good fellowship.
>
> The house which this harlotry dwelleth in, hath many in-lets, five doores open for their guests to come in at. These five doores are the five sences.[2]

After completing the setting in great allegorical detail, Bernard proceeds in his second part to narrate the trial of Sin. Of the Isle of Man, Christ is the king, Conscience the judge, Religion the sheriff, and Resolution the under-sheriff. There is a splendid passage describing the province of the individual conscience, a passage representing one of the finest sides of Protestantism:

> The *Circuit* of this Judge is his own *Soule*, he is not to sit and judge of other mens thoughts, words or deeds, but of the thoughts, words, and deeds of that man, wherein he is. A mans owne Conscience is Judge of himselfe; to judge another is out of his circuit, neither hath he any Authority from the King of Heaven to enable him so to doe. Knowledge may goe out to see and discerne of other mens waies, but conscience keepeth ever at home, and sits within to judge of that mans courses, whose conscience he is.[3]

The prisoners are various Sins, the Old Man, Mrs Heart and her maids, and Will, her man. Old Man is tried first, and Scripture gives much evidence against him. For his Original Sin he is condemned to mortification, and crucifixion. Mrs Heart is found guilty and put under the perpetual custody of New Man. Then Captain Reason complains that Wilful Will is no longer under his control. Will has

---

[1] Twelfth edition (1648) 10. [2] *Ib.* 50-1. [3] *Ib.* 96-7.

allowed the weapons of the spiritual warfare to decay. To Reason's complaints Will says he was born free and not under Reason's absolute command. But he ends by admitting his faults:

I doe here (my Lord) ingeniously confesse the truth of all that which these witnesses have spoken against me, for which I heartily crave pardon. I also do freely acknowledg that I stood too much upon my birth and gentry, as too many at this day doe, having never a good quality besides to boast or brag of. I took it for granted, that my gentrie stood in idlenesse, pleasurable delights, Hawking, Hunting, and haunting Taverne, drinking of Healths, whiffing the Tobacco pipe, putting on of new and variety of fashions, in Hat and in Haire, in Cloathes and in Shoe-ties, in Bootes and in Spurres, in Boasting and Bragging, in Cracking of Oathes, in big lookes, great words, and in some out bearing gestures the formes of Gentry: which I verily suppose should sufficiently of it selfe have born me out, in all my extravagant courses, in my licentious liberty, and lascivious wantonnesse in Mistresse *Hearts* house, through which I was brought into all these rebellious disorders, for which I justly deserved my Soveraignes indignation.[1]

Since Will admits his fault, his judge suspends sentence and puts him under the custody of New Man. Finally Covetousness and Idolatry are tried; and it is here that the preacher quite displaces the artist. Nevertheless the interest remains; for some of the writing is graphic, and the invective against covetousness takes us straight to similar invectives in the Middle Ages. Here is a descendant of Langland's attack on Lady Meed.

In the second quarter of the seventeenth century (to which the *Isle of Man* belongs) the greatest vitality lay with the Puritans. They had the strength of a simplified creed, and while their preachers inherited much from the Middle Ages, they were the new men in the increasingly important departments of trade and industry. And though their vitality was partly kept in check by a hostile government and was forced to seek an outlet in America in compensation, it flourished in England nevertheless. If it could have been given high artistic form it would have had a better chance of attaining epic embodiment than any other spiritual trend. The forces that anim- ated the Metaphysical poets and the Caroline drama were not of the epic kind. However much complication the epic can thrive on, it must retain a basic simplicity, it must be ruled by certain strong and steady notions. The Metaphysical poets were too self-involved or sophisticated or rarefied or pretty to have a kinship with the epic; the pleasant social observation of Caroline comedy was too small a thing

[1] *Ib.* 156-7.

to be able to serve it. Only the Puritans had the drive adequate to one of the greatest forms. But the preponderant Puritan form was the sermon and not any objective work of art. Bernard attempted such a work, and showed in the process a little artistic skill and much vitality. And though he did not write a great narrative he showed the form it could have taken, had a sufficient artist been found among the Puritans.

I have grossly over-simplified puritanism in this section, treating it as if it were solely a religious matter. Its core of strength was indeed religious, but various peripheral matters attached themselves to that core. Our imaginary Puritan writer of epic about the year 1626 would inevitably have introduced those peripheral matters. For instance, he would have had middle-class rather than aristocratic sympathies and would have continued the bias in that direction already noted in Sylvester's translation and adaptation of Du Bartas. He might also have shown a sympathy with the lowly that approximated him to *Piers Plowman* rather than to *Arcadia*. In the *Isle of Man* Bernard shows a great sympathy with the plight of the poor at the hands of the covetous. Covetousness induced usurers to pauperise honest men and then tempted the paupers to mischief. This is the poor men's evidence against Covetousness at his trial:

> When we have wanted reliefe, and begged of him, he hath counselled us to shift for our selves, and steale out of the stacks of Corne in gleaning time for bread, to breake hedges, to steale wood or cole in the night to make us fires, to pluck sheep, or sheere off their wooll for cloathing, to rob Orchards for fruit, to steale geese, hennes, duckes, pigges, and sheepe, for flesh meat, to cousen men that set us on worke, and to make us poore people hatefull to God and man.[1]

That gives the type of homely sensitiveness that would have formed part of a Puritan epic. But a more grandiose motive would have entered, and with gathering force as events evolved towards the civil war. To this I now go on.

In my account of Puritan mythology above I hinted at a political as well as the individual side of it. The centre of the Puritan drama was God's dealings with the Isle of Man, the individual soul. But those dealings had implications beyond the individual. God's choice of the company of the saved had nothing to do with the human hierarchies. It was thus a levelling choice, joining ruler and pauper in a common salvation or damnation, and hence calculated to foster levelling ideas even in this life. Further, though the Puritan was terrifyingly aware of his possible fate in the next world, he did not rule out the possibility of exciting developments in this. With the

[1] *Ib.* 185.

Book of Revelation to draw on as the repository of prophetic truth, he could fabricate schemes of future world history; and he did in fact believe that with the increased number of the elect in the era of Christ some startling human betterment, some kingdom of the Saints on earth, was possible. Such hopes did not apply to Bunyan, who wrote when the Saints had been defeated, but they animated the period leading to the Civil War and the first years of the war itself. And they were the potential material of high poetry.

I must now ask the reader to cast his mind back to my remarks on Foxe and the theory of history found in his *Book of Martyrs*. Here, however fantastic the process of its creation may have been, was a scheme simple in its great outlines and thrilling to the imagination because its majestic shape was incomplete and might even now be in process of completion. It was in fact not static but a plan of campaign or of pilgrimage, not in this case for the single human soul, but for the true Church militant on earth. I have already mentioned the persistent popularity of the *Book of Martyrs* and how in 1632 it was enlarged to include further evidence of God's favour to England, through a comparative view of England and France. Also, to the great events in the latest phase of history were now added the defeat of the Spanish Armada and the prevention of the Gunpowder Plot, evidence at once of the persistent machinations of Antichrist, the Pope, and of God's favour to England in causing them to be thwarted. But though God had thus shown his favour he was also pleased to test the endurance of his elect by allowing the counsellors of Charles I to oppress them. In particular they curtailed the liberty of preaching: a monstrous act of oppression, for, according to a principal Puritan tenet, it was the zealous preacher above all who awoke the unconverted man's conscience, propelled him on the spiritual pilgrimage, and kept him to his path.[1] Further, without the utmost activity of the preachers, there was no chance of the great historical process set forth by Foxe being consummated.

In 1640, with the summoning of the Long Parliament, the preachers were given their head, and the land began to throb with hopes of the millennium. Haller[2] has pointed out that the *Book of Martyrs* gave some of these a definite shape. The immediate practical issue was the episcopacy, and some kind of historical justification for attacking it was desirable. Foxe's *Book of Martyrs* served as a starting-point from which to provide it. To quote Haller:

> The preachers had to make clear that their demands were in accord not only with scripture but also with divine intention as revealed in the history of the church and of the realm of England.

[1] See for instance the *Plain Man's Path-way to Heaven*, the Table, 'Preaching, a matter of absolute necessitie unto eternall life.'

[2] In the article on Foxe mentioned above, p. 362.

This they found not difficult. They brought into the pulpit, adapted to their own purposes, the ideas which the English people had been imbibing from Foxe for the past eighty years. Everybody knew, or at any rate few were prepared to deny, that Antichrist in one guise or another, had for a long time been endeavouring to stifle the preaching of the word in England. For he knew that, if the word were preached in England, his power everywhere would presently come to an end. But the great bulwark of free preaching in England had been the independence of the English crown. Therefore papists, foreign and homebred, had labored to subject English monarchs to the will of the pope. Now, however, the repressors of free preaching were the English bishops, who had misled the king and were attempting to thwart the will of Parliament.[1]

Once the bishops were suppressed and free preaching secured, God would further indulge his habit of using England to promote a great advance of the true Church militant.

All this may sound remote from the epic, but first it does show an element that would have been present in a Puritan epic near the beginning of the Civil War, and secondly it leads to Milton and to his epic plans at that period.

Milton at the time of *Lycidas* and his Italian journey seems to have contemplated an epic on Arthur, a patriotic poem of vast range including the Trojans in Britain at one end and the defeat of the Spanish Armada at the other.[2] When he returned to England from Italy he was caught up in the religious enthusiasm of the Parliament and its party and joined in the campaign against the bishops. In his anti-episcopal pamphlets (and especially in the first of these, *Of Reformation in England*) he showed himself the heir of Foxe's conception of history.[3] England had always been in the forefront of any great religious betterment: and in particular Wycliffe had initiated the Reformation. But in one way Milton differed from Foxe. While Foxe had in mind the miracle of Elizabeth's succeeding Mary and accepted the Elizabethan form of Protestantism, being mainly interested in its permanence, Milton was one of those who believed that the early reformers in England had left their work half done and that now the wonderful moment had come for England to perfect her reformation and to shine out as the holiest nation of the world. And this hope kindled his highly poetical imagination. Not only did he embody this hope in passionate prose, but he pictured himself as the poet of the new and perfected England.

Then amidst the *Hymns* and *Halleluiahs* of *Saints* some one may perhaps bee heard offering at high *strains* in new and lofty *Measures*

[1] *Ib.* 219-20.
[2] See my *Miltonic Setting* (Cambridge 1938 and London 1947) 185-93.
[3] See Haller, *loc. cit.* 222-4.

to sing and celebrate thy *divine Mercies*, and *marvelous Judgements* in this land throughout all Ages; whereby this great and Warlike Nation instructed and inur'd to the fervent and continuall practice of *Truth* and *Righteousnesse*, and casting farre from her the *rags* of her old *vices* may presse on hard to that *high* and *happy* emulation to be found the *soberest, wisest*, and *most Christian People* at that day when thou the Eternall and shortly-expected King shalt open the Clouds to judge the several Kingdomes of the World, and distributing *Nationall Honours* and *Rewards* to Religious and just *Commonwealths*, shalt put an end to all Earthly *Tyrannies*, proclaiming thy universal and milde *Monarchy* through Heaven and Earth.[1]

And a little later, in the *Animadversions upon the Remonstrants Defence*, Milton speaks of taking a harp and singing God 'an elaborate song to Generations'.[2] In referring to God's judgements in England throughout all ages Milton is certainly thinking of some scheme of history on the model of Foxe and is probably thinking of a full-scale epic. Whether Milton did more than think vaguely of such a poem, whether he intended it to supersede his projected Arthuriad is uncertain; but one scholar,[3] on the evidence of a passage from *Of Reformation in England* just preceding the one quoted, has constructed Milton's plot as follows: the five invasions of Britain from Brutus to William I; the Reformation, beginning with Wycliffe and including the Armada and the Gunpowder Plot; the glorious future of a reformed Britain. Whether or not Milton had pushed his plans so far, he had all this material in mind and much of it he had inherited from Foxe. But the utmost poetic embodiment that Foxe's majestic, though Procrustean, theme received were a few passages in Milton's antiepiscopal tracts and in *Areopagitica*. It is in *Areopagitica* that Milton speaks of his country most worthily. The fever of the first antiepiscopal tracts has subsided; a sweet reasonableness has asserted itself; but the fine ardour remains.

> Methinks I see in my mind a noble and puissant Nation rousing herself like a strong man after sleep, and shaking her invincible locks: Methinks I see her as an Eagle muing her mighty youth, and kindling her undazl'd eyes at the full midday beam; purging and unscaling her long abused sight at the fountain itself of heav'nly radiance.

That side of Puritan emotion died during the Commonwealth. Bunyan, the one Puritan writer of epic, came too late to use it. Forced to abandon the national theme, he confined himself to the medieval inheritance of the spiritual warfare and pilgrimage.

[1] From the last paragraph of *Of Reformation in England*, Columbia Milton, iii. 1. 78-9.
[2] *Ib.* 148.   [3] H. Mutschmann, *Milton's Projected Epic* (Tartu 1936).

CHAPTER II

BUNYAN

Fremit et discordibus armis
Non simplex natura hominis.   (Prudentius)

They could not have thought that such rarities could have been couched in so few and such ordinary words.

(Bunyan, *The Holy War*)

The Holy War *is a construction, not a vision. The* Pilgrim's
Progress *came to Bunyan unsought.*   (Charles Firth)

1. GENERAL

BUNYAN was greatly gifted. He had to an exceptional degree spiritual vision, an eye for the things around him, and a mastery of the English language in its prose arrangement. But, through conditions beyond his control, he could not put those gifts to the fullest use of which they were capable. He was hindered by lack of education; and the Puritan phase of thought, which gave him his material, was past its zenith when he began to write and could provide him with only a part of the inspiration it had commanded earlier.

I said in my introduction that ideally the epic writer must be open to the widest range of normal human feelings, from the simple sensualities to a susceptibility to the numinous. Whatever Bunyan's shortcomings in filling the area between these extremes, he was supremely well versed in the extremes themselves. Indeed, at one extreme, his aptitude for the numinous may extend from the normal to the pathological. Rosemary Freeman has described that aptitude in words that are not likely to be bettered. They refer to the *Pilgrim's Progress*, but they are valid for Bunyan's whole quality of mind.

The *Pilgrim's Progress* springs from a tragic vision of life which is Bunyan's own. It is a vision engendered by his piercing insight into the depths and subtleties of spiritual wickedness, and at the same time, for it is tragic not satiric, by his profoundly imaginative apprehension of the goodness as well as the power of God. 'Man crumbles to dust at the presence of God; yea though he shows himself to us in his robes of salvation'—the sternness of the first part of the book, the compassion of the second, are the dual expression of that sad certainty.[1]

[1] *English Emblem Books*, 208.

GENERAL

Such 'crumbling to dust at the presence of God' approximates Bunyan to Dante and to a lesser degree to Langland. But it may do so even more to Virgil. Different as were his God and Virgil's, he would have understood through every fibre of his being, as perhaps no other epic writer mentioned in this book, the terrifying episodes of the *Aeneid*: Venus's revelation to her Aeneas during the fall of Troy that the greatest gods, and even Jupiter himself, are fighting unseen on the Greek side; and the great Fury, sent by Jupiter to baffle Turnus, shrunk to the shape of a small bird of ill omen. The sensitiveness that admits of such apprehensions and the strength to survive them, when combined (as they were in Bunyan), argue a great nature. So much, at present, for Bunyan's spiritual vision.

In his preface to *Mr Badman* Bunyan testifies to his own closeness to the things around him:

> All the things that here I discourse of, I mean as to matter of fact, have been acted upon the stage of this World, even many times before mine eyes.[1]

In his best-known work Bunyan nearly always subordinates his interest in life to his religious doctrine. It animates the doctrine but rarely exists in its own right. Yet once or twice it reveals its inherent power by breaking loose from its subordination, as when in the second part of the *Pilgrim's Progress* Mercy, whose rigid piety has cut short the courtship of Mr Brisk, cannot refrain from letting Prudence know that she is not in herself ineligible:

> I might a had Husbands afore now, tho' I spake not of it to any; but they were such as did not like my Conditions, though never did any of them find fault with my Person: So they and I could never agree.[2]

Here Bunyan's natural observation, his instinct for realism, has made him abandon his usual strict adherence to his allegory.

In *Mr Badman* there are several short stories, all, it is true, inserted as *exempla* in the medieval tradition to illustrate a moral, which show Bunyan quite caught up in the sheer and self-sufficient interest in the thing he describes and which thereby reveal his primal gift of whole-hearted absorption into the things around him. Here is one of the most striking, professing to illustrate the horror of the sin of uncleanness yet in its essence just a superbly good story:

> An ancient man, a man of good credit in our Country, had a

---

[1] Quotations from Bunyan are from the two volumes of John Brown's edition of the major works in the Cambridge English Classics: the earlier volume (Cambridge 1905) containing the *Life and Death of Mr Badman* and the *Holy War*: the later volume (Cambridge 1907) containing *Grace Abounding* and the *Pilgrim's Progress*. The quotation in the text above is on p. 3 in this edition.

[2] *Ed. cit.* 341.

Mother that was a Midwife: who was mostly imployed in laying great persons. To this womans house, upon a time, comes a brave young Gallant on horseback, to fetch her to lay a young Lady. So she addresses herself to go with him; wherefore, he takes her up behind him, and away they ride in the night. Now they had not rid far, but the Gentleman litt off his horse, and taking the old Midwife in his arms from the horse, turned round with her several times, and then set her up again; then he got up, and away they went till they came at a stately house, into which he had her and so into a Chamber where the young Lady was in her pains: He then bid the Midwife do her Office, and she demanded help, but he drew out his Sword and told her, if she did not make speed to do her Office without, she must look for nothing but death. Well, to be short, this old Midwife laid the young Lady, and a fine sweet Babe she had: Now there was made in a Room hard by, a very great Fire: so the Gentleman took up the Babe, went and drew the coals from the stock, cast the Child in, and covered it up, and there was an end of that. So when the Midwife had done her work, he paid her well for her pains, but shut her up in a dark room all day, and when night came, took her up behind him again, and carried her away, till she came almost at home; then he turned her round, and round, as he did before, and had her to her house, set her down, bid her Farewell, and away he went: And she could never tell who it was.[1]

That is the perfection of one kind of art, but it is also the work of a man not only of a vivid imagination but of exceptional powers of observation who delighted in the use of those powers.

I come to the third thing in which Bunyan was greatly endowed: his command of words. Bunyan's prose style is indeed one of the miracles of English literature. That he owed much to the prose of the authorised version of the Bible is obvious, but unless the debt is defined this obvious truth may mislead rather than illumine. The cadences of Bunyan's prose do not strike me as predominantly biblical. Certainly some are more like the rhythms of speech that come natural to people who are very close to life and who talk and listen much and read little. But the Bible taught Bunyan that prose could worthily express matters that custom had hitherto confined to the form of verse. He had in fact the model of a prose where every word and every rhythm had been weighed after a fashion usually practised by the most zealous poets alone. We may guess that like other people of humble education he read slowly and that the words of the few books he did read sank into his mind in a way scarcely imaginable by those who accept as normal today's habit of superficial reading.

[1] 56-7.

Whether or not he consciously aimed at it, Bunyan's prose, for all its simplicity, has the tautness and the rightness of poetry. Saintsbury, who described Bunyan's gifts extremely well,[1] cites Latimer and Cobbett as 'his two chief analogues in English prose-writing'. But I doubt if a true English analogue exists; and I am much more nearly reminded of Herodotus. Both Herodotus and Bunyan command a prose at once pellucid and easy but taut and poetical. Both, though entirely themselves in their style, had behind them a great work of imaginative literature: behind Herodotus Homer, behind Bunyan the English Bible. Both too, though for very different reasons, had to rely greatly on themselves in creating their literary instruments. For what they did they had no direct precedents; Herodotus because Greek prose was in its infancy, Bunyan because he lacked education and the chance of wide reading. Commanding so perfectly wrought a medium both authors, or rather Herodotus always and Bunyan at his best, stand up to constant re-reading. Most of the *Pilgrim's Progress* survives such an ordeal, and here is a passage, no better and no worse than many others, that can illustrate such a survival. It is the account of Discretion receiving Christian as he arrives at the House Beautiful:

> Then she asked him whence he was, and whither he was going? and he told her. She asked also, how he got in the way? and he told her. Then she asked him, What he had seen and met with in the way? and he told her. And last, she asked his Name? so he said, It is *Christian*, and I have so much the more a desire to lodge here to night, because, by what I perceive, this place was built by the Lord of the Hill, for the relief and security of Pilgrims: So she smiled, but the water stood in her Eyes: And after a little pause, she said, I will call forth two or three more of the Family. So she ran to the Door and called out *Prudence*, *Piety* and *Charity*, who after a little more discourse with him, had him into the Family; and many of them meeting him at the threshold of the house, said, Come in, thou blessed of the Lord; this house was built by the Lord of the Hill, on purpose to entertain such Pilgrims in. Then he bowed his head and followed them into the House.[2]

The great simplicity of the language heads us off the rhetorical cunning and the economy of the texture. But a very little examination reveals them. For instance, Discretion's interrogation at the beginning is strongly patterned. The first question is quite general, almost casual. The second is brief and clear but more particular and personal. The third is longer and invites intimacy. And it leads to the final intimacy of her asking Christian's name. But these different questions are counterpointed, the first three of them, by the same answer: *and he*

[1] In *A Short History of English Literature* (London 1908) 513-17.
[2] 176.

told her. And this sameness has at least two functions. It crosses the realism of the questions by the immemorial repetitiveness of the folk-tale and it expresses Christian's anxiety and nervous desire to be admitted. Our feeling, as we read, that the repetitions may go on for ever is also Christian's feeling that he may be kept waiting for ever. When Discretion asks his name, the tension breaks. We know and he knows that he has satisfied her; and instead of *and he told her* we get Christian's free speech about his desires. And when the water stands in Discretion's eyes we know that it is on account of her sympathy with that anxiety and that relief in Christian's mind of which not a word has been said directly. Such an oblique way of working is essentially the poetic way, and it is normal in Bunyan's best writing. Further, in spite of the apparent ingenuousness it is the way of the greatest weight and concentration of language: a way which, though suited by a kind of native right to the plain and homely things, can easily extend to the greatest emotional intensity. Its case is precisely the opposite of the contemporary heroic couplet which chose, in heroic writing, to make high pomp its norm and whose problem was to deal with smaller things convincingly. Bunyan's prose was more flexible than the heroic couplet. It could rise to majesty or to intense feeling more successfully than the couplet could descend from its resonant pomp to the subtle, the delicate, or the minute; witness Dryden's *Aeneid.*

Bunyan, then, in combining spiritual insight with worldly observation to an eminent degree and in having great power over words, was naturally equipped for the highest works of literature. But it would be foolish to belittle the disadvantages under which he laboured. First, there was his lack of education that restricted the range of topics on which he could exercise his talents. Secondly, throughout his career as a writer his social life was set in a religious sect that not only held a rigid creed but which, through being constantly in opposition to the larger world if not actively persecuted, fastened on to that creed with a passionate and exclusive concentration. Such a setting could not but restrict Bunyan's artistic range. We have only to think of Langland to perceive this. Langland, like Bunyan owing so much to the contemporary lore of the preacher and favouring the side of the poor against the rich, is yet able to include every social class within his survey. He criticises the government, he gives it drastic advice, but he is not against it. He has in fact that sense of responsibility marking the party in power which Bunyan, forced to the irresponsibility of being in constant opposition, all too obviously lacks. And through that responsibility Langland touches areas of life—political, social, and moral—that Bunyan, however well equipped in himself to touch them, cannot. When Langland reproves the baronial class for dining apart in their private rooms instead of dining in hall with the lower orders of the community he is doing something beyond Bunyan's scope, and something that helps to fill in the ground between intense spirituality and sheer observation of what lies there within view. Bunyan was denied the means of filling in that ground, to the serious impoverishment of his art.

Not only was Bunyan forced into a puritanism cut off from the larger world; he was also denied an important part of what were essentially Puritan concerns. There is little certainty and there has been much conjecture about the books Bunyan read. But besides the *Plain Man's Path-way to Heaven*, already mentioned, Foxe's *Book of Martyrs* was one of the books we know he read and studied. He bought it while in prison and refers to it frequently in his religious writings. Moreover, it has been plausibly suggested that the speeches of the various persons in the *Pilgrim's Progress* before they enter the River of Death were modelled on the farewell speeches of Foxe's Protestant martyrs.[1] I described earlier the majestic scheme of world history that Foxe advances, a scheme that makes his book so much more than a vast hand-book of Protestant martyrology, and I mentioned a few pages back the renewed vogue of Foxe's scheme in the years round the beginning of the Civil War. It was Bunyan's misfortune that he began writing too late to be able to use for his art those positive hopes of a holy community in England that had earlier held men's minds. These hopes, had Bunyan been able to embrace them, would have forced him to be political and to share in the responsibility that a man incurs through advocating definite lines of political action. In these matters Bunyan comes out poorly compared with Milton. Too idealistic and high-minded and sanguine to be an effective practical politician, Milton did nevertheless add greatly to his human stature by participating actively in politics. He committed himself utterly, he accepted complete responsibility; and he could never have made his epic so grand if he had not been of the temper, in the very act of writing that epic, to defy in a last pamphlet the popular voices which were insisting with an overwhelming force that the Stuarts must be restored. That Bunyan should compare poorly with Milton in this matter was not his fault. He merely had the misfortune to have been born too late and to reach his creative period at a date when as an active political force puritanism was dead, however powerful its undeclared and pervasive influence was on the manners and morals of England. It is true that there were millenarians in Bunyan's day and that Bunyan was influenced by millenarian hopes. But these hopes were forlorn, anachronistic, unable to mould the great shape of his mind and experience.

It thus happened that for the material of his art Bunyan was pretty well confined to two subjects: the great religious drama of human

[1] See Charles Firth, *Essays Historical and Literary* (Oxford 1938) 137-8.

salvation or damnation and the ordinary scene of men and things around him. To suggest that these should not suffice a man is to a certain type of believer (of which Bunyan himself was one) blasphemy and to certain easy-going folk pedantry. And it is true that by rendering the religious drama with surpassing force and by fathering the realistic novel Bunyan did both accomplish great things and satisfy the respective claims of 'Saint' and easy-goer. But the epic of its nature covers a great area of human life, concerning itself with middle ground as well as with extremes. Without the religious sense it is indeed defective, but it does not readily confine itself to religion. Bunyan, naturally equipped for the epic, could not find full scope for his aptitude.

Nevertheless, he did accomplish something in the epic line. Though Calvinism, or the Puritan myth, or whatever you wish to call it, excluded big areas of life, it attracted a large number of people; and anyone who could be its artistic interpreter was sure of a great body of supporters. I believe Bunyan to have been the true interpreter, I should even say poet, of the Puritan myth; the myth, that is, not of the course of history as predicted in *Revelation*, but of the holy life of the individual with its stages of election, vocation, justification, sanctification, glorification, and all the vicissitudes between those stages. And if he was foiled of the true epic amplitude in being forced to confine himself to this myth, he was, in so being, assured of the genuine choric character of his work. And that was no small help in giving it some epic quality at least. What this epic quality finally amounts to will depend on another part of Bunyan's equipment, the quality of his will. But this matter can be treated more aptly as manifested in the specific works, in fact in those works that have the strongest epic claim.

Of the four main works of Bunyan, two, *Grace Abounding* and *Mr Badman*, are the least epic. The first is autobiography and in its poignant personal vividness remote from the objective dignity of the major literary forms. It is Bunyan, not *homo*, who here holds our thoughts; and of all Bunyan's books this contains most of the pathological. I cannot agree with a recent opinion that *Mr Badman* is a masterpiece. Of all Bunyan's major works it contains the greatest amount of untransmuted sermon-material. Much of it is very dull reading. When it comes to the book's great and undoubted merits some of the best of it looks back to the medieval *exemplum*[1] and the rest looks forward to the realistic novel of Defoe. The actual history of Mr Badman counts for little compared with the details for which it is the excuse. There is no case here for the epic. The *Pilgrim's Progress* was written and published in two parts; the first part, com-

---

[1] See *English*, vii. 165-7, where Maurice Hussey calls *Mr Badman* a masterpiece and enlarges interestingly on its connection with the medieval *exemplum*.

plete in itself, in 1678: between it and the second part, not published till 1684, were written *Mr Badman* and the *Holy War*. This second part has superlative merits, but they are merits mainly of detail in the modes of the *exemplum* and the emblem. Structurally it rests on the scheme of the first part and is not self-sufficient. It forfeits in fact those things that constitute the chief claim of the first part to rank as epic. I conclude therefore that the two works of Bunyan that remain to be considered as epic writing are the first part of the *Pilgrim's Progress* and the *Holy War*. I now turn to these two works, dealing with them generally but also bearing in mind the special matters of the will and the construction.

2. THE PILGRIM'S PROGRESS

It is doubtful if Bunyan had read Lydgate's or any other version of Deguileville's *Pelerinage de la Vie humaine*,[1] but it is certain that he knew this medieval tradition. There is no need to seek further sources than the pulpit, where the imagery of the pilgrimage was an inherited commonplace, the conversation of the pious, and Dent's *Plain Man's Path-way to Heaven*. But though Bunyan inherited a medieval notion, he gave it in writing the *Pilgrim's Progress* a Calvinist[2] turn, being at once traditional and contemporary. Deguileville's pilgrim when he meets various allegorical characters is just like Bunyan's, but when he begins as an infant and is baptised and when he enters a house of religion he is different. For Bunyan the pilgrimage is mental only; it is the journey of the lonely soul scarcely aided by ecclesiastical mechanism; for Deguileville the pilgrimage is only partly the affair of the lonely soul, being largely the passage through the prescribed stages of an education in holiness by means of concrete religious acts. Not that Bunyan's pilgrim discovered a new road for himself. The stages of his journey had, he believed, been definitively fixed by Scripture, and, whatever his individual vicissitudes, were those of election, vocation, justification, sanctification, and glorification. But all these were matters not of ecclesiastical contrivance but of immediate traffic between the soul and its creator. The plot of the *Pilgrim's Progress* is in its skeleton the progress to salvation as pictured in Calvinist theology. The awakening of Christian's conscience, the torments he suffered in the City of Destruction were evidence, little as he knew it, that he was one of God's elect. The actual call to pilgrimage came through Evangelist. Burdened with sin, Christian knew he must seek justification, and after getting through the Slough of

[1] See J. B. Wharey, *A Study of the Sources of Bunyan's Allegories* (Baltimore 1904).
[2] See R. Sharrock, *Spiritual Autobiography in 'The Pilgrim's Progress'*, in *Review of English Studies*, 1948, pp. 102-20.

Despond he was seduced by Worldly Wiseman and persuaded to seek justification through the offices of Mr Legality. Threatened by destruction from the Mountain of the Law, Evangelist rescued him, explaining his error:

> This *Legality* is not able to set thee free from thy Burden. No man was as yet ever rid of his Burden to him, no, nor ever is like to be: ye cannot be justified by the works of the Law; for by the deeds of the Law no man living can be rid of his Burden.[1]

Entering the pilgrim's way through the wicket-gate and having been instructed in the House of the Interpreter, Christian attained to justification and was relieved of his burden when he encountered the cross of Christ. Most of the rest of the book recounts the process of sanctification with its many ups and downs. The battle with Apollyon, the passage through the Valley of the Shadow of Death, the ordeal of Vanity Fair are great landmarks in this process. Christian's companion after the Valley, Faithful, through suffering martyrdom in Vanity Fair, consummates his sanctification and is glorified simultaneously. Christian is fully sanctified only when he has escaped from Doubting Castle and has reached the land of Beulah:

> Now I saw in my Dream, that by this time the Pilgrims were got over the Inchanted ground, and entering into the Country of Beulah whose Air was very sweet and pleasant, the way lying directly through it, they solaced themselves there for a season. Yea here they heard continually the singing of Birds, and saw every day the flowers appear in the Earth; and heard the voice of the Turtle in the Land. In this Country the Sun shineth night and day; wherefore this was beyond the Valley of the *shadow of Death*, and also out of the reach of *Giant Despair*, neither could they from this place so much as see *Doubting-Castle*.[2]

Christian is finally glorified when he has passed the river of death and is conducted up to heaven.

Such is the Puritan theological skeleton of the *Pilgrim's Progress* and it corresponds to the phases of Bunyan's own spiritual voyaging as recounted in the direct narrative of *Grace Abounding*. But the form of the allegory into which Bunyan translated the Puritan myth was derived from places quite the reverse of theological. Harold Golder in a series of articles on the origin of the various incidents in the *Pilgrim's Progress* has shown how many of them go back to those medieval romances that, printed in London, were sold in the villages of England to simple people by pedlars. In his youth, before his conversion, it would have been the most natural thing in the world for Bunyan to have bought *Arthur of Little Britain*, the *Mirrour of Knighthood*, and

[1] 155.   [2] 272.

Richard Johnson's version of the *Seven Champions*; not to speak of the possibility of his borrowing such volumes from neighbours or hearing them read. This is not to deny the influence of the Bible; but that influence was ornamental, it did not dictate the form of the main episodes. For these,

> memories of old romances, forbidden food for conscious thought, came unbidden—but came blended with the familiar phrases of the Bible, and invested with religious significance that made them natural elements in the allegory.[1]

It is this blending of the three elements, the majesty and terror of the Puritan myth, the primary imaginative appeal of the romance-matter, possession of the folk, and the prophetic brilliance of *Isaiah* or *Revelation*, that gives the *Pilgrim's Progress* its high and unique quality.

But, granted the attraction and uniqueness of the blend, how in fact is the *Pilgrim's Progress* shaped, with what steadiness did Bunyan apply his conscious will? Critics (witness the sentence of Charles Firth printed as one of the captions of this chapter) have taken very literally Bunyan's own words about the surprise and suddenness of his inspiration in his prefatory verses. While occupied with another piece of writing he

> *Fell suddenly into an Allegory*
> *About their Journey, and the way to Glory,*
> *In more than Twenty things, which I set down:*
> *This done, I Twenty more had in my Crown;*
> *And they again began to multiply,*
> *Like sparks that from the coals of fire do fly.*

But need these words imply an unbridled spontaneity any more than these of Bunyan's near contemporary, Dryden?

> Thoughts, such as they are, come crowding in so fast upon me, that my only difficulty is to choose or to reject, to run them into verse, or to give them the other harmony of prose.[2]

Bunyan need only be recording an experience which is the rule rather than the exception in literary creation; and the question still remains how in fact he shaped the notions his brain so ardently threw out. We may get the hint of an answer if we consider the succession of Bunyan's major works. All great art has its origin in the compelling experience of the man who creates it. But art can exist at many

---

[1] From Harold Golder's article *Bunyan's Valley of the Shadow* in *Modern Philology*, 1929, pp. 55-72. This is the most helpful of Golder's articles. For the other articles and for recent select bibliography of Bunyan see Henri Talon, *John Bunyan, L'Homme et L'Œuvre* (Paris 1948). I should like to express my appreciation of Talon's thorough, sane, and sensitive book.

[2] *Essays*, ed. Ker, ii. 249.

degrees of distance from its origin. The less personal it is and the further it has moved from its origin, the less chance there is of its being entirely spontaneous and the more chance there is of the conscious will's cooperating to give the work a significant shape. Bunyan's compelling experiences consisted of or were forcibly attached to his religious life. There was really nothing else for him to talk of, but there were different ways of talking. He began in *Grace Abounding* with a direct personal account of his life before, during, and after his religious conversion. This book alone would have given Bunyan a place among the classic writers of England. But, naturally an artist, his instincts prompted him to put his private experiences into a public objective form. The result was the *Pilgrim's Progress*. Now, though its method is different, it retained marks of its personal origin. What was so terrible in Bunyan's religious experience was the number of times he fell from attainment to doubt, from high hope to despair. The main plot of the *Pilgrim's Progress* is true to this peculiarity of personal experience and, at times even, Bunyan fails to transmute the particularity of his own case into objective allegorical form. For instance, after Christian's passage through the Valley of the Shadow of Death, so perfectly a part of the story Bunyan has to tell, he adds this:

> One thing I would not let slip, I took notice that now poor *Christian* was so confounded, that he did not know his own voice; and thus I perceived it: Just when he was come over against the mouth of the burning Pit, one of the wicked ones got behind him, and stept softly to him, and whisperingly suggested many grievous blasphemies to him, which he verily thought had proceeded from his own mind. This put *Christian* more to it than any thing that he met with before, even to think that he should now blaspheme him, that he loved so much before.[1]

Here Bunyan puts in other words an experience already recorded in *Grace Abounding*, an experience more private to himself than common to all pilgrims of religion. Put in the form of a postscript to a piece of action, it is not out of place in the *Pilgrim's Progress*; but it shows Bunyan still close to his own case, for all the objectivity of the form he uses. And this small hangover from *Grace Abounding*, trivial in itself, is significant as a symptom. The main point in the relation between the two works is that by allowing the many (though similar) vicissitudes of experience in *Grace Abounding* to influence the plot of the *Pilgrim's Progress* Bunyan did shape his plot in an accidental and not an organic way. Luckily his very subject provided some sort of shape. The Christian's narrow way has an entrance and an end; or one may call it the single thread on which Bunyan can string his beads. But the beads are not perfectly chosen or arranged in the best

[1] 191.

possible way. And the necklace metaphor is in itself not inept, for the *Pilgrim's Progress* lacks the great sweep of plot and works through small and often repetitive units. The Valley of the Shadow of Death and Doubting Castle provide superb separate episodes, but much of their material is common to both. It seems wanton to say a word against them, and who could actually wish them other than they are? But it would have been a greater achievement to fuse them into a single unit. There is another structural defect. Working in this rather miniature manner, Bunyan was constrained to enlarge a slight work by inserting a good deal of unassimilated sermon-stuff. Examples of this are parts of Evangelist's talk about Worldly Wiseman, of the episode of Talkative, of Christian's talk of Little Faith and Great Grace, and of Hopeful's account of how he came to be a pilgrim. These do not mean that Bunyan was not elsewhere astonishingly successful in transmuting doctrine into action, but they do impair the structural economy. I conclude therefore that the *Pilgrim's Progress* is loosely constructed and that Bunyan did not fully exercise his will in the process.

What claims then has the *Pilgrim's Progress* to be an epic? The answer is not unlike the one I gave to the same question as put to Xenophon's *Anabasis*. By good fortune part of that story had a natural shape; and that natural shape was sufficient to allow the great choric sentiments Xenophon represented to have partial scope. In Bunyan's plot of the human soul's progress to heaven or hell there was sufficient natural coherence to make partially effective a great spiritual movement which for a long period of time held strong sway over men's minds throughout the whole of northern Europe.

3. THE HOLY WAR

The substance of the *Holy War* is the same as that of *Grace Abounding*. It is the struggle of the soul at war with itself and pulled this way and that by God and the Devil. And this traditional struggle again embodies the later Puritan myth. The theme itself goes right back to the fourth century A.D. and to the *Psychomachia* of Prudentius. Owst[1] has shown how the medieval preachers continued the Prudentian theme using various allegories to give the setting of the soul's battle. The soul could be a ship. It could also be a castle or fort, with the five senses the defending gates. Further, the castle could stand for man individually or the world collectively. We have seen how Bernard in the *Isle of Man* used this allegory. He was doubtless familiar with Prudentius, but he probably derived his allegory in the first instance

[1] *Literature and Pulpit in Medieval England*, 68-86.

from the tradition of preaching. Bunyan, certainly indebted to Bernard in the *Holy War*, was also mainly the heir of the preachers.

The *Psychomachia* is crude and it evoked a stricture on the holy war as a poetic subject from C. S. Lewis, which I quoted in my chapter on medieval allegory (p. 136). Though Lewis may have been right in crying down this subject as executed by Prudentius, he exaggerates the superiority of the pilgrimage over warfare as a subject for allegory. The theme of war admits of many topics other than battle, for instance of negotiations, truces, imprisonments, escapes, intrigues; and it would be easy to retort that the pilgrimage subject encourages diffuseness and endless episodes, whereas the martial subject encourages concentration. The point is important, because the reader should not be allowed to begin on the *Holy War* with a prejudice against it.

But even if the reader grants that the holy war is not in itself necessarily inferior to the spiritual pilgrimage as a subject, he needs to beware of another popular error, the tacit assumption that the *Pilgrim's Progress* is Bunyan's norm and that the *Holy War* is inferior wherever it diverges from it. Firth's pronouncement, which I have used as one of my captions, that the *Holy War* is a construction, not a vision, and that the *Pilgrim's Progress* came to Bunyan unsought, is a good example of this error. I have used it as a caption because out of its context it states a truth I wish to underline all I can. In its context it implies that the *Holy War* is inferior; first because it is different, and secondly because spontaneity is better than reflection and conscious shaping. Nothing could illustrate better than Firth's pronouncement the prejudice against the long poem, based on the extraordinary fallacy that inspiration and the exercise of the conscious will are incompatible: a fallacy against which I hope this whole book is a protest. Turning to the pronouncement as it stands in isolation, I should expand it by saying that through being a construction the *Holy War* both differs from the *Pilgrim's Progress* and achieves its characteristic excellence. By viewing his own basic experiences at a greater distance and by spending much longer—two whole years—on building up and amplifying this his third version of it, Bunyan came nearer than he ever did to creating a great organic work of art. Thereby he did indeed forfeit much that made the *Pilgrim's Progress* popular, but he also revealed an instinct to perfect his art which, his environment considered, is quite astonishing and which adds vastly to his literary stature.

It is in its plot that the *Holy War* differs most from the *Pilgrim's Progress*. The plot of the *Pilgrim's Progress* is a string of loosely connected episodes, some more important or exciting than others but not shaped in any obvious, culminating rhythm. The plot of the *Holy War* is shaped far more tightly, with the action grouped round a few great martial events. True, this plot does not altogether succeed, but for reasons that have nothing to do with architectonic power. Matching this grander sweep of plot is a different rhetoric, a style rather more periodic and further from the cadences of ordinary conversation. I shall have something to say on both topics; and since the *Holy War* is little read today I had better give a short account of the action in illustration of its tighter texture.

First, though covering most of the same ground of doctrine, the *Holy War* sets its action in a portion of the religious drama slightly different from that of the *Pilgrim's Progress*. In the *Pilgrim's Progress* man is already fallen, he inhabits the City of Destruction, and he prolongs his pilgrimage from it till beyond death. The action of the *Holy War* begins with Adam's state of innocence and ends before death and the glorification of the warfaring soul. Mansoul is different from Christian in representing both unfallen and fallen man. He is thus a less realistic and a more complex conception. Nor was he meant to be anything else, for he is conceived of as a town and not as a person. We must beware of condemning Bunyan's Mansoul for being different from his Christian; and if we must make comparisons we had better make them not with the *Pilgrim's Progress* but with the more usual and more shifting form of allegory found in the *Faerie Queene*. In the *Pilgrim's Progress* Bunyan had followed the unusual allegorical method of conceiving his allegorical figures in the first place as persons. He was under no obligation thus to continue; and he was at liberty to resemble Spenser by using different methods; sometimes beginning in the personal sometimes in the allegorical way, and then either continuing such beginnings or thinning a person into an abstraction or condensing an abstraction into a person. We must in fact judge the allegory of the *Holy War* for what it is.

Of the great continent of Universe, the fairest part was the town of Mansoul. God, whom Bunyan calls Shaddai, built it for his delight and gave it rule over its surroundings. There was the castle of the heart in the middle of it, which Shaddai intended to occupy, and there were five gates, Ear-gate, Eye-gate, and so on. The inhabitants of Mansoul had it in their own power to choose who should occupy the castle. In the beginning Shaddai was in occupation, and every citizen was content. Later the great giant, Diabolus, coveted the town and succeeded in deceiving the inhabitants into believing that Shaddai was a tyrant. They opened their gates to him and Diabolus occupied the town and proceeded to model it anew. He dismissed the Lord Mayor, Mr Understanding, and the Recorder, Mr Conscience, from their offices, and forced them to live in obscurity. In their places he elected Lord Lustings and Mr Forget-Good. Lord Willbewill, the town's most powerful nobleman, he made governor of the castle, having completely gained him over to his side. He found appropriate holders for the other offices. Meanwhile Shaddai and his son Emanuel resolved that Mansoul must be recaptured. Emanuel will himself be the instrument and the Lord Chief Secretary, the third of the Trinity, drew up a deed that said:

> Let all men know who are concerned, That the Son of *Shaddai* the great King, is ingaged by Covenant to his Father, to bring his *Mansoul* to him again; Yea and to put *Mansoul* too, through the power of his matchless love, into a far better, and more happy condition than 'twas in before it was taken by *Diabolus*.[1]

But Emanuel did not at first make war in his own person. Instead, Shaddai sent an army under Captains Boanerges, Conviction, Judgement, and Execution. Satan is alarmed and seeks to strengthen Mansoul against any good motion. There follows a long section recounting marchings, parleys, terror, and civil war within the town, and the gradual breakdown of it into despair. But Shaddai's captains cannot by themselves capture the town. The conviction of sin and the fear of punishment are not enough by themselves to dislodge Diabolus. Then Emanuel leads a second army to capture Mansoul, having as captains Credence, Goodhope, Charity, Innocent, and Patience. There follows another long section of siege-actions, parleyings, embassies, petitions, with the final issue that Diabolus withdraws and that Mansoul throws itself utterly on the mercy of Emanuel. Petitioners from the town with ropes round their necks wait on him expecting death for themselves and destruction for their town. Instead they receive a complete pardon; and Emanuel enters the town with music and triumph.

This is the first climax and it has as its natural sequel the displacement and trial of the diabolonian officers and the proper ordering of the town. Froude thought that the *Holy War* should have ended here:

> Here, as a work of art, the 'Holy War' should have its natural end. Mansoul had been created pure and happy. The Devil plotted against it, took it, defiled it. The Lord of the town came to the rescue, drove the Devil out, executed his officers and destroyed his works. Mansoul, according to Emanuel's promise, was put into a better condition than that in which it was originally placed. . . . Thus we have all the parts of a complete drama—the fair beginning, the perils, the struggles, and the final victory of good. At this point, for the purposes of art, the curtain ought to fall.[2]

Froude goes on to say that the same does not hold good for the purposes of truth, for in fact the struggle between Emanuel and Diabolus never ends in this world. I doubt if one need thus separate art and truth. The action up to this point is indeed majestically shaped; but a long work admits of more shapes than one. A. C.

[1] 210-11.   [2] J. A. Froude, *Bunyan* (London 1880) 142.

Bradley has pointed out how Shakespeare habitually works up to a climax nearly half way through a play, then sinks, and finally works up new motives into a second climax near the end. Bunyan needed to express not only the triumph of God's first entry into the soul, but the long subsequent process of sanctification with the perils of back-sliding and the need for perpetual vigilance. And he chose his form as Shakespeare had done.

Bunyan's first motion after the climax was masterly. The first diabolonian attack had been thoroughly organised and resoundingly put into action. In contrast he introduces and sets going the next one with deliberately casual quiet and through the agency of a single character, Mr Carnal Security. Here is a quite new accent, and the novelty at once dissipates any thought we may have had that Bunyan should have ended. By corrupting Mansoul from within, Carnal Security caused Emanuel to end his favours and to withdraw, and Diabolus to think a new attack worth making. Diabolus collects an army of Doubters and in the end breaks into the town, but not into the citadel, where Lord Willbewill, now the faithful servant of Emanuel, is in command and holds out. Also messengers can always find a way from the castle through the diabolonian occupants to the home of Shaddai and Emanuel. For a long time Emanuel refuses help and the town thinks itself lost, but in the end he returns with an army and kills the Doubters. Diabolus makes a last attack with an army of Bloodmen whose nature is apparent from their captains: Cain, Nimrod, Ishmael, Esau, Saul, Absalom, Judas, and Pope. To these are attached fresh contingents of Doubters. This second diabolonian army is also defeated and the Bloodmen are captured and reserved for judgement. A few Doubters, however, infiltrate into the town and hatch a plot. They are discovered and tried. The book ends with Emanuel addressing the town, promising it a fuller life hereafter when it shall 'no more hear the noise of the *Diabolonian* Drum'. Meanwhile, he explains, he cannot clear the town of every Diabolonian, for these serve to keep it aware of its perils and to prevent it from falling into a false tranquillity.

From this account it must appear that though Bunyan began his final episodes brilliantly with the introduction of Carnal Security he commits an artistic mistake in making the later episodes too like the earlier ones. We have had war and the trial of malefactors and we get them again. I believe the reason to be not any defect in Bunyan's architectonic sense—he knew where to locate his culminating places —but a simple lack of substance. As asserted above, Bunyan was deficient in the middle ground between the spiritual and the quo-tidian. With more knowledge he could for instance have given his Bloodmen a political meaning and made their attack something different from anything that had gone before. As things are, it adds little. In its structure therefore the *Holy War* has a serious deficiency: it is repetitive. Yet this is a detail, and the total conception has a grandeur possessed by no other of Bunyan's works.

But I must not pass by the charge of a more radical defect in the plot of the *Holy War*. Talon, while admitting the spiritual struggle of individual man as a main theme, enumerates three others: the biblical fall and resurrection of mankind, references to contemporary events, and the adumbration of the New Jerusalem.[1] And he thinks that these themes do not harmonise. I cannot agree. The action begins with the fall of mankind; and here there is no intrusion of any contemporary theme. But once man is fallen, the theme does indeed become double. And why not? Though the individual man of this world cannot also be Adam innocent, he can very well be also Adam fallen. The redeeming process was the same for both. How then can there be conflict? The other two themes are definitely subordinate and serve to support not to detract from the two first. Indeed, any contemporary references are valuable in doing something to fill in the middle ground. For instance, this passage, obviously based on memories of Bunyan's military service, describing Emanuel's troops after entering Mansoul, serves to enliven still more an already brilliant and exciting description:

> They marched, they counter-marched, they opened to the right and left, they divided, and subdivided, they closed, they wheeled, made good their front and rear with their right and left wings, and twenty things more, with that aptness, and then were all as they were again, that they took, yea ravished the hearts that were in Mansoul to behold it. *But add to this*, the handling of their arms, the managing of their weapons of war, were marvellous taking to Mansoul and me.[2]

Talon has another stricture on the *Holy War* with which I cannot agree.[3] In the civil strife early in the book there is some homely writing at the expense of Mr Prejudice and Mr Anything[4]: 'it made me laugh to see how old Mr Prejudice was kickt and tumbled about in the dirt'. And Talon comments that these broils appear puerile in an epic and fail to render the sad division of the human heart which the duel between Christian and Apollyon rendered so finely. Now this is a false comparison: for Christian's fight was a main piece of action; while the misfortunes of Prejudice and Anything are a small addition of subsidiary comic detail, they are not intended to render the great theme. When Bunyan did want to render it in the *Holy War* he knew very well how, witness the following passage:

> In those days, as I was informed, new thoughts, and thoughts that began to run counter one to another, began to possess the

---

[1] *Op. cit.* 284-5.　　　[2] 293.　　　[3] *Op. cit.* 292-3.　　　[4] 243.

minds of the men of the Town of *Mansoul*. Some would say, *there is no living thus:* others would then reply, *this will be over shortly:* then would a third stand up and answer, *let us turn to the King Shaddai, and so put an end to these troubles:* And a fourth would come in with a fear saying, *I doubt he will not receive us.* The old Gentleman too, the Recorder, that was so before *Diabolus* took *Mansoul*; he also began to talk aloud, and his words were now to the Town of *Mansoul*, as if they were *great claps of thunder.* No noise now, so terrible to *Mansoul*, as was his, with the noise of the Souldiers and shoutings of the Captains.[1]

In sum, no defect I recognise in the *Holy War* and no adverse criticism of it I have read can persuade me that the book is not grandly fashioned.

I come now to the style. And here I can agree with Talon's excellent tribute to its ampler rhetoric.[2] In the *Pilgrim's Progress* Bunyan picks his way with a most intense concentration. He achieves the keenest point and the finest economy. In the *Holy War* Bunyan travels rather than picks his way. What he loses in refinement he makes up in motion. A full-size technique has superseded a miniature one. For illustration I need not go further than the one immediately before the passage just quoted: a passage to which the repetitions of the words *alarms* and *sometimes* succeed in adding wings:

> For now could not *Mansoul* sleep securely as before, nor could they now go to their debaucheries with that quietness as in times past. For they had from the Camp of *Shaddai* such frequent, warm, and terrifying alarms; yea, alarms upon alarms, first at one *Gate* and then at another, and again, at all the gates at once, that they were broken as to former peace. Yea, they had their alarms so frequently, and that when the nights were at longest, the weather coldest, and so consequently the *season* most *unseasonable*; that that Winter was to the Town of *Mansoul* a Winter by it self. Sometimes the Trumpets would sound, sometimes the slings would whorle the stones into the Town. Sometimes ten thousand of the Kings Souldiers would be running round the walls of *Mansoul* at midnight, shouting, and lifting up the voice for the battel. Sometimes again, some of them in the Town would be wounded, and their cry and lamentable voice would be heard, to the great molestation of the now languishing Town of *Mansoul*. Yea so distressed, with those that laid siege against them, were they, that I dare say, *Diabolus* their King had in these days his rest much broken.

Or take the momentum of this part of Emanuel's speech to Diabolus, who has offered him the possession of Mansoul provided he may remain there as his deputy. It may be less like the Bunyan of the *Pilgrim's Progress* and more like the rhetoric of the contemporary pulpit. But it is magnificent and it typifies an expansion of Bunyan's powers, a deepening of his art, and an attempt at a more public form of utterance.

Thou talkest of subjecting of this Town to good, when none desireth it at thy hands. I am sent by my Father to possess it my self, and to guide it by the skilfulness of my hands into such a conformity to him as shall be pleasing in his sight. I will therefore possess it my self, I will dispossess and cast thee out: I will set up mine own standard in the midst of them: I will also govern them by new Laws, new Officers, new motives, and new ways; Yea, I will pull down this Town, and build it again, and it shall be as though it had not been, and it shall then be the glory of the whole Universe.[1]

Let me recapitulate my main points about the *Holy War*. It embodies Bunyan's authentic experience as surely as *Grace Abounding* and the *Pilgrim's Progress* but at a further remove from it. The method of conveying it lacks the homeliness of the earlier allegory; yet it admits plenty of homely touches, reassuring us that Bunyan has not lost the earlier skill. The *Holy War* gives a version of the same Puritan myth that is the skeleton of the *Pilgrim's Progress*, but Bunyan applied his shaping will to creating that version with a more prolonged concentration, seeking thereby to give it a grander outline and a more sustained rhetoric. How far this final version succeeded remains to be assessed. But Bunyan's aim at least gave to the *Holy War* a truer epic quality than the *Pilgrim's Progress* could aspire to. If the *Pilgrim's Progress* is a Puritan epic, it is so partly through luck. The *Holy War* is an epic by design.

And now how does the book succeed? Better by far than is usually allowed. Let me give samples of success. The rapture with which Bunyan describes the arrival of Christian and Hopeful in heaven is wonderful indeed. But the rapture with which he describes the entry of Emanuel into Mansoul is not less so. Yet while the first is classic, the second is scarcely known to the common reader. Further, the second is part of a large and complicated organism; the culmination of a long and sustained process. It says things which the first description does not try to say. There is the danger in sustained writing, in the long unit of action, of monotony, of the too solemn. And it is true that the *Holy War* lacks the quick turns of the *Pilgrim's Progress* and makes a greater demand on the reader's staying-power. But the power to turn and to surprise is there in an eminent degree. One example must suffice: the passage that recounts the final stage of

[1] 267.

Mansoul's felicity after Emanuel has reformed it and the sudden entrance of Carnal Security:

> The blessed Prince did also ordain a new Officer in the Town, and a goodly person he was, his name was Mr Gods-peace. Himself was not a native of it, but came with the Prince *Emanuel* from the Court. This man, as I said, was made Governour of the Town in general, specially over the Castle, and Captain *Credence* was to help him there. And I made great observation of it, that so long as all things went in *Mansoul* as this sweet natured *Gentleman* would, the Town was in most happy condition. Now there were no jars, no chiding, no interferings, no unfaithful doings in all the Town of *Mansoul*; every man in *Mansoul* kept close to his own imployment. The Gentry, the Officers, the Soldiers, and all in place observed their order. And as for the Women and Children of the Town, they followed their business joyfully, they would *work* and *sing*, *work* and *sing* from morning till night; so that quite through the Town of *Mansoul* now, nothing was to be found but harmony, quietness, joy and health. And this lasted all that Summer.
>
> But there was a man in the Town of *Mansoul*, and his name was Mr Carnal Security, this man did after all the mercy bestowed on this Corporation, bring the Town of *Mansoul* into great and grievous slavery and bondage. A brief account of him and his doings take as followeth.[1]

The force of the surprise is vastly heightened by the quiet stealthy way Bunyan introduces his sinister new character; it is a superb stroke of art. But the passage will serve to illustrate not only Bunyan's command of the sudden turn in the *Holy War* but other matters I have mentioned or have still to mention. The singing women and children show Bunyan still a master of homely realism. But above all this account of order in the town of Mansoul illustrates Bunyan's attempt, instinctive or other, to give the *Holy War* a social content that the *Pilgrim's Progress* lacked. Puritan though he was in an age when puritanism had become identified with a humble section of society, Bunyan was yet open to the all-inclusive hierarchical conception of the world that was still dominant in the age of Elizabeth. In his opening paragraph he compares the differences within the universe to the differences among the planets; and the allegory itself is one of the many traditional correspondences between the human and another cosmic organism. And Bunyan wants his town to be not only the human soul in its isolated exposure to God and the Devil but also the whole human society with its potentialities of godly discipline and devilish chaos. To fulfil his want he draws on any

[1] 331-2.

experience of social and political life he had. What served him best was his memory of his own military service and of the Civil War generally. I illustrated the first by the description of Emanuel's troops drilling. I could have illustrated the second from the description of the pitiful divided state of beleaguered Mansoul quoted for another purpose. Anyhow, much of the martial stuff is drawn from real experience whether felt in person or heard by report, and it helps to validate the attempted social scope of the book. Unfortunately, as already observed, Bunyan knew little of politics and he could not satisfactorily fill the middle ground between personal religious experience and the homely things he could see around him. But he did partially fill it in the *Holy War*; and this partial success does partially enable the other conspicuous virtues of the book to tell.

Until taste changes, until the grand shape attracts equally with the immediate brilliant perception, readers will prefer the *Pilgrim's Progress* to the *Holy War*. But each allegory offers things that the other cannot; and of the special marks of the epic the *Holy War* offers most. No other work has so good a claim to be called England's Puritan epic.

CHAPTER III

THE BEGINNINGS OF
NEO-CLASSICISM

1. TORQUATO TASSO

Tasso . . . is held, both in time and merit, the first of the Moderns.
(Davenant, *Preface to Gondibert*)

Speron Speron, *thinking Tasso's exquisite work of* Godfred *to
be too full of rich Conceits, and more dainty than did become the
Gravity of such Work, said, That it was a Heroick Poem written in*
Madrigals. (Sir William Alexander, *Anacrisis*)

Tasso . . . *his* Gierusalem liberata . . . *an excellent pile of
meerely Morall Philosophy.* (Henry Reynolds, *Mythomystes*)

TASSO'S *Gerusalemme Liberata* is clearly a work of transition
belonging at once to the less rigorous world of the Renaissance
and the more rigorous one of neo-classicism. In spite of his conscientious classicism he had written tolerantly and sympathetically of the
Italian verse-romance; and the abounding energy of his poem, with
its lavish descriptions and long-sustained speeches, is in keeping with
the age that was closing and of which his *Jerusalem* was in one way
the poetical epitaph. But on a balance Tasso certainly looks forward,
and his great poem is more like the one possible epic success of the
neo-classic age on the Continent, Fénelon's *Télémaque*, published a
century and a quarter later, than it is like the *Lusiad*, published only
three years before.

Camoens, though he lived long enough to sample the different
world into which his country was forced by the defeat at Alcazar,
wrote his epic on the older world of expansion, little troubled, though
he deplores them, by the religious divisions in Europe. His literary
models and his critical guides were simpler than Tasso's. He was
nurtured on the doctrine of Virgil-imitation advocated by Vida.
And this simplicity, for all its seemingly barren academicism, suited
the singleness of purpose that a life of action breeds in a man. Tasso
was the heir, perhaps in his fits of mania the victim, of the spiritual
and social complications and exactions of the Counter-Reformation.
Violence was a part of Camoens's world, but it was more casual and less
taut than the corresponding violence in Tasso's. Camoens had greater
option of choice. Through the old man watching Gama's fleet leave

Lisbon he can set forth the opinion that gainsays all the values on which the voyage relies; and both proposition and denial are allowed full scope and the assurance of survival. After the Counter-Reformation no such options are allowed. Men must submit to the right opinions, even at the price of strained or shattered nerves. The sensitive and ardent courtier of Ferrara was in the same case as the Archbishop of Cambrai; and their cases differ jointly from that of Camoens. In somewhat the same way Tasso's critical obligations were severer than Camoens's. He had to show himself more learned. There was no escaping with only the Latin poets as models. Homer, not to speak of Heliodorus, must be added. True, Tasso had not arrived at the fantastic lengths to which Fénelon pushed his obligation to work everything in; but that obligation is a real obligation and not a free choice, allying him to Fénelon and not to Camoens, whose motive in imitating Virgil was largely that he simply adored doing so. Tasso founded his poem as much on Homer as on Virgil and with a grim conscientiousness that called forth the ridicule of Dryden:

> Tasso . . . imitates Homer so very servilely, that (for example) he gives the King of Jerusalem fifty sons, only because Homer had bestowed the like number on King Priam; he kills the youngest in the same manner, and has provided his hero with a Patroclus, under another name, only to bring him back to the wars, when his friend was killed.[1]

Dryden may be right in using the word *servile*, but he was wrong in adopting a tone of light ridicule. Tasso's servility was a thorough-going affair; no light or conventional or cynical acquiescence; but as it were the passionate kissing of a critical rod.

Spenser, though a younger man than Tasso and his imitator, belongs to the earlier world. The contrast comes out clearly enough where the two poets overlap: in their treatment of the temptation of the senses through enchanting women. Tasso's Armida is the great temptress, living in a realm of magic beauty, who for a time held Rinaldo, the Achilles of the poem, from his duty. She turns into another Dido, craving revenge, when he leaves her, but at the very end of the poem submits herself body and soul to the conqueror. Bowra has an interesting and cogent defence of this surprising and scantily motivated reversal.[2] The Counter-Reformation made much of the beauty of late repentance and had a weakness for the type of penitence figured in Mary Magdalene. The greatness of Armida's faults and the power of her beauty (which Tasso certainly succeeds in conveying) would heighten for his contemporaries the interest in her conversion. Spenser copied Armida and her setting in Acrasia

[1] From the *Original and Progress of Satire*. W. P. Ker, *Essays of John Dryden*, ii. 27-8.
[2] *From Virgil to Milton*, 187-8.

and the Bower of Bliss. But he differs from Tasso in making Sir Guyon resist Acrasia from the beginning and break up her enchanted dwelling. Bowra puts these differences in terms of Catholic and Puritan doctrines concerning the sins of the flesh. But his antithesis is invalid, because he does not take into account what C. S. Lewis and others have made clear: that Spenser's Bower of Bliss must be associated and contrasted with his Garden of Adonis. To the latter Bowra's 'horror of the flesh', that marks the Protestant, is inept. In his way Spenser was as great a sensualist as Tasso, even if they may not have drawn the line between good and bad sensuality in the same place. The difference in the way Tasso and Spenser deal with their enchantress is not of sex morality but of method. Spenser is diffuse and easy-going; he works by juxtaposition and by leaving the reader to draw his inferences. Once Acrasia has failed to seduce Guyon and has suffered the destruction of her bower, she fades out of the poem. Later, in constructing his great picture of the Garden of Adonis Spenser nowhere *states* that it is the counterpart of the Bower of Bliss. He is the philosophical showman, where Tasso, as required by the greater doctrinal fierceness of Counter-Reformation Catholicism, is the conscientious organiser. There must be no vagueness, no unsettled details. The King of Jerusalem must, like Priam, have his fifty sons; and the enchantments and sins of Armida must be rounded off by conversion to the true religion and a husband. All this implies the spirit of neo-classicism: the spirit shown in France by the critics who turned the hints of Aristotle and the tentative findings of the Italian critics into the Three Unities and the other parts of an elaborate dramatic code; or the spirit of Davenant and Dryden, who, finding Shakespeare's *Tempest* too simple, added in their own version a confidant to Miranda on the one hand and on the other a man who had never seen a woman.

Armida's conversion points to another thing in both the poetry and the criticism of Tasso that was powerful in neo-classic literature. This conversion was surprising, indeed something of a miracle. In his *Discorsi* Tasso pronounced that admiration not pity and fear should be the chief feeling aroused by the epic; and in his *Jerusalem Delivered* he entirely made good his pronouncement. Armida's conversion is but one of many amazing and strained episodes. In itself the presence of the amazing means nothing. Medieval and Ariostan romance were full of it. But medieval romance was less serious than medieval religious allegory; and the amazing in Ariosto is comic. Tasso's innovation and a source of his great influence for the next hundred years was that he gave the amazing a central position, a new kind of seriousness. The episode of Olindo and Sophronia from the second book will do for an illustration. In it Tasso risks a very startling juxtaposition of Petrarchian love and the theme of martyrdom. Olindo and Sophronia are Christians living under infidel rule in Jerusalem. He is the bashful, hopeless lover, unable to come to a declaration. To shield other Christians they confess in turn to the theft of an image of the Virgin from a mosque (which neither has committed) and end up tied back to back on the pyre of execution. In this situation Olindo is at last able to declare his love. It is the kind of story that passed perfectly easily and with no particular grimness into medieval lives of saints, that Ariosto could have turned into airy burlesque, and that we today are apt to titter at. Tasso, in telling the tale, drenches it with enthusiasm. Our titters never reach our lips; and we are forced into acceptance. In Tasso's own day and for a hundred years after there was of course no temptation to titter. He gave men what they wanted and he set a genuine and powerful and widespread fashion of appealing to the sense of admiration.

When in the *Critic* Dangle commented on 'The father softens— but the governor is fix'd' with the remark that this antithesis of persons was a most established figure, he was of course speaking the truth. It may well be that Tasso did more than any man to establish it. The theme of duty against nature, present in all literature, received in the neo-classic age its most thorough and blatant exploitation. And the blatancy comes through the abstract rigour with which the theme is exploited. It is as if the great theme was there in powerful and in-escapable abstraction forcing the little men who chose to write on great matters to put it to the fore. There are the beginnings of this blatancy in Tasso, and his great influence must have contributed powerfully to making the love and honour theme inescapable in the neo-classic age. That the theme did really receive new treatment in Tasso comes out when you compare him with Virgil. Virgil's Aeneas is first of all a human being, and it is only in the second place that he finds himself in the unhappy position of having to choose between his entanglement with Dido and his patriotic duty. Tasso, for instance in the matter of Erminia's love for Tancred in Book Six, works the other way round; he makes the idea more important than the char-acters who embody it. The story of Erminia is in itself one of wild and absurd romance. Erminia, an infidel princess, has been be-friended by Tancred and falls in love with him. Confined to Jerusalem, she longs to visit him in the Christian camp. Love impels her, but honour and virgin modesty hold her back. Distracted she decides to don the armour of the woman-commander Chlorinda to gain exit from Jerusalem; a decision that leads to various improbable ad-ventures. As always Tasso is serious and forceful, but the seriousness arises not from the actions of the people but from the author's pre-existing passion on the abstract matter of the struggle between love and duty. And Tasso's method is generally typical of the age to come, even if a Racine can treat the theme so splendidly that abstract passion and present reality of the persons' feelings co-exist, with equal power and without mutual interference.

For those reasons I have chosen, and I am confident rightly, to put Tasso as the pioneer exponent of the neo-classic epic.

That Tasso wrote a fine and popular poem on a heroic subject is undoubted. Whether this poem fulfils the requirements of the epic as I have defined them is less certain. Luckily, my subject being the English epic, I need not give any clear and confident opinion. In style Tasso seems to have succeeded. His verse is vigorous as well as brilliant and melodious and carries the reader on through the length of a complicated plot. The language has colour but is not held up by conceits and witticisms: it is generally simple. Though Tasso finished his poem by the time he was thirty he had spent himself fiercely on it and had concentrated his will on the composition. As the great poem of the Counter-Reformation it voiced a large body of thought. But on the side of variety it may be lacking. It expresses a mind less ample than Camoens's or Spenser's: possibly not through any lack of natural endowment but through a narrower experience of living and a too early beginning.

On the English epic the *Jerusalem Delivered* had less effect than might have been expected. English opinion accepted it as the one great correct epic after the classical. It may have encouraged the neo-classicism of Daniel. It may have encouraged Cowley and Milton, both admirers of Spenser, to forsake the lax form of the *Faerie Queene* and to accept neo-classic requirements. In *Reason of Church Government*, *Jerusalem Delivered* and the *Book of Job* are the two works that Milton allows to figure alongside Homer and Virgil as models for the epic; and if he had written his Arthuriad he might have owed much to Tasso. But *Paradise Lost* with its extremes of free imagination and the human simplicities is remote from Tasso's impassioned orthodoxies. There may be debts of detail—Milton may have borrowed from the description of Hell and from Pluto's speech in the fourth book of *Jerusalem*—but there is no general debt beyond an encouragement to be classical in structure. On Cowley *Jerusalem* may have had a more pervasive influence.

Tasso's major sphere of influence in English literature was not the epic but the heroic play. Not only was this type of play founded on Tasso's theory of admiration, but the plays themselves keep on reminding us of him. Dryden said that Achilles and Rinaldo were his models for Almanzor in the *Conquest of Granada*; but of the two Rinaldo is much more to the point. Achilles's excesses seem to grow out of him; those of Rinaldo and Almanzor (in themselves greater) seem preconceived and inserted.

Great as was Dryden's debt to Tasso in his heroic plays, it is difficult to say how great it would have been if he had written his projected epic on King Arthur or the Black Prince. He began by giving Tasso the highest honour as an epic poet, calling him 'the most excellent of modern poets, and whom I reverence next to Virgil'.[1] This he said in 1671, in the preface to the *Mock Astrologer*; after the publication of *Paradise Lost* but before he came under the sway of that poem. By 1677 Dryden grouped Milton with Homer, Virgil, and Tasso.[2] In 1693 in the *Original and Progress of Satire* Dryden said hard things of Tasso, blaming the episodes of Sophronia, Erminia, and Armida for lack of heroic dignity, and the poem's style for being forced.[3] For all that it is surely significant that for his libretto for Purcell's *Arthur* he borrowed Tasso's enchanted wood. Even though *Absalom and Achitophel* has evident signs of Milton's influence, the more heroic stories in the *Fables* are much nearer in spirit to Tasso. If Dryden had written his epic, the odds are that, whether he willed it or not, he would have drawn principally on the *Jerusalem Delivered*.

But since the two chief poets of the seventeenth century in England never wrote their Arthuriads, Tasso was, apart from Cowley, more a potential than an actual influence on the English epic.

2. THE CRITICS

At this time with us many great Wits flourished, but Ben Johnson, *I think, had all the Critical learning to himself; and till of late years* England *was as free from Criticks as it is from Wolves, that a harmless well-meaning Book might pass without any danger.*

(Thomas Rymer, *Preface to Rapin*)

When does the neo-classic age begin for the epic in England? Not in general till the Restoration. There had of course been exceptions. Daniel, Shakespeare's senior, had begun his neo-classic epic a decade before the death of Elizabeth. In spite of the powerful overflow from the past, of the Spenserians and Puritans, there were partial manifestations of neo-classicism in the seventeenth century before the Civil War. May wrote his *Henry II* and Cowley began his *Davideis* well before that event. Tasso, though not generally imitated, was yet admired and considered correct. Jonson was the authoritative exponent of ideas of the epic that were not in fact put into practice. On the Continent neo-classic theory was really beginning to take shape; and though little followed it was not quite unknown in England.

Most of the components of neo-classic authority were ready to hand in the Renaissance. Neo-classicism made something new of them, first by fitting them into a set pattern and second by using this pattern to direct and control authors. But there were newer

---

[1] *Essays*, i. 145.   [2] *Ib*. 182.   [3] *Ib*. ii. 27.

elements too in neo-classicism. These were principally the spirit of
scientific inquiry and the assertion of modern against ancient orthodoxy in literary production and literary criticism. They are matters
that most concern the latter half of the century and they must therefore be held over for the moment. But inasmuch as they partly
originated in Bacon,[1] they come into the kind of English thought
which, between 1615 and the Civil War, concerned itself with the
epic in England.

The man who applied Baconian notions to criticism was Jonson;
and it was he who by the force of his personality and his growing
influence was the characteristic critic in the period now under review.
Other writers who touch on poetry are much smaller folk and they
say nothing new, merely continuing the commonplaces already established. It is Jonson, conservative though he was in his politics and his
hatred of usury, who ushered in a new way of thinking. His criticism
is indeed scanty but it is sufficient to make its point and it represents
a large quantity of influential talk. From Jonson's *Discoveries*, his
jottings, if not his lecture-notes, belonging to his later years, we learn
first his high admiration of Bacon and second his concern, identical
with Bacon's, about the status of ancient and modern learning. And
if we can trust a short entry, he was on the optimistic side in the
current dispute whether or not the universe was running down to its
close; a dispute which was connected with the question whether the
moderns could excel the ancients; for plainly if the world was near
its death pangs it was not likely to better the productions of Greece
and Rome.

> I cannot thinke *Nature* is so spent, and decay'd, that she can
> bring forth nothing worth her former yeares. She is alwayes the
> same, like her selfe; And when she collects her strength, is abler
> still. Men are decay'd, and *studies*: Shee is not.[2]

And in the next section he lays down the principle governing the
way a modern should take the ancients:

> I know *Nothing* can conduce more to letters, then to examine the
> writings of the *Ancients*, and not to rest in their sole Authority, or
> take all upon trust from them; provided the plagues of *Judging*,
> and *Pronouncing* against them, be away; such as are *envy, bitternesse,
> precipitation, impudence*, and *scurrile scoffing*. For to all the observations
> of the *Ancients* wee have our owne experience: which, if wee will
> use and apply, wee have better meanes to pronounce. It is true they
> open'd the gates, and made the way that went before us: but as
> Guides, not Commanders.

[1] For Bacon's indirect contribution to criticism through the countenance he gave
to modern learning see Richard Foster Jones, *The Seventeenth Century*, 10 ff.
[2] Ed. Herford and Simpson, viii. (Oxford 1947) 567.

In another passage to the same effect he actually takes off from Bacon's pronouncements on the three chief distempers of learning and repeats Bacon's doctrine on how you should take Aristotle.

> Nothing is more ridiculous, than to make an Author a *Dictator*, as the schooles have done *Aristotle*. The dammage is infinite, knowledge receives by it. . . . Let *Aristotle*, and others have their dues; but if we can make farther Discoveries of truth and fitnesse then they, why are we envied?[1]

That is one side, but such a vindication of the moderns' rights must not tempt a man to set up a party against the ancients. And Jonson defines the proper middle course:

> Let us beware, while we strive to adde, wee doe not diminish, or deface; wee may improve, but not augment—Wee must calmely study the separation of opinions, find the errours have intervened, awake Antiquity, call former times into question; but make no parties with the present, nor follow any fierce undertakers, mingle no matter of doubtfull credit with the simplicity of truth, but gently stirre the mould about the root of the Question.

Jonson's doctrine is truly neo-classic. It does not follow the uncritical adoration of antiquity and the simple desire to imitate the object of adoration that animated Renaissance classicisers, but it seeks to regularise antiquity by criticising it and it hopes in the process to do things that the ancients did not do. But you could not do them unless you began by making the ancients your guides. The novelty Jonson advocates may be limited, but it counts very greatly and it allies him with Bacon and those who had visions of great areas of achievement the ancients were unaware of, and it makes him more up to date than the writers who prolonged the more ingenuous enthusiasms of the Renaissance.

It is through this considered neo-classic doctrine that Jonson's scanty references to the epic take on a significance out of proportion to their bulk. These occur principally near the end of *Discoveries* in the section on the *Fable, Epicke, or Dramatick*.[2] It adopts the then recent comparison by Heinsius of the epic to a 'Court or Kings Palace', which 'requires other dimensions than a private house', and it expands Aristotle's idea of the unity of action. Now Heinsius, whose *De Tragoediae Constitutione* was published in Leyden 1611, was one of the instruments of drawing together the scattered assertions of the Italian critics into a definite system, the successor of Scaliger, the bridge between the Renaissance and the full rigidity of French neo-classic orthodoxy.[3] We can be certain that Jonson, in using Heinsius so freely, postulated a severely classical form of epic very

---

[1] *Ib.* 627.   [2] *Ed. cit.* 645.   [3] See Spingarn, *op. cit.* i. xvii.

different from the diffuse form of Spenser. But he would have wanted the epic writer to be critical of the ancient epics and not to assume they were uniformly good. By criticising them and sifting the bad elements from the good the epic writer might be guided to an even better epic form. There are a few hints in Jonson's talk with Drummond of the form he thought a modern English epic should take. He records that he had begun a patriotic epic on the British worthies and that it was in couplets; and in another place he said that for an epic 'ther was no such Ground as King Arthurs fiction'. From these various hints we can conjecture that Jonson's ideal English epic was one which began by closely imitating classical form with a severely shaped plot adorned with sufficient but not too abundant episodes, but that it improved on the ancients by having a Christian subject and by being in rhyme. It would be more severe than Tasso's *Jerusalem Delivered*, being more sparing of episodes and using the couplet and not the more sprawling form of the long stanza of which Jonson spoke to Drummond with disapproval. And the perfect subject was that of the great Christian hero of Britain, Arthur. The great patriotic and didactic value of such a poem in Jonson's eyes is obvious.

3. THOMAS MAY

Thomas May[1] was the first of the Jacobean and Caroline generation of poets to continue the classicising of Daniel's *Civil Wars* and to put the current neo-classic ideas of the epic into practice. He was born in 1595, ten years after Giles Fletcher, and like the brothers Fletcher he was Cambridge bred. But his sober competence is remote from their baroque enthusiasms. Later he was admitted to Gray's Inn and became a member of the literary set that was centred in Ben Jonson. When the Civil War came he forsook his fellows and joined the side of the Parliament. How soon he became Jonson's friend we do not know, but in his commendatory verses to May's Lucan Jonson calls May his 'chosen friend'. After a well-received comedy, the *Heir*, in 1620, May wrote three classicising tragedies under the influence of Jonson's *Sejanus* and *Catiline*. These were not successful, and it was through his translation of Lucan's *Pharsalia* into couplets in 1627 that he first gained the poetical reputation that put him in the running for the laureateship after Jonson's death. May's Lucan is one of the good translations of the Classics into English verse, and should itself rank as a minor classic. It represents the Latin faithfully and it is written in easy and dignified couplets: couplets sufficiently run on to ensure a forward movement but not so frequently run on as to lose the

[1] For the known facts about May see A. G. Chester, *Thomas May, Man of Letters 1595-1650* (Philadelphia 1932).

crispness which is one of the metre's characteristic virtues. I give as
a sample May's version of Lucan's passage describing Cato's austere
standards of life, a passage quoted above p. 95:

> *These were his manners, this sowre* Cato's *sect,*
> *To keep a meane, hold fast the end, and make*
> *Nature his guide, dye for his Countreys sake.*
> *For all the world, not him, his life was lent*
> *He thinks: his feasts but hungers banishment;*
> *His choicest buildings were but fence for cold:*
> *His best attire rough gownes, such as of old*
> *Was Roman weare; and nothing but desire*
> *Of progeny in him warm'd* Venus *fire:*
> *Father, and husband both to Rome was he*
> *Servant to justice, and strict honesty:*
> *For th'publike good, in none of* Catoes *acts*
> *Creepes selfe born pleasure, or her share exacts.*

May's Lucan brought him into favour with Charles I and his queen.
Encouraged by his success, he continued Lucan in English couplets
in seven books up to the death of Caesar. Then at the command of
Charles he wrote two heroic poems on English history, one on Henry
II, the other on Edward III, in 1633 and 1635. The second is inferior,
and I should say that May did not have his heart in its composition.
It is also less interesting technically, being more a historical narrative
than a poem on the neo-classic plan. But the *Reigne of King Henry the
Second, written in seaven bookes* has some merit in itself and considerable
historical interest as the next regular neo-classic epic in English after
Daniel's.

Since this poem has never been reprinted and the original edition
is rare, I will give a short account of it. At the end of the poem there
is a 'description of Henry II' in prose. Here May divides Henry's life
into five acts, thus showing that he tried to see that life as a whole.
He begins his first book in the full heroic style:

> *The second* Henry, *first* Plantagenet,
> *The first of Englands royall Kings, that set*
> *Victorious footing on the Irish-shore,*
> *And taught that warrelike nation to adore*
> *A forreine Scepter, sound ye Muses foorth.*
> *Declare how much his high Heroike worth,*
> *By stormes of spitefull fortune oft assail'd,*
> *As oft 'gainst fortunes spitefull stormes prevail'd.*

The first book then proceeds factually but in clear and sensible
couplets. As in Shakespeare's History Plays and Daniel's *Civil Wars*
there is a pervading moral motive. Henry, though a good king, broke

his oath in taking Anjou from his brother; and God punished his crime in the disloyalty of his sons. And May's recurrent motive is high prosperity constantly disturbed and regained. He recounts how Henry subdued Wales:

> *Not all her great*
> *Rough woods could yield her souldiers safe retreat;*
> *Nor could those high and craggy mountaines bee*
> *Of proofe 'gainst* Henry's *Magnanimity.*

The world is now at peace, and Enyo (the Greek version of the war-goddess) is furious. She descends into a hell very classical in some ways but inhabited by various Master-vices who are free to ascend to earth and cause private calamities but who must get Jove's permission before they can stage any great public upheaval. Enyo finds Lucifer (who is in charge of the Master-vices) and recalls with delight the civil wars in England under King Stephen. This recollection turns into a regular narrative of past events before Henry II came to the throne, in the traditional epic form. The narrative includes a fine description of Matilda escaping in the snow from Oxford. Having narrated past events, Enyo tells Lucifer that, if this peace in Europe continues, Henry will lead a crusade, to the great loss of Lucifer's empire on earth. Lucifer shows her the vices that will undermine Henry: Luxury, Ambition, Revenge, Sedition, Impiety, and chooses out Impiety (or lack of dutifulness) with which to infect Henry's sons. The first book ends with a reference to the enmity between Henry and Becket, a potential cause of strife.

In the second book May introduces the classical motive of *hubris*. Henry II rashly causes his eldest son to be crowned but without delegating any power. At the feast that follows the coronation he is wanton with excess of joy and upsets hierarchical fitness by waiting upon his son. The prince retorts arrogantly and ungratefully. But Henry was open to another weakness at this feast, for Venus herself had troubled to attend:

> *They say the beauteous Queene*
> *Of Love her selfe upon that day was seene*
> *Approching London; up cleare Thames his streame*
> *Borne on a sounding* Triton's *backe she came.*
> *The River smooth'd his face to entertaine*
> *The Queene of Love with her light-footed traine.*
> *The silver Swans ador'de her all the way,*
> *And churking did their snow-white wings display.*
> *The river-nymphes, that saw her comming, thought*
> *Some sweete atchievement now was to be wrought,*
> *That* Cupid *sure had promis'd her to see*
> *Some high exploit, some royall victory.*

The result of Venus's visit was that Henry fell in love with Rosamund. But he does not yet fall into amorous idleness. As he sleeps in a garden after the revels it is not Venus who appears in his dreams but Honour, or rather its personification in Athena, sent by Jove:

> *But Heaven was more propitious to his fame,*
> *And for Love-dreames, a Nobler vision came.*
> *Honours bright Goddesse, that heroike maide*
> *That issu'de from the braine of* Jove, *array'de*
> *In all her radiant gloryes came, before*
> *Whose face the* Cupids *fledd; her right hand bore*
> *The warlike Lance, her left* Medusaes *head;*
> *Her golden plumed Helme, both full of dread*
> *And Majesty, Such rayes of splendour yeilds*
> *As rising Phoebus, when farre off he guilds*
> *The Easterne Cloudes; her eyes wore Starry light;*
> *But fixt, not twinckling, like weake humane sight,*
> *Nor did she seeme by stepps at all to goe,*
> *Or stirring severall Limmes, as mortalls doe,*
> *But one sole motion through the ayre to make.*

Athena tells him he must conquer Ireland, granted to him ten years since by Pope Adrian. She then fulfils another part of the mechanism of the neo-classic epic by sketching the future of England for him: its loss of France, its conversion into Great Britain and Ireland, and its present felicity under Charles I.

The third book reverts to the loves of Henry and Rosamund. May invokes Erato and reminds us of the love-tragedies of classical mythology. There is a lifelike account of an old woman set to break down Rosamund's resistance. Henry is recalled from love to politics by the Pope's insisting that Becket, now in exile in France, be recalled. May inserts here another piece of past history, the previous contests between King and Clergy. And the continuance of the struggle beyond the time of the present action is hinted at in the mention of King John.

The fourth book shows Henry turning from business in France to business in Ireland. There is a fine homiletic passage on the importance of good subordinates. Ireland was largely won by their deeds. They often do the work for which kings get the credit (perhaps this passage foretells May's future choice of the Parliamentary side in the Civil War). Among Irish affairs the death of Becket is interposed. It is told briefly, with Henry's share in it minimised. To an Ireland already nearly subdued Henry goes and annexes it without needing to fight. At the feast to celebrate the annexation, which is beautifully described, Henry asks the Bishop of Dublin to tell him about the land.

THOMAS MAY

Ireland is a wonderful land, and the Bishop utters some good homiletic verse, prophetic of Dryden,[1] on nature and miracles:

> *Yet there let nought seeme strange, where we unfold*
> *The workes of him that could doe what he would;*
> *Nor let us say some things 'gainst nature be,*
> *Because such things as those we seldome see:*
> *We know not what is naturall, but call*
> *Those acts, which God does often, naturall;*
> *Where if we weigh'd with a religious eye*
> *The power of doing, not the frequency,*
> *All things alike in strangenesse to our thought*
> *Would be, which he in the creation wrought.*

Then the Bishop describes the wonders of Ireland and ends in a classical vein by painting its simple pastoral nature.

The fifth book turns from prosperity in Ireland to tragedy. Impiety, roused by Lucifer in the first book, now gets busy and stirs up Henry's sons against him. May compares this conflict to those in the houses of Thebes and Mycenae but describes the conflict itself tamely. He then recounts the domestic tragedy of Rosamund's murder by Queen Eleanor, in a way that reminds us of Drayton's treatment of the same theme.

The sixth book shows Henry at the height of his prosperity. His sons submit; peace is made; and the two Henries, father and son, make a triumphal progress through England. May recounts and applauds Henry's legal acts and particularly his institution of itinerant justices. But good fortune does not last. His eldest son, Henry, dies of sickness, another, Godfrey, from an accident in a tournament.

The seventh, and last, book repeats the poem's recurrent theme: prosperity and its sudden reversal. Henry has triumphed in Ireland and in England. He now meets King Philip in France. A prelate advises them to compose their differences and to join in a crusade. May writes eloquently of how these exploits will be more renowned in song than Troy because of the holiness of the soil on which they will be transacted. Henry and Philip agree. But their plans miscarry. Henry's son, Richard, proves unruly; and Henry and Philip fall out. Richard sides with Philip, and Henry is humiliated. The final stroke of fortune is the news that John is disloyal. Impiety has done its work. After this news Henry dies, and the poem ends. The last lines are worth quoting to show what May can achieve at his best.

> *And of so great a Monarch now remaines*
> *No more on earth, then what a tombe containes,*

---

[1] On another connection between May and Dryden see A. G. Chester in *Times Literary Supplement*, 19 July 1934. Chester states that in his translation of Virgil's *Georgics* Dryden used some hundred lines of May's translation.

Who lately ore so many Lands did reigne,
From Scotlands *bounds, to farthest* Aquitaine.
A Prince in peace of highest Majesty;
In warre too great to finde an enemy:
In power above his neighbour Princes farre;
Who, though his sword were often drawne to warre,
His owne conditions without battels wrought,
Liv'd still victorious, though he seldome fought,
And might have seem'd above the reach of Fate,
But that himselfe his greatest foes begate;
Wrong'd by that power which he had made, and crost
By those of whom he had deserved most;
Blest oft miraculously; oft againe
Beyond beleefe deprest; his various reigne
Temper'd with all extremities of Fate;
And though triumphant, yet unfortunate.

From this account it will have become clear that May's *Henry II* is more of a chronicle-poem than an epic. It includes a great many events. Nevertheless, May never abandons the effort to bind them together. Though he fails to pursue immediately the ruling subject of Impiety set forth in the first book, he reverts to it in the last three and ends on it strongly. And by repeating throughout the theme of prosperity followed by a reversal he does impose some shape. If he does not show the grade of will-power needed for the true epic, at least he shows thoughtfulness and tenacity of a sort. Nor does his poem lack variety. May inherits not only the plain and forthright narrative sincerity of Daniel but the dulcet lyrical strain of the Elizabethans as exemplified in Marlowe's *Hero and Leander* and in parts of Drayton's *Heroical Epistles* and *Barons' Wars*. Added to this is a newer vein of lucid homily, a vein suggesting the argumentative virtues of the Augustans. Thus May's deficiency is not that he was not on the right lines. *Henry II* is a praiseworthy effort and shows what its author was good for. Its deficiency is in himself. He is a minor poet. But he is a much better one than the various authors whose narrative poems Saintsbury reprinted in his *Caroline Poets*; and it is a pity that *Henry II* has not had the praise (moderate though it is) which it deserves.

Historically *Henry II* is interesting. Attempts at the neo-classic epic in the vernacular had been usual on the Continent since Trissino's *Italia Liberata*. But England held back. Daniel indeed had made a beginning and Sylvester had translated the *Judith* of Du Bartas. May gives us the second and rather more markedly neo-classic attempt in an English original. When we consider how little he had to go on, we may be the readier to give him some praise.

I have said that the theories of Ben Jonson were behind May. It is also possible that he was encouraged to classicise through the influence of Charles's French queen. Anyhow, in the court writers of this time we may expect some French influence to begin to make itself felt.

4. COWLEY

> . . . . *In the epic or lyric way . . . so elevated, so copious, and full of spirit as Mr Cowley.* (Dryden)

> *Who now reads Cowley? if he pleases yet,*
> *His Moral pleases, not his pointed wit;*
> *Forgot his Epic. . . .* (Pope)

> *Fin et subtil plus que robuste, il n'est pas taillé pour l'épopée.*
> (Jean Loiseau)

Cowley, born in 1618, was twenty-three years younger than May and ten years than Milton. But his precociousness brought his one attempt at the epic, the *Davideis*, within easy distance of *Henry II* and alongside Milton's plans for an Arthuriad. While yet at Westminster School in 1633, he published a volume of miscellaneous verse entitled *Poeticall Blossoms* and wrote a comedy, *Love's Riddle*, published in 1638 after he had left school. He entered Trinity College, Cambridge, in 1637. *Poeticall Blossoms* contained two short narratives in stanza form, and his comedy was a pastoral; and it is likely, though there is not the slightest proof, that already at school Cowley pictured himself as destined to be the English Virgil, for Virgil had written minor narrative and pastoral before going on to the *Aeneid*, and Spenser, who, it is recorded, first inspired Cowley to poetry, had followed Virgil in preparing for his epic by the pastoral of the *Shepheardes Calender*. Be that as it may, his precociousness is confirmed by Sprat, who, in his life of Cowley (attached to the 1668 collected edition of Cowley's poems and addressed to a Mr Clifford) stated that the *Davideis* belonged to his Cambridge days:

> His *Davideis* was wholly written in so young an Age; that if we shall reflect on the vastness of the Argument, and his manner of handling it, he may seem like one of the Miracles, that he there adorns, like a Boy attempting *Goliah*. I have often heard you declare that he had finish'd the greatest part of it, while he was yet a young Student at *Cambridge*.

This passage matters, because without it, Cowley not having published the *Davideis* till 1656 and having lived in France from 1644 to 1656, we should suppose him to have written under the influence of the new French neo-classic theories. Through Sprat's information we know, even if he touched up his poem in France, that he must have derived the neo-classicism that shaped it from sources available in England just before the Civil War. Before inquiring into these sources I must say a little about the scope of the poem itself.

As we have it, the *Davideis* is a fragment; four books out of the twelve which Cowley in his preface said he projected in imitation of Virgil. The whole action would have comprised the history of David, as told in the Bible, from a lull in Saul's hostility to him till the deaths of Saul and Jonathan at the battle of Gilboa. But the earlier history of Saul and David and much other earlier and later history was to be recounted episodically in the Virgilian manner. The *Davideis* is thus the first regular neo-classic epic in English on the Virgilian plan, differing from Daniel's *Civil Wars* by being on the stricter model of the *Aeneid* and not on the chronicle model of the *Pharsalia* and by using the heroic couplet and not a stanza; differing from Sylvester's *Judith* by being a full-scale epic and not an epic episode and by being an original and not a translation; and differing from May's *Henry II* by being a more set and solemn and thought-out attempt to transpose Virgil into English. The *Davideis* is in fact the first attempt in English fully corresponding to those of Trissino and Tasso in Italian, Ronsard in French, and Camoens in Portuguese: the attempt to embody the epic idea in your own tongue on the model of the greatest classical poets, Homer and above all Virgil, the ancient poets who had been entirely successful. And Cowley himself knew it to be such, for in his preface to his poems (1656) he said of it that 'there is nothing yet in our *Language* that is in any degree answerable to the *Idea* that I conceive of it'. The four extant books do not carry the action far. They recount only Saul's jealousy and attempts on David's life and David's successive searches for asylum in Samuel's philosophical college, the land of the Philistines where he is discovered and escapes by feigning madness, and the court of the King of Moab. But much more is recounted episodically: the early history of David and Saul, including an elaborate account of David's duel with Goliath and a sketch of Jewish history up to the Incarnation.

Now, so thorough a piece of neo-classicism as the *Davideis* would not be surprising in England after 1660 or from the pen of an English exile in Paris during the Civil War. How was it that Cowley, perhaps even before he entered Cambridge in 1637, decided to take with full seriousness those rules for the strict epic which in the first half of the seventeenth century, though commonly enough known, were not followed?

Like May, Cowley was certainly influenced by Ben Jonson. The question of personal contact is doubtful, but the literary contact is certain. Clarendon in his *Life*[1] says that Cowley acknowledged his

---

[1] See A. H. Nethercot, *Abraham Cowley* (London 1931) 30.

poetical debt to Jonson, and Nicholas Oldisworth wrote this quatrain[1] on the volume of verse Cowley published while still at school:

> *Ben Jonson's wombe was great; and wee*
> *Did doubt, what might the issue bee:*
> *But now he brings forth to his praise,*
> *And loe, an Infant crown'd with Baies.*

Further, it is hard to see how Ben Jonson could not have been talked about at Westminster School, or how the brighter boys there could have been ignorant of his critical doctrine. Certainly some things in the part of Cowley's own preface (1656) referring to his *Davideis* are close to Jonson's pronouncements in his *Discoveries*; and, though they were written many years after he planned the poem, they are not likely to go against the principles on which it was conceived. Jonson, as pointed out above, was for using a strictly classical form through which to express a new substance. The world was not played out; innovations were possible; but you needed ancient guidance to enable you to make best use of what the ancients had not got. Cowley in his preface expresses entire loyalty to ancient form ('the examples of *Homer* and *Virgil*, whom we should do ill to forsake to imitate others') but protests passionately that the substance of classical epic is now outworn and that Scripture offers to the poet the most superb repertory of subjects ('when I consider this, and how many other bright and magnificent subjects of the like nature the *Holy Scripture* affords and *proffers*, as it were, to *Poesie* . . .'). But for the addition of a biblical to Jonson's more generally Christian subject (he had called the deeds of Arthur the perfect epic material), Cowley's doctrine is identical with Jonson's; and Jonson may be the prompter of the neo-classicism of the *Davideis*.

J. McL. McBryde in his study of the *Davideis*[2] makes much of the influence of Du Bartas. He thinks that the remarks of Du Bartas's editor prefixed to one of the books of the *Semaines* gave Cowley his subject:

> Une Davideide vaudroit bien le cours d'une Eneide, ou le nombre des livres de l'Iliade et de l'Odyssee ensemble si quelque Chrestien et docte poete Francois vouloit y employer le temps et l'estude.

In *Judith* Cowley found the precedent for an epic both scriptural and cast in a neo-classic form. Loiseau in his long book on Cowley admits a debt to Du Bartas but considers that to Tasso more important.[3] Here again are very probable influences. Sylvester's Du Bartas was greatly read in the kind of pious home to which Cowley belonged;

---

[1] Published by Nethercot in *Modern Language Notes*, 1934, p. 158.
[2] *Journal of Germanic Philology*, ii. 454-527.
[3] Jean Loiseau, *Abraham Cowley, sa Vie, son Œuvre* (Paris 1931) 327 ff.

the high-pitched heroic tone of the *Davideis*, prophetic of the heroic play, has a strong superficial resemblance to Tasso's. There can be little doubt that Tasso's vehement advocacy of a Christian as against a pagan subject and the example of Du Bartas swayed Cowley strongly in his decision to go to Scripture for the subject of his epic.

But probably the strongest inducement to a strict neo-classic form was simple academicism. Cowley was precocious not only as a poet but as a scholar. He was the brilliant boy at school and he loved his University and College. Only his loyalty to Charles caused him to be uprooted. Thus up to the time of his planning and writing most of his *Davideis* Cowley was in a setting very different from that of the Court or the Mermaid in London, or from that of the Royalist exiles in Paris he was later to know. In his setting, imitation of the Classics was a ruling habit; and he himself wrote in Latin nearly as easily as in English. The academic setting was in itself sufficient to induce Cowley, when he made his ambitious attempt, to model himself not on Spenser but principally on Virgil. And this is indeed what he did. Not only is the general form Virgilian but the specific imitations very many. Indeed, if one were seeking more origins, the *Christiad* of Vida, so subservient to Virgil, is the most obvious place of all to go to. But, Virgil apart, definite origins are dangerous to conjecture. Cowley was using a stock of motives which had been used and re-used so often that they had become a great common academic possession. For instance, the motive of sending from Hell an emissary of mischief to disturb an existing concord is always appearing in classical or classicising epic. Its origin is in the seventh book of the *Aeneid*, but who is to say whether Cowley derived it from there or from Tasso or from May's *Henry II* or from Milton's Latin poem on the Gunpowder Plot (which may have been well known in Cowley's Cambridge) or from other possible places or from several at once? The motive was there, available, and any author was free to help himself to it. And at a University it was not only available but unusually obvious.

However, Cambridge was more to Cowley than a place of learning predisposing him, when writing in a traditional form, to a strict classicism. It was Cambridge that brought him in touch with Crashaw; and Crashaw may well have added his own persuasions to the example of Du Bartas in favour of a sacred subject. In 1623 Marino published his narrative poem on the massacre of the Innocents. Crashaw at some time translated the first book of Marino's poem, *Sospetto d'Herode*, and published it in *Steps to the Temple*, 1646, ten years before Cowley published the *Davideis*. There are passages so alike in Crashaw's translation and Cowley's epic that borrowing is certain; and the probabilities are that Cowley borrowed from his senior, Crashaw.[1]

[1] For Cowley and Crashaw see McBryde, *loc. cit.* 503-12.

From these remarks it should be clear that Cowley, being a learned poet and academically inclined, would naturally welcome a neo-classic method and that he had available a sufficient variety of example and precept to guide him in the details of his composition. He prolongs and completes the English neo-classic strain begun in Daniel, fostered by Ben Jonson, and partially practised by May. His choice of a biblical subject, however, owes nothing to these men. But it need not have a foreign origin. He had the precedent of Sylvester's Du Bartas, in particular *Judith*, various narrative poems of Quarles, and probably the *Sospetto d'Herode* of Crashaw.

Such then is the setting of the *Davideis*. I now turn to the poem itself.

Cowley was an amiable man and he had a quick, sensitive, and acquisitive mind. He was not greatly original and he did not have great staying-power. His talent was to adapt himself to prevailing fashions and in a small way to interpret and further them. He readily picked up the Metaphysical idiom, simplified the mental content that had engendered it, and in so doing gave it a wider popularity than it would otherwise have enjoyed. This acquisitive talent applied to a long poem produced a certain kind of variety. The *Davideis* reminds us of several current ways or traditions of writing. The characters of Saul and Jonathan in the fourth book[1] recall in their heightened tone the heroic strain of Tasso and of the tragedy or tragi-comedy of Fletcher, and in their set elaboration the current vogue of character-writing. Here is part of the character of Saul:

> *Such* Beauty *as great* Strength *thinks no disgrace*
> *Smil'd in the manly features of his Face.*
> *His large black Eyes, fill'd with a sprightful light,*
> *Shot forth such lively and* illustrious Night,
> *As the* Sun *beams on* Jet *reflecting show,*
> *His Hair, as black, in long curl'd waves did flow.*
> *His tall, strait* Body *amidst thousands stood,*
> *Like some fair* Pine *o'relooking all th'ignobler* Wood.
> Rest *was his* Toil, Labours *his* Lust *and* Game;
> *No natural wants could his fierce diligence tame,*
> *Not* Thirst, *nor* Hunger; *he would journeys go*
> *Through raging* Heats, *and take repose in* Snow.
> *His* Soul *was ne're unbent from weighty care;*
> *But active as some* Mind *that turns a* Sphere.
> *His way once chose, he forward thrust outright.*
> *Nor stept aside for* Dangers *or* Delight.
> *Yet was he wise all dangers to foresee;*
> *But born t'affright, and not to fear was* He.

[1] References to A. R. Waller's edition of *Poems* (Cambridge 1905). Since lines are not given, I refer to pages. For Saul and Jonathan see pp. 373 and 377 respectively.

This is not poetry of an epic pitch, but it shows Cowley's acquisitive talent and it looks forward. It recalls Livy's character of Hannibal as well as the heroic strains already mentioned and it leads on to Dryden's satirically heroic characters in *Absalom and Achitophel*. Cowley had the knack of being right on the highway of English letters. Another inherited strain is that of Sylvester's Du Bartas. At the end of the first book[1] there is a detailed account of the College, 'by *Samuel* built and moderately endow'd', where David took refuge. Here Cowley uses a more homely and familiar style, and though he fails to emulate the engaging middle-class bathos of Sylvester, he writes in his tradition:

> *The* Schollars, Doctors *and* Companions *here*
> *Lodged all apart in neat small chambers were:*
> Well-furnisht-Chambers, *for in each there stood*
> *A narrow* Couch, Table *and* Chair *of wood;*
> *More is but clog where* use *does bound* delight;
> *And those are rich whose* Wealth's *proportioned right*
> *To their* Lifes Form.

But Cowley's variety is that of quick and clever accumulation not the epic amplitude betokening wealth of mind. There can be no question of his having it in him to be an epic poet. The same thing appears in his construction. Though he adopts the form of the neo-classic epic, he lacks the architectonic grasp that gives reason to the form. For instance, he begins with a violent scene in Hell where Satan rages at the reconciliation of Saul and David, and Envy is dispatched to wreck it. Envy does indeed corrupt Saul; but as the poem proceeds, we soon forget the scene in Hell, for Cowley fails to create in the reader any sense of pervasive evil. Episode follows episode with no organic continuity.

Is then the *Davideis* quite irrelevant to the English epic in itself, and merely relevant to epic history through what it tried to do? No, for it has a certain virtue as an experiment in epic metre and style. There is of course no great authentic English epic in the heroic couplet: but there might have been, if events had given Dryden more encouragement; and Pope's Homer is a translation so great and individual as to be almost a poem in its own right. Cowley's *Davideis* marks a true stage in fitting the couplet to the task of high narrative.

We do not know how Cowley composed the *Davideis*, whether he wrote the books in the order in which they stand and whether he rewrote certain parts. But, as it is, it shows an increasing command of the couplet and a narrative skill which, stiff at first, grows suppler

---

[1] *Ed. cit.* 258.

in the third and fourth books. On the face of it Cowley learnt some of his job in the course of writing. A good example of what he could do is his description in the third book of the tapestries at the Moabite court and the song the minstrel, Melchor, sang there.[1] Among the pictures on the tapestries is the destruction of Sodom; and the fate of Lot's wife is described with consummate virtuosity:

> *Men thought, so much a* Flame *by Art was shown,*
> *The* Pictures *self would fall in ashes down.*
> *Afar old* Lot *toward little* Zoar *hies,*
> *And dares not move (good man) his weeping eyes.*
> *Behind his* Wife *stood ever fixt alone;*
> *No more a* Woman, *nor yet quite a* stone.
> *A lasting* Death *seiz'd on her turning head;*
> *One cheek was rough and white, the other red,*
> *And yet a* Cheek; *in vain to speak she strove;*
> *Her lips, though stone, a little seem'd to move.*
> *One eye was closed, surprised by sudden night,*
> *The other trembled still with parting light.*
> *The wind admired which her hair loosely bore,*
> *Why it grew stiff, and now would play no more.*
> *To heaven she lifted up her freezing hands,*
> *And to this day a* Suppliant Pillar *stands.*
> *She tryed her heavy foot from ground to rear,*
> *And rais'd the* Heel, *but her* Toe's *rooted there:*
> *Ah foolish woman! who must always be*
> *A sight more* strange *then that she turn'd to see!*

Such a passage had many virtues for Cowley's contemporaries. It was a metamorphosis in the classical style, but by being biblical it beat the ancients on their own ground. It was both lucid and witty: superior to the couplets of Donne by its lucidity and to those of Browne or Sylvester by its wit. It was packed far more closely, both in sense and in rhythm, than the sprawling periods of Chamberlayne. Here in fact was verse that a civilised modern could admire. And the moderns both admired and imitated. Above all, the great Dryden praised Cowley's poems, the *Davideis* included, extravagantly; and perhaps the greatest honour for the poem is that passage after passage in it reminds us of Dryden himself. Nor was its influence confined to Dryden, for it helped generally to mould the heroic verse of the Restoration. It is solidly behind the Heroic Play. But above all, if Dryden had written his epic he would have used a couplet that owed some at least of its qualities to Cowley.

---

[1] *Ib.* 329-31.

5. DAVENANT

The desire for a certain kind of product tends to beget the illusion that it has been produced. . . . Certain cultured contemporary verdicts on Gondibert *naturally occur to the mind.*

(C. S. Lewis)

I have found it difficult to decide where Davenant's fragmentary *Gondibert* belongs. It was a deliberate attempt at a great heroic poem, with whose rules and high dignity Davenant thought himself fully acquainted. He wrote it in exile, and in France at a time when the status of the epic was at the height and writers strove feverishly to create a French *Aeneid*. He met Cowley in France, and the *Davideis* may have encouraged him to make his own attempt at the epic.[1] His preface to *Gondibert* is one of the landmarks of seventeenth-century criticism and contains the earliest English statement of certain neo-classic epic doctrines. All these matters point to Davenant's belonging not to the beginning but to the maturity of neo-classicism. But *Gondibert* itself does not answer our expectations. It is indeed very different from what parts of its preface would suggest. It is remote from the neo-classic austerity of form common to the *Davideis* and *Paradise Lost* and destined to rule the full neo-classic age, and it is closer to the post-medieval arcadianisms of Sidney and D'Urfé and Chamberlayne. To quote Harbage:

> The real source of *Gondibert* is the wave of 'neo-romantic' themes and ideals which inundated Europe, especially France, during the seventeenth century. *Gondibert* should be viewed in relation not to historical and epic literature but to Davenant's own *Siege of Rhodes* and the heroic romances of Scudéry and her kind.[2]

Thus for all his classicising pretensions Davenant does not look forward.

As a poem *Gondibert* has no essential claim to be an epic, nor has it an important place in the history of the epic form. The alternately rhymed quatrain, put to such fine didactic and elegiac use in Davies's *Nosce Teipsum* and Gray's *Elegy*, is intolerably monotonous as the narrative measure of a long poem. As the vehicle of a highly involved plot it is especially inept. The historical importance of *Gondibert* is that it prompted Dryden to use its metre for *Annus Mirabilis*. There, applied with great skill to two plain pieces of recent history, it produced a pleasing though not specially epic effect.

This is not to say that Davenant is a negligible poet or that there are not good things in *Gondibert*. He had a tough and wakeful intellect

---

[1] See A. Harbage, *Sir William Davenant* (Philadelphia 1936) 108-9.
[2] *Ib.* 186.

and is no mean heir of the Metaphysical strain. But the kind of thing he was good at has nothing to do with the proper qualities of the epic. Here is an example of what he can do: a slightly cynical comment on the reason for the pomp of the marriage ceremony:

> Such dayes of joy, before the marriage day,
>   The Lombards long by custome had embrac't;
> Custom, which all, rather than Law obey,
>   For Lawes by force, Customes by pleasure last.
>
> And wisely Ancients by this needfull snare
>   Of gilded joys did hide such bitterness
> As most in marriage swallow with that care,
>   Which bashfully the wise will ne'r confess.
>
> 'Tis Statesmens musick, who States Fowlers be
>   And singing Birds, to catch the wilder, set;
> So bring in more to tame society;
>   For wedlock, to the wilde, is the States Net.
>
> And this loud joy, before the marriage Rites,
>   Like Battails Musick which to fights prepare,
> Many to strife and sad success invites;
>   For marriage is too oft but civil Warr.[1]

Though commonly coupled with the *Davideis* as the epic of the 1650's worth a mention, *Gondibert*, regarded as epic, is very much the less important.

[1] iii. 1. 39-42.

CHAPTER IV

MILTON

THE last great English writer I dealt with was Bunyan. To him in most ways Milton makes the most patent contrast. Bunyan was, as epic writer, confined to a single traditional theme, the Puritan myth, and he had no successor in his allegorical mode. In one way or another Milton touched nearly all the writers of epic so far mentioned in this book. And no epic writing in English after him could escape his influence. Milton is indeed the nodal figure in English epic, corresponding to Virgil in Latin. The old strands met in him; and out of him new strands emanated. I will try to describe Milton's nodal position.

First I must mention one strand that Milton did not include. In writing of Davenant I mentioned the influence of the French romance, an influence that existed in England partly through the accident of Charles I having a French wife. To French influence, so powerful in England in the latter part of his life, Milton was impervious. He never recognised that the cultural centre of Europe shifted during the seventeenth century away from Italy, and, if principally anywhither, then to France. In *Of Education* Milton showed himself doubtful of the educational benefits of foreign travel, recommending rather a knowledge of the home country. In particular he advised against travel in France.

> Nor shall we then need the *Monsieurs* of *Paris* to take our hopefull Youth into their slight and prodigal custodies and send them back again transform'd into Mimicks, Apes and Kicshoes.[1]

And in the same pamphlet he shows that he still looks to Italy for modern critical theory. He speaks of

> that sublime Art which in *Aristotles Poetics*, in *Horace*, and the *Italian* Commentaries of *Castelvetro*, *Tasso*, *Mazzoni*, and others, teaches what the laws are of a true *Epic* poem, what of a *Dramatic*, what of a *Lyric*, what Decorum is, which is the grand master-piece to observe.[2]

Milton's neo-classicism, then, is of the older Italian not of the newer Gallic type, strengthened, we may guess, by that of Jonson, which we have found influencing two of Milton's fellow-Cantabrigians, May and Cowley. It is because of these facts that I have placed this chapter at this point and not later within the scope of the neo-classic climax.

[1] iv. 290.   [2] *Ib.* 286.

But though Milton was a convinced neo-classic, though in *Reason of Church Government* he admits of modern epics fit for imitation only Tasso's *Jerusalem Delivered*, he is entirely open to the impact of other epicising works, whether or not they have a strictly classical form. And it was because he was so open that he was not at a loss when he found himself unable, through the trend of politics, to write the kind of Renaissance heroic poem he had planned. In the many kinds of long poem with which his mind was stored he had precedents enough to suffice for any changes of form he was compelled to make. Having written at length elsewhere[1] of the different epic strands with which Milton was familiar, and of the various changes of his epic plans, I will here do no more than summarise.

It seems scarcely worth mentioning that Milton was open to the influence of the classical epic. But he was so in a way denied to all his predecessors except Cowley. For these the Classics were virtually Latin. Milton could read Greek with ease; and it looks as if the *Odyssey* was his favourite epic. Along with the Classics went naturally the poets of the Italian Renaissance, whether they wrote in Latin or the vernacular. Milton knew Petrarch and Vida, Boiardo Ariosto and Tasso. From *Paradise Lost* it is clear that he knew the *Lusiad*, whether the original or the translation of Fanshawe, his contemporary at Cambridge. And along with the Italianate epic itself went the critical theories of the epic evolved in Italy. On this topic it is hard to be emphatic without being trite and repetitive. But let me here assure the reader that Milton did indeed inherit, accept, and try to put in practice all those Renaissance commonplaces about the epic which I have had to refer to over and over again: the almost mystical belief in the virtue of embodying the great literary forms worthily in a work of literature; the supremacy of the epic form, its high didactic and exemplary function; the patriotic virtue of using your native language for the great work; the need for decorum, for fitting your language and your characters to the high requirements of the epic. It is in the personal passage in *Reason of Church Government* that Milton informs us explicitly of most of these things. But here are a few lines from *Paradise Lost* that testify even more strongly to the seriousness with which Milton took the critical principles of the Renaissance. They are perfectly apt to their context yet they embody one of the commonest of all these principles: the obligation of epic and tragedy to teach through the example. The very casualness with which Milton slips in this principle proves how ingrained in him it was.

> *Say Goddess, what ensu'd when* Raphael,
> *The affable Arch-Angel, had forewarn'd*
> Adam *by dire example to beware*

[1] In the *Miltonic Setting*, 168-204.

Apostasie, by what befell in Heaven
To those Apostates, least the like befall
In Paradise to Adam *or his Race,*
Charg'd not to touch the interdicted Tree.[1]

But Milton was as open to the literature and the urges of his own country as to those of Italy. He saw himself from early years as the third great narrative poet in English after Chaucer and Spenser; and he accepted the Tudor myth as formulated by Hall and developed by the Elizabethan poets. His early poems are full of references to the early British legends of Geoffrey of Monmouth; and till the course of the Civil War altered his whole disposition towards his country he was resolved to have a British hero for his epic. As the strain between Puritan and High Church, between King and Parliament intensified, Milton gave the patriotism he inherited from the Elizabethans a contemporary turn. He added the heritage of Foxe, now brought up to date, to the heritage of Hall; and he planned to celebrate the great destiny of his country not only as confirmed by the defeat of the Spanish Armada but as establishing a holy community on earth. But this additional heritage must not make us forget that, however much Milton favoured a strict neo-classic form, Spenser supplied him with his chief poetical aliment in English.

Spenser introduces the other main type of influence to which Milton was open: the medieval. And that influence, through whatever channels, was powerful. We should remember first that Milton was brought up in the Puritan section of the Anglican church, the section which was most addicted to hearing sermons. Like Bunyan, Milton must have absorbed much medievalism from the preachers. He had read Dante; he quotes and presumably had read Langland; he had read Chaucer. He knew the medieval theme of the soul's pilgrimage from the first two books of the *Faerie Queene*. Phineas Fletcher, if no one else, taught him the allegorical fight of God and Devil for man's soul. The Morality Play lingered in the provinces; and the puppet-show of Adam, to which Milton refers in *Areopagitica*, was an inheritance from the medieval Miracle Play. Finally there was Sylvester's Du Bartas, the reading of his youth, that great repository of medieval lore, encyclopaedic and historical.

Such are the main strains of narrative poem to which Milton was open. But, naturally, he was not equally open to all of them at the same time. Before and during his Italian journey, that is just before the Civil War, he planned an Arthuriad. Because of the war he never wrote it, but from the hints he drops it is clear that it would have been a regular heroic poem in the Renaissance manner. He planned it as a patriotic poem of vast range, beginning with the Trojans in Britain,

[1] vii. 40-6.

dealing with British history up to the defeat of the Spanish Armada, and having Arthur as its hero and as the model on whom a gentleman could be fashioned. It was to be strongly Protestant in tone, like the *Faerie Queene*. Arthur would represent the genius of the English people. The form into which this vast material was cast was to be neo-classic. Milton would have improved on Spenser's form as Tasso did on Ariosto's, and his poem would have been shorter than the *Faerie Queene* and confined to a single great action. Early in the Civil War Milton planned to celebrate the deeds of his own party in freeing England from tyranny and perfecting the Reformation. Whether he could have used the projected Arthuriad for this purpose we do not know, but, whether or not, he would have borrowed freely from Foxe's great historical scheme.

But Milton was not destined to write a heroic poem in the patriotic vein of the Renaissance at all. England failed to ratify and support the heroic action of the Cromwellian extremists whom he supported and could no longer provide the central theme of his song. Foiled of a patriotic subject, too young and too Gallophobe to use the doctrine of human progress that gathered strength in the later seventeenth century, he went back behind the Renaissance and took his theme from an age in Europe that antedated the rise of militant nationalism: the old Morality theme of mankind fought over by the powers of Heaven and Hell and the old medieval theme of universal history. It may be that Milton, like any nineteenth-century critic of him, thought that he was changing a secular for a biblical theme. But if so he was also using a medieval tradition, however derived, to provide the essential shape for the bare biblical story. Adam and Eve are Everyman, ourselves; and *Paradise Lost* concerns both the mental pilgrimage of the individual and the course through historical time of the whole human race.

Milton in making a medieval subject central in his epic did not forfeit the rest of his heritage. Apart from the richness of classical allusion he modelled his plot on classical epic and above all on the *Odyssey*. Just as in the *Odyssey* the two large themes of Odysseus and Telemachus on their travels unite on Ithaca, so in *Paradise Lost* the forces of Heaven and Hell converge on Paradise for their culminating struggle. And as the motive of conflict narrows to the domestic struggle between Odysseus's family and Penelope's suitors, so the conflict in *Paradise Lost* is turned from the cosmic to the domestic.[1] Nor did Milton's rejection of nationalism mean that he rejected the rest of what the Renaissance stood for. Adam going out in naked dignity to meet Raphael is a Renaissance figure; Satan is partly a Renaissance tyrant. Though Milton, like Bunyan, could not use the

---

[1] For confirmation and added details see letter from D. S. Robertson on the *Odyssey* and *Paradise Lost* in *Times Literary Supplement*, 4 May 1940.

historical mythology of Foxe, he is essentially of the Renaissance through his Protestant individualism.

Milton, then, did not cramp or starve himself by his surprising recourse to an old medieval theme. On the contrary he added what was for him a new element to those he had originally selected for the substance of his epic: an element of greater moment than the patriotic one he was constrained to reject. Also he showed daring and original-ity both in bringing in so much and in blending it in an unheard of way. If he made *Paradise Lost* nodal by assembling so much in it, he was very much himself in the way he did so.

But Milton did more than select and blend the things he inherited. He was revolutionary as well as traditional. And first in his verse. Not all readers perceive how unconventional Milton was in choosing to write *Paradise Lost* in blank verse, how violently he went against his age in so doing. A masterpiece is bound to create its own standards and conventions, and for later ages to realise that these did not exist before it was published is almost impossible. We cannot help thinking of the masterpiece as *being* the norm while all the time it *created* the norm, doing thereby an original, maybe a daring thing. Now when Milton embarked on *Paradise Lost*, one of the conventions was that whereas blank verse had been proved the correct metre for the drama, the epic demanded the added dignity of rhyme. The con-vention had been created by the Continental writers: Ariosto, Camoens, and Tasso had used a stanza for their would-be epics. Then Spenser invented his own special stanza, based on the eight-line stanza of Ariosto, for the *Faerie Queene,* which quickly was accounted the one English poem to approach the epic status. The great mass of narrative poetry between Spenser and Milton was all either in coup-lets or in one among a variety of stanzas. But whatever the differences, all these poems agreed in adding to verse the dignity of rhyme. Now this was not a light matter. The idea of propriety was paramount in the seventeenth century. Just as a labourer wore one kind of dress, a merchant a second, a clergyman a third, and a nobleman a fourth, so different types of poetry were required to be presented in different verbal and prosodic forms. To deny rhyme to the epic was as bad as taking a sword away from the dress of a nobleman. Now Milton knew that when he was most serious, when he had to draw on all the re-sources he commanded, he could not write in a medium that imposed a restraint on the ardour that was proper to him. His genius was the reverse of epigrammatic, he needed elbow-room; to put the matter in terms of rhetoric, he needed the long period. Now rhyme, creating one kind of finality, does do something to abbreviate the period; and Milton knew that he must discard it. But it was a daring, even a defiant thing to do, an enforced piece of rebellion. He did, however, con-sider convention sufficiently to give notice of what he was doing and to defend his action in a short prefatory note to the verse. That he speaks so confidently is no sign that he was not uneasy at flouting convention: rather the reverse.

Milton's other revolutionary act was to domesticate his crisis. In the preface to the ninth book of *Paradise Lost* he gave notice of this by attacking the traditional heroic theme common to all the great classicising epics and by claiming that those of 'Patience and Heroic Martyrdom' were superior. But opinions differ on where the crisis of the poem occurs, and it is useless to say that Milton domesticated it unless I can persuade the reader that I am right in putting it where I do. Having written at length on this topic elsewhere,[1] I will only summarise my conclusions: conclusions which go beyond the crisis and concern the general interpretation of the poem. The usual assumption is that Eve's eating the apple is the point up to which all previous acts lead and from which all sequent action descends. This, as I think wrong, assumption goes back at least to Dryden, who said in 1697 that Milton would have a better claim to have written a genuine epic, 'if the Devil had not been his hero instead of Adam, if the giant had not foiled the knight and driven him out of his strong-hold to wander through the world with his lady errant'. There you have that undue narrowing of the poem's scope to the triumph of Satan through the episode of the Fall: a narrowing that has become traditional and still continues to close the eyes of many readers and critics to the poem's full significance. It is true that Milton himself gave countenance to this narrowing by naming the poem as he did, though I sometimes think that he was being ironical and meant us to think of *Lost* as in inverted commas. But Dryden's witty contention that the giant foiled the knight is quite at odds with the poem itself.

Paradise Lost in its grand outlines is founded on a simple irony. And we need not be surprised, for irony is one of the qualities Milton gives to God the Father himself. When near the beginning of the third book the Father looks down and sees Satan 'coasting the wall of Heav'n' and about to penetrate the universe, he addresses the Son as follows:

> *Only begotten Son, seest thou what rage*
> *Transports our adversarie, whom no bounds*
> *Prescrib'd, nor barrs of Hell, nor all the chains*
> *Heapt on him there, nor yet the main Abyss*
> *Wide interrupt can hold?*

One critic accused Milton here of inconsistency because when in the first book Satan raised himself from the burning lake Milton tells us he did so only through the 'will and high permission of all-ruling Heaven'. Of course there is no inconsistency, for in the passage quoted

---

[1] In *Studies in Milton* (London 1951) 8-52.

the Father speaks ironically, adopting Satan's own foolish assumption that he raised himself from the lake and set out to ruin mankind on his own initiative and responsibility alone. If we grasp God's ironical words at Satan's expense we may be the readier to believe that irony is central to the whole plot. The irony is as follows. Satan succeeds in tempting mankind to transgress God's commandment and he believes that his success can have only one result: namely that as Satan and his fellows have brought ruin on themselves by disobedience, so must Adam and Eve do by theirs. But he has made a false comparison. Satan's sin was self-motivated, that of Adam and Eve was partly motivated from without. For Satan there is no hope, because he is corrupt throughout his whole being; for Adam and Eve there is hope, because theirs was not the whole responsibility. And in the end humanity finds itself able to attain an inner paradise better than the paradise they must give up; Dryden's knight and lady errant have in fact the key to a better stronghold than the one from which the giant has driven them out. Such is the irony at Satan's expense. There is the further irony that Adam and Eve are as mistaken as Satan about their ultimate fate. When, exhausted by their quarrels and bereft of their pride, they become reconciled in very simple human companionship and fellow-feeling, they are unaware that they are following the promptings both of Heaven and of the residue of good thoughts that have survived the Fall and that by so following they have attained salvation: just as the Ancient Mariner blessed the water-snakes unawares, not knowing that thereby he had broken the evil spell.

The consequence of this fundamental irony is that the weight of the plot is put not on the mere episode of Eve eating the apple in the ninth book but on the whole process of temptation, Fall, the judgement of the Serpent Adam and Eve by the Son, the corruption of the world through the entry of Sin and the consequent despair of Adam and Eve, and then, unexpectedly evolved out of all these varied and vast happenings, their mutual reconciliation, their penitence before God, and their salvation. These happenings occupy the whole of Books Nine and Ten. Such a weighting of the plot is of the first moment. The fall of Eve, adequate in a larger ironic context, is nowhere near weighty enough, as described by Milton, to be the centre of the poem, the point to which all earlier happenings lead and from which all subsequent happenings derive. But read Books Nine and Ten as a unit, treat the events after the Fall not as appendices to a completed climax but as a sequence leading up to the real climax in man's regeneration, and you find them a brilliantly diversified and massive area of high poetry. It may be asked whether the climax as thus described will really bear the weight put on it any more than the traditionally assumed climax, the eating of the apple. Can this purely human scene of man and wife forgetting their quarrels, coming together again, and confessing their sin to God stand the tremendous test? First, it can be retorted that Milton undoubtedly intended it to do so. Near the end of the poem there is a conversation between Adam and Michael which follows on the vision of future world history Michael has given to Adam for his instruction. From its all-important position and its intensely concentrated and earnest tone it is clearly crucial to the poem's meaning. Adam has at last learnt wisdom, and this is his statement of some of the things hard experience has taught him:

> Henceforth I learne, that to obey is best,
> And love with feare the onely God, to walk
> As in his presence, ever to observe
> His providence, and on him sole depend,
> Merciful over all his works, with good
> Still overcoming evil, and by small
> Accomplishing great things, by things deemd weak
> Subverting worldly strong, and worldly wise
> By simply meek.

This is high moralising verse that would be irrelevant in a narrative poem if it did not repeat in its own abstract form what had already been transacted in concrete, dramatic action; and it points precisely to the poem's true climax where by their 'small' decent action Adam and Eve 'accomplish great things' and in their apparent 'weakness subvert' the apparently 'strong' machinations of the Prince of this world. The pair's noble self-extrication from the slough of inertia and despair (matching Satan's self-elevation from the burning lake) is Milton's version of the patience which in the opening of Book Nine he declared was more heroic than the traditional epic deeds of martial prowess. Whether Milton not only intended to make this part of the poem his climax but succeeded in making it a worthy one can only be decided by the verdict of competent readers; but to me at least the account of Adam's black despair, his ferocious and cruel repulse of Eve, her persistence, Adam's softening towards her, their coming together, Eve's still distraught state of mind and inclination to suicide, Adam's strong and comforting words, and their final resolution to confess their sins to God is true to the fundamental simplicities of human nature and composes one of the most moving dramatic episodes in literature; it can bear a very heavy weight.

Well, if Milton made the reconciliation of Adam and Eve his crisis he was doing something very bold and very new. Two analogies may help us to understand his act. The French Impressionist painters were innovators in subject-matter as well as in technique. They forsook officialdom and war for ordinary folk and the ordinary scene whether in town or country. Shakespeare in the course of his Histories and Tragedies moved from an official type of historical play to a type where people are first and politics second. Milton in moving from the official heroic epic to domestic life did much the same. But working in a more solemn tradition than that of the Elizabethan drama he showed the greater daring.

Not that he was without ancient precedent or contemporary encouragement. His favourite epic, the *Odyssey*, though it may have as its climax the killing of the suitors, contains close by the most lovely domestic scenes, including the meeting of Odysseus and Penelope. Just as Collins was probably glad to have as metrical precedent for the great innovation of his *Ode to Evening* Milton's translation of Horace's ode to Pyrrha; so Milton was probably glad to have in reserve the Odyssean precedent to satisfy any critic who attacked his departure from the heroic norm. Nearer to his day he had the precedent of the homely scenes in Du Bartas's *Judith* and their even more homely guise in Sylvester's rendering: a precedent particularly strong in view of this poem's correctly neo-classic form. More powerful was the general puritanism of which Sylvester's homeliness was a part. Though Milton was a natural aristocrat, though in *Areopagitica* he mocks the careful merchant with his pastor to see to his religion by proxy, and in *Paradise Lost* the citizen who is robbed by a cat-burglar, he was the son of a scrivener and he doubtless approved of the Puritan's high standard of family life. And though Taine may have been ridiculous in turning Milton's Adam into the heavy Puritan husband, he may have perceived a small portion of the truth. Anyhow, in abandoning wars and officialdom for the religion of the individual and for the domestic, Milton could have been sure of moral support from a section of the community in his own day and of even wider prospective support from Addison and his kind. Adam has yet another side to him that not only appealed to the practical bent of the Puritan but that looked forward. Once he knows that God will spare him and Eve after the Fall, he begins to have ideas: practical ones of how to make life on earth more tolerable, plans for the future. He has in fact, among many others, the Robinson Crusoe bent. And this may have helped to endear him to the eighteenth century.

My main conclusion so far is this. In the story of the epic in England Milton is both a great inheritor and a great innovator. With his vast learning he had all the best of the European past to draw on; with his reverence for that past he was careful to draw on it freely; but the way he arranged his borrowings was all his own, and when he needed to perpetrate startling innovations he did not hesitate to do so.

In describing Milton's position in the history of the English epic I have not escaped implying some judgements of value also. It is now time to pass explicitly to these and to ask how successfully Milton does in fact fulfil these epic plans which he so deliberately pursued.

There is no need to talk of Milton's distinction of style in *Paradise Lost*. Some distinction is allowed even by those who like him least. But there is the further question whether this distinction is such as to cope with all the variety of experience and emotion that the true epic includes. It is a question particularly pertinent today when the technique of assuming a variety of voices is in favour. For instance, in *Ulysses* and the *Waste Land* Joyce and Eliot seek to convey their sense of life's variety by sharp alternations of style or of imagined speaker. To a generation used to so self-declaring a technique the quieter one of variety within uniformity may appear tame or simply pass unnoticed. There are virtues in both methods. It is exhilarating to be smitten by the abrupt turn; it is peculiarly satisfying to detect a subtly understated one. An example of such understatement occurs in the passage of Spenser (quoted above p. 269) when into a smooth and apparently little rousing descriptive passage he inserts one lady's catty remark about the other lady's looking good enough if you did not eye her too closely. Here the reader's process of mind includes the thoughts, *could he have meant it? yes he must have done*, a process which has certain advantages over the more immediate apprehension. Milton, framing his epic in the great classical tradition and loyal to the contemporary doctrine of decorum, was committed from the first to a considerable dignity of style throughout. No requirement of variety must be allowed to break that dignity. His problem then was to indicate variety within limits. And it was most acute where he was the least conventional and traditional, where there was least dignity inherent in the subject-matter; above all where in his culminating scenes he introduced the domestic and the comic. It is not certain that he solved the problem. If I may be personal for a moment, I have to confess that I had known *Paradise Lost* well for many years before I perceived fully the comedy mixed with the domestic tragedy of Adam's dispute with Eve in the ninth book that led to their going different ways on the morning of the temptation. It would seem at first sight that, fearing for his dignity, Milton toned down his comedy too much. Against this we must set the extremely powerful reluctance of readers to allow Milton any variety outside the solemn and the sweet. It was through sharing this reluctance that I was so long in unstopping my ears to other tones of the Miltonic music. And could this initial prejudice be removed, I believe that Milton's variety need not wait very long to be detected. I will give two examples of the kind of comic or dramatic touch apt to be overlooked in the formal setting that he is committed to observe. In the argument between the human pair about joint or separate gardening Adam was unwise enough to say that it would be safer for Eve to stay at her husband's side. She regarded this as a slight; and Milton describes her air, and makes her begin her answer, in a dignified style that readers might consider inimical to comedy:

> *To whom the Virgin Majestie of* Eve,
> *As one who loves, and some unkindness meets,*
> *With sweet austeer composure thus reply'd.*
> *Ofspring of Heav'n and Earth, and all Earths Lord*—[1]

but a few lines later he is able by a small manipulation of rhythm to particularise the scene astonishingly and to create realistic comedy within the dignified epic framework. Eve says

> *But that thou shouldst my firmness therfore doubt*
> *To God or thee, because we have a foe*
> *May tempt it, I expected not to hear.*

The emphasis on *thou* and *my* in the first line, the carefully measured but taut evolution of the words create the picture of Eve, a little flushed and having her wits very much about her; knowing that Adam has put his foot in it, and resolved to exact full penance for his mistake.

Or take some lines from one of Satan's flattering speeches to Eve when he tempts her to eat the apple. He has been describing his survey of the beauties of the universe after his pretended eating of the forbidden fruit and suddenly switches his talk on to Eve herself with:

> *But all that fair and good in thy Divine*
> *Semblance, and in thy Beauties heav'nly Ray*
> *United I beheld; no Fair to thine*
> *Equivalent or second, which compel'd*
> *Mee thus, though importune perhaps, to come*
> *And gaze, and worship thee of right declar'd*
> *Sovran of Creatures, universal Dame.*[2]

Here is Milton using language in a way perhaps a little more inverted than usual, conscientiously fulfilling his obligations to be dignified and not casual; and it is only too easy to read the lines as a piece of Miltonic dignity and no more. Actually, it would take far too long to set forth all the shades of implication that reveal themselves to a close and leisured perusal. But they would, most of them, come under the dramatic act of Satan watching Eve out of the corner of his eye (he pauses after *Divine* in the first line to see how his words are getting home), assessing just how much flattery she can take, and deciding at the end (with Disraeli) that he can safely lay it on with a trowel.

In sum, if we can only begin unprejudiced and can really open

---

[1] ix. 270-3.   [2] ix. 606-12.

ourselves to all Milton's effects, we shall find that within the rhetorical ceremony to which he was committed there is a rich range of stylistic effect.

Through what I have just said about Milton's range of style and what I have said earlier about the different strains he inherited I have already implied something about his variety of substance. I will add a little about the freedom of choice his religious subject gave him. This will be to argue in a different sense from what was once commonly thought: that Milton succeeded not through but in spite of his Genesis-derived theme. It is difficult if not impossible to know what Milton thought of the Puritan myth (I mean the doctrinal not the historical myth) that he must have heard expounded over and over again in church from early years and that in a way he accepted.[1] Although he gave up the doctrine of predestination that was usually a part of it, he retained his allegiance to the all-sufficiency of Scripture and to the Protestant scheme of election, vocation, and so on. The political party to which he was devoted was essentially Puritan in religion. When he found that the country at large was slipping away from the righteous policy on which it had entered and that this defection made a patriotic subject impossible for his epic, he could so naturally, one thinks, have turned in passionate compensation to the form of religion, so ingrained in him, that dwelt on the wickedness of the many and the militant virtue of the few; he could in fact have chosen for his verse epic the theme Bunyan used for the *Holy War*. Foiled of his political aspirations in this world, he could among other things have hinted at a better fate for his own party, and a worse one for his enemies, in the next. And with Dante to help him he might have achieved a powerful work. But Milton never fitted into the genuine Puritan frame. Not only did he give up predestination, but he interpreted the authority of Scripture with a liberalism that was quite unpuritan, and he showed himself closer in temper to Cambridge Platonism than to Puritan orthodoxy.

Now, strange as it may seem at first, Milton left himself greater freedom by choosing a myth from *Genesis* as his skeleton-theme than if he had chosen a less myth-tied religious allegory. The spiritual progress as defined by the Puritans may stand in a way for any possible human pilgrimage; but it was too precisely charted to be ideal for this purpose and too inbred to reach out to all sorts of secular concerns. But the myth of *Genesis* strikes deep into the human mind, while one myth cannot but evoke the memory of others. There is never the least sense of strain when Milton crowds his story with ancient mythology, medieval romance or superstition, and the details of contemporary exploration. All these would have been much

[1] I have recorded some conjectures in this topic in my *Studies in Milton*, the section on theology and emotion in Milton's poetry.

less appropriate in a plot that was essentially more doctrinal and less primitive and mythical.

Nevertheless, Milton was, among so much else, loyal to the Puritan myth in *Paradise Lost*, but without some of the usual distressing adjuncts. He contrives matters so well that in reading we simply do not notice that Adam and Eve are at once their biblical selves, and Everyman traversing the stages of his spiritual journey; certainly better than Bunyan did with his Mansoul, which has the same double significance.[1] In one matter Milton's plot helped him in his obligation to recount the Puritan myth. Since Adam and Eve were unique, there could be no question of *election*. Or rather their very creation was a substitute. So one item in the long Puritan list was dispensed with. But Milton faithfully includes all the others, though sometimes with a tact which should surprise those who dislike the forthright dogmatic statements of God the Father. As to *vocation*, the Son called Adam and Eve to him when after pronouncing sentence on them he uttered a mitigating prophecy and showed pity by clothing them with skins. There was as yet no Mosaic Law, but Adam in his remorse after the Fall concludes that by the law of nature he is condemned and has no hope. He expresses what Bunyan expressed through the episode of Mr Legality. The Fall did not extinguish every trace of good in the pair's hearts, and their reconciliation was due in part to themselves. But their reconciliation to God and their *justification* depended on God's grace and Christ's expiatory sacrifice. The process is described in a beautiful passage at the beginning of the eleventh book:

> *Thus they in lowliest plight repentant stood*
> *Praying, for from the Mercie-seat above*
> *Prevenient Grace descending had remov'd*
> *The stonie from thir hearts, and made new flesh*
> *Regenerate grow instead.*

Sanctification comes to Adam through the didactic force of the visions shown him by Michael. He is a saved man by the end of the poem. And the state of glory after death is foretold more than once.

I will cite a single instance of how skilfully Milton satisfied a Puritan requirement and yet transformed it in the process. Puritan doctrine insisted on a great violence of repentance in the process of conversion, and in particular on a great profusion of tears. Such excessive display of sensibility was, we may be sure, distasteful to Milton. He solved his problem by duly making Adam and Eve weep, when they first ask God's pardon,

---

[1] It has been confidently stated and confidently denied that Bunyan knew and drew on *Paradise Lost* in his *Holy War*. I doubt if the matter has been thoroughly sifted. I fancy a thorough sifting would reveal a really large number of resemblances, though not necessarily of a kind to prove an actual debt.

with tears
Watering the ground, and with thir sighs the Air
Frequenting,

but also by making those tears the dramatically natural result of all the antecedent emotions. We have only to recall one of Bunyan's less happy characters, Mr Wet-Eyes, sent from Mansoul to plead with Emanuel, to see how masterly Milton subordinates a particular requirement to the poetic effect.

In setting forth the medieval Everyman theme through the myth of Adam and Eve Milton's Protestantism secured him one advantage. In medieval Catholic story Adam and Eve went after death to Hell, where they waited till Christ redeemed them by his death, and harrowed Hell to pull them out of it. Not committed to this story, which for Protestants brought with it the pernicious doctrine of Purgatory, Milton could contrive the salvation of Adam and Eve while they were still in Paradise, through Christ's promise of his future redeeming death, thereby tightening his action.

Thus it was that the bare myth of *Genesis* was actually propitious to Milton's urge to include within his poem a vast variety of substance.

I do not need to say much about Milton's will-power and the way he shaped his epic. There is no question of deficiency here. But I must recall the bearing that the position of the poem's crisis has on the shape. It has been usual to confine the greatest glory of *Paradise Lost* to the first two books. For this there is the simple reason that only a proportion of readers stay the course and read the whole poem, and that the parts they read when they are freshest, namely the first, will tend to make the deepest impression. But, even if we rule out the partial readers, so long as the crisis was confined to the temptation and the eating of the fruit, some disappointment with it was bound to be felt, and the complaint, covert or declared, must have existed that the crisis was feeble compared with the promise of the opening. To grasp the nature and extent of the crisis restores the balance. An analogy with Spenser may help. The episode of the Bower of Bliss, occurring earlier in the *Faerie Queene* than that of the Garden of Adonis, was both more read and given an exaggerated self-importance. Spenser was credited with, or accused of, an unadmitted sympathy with the Bower's sensualities much as Milton was with his Satan. Thanks mainly to C. S. Lewis we now know that the Garden of Adonis matches and condemns the Bower of Bliss, for it is the home of creative sensuality, while the sensuality of the Bower of Bliss was deceptive and barren. Each episode gains in the light of the other, but the Garden of Adonis becomes now the culminating one. Just so the regeneration of Adam and Eve, when allowed its full circumstantiation, matches and condemns the actions of Satan in the first two books. These actions gain rather than lose poetically by being related to the poem's crisis, while through that relation they fall into perfect place in the organisation of the whole.

Lastly, there is the question of the choric character of *Paradise Lost*; and the answer is not simple. In the generally transitional period of history through which Milton lived and especially in the divided state of his England he was debarred from being the undoubted voice of his age. Spenser, as I asserted, may have had his personal centre outside the ordinary human norm, but when he surveyed and interpreted the life outside him it was a life that represented the English majority; he did in a true sense speak for his age. Milton certainly wished to do the same; and his early writings, verse and prose, show him on the way to success. His verse shows him aware of the different social strata; and he pictures them as a complete and ordered hierarchy. Even when he attacked the clergy in *Lycidas*, the abuses of the Church not the Church itself were the target. And the reforms he dreamt of were intended to heal as well as to purify. From one of his Latin poems, from his letters and academic exercises, and from his later autobiographical passages we know that he was on the side of the optimists in the current dispute on whether the earth was in its last stage of decay, that he was one of the moderns who admired Bacon, and that he believed in a possible betterment even now of man and of society. He yearned after such a betterment for its own sake; and for his self's sake he wished both to promote it by his pen and to celebrate it as his country's spokesman. On looking back we can perceive that Milton's hopes were vain and that the country was actually more divided in the years before the Civil War than appeared. But Milton was one of a majority in being so deceived and should not be blamed. As the Civil War proceeded, reforming energy cooled, or was split into a number of forms with most of which Milton was out of sympathy. He had no belief in levelling projects, and if he came to favour an aristocratic government on Venetian lines he did so less because he was anti-Royalist than because he distrusted the Stuarts, while in doing so he was merely repeating a way of thinking that had a highly respectable Renaissance ancestry. In brief, most of the contemporary institutions or trends of activity he had believed in and might have been prepared to celebrate had in some way been corrupted. He had proposed to celebrate a Christian king in Arthur; and the Stuarts proved tyrannical and in exile found a home, spiritual as well as physical, in Catholic France. The small band of Cromwellian leaders he could have celebrated were spoilt for epic purposes by the lack of support they commanded in the country at large. His dreams of human progress, whether general or in the form of a holy society filling England, were rudely annihilated by the course of events. Baconian ideas of scientific progress were partial and pallid compared with his dream of religious progress and they were in greater part the property of his political opponents and most alive in France, the country for which he had least taste. In fact, events could seem to have taken a cruel delight in uniting to thwart Milton's desire to speak for his England as Spenser had done for the England of Elizabeth.

But it is possible to be choric in more ways than one. It is best of course for a poet to speak for a way of thinking that extends before and after him but which enjoys its most powerful and unanimous phase in his own day. Camoens, who suffered many personal misfortunes, was lucky in the span of his life. He was central to the adventurous expanding impulse of the whole Renaissance and he was the present voice of all his countrymen. But it is also possible to achieve the choric character necessary to the epic through expressing great and wide impulses that were at their height at periods just a little removed from the time of the man who expresses them.

Now Milton, although he could not celebrate his own day as its epic poet, was close to it and at least bore its imprint. And this closeness ensures for him a certain essential authenticity which keeps sweet and living his choric rendering of impulses that belonged more properly both a little before and a little later. What those impulses were is obvious enough, but still they have to be described.

First, he expressed better than any English writer the religious humanism of the English Renaissance in its Protestant form. With less aristocratic bravery and in a more reflective spirit he said about mankind the kind of things Sidney said in *Arcadia*, things which were the common intellectual or spiritual property of many men: for instance that man is a great adventurer in both body and spirit with the world all before him. There, self-responsible but with Providence his guide he has great scope for action good and bad. But if he is to act well he must put the state of mind before the result. The main characters in *Arcadia* all face the most unhappy results of their actions, but they all succeed in thinking that their minds' integrity matters more; Adam and Eve learn the same lesson through seeing what happens when they go against it. The greatest scope of the human spirit in deed and in thought, regulated by the rule of Christian humility and the subordination of that scope to the soundness of the state of mind—that is the kind of doctrine, truly choric because once so widely held and so genuinely vital, that *Paradise Lost* contains. At no time in history was this doctrine convincingly borne out by the actual deeds of men; but it was a little less remote from fact in Sidney's day. Milton had the more difficult task to believe in it, but he succeeded all the same. He was compelled to divest it of any political application, but he conveyed the doctrine in its general human form and in so doing he made his poem choric. I could give other instances of how Milton expressed the generally held doctrines of a slightly earlier age, but I think this sample serves to make my point.

It is hard to speak of the anticipatory choric quality of *Paradise Lost* without being unfair to Milton. Just as eighteenth-century Miltonic blank verse derives from only a fraction of Milton's prosodic genius, so when he speaks for certain sides of the eighteenth century he does so with only a fraction of himself. And that fraction is very different in its true context from what it is in isolation. Nevertheless, as Havens[1] has shown us, Milton was very widely read in the eighteenth century, especially by the middle classes. *Paradise Lost* was so popular partly through the adventitious reason that in pious families it was authorised Sunday reading along with the Bible and the *Pilgrim's Progress*. But this would not explain all Milton's popularity, and a large part of the reason for it was that many people then felt that he spoke for them. Through what portion of his utterance did he do this? I have given some kind of answer in what I have said already about the Puritan support Milton could have counted on when he substituted a domestic for a heroic setting in which to site his crisis in *Paradise Lost* and about the Robinson Crusoe side of Adam's character. Milton was a natural aristocrat and he had no objection to pomp in itself, but such a disposition was checked by the powerful proviso that there must be no nonsense about the pomp and the aristocracy. As he grew older the side of him that valued simplicity, candour, and no nonsense grew stronger. His position comes out clearly in the description of Adam going out to meet Raphael:

> *Mean while our Primitive great Sire, to meet*
> *His god-like Guest, walks forth, without more train*
> *Accompani'd then with his own compleat*
> *Perfections, in himself was all his state,*
> *More solemn then the tedious pomp that waits*
> *On Princes, when thir rich Retinue long*
> *Of Horses led, and Grooms besmeard with Gold*
> *Dazles the croud and sets them all agape.*[2]

I have already cited this description as the expression of feelings peculiarly proper to the Renaissance, but it also looks forward to the modified Puritan sobriety of the pious middle classes in the eighteenth century. It is of course unfair to separate the component parts of such a passage and to fasten on one part to the detriment or ignoring of the other. But it is the kind of unfairness that every age and most readers perpetrate. People insist on getting out of the objects of their study the things they want. Anyhow, eighteenth-century readers found in Milton a genuineness, a forthrightness, a reasonableness, an honest

---

[1] R. D. Havens, *The Influence of Milton on English Poetry* (Cambridge, Mass., 1922).
[2] v. 350-7.

warmth that answered their own liking for these qualities. However partial and unjust a finding this is, it points to another kind of choric quality in *Paradise Lost*.

It is by thinking of the way *Paradise Lost* reaches both back and forward that we can do justice to its great scope. We see that it could speak for a bigger range of group opinion than if it had been better attuned to its immediate setting. Further, even if it was denied that attunement, it did through its Januslike character speak for the whole century to which it belongs.

I turn finally to *Paradise Regained* only to give reasons for passing it over. How this poem should be labelled is doubtful. None of the traditional categories fit it. And the epic category fails to fit it most conspicuously. It is too short, confined, and simplified for the necessary epic variety and it quite lacks choric character. This is not to condemn the poem, which has its own perfection, but it is to assert that it has no place in the present context.

CHAPTER V

CLARENDON

It was in the peaceful reign of Augustus, *after the conclusion of their long Civil Wars, that most of their perfect* Historians *appear'd. And it seems to me, that we may expect the same progress amongst us. There lye now ready in Bank, the most memorable Actions of Twenty years: a Subject of as great Dignity, and Variety, as ever pass'd under any Mans hands: the peace which we injoy, gives leisure and incouragement enough: The effects of such a Work could be wonderfully advantageous, to the safety of our Country, and to* His Majesty's *Interest: for there can be no better means to preserve his Subjects in obedience for the future, than to give them a full view of the miseries, that attended rebellion.*

(Thomas Sprat, *History of the Royal Society*, 1667)

The historian is not at liberty to dispose his fable as he would wish. If, in fact, the mountains travailed and a mouse was born, his narrative must be content with the anticlimax.

AFTER Raleigh, Clarendon is the only English historian of the seventeenth century I need to take into account. As C. H. Firth[1] pointed out, Burnet, the other great historian of the century, had a better sense of historical motivation, believing steadily in the divine ordering of the evolution of Protestantism and referring the details of history to this grand belief. But his style, clear and dry, has no special dignity and disqualifies his work as epic from the outset. Clarendon's style, uneven as it is, is warm and ample and conveys the sense of immediate, urgent action; plainly equal to great events and to great actors on the stage of history. It has qualities apt to the epic, and as it were demands that the achievements of which it was the instrument should at least be examined.

Unfortunately the achievements themselves suffer from defective organisation. Clarendon devoted some years of his life to his great historical work: but he did not construct it as a whole from the beginning; instead he patched and improvised. One of the chief Royalist members of the Long Parliament and one of King Charles's ministers during the early years of the Civil War, he had as good a first-hand knowledge of events as any man, up to the decisive victory of Parliament at Naseby in 1645. He then fled from England and began his history of the war and its causes in the spring of 1646 in the

---

[1] *Essays Historical and Literary*, 207-9.

Scilly Isles, continuing in Jersey till the spring of 1648.[1] Doubtless he thought of himself as the English Thucydides: the man who was close to the events and who wrote of a great phase of history even while that phase was in process of transaction. But he sees events in the light of contemporary not classical piety. The rebellion arose from man's sin and God's punishment; it is a classic instance of the recurrent rhythm of history, for he finds

> all the bulk of misery to have proceeded and to have been brought upon us from the same natural causes and means which have usually attended Kingdoms swoln with long plenty, pride, and excess, toward some signal mortification and castigation of Heaven[2]:

a sentiment echoed, it is interesting to recollect, by Clarendon's political adversary, Milton, at the very same time, in his Latin ode to Rouse. But though in his preface Clarendon professed to see history in this philosophic spirit, he wrote his narrative primarily for the instruction of his master, and his peculiar talent was for seeing events from near by and not for generalising and distancing them. He did indeed hope that current events would be shaped into an end, when the country's sins should be expiated and peace restored; and he did seek the causes of the rebellion in past events: thus making some show of setting the things he had experienced or learnt of at first hand in a larger context. But, when it comes to the fabric of the history, that show counts for little. The country had, as it were, contracted a terrible disease. Clarendon described the progress of the disease and wanted to discover how it was caught, but he was not really interested in the general nature of disease of which this was a specific example. Why should he be, when he was fresh from the events themselves and full of their excitement and urgency? The point is that his first instalment of history, written in Scilly and Jersey, was by the circumstances of its composition primarily a matter of reporting and hence un-epic.

Clarendon wrote no more history for twenty years. In 1667, out of favour with his second master, Charles II, he fled to France and between 1668 and 1670 wrote his autobiography from boyhood to the Restoration. This work contained much history, but it differed from his first historical fragment by dwelling more on the characters of men and less on the sequence of events. In the next year, 1671, Clarendon re-read his historical fragment and then decided to construct a third work through the processes of conflation and of addition. He transferred to the original fragment the relevant character-sketches from his autobiography; he used the historical portions of his autobiography to bring his story down to the Restoration; he added portions to join and to complete the two components;

---

[1] For a summary of how Clarendon composed his historical work see Firth, *op. cit.* 114 ff.

[2] *History of the Rebellion*, ed. W. D. Macray (Oxford 1888) i. 2.

and he called the whole the *History of the Rebellion*. He also prolonged his autobiography beyond the Restoration, seeking to justify his career as Lord Chancellor under Charles II.

Clarendon's *Life*, little known or read compared with his *History of the Rebellion*, is shorter and less given to detail and hence the more likely to have an artistic shape. But it is more personal and less detached and hence remoter from a great objective literary form. It is on his *History of the Rebellion* that Clarendon as possible epic writer must be judged. That Clarendon in building up this book meant to compete with the great historians of antiquity cannot be doubted. If he originally saw himself as the English Thucydides through his closeness to the events he narrated, he sometimes throws in an epigram to show that he had his eye on Tacitus also. Speaking of Sir John Coke, he said that 'his cardinal perfection was industry and his most eminent infirmity covetousness'.[1] There is even the chance that when he inserted the great character-sketches into the original portion of the history written in Scilly and Jersey he had an eye to the way Homer conducted the *Iliad*. As Homer began with the origin of the Greeks' trouble in the quarrel of Agamemnon and Achilles, so Clarendon began with the fatal influence of the Duke of Buckingham in getting Parliament dissolved and alienating men's affections from the King. And just as Homer put his catalogues of forces and descriptions of leaders in the pause after the main motivating action had been recounted, so Clarendon introduced his characters of the main actors after he had finished his account of the origins of the rebellion. Not only does Clarendon up to this point construct homerically, he resembles Homer in endowing his characters with much power over events. Men for him are not the mere victims of events; it is rather the virtues and the vices of great men that cause things to happen thus and thus. If men are victims, it is of the vices of their most powerful and responsible representatives. Thus in the first shapings of his plot and in a kind of heroic significance he imparts to his characters Clarendon does show an epic quality.

Nevertheless, Clarendon's *History of the Rebellion* cannot bear sustained comparison with those renderings of history that we have found to reach closest to the epic: the history of Herodotus, the first books of Xenophon's *Anabasis*, and the *Lusiad* of Camoens. First, Clarendon fails to maintain the Homeric shape of his composition. The mass of fact he has to convey loses form and direction. He is indeed horrified at the stupidity that allowed events to take the turn they did, and his sense of events being transacted on a great stage before the eye of God is both magnificent in itself and an inheritance from an earlier habit of thought. But he fails to give any meaning to the mass of vivid detail he includes, lacking any overriding or

[1] *Ed. cit.* i. 81.

permeating philosophy of history. This failure comes out most of all in his lack of sympathy with his opponents. That these could have been animated by any large principles he cannot see. In particular he is blind to the amount of genuine religious fervour that inspired the Roundheads. Seeing only their extravagances and violence and hypocrisy, he misses the positive values for which they stood. Herodotus and Xenophon are passionately patriotic, but they recognised the grand scale of the Persian empire; Camoens could be both for and against the expedition of Gama to India. Clarendon is more the partisan, and, in so far as he is, fails in the mental amplitude proper to the epic. The Restoration was a grand consummation, and yet of what was it a consummation? Clarendon has no sufficient answer. He possesses no clear conception of the way history evolves, after the fashion of Foxe before and Burnet after. And this lack is fatal to a general epic effect.

Clarendon is a great writer, but in the present context the most that can be said is that he showed epic promise at the outset and that he gave an epic impression in some places.

CHAPTER VI

THE APEX OF NEO-CLASSICISM

NEO-CLASSICISM is an apter word than its inventors intended. Meaning at the beginning no more than the practice of imitating the ancients in modern days, it easily acquires a connotation that is generally true of the neo-classic ages. The notion of *new* more often than not implies that of *better* (unless it did, public houses would not boast of being under entirely new management); and a principal mark of the achieved neo-classic age was that it believed, for all its reverence for ancient achievements, that it had gone or could go beyond them. In the Renaissance men imitated the ancients with joy and admiration rather than in competition. Their spirit was that of discoverers rather than of critics; and antiquity was not the only thing they had discovered. But this spirit could not last indefinitely; and it went stale, or was crossed by doubts. Certainly it became more critical, both of self and of the things it had enjoyed or discovered. The process of what has recently been called the Counter-Renaissance[1] set in. But moral disillusion and the critical spirit could not destroy the sheer fact of certain achievements beyond those of antiquity and the prospect of more to come. Those nations and those men to whom these achievements were most congenial and emotionally attractive were bound to be touched by a new thrill and a new certitude; and they were the true neo-classics. Not that they repudiated antiquity; it was only the extreme revolutionaries, a tiny minority (like a few of the Levellers in England), who could dream of doing so. Allegiance to it was overwhelming. Yet the leading spirits believed that through that necessary allegiance you could go beyond the very authority to which you owed it.

I noted traces of this neo-classic treatment of antiquity in Ben Jonson. But he was exceptional in his day. The first half of the seventeenth century in England belongs mainly to the reaction from the Renaissance; and the true neo-classic age does not begin till 1660, and then partly through the influence of France. Doubtless, without France, the factors making for neo-classicism already mentioned, Tasso, Bacon, and Cowley (not Milton, for his influence came later) would have promoted a partial neo-classicism at the Restoration. But the full neo-classic spirit was French, and it was only through French influence that it could approach plenitude in other countries. Thus in explaining the circumstances governing the neo-classic epic in England I shall have to begin with conditions in France.

---

[1] Hiram Haydn, *The Counter-Renaissance* (New York 1950).

THE APEX OF NEO-CLASSICISM

What most determined the nature of the neo-classic age in northern Europe (where the greatest vitality resided by the middle of the seventeenth century) was a new temper in France at the century's beginning. Out of the weariness and miseries of the wars of religion emerged a new desire for discipline and stability accompanied not by a weary and sterile acquiescence but by a resurgence of vitality. After the confusion and unleashed passions of civil war men demanded discipline; after the lushness and amplitude of French Renaissance literature men demanded a principle of simplicity. But it is best to use a Frenchman to state a generalisation about the temper of his own country at the beginning of the seventeenth century:

> C'est pour moi, je l'avoue, une source toujours nouvelle de plaisir et d'admiration que de voir comment, en France, dès les premières années du dix-septième siècle, tous les efforts convergent par des chemins divers vers un même idéal, celui de la raison, maîtresse du monde. Les rois de France, leurs ministres, les poètes, les philosophes, et mêmes ces femmes qu'on méconnaît trop sous le nom de 'précieuses', tous s'appliquent à reconnaître, et à réaliser dans la vie de l'Etat et dans celle des individus, ces lois de logique qui régissent l'univers entier. . . . Mais ce que j'admire plus que l'idéal lui-même, c'est l'*effort* commun et spontané de tout un peuple; après une longue crise politique, religieuse et intellectuelle, après avoir reçu de tous côtés des éléments nouveaux, ce peuple se rajeunit, se ressaisit, prend conscience de sa destinée et crée dans tous les domaines une œuvre qui lui assure une suprématie séculaire.[1]

It is the last sentence that English readers should most take to heart, for they find it hard to believe that the critical austerities of Rapin and Boileau crown an epoch not of restriction but of vitality; that they represent not timidity or lethargy but effort.

Of this general striving in France after simplicity, codification, the common aim, the universal principle of reason, or however you like to put it, literary theory and in particular that of the epic was a part. Deriving the bulk of their critical creed from the Italian commentators on Aristotle and encouraged in their codifying task by a parallel movement in Holland (mentioned above in connection with Ben Jonson), the French critics sought to reduce it to shape and system. It does not matter in this context who began the process, but Brunetière and other French critics make Chapelain's preface to Marino's *Adone* a landmark in it. Here are found an intense awareness of the literary kinds with their own separate rules, the doctrine of verisimilitude that condemns improbabilities and monstrosity, that of the consistency of characters throughout a work, the social utility of poetry with its principal aim of bettering mankind, the imitation of

[1] E. Bovet, *La Préface de Chapelain à l'Adonis* in *Heinrich Morf Festschrift* (Halle 1905) 19.

classical antiquity and an allegiance to Aristotle not because there is anything sacrosanct about the ancients but because they could never have stood the test of time had they not founded their poems or their rules on a universal principle of reason. It is this emphasis on the social function of literature and this adjustment of the ancients and reason that form the chief novelty and strength of French neo-classicism. By making literature social the French knit it into their general scheme of life. By adjusting the ancients and reason as they did they escaped too extreme a subservience to the past and left open the possibility of progress. Speaking of the rule of the Unity of Time, Corneille wrote in his *Discours des Trois Unités*:

> Beaucoup déclament contre cette règle, qu'ils nomment tyran-nique, et auroient raison, si elle n'étoit fondée que sur l'autorité d'Aristote; mais ce qui la doit faire accepter, c'est la raison naturelle qui lui sert d'appui.[1]

In so writing he was speaking for most of his age. You must not treat Aristotle as a dictator. He was usually right, for his rules rested on the larger authority of reason. But he could be wrong (Chapelain on one point disagreed with him), and, if he could, his successors might improve on him. And such possible improvement was a kind of pledge of possible progress generally.

When at the beginning of this chapter I spoke of the sheer fact of certain things achieved during the Renaissance I was of course referring to natural philosophy. I shall need to say more on this topic, for the discoveries of the scientists have their bearing on the epic, but I can do so more conveniently when I get back to England. In this place, before I turn to specific theories of the epic, it remains to point out how the philosophy of Descartes answered and reinforced the adjustment between antiquity and modern literary production I have just described. The theological innovation in Descartes was not that he attempted to destroy any part of orthodox doctrine; it was that he invented a new route into orthodoxy. Unsupported authoritarianism did not justify dogma; the further support of human reason was needed. It turned out that human reason did in fact substantiate orthodox conceptions of God to (as was then thought) the great benefit of orthodoxy. Nevertheless, to put what had been primarily a matter of revelation in terms of the dictates of the human mind did imply a new kind of freedom and the possibility of further discoveries. In theory, if Descartes had found orthodoxy and reason at odds, he was free to modify orthodoxy. In the same way the most advanced neo-classic critics in France (of whom Boileau was one) were free to disagree with and improve on Aristotle if they found any conflict between his rules and the reasoning powers of man.

[1] *Works*, ed. C. Marty-Laveaux (Paris 1862) i. 113.

Although the classic French writings on the epic, Rapin's *Réflexions sur la Poétique d'Aristote*, Le Bossu's *Traité du Poeme épique*, and Dacier's commentary to his translation of Aristotle's *Poetics* belong to the end of the century (1674, 1675, and 1692 respectively), the doctrines they embody had been recognised and uttered soon after the foundation of the French Academy. They can be seen for instance in the prefaces that Georges de Scudéry wrote for his sister's romance *Ibrahim ou l'illustre Bassa* (1641) and for his own epic *Alaric* (1654), or in the *Dissertatio peripatetica de epico Carmine* (1652) of the Jesuit, Pierre Mambrun. The doctrines themselves derive from Aristotle and his Italian commentators, but the codifying zeal with which they are presented is new. In his earlier preface Scudéry wrote: 'Chaque Art a ses regles certaines, qui par des moyens infaillibles, menent à la fin que l'on se propose.' Human frailty may lead to failure, but there *cannot* be anything wrong in the method itself and it is unique. Further, this passage illustrates a thing of which I spoke, in the very first pages of this book, as characterising the temper of mature neo-classicism: the almost religious adoration of an abstraction. The rules exist in a kind of heaven of Platonic essences, and the poet's aim is to exemplify them in his concrete work of art. In that same heaven are the essences of the various literary kinds, and it is the poet's task, having chosen his kind, to give it a concrete embodiment in a poem as near to its divine prototype as human frailty allows. In the preface to his *Alaric* Scudéry says the same kind of thing but enters into more detail. Here are his main points. The epic must have a matter of the greatest potentiality, a form to answer this greatness, and the finest ornamentation. Better a true than a feigned subject: hence his Alaric, a historical personage, and therefore more easily to be believed in. A pagan subject is no longer admitted, and the best is Christian without being scriptural. Such a subject admits of machines and the marvellous (see Tasso). But you must have a pervading allegorical theme in addition to the historical for the purpose of the highest instruction. His Alaric is not only the historical king but the soul of man, and his capture of Rome symbolises the victory of reason over the senses. The modern epic must also contain scientific lore, but in a less crude form than in the schools. Alaric himself exemplifies the rule of the greatest potentiality of matter, for he combines the virtues of the previous great epic heroes. But wealth of substance can be over-done, and if you overdo it you risk becoming too much of a historian, like Lucan. In choosing a historical subject the epic poet does not tie himself to literal truth. His law is that of verisimilitude. 'J'ay plus consulté ma raison que Procope.' Unity of action is necessary; and everything in his epic converges on the capture of Rome. He had already in his preface to *Ibrahim* insisted on the now accepted epic Unity of Time of a single year. There are three kinds of style, high, middle, and low; and the first is proper to the epic. But the other two can be admitted in a small way.

Scudéry's prefaces contain matters of debate: whether you may admit 'machines', whether a scriptural is better than a merely Christian subject, exactly which previous epics make the grade. And his own preferences are not necessarily those of the majority. But in general he is true to the full Gallic neo-classicism; and to his substance later critics add little. But Scudéry is less a critic than the retailer of critical commonplaces on the epic; and later and greater writers can put the same commonplaces more effectively and enhance their significance by inserting them into a larger context. The French critic who does this pre-eminently is Rapin in his *Réflexions*.[1] The year 1674, when Boileau's *Art Poétique* was also published, has the best claim to be that in which neo-classicism combined maturity with still potent vitality; and it is in Rapin's work that these two qualities are most eminently combined. There is something to be said for all the main critical systems throughout the ages, but these vary in effectiveness according to the talents of their exponents. In the hands of its greatest exponents every critical creed takes on grace, dignity, and reasonableness. In Rapin are found all the stock neo-classic commonplaces, and yet in him they are not commonplaces but living principles never separated from the works of art to which they apply. There is nothing like Rapin in English. Rymer in translating his book and adopting his principles coarsened them and destroyed their point. Dryden only half accepts Rapin's creed and is at his best when he escapes from it. Rapin really believed in the doctrines of his age; it will be through them and not through any other that literature will flourish. And his tone is magisterial, not like Scaliger's through his knowledge of his own learning and his comfortable assurance of the strong academic snobbery of his age, but through the sheer conviction and urgency of his beliefs. When Rapin repeats the age's commonplace that the epic 'c'est l'ouvrage le plus accomply de l'esprit humain', he does so in full realisation of the phrase's implications. The epic requires the most formidable combination of human qualities. It requires all knowledge and not mere imagination but something much more, genius. And genius is both a divine, undefinable gift and a sublime art of control far transcending the simple *furor poeticus*.[2] And when he condemns poets for not rising to the true epic height he does so not in any querulous spirit as if he were failing them in an examination but through his insistent sense of the vastly exacting standards of the greatest of all literary forms. Petrarch, Ariosto,[3] Du Bartas, and Statius[4] all failed: the first two because they

---

[1] Father René Rapin, *Réflexions sur la Poëtique d'Aristote et sur les Ouvrages des Poëtes anciens et modernes* (Paris 1674).

[2] 2-11.   [3] 24.   [4] 39.

did not heed the rules, the other two because they thought verbal grandeur sufficient without structural grandeur. But at the same time he makes you feel that they were very great spirits for all their failure. Yet he cannot pretend that they did not fail or that success is to be attained by anyone who cannot compass one great design in which there is the secret co-operation of all the parts. Only Homer and Virgil have so far succeeded, though of the moderns Tasso has come nearest success.[1] Neo-classic though he may be, Rapin's *Réflexions* joins with Tasso's *Discorsi* in giving the noblest expression of the true epic temper. Rapin's enthusiasm for the epic form is the more remarkable if we bear in mind that between 1650 and 1670 French poets produced as many as forty epic poems,[2] all of them failures.

In turning to English opinions and expectations of the epic let me recapitulate the kinds of pressure France, then the headquarters of European culture, exercised. There was the urge to simplicity and codification; the confidence that the moderns could extend or even improve on the achievements of antiquity; the mystical belief in the virtue of the abstract epic form and the passionate hope that by keeping the rules of the epic game a poet had a chance of repeating the miracles of Homer and Virgil.

According to Spingarn[3] it was Tassoni in the tenth book of his *Pensieri Diversi* (1612) who set the model for the controversy about ancient and modern learning and art that occupied Europe through the seventeenth century, and who prompted men to consider the whole problem of human progress. The great influence of Bacon, however, gave the problem a rather different form in England. Bacon indicated an experimental method which promised grand and revolutionary results beyond the dreams or capacity of the ancients; and his faith, accepted by the liveliest thinkers of the Restoration, helped to dictate the form which any true epic of that time was bound to assume. Apart from Bacon, there was conducted early in the century a controversy on whether or not the world was falling into decay. In 1616 Godfrey Goodman published his *Fall of Man*, arguing on the pessimistic side. In 1627 George Hakewill published a reply to Goodman, *An Apologie of the Power and Providence of God*. Goodman retorted, and his retort together with Hakewill's comment on it were appended to the third edition of *An Apologie* in 1635.[4] The dispute was largely theological, but Hakewill included a survey of concrete attainments in which he thought the moderns could compete

[1] 41.
[2] See T. W. Russell, *Voltaire, Dryden, and Heroic Tragedy* (New York 1946) 1.
[3] *Critical Essays of the Seventeenth Century*, i. lxxxix.
[4] Victor Harris's *All Coherence Gone* (Chicago 1949) expounds the controversy and its subsequent history and influence in the seventeenth century. For the relation of science and the doctrine of progress see Richard Foster Jones, *Ancients and Moderns: A Study of the Background of the Battle of Books* (Seattle 1936).

with or surpass the ancients. Du Bartas, Tasso, Spenser, and Sidney can compete with Homer and Virgil; modern mathematics, astronomy, and anatomy have surpassed their predecessors. Not to speak of the superiority of the Christian to the pagan religion. The controversy between Goodman and Hakewill is best known through Milton, who in a Latin poem professed himself on the side of progress. And naturally it was to the Puritan reformers, the followers of Foxe in his conceptions of Protestant evolution, that the general doctrine of progress would be most likely to appeal in the years before the Civil War and in the first years of the Civil War itself. It is true that Milton, while at Cambridge, shared Bacon's hostility to the scholastic philosophy and supported his plea for including positive studies such as history in the University curriculum and that later he was an educational reformer, but he did not share Bacon's thrill at the prospect of scientific discovery and of the yoking of nature to the commands of man. The new world whose prospect dazzled him in the early days of the Civil War was theological and political. And the kind of progress he dreamt of as possible in the great poem he planned at that time was religious. He decided to write it in English in order to serve his country,

> that what the greatest and choycest wits of *Athens*, *Rome*, or modern *Italy*, and those Hebrews of old did for their country, I in my proportion with this over and above of being a Christian, might doe for mine.[1]

By *Christian* Milton meant here not just that but 'Protestant Christian belonging to that portion of the Protestant Church in England now in process of a more perfect reformation than had ever before been effected'. With the Restoration Milton's belief in progress, theological and political as it was, was either destroyed or made relevant only to a future which he personally knew he would never see and the nature of which it was vain to predict. About the time when Sprat was writing his history of the Royal Society and Dryden his *Annus Mirabilis*, Milton in a letter to Peter Heimbach protested that he had virtually no country. The recent advances of science now left him cold.

The true Baconians, then, the men who were emotionally touched by the prospect of dominating nature, were not the Puritans but the Royalists; and Bacon came into his own in 1660, when the Royalist party was dominant once more. But I must go back a little before speaking of Sprat's *History of the Royal Society* (1667), a work that shows better than any I know something of the temper that must have animated any authentic epic in the first few years of the Restoration and to a lesser degree for the rest of the century. When after the battle

[1] From *Reason of Church Government*. *Works*, iii. i. 236.

of Naseby some of the Royalists took refuge in France, they were in a peculiarly receptive state of mind. Their own country had taken a fatally wrong turn; and France had emerged from her own troubles into a period of certitude and had plainly much to teach her unfortunate neighbour. Two pieces of criticism written by English refugees in France show the influence of that country and make something of a bridge between the old England of before the Civil War and the new England of the Restoration. These are Davenant's *Preface to Gondibert* (1650) and Hobbes's *Answer* (1651). Davenant's *Preface* is transitional. It purports to deal with the epic, but the last portion is mainly a defence of poetry in general. The tenour of that defence is antique and Sidneian and not modern and Gallic; and the prose style of most of the treatise is antique in its cumbrous syntax and frequent obscurity. But in parts the *Preface* is modern. It echoes the doctrine that the epic is the supreme form, as any writer might have done before or after him, but it is austere in its selection of poets who have succeeded in the epic. They are Homer, Virgil, Lucan, Statius, Tasso, and Spenser.[1] And Spenser is defective. Where a modern poet can improve on an ancient is in discarding the supernatural. This element could be excused in the ancients but is now inept, and Tasso was to blame in letting it in. Davenant here is with the French and their preference for what is reasonable. When he speaks of the epic in terms of politics and of the aristocracy he does not thereby go beyond Sidney and the Renaissance generally. But when he says that the epic must serve the needs of the ruling class and must deal with the passions proper to that class and then goes on to say just what those passions are he codifies in a more modern and probably in a French manner. I conjecture that he looked to France also in the most interesting part of his general defence of poetry.[2] His general thesis there is that the 'four chief aids of government' are religion, arms, policy, and law. Between them there is usually rivalry and strife. Poetry is something that can mitigate such strife. It steals insensibly into men's minds, softening them and making them more reasonable. If the epic educates the ruling class, the drama is suited to educating the populace. Poetical drama and music too, by amusing the populace, make it more amenable to the absolute ruler. In a way Davenant here repeats the old Renaissance notion of poetry fashioning the ruler. But he is modern and Gallic in picturing the polity to which poetry applies as closely knit and powerfully centralised.

I have assumed Gallic influence in the way Davenant joins poetry and politics. But that of his friend Hobbes is also possible here. As

[1] Davenant's *Preface* and Hobbes's *Answer* are conveniently accessible in Spingarn, *Critical Essays of the Seventeenth Century*, ii. Discussion on correct epics and need to avoid the supernatural, pp. 1-7.

[2] Spingarn, *op. cit.* ii. 44-7.

one passes from Davenant's *Preface* to Hobbes's *Answer* it is hard to realise that Davenant was the younger by eighteen years. There is nothing Sidneian about Hobbes's disposition or opinions, and his dry style, though lacking the elegance that marked the best Restoration prose, is much more reasonable and lucid than most prose of the middle of the century, Davenant's most emphatically included. For all his years, he is much more modern than his friend in both substance and style. Hobbes's *Answer* is short, but it contains or hints at a great deal. It resembles Davenant's preface in its dislike of improbabilities in the epic, but it somehow makes that dislike more weighty, treating it not only as a separate point but as part of a wider creed of materialism and curtailment. Not only does Hobbes dislike the improbabilities of Ariosto and Spenser; he repudiates the poem in prose, meaning presumably the Heliodoran tradition of the prose epic. In fact, he insists on things keeping strictly to their ordained limits. He loves arbitrary categories: there are six kinds of poetry and no more; or if there are more they are too trivial to count. Judgement and fancy are the creative agents of poetry; and of the two, judgement matters most because it builds the essential groundwork. Truth bounds history, verisimilitude poetry. That of course is a stock sentiment, especially dear to the French under the terms *vrai* and *vraisemblable*. But Hobbes makes one feel he means it in his own way.[1] In heathen days the bounds of verisimilitude were different; and strange fictions, corresponding to the extravagances of their religion, could be allowed. But in these days of enlightened religion (and Hobbes lets us think that religion has become more reasonable in very recent years) those bounds are narrower. 'Beyond the actual works of nature a Poet may now go; but beyond the conceived possibility of nature, never.' Hobbes has an austere standard of decorum (which he establishes by ruling out a number of what he calls 'indecencies') and of the epic form. Admiration is the emotion of the epic and that of mirth is ruled out. Hobbes rated the ancient poets very high. You cannot say that he was on the side of the moderns against the ancients. But he makes it perfectly clear, though he never states it, that his own age has progressed far beyond its immediate predecessors, replacing irregularity by order and a wanton fancy by a self-conscious reason. He looks right forward to the Royal Society and its historian.

At this point I refer the reader to Basil Willey's chapter on the heroic poem in a scientific age, the tenth in his *Seventeenth Century Background*.[2] The connecting theme of this book is the change that took place in what was meant by *truth* in the seventeenth century. All the trends of thought so far mentioned in this chapter would be specific details in this general change. Men decided to think of truth purely

[1] Spingarn, *op. cit.* ii. 62.   [2] London 1934.

in terms of fact verifiable by the reason, refusing to admit what was merely congenial to the imagination. Hence such a detail as that just mentioned in Davenant and Hobbes: the dislike of supernatural fictions in the modern epic. Willey attributes Milton's abandonment of the subject of Arthur for a scriptural to the pressure of scientific standards of truth. The pagan fictions were exploded, the historicity of Arthur was questioned; but Scripture at present was free from the probings of the critics, its truth was not impugned. Milton could find in the Bible both a varied mythology and an area of truth beyond the disintegrating processes set going by the scientists. It is very probable that Milton was thus prompted, but this is not to deny that in addition he turned away from all national subjects because he thought his country had failed in its duty.

For the changes in the status of poetry caused in the early years of the Restoration by the new scientific spirit and by the new conception of truth, Willey rightly considers Sprat's *History of the Royal Society* (1667) very important evidence. Sprat spoke for a large and influential body of opinion, the dominant opinion indeed of his age. Davenant and Hobbes had objected to 'fictions' in modern poetry. Sprat makes it especially clear of what larger movement of thought such objection was a part. He and his mental kin thought that until recently life had been conducted largely by the rule of inherited principles which had no foundation in truth. Learning had been clogged by false assumptions, daily life degraded by superstitions. And the cure is the new experimental science that brings man face to face with truth:

> *Experimental Philosophy* will prevent mens spending the strength of their thoughts about *Disputes*, by turning them to Works . . . it will cure our minds of *Romantic swelling*, by shewing all things familiarly to them, just as large as they are . . . it will free them from *perversity*, by not permitting them to be too peremptory in their *Conclusions*.[1]

The pagans had stocked nature with imaginary powers and the Middle Ages had made the mistake of continuing the belief in their existence. And it was the poets who had originally been responsible for disseminating the false doctrine:

> The *Poets* began of old to impose the deceit. They to make all things look more venerable than they were, devis'd a thousand false *Chimaeras*; on every *Field*, *River*, *Grove*, and *Cave*, they bestow'd a *Fantasm* of their own making: With these they amaz'd the world; these they cloath'd with what shapes they pleas'd; by these they pretended, that all Wars, and Counsels, and Actions of men were

---

[1] *The History of the Royal Society of London,* the second edition corrected (London 1702) 341.

administred. And in the modern *Ages* these *Fantastical Forms* were reviv'd and possess'd *Christendom*, in the very height of the Scholemens time: An infinite number of *Fairies* haunted every house; all Churches were fill'd with *Apparitions*; men began to be frighted from their *Cradles*, which fright continued to their *Graves*. . . . All which abuses if those acute Philosophers did not promote, yet they were never able to overcome; nay, even not so much as King *Oberon* and his invisible *Army*. But from the time in which the *Real Philosophy* has appear'd there is scarce any whisper remaining of such *horrors*: Every man is unshaken at those Tales at which his *Ancestors* trembled: The cours of things goes quietly along, on its own true channel of *Natural Causes* and *Effects*. For this we are beholden to *Experiments*.[1]

The case here is not that of putting up Science in opposition to Poetry but of rescuing poetry from its false and anachronistic accretions. There were various excuses for the fictions of the classical poets; there could be none for the poets living in the age of the new enlightenment. To introduce fictions *now* was to ignore the most precious acquisition of the new age. I am not denying that the new doctrines of truth may have been harmful ultimately to the status of poetry, as Willey argues; but those who applied them to poetry might do so in the belief that they were doing it the highest service.

Of these, Sprat was one. Far from curtailing letters, experimental science, he thought, opened out new places for them. Near the end of his book (part 3, section 35) he enlarges on the topic: *Experiments will be beneficial to our wits and Writers*.[2] Here Sprat seeks to prove that though experimental science has rendered some of the material of letters useless it has on a balance enlarged it very greatly. The whole passage expresses so well the positive hopes for new writing in the age of the Restoration (and indeed in most of the Augustan age in England) that I had better give a summary of it to serve as the setting of my subsequent chapters. Sprat's thesis is that 'there is in the *Works of Nature* an inexhaustible Treasure of *Fancy*, and *Invention*, which will be reveal'd proportionably to the increas of their *Knowledge*'. He goes on to review the main sources of creative writing. First, there are the fables and religions of the ancients. These are outworn (as he has already explained) and have served the poets long enough. They must be abandoned. 'Civil history' comes next, a source of writing not yet fully exploited in England and full of promise. The manners of men have already been well exploited, witness the high quality of the drama in England. The Bible provides inexhaustible material, which 'may be us'd and allow'd without any danger of prophaneness'. Logic and Metaphysics make poor material for writing; but 'the *Wit*

---

[1] *Ib*. 340. [2] *Ib*. 413 ff.

that is founded on the *Arts* of mens hands, is masculine and durable', and as these arts may be improved by experiment so may they offer a more abundant material to the writer. Finally Sprat comes to his climax, the works of nature; and it is here that the modern writer can find the most enlarged scope and can best go beyond the ancients:

> The defect of the *Antients* in *Natural Knowlege* did also streighten their *Fancies*: Those few things which they knew, they us'd so much, and appli'd so often, that they even almost wore them away by their using. The sweetness of Flowers, and Fruits, and Herbs, they had quite devour'd: They had tir'd out the *Sun*, and *Moon*, and *Stars* with their Similitudes, more than they fancy them to be wearied by their daily journys round the *Hevens*.

Natural philosophy will soon put this poverty of matter right through experiments:

> The comparisons which these may afford will be intelligible to all, because they proceed from things that enter into all mens Senses. These will make the most vigorous Impressions on mens *Fancies*, because they do even touch their *Eyes*, and are nearest to their *Nature*. Of these the variety will be infinite.

Thus the new standard of truth and the new experimental science not only will not damage letters but will present a vast new scope to them.

Finally Sprat asks what are the prospects of his own country, and he is optimistic. 'There are very many things in the *Natural Genius* of the *English*, which qualify them above any other for a *Governing Nation*.' Corresponding to this genius there is scope for writers to guide it aright by their works. And we must here bear in mind that the literary form specifically apt to the governing class was then considered the epic. Not only did Sprat express a general confidence in his country; he mentions too an instance of how high it could rise. About a third of the way through his book, at the end of the twentieth section of the first part, he says that his work has been interrupted by the year of plague and fire and he pauses to comment on these disasters. After pointing to the wonderful fortitude of the people in resuming normal life after the plague and in bearing the loss of all their goods through the fire, he goes on thus:

> Yet still there is one *circumstance* behind, which may raise our wonder higher: and that is, that amidst such horrible *ruines*, they still prosecuted the *War* with the same *vigour*, and *courage*, against three of the most powerful States of all *Europe*. What Records of Time, or Memory of past Ages, can shew us a greater testimony of an invincible and heroick *Genius*, than this, of which I now speak?

that the sound of the *Heralds* proclaiming new *Wars*, should be pleasant to the people, when the sad voice of the *Bell-man* was scarce gone out of their ears.[1]

Sprat could have had no doubt in his mind that the time was propitious for a patriotic epic.

He was not the only person who thought thus, for the plague, the fire, and the war, the three things that brought out the high temper of the English people, were the subject of Dryden's first attempt at the epic, *Annus Mirabilis*. Indeed, this poem reads almost like an answer to Sprat's implicit challenge. Anyhow, the point to which I have brought neo-classic ideas in general and those on the epic in particular, namely the patriotic optimism of Sprat, leads naturally to my next chapter, on Dryden.

But before I begin it let me recapitulate, for Dryden was open to all the movements of thought I have touched on in this chapter. These were the urge to simplify, to ground the fundamental truths not only on inherited authority but on the reasoning powers of the human mind; the belief generally in verifiable truth with its specific effects, namely the repudiation of fictions in literature and the pursuit of scientific experiment; and arising from all these a new way of thinking about past and future. Great as had been the achievements of classical antiquity, necessary as it was to copy them and not the fallacies and meaningless obscurities of the scholastic ages, the new age had proved that it could go beyond the ancients in some things and there were strong hopes of going further in the future. And in addition there was the thought at the back of men's minds that all these movements were especially strong in the neighbouring land of France.

[1] *Ib.* 121-2.

CHAPTER VII

DRYDEN

The Virgil *and the* Fables *seem to-day to stand astride of the interval between* Paradise Lost *and Pope's* Homer.

(Mark Van Doren, *The Poetry of John Dryden*)

Dryden's creative energy was diverted from his great ambition, to write an epic, and dissipated in a multitude of miscellaneous tasks. . . . In spite of his love for literature and his desire for fame in it, he was not heroic enough to achieve what he thought should be his greatest work.

(L. I. Bredvold)

DRYDEN indicates what Englishmen thought about the epic in the last forty years of the seventeenth century and what form it would have assumed had there been a poet able to rise to it. But he also achieved in some of his own writings the nearest approach to the epic that there was. From this statement I exclude Milton and Bunyan because, though their great narratives fall within the age, they do not represent the main course of it, which had to do with the restored monarchy.

I do not need to add much here to what I said in my last chapter, for, however licentious English practice was, the age of the Restoration did accept the main tenets of French neo-classicism as correct theory. Rapin, Boileau, and Le Bossu were quickly translated into English and were highly respected; and Dryden stated categorically that, though English creative writing was superior to the French on account of its vigour, French criticism was supreme. In fact, what I said about French neo-classicism holds good generally for English. I will limit myself to indicating how English critical opinion (for which Dryden can mainly speak) regarded the epic form. Even so, I cannot avoid some repetition.

A main article of faith in the years under consideration was the supremacy of the epic form. The Earl of Mulgrave spoke for his age when in his verse *Essay upon Poetry* (1682) he placed the epic poets on the summit of Parnassus with all the rest on the slopes below:

> *By painfull steps we are at last got up*
> *Parnassus hill, upon whose Airy top*
> *The* Epick *Poets so divinely show,*
> *And with just pride behold the rest below.*
> *Heroick Poems have a just pretence*
> *To be the chief effort of humane sence,*

THE ENGLISH EPIC AND ITS BACKGROUND

A work of such inestimable worth,
There are but two the world has yet brought forth,
Homer *and* Virgil.[1]

Dryden, whether describing the nature of Heroic Plays, or speaking of the epic in the abstract, or commenting on Virgil, iterates his belief in the supremacy of the epic form. It is 'the most noble, the most pleasant, and the most instructive way of writing in verse, and withal the highest pattern of human life' and 'undoubtedly the greatest work which the soul of man is capable to perform', to give but two instances of his testimony. Further, Dryden shows that he accepts other portions of neo-classic theory concerning the epic. In the second of his prefaces, that to *Annus Mirabilis*, he says that the proper object of the descriptions of heroic poetry is to 'beget admiration', and much later in his *Dedication of Examen Poeticum* prefixed to the *Third Miscellany* (1693) he says that 'to cause admiration is the proper and adequate design of an Epic Poem'. In his *Apology for Heroic Poetry*, the preface to the *State of Innocence* (1677), he enlarges on the need of a heightened style to match the epic's high aims and duties. Dryden also believed in the patriotic value of writing an epic. He mentioned it when, in a passage I shall refer to below, he spoke of his own epic plans, and when, in writing to Charles Montague about his plans for translating the *Iliad*, he said he would execute them 'for my Country's honour as well as my own'.[2] And though he may have written with less solemnity than Milton, he did agree with him on the poet's need of a comprehensive background of learning and experience, for in his brilliant little postscript to the *Remarks* on Settle's *Empress of Morocco*[3] he contrasts Settle's mean and narrow fancifulness with the comprehensive character of the real poet. Though he does not refer explicitly to epic poetry he certainly included it in his statement; for he speaks of a 'complete and excellent poet' and we know he thought the epic the most complete and excellent part of poetry:

> A man should be learned in several sciences and should have a reasonable, philosophical, and in some measure a mathematical head, to be a complete and excellent poet; and besides this, should have experience in all sorts of humours and manners of men; should be thoroughly skilled in conversation, and should have a great knowledge of mankind in general.

Finally Dryden by his frequent and almost effusive references to the epic form shows himself fully open to the awe of it as an abstraction,

---

[1] Spingarn, *Critical Essays of the Seventeenth Century*, ii. 295.
[2] Letters ed. Charles E. Ward (Durham, North Carolina, 1942) 121.
[3] Not in Ker's *Essays of John Dryden*. The passage is from Walter Scott's edition (London 1808) xv. 411.

to which I have referred before. In all these matters he spoke for his age.

In the dispute between ancients and moderns Dryden chose a middle and, we may conjecture, representative position. And this dispute had its bearing on the epic. If the ancients were not yet rivalled and could never be, there was little inducement to a modern to trespass on their special departments of culture. They had excelled above all in the epic; hence this was the last thing in which a modern should try to compete. Dryden's position can be inferred with some probability from his *Essay of Dramatic Poesy*, where the topic of ancients and moderns is a main part of the discussion. But one is on surer ground in the essays where he speaks entirely in his own person. In the *Essay of Dramatic Poesy* Crites had advanced the theory that every age had its own genius; that of the ancients was poetical, that of today scientific. And Eugenius had retorted with the now classic plea that not only has the present age excelled in science but it may excel in poetry by following and bettering the ancients' example. We can guess that Dryden himself agreed with Eugenius. But for his mature and certain opinion we can find evidence in the *Dedication of Examen Poeticum* and the *Preface to Juvenal*, otherwise known as the *Discourse concerning Satire*. Here he repudiates the militant modernity of Perrault,[1] who claimed that *Astrée* and other French romances had far surpassed the *Iliad* in the wealth of their invention, but he thinks that English drama had improved on the ancient. Further, we must not despair of matching even Homer and Virgil:

> For good sense is the same in all or most ages; and course of time rather improves Nature, than impairs her. What has been, may be again: another Homer, and another Virgil, may possibly arise from those very causes which produced the first; though it would be impudence to affirm, that any such have yet appeared.[2]

In sum, Dryden and his age held the main ideas on the epic current in western Europe, ideas that had prompted and were prompting the French to abundant epic attempts, and did not despair of embodying them in the English tongue. But in some respect the cases of France and England differed greatly. The political and social situation was more propitious to epic writing in France than in England; but none of the French writers of epic had the literary stature of the Englishman who planned an epic but never actually wrote it. In passing now to the bearing of the English political and social position on the prospect of English epic writing I shall

[1] W. P. Ker, *Essays of John Dryden*, ii. 6.
[2] *Ib.* 25. R. A. Brower (*Dryden's Epic Manner and Virgil* in *Publications of the Modern Language Association*, 1940, pp. 119-38) shows that in his more heightened verse Dryden owed many details to Virgil. But the debt is relatively small in *King Arthur* and the *Fables*.

include Dryden's own epic plans, for the two topics are closely connected.

At the end of last chapter I wrote of the high hopes Sprat expressed for the future of English poetry, in his *History of the Royal Society*. That book centred in point of time on the wonderful year of plague, fire, and naval victory; and the tough courage which the country displayed through its many trials was the cause in Sprat of confidence in its future. But this confidence was bred not only of the wonderful year. The spirit of disillusion and uncertainty usually attributed to the period of the later Stuarts did not prevail in the first years of the Restoration. Although Charles, constrained by Parliament and a strong section of opinion in the country, was forced into an intolerance of nonconformist religion that he personally disliked and that drove a section of the country into a resentment it would not otherwise have felt, the prevailing temper was one of relief at the end of civil war and of hope for an assertion of British strength. Dryden himself in *Astraea Redux*, celebrating Charles's return, had exclaimed:

> *Tremble ye Nations who secure before,*
> *Laught at those Arms that 'gainst ourselves we bore;*
> *Rous'd by the lash of his own stubborn Tail,*
> *Our Lion now will foreign Foes assail.*[1]

And later in the poem Dryden celebrates the country's bright prospects for the future:

> *And now times whiter Series is begun,*
> *Which in soft Centuries shall smoothly run;*
> *Those Clouds that overcast your Morn shall fly,*
> *Dispell'd to farthest corners of the Sky.*
> *Our nation, with united Int'rest blest,*
> *Not now content to poize, shall sway, the rest.*
> *Abroad your Empire shall no Limits know,*
> *But like the Sea in boundless Circles flow.*[2]

Dryden's *Annus Mirabilis*, too, written to celebrate and describe the naval campaigns against the Dutch and the great fire of London (and in a minor way the plague) of the year 1666, not only links up with Sprat but prolongs the strain of existing optimism.

The connection with Sprat is remarkable enough to merit further illustration. In the 155th stanza Dryden inserts a 'digression concerning shipping and navigation' and ends this with an 'apostrophe to the Royal Society', the climax of the advancement of knowledge. Having described the coming marvels of navigation he goes on:

---

[1] 115-18. I use John Sargeaunt's edition of the poems (London 1925) as far as this reaches; otherwise Scott-Saintsbury or the original Scott.
[2] 292-9.

This I fore-tel from your auspicious Care,
*   Who great in search of God and Nature grow;*
Who best your wise Creator's Praise declare,
*   Since best to praise his works is best to know.*

O truly Royal! who behold the Law,
*   And rule of Beings in your Makers mind:*
And thence, like Limbecks, rich Idea's draw,
*   To fit the levell'd use of Human-kind.*

In his 289th stanza Dryden duplicates Sprat in referring to the country's courage in persisting in the war in spite of the fire:

They have not lost their Loyalty by Fire;
*   Nor is their Courage or their Wealth so low,*
That from his Wars they poorly would retire,
*   Or beg the Pity of a vanquish'd Foe.*

And the poem ends with the boast—very soon to be falsified—of good fortune to come:

Already we have conquer'd half the War,
*   And the less dang'rous part is left behind:*
Our Trouble now is but to make them dare,
*   And not so great to Vanquish as to Find.*

Thus to the Eastern wealth through Storms we go,
*   But now, the Cape once doubled, fear no more:*
A constant Trade-wind will securely blow
*   And gently lay us on the Spicy shore.*

And not only was Britain to be more powerful, but her capital city was to arise from its ashes nobler and more civilised:

More great than human now, and more August,
*   New deified she from her Fires does rise:*
Her widening Streets on new Foundations trust,
*   And, opening, into larger parts she flies.*[1]

But early hopes were soon to be disappointed. In the very year, 1667, Dryden published *Annus Mirabilis*, the English navy fell into disrepair, the Dutch raided the Medway, and the peace of Breda, regarded as humiliating, was concluded. Clarendon, the Chancellor, a steadying influence even if out of tune with the new epoch, was dismissed, and the uneasy period of the Cabal succeeded. Charles himself, less active in business and more given to his pleasures, had lost his initial favour with the mass of the population. London indeed

[1] Stanza 295.

was rebuilt swiftly and to the admiration of Europe. But Dryden's prophecy, taken up by Wren's plans for rebuilding the city, was never worthily fulfilled. And generally a simple hope expired in an epoch of cross-purposes and frustrations. There was no analogy between France and England in their conditions after their civil wars. France achieved a sense of agreed direction; England failed for years to decide where she really meant to go. Even after the different sections of the community had united to promote the revolution of 1688, England did not at once reach such a decision, and Dryden's *Secular Masque*, his epilogue to the century, proclaiming the weariness of the expiring age and the need to begin the next, was not the mere pessimism of an old man. It was only in the next century that the union with Scotland, Britain's hegemony in Europe under Marl-borough, and the triumph of Newton's philosophy helped with other things to make Britain feel at ease with herself. Politically and socially, with confusion in its counsels of state and the suppression of the nonconforming sections of the community, England after 1667 was not propitious to epic writing. It was not an epic area like the England of Elizabeth.

For all that, the convention of heroic writing was too strong to be dropped. Dryden exploited it in *Annus Mirabilis*, he and others did the same in the heroic play, and the formal ode, heroic in tone, flourished exceedingly. Such writing might have a direct correspond-ence with reality in the first few years of Charles's reign. Later it could have only an indirect one; and it is worth trying to describe this indirect correspondence. First, the heroic mode could be a convention, betokening at its best a belief in the value of accepted forms and manners generally. Next, it could be a compensation, in the modern psychological sense, for those true heroic qualities which it became gradually obvious the age conspicuously lacked. Thirdly, though the heroic vein did not apply generally to the age, it did in a limited way represent the temper of the courtier class. C. S. Lewis is of course right when he points to the vulgar side of that temper and its falsity to the genuine English aristocratic tradition:

> We in England had had an aristocratic tradition of our own, to be sure; a tradition at once more sober and more tenderly romantic than the French, obeying a code of honour less dissociated from piety. . . . But Dryden seems to know nothing of it. He and his audiences look to Versailles, and feel for it that pathetic yet un-profitable yearning which vulgarity so often feels for unattainable graces. But the yearning does not teach them the secret. Where their model was brilliant they are flashy; where the *Cid* was brave, Almansor swaggers.[1]

[1] *Rehabilitations* (London 1939) 13.

But he goes too far; and the excesses of English heroic writing did express something, even if it obscured much, of certain standards of distinction required by the best of the ruling class. Those standards are far better expressed by Congreve in the *Way of the World* than by Dryden in his heroic writing. Mirabel and Millamant are really superior people with very high standards of conduct and intellect; and they take as much trouble to pretend to take them lightly as the heroes of heroic tragedy to advertise their excessive audacity. But the same idea is behind them all, and Dryden though he vulgarised did not quite destroy it. The egoism of Albemarle's speech in *Annus Mirabilis* when he laments his separation from the rest of the fleet and his inability to renew the fight on the third day is not exempt from ridicule, yet it does express a resolve to measure himself by high standards:

> *That happy Sun, said he, will rise again,*
> *Who twice victorious did our Navy see:*
> *And I alone must view him rise in vain,*
> *Without one ray of all his Star for me.*

> *Yet like an* English *Gen'ral will I die,*
> *And all the Ocean make my spatious grave:*
> *Women and Cowards on the Land may lie,*
> *The Sea's a Tomb that's proper for the Brave.*[1]

But though I go as far as this in allowing a direct meaning to the heroic vein, I am far from allowing it any comprehensive application to the whole age.

Not that the age lacked its convictions, but they were not of the positive, ardent kind. If hopes of national greatness were disappointed, the genuine distrust of 'enthusiasm', of acts urged by an excess of passion, remained. If the general temper was sceptical and critical and suspicious of anything in the least utopian, it did believe in the wisdom of making the best of what was there already, of giving it a decent order. And though the age had turned out worse than it should be, at least it was more civilised, sophisticated, and enlightened than what had gone before, and especially through its advance in science. Such a temper did not actively encourage epic writing, did not, as I have said, create an epic area, but it did not necessarily exclude feelings of an epic nobility. It is possible to feel strongly about the importance of order, decorum, and of taking thought before acting, as Wren proved through the best of his architecture. Meditating on his twin towers at Greenwich, we may conclude that an epic poem was not impossible in this age. And when we turn to Dryden's failure to realise his epic ambition, we must not allow his age to bear the whole blame for it.

[1] Stanzas 100-1.

There is no doubt about Dryden's ambition to be an epic poet
Nor did he have any illusions about the magnitude of the task. There
was no danger of his making a premature attempt. His first epicising
poem was *Annus Mirabilis*, but it is modestly experimental. From the
preface it is clear that he had already given thought to epic theory
and practice. He mentions, as well as classical, contemporary French
epic, *Gondibert* (whose metre he borrowed), and Chapman's Homer,
showing that he was alive to most precedents and possibilities. But
he is modest in his claims for his own poem. It is not epic, he says,
but historical. Epic is too bold a title for a poem of about the length
of a single book of the classical epics; moreover, the action is not
one. So, while admitting a general debt to Virgil, he classes his
poem with the looser structural form of Lucan. But, though he is
modest, his experiment is serious enough in point both of subject
and of style. He believes in his patriotic theme, the military,
scientific, and moral prowess of his country; and he exalts the stanza
of *Gondibert* to a grandeur far above anything that Davenant could
compass. In its restricted way the poem does represent the larger
affair of which Dryden was really capable had he felt that the true
moment had come for him to put forth all his strength. It should not
be dismissed from all epic pretensions as mere immature work.

There is another side to *Annus Mirabilis*, the prophetic. Though
Dryden was to do better, he showed in it where his special gifts lay.
Throughout his maturity Dryden was a master of grand writing, but
only under special conditions. Those conditions may be indicated
generally by the idea of distortion. When he attempted simple
description he was either flat or ridiculous or both. Take the stanza
(238) which introduces the King, a stanza which is simple and
should have been sublime:

> *Now Day appears, and with the day the King,*
> *Whose early Care had robb'd him of his rest:*
> *Far off the Cracks of Falling houses ring,*
> *And Shrieks of Subjects pierce his tender Breast.*

When Dryden had an argument to conduct, when he could find
refuge from the plain root-feelings of men in intellectual exercise, he
could be exquisitely simple. But when he had no such refuge, either
he failed, as in this stanza, or he had to distort, he had to forsake a
simple treatment. Later he was to achieve greatness through the
exaggeration that is proper to satire and through the conventional
fantasies of the elaborate ode. In *Annus Mirabilis* Dryden is most
sublime where he most exaggerates. The heroic egoism of Albemarle,
already referred to, is slightly ridiculous in its distortion from reality
but is sublimely expressed. Take another example. Dryden was incapable of expressing simply and directly the feelings of the populace

in the great fire, but by exploiting outrageously the 'pathetic fallacy', attributing feeling and thought to the flames in stanza after stanza, he touches grandeur of expression and infects us with the sinister horror of the event:

> The Powder blows up all before the Fire:
> Th' amazed flames stand gather'd on a heap;
> And from the precipices-brink retire,
> Afraid to venture on so large a leap.
>
> Thus fighting Fires a while themselves consume,
> But streight like Turks, forc'd on to win or die,
> They first lay tender Bridges of their fume,
> And o're the Breach in unctuous vapours flie.
>
> Part stays for Passage, 'till a gust of wind
> Ships o're their Forces in a shining Sheet:
> Part, creeping under ground, their Journey blind,
> And, climbing from below, their Fellows meet.[1]

If Dryden was to have succeeded in his epic, it must have been in a style that included an element of the monstrous or the burlesque.

Now this addition of the burlesque to the serious, potentially Dryden's original contribution to the course of the English epic, was something true not only to Dryden but to his age. It implies a high degree of self-consciousness, the refusal to be ultimately committed, an advanced scepticism. The heroic postures of Homer and of Milton were not the same. But they had this in common: there was no escape from them. Indeed, they were far more than postures. The heroic posture of the Restoration was different from both. It was worth trying, but you must be able to abandon it. Thus Dryden can both be the age's leading creator of heroic drama and write thus:

> Homer . . . can move rage better than he can pity. He stirs up the irascible appetite, as our philosophers call it; he provokes to murder, and the destruction of God's images; he forms and equips those ungodly man-killers, whom we poets, when we flatter them, call heroes; a race of men who can never enjoy quiet in themselves, till they have taken it from all the world.[2]

To accuse Dryden of inconsistency and hypocrisy is to do much more than that: it is to indict a whole epoch. And wise men hesitate to go so far as that.

Every age has its own paradoxes. The Restoration at once exalted and doubted the heroic posture and the virtue of reason. And such a doubt went further in England than in France, where the belief in reason was animated by stronger and steadier emotions.

[1] 245-7.   [2] From the Dedication of Examen Poeticum, Ker, ii. 13.

L. I. Bredvold in his *Intellectual Milieu of John Dryden*[1] has described the sceptical temper of Restoration England very well and in so doing has made the position of Dryden in his age a great deal more intelligible. Here are some of his points. A dominant trend of thought was Pyrrhonist; and Sextus Empiricus, Montaigne, and Charron were favourite authors. Men had little trust in the rightness of mere human reason. But in compensation they put more trust in the institutions that happened to exist and in the revealed element of religion. The current scepticism of the age was opposed to the far-reaching materialism of Hobbes; for the leaders of the Royal Society, that representative institution, were pious and orthodox men, and professed a scepticism of the certainty of their own results compared with the superior certainty of revealed religion. Bredvold thinks that Dryden, though he shows himself acquainted through his plays with the determinism of Hobbes, was (against some modern opinion) himself against Hobbes and on the side of the Royal Society. Dryden's membership of that society was not nugatory and he understood roughly the principles that animated it: the Baconian belief in collecting data for experiment and the new mathematical principle of motion, that of replacing the old idea of an innate proneness to motion in things by a constant external measurable cause. To quote Bredvold,

> Dryden was interested in the Royal Society, understood its spirit, and recognised that he was like-minded with it; he understood the new philosophy of motion, vaguely perhaps in its scientific aspects, but with an acute interest in its deterministic implications regarding human nature; and he rejected the dogmatic materialism of Hobbes and Lucretius.[2]

Dryden was thus interested in the Royal Society and even confident in it and enthusiastic about its findings. But he tempered this feeling with a fundamental distrust of the human reason, with a philosophical scepticism; and it was this distrust that impelled him to conservatism and authority—ultimately Catholic authority—in religion and made a Tory of him in politics.

What, now, is the bearing of this on Dryden's poetry? Let me revert to the period of the *Annus Mirabilis* and consider the special conditions of that period and the general scepticism of the Restoration age together. If in 1666 Dryden had meditated a patriotic epic, events from 1667 must have caused him either to abandon or to postpone his intention, while the prevalent scepticism would have worked against his choosing for subject anything so forthright as England's emergence from civil war into the glories of restored monarchy. Anyhow, he recognised things as they were and turned his hand to

[1] Ann Arbor 1934.   [2] *Op. cit.* 72.

writing the kind of play that was then in demand. But his having to abandon or postpone his patriotic theme did not mean that he stopped thinking. And from the miscellany of his works between *Annus Mirabilis* and his next epicising attempt, his translation of the *Aeneid* in 1697, we can deduce the form his thoughts took. I mentioned above, using Bredvold's book, that the Pyrrhonist was prone to compensate his philosophical scepticism by a confidence in existing institutions. Dryden, suspicious of extravagant hopes and high motives both in themselves and as the driving power of poetry, compensated by centring his dearest interests in those parts of literature that were most obviously permanent, the language itself and its rhetoric. His highest boast at the end of his life was that he had improved the language; his criticism is concerned preponderantly with technique. Nor was such a compensation devoid of moral significance. If Dryden distrusted extravagance, he believed in cultivating to the utmost the things of which you were sure. Poetry was a craft, and to cultivate it honestly was to express a belief in the moral value of all sound workmanship. Poetry was also a discipline, and when the writer submitted to that discipline he was expressing his belief in culture against barbarism, order against arbitrary 'enthusiasm'. A single stanza from *Threnodia Augustalis*, Dryden's official ode on the death of Charles II, will illustrate the whole of my meaning in a very short space. It is the fifteenth and refers to the new king.

> *A Warlike Prince ascends the Regal State,*
> *A Prince, long exercis'd by Fate;*
> *Long may he keep, tho he obtains it late.*
> *Heroes in Heaven's peculiar Mold are cast,*
> *They and their Poets are not formed in hast;*
> *Man was the first in God's design, and Man was made the last.*
> *False Heroes, made by Flattery so,*
> *Heav'n can strike out, like Sparkles, at a blow;*
> *But e're a Prince is to Perfection brought,*
> *He costs Omnipotence a second thought.*
> > *With Toyl and Sweat,*
> > *With hardning Cold, and forming Heat,*
> > *The Cyclops did their strokes repeat,*
> *Before th' impenetrable Shield was wrought.*
> > *It looks as if the Maker wou'd not own*
> > *The Noble work for his,*
> *Before 'twas try'd and found a Masterpiece.*

Only in a most superficial sense is this a piece of flattery for the new king. It does indeed express a belief in royalism: 'kings are there and had better remain. And it is proper to play the game of writing them up and calling them demi-gods. And such writing up is one of a number of other necessary proprieties'. But more important than the belief in royalism is the belief in technique, in taking pains, in the culture symbolised by honest work. It is not James the stanza first concerns but the years that went to making him a true prince; those years being primarily not the years of James's life but all the periods of incubation of any human product that has any value. And it is worth here digressing to point out how, as in *Annus Mirabilis*, Dryden when he is really serious distorts and exaggerates. The oxymoron of Omnipotence's second thought is ridiculous and yet somehow sublime. And such a combination is the true index of Dryden's double feeling: his profoundly critical estimate of human nature and his profound belief in honest work and achieved culture.

These are the feelings that must have formed the core of any successful epic Dryden could have written. What promised the chance of his expressing those feelings worthily was his own mental and literary endowment. He had great energy of mind; he had, if you include his translations of Persius and Juvenal, the command of a very large vocabulary; and he had the command of considerable metrical resources. His mind was more energetic than rich, but if he had succeeded in putting the whole of himself into his epic he would have satisfied the condition of amplitude tolerably. Much would have depended on his directing his energy to the things he really could do. He needed a subject that admitted, besides action, of cool argument, of satire, and of studied exaltation: a subject capable of including the athletic, argumentative vein of *Religio Laici*, the high satire of *Absalom and Achitophel*, and the pompous rapture of the best of his odes.

The kind of action that suited him can be gathered best not from his plays but from the two pieces that crown the *Fables*, the first two of the versions of Boccaccio, *Sigismonda and Guiscardo* and *Theodore and Honoria*. Dryden's subtlety was intellectual only; his conception of the human passions was crude, but he was able to make crudity convincing by the energy with which he could describe them. Tancred and Sigismonda are harshly unpleasant characters, the father an inhuman tyrant and the daughter a self-willed and calculating sensualist. There is something a little monstrous about them both. Theodore and Honoria have very little character, but the exaggerated and distorted version of them and of their possible fate in the ghostly vision of Guido hunting his cruel mistress is terrifying and has a like monstrous quality. In both stories Dryden conveys through this very monstrousness the assurance of high and striking passions. Here, better than in *All for Love*, Dryden hits on the heroic vein that really suits him and finds the true outlet for his energy. This passage, for instance, where Sigismonda defends her love of Guiscardo, the lower-born, by an appeal to nature, rings true as the conventional heroics of *All for Love* do not:

DRYDEN

> *But leaving that: Search we the secret Springs,*
> *And backward trace the Principles of Things;*
> *There shall we find, that when the World began,*
> *One common Mass compos'd the Mould of Man;*
> *One Paste of Flesh on all Degrees bestow'd,*
> *And kneaded up alike with moistning Blood.*
> *The same Almighty Pow'r inspir'd the Frame*
> *With kindl'd Life, and form'd the Souls the same:*
> *The Faculties of Intellect, and Will,*
> *Dispens'd with equal Hand, dispos'd with equal Skill,*
> *Like Liberty indulg'd with choice of Good or Ill.*
> *Thus born alike, from Vertue first began*
> *The Diff'rence that distinguish'd Man from Man:*
> *He claim'd no Title from Descent of Blood,*
> *But that which made him Noble, made him Good:*
> *Warm'd with more Particles of Heav'nly Flame,*
> *He wing'd his upward Flight, and soar'd to Fame;*
> *The rest remain'd below, a Tribe without a Name.*[1]

Dryden's genius was truly at ease in Tancred's brutal obstinacy and Sigismonda's brazen defiance. And it is interesting to note that the year 1700 that saw the publication of the *Fables* saw also that of the *Way of the World*, the other product of the age that turned the heroic conception to the best account.

Whether the decasyllabic couplet was capable of holding all the elements that Dryden needed to bring together if he was to succeed in the epic is doubtful. (How, for instance, could it have compassed the high but measured and sophisticated rapture of the first and last verses of the *Ode on Anne Killigrew?*) It was the only metre then correct for the epic; and it is possible that Dryden shirked his ambition for no further reason than that he knew instinctively he lacked the tools for the work.

Had Dryden brought himself to carry the work through, I think that he would have been able to control it, to carry it in his head as a whole. And here the discipline of play-writing would have helped him, for it is not in architectonics that *All for Love* is lacking.

Last, Dryden could not have failed to speak for his age as far as the age permitted itself to be spoken for by any one person. He would have represented more of it than any other man was capable of doing. He had the best chance of any of being truly choric.

So much for my speculations on what Dryden might have done.

Of Dryden's actual plans we know little; and that little is found chiefly in his *Discourse concerning Satire*, prefixed to his translation of Juvenal (1693)[2]. There he gives the Earl of Dorset ('and by him the

---

[1] 499-515.   [2] Ker, ii. 37-8.

world') his general notions of the epic and an abstract of his own epic plans. These plans he had long revolved and had hoped to put in practice, leaving the stage, for which he says his genius is not truly inclined. His poem was to have been patriotic and to have concerned either Arthur's victories over the Saxons or the Black Prince restoring Don Pedro to his rightful throne in Spain. The second subject would have provided the occasion of many topical allusions. The English characters could have represented 'my living friends and patrons of the noblest families', and events could have 'shadowed the events of future ages, in the succession of our imperial line'. Charles had encouraged him, but only with words not with the punctual payment of his salary. And now it is too late, with age and want disabling him. Perhaps the chief interest of the passage is personal. Dryden makes it quite clear that he had intended his life's work to be an epic: it was to have been 'a work which would have taken up my life in the performance of it'. And the confession of failure is tragic in proportion to the magnitude of the aim.

But Dryden was not quite defeated. Very soon after this confession he began his translation of the *Aeneid*; and when we remember the high status of certain kinds of translation in the neo-classic ages we can see that his new venture represented the commutation rather than the abandonment of his epic plans. This Dryden's introduction to his translation makes clear enough. Here he reiterates his notions of the epic: its supremacy as a literary form, the difficulty of succeeding in it, and so on[1]; showing that his own ambitions are still haunting him. He protests that heroic poetry, if cultivated, *could* flourish in England. He laments that he has spent only three years on the translation, when he needs four more to improve it. But he ends by hoping that his translation will be (like the original epic, we may understand) to the honour of England.[2]

Spingarn in the fifth section of his introduction to his *Critical Essays of the Seventeenth Century* has written generally on theories of translation. What most has to be borne in mind is that throughout the Renaissance and neo-classic periods less value was put on originality and more on imitating the ancients than has been the case since the Romantic Revival. Hence the gap between an original poem and a translation was less. Within the art of translation various grades of fidelity to the original were distinguished. Dryden in his *Preface to Ovid's Epistles* mentions three, which he calls metaphrase, paraphrase, and imitation,[3] he himself favouring the middle method as being one that retains and best brings out the main features of the original but which also allows scope to the poetical gifts of the translator. He enunciates the same principle in his preface to his *Aeneid*,[4] though he uses his terms differently. His translation of the *Aeneid* would thus

[1] *Ib.* ii. 154-64.   [2] *Ib.* ii. 216-41.   [3] Ker, i. 237.   [4] ii. 228.

both represent the main Virgilian features and allow the translator considerable scope for invention. It would, if successful, be counted not a complete but a partial substitute for the epic on Arthur or the Black Prince Dryden had intended.

Dryden's *Aeneid* has very great merits and is the best English translation of that poem. If he had spent on it the four more years he said it needed, it would have expressed through its craft his belief in culture more fully; but even in its present form it is finely shaped. As a whole it is far more readable than Douglas and in spite of much unevenness it never flags throughout its long course. When Dryden has to deal with politics and strong action he usually succeeds; and there are so many opportunities for such success that he can get through to the end and leave a grand positive impression. I give two examples of what he can do. First, here is Anchises's famous account of the peculiar Roman genius, from the sixth book. Dryden does indeed fail to translate *parcere subiectis*, but that is a small matter compared with his ability to write nobly at this high point in the book:

> *Let others better mold the running Mass*
> *Of mettals, and inform the breathing Brass;*
> *And soften into Flesh a Marble Face:*
> *Plead better at the Bar; describe the Skies,*
> *And when the Stars descend, and when they rise.*
> *But, Rome, 'tis thine alone with awful sway,*
> *To Rule Mankind; and make the World obey;*
> *Disposing Peace, and War, thy own Majestic Way.*
> *To tame the Proud, the fetter'd Slave to free;*
> *These are Imperial Arts, and worthy thee.*[1]

And here is the account of Priam's death in the second book, an account giving Dryden's energy of utterance full scope:

> *This said, his feeble hand a Javelin threw,*
> *Which flutt'ring, seem'd to loiter as it flew:*
> *Just, and but barely, to the Mark it held,*
> *And faintly tinckl'd on the Brazen Shield.*
> *   Then Pyrrhus thus: Go thou from me to Fate;*
> *And to my Father my foul deeds relate.*
> *Now dye: with that he dragg'd the trembling Sire,*
> *Slidd'ring thro' clotter'd Blood, and holy Mire,*
> *(The mingl'd Paste his murder'd Son had made,)*
> *Haul'd from beneath the violated Shade;*
> *And on the Sacred Pile the Royal Victim laid.*
> *His right Hand held his bloody Fauchion bare;*

---

[1] Virgil's *Aeneis*, vi. 1169-78. Text used is that of Dryden's *Works of Virgil* (London 1697).

The left he twisted in his hoary Hair:
Then, with a speeding Thrust, his Heart he found:
The lukewarm Blood came rushing thro' the wound,
And sanguine Streams distain'd the sacred Ground.
Thus Priam fell: and shar'd one common Fate
With Troy in Ashes, and his ruin'd State:
He, who the Scepter of all Asia sway'd,
Whom Monarchs like domestic Slaves obey'd,
On the bleak Shoar now lies th' abandon'd King,
A headless Carcase, and a nameless thing.[1]

But with the less public and more individual sides of Virgil Dryden was unable to cope. His coarse energy and tendency to distort did constant violence to Virgil's subtle, pathetic, or mystical genius. One does not need to go far into the translation for instances. In my chapter on Virgil (p. 79) I quoted the account of Venus revealing herself to Aeneas in the first book and added that here Virgil intended some reference to a world of appearance and a world of superior truth. Dryden in translating not only misses all subtlety but, true to his instinct for distortion, complicates and vulgarises the direct description of the original:

Thus having said, she turn'd, and made appear
Her Neck refulgent, and dishevel'd Hair;
Which, flowing from her Shoulders, reach'd the Ground,
And widely spread Ambrosial Scents around:
In length of Train descends her sweeping Gown,
And by her graceful Walk, the Queen of Love is known.[2]

There is nothing in the original about Venus's hair being dishevelled or reaching the ground, or about her walk being graceful. Dryden, who had a positive genius for making nasty every aspect of the passion of love that was not nasty already, here transforms a goddess into a competitor in a beauty competition. He prolongs his vulgarisation into the subsequent account of Venus arriving at Paphos, where not only

A hundred Altars in her Temple Smoke,

but, with a gratuitous addition to his original,

A thousand bleeding Hearts her Pow'r invoke.

Dryden adored Virgil and criticised him superbly. And he knew he failed to do him justice, concluding at length, as he tells us in the *Preface to the Fables* and in his letter of about the same time to Charles Montague,[3] that he believed he was better suited to translate the *Iliad* than the *Aeneid*, better able to cope with Homer's 'fiery way of

---

[1] *Ib.* ii. 742-63.   [2] *Ib.* i. 556-61.   [3] Letters, ed. Ward, 121.

writing' than with 'the exactness and sobriety' of Virgil. There is no need to discuss this question. Here it suffices to say that Dryden was right in confessing his failure. The talents of Virgil and Dryden were so different that they possessed a strictly limited amount of common ground. Beyond those limits Dryden could never succeed; and his translation of the *Aeneid* could be epic only in a much more restricted sense than the plenitude of his genius (exemplified as I have said by some of the *Fables* and the Odes) could have accomplished in an original poem.

CHAPTER VIII

ARTHUR AND TELEMACHUS

1. BLACKMORE

I cannot believe my Imitation of Virgil *to be the least dishonour.*
Would the famous Sir Godfrey Kneller *think it a Reproach if any*
should say, that his Pencil too nearly follow'd that of Raphael
Urbin? *Or can it be imagin'd, that Sir* Christopher Wren
would be offended, if it should be objected to him, that in his building
of St. Paul's Church *he too much imitated* Michael Angelo.

(Richard Blackmore, Preface to *King Arthur*)

NEAR the end of the seventeenth century two writers produced
epics so striking both in their likenesses and differences that I
have put them in the same chapter. Blackmore and Fénelon were
close in age and they were engaged on their epics on Arthur and
Telemachus respectively in the same decade, the last of the century.
Both gloried in the utter correctness of what they wrote, in the lavish
completeness with which they imitated the best models; both were
enthusiastically orthodox believers in the neo-classic creed. Both were
obvious and sincere moralists, both pointed the clearest contemporary
lessons. Both were ambitious of making their morality reach the
highest places in the realm. There was a genuine identity of aim. But
Blackmore was a middle-class Englishman and a physician, Fénelon
an aristocratic Frenchman and an archbishop. Blackmore wrote in
the heroic couplet and failed to achieve the distinction of style
necessary for him even to be considered as an epic poet; Fénelon wrote
in prose and in a measure succeeded. Blackmore's two epics on
Arthur had some initial success but were soon discredited. *Télémaque*
quickly became a classic and was much read in England as well as
all over the Continent.

If Dryden had written an epic, he would doubtless have owed a
good deal to various models. (The enchanted wood in his own opera,
King Arthur, borrowed from Tasso, may well have been a part of his
abandoned epic plan.) But he would have exploited his own peculiar
genius with its energy and its critically burlesque tone so strongly as
to have made his debts a matter of detail rather than of substance.
Blackmore and Fénelon belong to the eclectic stage of neo-classicism,
where individual success comes about through the very excess of
imitative correctness. They put into action the doctrine which
animated the dispute on the merits of ancients and moderns: that by

both following nature and imitating the ancients you could achieve a new and superior correctness and beat the ancients on their own ground and through the very act of doing them homage.

I shall deal with Blackmore[1] not as an epic poet but as a pheno-menon in the history of English epic poetry. His *Prince Arthur* (1695) and *King Arthur* (1697) work like certain other long poems, for instance Young's *Night Thoughts* and Bailey's *Festus*. They at once reveal certain obvious talents in the author, leading the reader to think at first that they are better than usually reputed. Blackmore had a remarkable natural facility with verse and a lot of energy. But very soon the narrowness of his metrical range tells on the ear. The reader begins to weary, and nausea succeeds weariness with remark-able speed. The man declares himself a bore on a grand scale, and the only thing to do is to run away. But as an epic phenomenon, as the classic English example of excessive imitative correctness, he demands a little space in this book.

To his first epic, *Prince Arthur*, Blackmore added a preface. There is nothing new in it except an attack on the immorality of the English stage. But it is precisely his repetitiveness that is significant. He repeats every stale commonplace concerning the nature of the epic as fixed by the strict neo-classic creed and acknowledges his allegiance to Rapin, Dacier, and Le Bossu among the French critics, and Rymer among the English. Judged by their rules (and of course by those of Aristotle and Horace), no makers of epic have been correct except Homer and Virgil. Blackmore by following the rules of the best critics and by setting up Virgil as his chief model will try to improve on his non-classical predecessors: 'What *Homer* and *Virgil* have *perform'd* with Honour and universal Applause I have *attempted*: What they have been *able*, I have been *willing* to do'.

Blackmore's two poems are as overwhelmingly, one can say devastatingly, correct as his preface. Though he made Virgil his chief model, he reinforced the assurance of his imitative capacity by drawing on Spenser, Tasso, Milton, and Dryden as well. Tasso and Spenser had had their enchantresses, more subtle and sensual than Virgil's Dido; so Blackmore must have his Fascinia to try Arthur with her charms. A true epic should have more than one layer of meaning and should bear a contemporary significance. Arthur is not only the British King out of Geoffrey of Monmouth but William III himself, who crosses the Channel and restores the land to its true self. The Saxons, who reintroduced Paganism into Britain, are also the Catholics; and the Christianity of Arthur is also the Protestant faith of William III. *Prince Arthur* recounts Arthur's establishment in England, thereby shadowing the events of 1688 and 1689. *King*

---

[1] For a convenient account of Blackmore's poems on Arthur see R. Florence Brinkley, *Arthurian Legend in the Seventeenth Century*, 146-95. I am indebted to it in the pages that follow.

Arthur recounts Arthur's European wars culminating in the capture of Lutetia, thereby shadowing the French wars of William III. Blackmore aspired not only to be the correct epic poet among the moderns but the heroic poet of his own country. In his process of going through the proper motions he was wonderfully complete; and in that resides the whole of his interest.

2. FÉNELON[1]

Notre illustre Auteur a donc réuni dans son Poëme les plus grandes beautez des Anciens. Il a tout l'enthousiasme et l'abondance d'Homére, toute la magnificence et la régularité de Virgile.

(Mr de Ramsay, *Discours de la poësie épique et de l'Excellence du Poëme de Télémaque*)

Classique, si l'on veut, mais d'une façon si personelle que l'école hésitera toujours à le reconnaître pour sien. . . . Il n'est que lui-même, rare, délicat et complexe de nature comme de formation.

(Ely Carcassonne)

'Mr de Ramsay' was Andrew Ramsay, a Scotsman whom Fénelon converted to Catholicism and his intimate friend. He appended his *Discours* to the first authorised edition of *Télémaque* and is useful in confirming certain things one could reasonably conjecture. Though Fénelon would not have used prose for his epic attempt without the long tradition of Heliodorus and the French epicising romances, it is plain from Ramsay that Fénelon considered that he went straight to Homer and Virgil for his inspiration. Ramsay expressly condemns the modern romances for the extravagance of their marvels. The true epic works in a simpler and more natural way.[2] Again, when he meets the objection raised against *Télémaque* that it is in prose, he does not mention the precedent of Heliodorus but argues on general principles like those of Sidney concerning the same matter:

Ce qui fait la Poësie, n'est pas le nombre fixe et la cadence réglée des syllabes; mais le sentiment qui anime tout, la fiction vive, les figures hardies, la beauté et la variété des images.[3]

And he goes on to cite as precedent not the epicising prose romances but the epic poems that have dispensed with one of the chief attributes of verse, rhyme. And after mentioning Italian and Spanish precedent generally, he cites the example of Milton as strikingly successful. Fénelon was indeed uncompromising in the purity of his classicising: Homer and Virgil alone were good enough for his models; only

[1] For *Télémaque* I use the edition of 1734 printed in Holland. It contains Ramsay's *Discours*.
[2] P. iv.   [3] P. xiv.

through them could the road to success lie; and divagation was a poor evasion of the real issue. But, like Milton, he thought he had the chance of excelling, through the advantage of being a Christian. By the abundance and conscientiousness of his imitation he might equal his models in charm; by his morality he might go beyond them.

Another of the current objections to *Télémaque* and Ramsay's answer take us right into the essential quality of the book. Here is the objection:

> Quelques-uns croyent que l'Auteur du Télémaque épuise trop son sujet, par l'abondance et la richesse de son génie. Il dit tout, et ne laisse rien à penser aux autres.

To which Ramsay answers:

> Il est vrai que l'Imagination ne peut rien ajouter aux peintures de notre Poëte: mais l'esprit en suivant ses idées, s'ouvre, et s'étend. Quand il s'agit seulement de peindre, ses Tableaux sont parfaits, rien n'y manque. Quand il faut instruire, ses lumiéres sont fécondes, et nous y dévelopons une vaste étenduë de pensées. Il ne laisse rien à imaginer, mais il donne infiniment à penser.[1]

Whether it be virtue or vice, it is precisely this exhaustiveness that gives *Télémaque* an important part of its character. Just as Poussin in depicting a classical scene can make his figures more Greek than the Greeks, so Fénelon attains to a more than classical amplitude and correctness in the epic features he includes. Every feature in Homer and Virgil must be worked in somehow. It is inconceivable that Telemachus should not visit the lower world and that women should not attempt to burn a boat to stop the men taking a voyage the women dislike. There must be episodes, and Fénelon sees to it that his shall beat the epic poets in so doing. He devotes a book to the story of Philoctetes and has the advantage over Homer in being able to draw on Sophocles. Everything has to be of superlative quality. In this matter *Télémaque* reminds me of the Isabella Stewart Gardner museum in Boston; that resurrected Venetian palace, not only crammed with Old Masters but furnished throughout with first-quality treasures. The visitor is so browbeaten by masterpieces at every turn that he is tempted to put up a feeble resistance by falling into giggles; and he ends by suspecting that if he lifted the bed-coverlet in one of the bedrooms he would find a gold Cellini chamber-pot, the sight of which would turn giggles into positive hysterics. Even so the excess of *Télémaque* tempts us to giggle; but, unlike the Gardner museum, it achieves a heroic quality that ends by making the giggles irrelevant.

There is indeed something sublime about the way Fénelon sustains

[1] P. xvi. (misnumbered xxvi.).

his neo-classic correctness. It is the oblique expression of the austere morality that he preaches through the mouth of Mentor at such length and so explicitly: an obliquity that makes tolerable and often most acceptable an amount of direct didacticism that on the face of it would cause any work of art to founder. Fénelon, tutor of the prospective heir to the French throne, did indeed accept, and on behalf of a whole class express, the current doctrine of *noblesse oblige* with a success comparable to that achieved by the authors of *Le Cid* and *Bérénice*; and he did so with cumulative force over the extent of a long work.

Just as *Arcadia* was first concerned with the education of four princely young people, so *Télémaque* is concerned with fashioning a ruler. But Fénelon does not split his didacticism between several people, he concentrates it on one man, making it both the more sublime and scarcely tolerable to flesh and blood. But however exacting he was, he was tenderly aware of the exorbitance of his demands; and this combination of pity and insistence reveals a great nature. I can best illustrate from the conversation between Telemachus and Mentor just after the exquisite scene of Telemachus meeting his father for a moment without knowing him, in the last book of all. Mentor reads Telemachus a lesson on a king's need of serving the interests of his people, upon which Telemachus falls into a kind of despair at the hard lot of the ruler. It is his last spasm of revolt against the terrible duty to which he is being subjected:

> Pendant que Mentor parloit ainsi, Télémaque étoit plongé dans la tristesse et dans le chagrin, et il lui répondit avec un peu d'émotion: Si toutes ces choses sont vrayes, l'état d'un Roi est bien malheureux: il est l'esclave de tous ceux auxquels il paroît commander. Il n'est pas tant fait pour les commander, qu'il est fait pour eux: il se doit tout entier à eux, il est chargé de tous leurs besoins; il est l'homme de tout le peuple et de chacun en particulier. Il faut qu'il s'accommode à leurs foiblesses, qu'il les corrige en père, qu'il les rende sages et heureux. L'autorité qu'il paroît avoir n'est pas la sienne; il ne peut rien faire ni pour sa gloire, ni pour son plaisir: son autorité est celle des Loix, il faut qu'il leur obéisse pour en donner l'éxemple à ses Sujets. A proprement parler, il n'est que le défenseur des Loix pour les faire régner; il faut qu'il veille et qu'il travaille pour les maintenir: il est l'homme le moins libre et le moins tranquile de son Royaume. C'est un esclave qui sacrifie son repos et sa liberté, pour la liberté et la félicité publique.[1]

There is something sublime in Telemachus's imaginative recognition of what true royalty involves and in his final surrender to its demands;

[1] 408.

something which the heroic creed of Restoration England did not begin to approach.

Not only is Telemachus a great moral figure, he possesses, like his father in the little one sees of him, the social grace of the perfect aristocrat with its restrained assurance and highly trained sensitiveness to the things and people around him. There is something exquisitely apt and tactful, for instance, in the way Telemachus tells Mentor that he has found in Antiope, daughter of Idomeneus, the woman he knows he could marry. It was a difficult confession, for earlier Telemachus had fallen into a consuming passion for Eucharis, one of the train of Calypso: a passion that led to other violent emotions and an impossible situation, to be escaped from only by flight from Calypso's island. Now, Telemachus is quite certain of himself: he looks back on his old madness with clear eyes and a humble mind, sparing Mentor the slightest embarrassment as he makes his confession. The situation is that it is time to leave the land of the Salentines, where Idomeneus now rules, and Telemachus tells Mentor why he regrets this obligation:

> Aussitôt Télémaque ouvrit son cœur à son ami, mais avec quelque peine, sur un attachement qui lui faisoit regretter Salente. Vous me blâmerez peut-être, lui dit-il, de prendre trop facilement des inclinations dans les lieux où je passe; mais mon cœur me feroit des continuels reproches, si je vous cachois que j'aime Antiope fille d'Idomenée. Non, mon cher Mentor, ce n'est pas une passion aveugle comme celle dont vous m'avez guéri dans l'Isle de Calypso; j'ai bien reconnu la profondeur de la playe que l'amour m'avoit fait auprès d'Eucharis; je ne puis encore prononcer son nom sans être troublé; le tems et l'absence n'ont pu l'effacer. Cette expérience funeste m'apprend à me défier de moi-même: mais pour Antiope, ce que je ressens n'a rien de semblable; ce n'est point amour passioné, c'est goût, c'est estime, c'est persuasion que je serois heureux si je passois ma vie avec elle.[1]

Like the whole book of which he is hero, Telemachus here is profoundly correct: yet his is a living correctness of morals and breeding won by a noble nature from the hard school of experience.

In the above matters Fénelon voiced the best thought of his age. But he did also achieve the personal distinction that is necessary for validating his expression of it. Fénelon's style is all his own in its mixture of intellectual clarity and lyrical grace, and it corresponds to his unique quality of mind. He looks at humanity with an uncompromisingly disillusioned eye: 'il faut compter sur l'ingratitude des hommes' is one of his typical sentiments. And every man is his own

[1] 378-9.

enemy, witness Minerva's last words to Telemachus (Mentor was all along Minerva in disguise):

> Sur tout soyez en garde contre votre humeur. C'est un ennemi que vous porterez par tout avec vous jusqu'à la mort. Il entrera dans vos conseils, et vous trahira si vous l'écoutez. L'humeur fait perdre les occasions les plus importantes: elle donne des inclinations et des aversions d'enfant au préjudice des plus grands intérêts; elle fait décider les plus grandes affaires par les plus petites raisons: elle obscurcit tous les talens, rabaisse le courage, rend un homme inégal, foible, vil et insupportable. Défiez-vous de cet ennemi.[1]

And here is Mentor reproving Telemachus for having been led on by Calypso to enjoy talking about himself instead of pursuing the errand on which he had come:

> Elle s'étoit engagée à vous raconter des histoires, et à vous apprendre quelle a été la destinée d'Ulysse; elle a trouvé moyen de parler long-tems sans rien dire, et elle vous a engagé à lui expliquer tout ce qu'elle désire savoir; tel est l'art des femmes flateuses et passionées.[2]

But along with this disillusion exists an obstinate hope of a golden age.[3] And this hope is not only that of a pious archbishop thinking of heaven; it refers to the present life also. And it comes out in different ways throughout the book. Even if you can count on men's ingratitude you need not quite despair of wearing it down; and Fénelon modifies his disillusioned generalisation thus:

> Si la multitude est ingrate, il y a toujours des hommes vertueux qui sont touchez de votre vertu. La multitude même, quoique changeante et capricieuse, ne laisse pas de faire tôt ou tard une espéce de justice à la véritable vertu.[4]

He even mentions a golden age, as when Mentor congratulates Telemachus on his choice of Antiope for bride: she will be 'une épouse digne de l'âge d'or: fût-elle bergére dans la froide Algide, au lieu qu'elle est fille d'un Roi de Salerne; vous serez trop heureux de la posséder'. But Fénelon's utopian desires come out most beautifully in his accounts of pastoral felicity and in his strained, highly artificial imitations of classical imagery; imitations which ought to be ridiculous and are yet quite individual and delightful. The pastoral descriptions gain force through being traditional; they derive in part from the Arcadian prose romance: but they are also intensely serious pieces of economic propaganda. Fénelon hated the concentration of wealth

---

[1] 417-18.   [2] 55.

[3] For Fénelon's love of pastoral simplicity and his emotional urge towards a golden age see Ely Carcasonne, *Fénelon, L'Homme et L'Œuvre* (Paris 1946) 99-100.

[4] 409.

into the towns and believed that France could enter on a golden age if her rulers reversed the process and first ensured a prosperous agriculture. It is this mixture of practical earnestness and idyllic utopianism that makes his descriptions so memorable. Here is Mentor recommending strong measures for stopping bad and encouraging good husbandry, and their happy consequences:

> Mettez des taxes, des amendes, et même, s'il le faut, d'autres peines rigoureuses sur ceux qui négligent leurs champs, comme vous puniriez des Soldats qui abandonneroient leur poste dans la guerre. Au contraire donnez des grâces et des exemptions aux familles qui se multiplient; augmentez-les à proportion de la culture de leur terre. Bientôt leurs familles se multiplieront, et tout le monde s'animera au travail; il deviendra même honorable. La profession de Laboureur ne sera plus méprisée, n'étant plus accablée de tant de maux. On reverra en honneur la charruë maniée par des mains victorieuses qui auront défendu la patrie. Il ne sera pas moins beau de cultiver l'héritage de ses ancêtres pendant une heureuse paix, que de l'avoir défenduë généreusement pendant les troubles de la guerre; toute la campagne refleurira. Cérès se couronnera d'épics dorez. Bacchus foulant sur ses pieds les raisins, fera couler du penchant des montagnes des ruisseaux de vin plus doux que le nectar. Les creux vallons rententiront des concerts des Bergers, qui le long des clairs ruisseaux joindront leurs voix avec leurs flûtes, pendant que leurs troupeaux bondissans paîtront sur l'herbe et parmi les fleurs, sans craindre les loups.[1]

But it is the little passages of classicising ornament, in which the book abounds, that express most purely Fénelon's hope for an earthly paradise. Conventional in substance, remote from apparent actuality, they are yet highly individual and full of feeling, expressing in their unreality not the unreal but a state unrealised and yet not utterly beyond all hope of realisation. Here is one inserted suddenly into the wonderful passage in the last book where Telemachus sees his father but does not know him and his father sees him but may not make himself known. Telemachus has been told that this is a man called Cleomenes, a wanderer on the earth, destined to obtain a kingdom but not yet successful in fulfilling his destiny. Here is the account of Ulysses leaving the rocky islet where he and Telemachus have met:

> Cet inconnu avoit erré quelque tems au milieu de l'Isle, montant sur le sommet de tous les rochers, et considérant de là l'espace immense des mers avec une tristesse profonde.

Telemachus watches him, pitying the man's cruel fate of ceaseless wandering and forgetting his own smaller sorrows in this sympathy.

> Enfin cet homme voyant son vaisseau prêt, étoit descendu de ces rochers escarpez avec autant de vîtesse et d'agilité, qu'Apollon dans les forêts de la Lycie, ayant noué ses cheveux blonds, passe au travers des précipices pour aller percer de ses fléches les cerfs et les sangliers. Déja cet inconnu est dans le vaisseau qui fend l'onde amère, et qui s'éloigne de la terre.[1]

Ulysses has been presented to us as a fairly lifelike figure; and this comparison of him to a Greek god is startling in its remoteness and its imitative correctness. But it is more than a mere piece of classical imitation inserted to assure the reader that the author knows the rules of the game he is playing. It implies some new area of experience; and I think that area has to do with Fénelon's idealising proclivity, his insistence on the possibility of a better world than the one he sees around him.

I do not doubt Fénelon's success in creating a new medium of poetic prose[2] and in expressing both the heroic creed of the contemporary French aristocracy and a highly individual way of looking at life. What is less certain is whether he compassed a sufficient range of feeling to satisfy the requirement of epic amplitude. He has, for instance, been censured for failing to make his characters live. That is true in the sense that he does not individualise them strongly. But he does make them the successful vehicles of general ideas and of powerful feelings. An eminent example of his success is in the sixth book, where he recounts Telemachus's passion for Eucharis (already referred to), Calypso's jealousy of her, and the eventual flight of Mentor and Telemachus from the island. If Fénelon does not create characters, he here creates passion, beauty, and jealousy in an eminent degree. Telemachus is subjected to the conventional struggle between love and honour; but the struggle is so genuine that we have no thought for the conventionality and are entirely convinced when we hear that all the gods in Olympus gathered and sat in profound silence watching the fight between Venus and Minerva for the possession of the hero. Passion devastates him as another Frenchman pictured it devastating Manon Lescaut. And as to beauty, Fénelon endows Eucharis with it, but in the strictest accord with Lessing's principle of implication without the least statement or direct description. Having aroused in us a vivid sense of Telemachus's passion, he tells us that Telemachus and the nymphs were going hunting. Eucharis was of the party 'et elle étoit vêtuë comme Diane': perhaps the most evocative description of the female leg in literature. She has indeed no character, but of her beauty there can be no doubt.

[1] 412.   [2] See Carcassonne, *op. cit.* 109.

Calypso on her part expressed her jealousy to perfection by her change of front to Telemachus when she perceives his love for Eucharis. Previously bent on keeping him her enamoured slave in her island, she now accuses him of craven effeminacy:

> Ce Télémaque, qui a méprisé tous les plaisirs de l'Isle de Cypre, ne peut résister à la médiocre beauté d'une de mes Nymphes. Comment ose-t-il se vanter d'avoir fait tant d'actions merveilleuses, lui dont le cœur s'amolit lâchement par la volupté, et qui ne semble né que pour passer une vie obscure au milieu des femmes?[1]

And Fénelon can represent convincingly not only the separate passions but their cross-currents. There is an eminent example in the incident, short but extremely tense, of Telemachus, weakened by the terrible conflict between love and duty, committing the scandalous indiscretion of disclosing his passion in public. The position is complicated. Mentor has just finished building a ship (with Calypso's consent) which is to take both him and Telemachus from the island. Telemachus sees the ship and asks Calypso what it means. Calypso, jealous but still enamoured of him and wavering in her resolution to send him away, answers that it is to get rid of Mentor and his troublesome scruples. Telemachus jumps to the conclusion that Mentor is giving him up as hopeless:

> Mentor m'abandonne, c'est fait de moi, s'écria Télémaque! Eucharis, si Mentor me quitte, je n'ai plus que vous. Ces paroles lui échapérent dans le transport de sa passion: il vit le tort qu'il avoit eu en les disant: mais il n'avoit pas été libre de penser au sens de ses paroles. Toute la troupe étonnée demeura dans le silence. Eucharis rougissant, et baissant les yeux, demeuroit derriére toute interdite, sans oser se montrer. Mais pendant que la honte étoit sur son visage, la joie étoit au fond de son cœur.[2]

None of the persons has any marked individual character; and yet what a convincing complex of passions, how tense the human situation! In the reading we do not notice any particular deficiency in the author. What he provides is so good that we have no thought for what he does not.

Fénelon spent about nine years on *Télémaque* and showed a powerful controlling mind. His models helped him to construct, but his success in keeping all the details in solution in his mind at once was his own.

In a way *Télémaque* spoke for its age. Yet its choric quality was limited to the educated society to which it was addressed. For instance, in pleading for a revival of agriculture Fénelon did so from without. He does not voice the aspirations or the complaints of the peasants

[1] 105.   [2] 110.

themselves but gives them benevolent advice. Living in the society he did, he could hardly have achieved more in this way.

It would be vain to claim for Fénelon the scope of the very greatest, but his scope is sufficient, like that of Sidney, to admit him among the epic writers of a second order.

Télémaque was an immediate success and came soon to be considered the one French work worthy to be classed with the great epics. The anonymous writer of the interesting *Dissertation sur la Poësie Angloise* contained in the *Journal Literaire* for 1717, published at the Hague, gives the accepted verdict:

> Les François . . . entendent mieux les regles de l'Epopée qu'ils ne savent les mettre en pratique et ils critiquent très bien les Anciens, mais ils ne les égalent pas. Cependant si l'on veut bien mettre le *Telemaque* de l'Archevêque de Cambray au nombre des Poëmes Epiques, comme on le peut sans lui faire trop de grace, nous osons dire que cet Ouvrage seul peut tenir tête à tout ce que les Anciens et les Modernes ont fait de plus estimable dans le genre Heroïque. Une prose forte, hardie, mesurée et harmonieuse, n'est pas inférieure aux vers non rimez des Anglois.[1]

And later Voltaire was to follow Andrew Ramsay in putting it above the *Iliad*.[2] These extravagant verdicts are to be expected. *Télémaque* for all its imitative correctness was something new and surprising. It gave the abstract idea of the epic, still dominant in 1699 when the book was published, its last new turn. When the next century created the novel, thereby drawing the possibility of epic writing to a new mode, it destroyed the older abstraction. But some of the things *Télémaque* stood for were prolonged into the eighteenth century, and it is with these that I shall be concerned.

In England *Télémaque* soon became popular as none of the earlier French romances had done and was esteemed as an epic. In his 156th *Tatler*, for 8 April 1710, Steele commented at length on Telemachus's descent to the underworld and let fall a few general comments. He called the book a 'beautiful Romance' and added that the story was 'form'd altogether in the Spirit of Homer'. He excused himself for having confined himself to a single episode as follows:

> I have here only mention'd some Master-Touches of the admirable Piece, because the original it self is understood by the greater Part of my readers.

Two years later an anonymous writer translated the first book into couplets and reveals in his short preface in how high repute *Télémaque* then stood in England:

> The Adventures of Telemachus is a Book so well known and

---

[1] 177.
[2] See T. W. Russell, *Voltaire, Dryden, and Heroic Tragedy*, 149.

esteem'd, by Persons of the first Rank for Education, Wit, and good Sense; that to presume at a farther Recommendation of it, would look like refining upon their Judgment, and be almost as great a Breach of good Manners as to contradict 'em.

And the fortunes of *Télémaque* in England in the first half of the eighteenth century and in Europe generally are vividly described in the opening words of the preface to John Hawksworth's beautifully produced and widely patronised translation of 1768:

> The Telemachus of the celebrated archbishop of Cambray is a work of such reputation, that it would be scarce less absurd to recommend it, than to recommend the writings of Homer and Virgil: it holds the first class among the moral works of imagination in France, it has passed through innumerable editions, art has been exhausted to adorn it, and learning to illustrate its beauties; it has been translated into every language in Europe, the Turkish not excepted, and there are no less than five translations of it in our own.

Being so widely known, it was bound to have some influence, however indirect, on the attempts at the epic in eighteenth-century England. The details of this influence lie outside the scope of this book. What does concern me is that there is a strong affinity between *Télémaque* and Pope's *Iliad*, quite apart from any question of direct influence, an affinity very different from the more obvious one between Pope's translation and Dryden's *Aeneid*. And it is this concern that now takes me from seventeenth-century France to eighteenth-century England.

CHAPTER IX

EIGHTEENTH-CENTURY TRENDS

I AM nearing the end of my story of the English epic and I must give reasons why I go into less detail now than at the beginning. For my first reason I can use the words of Scott as he came to the last stages of *Waverley*. After describing the fall down a mountainside of a stone dislodged 'by an idle truant boy', slow at first and ever gaining speed till it comes to rest for ever, he goes on:

> Even such is the course of a narrative, like that which you are perusing; the earlier events are studiously dwelt upon, that you, kind reader, may be introduced to the character rather by narrative than by the duller medium of direct description; but when the story draws to its close, we hurry over the circumstances, however important, which your imagination must have forestalled, and leave you to suppose those things, which it would be abusing your patience to relate at length.

The other reason is that once a literary fashion is established it changes less rapidly than in the process of establishment. Critical theory of the epic in the sixteenth century was fluid and fluctuating and possessed the interest of uncertainty: which of a number of possible paths will it end by taking? But once Heinsius, Mambrun, Rapin, and Le Bossu had created an orthodoxy, there was no scope for change and unlimited scope for repetition. To describe these repetitions is pointless. May's *Henry II* is not a great poem, but just because it belongs to the formative stage of the English epic it is interesting and significant in a way that no mediocre epic of the eighteenth century can begin to be. Thus I have included it, while I shall not include Glover's *Leonidas*. It is only the great works still under the spell of the epic idea that are worth considering in a book of this kind.

That the serious urge to the verse epic in the traditional manner was losing its power appears from the vogue of the burlesque. It is not that the burlesque cannot co-exist with the strong flourishing of the mode to which it refers, witness the satyric drama in fifth-century Athens and Spenser's *Muiopotmos*; and there is no need to conclude that Boileau's *Le Lutrin* indicates a loss of faith in the serious epic consequent on the many failures in France to achieve it: but if it permeates or largely replaces, then the original mode has begun to decline, has begun to be beyond the men who would like to exploit it.

494

Butler's *Hudibras*, Cotton's *Scarronides*, and Dryden's admission of burlesque into his serious heroic writing show the beginnings of the process. But Pope's *Rape of the Lock* shows the burlesque given its own independent if miniature seriousness: a further process. Of whatever nature, the vogue of the burlesque heroic mode revealed a lack of confidence in the possibility of exploiting the mode itself in a straightforward way.

Another agent of change was a new critical spirit of the eighteenth century: the spirit that ultimately led to F. A. Wolf's *Prolegomena* in 1795, to which all subsequent disintegration of Homer's poems goes back. Before the eighteenth century (and of course for most men during it) Homer and Virgil had stood solidly together. But during the century the taste arose for the primitive, whether social, political, or literary, and it was bound to differentiate between the earlier and the later epic writers. A similar sentiment appears in conceptions of Shakespeare. Some people *liked* to think of him not as an ordinarily educated and sophisticated Elizabethan but as an illiterate genius. The idea of the illiterate Homer arose in the eighteenth century; and surprisingly early. In the preface to *A Collection of Old Ballads* published in London in 1723 occurs this sentence:

> The very Prince of Poets, old Homer . . . was nothing more than a blind Ballad-singer, who writ Songs of the Siege of Troy, and the Adventures of Ulysses; and playing the Tunes upon his Harp, sung 'em from Door to Door.[1]

Later in the century Homer was associated with the wild primitiveness of Ossian, and Blair said that both were equally ignorant of the laws of criticism.[2] Lois Whitney sums up the situation thus:

> The eighteenth century saw a change in the critical conception of the epic from that of the Aristotelian formalist at the beginning of the century to that of the primitivistic critic in the latter part. Critics of the former school regarded the epic, whether by Homer or Virgil, as the highest and most difficult form of literary art, the product of a sophisticated writer, who, as a conscious literary artist, followed certain prescribed regulations and wrote with a definite moral purpose. The primitivists, on the other hand, assumed that the epic was the product of the primitive bard, ignorant of rhetoric and the rules of the epic, who sang his lays to savage audiences on festival occasions.[3]

[1] I take this reference from Lois Whitney's article, *English Primitivistic Theories of Epic Origins* in *Modern Philology*, 1924, p. 366. I am indebted to this interesting article in this paragraph. In one place the authoress distorts her evidence. On p. 361 she makes out that Thomas Blackwell emphasised the tradition that Homer was a mere strolling bard. In actual fact Blackwell's main point is that the wandering poet was highly regarded, an important part of the community. 'Strolling bard' does not represent Blackwell's intention.

[2] *Ib.* 362.   [3] *Ib.* 327.

Once the partnership of Homer and Virgil as the two poets who had worthily realised the abstract idea of the epic was dissolved, the peculiar prestige of the epic could not but suffer a diminution.

An even more important indication of the way things were going was the appearance of *Robinson Crusoe* in 1719. The official epic of the age was uncompromisingly heroic and aristocratic. And here was a work, springing from a quite different area of ideas and society and yet containing not a few of the features that had in practice raised the epic to eminence. Looking back on the subsequent history of the novel we can see that Defoe began the transfer of the true epic instinct from the verse narrative, once its proper medium, to the middle-class prose romance. And the transfer was not merely that; it was a renovation. Defoe initiated something that was a new birth and which by its youthful vitality was bound to supplant the older thing with which it competed. Fielding both prolonged the vogue of the burlesque and continued the process begun by Defoe. Without in the least wishing to suppress the verse epic, he saw the weaknesses of the heroic convention of the Restoration and burlesqued it in *Tom Thumb the Great* and *Jonathan Wild*. On the other hand, in the preface to *Joseph Andrews* he argued for a new kind of prose epic. He considered *Télémaque* an example of it: serious, to be classed with the *Odyssey* and not with 'those voluminous works called Romances, namely Clelia, Cleopatra, Astraea, Cassandra, the Grand Cyrus, and innumerable others, which contain, as I apprehend, very little instruction or entertainment'. And then, on the analogy of the relation of comedy to tragedy, he postulated a comic form of epic to correspond to the solemn or tragic form.[1] To this form he considered *Joseph Andrews* to belong. Later, he called *Tom Jones* 'this heroic, historical, prosaic poem' and at the same time showed his sense of the continuity of his novel with the strict epic by, for instance, his burlesque classical introduction to his first picture of Sophia[2] and his comic treatise on the marvellous in literature.[3] This is not the place to discuss whether or not *Tom Jones* has the true epic qualities. The present point is that by enlarging the scope of serious narrative to embrace all sorts and conditions of men he helped to create for the novel epic possibilities that had come to be lacking in the official verse epic of the neo-classic tradition. He was really promoting the process begun by Defoe.

But a great movement does not die at once. Though conditions did not encourage any but fools to attempt the straight epic, the quasi-mystical veneration of the epic form persisted and could still produce indirect results. The prestige of Homer and Virgil remained enormous, and to translate them worthily was a secondary fulfilment

---

[1] Ethel M. Thornbury did a Ph.D. thesis on *Henry Fielding's Theory of the Comic Prose Epic*, published Madison 1931.

[2] Book iv. chap. 2.

[3] Book viii. chap. 1.

of the ever-beckoning task to glorify your country by an epic achievement. Dryden had translated the *Aeneid* well enough to rule out another attempt for many years, but Chapman's or Ogilby's Homer would not deter an Augustan. Here was an opening, and the first poet of the early part of the century was persuaded to profit by it. History had long been associated with the epic, but the production of history in the neo-classic age in England had lagged behind that of the Continent. Here was another opening, and the greatest historian of eighteenth-century England was inspired by the same kind of motives that prompted Pope to produce his *Iliad*. The *Decline and Fall of the Roman Empire* is the latest work of English literature to be conceived in the same manner as the *Faerie Queene* and *Paradise Lost*. Pope and Gibbon are then the two authors who remain to be described.

CHAPTER X

POPE'S ILIAD

That poetical wonder, the translation of the Iliad; *a performance which no age or nation can pretend to equal.*   (Samuel Johnson)

Pope's translation is a portrait endowed with every merit excepting that of likeness to the original.   (Gibbon)

POPE was untouched by the primitivist notion of the epic described in the last section and was fully open to the neo-classic doctrine of the eminence of that mode in itself and of Homer and Virgil as its great practitioners. I cannot do better than quote W. P. Ker on this point:

> Pope was haunted by the orthodox critical doctrine of the Epic Poem. Like Milton and Dryden, he had the epic ambition; he wrote *Alcander Prince of Rhodes* when he was a boy; he made the plan of *Brutus*, an epic, when he was older. He wrote for Steele's *Guardian* the comic receipt to make an epic poem which was incorporated in Martinus Scriblerus on the Art of Sinking in Poetry. But his preface to the *Iliad* goes over, seriously, the same divisions of the subject: Fable, Characters, Machines, Allegory. His plan of *Brutus* follows the receipt; the fable is taken from Geoffrey of Monmouth, the machines are guardian angels of kingdoms, such as Dryden had recommended. He puts the old allegories into his Homer. The revised version of the *Rape of the Lock*, the very successful 'machinery' of sylphs and gnomes, is something more than play; it is parody of one of the most important things in life for Pope, and his heroi-comical expedient, his most excellent lively burlesque substitute for the Olympians of Homer, is valued by him for its epic quality and its faithfulness to the epic idea.[1]

But I should go further than this and say that Pope's *Iliad* was itself the great popular neo-classic attempt to embody the epic idea in English verse. *Paradise Lost* was Milton's private, individual attempt. He had no popular backing during composition. With Pope's *Iliad* we have the queer picture of an unnaturally precocious poet spending six of the best years of his youth (from twenty-five to thirty) on his task, mainly in the country but with excursions into urban society, in a mood of quasi-religious fervour though punctuated with outbursts of flippancy and rebellion, aided by scholars, and as the work

[1] W. P. Ker, *The Art of Poetry* (Oxford 1923) 95-6.

498

progressed (it came out by instalments) attended by the awed expectancy of all the culture and aristocracy of England. Indeed it may be just to compare the genesis of Pope's *Iliad* with that of the *Aeneid* of Virgil. Propertius, Virgil's contemporary, wrote that something greater than the *Iliad* was being born: *nescioquid maius nascitur Iliade*.[1] If we knew as much of the petty details of literary men's lives in the age of Augustus as we do in the age of Queen Anne we might find the analogy very close indeed. True, *maius* may not be appropriate to the thoughts of Pope's contemporaries; but a version in some ways better, more correct and more civilised, was not out of the question.

I spoke of Pope's 'mood of quasi-religious fervour' and I want to dwell on it, for the notion is still prevalent that there is something frivolous in the way Pope tricked out the Homeric simplicity. First, Homer had impressed Pope deeply in childhood. He told Broome that Homer was the first author that made him as a child 'catch the itch of poetry'. And Spence records under his entries for the years 1742-3 that Pope still experienced a kind of rapture at the recollection of reading Ogilby's translation at the age of eight. Pope's early admiration of Homer continued into maturity. The preface to the *Iliad* and postscript to the *Odyssey* breathe an almost rapturous admiration. And Pope confesses himself 'utterly incapable of doing justice to Homer'. But it is perhaps in Pope's own notes that this appears most convincingly. For instance, in his note to the description of Athena arriving for battle (v. 904 ff. in his own *Iliad*) he says:

> Indeed there is a Greatness and Sublimity in the whole Passage, which is astonishing and superior to any Imagination but that of *Homer*, nor is there any that might better give occasion for that celebrated saying, That *he was the only Man who had seen the Forms of the Gods, or the only Man who had shewn them.* . . . But we shall not wonder at the unusual Majesty of all these Ideas, if we consider that they have a near Resemblance to some Descriptions of the same kind in the sacred Writings, where the Almighty is represented arm'd with Terror, and descending in Majesty to be aveng'd on his Enemies.

Pope in fact approached Homer a little as King James's translators approached Holy Writ. There is a famous comparison at the end of the eighth book of the camp-fires of the Trojans to the stars on a

[1] For an excellent brief account of the circumstances attending the production of Pope's *Iliad* see R. K. Root, *The Poetical Career of Alexander Pope* (Princeton 1938) chap. v. For a fully detailed account see George Sherburn, *The Early Career of Alexander Pope* (Oxford 1934). Pope's *Iliad* has more recently been the subject of an excellent monograph by Douglas Knight, *Pope and the Heroic Tradition* (New Haven 1951). Knight argues strongly for the work being not just a translation but part of the European heroic tradition. He also has valuable things to say about the epic generally.

clear night. Homer adds to the comparison the homely picture of the shepherd rejoicing at the fine weather; and Pope has been accused of degrading Homer by his rendering of Homer's simplicity:

> *The conscious Swains, rejoicing in the Sight,*
> *Eye the blue Vault, and bless the useful Light.*

But whatever the merits or demerits of Pope's translation, his note to the passage (viii. 687) testifies to his humility before his original:

> This Comparison is inferior to none in *Homer*. It is the most beautiful Night-piece to be found in Poetry. He presents you with a Prospect of the Heavens, the Seas, and the Earth: The Stars shine, the Air is serene, the World enlighten'd, and the Moon mounted in Glory.

Pope then showed a humility, a quasi-religious reverence, before Homer. But that did not prevent his thinking that the age of Queen Anne was more civilised than that of Greece of the heroic age. His aim was to serve Homer by presenting him to his countrymen in the best possible guise. Poetically he could not equal him: the one thing he could do was to civilise his setting. People complain that Pope degraded Homer by making his warriors talk like gentlemen: Pope on the contrary thought that by doing so he improved him, and thus served him, in the only way that lay open. The same is true about Homer's shepherd and Pope's 'conscious Swains'. Pope believed he could never equal the poetic beauty of Homer's night-piece. It was the most beautiful in poetry, unapproachable. But there was still the chance of bettering a detail. The mention of the plain shepherd was a piece of baldness characteristic of the uncouth age to which Homer belonged, and it could be improved on. The 'conscious Swains' who 'bless the useful light' are humble, practical, though remote, members of a civilised community.

This filling-out of Homer by Pope is the great English example of the age's general sentiments about ancients and moderns. There were many different opinions on the relations between them. But the preponderant opinion was that (whatever future events might bring forth) the ancients were at the present moment superior to the moderns in poetry and that the moderns were superior to them in science and philosophy. The ancients had more natural poetic genius, had produced the two chief poets, but the moderns were more civilised and sophisticated. Further, there were great possibilities today of advances in civilisation. Any creative writer in touch with his age was bound to render the double theme: the genius of the ancients, the superior and growing civilisation of the moderns. Now Fénelon had expressed it. He had done homage to Homer and Virgil by copying them so scrupulously; he had expressed the greater civilisation of his own age by the very exaggeration of his correctness. The

changes Pope made in his translation of Homer, the gentility added
to his warriors, the antitheses added to their sentiments, the regu-
larity added to the descriptions, correspond precisely to the exaggerated correctness of *Télémaque*.

Of the close spiritual kinship of Fénelon and Pope I have no doubt;
but Pope may not have been conscious of it, and the direct influence
of the French on the English writer, though possible, even probable,
cannot be proved. At least Pope was familiar with *Télémaque* and had
the highest regard for it. In his preface to the *Iliad* after citing Virgil
and Milton as the two poets to be compared with Homer he goes on:

> Next these, the Archbishop of *Cambray's Telemachus* may give
> him [the translator] the truest Idea of the Spirit and Turn of our
> Author.

And in his postscript to the *Odyssey* he calls *Télémaque* the greatest
example of epic narrative after the *Aeneid*. Further, Pope, through his
hereditary Catholicism, was aware of Catholic thought across the
channel and apt to heed it. And lastly he was the friend and corre-
spondent of Andrew Ramsay, already mentioned as intimate with
Fénelon and his panegyrist in the first authorised edition of *Télémaque*.[1] I should conjecture that Pope knew *Télémaque* well, was
prejudiced in its favour and apt to ponder on it, and that on account
of this familiarity was led unconsciously to express through the
medium of his translation the kind of things Fénelon expressed
through his prose romance.

I have been speaking of what Pope added to his original and by
so doing I have been going against the usual method of criticising
Pope's Homer. Most criticism tries to answer the question whether
Pope succeeded in translating Homer; but in this context far more
important is the question whether in translating Homer he succeeded
in translating his age. And this second question is important not only
for this book but for the history of English literature in general. How
flatly or blandly it has been ignored can be judged by this summary
dismissal of Pope's *Iliad* by Saintsbury. He wrote:

> Pope's *Iliad* has long become merely a curiosity, because if we
> want Homer we go either to himself or to a translator who has
> some sense of him.

Saintsbury assumes that the only reason for going to Pope's *Iliad* is
because we want Homer. Such an assumption goes clean against the
opinions of Pope's age. A large proportion of the many distinguished
subscribers to Pope's *Iliad* had the freedom of the original and went
to Pope for something other than Homer. And when Johnson called

---

[1] For Pope and his Catholic friends see E. Audra, *L'Influence Française dans l'Œuvre
de Pope* (Paris 1931) chap. iii.

it 'that poetical wonder', implying thereby a quality beyond that of fidelity to an original, he spoke not only for himself but for his age. And we neglect the verdict of an age at our peril.

But before I come to my main topic, how far Pope through his Homer succeeded in interpreting his age, I cannot refrain from divagating into a short defence of Pope as a translator.

Like the disintegrators of Shakespeare, the critics of translations usually fix their eye on the small detail, on the accuracy of the phrase or the short passage. The better tests of a long work are whether the translator has a durable rhetoric and whether he can follow the main undulations of his original. The modern debunking translators of Homer from Samuel Butler to E. V. Rieu have done good work in persuading the public that Homer was a man with the same basic feelings as our own. But their work is topical, it has no durable rhetoric. Take this from Rieu's *Iliad*:

> Picture a horde of wasps pouring out from the side of a road. They are used to being teased by boys, for the young fools provoke them every time they pass their wayside nest. The result is a public menace.

Writing like this has a good topical propaganda value. But it belongs to no solid school of writing and it omits any reference to one of the largest components of Homer's poetry: the formal, one might almost say hieratic quality of his verse. Pope's *Iliad* on the contrary is the only translation in English (apart from Dryden's fragments and perhaps one or two other fragments) that has got anywhere near the larger qualities of the original. Pope's poetical rhetoric is durable and he hardly ever fails to follow the undulations of his original. He is as energetic as Dryden as a translator and far more sensitive. He can describe a battle with Homer; he can be pathetic with him, as in the parting of Hector and Andromache and Priam's recovery of Hector's body from Achilles; and he can give the sense of urgency to a council-scene in the true Homeric manner. All these are large matters; and success in them, not attained by any other translator, immensely outweighs any possible defect of detail.

I come now to my main inquiry: how far in his translations of Homer Pope was able to interpret his age. It is an inquiry crucial to the question whether Pope's Homer had the choric character necessary for the true epic.

And first I must note what is simply a remarkable accident: that Homer's *Iliad* (but hardly his *Odyssey* as I shall point out) does present a society in some ways strangely analogous with that of the age of Queen Anne. The *Iliad* comprises all grades of society, but it confines itself in the main to the nobles who wield the real power in time of war. It pictures these as of strong and wilful but varied character. At their head is Agamemnon; but his power is limited and depends greatly on the voluntary co-operation of the nobles. There is the utmost freedom of speech in debate. In spite of quarrels and mistakes this Greek world was energetic and self-confident. In Troy the civilisation was similar, but Priam and his family had the power, and the allied nobles counted for less. Along with the aristocratic society depicted by Homer goes an apparently formal way of life. Objects are often given a standard epithet; the ordinary operations of eating and paying a visit and going to bed are described with a hieratic fixity. Most of these matters had a correlative in the age of Queen Anne. Since the beginning of the eighteenth century, with Blenheim, the union with Scotland, the acceptance of the Newtonian conception of the universe, with, generally, the recognition abroad of Britain as a power great and growing in military force and in culture, the temper of the country was analogous to the temper of the Greeks in their energetic prosecution of the Trojan War. Since 1688 the king had been reduced to a position not unlike that of Agamemnon. The British aristocracy, like the Greek, was the real wielder of power. And the quarrels between the Greek chiefs presented a ready analogy with the rivalry of Whigs and Tories, itself fostered by a corresponding freedom of speech. (Courthope in his life of Pope noted how in his *Iliad* Pope delighted in the Greek leaders' exchange of exhortation and invective and how he found for it a 'style springing naturally out of the genius of a free nation, and the lofty eloquence developed from free Parliamentary debate'.[1]) It would be wrong to suggest anything but the vaguest analogy between Troy and France. But probably the rivalry between Troy and Greece did just hint that between France and England.

With the *Odyssey* the life of the ruling classes in the age of Queen Anne is not so comparable. There the more democratic side of Homeric society comes out. Odysseus is on terms of intimacy with his crew very different from the relations of a great English landlord with his tenants and servants. While in the *Iliad* life was unusually concentrated and on a grander scale through the assembly of so many princes in a single army, in the *Odyssey* we see the miniature life of a small island state, an intimate patriarchal society remote from eighteenth-century England. I do not say that this is the reason why Pope took his translation of the *Odyssey* less seriously, working at it with a less concentrated intensity and delegating half of it to others. But it may well be that he had an unconscious notion that the *Odyssey* could not meet his requirements so well as the *Iliad*, which reinforced his sense that for the *Iliad* he had made his supreme effort and that he was not prepared to do the same a second time. Pope

---

[1] (London 1889) 167. This life is the fifth volume of the works of Pope edited by W. Elvin and W. J. Courthope.

translated some of the domestic scenes of the *Odyssey* exquisitely. But he does not show the same range as in the *Iliad*. Nor is it true that Pope's share and those of Broome and Fenton are not to be distinguished. Passing from the last book of the *Iliad* to the first of the *Odyssey* one notices a sharp fall in standard: a far more monotonous versification.[1] In view of all this I consider that the *Odyssey* does not come within my present scope and I shall not consider it further.

To return to the *Iliad*, my point is that the life there pictured by Homer presented sufficient analogies with life among the ruling classes in the age of Queen Anne to enable Pope, setting out to make his original more civilised, to reflect not just a vague notion of civilisation, but the actual civilisation in which he was set. I believe he succeeded in making his *Iliad* the great poetical interpretation of his age.

It is now time to reinforce my point by a few illustrations. And first for Pope's energy. Here indeed he is largely inspired by the infectious energy of his original. It is the quality he especially admired and which above all he strove to retain. Even so, he was helped in his desire to reproduce Homer's energy by the age's awareness of its own positive achievements. What is so remarkable about Pope's *Iliad* is not so much this or that energetic passage but his surprising sustention of energy throughout the poem. He hardly ever fails to rise to Homer. This sustention cannot be illustrated, but for one out of so many possible single examples of Pope's success I choose the account, from the thirteenth book, of the pick of the Greek leaders, rallied by Poseidon's exhortation, gathering together to resist Hector, now at the height of his martial prowess. Homer describes the Greeks pressed together in closest formation awaiting the impetus of Hector and the Trojans. Hector crashes into them like a great rock dislodged high up on a hillside and hurtling down till halted in the valley below. This is Pope's version:

> *A chosen Phalanx, firm, resolv'd as Fate,*
> *Descending Hector and his Battel wait;*
> *An Iron Scene gleams dreadful o'er the Fields,*
> *Armour in Armour lock'd, and Shields in Shields,*
> *Spears lean on Spears, on Targets Targets throng,*
> *Helms stuck to Helms, and Man drove Man along.*
> *The floating Plumes unnumber'd wave above,*
> *As when an Earthquake stirs the nodding Grove;*
> *And levell'd at the Skies with Pointing Rays,*
> *Their brandish'd Lances at each Motion blaze.*

[1] I make this observation with greater confidence because, when I first read Pope's *Odyssey*, Bk. i, I imagined, relying on the mendacious note at the end of the translation, that Pope himself was the translator. In spite of that I was struck by its inferiority. Actually it was Fenton who translated this book.

POPE'S ILIAD

Thus breathing Death, in terrible Array,
The close-compacted Legions urg'd their way:
Fierce they drove on, impatient to destroy;
Troy charg'd the first, and Hector first of Troy.
As from some Mountain's craggy Forehead torn,
A Rock's round Fragment flies, with Fury born,
(Which from the stubborn Stone a Torrent rends)
Precipitate the pond'rous Mass descends:
From Steep to Steep the rolling Ruin bounds;
At ev'ry Shock the crackling Wood resounds;
Still gath'ring Force, it smoaks; and, urg'd amain,
Whirls, leaps, and thunders down, impetuous to the Plain:
There stops—so Hector.[1]

Pope here as usual takes liberties with Homer. For instance, his
'resolv'd as Fate' and 'Iron Scene' are gratuitous additions, while he
suppressed (perhaps in the interests of modern theories of motion)
Homer's simplicity of the stone rolling no more, ἐσσύμενός περ,
although it wanted to go on. But it is the general effect that matters, and
this is impressive. The phalanx is indeed powerful and grim; the
stone's impetus is formidable. Pope in some sort has met the challenge
of Homer's vitality. I say 'in some sort', because, vitality apart, the
picture Pope gives is not Homer's. Homer is right on the spot, he
knows all about the thing he describes. Pope fabricates from without
a splendid picture of a battle scene. Homer feels the urgency of the
crisis: the best men of the Greeks get together to meet it. Pope's
'chosen Phalanx' is in comparison detached from reality. Yet what
a superb academic *picture* he creates. Dramatically he cannot compete
with Homer, but he has the energy to make his 'Iron Scene' live.

Or, to show Pope equally energetic but more faithful to his original,
take his rendering of the fight over the body of Patroclus, Greeks and
Trojans tugging at it like curriers working at a bull's skin:

But round the Corps, the Heroes pant for Breath,
And thick and heavy grows the Work of Death:
O'erlabour'd now, with Dust and Sweat and Gore,
Their Knees, their Legs, their Feet are cover'd o'er,
Drops follow Drops, the Clouds on Clouds arise,
And Carnage clogs their Hands, and Darkness fills their Eyes;
As when a slaughter'd Bull's yet reeking Hyde,
Strain'd with full Force, and tugg'd from Side to Side,
The brawny Curriers stretch; and labour o'er
Th'extended Surface, drunk with Fat and Gore;
So tugging round the Corps both Armies stood;
The mangled Body bath'd in Sweat and Blood:

[1] 177-99.

> *While* Greeks *and* Ilians *equal strength employ,*
> *Now to the Ships to force it, now to* Troy.
> *Not* Pallas' *self, her Breast when Fury warms,*
> *Nor He, whose Anger sets the World in Arms,*
> *Could blame this Scene; such Rage, such Horror reign'd;*
> *Such,* Jove *to honour the great Dead ordain'd.*[1]

But, though here Pope is pretty faithful to his original, he cannot forbear to add one significant touch. Humanitarian though Pope was, he was poet enough to glory in any activity superlatively carried out. It was a magnificent struggle, and Pope backs up Homer in his sense of it. But at the end he adds his own, gratuitous, justifying touch. It was to honour a great man, the dead Patroclus, that Zeus allowed the terrible display of evenly matched martial passions. And that somehow makes it a little more civilised than it is in Homer.

For another kind of transformation take Pope's rendering, in the eleventh book, of Zeus, regardless of the resentment of the other gods at his favouring the Trojans, sitting by himself in his own might and looking down on Troy, the Greek ships, the flash of bronze, killer and killed:

> *Meanwhile apart, superior, and alone,*
> *Th'eternal Monarch, on his awful Throne,*
> *Wrapt in the Blaze of boundless Glory sate;*
> *And fix'd, fulfill'd the just Decrees of Fate.*
> *On Earth, he turn'd his all-consid'ring Eyes,*
> *And mark'd the Spot where* Ilion's *Tow'rs arise;*
> *The Sea with Ships, the Fields with Armies spread,*
> *The Victor's Rage, the dying, and the dead.*[2]

This may not be Homer's Zeus, but (with Milton in the background) it is a superb rendering of the God of the eighteenth-century hymn-books. Best of all is the sense of God's pity for mankind conveyed through the falling rhythm of the last line: a pity entirely absent from the equally superb but non-committal Greek.

To illustrate Pope's zest for the council-scenes with their free disputes would take too much space; and it can readily be found early in the first book. But I will illustrate the gentility Pope added to the Homeric heroes by his translation of one of the most famous things, Sarpedon's speech in the twelfth book on the shortness of life and the reason for pursuing honour:

> *Why boast we,* Glaucus! *our extended Reign,*
> *Where* Xanthus' *Streams enrich the* Lycian *Plain,*
> *Our num'rous Herds that range the fruitful Field,*
> *And Hills where Vines their purple Harvest yield,*

[1] xvii. 444-61.   [2] 108-14.

Our foaming Bowls with purer Nectar crown'd,
Our Feasts enhanc'd with Music's sprightly Sound?
Why on those Shores are we with Joy survey'd,
Admir'd as Heroes, and as Gods obey'd?
Unless great Acts superior Merit prove,
And vindicate the bount'ous Pow'rs above.
'Tis ours, the Dignity they give, to grace;
The first in Valour, as the first in Place.
That when with wond'ring Eyes our martial Bands
Behold our Deeds transcending our Commands,
Such, they may cry, deserve the sov'reign State,
Whom those that envy, dare not imitate!
Could all our Care elude the gloomy Grave,
Which claims no less the fearful than the brave,
For Lust of Fame I should not vainly dare
In fighting Fields, nor urge thy Soul to War.
But since, alas! ignoble Age must come,
Disease, and Death's inexorable Doom;
The Life which others pay, let us bestow,
And give to Fame what we to Nature owe;
Brave tho' we fall, and honour'd if we live,
Or let us Glory gain, or Glory give.[1]

Pope here renders Homer's general sentiments justly enough, but he takes very great liberties with the details. Homer's Sarpedon described their home amenities briefly and set forth without epigram or antithesis his plea for the one crowded hour of glorious life. Pope has bestowed on Sarpedon the education of a great nobleman's house and of an English university. It would never do for his Sarpedon merely to get more meat and drink than the proletariat: decency required something more elaborate. So his herd must range the field, his vines yield a purple harvest, and his foaming bowls be crowned with purer nectar. Unlike Homer's, Pope's Sarpedon knew the meaning of the phrase to 'pay the debt to nature', and he shows his education and his wit by the original notion of paying that debt to fame instead. Homer's bare presentment of the solemn theme of death and decay and glory might serve in earlier days; it would not do in the age of Queen Anne: and Pope does not hesitate to add detail and fabricate antitheses. I say this not to decry Pope. On the contrary I think the passage magnificent eighteenth-century poetry, poetry which does not stale however often read. In spite of the liberties taken with Homer it remains the worthiest translation; but its first praise is to be the poetry of its own age. And why not? The sentiment of *noblesse oblige* animates all true aristocracies. That of Queen Anne's

[1] xii. 371-96.

day was less purely military than in Homer's. But it is easy enough, in reading this passage, to include the duties of government with those of war; and by such an inclusion it becomes perfectly apt to the eighteenth century. And though the solemnity of the last lines, on death, originated in Homer, why deny them their undoubted glory of anticipating the best that Gray attained to in his *Elegy?*

But even if it is granted that Pope's *Iliad* is fine Augustan poetry, the question whether it is epic remains to be answered. What I have said so far concerns mainly its choric quality. I have maintained that it does speak for the ruling classes: on the official side it is choric. It is when we consider the matter of amplitude that doubts arise. And here we are forced to ask: did Pope interpret a sufficient range of English life, and was his couplet a sufficiently inclusive medium, to give his *Iliad* the proper epic amplitude? It is vain to ignore the partiality of Pope's range. Pope lived in an age when society was divided: the legacy of the civil war of the last century. Pope's world is different from the more miscellaneous world of Defoe and the strict, Dissenting world of Watts. There is no need to go further for illustration than the 'night-piece' from the eighth book, mentioned earlier. This begins with a description of the moon, of the clarity of the sky

> *When not a Breath disturbs the deep Serene;*
> *And not a cloud o'ercasts the solemn Scene;*

and goes on to describe the stars and their light. Then

> *The conscious Swains, rejoicing in the Sight,*
> *Eye the blue Vault, and bless the useful Light.*[1]

Pope has a sincere and direct appreciation of the beauties of a moonlight night in the hills, which animates the formalities of a carefully staged and much corrected description. But the shepherds are outside that direct appreciation. This is not just because he calls them 'conscious Swains'; it is perfectly possible to get used to such a circumlocution. If he had allowed his swains merely to rejoice (like Homer's shepherd), they might have been a living part of the scene. It is their further activities that separate them and declare them an alien insertion. Think of Shakespeare's 'Looke, th' unfolding Starre calles up the Shepheard', think of Milton's

> *The Star that bids the Shepherd fold*
> *Now the top of Heav'n doth hold,*

and see the difference. *Their* shepherds were a part of total society in a way they had ceased to be in the age of Pope. And Pope's own scope is narrowed accordingly. It is not to Pope's but to a portion of Defoe's world that shepherds belonged.

[1] viii. 689-90,69 7-9.

Pope's couplet has a wider range than has usually been supposed, and Miss Sitwell has done good work in making this clear. But compared with the Homeric hexameter it is restricted; and its restrictions correspond neatly enough with the partiality of the English society for which he wrote. It could not have dealt with the total society of Homer; but for the society of the ruling classes in the age of Queen Anne it was amazingly appropriate. It can compass this society's energy and political self-confidence, its critical sophistication, its elegance, and its satirical coarseness (see the picture of Thersites in the second book). It is perfectly adequate to the only job that was open to it.

Pope had little architectonic power but great tenacity of purpose. His natural unit of composition was small. The *Iliad* provided the architectonic frame, and Pope exhibited a superb power of will in persisting with the laborious process of filling it in. That he did so persist may have been in part an accident. Doubtless he did show a wonderful courage in an exacting task; but who knows if he would have persisted in it if he had not committed himself to satisfying his subscribers? But it is the result that counts, not the accident by which it was brought about. It is not on the side of the conscious will that Pope's *Iliad* will be deficient.

To sum up is hard. And about a translation people will not be likely to agree. Pope's failure to present a total society was not his fault, and yet I doubt his ability to do so had the possibility been there. There is no case for counting Pope's *Iliad* as a major epic. But it remains the great long poem of its age, and, however different in other ways, achieves the same relative approximation to the major epics as do Sidney's *Arcadia* and Bunyan's *Holy War*.

CHAPTER XI

GIBBON

*L'historien doit embrasser et posséder toute son histoire . . . il faut
qu'il la tourne et retourne de tous côtés jusqu'à ce qu'il ait trouvé son
vrai point de vue.* (Fénelon)

*My lot might have been that of a slave, a savage, or a peasant; nor
can I reflect without pleasure on the bounty of nature, which cast my
birth in a free and civilised country, in an age of science and philosophy, in a family of honourable rank, and decently endowed with
the gifts of fortune.*

(Edward Gibbon, *Memoirs of my Life and Writings*)

*However far his eye may range, the clue is always firmly in his
fingers, and the conclusion of the third volume was in draft before the
first volume was written.* (G. M. Young, *Gibbon*)

THE notion, propounded by Quintilian, that the province of
history lay close to, or even overlapped, that of poetry was strong
in the Renaissance and continued throughout the neo-classic age.
Gibbon was open to it and conceived of his own great historical work
much as an epic writer of the same school conceived of his heroic
poem. I can lead up to Gibbon's own testimony concerning the
relations of poetry and history and to the principles of his composition
by what two earlier writers said about history. It is apt to Gibbon's
international spirit that one of these should be English and the other
French.

In his *History of the Royal Society*[1] Sprat proposed the creation of an
English academy. Its first concern was to be with the English language, which Sprat thought demanded immediate improvement.
But it could also foster the production of literature; and he goes on to
say of what species of literature there is now the greatest need:

> Of all the Labors of mens Wit, and Industry, I scarce know any,
> that can be more useful to the World, then *Civil History*: if it were
> written, with that sincerity and majesty, as it ought to be, as a
> faithful Idea of humane Actions. And it is observable, that almost
> in all civiliz'd Countries, it has been the last thing, that has come
> to perfection.

Sprat then goes on, in a passage full of hope, to say that the time is
propitious for an advance in the art of history and that in the recent

[1] The passages I here refer to are on pp. 40-5 of the 1702 edition.

civil war a great subject is to hand. It almost looks as if Clarendon intended his history as an answer to Sprat's challenge. But that is not to the point here, for Gibbon did not consider Clarendon a great historian: for him the void in English historical writing remained till his near-contemporaries, Robertson and Hume; and they had not at all exhausted the subject. Gibbon both inherits Sprat's belief in the virtue of scientific discovery, and agrees with him in his estimate of history and in his calling it a literary mode that comes to perfection only in the late maturity of a culture. In his first published work, the *Essai sur l'Etude de la Littérature* (1759), he asserted that the great age of literature was past and that the present was the great age of natural philosophy.[1] But history, flourishing later than the other kinds of literature, was not yet exhausted and was still open to the aspirant to literary fame. Gibbon could never have been a poet; Clio was his sole proper mistress: but, living when he did, he could and did contemplate a work of history in the spirit in which poets had contemplated their epic poems.

Fénelon, in his *Lettre sur les Occupations de l'Académie Française* (1714), has a section on history which illustrates the close relation it had then with poetry and especially the epic. He repeats the old doctrine of the example, common to both epic and history; and one of the supreme manifestations of the art of history is the exemplary *Lives* of Plutarch. The following passage is typical:

> L'histoire est très-importante: c'est elle qui nous montre les grands exemples, qui fait servir les vices mêmes des méchans à l'instruction des bons, qui débrouille les origines, et qui explique par quel chemin les peuples ont passé d'une forme de gouvernement à une autre.[2]

The true historian is not a pedant or a compiler. He has his eye on his reader, and omits all but the vital facts.

> Le grand point est de mettre d'abord le lecteur dans le fond des choses, de lui en découvrir les liaisons, et de se hâter de le faire arriver au dénouement. L'histoire doit en ce point ressembler un peu au poème épique.[3]

History can reach its perfection only if it achieves unity of action:

> La principale perfection d'une histoire consiste dans l'ordre et dans l'arrangement.[4]

And Fénelon goes on to say that the rules Horace lays down for the epic apply equally to history. From his autobiography and still more from some of the miscellaneous writings it is certain that Gibbon agreed entirely with Fénelon.

[1] *Miscellaneous Works*, ed. Lord Sheffield (London 1796) ii. 450.
[2] *Works* (Paris 1824) xxi. 227.   [3] *Ib.* 228.   [4] *Ib.* 229.

To consider these writings more generally, what first emerges is that Gibbon was thoroughly aware of the orthodox neo-classic ideas on literature and entirel yin sympathy with them. In his *Essai sur l'Etude de la Littérature* he cites the orthodox French critics of the seventeenth century—Le Bossu, Boileau, Rapin, Brumoy—as the undoubted masters; and he shows himself well acquainted with the disputes about ancients and moderns. There is much about Homer and Virgil, who are for him without question the great poets. In fact, Gibbon sees himself first of all as a man of letters, of general culture; and history is but one of a number of other Muses.

Secondly, Gibbon shows a marked interest in the epic form. In his *Memoirs of my Life and Writing*, commonly know as his autobiography, he records his very early acquaintance with Pope's Homer and Dryden's Virgil, and his partiality for Pope. And later, after he had learnt Greek, he read and re-read Homer in the original. Included in his commentary on Hurd's edition of Horace's *Epistles* is a section on the epic practice of putting important parts of the action in the form of reported narrative. Here he includes Fénelon and Voltaire among epic writers, showing that he has meditated on the epic throughout the ages. Gibbon also wrote essays on the epic practice of catalogues of armies and on the sixth book of the *Aeneid*. Near the end of the *Decline and Fall of the Roman Empire*, at the beginning of the seventieth chapter he revealed casually his predilection for the epic form. Commenting on the popularity of Petrarch's sonnets and elegies, he asserts that these do not compare with 'the sublime composition of their [the Italians'] epic muse, the original wildness of Dante, the regular beauties of Tasso, and the boundless variety of the incomparable Ariosto'.

Thirdly, Gibbon does mention history along with the epic. For instance, in his commentary on Hurd's Horace he writes:

> As an epic poem must preserve an unity of hero, and of action, every event, instead of being related at full length, need only occupy a place proportionate with its importance and degree of connection with the principal subject. This is at least the rule of history.

And he adds a footnote to the effect that Lord Bacon and Hurd agree that poetry is an imitation of history and 'should only deviate from it, for the sake of making the fable one, connected, marvellous, heroic, and answering to our notion of justice.'[1] Gibbon's literary criticism is too factual and rationalistic to be valuable in elucidating poetry, but it is most valuable in showing how complete a part of literature he thought history was and how close to the epic.

Lastly Gibbon's accounts of how he came to choose the theme of

---

[1] *Miscellaneous Works*, ii. 34.

his great work show him casting round for it in precisely the way of an epic poet. There is one in the autobiography,[1] where he transcribes relevant passages from his diaries. His early subjects were mainly single men; and his first choice was Sir Walter Raleigh. Of him he wrote 'I am afraid of being reduced to drop my hero'; and in its context the word *hero* reveals Gibbon conceiving of history as a kind of heroic poem. Then he thought of the *History of the Liberty of the Swiss*; and this he conceived in just the exemplary spirit of the epic illustrated from Fénelon:

> From such a theme, so full of public spirit, of military glory, of examples of virtue, of lessons of government, the dullest stranger would catch fire: what might not *I* hope, whose talents, whatsoever they may be, would be inflamed with the zeal of patriotism.

But the most revealing account of all is a fragment written in French, when Gibbon was in camp with the militia at Winchester, called *Idée de quelques Sujets pour une Composition historique*.[2] Here Gibbon first confesses that though he has his eye on the reader he cannot put off personal ambition. Like Fénelon he considers the part of the real historian glorious, that of the mere chronicler contemptible. He will aspire to the first part. Then he reviews the subject of Richard I leading French and English troops on a crusade against the Saracens. And he says that this subject 'plairoit du côté du merveilleux'. Now the marvellous was the accepted business of the epic; and Gibbon's mention of it here shows with what unconscious thoroughness he accepted the proximity of epic and history. Gibbon conceived of his history as a great moral and exemplary work to which the best efforts of a man's life should be devoted. He was in his way the heir of Spenser, Milton, and Pope.

It was a good thing that Gibbon did not persist with his early idea of centring history in a person. He liked society and in one way or another had met and considered many kinds of people. But the realm in which he excelled was not that of people but of ideas. His peculiar glory was to unite an almost matchless gift for details with the gift of reducing them to the sway of a few great overruling ideas. This glory was a matter not only of endowment but of conviction and of a deliberate policy. At the beginning of the last third[3] of the *Decline and Fall* Gibbon announces that he will now change his plan and go more quickly; and the reason is that through the nature of his

[1] Everyman Edition (London, not dated) 108-12.
[2] *Miscellaneous Works*, ii. 23-4.
[3] I use the original editions in six volumes in my references to the *Decline and Fall of the Roman Empire*. These are i (chaps. 1-16) 1776; ii (chaps. 17-26) and iii (chaps. 27-38) 1781 (these take the story down to the extinction of the Roman Empire of the west and comprise Gibbon's history as first projected); iv (chaps. 39-47), v (chaps. 48-57), and vi (chaps. 58-71) 1788.

material from now on he is forced to a new adjustment between detail and general idea:

> Should I persevere in the same course, should I observe the same measure, a prolix and slender thread would be spun through many a volume nor would the patient reader find an adequate reward of instruction or amusement. At every step, as we sink deeper in the decline and fall of the Eastern empire, the annals of each succeeding reign would impose a more ungrateful and melancholy task. These annals must continue to repeat a tedious and uniform tale of weakness and misery; the natural connection of causes and events would be broken by frequent and hasty transitions, and a minute accumulation of circumstance must destroy the light and effect of those general pictures which compose the use and ornament of a remote history.[1]

Gibbon then reflects on the significance of the small number of Athenians at the time of their city's freedom and eminence and on the insignificance of the much greater number of Byzantines under a tyrannical ruler:

> The subjects of the Byzantine empire, who assume and dishonour the names both of Greeks and Romans, present a dead uniformity of abject vices, which are neither softened by the weakness of humanity, nor animated by the vigour of memorable crimes.[2]

And he has no doubt that detail is only admissible as it is varied and significant and subserves a worthy general truth or large event.

The general truths that Gibbon had to convey through the *Decline and Fall* had no exclusive connection with that theme. Had he settled on the rise of the Swiss nation or on the history of Florence under the Medicis instead, they would have been the same. And they were simply the great commonplaces, inherited from the revolution of 1688, that were the moral and intellectual staple of the section of society in the late eighteenth century to which he belonged. Voracious though Gibbon's appetite was for the facts of history, it yet remains true that the first principle of the *Decline and Fall* was that it should express certain great moral truths. And for this there is evidence both in his history and in his autobiography. The passage, cited a little earlier, about a Swiss theme and its moral worth is confirmed immediately after when he considers the alternative subject of the rise and decline of Florence under the Medicis. Both lessons, he says, the Swiss and the Italian, are equally instructive. And the *Decline and Fall* is remarkable for the consistency with which Gibbon reverts to the great moral lessons that emerge from his theme. His process

---

[1] v. 2 (beginning of chap. 48).   [2] *Ib.* 3.

was not one of drawing any odd moral lessons that successive episodes of history happened to suggest but of having begun from a series of great moral principles and of recalling the reader's attention to them as they have been illustrated by the course of events. Like the epic, history was for Gibbon a solemn affair, offering large general lessons in morality.

I come now to the lessons themselves or to the commonplaces associated with them.

First, there is that unique eighteenth-century combination of a disillusioned view of humanity with a tempered belief in human progress: that apparent paradox in what is supposed the least paradoxical age. One could cite passages from all over the *Decline and Fall* to illustrate Gibbon's readiness to acknowledge human depravity and to qualify any human claim to perfection. But there is one passage at least that sums up his feelings so well and is in such perfect tune with its age that it deserves quotation at length. It is the account of the seven pagan philosophers, who, when Justinian closed the schools of Athens, sought a home in the court of Chosroes, King of Persia. They were of the neo-platonic persuasion and

they had heard, and they credulously believed that the republic of Plato was realized in the despotic government of Persia, and that a patriot king reigned over the happiest and most virtuous of nations. They were soon astonished by the natural discovery, that Persia resembled the other countries of the globe; that Chosroes, who affected the name of philosopher, was vain, cruel, and ambitious; that bigotry, and a spirit of intolerance, prevailed among the Magi; that the nobles were haughty, the courtiers servile, and the magistrates unjust; that the guilty sometimes escaped, and that the innocent were often oppressed. The disappointment of the philosophers provoked them to overlook the real virtues of the Persians; and they were scandalized, more deeply perhaps than became their profession, with the plurality of wives and concubines, the incestuous marriages, and the custom of exposing dead bodies to dogs and vultures, instead of hiding them in the earth, or consuming them with fire. Their repentance was expressed by a precipitate return, and they loudly declared that they had rather die on the borders of the empire, than enjoy the wealth and favour of the Barbarian. From this journey, however, they derived a benefit which reflects the purest lustre on the character of Chosroes. He required that the seven sages who had visited the court of Persia, should be exempted from the penal laws which Justinian enacted against his Pagan subjects. Simplicius and his friends ended their lives in peace and obscurity.[1]

[1] iv. 118-19 (chap. 40).

Gibbon is delighted that these neo-platonic enthusiasts should have their illusions about mankind upset, but he is equally delighted that the Persian tyrant should have behaved generously and have upset their expectations in the other direction. He does not want men to be bad, but he refuses to pretend they are better than they are. Or take this comment on Trajan:

> Trajan was ambitious of fame; and as long as mankind shall continue to bestow more liberal applause on their destroyers than on their benefactors, the thirst for military glory will ever be the vice of the most exalted characters.

Gibbon does not like the type of conqueror, but he refuses to ignore the feelings of humanity about it. In a measure he acquiesces with those feelings, for he has a powerful social sense, but he does not exclude the possibility that one day they may alter. In just the same way he admits the prevailing vulgar principle of an exclusive patriotism but would like to go beyond it:

> It is the duty of a patriot to prefer and promote the exclusive interest and glory of his native country: but a philosopher may be permitted to enlarge his views, and to consider Europe as one great republic, whose various inhabitants have attained almost the same level of politeness and cultivation.[1]

And he goes on to say that though the balance of power will fluctuate, the wars within the republic are partial affairs and will not upset civilisation like the barbarian invasions, of which now there is a far smaller danger than in the days of the Roman Empire. In all these matters he represents the sceptical benevolence of his age.

Gibbon's belief in progress is in the central tradition inherited from the older controversy concerning the merits of ancients and moderns. Whatever the attainments of the ancients in art, the moderns have gone beyond them in the sciences, of whose beneficent influence he has not the least doubt. It is in the splendid epilogue to the first division of his history, the division that fulfils his original plan of the course of the Roman Empire till its termination in the west, that Gibbon expatiates most freely on the world's destiny. He is comforted at the thought of further barbarian invasions being improbable; but he is elated at the advance of science and at the hope that this advance may represent, in spite of fluctuations, a constant process from barbarism to higher civilisation:

> The discoveries of ancient and modern navigators, and the domestic history, or tradition, of the most enlightened nations, represent the *human savage*, naked both in mind and body, and

[1] iii. 633-4.

destitute of laws, of arts, of ideas, and almost of language. From this abject condition, perhaps the primitive and universal state of man, he has gradually arisen to command the animals, to fertilise the earth, to traverse the ocean, and to measure the heavens. His progress in the improvement and exercise of his mental and corporeal faculties has been irregular and various; infinitely slow in the beginning, and increasing by degrees with redoubled velocity: ages of laborious ascent have been followed by a moment of rapid downfall; and the several climates of the globe have felt the vicissitudes of light and darkness. Yet the experience of four thousand years should enlarge our hopes, and diminish our apprehensions: we cannot determine to what height the human species may aspire in their advances towards perfection; but it may safely be presumed that no people, unless the face of nature is changed, will relapse into their original barbarism.[1]

Such is Gibbon's optimism, tempered by his never-sleeping awareness of human frailty but based, as he thought, on a just observation of the facts of history.

When it comes to the means by which the human race has progressed and may continue to do so, Gibbon like many others of his age summed them up in the two evocative words, *liberty* and *enlightenment*. In his autobiography he congratulated himself on having been born in a 'free and enlightened country' and he recounted how when he had returned from his first long residence in Lausanne, 'the favorite companions of my leisure were our English writers since the Revolution: they breathe the spirit of reason and liberty'. And the references could be multiplied. Liberty for Gibbon was that of the revolution of 1688, not that of the American colonies to demand a bigger say in the disposal of their taxes. But he believed in it passionately in his own way. A limited monarchy ensured the maximum of liberty compatible with human nature, and like Burke (but without Burke's mystical feelings in this matter) he believed in the hereditary principle: a principle open to abuse but less so than any other. Enlightenment consisted mainly in resisting the impulse to wild passions and superstitious fears and in trusting the steady and laborious results of human reason. I know no passage in Gibbon that conveys his feelings better than his comment on the appearance of two comets (including Halley's) in the age of Justinian. When they then appeared,

the nations, who gazed with astonishment, expected wars and calamities from their baleful influence; and their expectations were abundantly fulfilled. The astronomers dissembled their ignorance of the nature of these blazing stars, which they affected to represent as the floating meteors of the air; and few among them embraced

[1] iii. 638-9.

the simple notion of Seneca and the Chaldaeans, that they are only planets of a longer period and more eccentric motion. Time and science have justified the conjectures and predictions of the Roman sage: the telescope has opened new worlds to the eyes of astronomers; and, in the narrow space of history and fable, one and the same comet is already found to have revisited the earth in *seven* equal revolutions of five hundred and seventy-five years.[1]

Gibbon goes on to enumerate the different appearances. After the sixth he says:

> The *seventh* phaenomenon, of one thousand six hundred and eighty, was presented to the eyes of an enlightened age. The philosophy of Bayle dispelled a prejudice which Milton's muse had so recently adorned, that the comet 'from its horrid hair shakes pestilence and war'. Its road in the heavens was observed with exquisite skill by Flamstead and Cassini; and the mathematical science of Bernouilli, Newton, and Halley, investigated the laws of its revolutions. At the *eighth* period, in the year two thousand three hundred and fifty-five, their calculations may perhaps be verified by the astronomers of some future capital in the Siberian or American wilderness.

The condition of liberty is courage; and Gibbon was as convinced as his fellow-aristocrats in eighteenth-century England and as the citizens of Lausanne that a man must be prepared to die for it, if necessary. Such a statement may surprise those who found their conception of Gibbon's character on his physical qualities: on his huge head and weak legs, his childhood sicknesses, and his lack of interest in sports and exercise. It should not do so, for plainly in his own way he possessed a toughness entirely worthy of his tough age. We should derive our conception of him not from his sickly childhood but from his intense application to study, his successful resolution in carrying through one of the most laborious pieces of work undertaken by a man, and the astonishing cheerfulness and carelessness with which he met his last illness. He had a perfect right to assert the doctrine that liberty depends on courage.

As courage, liberty, and enlightenment make for progress, so cowardice, slavery, barbarism, and fanaticism make for chaos. Gibbon thought of slavery as the cringing subservience of men to a tyrannical master. Barbarism and fanaticism are both the opposites of enlightenment.

> If we contemplate a savage nation in any part of the globe, a supine indolence and carelessness of futurity will be found to constitute their general character. In a civilized state, every faculty

[1] iv. 323 (chap. 43).

of man is expanded and exercised, and the great chain of mutual dependence connects and embraces the several members of society.[1]

Fanaticism is the by-product of any religion that claims absolute truth of dogma. But it can also infect the remote cerebrations of metaphysical philosophers, like the neo-platonists, with whom Gibbon is very much out of sympathy.

I have spent so long on these commonplace topics because by so doing I can make emphatic this most necessary truth: that Gibbon's first aim was to assert these general matters; general both in the sense of being wide-embracing and in that of being widely received. His history was first of all his way of asserting great commonplaces just as a serious poem can be similarly simplified and resolved.[2]

Coming now from these commonplaces to the pattern of human events exemplifying them, I find Gibbon equally at one with his age. A perfectly good place to find it is Collins's *Ode to Liberty* (published 1746). Collins traces the origin of political liberty to Greece, records its transfer to Rome and its ruin there by the Goths:

> *No, Freedom, no, I will not tell,*
> *How Rome, before thy weeping Face,*
> *With heaviest sound, a Giant-statue, fell,*
> *Push'd by a wild and artless Race,*
> *From off its wide ambitious Base,*
> *When Time his Northern Sons of Spoil awoke,*
>   *And all the blended Work of Strength and Grace,*
>   *With many a rude repeated Stroke,*
> *And many a barb'rous Yell, to thousand Fragments broke.*

But some remnants of liberty lingered, to be fostered and improved by Florence and other Italian towns, by Switzerland, by Holland, till at last they blossomed to perfection in Britain, aided by the liberty that was endemic there. It is interesting that all the subjects Gibbon contemplated most seriously, the history of Swiss liberty, the history of Florence under the Medicis, the decline and fall of Rome, occur prominently in Collins's *Ode*. The interest is not that Gibbon drew on Collins; it is that the occurrence of these themes in both contexts shows how accepted they were, how central to the eighteenth century.

I now come to the *Decline and Fall* itself as the means of expressing these wide commonplaces. Like *Paradise Lost*, the *Decline and Fall* includes more than its title declares. Like the *Iliad*, it implies many things both before and after the temporal scope of the fable. It really begins in republican Rome and ends in the freedom and enlightenment of the eighteenth century. The golden age of the Antonines was

---

[1] This occurs in chap. 9, on Germany, i. 224.
[2] For the great commonplaces in poetry see my *Poetry Direct and Oblique* (London 1945) 39-49.

engendered by the severe virtues of the early Romans and bore within itself the marks of decay. Fallen Rome and the barbarian kingdoms that grew up on its ruins themselves contained the seeds of a new and superior age. To enumerate all the places where Gibbon presents or implies these processes would take many pages, for he does so constantly throughout his book. A very few instances must suffice. In the general chapters on the Roman army and the legal codes of Justinian, Gibbon goes right back to the early days of Rome, finding there the sources of these great monuments of Roman genius and activity. In his general observations that follow the fall of the Roman Empire of the west he expatiates through the text of Polybius on the 'deep foundations of the greatness of Rome'. At the time of the Punic Wars there was a satisfactory constitutional adjustment between the different elements in the state; and the individual citizen was bound to the protection of his country or to the enlargement of its borders. It is in such a state of Rome that Gibbon's history really begins.

Contrariwise, Gibbon underlines any signs within the decadent Roman Empire of a new growth; a growth culminating in the enlightenment of modern Europe. As early as the second chapter, which deals both with the grandeur of the Empire in its golden age of the Antonines and the corruptions that were bound to be its ruin, he introduces the theme of revival. Compared with their great ancestors, the individual Romans were insignificant:

> This diminutive stature of mankind was daily sinking below the old standard, and the Roman world was indeed peopled by a race of pygmies: when the fierce giants of the north broke in, and mended the puny breed. They restored a manly spirit of freedom; and after the revolution of ten centuries, freedom became the happy parent of taste and science.[1]

In a similar context, Gibbon reflects on the instability of the peace of the Antonines through the susceptibility of all absolute monarchies to the freaks of fortune. The Antonines, he says,

> must often have recollected the instability of a happiness which depended on the character of a single man. The fatal moment was perhaps approaching, when some licentious youth, or some jealous tyrant, would abuse, to the destruction, that absolute power, which they had exerted for the benefit of their people.[2]

Here Gibbon wishes us to think (though through implication only) of the happy state enjoyed by England through the revolution of 1688. In the splendid thirty-sixth chapter describing the first irruption of the Goths into the Roman Empire Gibbon comments on the comparative humanity and the gratifying restriction of the wars of his

[1] i. 59.   [2] i. 80-1 (chap. 3).

own day, so alien to the total war he is about to describe. When Gibbon described the establishment of the French monarchy in Gaul in 536, he added this comment on a Greek historian who praised its subjects' 'politeness and urbanity'.

> Perhaps the Franks already displayed the social disposition, and lively graces, which in every age have disguised their vices, and sometimes concealed their intrinsic merit.[1]

In the forty-fourth chapter Gibbon enlarges on the Paulician heretics (who flourished in Asia Minor from 660) and on how, transferred two centuries later to Bulgaria, they engendered the first movement of reform in the west, a movement not without its connection with the actual Reformation. And as a final example, Gibbon detects in the history of Rienzi in Rome and Petrarch's support of him an attempt to recreate in Rome itself a new spirit and a new order not unworthy of the ancient republic. For all his interest in detail, in sheer historical fact, Gibbon never forgets the new age of enlightenment which was destined to emerge from the epoch of the invasions.

In the great story of the loss and re-emergence of freedom and enlightenment the Christian religion is prominent. While having a sincere regard for the simple morality of the Gospels, Gibbon thought of the Christian religion in terms of its later growth. For him it meant superstition, monasticism, and fanatical religious controversy. The reforms of Luther were on a balance beneficial (as he tells us at length near the end of the *Decline and Fall*) for they did ultimately lead to the rationalism of a later age. But Gibbon's scepticism co-existed with a passionate interest in the tangles of theological dispute and with a firm belief in the importance of theology as a force in the shaping of events. And when in his autobiography he gave his famous account of having first conceived of his great theme as he 'sat musing amidst the ruins of the Capitol, while the barefooted friars were singing vespers in the temple of Jupiter', he was not merely recording an accident but indicating an essential part of his theme. Indeed, he was explicit on this topic in the same work, where he declared:

> I believed, and . . . I still believe, that the propagation of the Gospel, and the triumph of the church, are inseparably connected with the decline of the Roman monarchy.[2]

He saw the connection roughly as follows. A strong age like the Roman in its prime could afford to be tolerant in matters of religion. But weakness engendered fear, and fear fanaticism, or alternatively the desire to escape. The stronger spirits tended to fierce religious intolerance, the weaker to an escape from the terrors of civil responsibilities in a dangerous age into the less dangerous discomforts of a

---

[1] iii. 581 (chap. 38). [2] *Memoirs, ed. cit.* 136.

monastic life. One of the great connecting threads of Gibbon's history is the disintegrating force of religious strife. The final supreme example was the dispute between the western and the eastern Churches on the use of unleavened or leavened bread in the sacrament, which brought to nothing a proposed alliance and the provision of military aid shortly before the fall of Constantinople.

Even so tolerant a critic as Sainte-Beuve is shocked at the parochialism of Gibbon's view of Christianity. But the fault is not Gibbon's alone, for it belongs to the community of which he was a member, and it applied to the orthodox and the sceptical alike. All sections of this community agreed in their dislike of metaphysics, mysticism, and enthusiasm and had as little use for John Wesley as for Plotinus. Gibbon's sceptical view of Christianity, no less than Paley's defence of it on purely rational grounds, is central to its period.

In stressing the general ideas that animate Gibbon's *Decline and Fall* I must not overlook its wealth of detail. Often Gibbon allows his general ideas to recede to the back of his brain while he summons his powers to marshal and present agreeably a great mass of facts. It is his triumphant success in this matter that largely contributes to expressing two of his great qualities: his general courage and vitality (including a passionate intellectual vitality) and an uncommon staying power and grasp. Gibbon was blessed with that gift necessary for the very great historian, a phenomenal memory. But he had the courage and the pertinacity to put that gift to a creative use; to choose, reject, select, and grade the things his memory offered and finally to present them to the reader in a form of never-failing freshness and charm. Such success enhances the whole book. In the act of mastering detail Gibbon displays qualities of mind that serve to animate the general truths which are his first concern. Delighted by the way Gibbon conducts his factual narrative, the reader finds that the generalities to which it leads have ceased to be mere moral abstractions and have taken on a powerful life of their own.

Gibbon's style is one of the puzzles of English letters. With its elaborate scheme of balances it should prove intolerably monotonous; but having read half of the *Decline and Fall* aloud without weariness and with ever renewed appetite I can testify with emphasis to the exact opposite. Part of the charm consists in exploiting one of the great basic potentialities of the English language: the playing off of the Saxon or at least the simple against the obviously Latin element. Let me take a single paragraph: once again from that splendid ending to the history as first projected, already referred to.

Fortunately for mankind, the more useful, or, at least, more necessary arts, can be performed without superior talents, or national subordination; without the powers of *one*, or the union of *many*. Each village, each family, each individual, must always possess both ability and inclination, to perpetuate the use of fire and of metals; the propagation and service of domestic animals; the methods of hunting and fishing; the rudiments of navigation; the imperfect cultivation of corn, or other nutritive grain; and the simple practice of the mechanic trades. Private genius and public industry may be extirpated; but these hardy plants survive the tempest, and strike an everlasting root into the most unfavourable soil. The splendid days of Augustus and Trajan were eclipsed by a cloud of ignorance; and the Barbarians subverted the laws and palaces of Rome. But the scythe, the invention or emblem of Saturn, still continued annually to mow the harvests of Italy; and the human feasts of the Laestrigons have never been renewed on the coast of Campania.[1]

Here there is a happy alternation of pomp and simplicity leading up to the magnificent homeliness and concreteness of the *scythe mowing* the harvests of Italy. But all detailed observation on Gibbon's style should be subordinated to the one general truth that it is positive and original. By that I mean that it is animated by Gibbon's own very lively faith. By 1788 the eighteenth century is supposed to have been running down, its scepticisms and its belief in reason and tolerance and compromise are supposed to have gone stale; and indeed the movements in the other direction were gathering force. But Gibbon was unaware of these movements, or, if aware, not at all impressed by them; and his faith in the existing ways of thought was fresh and powerful. And that is one reason why his style never wearies and why it is not unworthy of a matter conceived in the spirit and influenced by the method of an epic poet.

But though Gibbon believed in his philosophy of freedom and enlightenment, has it, we may ask, the breadth necessary for the effect of the epic? It is easy enough to see its shortcomings; and I have already indicated some of them by what I said about Gibbon's exclusion from his vision and from his interests of what Plotinus and Wesley represent. Nevertheless there are compensations. One is his successful cosmopolitanism. He became acclimatised to the Continent in a way Shelley and Landor and Browning never could. He was a genuine resident, not a refugee or a sightseer. And this without ceasing to be very much of an Englishman. Another is the variety of his interests. Of all the writers whom I have seriously considered as epic, Gibbon is far the most intellectual. No amount of cerebral effort tired him or dulled the freshness of his mind. He reads and re-reads the classics of various languages. He follows many highways and byways of scholarship. He is passionately interested in law; and a

[1] iii. 639-40.

typical note in his autobiography is that at a certain date he read Blackstone's *Commentaries* for the third time, making an abstract. Such tirelessness and vigilance bespeak a strong emotional urge and may largely compensate the lack of some more common interests or passions. But the best answer to a charge of narrowness is that the kind he suffered from was that of a whole phase of European thought and that to condemn any such phase of thought is perilous.

I have already said by implication a good deal about Gibbon's strength of will and power of shaping his material. He spent twenty years on his work and he ended as strongly as he began. He gave coherence to an immense body of sheer facts. But something remains to be said about the way he shaped his nominal and more restricted theme, the actual decline and fall of Rome. The matter is the less simple because Gibbon did not settle his total plan in advance. While not excluding a work that would include the whole span of the Byzantine Empire and the beginning of the revival of learning, he planned definitely only as far as the extinction of the empire of the west. This first plan occupies half of the history as ultimately completed; and this half could be considered as a separate artistic unit except for certain anticipatory insertions designed to lead on to the second half. It occupied three volumes. The fourth volume treats mainly of the great emperors Theodoric and Justinian. Here Gibbon allows his interest in the period to make him enlarge his scale. It could be argued that he thus was untrue to the proportions of what had gone before; but in actual fact the variety of treatment may help out so long a book. The remaining volumes deal with the period when the empire of the east was shrunk to a small proportion of its old self by the irruption of the Arabs. And for the last two volumes Gibbon adopts a much abbreviated form to suit a long but less important span of years. The *Decline and Fall* then was conceived by stages, and it is only in the first half that we can expect a plan closely comparable to that of a neo-classic epic. Not that Gibbon at all forgets his main theme in the last half or that he has not got a coherent plan. It is merely that the whole six volumes do not have the close and even coherence of the first three. Thus I shall be most apt to my subject if I confine my remarks on structure to Gibbon's history as originally planned, though before I turn to this I will choose from the second half a single example of planning in the grand manner. The actual fall of the Roman Empire was consummated by the capture of Constantinople in 1453. But Gibbon is too good an artist to end his book there. He begins his next chapter with the statement that 'in the first ages of the decline and fall of the Roman empire, our eye is invariably fixed on the royal city' and now he returns to Rome, recounting any signs of reviving liberty that showed themselves there in the Middle Ages and ending with an account of the great monuments surviving from imperial times. It was in their midst that he had conceived his theme and it is in the same place that he knows he must end. Gibbon's concluding technique resembles Homer's in both his poems, more particularly the *Odyssey*.

I turn now to the structure of Gibbon's first instalment. Apart from the anticipatory matter inserted to lead on to the prolongation of his theme, the strict action extends from the eighty years of prosperity under the good emperors—Nerva, Trajan, Hadrian, and the two Antonines—to the deposition in 476 of Augustulus, the last emperor of the west. But, like the epic poet who begins in the middle of things, Gibbon looks back telling us much of the past and looks prophetically into the future. The period of stability he begins from both summed up the past and shadowed the future. It crowned the period of Roman expansion through Trajan's conquest of Dacia, and yet the heart of Rome was degenerate, and she was ready to be the prey of the barbarians. In describing the generally pacific policy of the five emperors, Gibbon looks back to the wisely unambitious policy of Augustus; and his account of what wars there were leads naturally to a disquisition on the Roman army and provincial system. This disquisition is partly retrospective and takes us back to the very beginnings of Rome's greatness in republican days. But he ends his first chapter by switching us deftly from past to future, from the majestic organisation of the provinces to what lay beyond them:

> This long enumeration of provinces, whose broken fragments have formed so many powerful kingdoms, might almost induce us to forgive the vanity or ignorance of the ancients. Dazzled with the extensive sway, the irresistible strength, and the real or affected moderation of the emperors, they permitted themselves to despise, and sometimes to forget, the outlying countries which had been left in the enjoyment of a barbarous independence; and they gradually usurped the licence of confounding the Roman monarchy with the globe of the earth.[1]

The next two chapters continue to set the stage in the same masterly way, with the same retrospective technique, and the same shadowing of the future. But the third chapter performs the last function at greater length and more solemnly than the other two had done. It dwells on the felicity of the human race under the Antonines, and points out the terrible precariousness of it when it depends on a single man: a sentiment that leads on to the vices of the next emperor, Commodus, and the beginning of the narrative proper.

From now on Gibbon has an immense quantity of fact to present; he cannot escape a great deal of sheer narrative. But he has his eye

---

[1] i. 27.

ever on the great theme and delights to mark every stage in it. He never lets detail swamp him. He also shows high literary skill in introducing new topics. Indeed, he can work like a dramatist, holding back a topic as the dramatist does a main character till the most effective moment for entry. Thus Gibbon says almost nothing about Christianity till the rise and conversion of Constantine. Withheld in this way, his two notorious chapters on Christianity come the more surprisingly and, our appetite for narrative having been satisfied, are acceptable as the contrasting counterpart of the static chapters on the age of the Antonines. It would take far too long to point out all the stages in the decline of Rome that Gibbon detects. I will confine myself to one, and perhaps the most notable. If one were forced to point to the most spectacular event in the long process of the fall of the western empire, one could hardly avoid choosing the first capture and sack of Rome, that by Alaric in 410, an event memorable not only in itself but for the impression it made on the mind of Augustine, as recorded in the *City of God*. Gibbon does not fail to rise to it, prefacing it by an account of the senate and people of the city itself and following it by an account (plainly meant to be prophetic) of the surprising establishment of certain free institutions in Gaul. But Gibbon is at least as interested in symptoms as in their realisation, and for him the really fatal moment in the fortunes of Rome was that when the Goths, in flight from the pressure of the Huns, were allowed to cross the Danube. Gibbon describes the episode in his twenty-sixth chapter. Through the weakness of the emperor Valens, the Goths were given leave to cross the Danube on condition of surrendering their arms. Through the corruption of the Roman guards they succeeded in evading the condition. The fatal battle of Adrianople was the result. It is a wonderful chapter, deeply felt, highly dramatic in the way it brings out the fatality of the events and perfectly expressive of the principles Gibbon had most at heart: a worthy turning-point in the process of decline and fall. The magnificence of this chapter may be partly due to Gibbon's long acquaintance with the theme. In his autobiography he recounts the following happenings to himself at the age of fourteen:

In the summer of 1751 I accompanied my father on a visit to Mr Hoare's, in Wiltshire; but I was less delighted with the beauties of Stourhead than with discovering in the library a common book, the *Continuation of Echard's Roman History*. . . . To me the reigns of the successors of Constantine were absolutely new; and I was immersed in the passage of the Goths over the Danube, when the summons of the dinner-bell reluctantly dragged me from my intellectual feast.[1]

[1] 35.

The twenty-sixth chapter comes about two-thirds of the way through Gibbon's work, as first planned, a fitting position for the decisive turning-point. Both its quality and its position argue that Gibbon shaped his material as a poet shapes his epic.

The question of Gibbon's choric quality has already been answered. I have asserted that he did represent a large body of opinion in England and abroad. That this opinion was restricted and ignored many sides of contemporary life simply cannot be denied. But I do not think that some restriction need be fatal to the epic effect. Since the seventeenth century the classes of society have so fallen apart and the departments of learning so multiplied that no one man can master the totality. All art, however great, was now bound to be partial. There are epic qualities in *Robinson Crusoe* and in the *Heart of Midlothian*, but can one maintain that they include more areas of the human spirit than the *Decline and Fall of the Roman Empire*?

It would be vain to argue that Gibbon was epic in the manner of Langland or Milton. History in a strict sense can never be more than partial epic. It must ever yield much to the pressure of facts; and the battle for unity must always be fought against odds. Gibbon fought that battle as well as a man can; and his history, restricted though it may be as literature, is yet the one English work that expresses the temper of eighteenth-century Britain in the age of Hume in something of an epic manner.

EPILOGUE

I

Far better never to have heard the name
Of zeal and just ambition, than to live
Thus baffled by a mind that every hour
Turns recreant to her task, takes heart again,
Then feels immediately some hollow thought
Hang like an interdict upon her hopes.

(Wordsworth, *The Prelude*, 1805)

THESE lines of Wordsworth occur after his review, early in the *Prelude*, of the various subjects he had toyed with for the epic poem which he assumed was the natural aim of any poet ambitious of great achievements other than dramatic. And they express not only his own experience of bafflement but that of any poet who then attempted to prolong the neo-classic tradition of the epic last made use of by Pope and Gibbon. The name of the epic still remained, but the animating idea had perished by the beginning of the nineteenth century. Wordsworth's proposals, with their extraordinary range of possible subjects, British (which may have meant Arthurian), medieval, classical, classical-cum-Gothic, Scottish and others, should be set alongside Gibbon's proposals for his great work of history. Wordsworth had all the world to choose from and had no particular reason to take this subject rather than that. Gibbon had a smaller range of subject initially and enjoyed the firm directions of his own capacities and of his set ethical and political principles. He must have a subject whose documentary sources were intelligible and congenial (the history of Swiss liberty, otherwise excellent, came short on this score) and he must be able to express the principles of 1688 worthily through its means. And he was not long in finding the right one and sticking to it with complete faith. What, we may ask, had happened in the interval to make a thing possible for Gibbon impossible for Wordsworth?

First, we must not forget that Gibbon himself was something of a freak, a decided anachronism. The values he celebrated were those of but a part, and the most antique part, of his age and he succeeded in celebrating them only by means of ignoring many, and those the newer trends of thought. That he should have succeeded was itself marvellous; that anyone after him should succeed in the same way was impossible.

But there were other and broader reasons for the same result. First, the French Revolution destroyed the relevance of the milder English

EPILOGUE

revolution of a century before as a living epic theme. You could not
keep the French Revolution out of English political thought; and
once you let it in you became a partisan and had no chance of being
the steady and settled voice of a large body of men. Or, if you tried
to be reasonable, you risked being tame or at least unwarmed by the
proper epic fire. Burke was open to more sides of his age than Gibbon,
yet his *Reflections on the French Revolution*, with its stormy and afflicted
tone, does not point the way a possible epic could have taken. Crabbe
too had the same advantage over Gibbon; but he suffered from the
opposite drawback to Burke's in that he sacrificed partisan intensity
to a reasonableness which, however admirable and charming, lacked
the fire of the highest poetry. It is interesting that Crabbe knew the
nature of his poetry and that he set it in a just relation to the epic.
True, he put the thing in terms of the characters about whom he told
his stories, but it is easy to apply his principle to the moral and
political ideas these stories do so easily and naturally reveal. In his
preface to his *Tales* (1812) he called his characters

> beings of whom might be formed groups and smaller societies, the
> relations of whose adventures and pursuits might bear that kind of
> similitude to an Heroic Poem, which these minor associations of
> men (as pilgrims on the way to their saint, or parties in search of
> amusement, travellers excited by curiosity, or adventurers in pur-
> suit of gain) have in points of connexion and importance with a
> regular and disciplined army.[1]

Crabbe knew that his characters and his ideas, while possessing some
common trend, were not organised into the kind of hierarchy that
gives an epic strength. He was thus well attuned to his age; and he
was in his way lucky in possessing and in knowing he possessed a
mediocrity of talent that spared him the futile struggle to compass a
great end, impossible of attainment in the ineluctable conditions of
his time.

Second, the forces urging an ambitious poet to try the epic form
were weaker. The old mystical idea of the epic, still powerful in
Gibbon's youth, had lost ground by the nineteenth century. That idea
had partly been derived from, and certainly rested on, the acknowledged supremacy of Homer and Virgil. These two poets had hallowed
the poetic form into which they had cast their great works. During
the eighteenth century in England first Shakespeare and then Dante
obtruded into the class where once only Homer and Virgil had
reigned. Further, men had begun to speculate about Homer and to
associate him not with Virgil alone but with the primitive bards of
other races. By associating him with Ossian, in particular, whatever
their intentions, they did make him more common, they did subtract

[1] *Poems*, ed. A. W. Ward, ii. (Cambridge 1906) 6.

529

something of his awe. It was this subtraction of awe that made possible the influence and popularity of the disintegrating critics of Homer, the earliest of whom, W. A. Wolf, published his *Prolegomena* in 1795. Once the common authorship of the *Iliad* and *Odyssey* was questioned, not to speak of the single authorship of the separate poems, the old neo-classic glamour investing Homer (and hence the verse epic) was doomed.

For these different reasons, then, the epic tradition I have been describing in the last third of this book had perished before the end of the eighteenth century. And it was a set of genuine facts and not a mere arbitrary hankering after tidiness that induced me, having begun my book with Homer and Herodotus's history of the Persian Wars, to bring it to rest with Pope's *Iliad* and Gibbon's account of the decline and fall of the Roman Empire.

2

Finally, I do not wish to imply that, because a certain epic tradition expired in the eighteenth century, the possibility of epic writing in a different tradition was shut out. What happened in the eighteenth century (if not in the second half of the seventeenth) was this. Life had become so complicated, so much had been added to the stock of human learning, there was so much ecumenical freedom to exchange ideas, that the epic spanning a total society, like Homer's or Dante's, became impossible. Any great work of literature, however ambitious of universality, was forced to be in some degree specialist.

Now the speciality that turned out most propitious for the epic effect was the middle-class novel that began to flourish in the eighteenth century. In my chapter on Milton I wrote of the middle-class side (among other and more important sides) of *Paradise Lost*: how by substituting a domestic for a heroic crisis he looked forward to one proclivity of the eighteenth century, and how Adam displayed a Robinson Crusoe element in his character. In these matters Milton appealed to new forces of life in the English community, forces that were to outlast the Renaissance and neo-classic tradition that actually dominated *Paradise Lost*. These forces were of course old as well as new, inheriting for instance the old spirit of Elizabethan adventure as well as embodying the new Puritan spirit of commercial enterprise. They thus included a large and rich area of life. Though these forces created no undoubted epic they served to animate works that did in fact go some way towards the epic goal and which showed that this way was indeed a right and possible one. Along with Pope's *Iliad* and Gibbon's *Decline and Fall*, Defoe's *Robinson Crusoe* (the first part) is the nearest approach to the epic, as I conceive it, in the eighteenth century.

EPILOGUE

By the nineteenth century the real course of the epic had forsaken the traditional verse form for the novel. And the two British efforts that come nearest success as epics are solidly rooted in the middle-class movement of the eighteenth century. There is no one of Scott's novels that can be called roundly epic, though the *Heart of Midlothian* comes nearest. But the first few of the Waverley Novels constitute an epic area. There, the great themes are: English and Scottish, British and Continental, Highland and Lowland, antique romance and modern commerce[1]; wide themes not only dear to Scott but newly brought into common consciousness by the particular stage of history in which Scotland found itself. And here, in these first works, whatever the complications of Scott's sympathies, he is on the side (since he felt compelled to choose) of modern middle-class reasonableness and he inherits the cool observation and the domestic inclinations of the great English novelists of the eighteenth century. And it is Jeanie Deans, the thrifty Puritan woman, who is his great epic heroine, the symbol of all southern Scotland. Later in the century it was through a wide middle-class setting, part country part provincial town, that George Eliot in *Middlemarch* was able to get nearer to the epic than any other of the great Victorian novelists.

Round the turn of the centuries the possible epic successes cannot be attributed to any one literary kind or tradition. *Travels in Arabia Deserta* and the *Dynasts* stand apart; and the affinities of *Nostromo* are not with *Middlemarch* or the *Heart of Midlothian*.

To conjecture what will be the fate of the epic in the near future would be an act of quite uncommon stupidity. All I can say is that it would be strange if the impulses that have found vent in past epics did not at some points of man's future history find vent in forms which, though superficially alien, may, deeper down, have a kinship with *Piers Plowman*, the *Faerie Queene*, *Arcadia*, the *Holy War*, or *Paradise Lost*.

---

[1] For this see David Daiches's two articles, in *Nineteenth-Century Fiction*, 1951, pp. 81-95, 153-73.

INDEX

Main references in *italic* figures

INDEX

INDEX

Dawson, Christopher, on Corippus, 116

Dearing, Bruce, on Gavin Douglas, 338 n

De Contemptu Mundi, Boccaccio's use of, 196, 198

Defoe, Daniel, relation to Bunyan, 392
  Robinson Crusoe, epic qualities, 527
    as forerunner of ' middle-class ' novel, 496
  ' Robinson Crusoe element ' in Milton's Adam, 438, 530

Degree, 143, 160, 287-90, 330
  Scaliger's theory of epic, 229
  Tasso's theory of epic, 231
  ' Chain of Being ', 193

Deguileville, *Pelerinage de la Vie Humaine*, 149
  relation to Bunyan, 393
  hierarchical idea in, 143
  translation by Lydgate, 173-6
  debt to *Roman de la Rose*, 173-4
  influence on Spenser, 283

Dent, Arthur, *The Plain Man's Path-way to Heaven*, influence on Bunyan, 377-8, 393
  emphasis on religion, 378-9
  style, 377

Descartes, René, relation to neo-classic theories of epic, 454

Digby, Sir Kenelm, on Spenser, 264-5

Dionysius of Halicarnassus, on Herodotus, 41
  on Thucydides, 40
  on Xenophon, 52

Dissertation sur la Poësie Angloise, on Fénelon, 492

Dobrée, Bonamy, on Sylvester, 353

Donaldson, E. T., on *Piers Plowman*, 151 n, 169 n

Donne, John, 5, 270, 300, 427

Dos Passos, 62

Doughty, Charles, *Travels in Arabia Deserta*, 54, 531

Douglas, Gavin, *Aeneid*, 14, *338-44*
  choric quality, 343, 344
  control, 342
  compared with Dryden, 479
  epic qualities, 340-3, 344
  compared with Harington, 347
  view of history as example, 343
  prosody, 338-40, 342
  vitality, 340, 342, 344

Dowlin, C. M., on Sidney, 305 n

Drayton, Michael, *Barons' Wars*, 321, 420
  Heroical Epistles, 420
  Mortimeriados, 321
  Poly-Olbion, 258, 321

Dream of the Rood, 163

Dreiser, Theodore, 62

Drummond, William, on Drayton, 258

Dryden, John, 20, 395, *465-81*
  amplitude, 476
  burlesque, 473, 495

on Chapman's Homer, 351
choric quality, 477
relation to Cowley, 426, 427
control, 477
distinction, 472-3
idea of epic, 465-7, 478
projected epic, 466, 472-9 *passim*, 482
on Homer, 480-1
connection with May, 419 and n
influence of Milton, 412
on Milton, 435
on qualification of poet, 466
relation to Rapin, 456
political and social situation at time, 468-71
scepticism, 473-5
connection with Sprat, 468-9
relation to Sylvester, 352-3, 360
on Tasso, 408, 411
interest in technique, 475-6
on Virgil, 67-8, 480-1
Absalom and Achitophel, 426, 476
Aeneid, 390, 475, 478, *479-81*
All for Love, 476
Annus Mirabilis, 458, 466-76 *passim*
Apology for Heroic Poetry, 466
Astraea Redux, 468
Conquest of Granada, 411
Essay of Dramatic Poetry, 467
Examen Poeticum (Dedication), 466, 467
Fables, 476, 480, 481
translation of Juvenal, 476
translation of Juvenal (Preface) (*Discourse concerning Satire*), 467, 477-8
Odes, 476, 477, 481
Ovid's *Epistles* (*Preface*), 478
translation of Persius, 476
Religio Laici, 476
Remarks on Settle's Empress of Morocco 466
Secular Masque, 470
Threnodia Augustalis, 475

Du Bartas, 423, 456-7
and see Sylvester

Du Bellay, 234-5, 251

D'Urfé, *Astrée*, 374-5, 428, 467

EDUCATION of prince or gentlemen as object or theme of epic, 178, 183, 261, 307, 309-10, 311, 320, 459, 486
  as object of histories, 211-2, 343
  and see Example, Moral

Egger, E., on Peletier, 235 n

Ekkehart, *Waltharius*, 119

Eliot, George, *Middlemarch*, 531

Eliot, T. S., on Virgil, 68
  on Sidney, 301
  Waste Land, 439

Elyot, *Governour*, 211
  Image of Governance, 14, 211

Ennius, 62, 70, 98, 109, 191

INDEX

Printed in Great Britain
at Hopetoun Street, Edinburgh,
by T. and A. CONSTABLE LTD.
Printers to the University of Edinburgh